LEEDS UNITED

1919 — 2019

100 YEARS

An Official History of
LEEDS UNITED

ANDREW DALTON

First Published in Great Britain in 2019 by DB Publishing,
an imprint of JMD Media Ltd

© Andrew Dalton, 2019

All Rights Reserved. No part of this publication may be reproduced, stored in a retrieval system, or transmitted in any form, or by any means, electronic, mechanical, photocopying, recording or otherwise without the prior permission in writing of the copyright holders, nor be otherwise circulated in any form or binding or cover other than in which it is published and without a similar condition being imposed on the subsequent publisher.

ISBN 9781780915845

Printed and bound by OZGraf, Poland.

CONTENTS

Dedication 6
Introduction 7
Foreword by Phil Hay 9

The 1920s
Getting started 10
Debutants in 1920s 16
Managers appointed in the 1920s 24

1930s
Going Down, Going Up, Being consistent . 37
Debutants in the 1930s 41
Managers appointed in the 1930s 49

The 1940s
A time to forget 60
Debutants in 1940s 62
Managers appointed in the 1940s 73

1950s
Arise Sir John 81
Debutants in 1950s 87
Managers appointed in the 1950s 99

The 1960s
The Don takes charge 113
Debutants in 1960s 125
Managers appointed in the 1960s 148

The 1970s
From Revie to Clough to Armfield to Adamson to Stein 165
Debutants in 1970s 179
Managers appointed in the 1970s 193

The 1980s
Down Down Deeper and down and back up again 219
Debutants in the 1980s 232
Managers appointed in the 1980s 248

The 1990s
Time flies when you are having fun . . . 275
Debutants of the 90s 289
Managers appointed in the 1990s 304

The 2000s
From the sublime to the ridiculous . . . 323
Debutants in the 2000s 329
Managers appointed in the 00s 341

The 2010s
Changes, changes and more changes . 381
Debutants in 2010 onwards 394
Managers appointed in the 2010s 409

Shirts, shorts and all 458
Leeds United 100 years concert 470
Memorabilia 474
Fans on their Leeds United 476
Media memories 483
LUFC 2019 tweets 497
Bibliography 510

DEDICATION

I would like to thank everyone who has helped me make this book possible:

Mum and Dad, who I love very much.

Leeds United Football Club, in particular the media team, James Mooney, Jordan Owens, Craig Wilson, Dominque Grant and photographer Andrew Varley

Everyone who agreed to take part and help me with it.

All my friends who have kept me going through the good and bad times.

To those close to me who are no longer with us, most importantly my loving Grandma Jeanne and Grandpa Arnold

Phil Hay for doing the Foreword. Good Luck in the new job.

Finally, Steve Caron and Michelle Grainger from DB publishing, whom without their support this could not have been possible.

INTRODUCTION

Leeds United Football Club is like no other: a one city club, fuelled on passion, commitment, desire and the will to win. A club that has faced so many trials and tribulations, you can take a trip down memory lane in this comprehensive book celebrating 100 years of this great club.

From the start of Arthur Fairclough's tenure right through to Marcelo Bielsa taking on the role of head coach, every manager, including caretakers, are included in this book. You can also read about Leeds United's kit history written by True Colours author John Devlin, as well as thoughts and interviews conducted by Heidi Haigh.

Relive every season, the games, the players that mattered, the memorabilia, the fans and every competitive result since the opening day against Port Vale in season 1920-21.

For Leeds United supporters Leeds United is just a way of life. We have all lived through the title-winning seasons, the relegations, the European tours, the League One years, the 'oh so nearly years', the controversies and much much more. Take a tour through the decades as we celebrate 100 years of Leeds United.

Marching on Together

Leeds Leeds Leeds

FOREWORD

PHIL HAY

I started covering the club in 2006-07 season, predominately in the Championship, with it being the post-Premier League years and have seen changes at the club. The first year saw Blackwell and Leeds struggle and it became apparent very early on that the side wouldn't be competitive and it was no surprise that the side were relegated and administration was an inevitability. You only have to look at the number of players that came in on short-term contracts. That summer was the most fascinating as there was so much going on, especially with the legal side of things. We didn't know if the club were going to be punished and you had to have an understanding of financial law as well as the Football League rules, the appeal process and the counter-appeal process. I remember coming back to do a presser with Dennis Wise (manager at the time) and he had photocopies from the *Yorkshire Evening Post* on his desk and the top one read 'United Home in Disgrace' after they came back from the tour of Germany in the summer of 2007. I had a bit of set too with Wise but these things are part and parcel of the job, the same being with managerial sackings. It is something that with more experience you learn how to deal with. The League One years were a novelty but by the end of the third season, you knew that we had to go up otherwise there would be changes. The Bristol Rovers game stands out and even though it is not our job to bounce up and down in the press box you can't help it when you cover the possible consequences of a fourth season in League One. From a professional point of view, you want to be covering the side at the highest level possible and seeing Leeds test themselves against likes of Guardiola at Manchester City and Klopp at Liverpool. One date that will always stick in my mind was that of 31 January 2014, when GFH told Massimo Cellino that the club was effectively his and he moved to sack Brian McDermott. We had done a pre-match press conference early that day (ahead of the Huddersfield Town game) and he knew that the first thing Cellino was going to do was sack him. At 6pm that night he was gone, but there was even talk of McDermott watching the game from one of the boxes in the East Stand and it was GFH who effectively reinstated him midway through the game. It was a sign of things to come under Cellino.

The introduction of social media has certainly put more pressure on journalists, especially now that everything is so instant nowadays and you have to keep on top of that. It is a challenge for everyone but it is a sign of the times as everything moves at such a pace.

I always liked working with Simon Grayson due to the results under him and he was a manager that came in, wanted to do things, promised to do things and delivered. Brian McDermott as well, fantastic guy to deal with, understood our jobs, understood where we were coming from and when things went wrong under him. The most fascinating head coach to work with has been Bielsa. It is like dealing with a manager you shouldn't be dealing with in the Championship. It is interacting with someone who you wouldn't have put any money on him deciding to come down to this level.

THE 1920s
GETTING STARTED

Much has been written about the demise of Leeds City, which led to the creation of Leeds United all those years ago. When Joe Henry Junior was appointed as chairman adverts started to appear in the local press asking for players. Dick Ray was the manager initially as the new side replaced Leeds City in the Midland League. Leeds United Football Club was founded on Friday 17 October 1919.

Hilton Crowther, who was Huddersfield Town's chairman at that time, had suggested moving Huddersfield to Elland Road due to problems at the club, but it was then that the Football League decided on the next move, and in the end, Town supporters demanded to buy Crowther's £25,000 stake in the club, and Crowther became Leeds United's new chairman as he canvassed votes to gain election to the Football League. The side polled the highest number of votes and status was achieved on 31 May 1920. Leeds United were off...

So this was a season of firsts for Leeds United. Their first-ever season in the English Football League saw Arthur Fairclough appointed as the club's first-ever Football League manager, and Jim Baker was appointed as the club's first-ever captain, with their colours being blue-and-white striped shirts and white shorts. Their first-ever game was a 2-0 defeat away at Port Vale on 28 August 1920. Len Armitage then went down in the club's record books, scoring the first-ever goal in a 2-1 home defeat to South Shields at Elland Road. The first win came on 4 September 1920 at home to Port Vale, with Merton Elston scoring a brace, and the first FA Cup tie took place at Elland Road against Boothtown, who were beaten 5-2, with Eugene O'Doherty scoring the first hat-trick. Despite beating Leeds Steelworks 7-0, Leeds withdrew from the competition. They ended the season in 14th place, with Robert Thompson finishing as top scorer with 12 goals, and Baker, Billy Down and Albert Dudfield playing in every game.

Their second season in existence saw Fred Whalley join as the new goalkeeper, as well as Harry Sherwin and Ralph Coates. They made a flying start and were top of the table after winning three and drawing one of their first four games, with Tommy Howarth scoring four goals. They were still second following a 1-0 away win over Bradford Park Avenue thanks to that man Howarth, but that was as good as it would get as results proved to be inconsistent and they slipped as low as tenth following a goalless draw at home to West Ham United. The FA Cup came and went in a 2-1 away defeat to Swindon Town, but the side captured some consistency to finish eighth. Howarth

Joe Harris, Leeds Utd, 1920s

Leeds Utd Team, 1920-21, J Baker, R Murrel Trainer, Ernie Hart, W Lownes, Mr Barker Director, R Rogerson, H Crowther President, J Walton, FR - G Mason, B Duffield, T Howarth, M Ellson, B Wood, J Trew.

finished top of the scoring pile with 13 and skipper Baker was yet to miss a game since the start of the previous season.

During the summer Joe Harris joined from Bristol City and he scored the winner in his fourth game for the side in a 1-0 win over Southampton at Elland Road at the start of September. However, the side only won five out of their opening 12 games and new blood was needed. The manager bought Percy Whipp for £750 from Sunderland. It paid immediate dividends as he scored a hat-trick on his debut in a 3-0 home win against West Ham United at the start of November. The side then crept up to third in the league by the New Year, with Whipp scoring ten goals. Leeds made it through the first round of the FA Cup with a 3-1 replay win over Portsmouth, before being knocked out by Bolton Wanderers (2-1) at Burden Park. Despite looking like they would challenge for promotion, a bid faltered as the side finished in seventh place with Whipp top scoring with 16 goals and Jim Baker still keeping up his impeccable record of not missing a game.

Percy Whipp, Leeds Utd, 1920s

Leeds Utd Team, 1923-24, HS, Shirwin, Duffield, Down, Armand, Menzies, FR-Coates, Whipp, Richmond, Baker, Swan, Harrin, Hart

After having three players to adjust to the Football League, hopes were finally high in West Yorkshire that a promotion challenge could be mounted. But early season optimism gave way to a sense of reality as the side won only one of their first six league games and found themselves in 14th place. A 2-1 win at Hull City in which Jack Swann scored a brace set Leeds on the way to seven straight wins and propelled them into top spot following a 1-0 win over Bradford City at Elland Road. On Boxing Day 1923, they produced a season's best to defeat Oldham Athletic 5-0 at Elland Road, thanks to braces from Swan, Richmond and one from Whipp. Despite a 2-0 defeat at South Shields at the start of 1924 and being knocked out of the FA Cup by Aston Villa, six straight league wins kept Leeds top of the pile. However, two wins in nine games looked to have derailed things, promotion was clinched with a 4-0 win over Stockport County at Elland Road after Bury lost at Barnsley. The Championship was then clinched with a 1-0 home win over Nelson, coupled with Derby County's 3-0 defeat at Leicester. Baker finally lost his ever-present task and Swan finished as top scorer with 18.

Hilton Crowther was replaced by Major Albert Braithwaite in the off season and over 33,000 fans flocked to Elland Road

Jack Swann, Leeds Utd, 1920s

Tom Jennings in action against Aston Villa

to watch the first ever top-flight game against Sunderland. It turned out to be a tough season for the side with only two wins in the opening 10 games, with one of them being a 4-0 home win against Preston North End. They did win three in a row: Tottenham Hotspur 1-0 at Elland Road, Blackburn Rovers 3-2 at Ewood Park and 2-1 at home to West Ham United, which took Leeds up to 10th, but they never looked like serious championship challengers. A season's best 6-0 win over Aston Villa on Christmas Day saw Percy Whipp score a hat-trick, but a day later Villa got their revenge in a 1-0 win. Liverpool knocked Leeds out of the FA Cup and league form stuttered until a 4-1 win at Elland Road over the same side on 28 March in which Tom Jennings scored his first goal for the club. Leeds finished the campaign in 16th place with Swan again top scoring, and the season saw a notable debutant, Willis Edwards, who would go on to play a massive part in the club's history.

In came Bobby Turnbull, Jim Allen, Tom Townsley and Bill Johnson as Fairclough looked to strengthen his side and become more competitive. Following a 5-2 win over West Ham United at Elland Road in mid-September, Leeds were second in the league, with Jennings having scored seven goals in the first seven games, and hopes were high. A week later Arsenal won 4-1 at Highbury and Leeds dropped to seventh. Three straight defeats in October, 4-0 at home to Huddersfield Town, 4-2 at Everton and 3-2 at home to Bury, sent Leeds down to 15th. But worse was to come as Leeds hit rock bottom following a 6-3 defeat away to Burnley and it looked like a relegation battle was on the cards. Thankfully for the side,

Tom Townsley, Leeds Utd, 1920s

Billy Down and his defenders deal with a West Ham attack in the FA Cup in 1924.

they crept away from the scrap zone and a 1-0 win over Leicester City at the end of January saw Leeds in 17th place. Better results followed with a 4-2 home win over Arsenal at the start of February which saw the Whites in 15th place. Three straight defeats at the start of April saw the worries return, but on the last day of the season a 4-1 win over Tottenham Hotspur with a brace from Jennings saw Leeds survive and finish in 19th place. Jennings finished as top scorer with 26 goals and Willis Edwards became the first Leeds United player to represent England. Middlesbrough knocked Leeds out of the FA Cup in the third round with a 5-1 win.

Season 1926-27 saw Leeds as one of the favourites for the drop, but one man had different ideas. Tom Jennings became the first ever Leeds United player to score four in a game in a 4-2 home win against Liverpool at Anfield at the start of October. He then backed it up with another four-goal haul a week later in a 4-1 home win against Blackburn Rovers. He then scored a hat-trick in another 4-1 home win, this time against Bury, which propelled Leeds up to ninth place in the First Division. By Jennings standard his goals dried up with only two goals in the next seven and results suffered. By the middle of January, Leeds were in 19th place and looking at a relegation battle. Bolton Wanderers knocked the side out of the FA Cup and a 6-2 horror show away at Sunderland in the March followed, which saw Leeds 22nd in the league and staring relegation in the face. Jennings did keep scoring and ended up with 37, but it was too no avail as a 1-0 defeat to Sheffield Wednesday saw the Whites sent back to the Second Division following three years in the top flight. Arthur Fairclough left the side at the end of the campaign.

Former Leeds City captain Dick Ray was then appointed as the new manager and his remit was to gain promotion. His first signing would be Charlie Keetley who, like Jennings, would play an important part in the club's history. A 5-1 win over South Shields set the tone for the season and they scored in every league bar three, with the run coming to an end at the start of March. Nottingham Forest were beaten 4-0 at Elland Road and Swansea Town 5-1 and Jennings kept up his scoring, with another four goal haul in a 5-0 win over Chelsea, two weeks before Christmas. Going into the New Year Leeds had won seven straight league games, which saw them in third place. The FA Cup disappeared in a 1-0 defeat away at Manchester City, which left Leeds to concentrate on promotion. Following a 4-2 defeat away at Preston North End, Leeds were fourth, but five straight wins saw Leeds up to second and looked like they may win the title. A defeat at home to Manchester City cost Leeds the title, but promotion was secured, with Jennings scoring 21 and the side in total scoring 98 in the league.

Back in the top flight at the first attempt, Leeds made an excellent start, winning eight of their opening 12 games, and following a 3-2 home win over Portsmouth, with goals from Russell Wainscoat, Tom Jennings and John White, Leeds were in third position and a possible tilt at the First Division title. Sadly for Leeds, goalscoring hero Jennings would be sidelined for almost three months and all hopes vanished. New signings were brought in, Tom Cochrane and George Milburn, but results were too hit and miss for Leeds to make any impact. They suffered a record 8-2 loss at West Ham United, and a 5-0 defeat at Burnley dropped Leeds to sixth. A run of five defeats in the last six saw the side finish in 13th position. Charlie Keetley finished as top scorer with 22 and Ernie Hart became the second Leeds player to represent England alongside Willis Edwards.

The final season of the decade again saw no major changes. Jennings was back to full fitness and Willis Edwards took over the captaincy from Tom Townsley. Following an inconsistent start, two wins, two defeats and one draw, Leeds then embarked on a seven-game winning run, which took them to the top of the pile, the last win being a 6-0 win over Grimsby Town, in which Russell Wainscoat scored a brace. They stayed top despite a 3-2 defeat away at Sheffield United. A run of three wins from the next eight saw the side drop to fifth, but they then recorded the best victory to date in a 8-1 FA Cup third-round win over Crystal Palace, in which Wainscoat scored a hat-trick. Back-to-back wins over Burnley 3-0 at Turf Moor and 5-0 at home to Sunderland saw Leeds in fourth position, but three consecutive defeats meant Leeds dropped to seventh. In the end they won four out of the last seven to finish in a best-ever fifth place. Wainscoat finished with 18 goals and the FA Cup run was ended at West Ham United in the fourth round.

DEBUTANTS IN 1920s

JIM BAKER

Debut: Port Vale (A) 28 August 1920
Appearances: 208
Goals: 2

Born in Staffordshire in 1891, Baker was one of three brothers who played league football. He started his early career with Eastwood Rangers and Ilkeston Town before joining Derby County as an amateur. Baker then moved to Hartlepool United and he made his debut away at Gateshead. He was almost an ever-present for Hartlepool before joining his first west Yorkshire club in Huddersfield Town. He helped the Terriers win promotion to the top flight in the 1919-20 season, who were then managed by Arthur Fairclough. Fairclough would then become Leeds United's first-ever manager and Baker came with him. He was named the club's first-ever captain and would go on to play 149 consecutive games for the side, scoring two goals, both in United's first-ever season at home to Birmingham City on New Year's Day and in a 2-1 win at home to Clapton Orient at the start of March 1921. In total, Baker would make 208 appearances, captaining the side to promotion in the 1923-24 season. He left for Nelson in June 1926 for £125. He passed away in Leeds aged 75 on 13 December 1966.

ERNIE HART

Debut: Boothtown (H) 11 September 1920
Appearances: 472
Goals: 15

Hart was born in Overseal, near Burton on Trent, and went to Overseal school, where he played for Overseal Juniors before joining Leeds United in 1920 when the side was formed. He made his debut for the club in an FA Cup tie at home to Boothtown, with Leeds playing two games on the same day. He scored his first goal for the side in the next round against Boothtown and went on to net another eight times in his first season. The following season, and the Whites second, saw Hart start to became part of the first team, making 32 appearances, and the following season he improved his appearance rate with 44 and scored in a 1-0 win over Wolverhampton Wanderers. Thirty-two, 28 and 26 starts followed in the next three seasons, as Leeds won promotion to the First Division in 1923-24. Despite relegation in 1926-27, when Hart played only five games, Leeds and Hart bounced back the following campaign as they returned to the top flight, and Hart played in 31 games for the Peacocks. He became captain in September 1932 and a third promotion followed after relegation in 1931. He left for Mansfield in 1936 and passed away aged 52 in July 1954.

BILL MENZIES

Debut: Oldham Athletic (A) 25 December 1923
Appearances: 258
Goals: 2

Menzies was born in Bucksburn, near Aberdeen, in July 1901, and joined Leeds from Mugieumoss in 1922 after a brief trial. He made his debut away at Oldham Athletic on Christmas day 1923, and his first campaign saw him feature on 18 occasions as Leeds won promotion to the First Division. The 1924-25 season saw the left-back play on 41 occasions as Leeds finished in 18th place in the top flight, and the following year he made 36 appearances for the club as they finished a position below but kept their heads above water. As Leeds finished bottom the following campaign, Menzies made 32 appearances, scoring his first goal away at West Ham United. Two more promotions followed in 1927-28 and 1931-32 and Menzies captained the side on five occasions when injuries dictated, and he made his last appearance for the club on the final day of the 1931-32 season at home to Port Vale. He went on to join Goole Town in September 1933. He was 69 when he passed away on 3 January 1970.

TOM JENNINGS

Debut: Sheffield United (H) 14 March 1925
Appearances: 174
Goals: 117

The Whites' first goalscoring hero, Jennings started his career at Strathaven Academy and had trials at Tottenham Hotspur before being rejected, so from the south of the border he travelled north to join Raith Rovers. He joined Leeds in March 1925 and what a signing he went on to be. He scored three goals in ten games at the back of that season and the following campaign he hit 26 goals in 43 games, including a hat-trick in a 4-2 win at home against Arsenal. This was part of a run that saw Jennings score eight in five games. His best ever season in Leeds colours came the following year when he hit 37 goals in 44 games, which included a hat-trick at home to Arsenal (again) and a pair of four-goal hauls away at Liverpool and at home to Blackburn Rovers. To make the achievement even better, the feat came in three consecutive games. Twenty-one goals in 27 games followed as he helped Leeds win promotion in 1927-

28 and he kept on scoring right until his last game away at Liverpool in February 1931. He joined Chester City in June 1931. He died aged 71 in July 1973.

RUSSELL WAINSCOAT

Debut: Newcastle United (A) 21 March 1925
Appearances: 226
Goals: 93

Born in East Retford in Nottinghamshire in 1898, Wainscoat began his career with his local side Maltby Main Colliery Welfare before joining Barnsley in March 1920. From Barnsley he joined Middlesbrough when they paid £4,000 to sign him. Leeds paid Middlesbrough half of that fee when he joined the side in March 1925 and he would become an important part of the side. He made his debut away at Newcastle in March 1925 and went on to score four goals in the nine games he played that season. Eight more goals followed in 1925-26 in 25 games, but every season after that, bar the three games Wainscoat played in 1931-32, he reached double figures for the side. He hit 11 in 1926-27, including four in a 6-3 win over West Ham United at the back end of the campaign, and would become a vital part of the side that won promotion to the First Division the following season. He hit 18 goals as Leeds finished second and went one better the following year with 19 goals in 41 games. Thirty-three goals in 81 games followed before Wainscoat left the Whites for the Humber and Hull City in October 1931. He passed away in Worthing in July 1967.

WILLIS EDWARDS

Debut: Newcastle United (A) 21 March 1925
Appearances: 444
Goals: 6

Edwards, who became the first-ever Leeds player to be capped by England, had a 35-year association with the club as player, manager and trainer. Born in Newton, near Alfreton, he started his career with Newton Rangers, before joining Chesterfield for £10. He joined Leeds in March 1925 for £1,500 and it would be the start of an illustrious career at Elland Road. He made nine appearances in 1924-25 after making his debut away at West Ham United. The following season saw him start 41 games and an even bigger honour was just around the corner when he made his England debut on 1 March 1926 against Wales. Despite being relegated in 1926-27, Edwards made 40 appearances, scoring his first goal in a 4-1 win over the Wednesday in December 1926. He helped the side win back their place in the First Division the following year with 33 appearances and captained the side for three games in the absence of Tom Townsley the following year. He was made permanent captain the following season, missing just five games over the next two seasons. He would be a mainstay throughout the 1930s and also represented the Football League on 11 occasions. He retired from playing in May 1939, with his last and 444th appearance for the side coming on the last day of the 1938-39 season at home to Stoke City. He would join the coaching staff before becoming manager in April 1947.

JIMMY POTTS

Debut: Huddersfield Town (A) 27 February 1926
Appearances: 262

Born in Morpeth, Northumberland, in January 1904, Potts was the brother-in-law of the Milburns, with his sister having married Jack Milburn. He started his career at Blyth Spartans and he stayed in the North East until February 1926, when Leeds met Blyth officials looking to secure his services. He joined Leeds for a fee of £200 and he made his debut away at

Huddersfield Town within a couple of days of signing. He kept five clean sheets in his first 12 games at the back end of the 1925-26 campaign. He was an ever-present the following year as Leeds were relegated from the top flight, but he played a massive part the following campaign as Leeds bounced back to the First Division at the very first attempt, with Potts keeping 18 cleans sheets. He missed only four games in the 1928-29 season back in Division One, but Bill replaced him, as he played the majority of games at the back end of the decade. In his last three campaigns at the club he made a further 100 appearances and was eventually replaced by Stan Moore, before moving to Burslam to join Port Vale at the age of 35. He died in his home county of Northumberland aged 82 in 1986.

CHARLIE KEETLEY

Debut: South Shields (H) 31 December 1927
Appearances: 169
Goals: 110

Keetley was a former Rolls-Royce worker and the youngest of a set of Derbyshire brothers who played League Football between the wars. He hammered in 80 goals for Alvaston and Boulton in 1926-27 before joining Leeds in July 1927. He may have only featured 16 times in the promotion year of 1927-28, but he hit 18 goals as Leeds scored 98 in total and finished runners-up in the Second Division. He hit three hat-tricks, all at Elland Road, against Bristol City, Notts County and Clapton Orient respectively. He went on to top the goalscoring charts in 1928-29 with 23, starting the season with another hat-trick again at home, this time against Aston Villa. Two more three-goal hauls followed at home to Leicester City and at home to Everton as Leeds finished in 13th place back in the First Division. He kept on scoring goals and hit double figures every season bar his last full one in 1933-34, when he hit seven, though that was in 16 games. He ended his Leeds career with a goal ratio of 1.5 goals per game. He left Leeds for west Yorkshire rivals Bradford City in October 1934 and passed away in 1979.

TOM COCHRANE

Debut: Manchester City (H) 20 October 1928
Appearances: 259
Goals: 27

Born in Newcastle, Cochrane had trials with Hull City and Sheffield Wednesday before joining Leeds in August 1928. He was spotted at his first club St Peters Albion by Dick Ray, who by this time was the manager at Leeds and remembered Cochrane's display. An outside-left, he made 13 appearances as Leeds adjusted to life back in the First Division, scoring in a 5-1 hammering over Exeter City in an FA Cup third-round replay at Elland Road. Ten appearances followed in the last season of the decade before he started to establish himself at the start of the 1930s. Three goals in 28 games was his return in 1930-31, but his best season came in 1931-32 as Leeds finished runners-up in the Second Division. He scored nine goals in 42 games, including a brace in a 5-0 win over Burnley at Turf Moor in November 1931. He became a regular over the next four seasons, helping Leeds to win promotion in 1932, building a vital partnership with Billy Furness, missing just three games between August 1934 and May 1936. His final game for Leeds was a 3-0 defeat away to Huddersfield at the start of October 1936 and he went onto to join Middlesbrough for £2,500 that same month. He died in Cleveland in 1976.

JACK MILBURN

Debut: The Wednesday (H) 17 November 1928
Appearances: 413
Goals: 30

The oldest of the Milburn clan to play for Leeds United, Milburn had two spells with the Whites, playing for the club during the Second World War. His famous cousin was Jackie Milburn who had a fantastic career at Newcastle United and his nephews were a certain Bobby and Jack Charlton. To add intrigue, Milburn was married to goalkeeper Jimmy Potts's sister. He started his career at Spen Black and White before signing for Leeds in November 1928 and made his debut at home to The Wednesday, but only featured five times that season. It would be the 1929-30 season when Milburn would settle in to the first team, making 40 appearances as Leeds finished in their highest position of fifth in the First Division. He became a mainstay in the Leeds side, making at least 30 appearances every season bar his last, and he captained the side on 80 occasions. He became a member of the 400-appearance club, scoring 30 goals along the way before joining Norwich City in February 1939. With the start of the Second World War, Milburn returned to Leeds as he guested for the Whites in 64 war-time games before suffering a broken leg against Barnsley. Milburn passed away in Leeds aged 71 in August 1979.

MANAGERS APPOINTED IN THE 1920s

ARTHUR FAIRCLOUGH

First game in charge: Port Vale (A) 28 August 1920
Last game in charge: The Wednesday (A) 7 May 1927
Games 309
Won 111
Drawn 77
Lost 121

The first ever incumbent in the manager's hot seat at Elland Road, Fairclough was officially appointed by the board of directors on 26 February 1920. Previous experience listed was player-secretary of a Barnsley junior side and he then became club secretary of Barnsley football club. In 1904 he was given the role of manager-secretary at the south Yorkshire club and led the Tykes to the 1910 FA Cup Final, which they lost 2-0 to Newcastle after a replay. Two years later he succeeded, beating West Bromwich Albion after a replay. Come April 1912, Fairclough had moved to neighbours Huddersfield Town, whilst Hilton Crowther was chairman. Following the dismissal of Leeds City and Crowther's move to Leeds, Fairclough resigned at Huddersfield to join Leeds. Fairclough had taken over from Dick Ray, who had held the position whilst the side were in the Midland League and Ray was subsequently appointed Fairclough's assistant. His first-ever game in charge of the Whites was a 2-0 loss away at Port Vale and his first-ever captain at Elland Road was Jim Baker.

In his first season at the club the side ended up in 14th place, with Robert Thompson being the first top scorer under his leadership with 11 goals. His second season in charge saw an improvement as Leeds finished in eighth place in the Second Division, this time with Tommy Howarth top of the charts with 13 goals. Further improvement was seen 12 months later as the side finished seventh, only six points off the top spot.

By the end of his third campaign, Ray had left the club to join Yorkshire rivals Doncaster Rovers, who had just been elected into Division Three North. Fairclough replaced him with Blackpool manager Dick Norman and the partnership, which had worked so well at Barnsley, once again worked wonders as Leeds, in only their fourth competitive season, won the Second Division, finishing three points clear of nearest rivals Bury. Jack Swann top scored with 18 goals, with Joe Richmond 15 goals and Percy Whipp 11 goals nipping in just behind.

Fairclough's first season in the top flight saw the side struggle at first, but thanks to the signings of Russell Wainscoat, Tom Jennings and Willis Edwards they finished in 18th place. The following season was more of the same as the side finished in 19th place, a point ahead of the drop zone, and worse was to follow 12 months later as the side were relegated, finishing in 21st place, four points adrift of safety. Fairclough resigned at the end of that season and was replaced by his former assistant Dick Ray. He passed away aged 74 in Sheffield on 19 March 1947.

Arthur Fairclough's first line up: Port Vale (A) 28 August 1920: Down, Duffield, Tillotson, Musgrove, Baker, Walton, Mason, Goldthorpe, Thompson, Lyon, Best.

Arthur Fairclough's last line up: Sheffield Wednesday (A) 7 May 1927: Potts, Roberts, Allan, Edwards, Townsley, Reed, Turnbull, White, Jennings, Wainscoat, Mitchell.

DICK RAY

First game in charge: South Shields (A) 27 August 1927
Last game in charge: Portsmouth (H) 2 March 1935
Games: 345
Won: 144
Drawn: 73
Lost: 128

Following Fairclough's decision to quit the job at the end of the 1926-27 season, Ray, who played for Leeds City and ran the side during the 1919-20 campaign when they competed in the Midland League, was appointed as secretary-manager at Elland Road. Ray was born in Newcastle-Under-Lyne on 4 February 1876 and he began his playing career at Macclesfield and would take in such clubs as Burslem Port Vale, Crewe Alexandra, Manchester City, Stockport County and eventually Leeds City.

As mentioned in Fairclough's biography, he was appointed his assistant manager before a move to Doncaster Rovers. His first task when appointed was to achieve promotion back to the top flight, and he did this in style as the club finished on 57 points, two goals shy of the century. Tom Jennings hit 21 goals in 26 games, Charlie Keetley 18 in 16 and Russell Wainscoat with another 18 as Leeds returned to the top flight at the very first attempt.

The Whites first season back in England's top table saw the side finish in a respectable 13th place and the following year would be even better as they finished in the top five for the first time in the club's history. This was a record that would not be bettered until the arrival of a certain Don Revie. The following season proved to be a disappointing one for Ray and Leeds, despite the goals of Charlie Keetley, who finished with 16, they were relegated to the Second Division. However, just like in his first season in charge, they bounced back immediately as they finished second, two points behind champions Wolverhampton Wanderers, with that man Keetley top scorer once more with 23 goals. Ray consolidated the side in the First Division, finishing in a credible eighth place and completing an FA Cup run to the last 16 that was ended by Everton in front of over 58,000 fans at Goodison Park. He followed this up with a ninth-place finish in season 1933-34, but he resigned on 5 March 1935 and the following month was installed as Bradford City's new manager. The Football League appointed Ray as their first-ever manager of a Football League representative team for a 2-2 draw with the Scottish League at Ibrox. He also worked as chief scout for Millwall in his later years and ran a garage business and billiard clubs. He died aged 76 on 28 December 1952.

Dick Ray's first line up: South Shields (A) 27 August 1927: Potts, Roberts, Menzies, Edwards, Townsley, Reed, Turnbull, White, Jennings, Wainscoat, Mitchell.

Dick Ray's last line up: Portsmouth (H) 2 March 1935: Savage, G. Milburn, J. Milburn, Edwards, Hart, Hornby, Duggan, J. Kelly, Hydes, Stephenson, Mahon.

DIVISION TWO

1920–21

Date	Opposition	Competition	Score
28/08/1920	Port Vale	Division Two	0-2
01/09/1920	South Shields	Division Two	1-2
04/09/1920	Port Vale	Division Two	3-1
08/09/1920	South Shields	Division Two	0-3
11/09/1920	Leicester City	Division Two	1-1
11/09/1920	Boothtown	FA Cup 1st Qualifying Round	5-2
18/09/1920	Leicester City	Division Two	3-1
25/09/1920	Blackpool	Division Two	0-1
25/09/1920	Leeds Steelworks*	FA Cup 2nd Qualifying Round**	7-0
02/10/1920	Blackpool	Division Two	2-0
09/10/1920	Sheffield Wednesday	Division Two	0-2
16/10/1920	Sheffield Wednesday	Division Two	2-0
23/10/1920	Hull City	Division Two	1-0
30/10/1920	Hull City	Division Two	1-1
06/11/1920	Stoke City	Division Two	0-4
13/11/1920	Stoke City	Division Two	0-0
27/11/1920	Coventry City	Division Two	1-1
01/12/1920	Coventry City	Division Two	4-0
04/12/1920	Notts County	Division Two	2-1
11/12/1920	Notts County	Division Two	3-0
18/12/1920	Birmingham City	Division Two	0-1
25/12/1920	Fulham	Division Two	0-0
27/12/2020	Fulham	Division Two	0-1
01/01/1921	Birmingham City	Division Two	1-0
08/01/1921	Rotherham County	Division Two	1-0
15/01/1921	Wolverhampton Wanderers	Division Two	0-3
22/01/1921	Wolverhampton Wanderers	Division Two	3-0
29/01/1921	West Ham United	Division Two	1-2
05/02/1921	West Ham United	Division Two	0-3
12/02/1921	Stockport County	Division Two	1-3
19/02/1921	Stockport County	Division Two	0-2
26/02/1921	Clapton Orient	Division Two	0-1
05/03/1921	Clapton Orient	Division Two	2-1
12/03/1921	Bury	Division Two	1-1
19/03/1921	Bury	Division Two	1-0
26/03/1921	Bristol City	Division Two	0-1
28/03/1921	Cardiff City	Division Two	0-1
29/03/1921	Cardiff City	Division Two	1-2
02/04/1921	Bristol City	Division Two	0-0
13/04/1921	Barnsley	Division Two	0-0
16/04/1921	Barnsley	Division Two	1-1
23/04/1921	Nottingham Forest	Division Two	1-1
30/04/1921	Nottingham Forest	Division Two	0-1
07/05/1921	Rotherham County	Division Two	2-0

Team	Pld	W	D	L	GF	GA	Pts
Birmingham	42	24	10	8	79	38	58
Cardiff City	42	24	10	8	59	32	58
Bristol City	42	19	13	10	49	29	51
Blackpool	42	20	10	12	54	42	50
West Ham United	42	19	10	13	51	30	48
Notts County	42	18	11	13	55	40	47
Clapton Orient	42	16	13	13	43	42	45
South Shields	42	17	10	15	61	46	44
Fulham	42	16	10	16	43	47	42
Sheffield Wednesday	42	15	11	16	48	48	41
Bury	42	15	10	17	45	49	40
Leicester City	42	12	16	14	39	46	40
Hull City	42	10	20	12	43	53	40
Leeds United	42	14	10	18	40	45	38
Wolverhampton W	42	16	6	20	49	66	38
Barnsley	42	10	16	16	48	50	36
Port Vale	42	11	14	17	43	49	36
Nottingham Forest	42	12	12	18	48	55	36
Rotherham County	42	12	12	18	37	53	36
Stoke	42	12	11	19	46	56	35
Coventry City	42	12	11	19	39	70	35
Stockport County	42	9	12	21	42	75	30

Leeds first-ever season in the football League saw a new captain, Jim Baker.

The club's first-ever colours were blue-and-white striped shirts and white shorts.

Jim Baker, alongside Billy Down and Albert Dudfield, were ever-presents (apart from the FA Cup ties which were played on the same day).

Leeds withdrew from the FA Cup after they were unwilling to compete in eight games to reach the first round proper.

Len Armitage created history as he became the side's first-ever goalscorer in a 2-1 home defeat against South Shields.

Fixture list
Home Fixtures
Away Fixtures

1921–22

DIVISION TWO

Team	Pld	W	D	L	GF	GA	Pts
Nottingham Forest	42	22	12	8	51	30	56
Stoke	42	18	16	8	60	44	52
Barnsley	42	22	8	12	67	52	52
West Ham United	42	20	8	14	52	39	48
Hull City	42	19	10	13	51	41	48
South Shields	42	17	12	13	43	38	46
Fulham	42	18	9	15	57	38	45
Leeds United	42	16	13	13	48	38	45
Leicester City	42	14	17	11	39	34	45
Sheffield Wednesday	42	15	14	13	47	50	44
Bury	42	15	10	17	54	55	40
Derby County	42	15	9	18	60	64	39
Notts County	42	12	15	15	47	51	39
Crystal Palace	42	13	13	16	45	51	39
Clapton Orient	42	15	9	18	43	50	39
Rotherham County	42	14	11	17	32	43	39
Wolverhampton W	42	13	11	18	44	49	37
Port Vale	42	14	8	20	43	57	36
Blackpool	42	15	5	22	44	57	35
Coventry City	42	12	10	20	51	60	34
Bradford Park Avenue	42	12	9	21	46	62	33
Bristol City	42	12	9	21	37	58	33

Captain Jim Baker kept up his ever-present tag from last season by repeating the feat 12 months later.

Billy Poyntz created unwanted history away at Bury when he became the first Leeds United player to be sent off.

Just nine days later it was a complete turnaround as he scored a hat-trick at home to Leicester City just hours affter getting married.

Leeds used three goalkeepers, Fred Whalley, Billy Down and Harold Jacklin.

Following their withdrawal the previous season from the FA Cup, Leeds entered the competition at the first-round stage, losing 2-1 away at Swindon Town.

Date	Opposition	Competition	Score
27/08/1921	**Port Vale**	**Division Two**	**2-1**
29/08/1921	Bristol City	Division Two	0-0
03/09/2021	Port Vale	Division Two	1-0
05/09/1921	**Bristol City**	**Division Two**	**3-0**
10/09/1921	**Blackpool**	**Division Two**	**0-0**
17/09/1921	Blackpool	Division Two	3-1
24/09/1921	**Clapton Orient**	**Division Two**	**2-0**
01/10/1921	Clapton Orient	Division Two	2-4
08/10/1921	**South Shields**	**Division Two**	**0-0**
15/10/1921	South Shields	Division Two	1-0
22/10/1921	**Stoke**	**Division Two**	**1-2**
29/10/1921	Stoke	Division Two	0-3
05/11/1921	**Bradford Park Avenue**	**Division Two**	**3-0**
12/11/1921	Bradford Park Avenue	Division Two	1-0
19/11/1921	Hull City	Division Two	0-1
26/11/1921	**Hull City**	**Division Two**	**0-2**
03/12/1921	Notts County	Division Two	1-4
10/12/1921	**Notts County**	**Division Two**	**1-1**
17/12/1921	**Crystal Palace**	**Division Two**	**0-0**
24/12/1921	Crystal Palace	Division Two	2-1
26/12/1921	**The Wednesday**	**Division Two**	**1-1**
27/12/1921	The Wednesday	Division Two	1-2
31/12/1921	**Rotherham County**	**Division Two**	**0-2**
07/01/1922	Swindon Town	FA Cup 1st Round	1-2
14/01/1922	Rotherham County	Division Two	0-1
21/01/1922	**West Ham United**	**Division Two**	**0-0**
28/01/1922	West Ham United	Division Two	1-1
04/02/1922	**Bury**	**Division Two**	**2-0**
11/02/1922	Bury	Division Two	1-2
20/02/1922	**Leicester City**	**Division Two**	**3-0**
25/02/1922	Leicester City	Division Two	0-0
04/03/1922	**Derby County**	**Division Two**	**2-1**
11/03/1922	Derby County	Division Two	0-2
18/03/1922	Coventry City	Division Two	0-1
25/03/1922	**Coventry City**	**Division Two**	**5-2**
01/04/1922	Barnsley	Division Two	2-2
08/04/1922	**Barnsley**	**Division Two**	**4-0**
14/04/1922	**Fulham**	**Division Two**	**2-0**
15/04/1922	Wolverhampton Wanderers	Division Two	0-0
17/04/1922	Fulham	Division Two	1-0
22/04/1922	**Wolverhampton Wanderers**	**Division Two**	**0-0**
29/04/1922	Nottingham Forest	Division Two	0-1
06/02/1922	**Nottingham Forest**	**Division Two**	**0-0**

Arthur Fairclough

DIVISION TWO
1922–23

Date	Opposition	Competition	Score
26/08/1922	Blackpool	Division Two	1-1
28/08/1922	Southampton	Division Two	1-0
02/09/1922	Blackpool	Division Two	0-1
04/09/1922	Southampton	Division Two	1-0
09/09/1922	Stockport County	Division Two	2-0
16/09/1922	Stockport County	Division Two	1-2
23/09/1922	Bradford City	Division Two	1-0
30/09/1922	Bradford City	Division Two	2-0
07/10/1922	Clapton Orient	Division Two	0-3
14/10/1922	Clapton Orient	Division Two	0-0
21/10/1922	Leicester City	Division Two	0-0
28/10/1922	Leicester City	Division Two	1-2
04/11/1922	West Ham United	Division Two	3-1
11/11/1922	West Ham United	Division Two	0-0
18/11/1922	South Shields	Division Two	0-1
25/11/1922	South Shields	Division Two	2-0
02/12/1922	Wolverhampton Wanderers	Division Two	1-0
09/12/1922	Wolverhampton Wanderers	Division Two	1-0
16/12/1922	Coventry City	Division Two	2-1
23/12/1922	Coventry City	Division Two	1-0
25/12/1922	Bury	Division Two	1-1
26/12/1922	Bury	Division Two	0-0
30/12/1922	Port Vale	Division Two	2-1
06/01/1923	Port Vale	Division Two	2-1
13/01/1923	Portsmouth	FA Cup 1st Round	0-0
17/01/1923	Portsmouth	FA Cup 1st Round Replay	3-1
20/01/1923	Manchester United	Division Two	0-0
27/01/1923	Manchester United	Division Two	0-1
03/02/1923	Bolton Wanderers	FA Cup 2nd Round	1-3
10/02/1923	Barnsley	Division Two	0-1
17/02/1923	The Wednesday	Division Two	0-0
24/02/1923	Barnsley	Division Two	1-1
03/03/1923	Hull City	Division Two	2-2
10/03/1923	Hull City	Division Two	1-3
17/03/1923	Crystal Palace	Division Two	0-1
19/03/1923	The Wednesday	Division Two	1-3
24/03/1923	Crystal Palace	Division Two	4-1
30/03/1923	Rotherham County	Division Two	2-0
31/03/1923	Fulham	Division Two	0-3
02/04/1923	Rotherham County	Division Two	1-3
07/04/1923	Fulham	Division Two	1-1
14/04/1923	Notts County	Division Two	0-1
21/04/1923	Notts County	Division Two	3-0
28/04/1923	Derby County	Division Two	1-0
05/05/1923	Derby County	Division Two	1-0

Team	Pld	W	D	L	GF	GA	Pts
Notts County	42	23	7	12	46	34	53
West Ham United	42	20	11	11	63	38	51
Leicester City	42	21	9	12	65	44	51
Manchester United	42	17	14	11	51	36	48
Blackpool	42	18	11	13	60	43	47
Bury	42	18	11	13	55	46	47
Leeds United	42	18	11	13	43	36	47
Sheffield Wednesday	42	17	12	13	54	47	46
Barnsley	42	17	11	14	62	51	45
Fulham	42	16	12	14	43	32	44
Southampton	42	14	14	14	40	40	42
Hull City	42	14	14	14	43	45	42
South Shields	42	15	10	17	35	44	40
Derby County	42	14	11	17	46	50	39
Bradford City	42	12	13	17	41	45	37
Crystal Palace	42	13	11	18	54	62	37
Port Vale	42	14	9	19	39	51	37
Coventry City	42	15	7	20	46	63	37
Clapton Orient	42	12	12	18	40	50	36
Stockport County	42	14	8	20	43	58	36
Rotherham County	42	13	9	20	44	63	35
Wolverhampton W	42	9	9	24	42	77	27

Captain Jim Baker made it three ever-presents in a row playing in 130 consecutive games by the end of the campaign.

Goalkeeper Fred Whalley was also an ever-present for the side.

Percy Whipp who finished as top scorer with 16, joined the club from Sunderland for a fee of £750!

Striker Joe Harris joined from Bristol City and finishd with five goals in his debut campaign for Leeds.

After a 0-0 draw at Old Trafford v Manchester United, Leeds actually topped the table, but went on to win only five of their last 17 League games.

1923–24

DIVISION TWO

Team	Pld	W	D	L	GF	GA	Pts
Leeds United	42	21	12	9	61	35	54
Bury	42	21	9	12	63	35	51
Derby County	42	21	9	12	75	42	51
Blackpool	42	18	13	11	72	47	49
Southampton	42	17	14	11	52	31	48
Stoke	42	14	18	10	44	42	46
Oldham Athletic	42	14	17	11	45	52	45
Sheffield Wednesday	42	16	12	14	54	51	44
South Shields	42	17	10	15	49	50	44
Clapton Orient	42	14	15	13	40	36	43
Barnsley	42	16	11	15	57	61	43
Leicester City	42	17	8	17	64	54	42
Stockport County	42	13	16	13	44	52	42
Manchester United	42	13	14	15	52	44	40
Crystal Palace	42	13	13	16	53	65	39
Port Vale	42	13	12	17	50	66	38
Hull City	42	10	17	15	46	51	37
Bradford City	42	11	15	16	35	48	37
Coventry City	42	11	13	18	52	68	35
Fulham	42	10	14	18	45	56	34
Nelson	42	10	13	19	40	74	33
Bristol City	42	7	15	20	32	65	29

Date	Opposition	Competition	Score
25/08/1923	Stoke	Division Two	1-1
27/08/1923	**Crystal Palace**	**Division Two**	**3-0**
01/09/1923	**Stoke**	**Division Two**	**0-0**
05/09/1923	Crystal Palace	Division Two	1-1
08/09/1923	Leicester City	Division Two	0-2
15/09/12923	**Leicester City**	**Division Two**	**1-2**
22/09/1923	Hull City	Division Two	2-1
29/09/1923	**Hull City**	**Division Two**	**5-2**
06/10/1923	Clapton Orient	Division Two	1-0
13/10/1923	**Clapton Orient**	**Division Two**	**1-0**
20/10/1923	Port Vale	Division Two	1-0
27/10/1923	**Port Vale**	**Division Two**	**3-0**
03/11/1923	**Bradford City**	**Division Two**	**1-0**
10/11/1923	Bradford City	Division Two	0-0
17/11/1923	**Barnsley**	**Division Two**	**3-1**
24/11/1923	Barnsley	Division Two	3-1
01/12/1923	**Manchester United**	**Division Two**	**0-0**
08/12/1923	Manchester United	Division Two	1-3
15/12/1923	**Bury**	**Division Two**	**1-2**
22/12/1923	Bury	Division Two	0-3
25/12/1923	Oldham Athletic	Division Two	2-2
26/12/1923	**Oldham Athletic**	**Division Two**	**5-0**
05/01/1924	South Shields	Division Two	0-2
12/01/1954	**Stoke**	**FA Cup 1st Round**	**1-0**
19/01/1924	The Wednesday	Division Two	0-0
26/01/1924	**The Wednesday**	**Division Two**	**1-0**
02/02/1924	West Ham United	FA Cup 2nd Round	1-1
06/02/1924	**West Ham United**	**FA Cup 2nd Round Replay**	**1-0**
09/02/1924	**Coventry City**	**Division Two**	**3-1**
16/02/1924	Bristol City	Division Two	1-0
23/02/1924	Aston Villa	FA Cup 3rd Round	0-3
27/02/1924	**South Shields**	**Division Two**	**2-1**
01/03/1924	Southampton	Division Two	1-0
08/03/1924	**Southampton**	**Division Two**	**3-0**
10/03/1924	Coventry City	Division Two	1-2
15/03/1924	**Fulham**	**Division Two**	**3-0**
19/03/1924	**Bristol City**	**Division Two**	**0-0**
22/03/1924	Fulham	Division Two	2-0
29/03/1924	**Blackpool**	**Division Two**	**0-0**
05/04/1924	Blackpool	Division Two	1-1
12/04/1924	**Derby County**	**Division Two**	**1-1**
18/04/1924	Stockport County	Division Two	1-1
19/04/1924	Derby County	Division Two	0-2
21/04/1924	**Stockport County**	**Division Two**	**4-0**
26/04/1924	**Nelson**	**Division Two**	**1-0**
03/05/1924	Nelson	Division Two	1-3

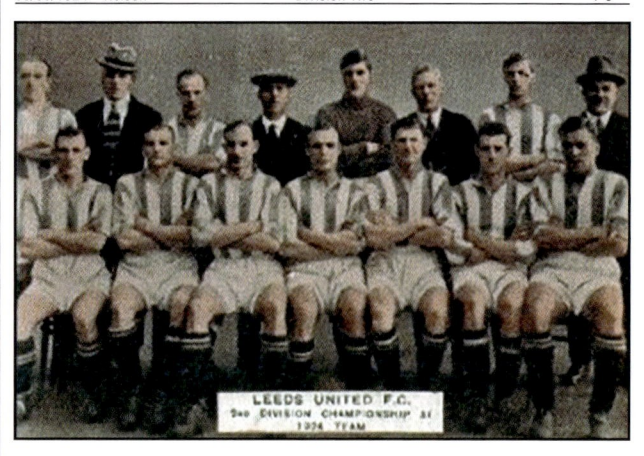

Before the season started assistant manager Dick Ray became manager at Doncaster Rovers and was replaced by Blackpool boss Bill Norman.

Jim Baker's proud run of consecutive games came to an end at 149 when he missed the 0-3 reverse at Bury.

This meant for the first time in the club's history they needed a new captain, and Bert Duffield took over.

With Duffield missing the next game at Oldham and Baker still out, Harry Sherwin lead the side.

As Leeds reached the top flight for the first time, Joe Harris was top of the appearance charts, missing just one game.

DIVISION ONE
1924–25

Date	Opposition	Competition	Score
30/08/1924	Sunderland	Division One	1-1
01/09/1924	Notts County	Division One	0-1
06/09/1924	Cardiff City	Division One	0-3
10/09/1924	Notts County	Division One	1-1
13/09/1924	Preston North End	Division One	4-0
17/09/1924	Everton	Division One	1-0
20/09/1924	Burnley	Division One	1-1
27/09/1924	Huddersfield Town	Division One	1-1
04/10/1924	Birmingham	Division One	0-1
11/10/1924	West Bromwich Albion	Division One	1-3
18/10/1924	Tottenham Hotspur	Division One	1-0
25/10/1924	Blackburn Rovers	Division One	3-2
01/11/1924	West Ham United	Division One	2-1
08/11/1924	Sheffield United	Division One	1-1
15/11/1924	Newcastle United	Division One	1-1
22/11/1924	Liverpool	Division One	0-1
29/11/1924	Nottingham Forest	Division One	1-1
06/12/1924	Bury	Division One	0-1
13/12/1924	Manchester City	Division One	0-3
20/12/1924	Arsenal	Division One	1-6
25/12/1924	Aston Villa	Division One	6-0
26/12/1924	Aston Villa	Division One	1-2
27/12/1924	Sunderland	Division One	1-2
03/01/1925	Cardiff City	Division One	0-0
10/01/1925	Liverpool	FA Cup 1st Round	0-1
17/01/1925	Preston North End	Division One	4-1
24/01/1925	Burnley	Division One	0-2
31/01/1925	Huddersfield Town	Division One	0-2
07/02/1925	Birmingham	Division One	0-0
14/02/1925	West Bromwich Albion	Division One	0-1
28/02/1925	Blackburn Rovers	Division One	1-1
07/03/1925	West Ham United	Division One	0-0
09/03/1925	Tottenham Hotspur	Division One	1-2
14/03/1925	Sheffield United	Division One	1-1
21/03/1925	Newcastle United	Division One	1-4
28/03/1925	Liverpool	Division One	4-1
04/04/1925	Nottingham Forest	Division One	0-4
10/04/1925	Bolton Wanderers	Division One	0-1
11/04/1925	Bury	Division One	1-0
14/04/1925	Bolton Wanderers	Division One	2-1
18/04/1925	Manchester City	Division One	2-4
25/04/1925	Arsenal	Division One	1-0
02/05/1925	Everton	Division One	0-1

Team	Pld	W	D	L	GF	GA	Pts
Huddersfield Town	42	21	16	5	69	28	58
West Bromwich Albion	42	23	10	9	58	34	56
Bolton Wanderers	42	22	11	9	76	34	55
Liverpool	42	20	10	12	63	55	50
Bury	42	17	15	10	54	51	49
Newcastle United	42	16	16	10	61	42	48
Sunderland	42	19	10	13	64	51	48
Birmingham	42	17	12	13	49	53	46
Notts County	42	16	13	13	42	31	45
Manchester City	42	17	9	16	76	68	43
Cardiff City	42	16	11	15	56	51	43
Tottenham Hotspur	42	15	12	15	52	43	42
West Ham United	42	15	12	15	62	60	42
Sheffield United	42	13	13	16	55	63	39
Aston Villa	42	13	13	16	58	71	39
Blackburn Rovers	42	11	13	18	53	66	35
Everton	42	12	11	19	40	60	35
Leeds United	42	11	12	19	46	59	34
Burnley	42	11	12	19	46	75	34
Arsenal	42	14	5	23	46	58	33
Preston North End	42	10	6	26	37	74	26
Nottingham Forest	42	6	12	24	29	65	24

Leeds had a new chairman at the helm as Major Albert Braithwaite replaced Hilton Crowther

As Leeds started their first-ever season in the First Division, a club-record crowd of 33,722 watched them on day one at home to Sunderland.

The side had just one ever-present with Joe Harris playing in every game.

Significant debuts half-way through the decade included Russell Wainscoat, Tom Jennings and Willis Edwards, who would all play a massive part in the club's future.

Like the previous season, Leeds had three captains when needed, Jim Baker, Bert Duffield and Harry Sherwin.

1925–26

DIVISION ONE

Team	Pld	W	D	L	GF	GA	Pts
Huddersfield Town	42	23	11	8	92	60	57
Arsenal	42	22	8	12	87	63	52
Sunderland	42	21	6	15	96	80	48
Bury	42	20	7	15	85	77	47
Sheffield United	42	19	8	15	102	82	46
Aston Villa	42	16	12	14	86	76	44
Liverpool	42	14	16	12	70	63	44
Bolton Wanderers	42	17	10	15	75	76	44
Manchester United	42	19	6	17	66	73	44
Newcastle United	42	16	10	16	84	75	42
Everton	42	12	18	12	72	70	42
Blackburn Rovers	42	15	11	16	91	80	41
West Bromwich Albion	42	16	8	18	79	78	40
Birmingham	42	16	8	18	66	81	40
Tottenham Hotspur	42	15	9	18	66	79	39
Cardiff City	42	16	7	19	61	76	39
Leicester City	42	14	10	18	70	80	38
West Ham United	42	15	7	20	63	76	37
Leeds United	42	14	8	20	64	76	36
Burnley	42	13	10	19	85	108	36
Manchester City	42	12	11	19	89	100	35
Notts County	42	13	7	22	54	74	33

Date	Opposition	Competition	Score
29/08/1925	Notts County	Division One	0-1
31/08/1925	Bolton Wanderers	Division One	2-1
05/09/1925	Aston Villa	Division One	2-2
07/09/1925	Bolton Wanderers	Division One	0-1
12/09/1925	Leicester City	Division One	3-1
16/09/1925	Newcastle United	Division One	2-0
19/09/1925	West Ham United	Division One	5-2
26/09/1925	Arsenal	Division One	1-4
03/10/1925	Manchester United	Division One	2-0
10/10/1925	Liverpool	Division One	1-1
17/10/1925	Huddersfield Town	Division One	0-4
24/10/1925	Everton	Division One	2-4
31/10/1925	Bury	Division One	2-3
07/11/1925	Blackburn Rovers	Division One	2-2
14/11/1925	Cardiff City	Division One	1-0
21/11/1925	Sheffield United	Division One	0-2
28/11/1925	West Bromwich Albion	Division One	0-1
05/12/1925	Birmingham	Division One	1-2
12/12/1925	Manchester City	Division One	3-4
19/12/1925	Tottenham Hotspur	Division One	2-3
25/12/1925	Burnley	Division One	2-2
26/12/1925	Burnley	Division One	3-6
01/01/1926	Sunderland	Division One	3-1
02/01/1926	Notts County	Division One	2-1
09/01/1926	Middlesbrough	FA Cup 3rd Round	1-5
23/01/1926	Leicester City	Division One	1-0
30/01/1926	West Ham United	Division One	2-4
03/02/1926	Aston Villa	Division One	1-3
06/02/1926	Arsenal	Division One	4-2
13/02/1926	Manchester United	Division One	1-2
20/02/1926	Liverpool	Division One	1-1
27/02/1926	Huddersfield Town	Division One	1-3
06/03/1926	Everton	Division One	1-1
13/03/1926	Bury	Division One	2-0
20/03/1926	Blackburn Rovers	Division One	2-0
27/03/1926	Cardiff City	Division One	0-0
03/04/1926	Sheffield United	Division One	2-0
05/04/1926	Newcastle United	Division One	0-3
06/04/1926	Sunderland	Division One	0-2
10/04/1926	West Bromwich Albion	Division One	0-3
17/04/1926	Birmingham	Division One	0-0
27/04/1926	Manchester City	Division One	1-2
01/05/1926	Tottenham Hotspur	Division One	4-1

Four players who had served the club so well during its early years, Jim Baker, Bert Duffield, Jack Swann and Joe Harris, would all depart the club during the season.

For the first time in the club's history, Leeds used six captains in a season, Duffield (3 games), Baker (9 games), Willis Edwards (1 game), Ernie Hart (5 games), Bill Menzies (5 games) and Tom Townsley (20 games).

Leeds used three different goalkeepers this term, Bill Johnson (30 games), Jimmy Potts (12 games) and Richard Thornton (1 game).

Top scorer Tom Jennings was the only ever-present for the side.

Willis Edwards became the first Leeds United player to be capped by England.

DIVISION ONE

1926–27

Date	Opposition	Competition	Score
28/08/1926	Bolton Wanderers	Division One	2-5
30/08/1926	Cardiff City	Division One	0-0
04/09/1926	Manchester United	Division One	2-2
06/09/1926	Cardiff City	Division One	1-3
11/09/1926	Derby County	Division One	1-0
15/09/1926	Aston Villa	Division One	3-1
18/09/1926	Sheffield United	Division One	0-1
25/09/1926	Arsenal	Division One	4-1
02/10/1926	Liverpool	Division One	4-2
09/10/1926	Blackburn Rovers	Division One	4-1
16/10/1926	Leicester City	Division One	2-3
23/10/1926	Everton	Division One	1-3
30/10/1926	Huddersfield Town	Division One	1-4
06/11/1926	Sunderland	Division One	2-2
13/11/1926	West Bromwich Albion	Division One	4-2
20/11/1926	Bury	Division One	4-1
27/11/1926	Birmingham	Division One	0-2
04/12/1926	Tottenham Hotspur	Division One	1-1
11/12/1926	West Ham United	Division One	2-3
18/12/1926	The Wednesday	Division One	4-1
27/12/1926	Newcastle United	Division One	1-2
28/12/1926	Aston Villa	Division One	1-5
01/01/1927	Newcastle United	Division One	0-1
08/01/1927	Sunderland	FA Cup 3rd Round	3-2
15/01/1927	Bolton Wanderers	Division One	0-3
22/01/1927	Manchester United	Division One	2-3
29/01/1927	Bolton Wanderers	FA Cup 4th Round	0-0
02/02/1927	Bolton Wanderers	FA Cup 4th Round Replay	0-3
05/02/1927	Sheffield United	Division One	1-1
12/02/1927	Arsenal	Division One	0-1
19/02/1927	Derby County	Division One	0-1
23/02/1927	Liverpool	Division One	0-0
26/02/1927	Blackburn Rovers	Division One	1-4
05/03/1927	Leicester City	Division One	1-1
12/03/1927	Everton	Division One	1-2
19/03/1927	Huddersfield Town	Division One	1-1
26/03/1927	Sunderland	Division One	2-6
02/04/1927	West Bromwich Albion	Division One	3-1
09/04/1927	Bury	Division One	2-4
15/04/1927	Burnley	Division One	2-3
16/04/1927	Birmingham	Division One	2-1
19/04/1927	Burnley	Division One	0-2
23/04/1927	Tottenham Hotspur	Division One	1-4
30/04/1927	West Ham United	Division One	6-3
07/05/1927	The Wednesday	Division One	0-1

Team	Pld	W	D	L	GF	GA	Pts
Newcastle United	42	25	6	11	96	58	56
Huddersfield Town	42	17	17	8	76	60	51
Sunderland	42	21	7	14	98	70	49
Bolton Wanderers	42	19	10	13	84	62	48
Burnley	42	19	9	14	91	80	47
West Ham United	42	19	8	15	86	70	46
Leicester City	42	17	12	13	85	70	46
Sheffield United	42	17	10	15	74	86	44
Liverpool	42	18	7	17	69	61	43
Aston Villa	42	18	7	17	81	83	43
Arsenal	42	17	9	16	77	86	43
Derby County	42	17	7	18	86	73	41
Tottenham Hotspur	42	16	9	17	76	78	41
Cardiff City	42	16	9	17	55	65	41
Manchester United	42	13	14	15	52	64	40
Sheffield Wednesday	42	15	9	18	75	92	39
Birmingham	42	17	4	21	64	73	38
Blackburn Rovers	42	15	8	19	77	96	38
Bury	42	12	12	18	68	77	36
Everton	42	12	10	20	64	90	34
Leeds United	42	11	8	23	69	88	30
West Bromwich Albion	42	11	8	23	65	86	30

Despite relegation back to the Second Division, Tom Jennings hit 37 goals, in a season where the club scored 72!

He became the first player to score four goals in back-to-back games for the side.

His three hat-tricks in consecutive games at home to Arsenal, away at Liverpool and at home to Blackburn Rovers is a record that still stands today.

Jimmy Potts and Tom Townsley were the side's only ever-presents.

Leeds broke their club record with the £5,600 purchase of inside-forward John White from Heart of Midlothian as they looked to escape relelgation.

1927–28

DIVISION TWO

Team	Pld	W	D	L	GF	GA	Pts
Manchester City	42	25	9	8	100	59	59
Leeds United	42	25	7	10	98	49	57
Chelsea	42	23	8	11	75	45	54
Preston North End	42	22	9	11	100	66	53
Stoke City	42	22	8	12	78	59	52
Swansea Town	42	18	12	12	75	63	48
Oldham Athletic	42	19	8	15	75	51	46
West Bromwich Albion	42	17	12	13	90	70	46
Port Vale	42	18	8	16	68	57	44
Nottingham Forest	42	15	10	17	83	84	40
Grimsby Town	42	14	12	16	69	83	40
Bristol City	42	15	9	18	76	79	39
Barnsley	42	14	11	17	65	85	39
Hull City	42	12	15	15	41	54	39
Notts County	42	13	12	17	68	74	38
Wolverhampton W	42	13	10	19	63	91	36
Southampton	42	14	7	21	68	77	35
Reading	42	11	13	18	53	75	35
Blackpool	42	13	8	21	83	101	34
Clapton Orient	42	11	12	19	55	85	34
Fulham	42	13	7	22	68	89	33
South Shields	42	7	9	26	56	111	23

Date	Opposition	Competition	Score
27/08/1927	South Shields	Division Two	5-1
29/08/1927	Barnsley	Division Two	2-2
03/09/1927	Southampton	Division Two	2-0
10/09/1927	Nottingham Forest	Division Two	4-0
17/09/1927	Manchester City	Division Two	1-2
24/09/1927	Hull City	Division Two	2-0
26/09/1927	Barnsley	Division Two	1-2
01/10/1927	Preston North End	Division Two	1-5
08/10/1927	Swansea Town	Division Two	5-0
15/10/1927	Fulham	Division Two	1-1
22/10/1927	Grimsby Town	Division Two	2-3
29/10/1927	Oldham Athletic	Division Two	1-0
05/11/1927	Notts County	Division Two	2-2
12/11/1927	Reading	Division Two	6-2
19/11/1927	Blackpool	Division Two	2-0
26/11/1927	West Bromwich Albion	Division Two	1-2
03/12/1927	Clapton Orient	Division Two	1-2
10/12/1927	Chelsea	Division Two	5-0
17/12/1927	Bristol City	Division Two	2-1
24/12/1927	Stoke City	Division Two	5-1
26/12/1927	Port Vale	Division Two	2-1
27/12/1927	Port Vale	Division Two	3-0
31/12/2027	South Shields	Division Two	3-0
07/01/1928	Southampton	Division Two	4-1
14/01/1928	Manchester City	FA Cup 3rd Round	0-1
21/01/1928	Nottingham Forest	Division Two	2-2
28/01/1928	Bristol City	Division Two	3-2
04/02/1928	Hull City	Division Two	1-3
11/02/1928	Preston North End	Division Two	2-4
18/02/1928	Swansea Town	Division Two	1-1
25/02/1928	Fulham	Division Two	2-1
03/03/1928	Grimsby Town	Division Two	0-0
10/03/1928	Oldham Athletic	Division Two	1-0
17/03/1928	Notts County	Division Two	6-0
24/03/1928	Reading	Division Two	1-0
31/03/1928	Blackpool	Division Two	4-0
07/04/1928	West Bromwich Albion	Division Two	1-0
09/04/1928	Wolverhampton Wanderers	Division Two	0-0
10/04/1928	Wolverhampton Wanderers	Division Two	3-0
14/04/1928	Clapton Orient	Division Two	4-0
21/04/1928	Chelsea	Division Two	3-2
25/04/1928	Manchester City	Division Two	0-1
05/05/1928	Stoke City	Division Two	1-5

Following relegation it was the end of the road for Arthur Fairclough and former Leeds City captain Dick Ray took over

Ray's first signing was Charlie Keetley who would go on to score 110 goals for the side.

Leeds scored 98 goals in the league as they returned to the top flight at the first attempt, the closest the side have got to a century of goals in a league season.

Tom Townsley, George Reed and Tom Mitchell were ever-presents.

Leeds used two goalkeepers, Jimmy Potts (39 games) and Bill Johnson (4 games).

BACK ROW: JOHN ARMAND, WILLIS EDWARDS, TOM TOWNSLEY, JIMMY POTTS, BILL MENZIES, GEORGE REED, ALLAN ORE (ASSISTANT TRAINER)
FRONT ROW: BOBBY TURNBULL, JOHN WHITE, CHARLIE KEETLEY, RUSSELL WAINSCOAT, TOM MITCHELL, ERNIE HART

DIVISION ONE

1928–29

Date	Opposition	Competition	Score
25/08/1928	Aston Villa	Division One	4-1
27/08/1928	Bury	Division One	3-1
01/09/1928	Leicester City	Division One	4-4
08/09/1928	Manchester United	Division One	3-2
15/09/1928	Huddersfield Town	Division One	1-6
22/09/1928	Liverpool	Division One	1-1
29/09/1928	West Ham United	Division One	4-1
06/10/1928	Newcastle United	Division One	2-3
13/10/1928	Burnley	Division One	2-1
20/10/1928	Manchester City	Division One	4-1
27/10/1928	Everton	Division One	1-0
03/11/1928	Portsmouth	Division One	3-2
10/11/1928	Bolton Wanderers	Division One	1-4
17/11/1928	The Wednesday	Division One	0-2
24/11/1928	Derby County	Division One	4-3
01/12/1928	Sunderland	Division One	0-3
08/12/1928	Blackburn Rovers	Division One	1-0
15/12/1928	Arsenal	Division One	1-1
22/12/1928	Birmingham	Division One	1-5
25/12/1928	Cardiff City	Division One	3-0
26/12/1928	Cardiff City	Division One	1-2
29/12/1928	Aston Villa	Division One	0-1
01/01/1929	Bury	Division One	2-2
05/01/1929	Leicester City	Division One	4-3
12/01/1929	Exeter City	FA Cup 3rd Round	2-2
16/01/1929	Exeter City	FA Cup 3rd Round Replay	5-1
19/01/1929	Manchester United	Division One	2-1
26/01/1929	Huddersfield Town	FA Cup 4th Round	0-3
02/02/1929	Liverpool	Division One	2-2
09/02/1929	West Ham United	Division One	2-8
16/02/1929	Newcastle United	Division One	0-0
23/02/1929	Burnley	Division One	0-5
02/03/1929	Manchester City	Division One	0-3
09/03/1929	Everton	Division One	3-1
16/03/1929	Portsmouth	Division One	2-0
30/03/1929	The Wednesday	Division One	2-4
01/04/1929	Sheffield United	Division One	1-1
02/04/1929	Sheffield United	Division One	2-0
06/04/1929	Derby County	Division One	1-1
13/04/1929	Sunderland	Division One	1-2
20/04/1929	Blackburn Rovers	Division One	0-1
27/04/1929	Arsenal	Division One	0-1
29/04/1929	Bolton Wanderers	Division One	2-2
01/05/1929	Huddersfield Town	Division One	1-2
04/05/1929	Birmingham	Division One	0-1

Team	Pld	W	D	L	GF	GA	Pts
Sheffield Wednesday	42	21	10	11	86	62	52
Leicester City	42	21	9	12	96	67	51
Aston Villa	42	23	4	15	98	81	50
Sunderland	42	20	7	15	93	75	47
Liverpool	42	17	12	13	90	64	46
Derby County	42	18	10	14	86	71	46
Blackburn Rovers	42	17	11	14	72	63	45
Manchester City	42	18	9	15	95	86	45
Arsenal	42	16	13	13	77	72	45
Newcastle United	42	19	6	17	70	72	44
Sheffield United	42	15	11	16	86	85	41
Manchester United	42	14	13	15	66	76	41
Leeds United	42	16	9	17	71	84	41
Bolton Wanderers	42	14	12	16	73	80	40
Birmingham	42	15	10	17	68	77	40
Huddersfield Town	42	14	11	17	70	61	39
West Ham United	42	15	9	18	86	96	39
Everton	42	17	4	21	63	75	38
Burnley	42	15	8	19	81	103	38
Portsmouth	42	15	6	21	56	80	36
Bury	42	12	7	23	62	99	31
Cardiff City	42	8	13	21	43	59	29

Leeds had three captains as they returned to the First Division, Tom Townsley (40 games), Willis Edwards (3 games) and Russell Wainscoat, who did the job on the last day of the season.

Willis Edwards became the first Leeds United player to captain England v Ireland.

Ernie Hart also represented England and lined up alongside Edwards, the first time two Leeds players had represented England.

The side had no ever-presents, with George Reed, Russell Wainscoat and Bobby Turnbull playing in 42 out of the 45 games.

Two important debutants this term were Tom Cochrane and George Milburn who would play important roles in the club's future.

1929–30

DIVISION ONE

Team	Pld	W	D	L	GF	GA	Pts
Sheffield Wednesday	42	26	8	8	105	57	60
Derby County	42	21	8	13	90	82	50
Manchester City	42	19	9	14	91	81	47
Aston Villa	42	21	5	16	92	83	47
Leeds United	42	20	6	16	79	63	46
Blackburn Rovers	42	19	7	16	99	93	45
West Ham United	42	19	5	18	86	79	43
Leicester City	42	17	9	16	86	90	43
Sunderland	42	18	7	17	76	80	43
Huddersfield Town	42	17	9	16	63	69	43
Birmingham	42	16	9	17	67	62	41
Liverpool	42	16	9	17	63	79	41
Portsmouth	42	15	10	17	66	62	40
Arsenal	42	14	11	17	78	66	39
Bolton Wanderers	42	15	9	18	74	74	39
Middlesbrough	42	16	6	20	82	84	38
Manchester United	42	15	8	19	67	88	38
Grimsby Town	42	15	7	20	73	89	37
Newcastle United	42	15	7	20	71	92	37
Sheffield United	42	15	6	21	91	96	36
Burnley	42	14	8	20	79	97	36
Everton	42	12	11	19	80	92	35

Date	Opposition	Competition	Score
31/08/1929	Arsenal	Division One	0-4
07/09/1929	Aston Villa	Division One	4-1
11/09/1929	Everton	Division One	1-1
14/09/1929	Huddersfield Town	Division One	0-1
16/09/1929	Everton	Division One	2-1
21/09/1929	Sheffield Wednesday	Division One	2-1
23/09/1929	Portsmouth	Division One	1-0
28/09/1929	Burnley	Division One	3-0
05/10/1929	Sunderland	Division One	4-1
12/10/1929	Bolton Wanderers	Division One	2-1
19/10/1929	Birmingham	Division One	1-0
26/10/1929	Leicester City	Division One	2-2
02/11/1929	Grimsby Town	Division One	6-0
09/11/1929	Sheffield United	Division One	2-3
16/11/1929	West Ham United	Division One	1-3
23/11/1929	Liverpool	Division One	0-1
30/11/1929	Middlesbrough	Division One	1-2
07/12/1929	Blackburn Rovers	Division One	1-2
14/12/1929	Newcastle United	Division One	5-2
21/12/1929	Manchester United	Division One	1-3
25/12/1929	Derby County	Division One	2-1
26/12/1929	Derby County	Division One	0-3
28/12/1929	Arsenal	Division One	2-0
04/01/1930	Aston Villa	Division One	4-3
11/01/1930	Crystal Palace	FA Cup 3rd Round	8-1
18/01/1930	Huddersfield Town	Division One	0-1
25/01/1930	West Ham United	FA Cup 4th Round	1-4
01/02/1930	Burnley	Division One	3-0
08/02/1930	Sunderland	Division One	5-0
15/02/1930	Bolton Wanderers	Division One	2-4
22/02/1930	Birmingham	Division One	0-1
01/03/1930	Leicester City	Division One	1-2
08/03/1930	Grimsby Town	Division One	2-1
15/03/1930	Sheffield United	Division One	2-2
22/03/1930	West Ham United	Division One	0-3
29/03/1930	Liverpool	Division One	1-1
05/04/1930	Middlesbrough	Division One	1-1
09/04/1930	Sheffield Wednesday	Division One	3-0
12/04/1930	Blackburn Rovers	Division One	4-2
19/04/1930	Newcastle United	Division One	1-2
21/04/1930	Manchester City	Division One	1-4
22/04/1930	Manchester City	Division One	3-2
26/04/1930	Manchester United	Division One	3-1
03/05/1930	Portsmouth	Division One	0-0

Willis Edwards took over the captaincy from Tom Townsley, with Townsley now filling in when Edwards was out.

Russell Wainscoat finished as both the top appearance maker with 42 and top scorer with 18.

In the 2-1 win over Aston Villa at Elland Road, Harry Roberts became the first Leeds player to score two penalties in a match.

Leeds finished the season in fifth place in Division One, a placing that would not be bettered until season 1964-65.

The side recorded a 8-1 win over Crystal Palace in the FA Cup, a record that would stand until Leeds beat Spora Luxembourg 9-0 in October 1967.

BACK ROW: DICK RAY (MANAGER), GEORGE REED, ERNIE HART, JIMMY POTTS, GEORGE MILBURN, GEORGE WILSON, TOM JENNINGS, ARTHUR CAMPEY (TRAINER)
FRONT ROW: POPPY TURNBULL, JOHN WHITE, WILLIS EDWARDS, HARRY ROBERTS, RUSSELL WAINSCOAT, TOM MITCHELL

1930s
GOING DOWN, GOING UP, BEING CONSISTENT

The second decade of Leeds United's illustrious history started with high hopes that the Whites could challenge for the top honours. Despite opening the season with a 2-2 draw at home to Portsmouth, a 7-3 away win at Blackpool in mid-September and a 7-0 home win against Middlesbrough, Leeds found themselves in 21st place heading into the festive season. A 5-0 win over Manchester United, in which Bobby Turnbull scored a hat-trick, saw a slow improvement in form and a 0-0 draw in the reverse fixture at old Trafford saw Leeds in 16th position. A terrible run of seven games without a win saw the side drop to 21st and staring relegation in the face. A Turnbull penalty saw off Newcastle United at Elland Road, but back-to-back defeats at home to Arsenal (2-1) and Sheffield Wednesday at Hillsborough (2-1) kept Leeds in trouble. A 4-0 home win over Sheffield United kept hopes alive, but defeats at Bolton Wanderers (2-0) and Aston Villa (2-0) left Leeds staring into the abyss. Despite a final day 3-1 win at home to Derby, Blackpool's leveller against Manchester City sent Leeds down. Wilf Copping was the side's only ever-present.

Leeds Utd Team Shot, 1931-32, Stacey, George Milburn, Moore, Jack Milburn, Wilf Copping, Duggan, Hornby, Keetley, Bennett, Cochrane, Hart.

The following season started with the hope that Leeds could bounce back straight away. They started with a 2-0 win at Swansea Town with goals from Firth and Green, and come the 24 October a 2-1 win away at Charlton Athletic sent Leeds top of the pile and they wouldn't leave the top two all season. Some notable victories included a 5-2 at Manchester United in which goals came from Duggan, two from Firth and one each from Keetley and Furness, as well as a 5-0 win away at Burnley, kept Leeds in pole position and back-to-back 3-2 wins at home to Bradford Park Avenue and Swansea Town kept the Whites top going into the FA Cup. The run ended at the first hurdle with a 3-1 defeat away at QPR, but promotion was the main priority. A 3-2 defeat away at Plymouth Argyle dropped Leeds to second,

Billy Furness, , Leeds Utd, 1930s

but they bounced back with four wins in the next six. The side only won two of their last ten games, but by the time Southampton were beaten 1-0 at Elland Road, promotion was already assured. 9,588 fans saw the last game of a successful season at home to Port Vale as the Whites bounced back at the first attempt.

The following season saw little transfer activity and despite losing their opening two games, Leeds went on a 14-game unbeaten run, including a Yorkshire derby win over Sheffield Wednesday in which Keetley scored a brace, that saw the Whites climb up to sixth place in the First Division. They then took seven points from eight between 17 and 27 December, which pushed the side up to fourth but they dropped down to sixth after a 5-1 loss away at Derby County. Leeds did progress to the fifth round of the FA Cup, but were knocked out by Everton at Goodison Park. League form was very up and down. On 8 April the side lost 6-0 at Chelsea before bouncing back with a 6-1 win at home to Newcastle United just a week later. In the end the side finish in a respectable eighth place with Arthur Hydes top-scoring with 20 goals.

The fourth season of the decade saw manager Dick Ray sign Bert Sproston, who would go on to represent England. The season started inconsistently with Leeds as far down as 16th following a 4-0 loss away at Birmingham. The side then won their next three, before losing the next three after that, which saw the side in 14th place. Festive football saw Leeds win only one of four (a 4-0 win at home to Blackburn Rovers) and adding to that with an FA Cup third-round defeat at home to Preston North End. League form did pick up in the second half of the season, including a record 8-0 home win against Leicester City, in which there were braces for Duggan, Mahon, Furness and Firth. A 3-1 win on the final day saw Leeds finish in ninth place and Hydes again top scorer with 16 goals.

Sadly for Leeds, Wilf Copping was sold to Arsenal and early form was disastrous. An 8-1 defeat away at Stoke City was followed up weeks later by a 6-3 defeat away at West Bromwich Albion and Leeds found themselves in 18th place. Form did improve slightly with a 5-2 home win against Chelsea, and a 4-3 win at home to Derby County saw Leeds up to 15th, but a run of three consecutive defeats saw the side drop to 19th. Ray resigned on 5 March 1935 and was replaced by Billy Hampson, who had played for Leeds City during World War One. Hampson saw Leeds home with three wins in the last six games and they would finish the season in 18th place.

Hampson was now set for his first full season at the helm and signed goalkeeper Albert McInory, Jock McDougall and Jack Kelly. Early results were a worry, with Leeds hitting the bottom of the league following a 1-0 defeat at Chelsea in mid-September. However, slowly but surely, results did start to pick up and a 4-2 win over Aston Villa saw Leeds in 13th place. A 7-2 hammering over Sheffield Wednesday in which Duggan scored a hat-trick and a 5-2 win over Bolton Wanderers saw the side creep up to 11th in the table. Festive results were inconsistent – a 2-1 Boxing Day defeat at Sunderland was followed up with a 4-1 win over Stoke City at Elland Road just two days later. Leeds did reach the dizzy heights of seventh place after a 2-0 win at home to Chelsea and they stayed there after a 2-1 win away at west

Leeds Utd Team Shot, 1937, Billy Hampson, Bert Sproston, Jim Makinson, Reg Savage, Jack Milburn, Bobby Browne, Tom Holley, Front - Sammy Armes, George Ousley, Gordon Hodgson, Eric Stephenson, Arthur Buckley.

Yorkshire rivals Huddersfield Town. In the end it was the inconsistency that cost the side during the season and despite being in 18th place as late as the end of March, they ended up in 11th. George Brown topped the charts with 20 goals.

The following campaign couldn't have started in worse fashion for Hampson and Leeds with three straight defeats and four more followed in the next seven games. They were rock bottom and needed a pick me up. This came in the form of a 3-0 win at home to Everton, and despite a 2-1 reverse in the next game at Bolton, results did pick up and by then end of November, and following a 2-1 win over Manchester United at Elland Road, Leeds were in 17th place. However, results proved to be very up and down and by the time the new year came around, Leeds were in 19th place and struggling in front of goal. Chelsea knocked the side out of the FA Cup at the third round stage, which left Leeds concentrating on the league. Leeds needed a striker and in came Gordon Hodgson from Liverpool for £1,500. He marked his debut with the side's only goal in an embarrassing 7-1 defeat at Everton, but he would go on to score seven more as Leeds battled against the drop. A 3-0 defeat away at West Bromwich Albion dropped Leeds to the bottom, and going into the last two games of the season they were still there. Leeds rose to the occasion and won both games 3-0 at home to Sunderland and 3-1 at home to Portsmouth as the side stayed up.

Hampson knew he had work to do to get the Whites up the table, and former player Willis Edwards joined the coaching team at Elland Road. Early signs of progression was evident as the side were second in the league at the end of the September following a 2-0 win over Liverpool. They kept in and around the top six, going into the new year, and Hodgson was proving a goalscoring hero and ended the season with 26. On Christmas Day Middlesbrough were beaten 5-3 at Elland Road but just two days later they got their revenge in a 2-0 win at Ayersome Park. Hodgson scored all four in a thrilling 4-4 draw at home to Everton, but the side then went on a win-less streak of seven games, which dropped them to 12th. They picked themselves up to finish in ninth position, which was a massive improvement following the previous season's battle against the drop.

The following campaign saw no new arrivals and Hodgson kept on scoring. He became the first and to date the only Leeds player to score five in a game in a 8-2 win over Leicester City at the start of October which saw Leeds in sixth place. They hit third place after a 2-1 win at Blackpool and hopes were high at Elland Road. A winless streak of seven league games saw any hopes of a title challenge disappear, and following a 2-0 loss at Portsmouth at the start of March the side dropped down to 16th. Five wins in the last 11 saw them finish in 13th place and Hodgson finished as top scorer with 21.

The following league season was abandoned after three games in which Leeds lost them all and were bottom of the league before Neville Chamberlain declared that Britain was at war.

DEBUTANTS IN THE 1930s

WILF COPPING

Debut: Portsmouth (H) 30 August 1930
Appearances: 183
Goals: 4

Copping was born in Barnsley and had two spells in the 1930s at Elland Road, signing from Middlecliffe Rovers in March 1930 despite having a trial with his home-town club the year before. He was nicknamed the 'Iron Man' of football as he rarely shaved before a game! He made his debut on the opening day of the 1930-31 season as Leeds were relegated to the Second Division, but Copping was an ever-present, scoring just the once in a 1-1 draw at home to Sheffield United at the start of March 1931. The following season was one of great success for both Copping and the side as they bounced back at the first attempt, finishing second, two points behind eventual champions Wolverhampton Wanderers. Copping missed just two games, a 3-1 win at home to Burnley and a 1-1 draw at Chesterfield. Season 1932-33 was more of the same as Copping missed just three games and this was same return 12 months later. He joined Arsenal in June 1934 for £6,000 and he would go on to win two League Championships and an FA Cup winner's medal with the north London club before returning north for a second spell at Elland Road. He played the first three games of the 1938-39 season before the league was abandoned due to the outbreak of World War Two.

During the war, Copping did feature 24 times as a war-time guest for Leeds. He passed away in Southend in June 1980.

ARTHUR HYDES

Debut: Huddersfield Town (H) 10 January 1931
Appearances: 137
Goals: 82

Born in Barnsley in 1911, Hydes started his career for Central School, Barnsley, before moving onto Ardsley United and then Barnsley in 1928-29. He had a brief trial at Southport at the start of the 1929-30 campaign, but he returned to play for Ardsley Recreation from where he would join Leeds in May 1930. He made a goalscoring debut in an FA Cup tie at home to Huddersfield Town in January 1931 and he would make four appearances in his first season, scoring one other goal a week later away to Blackburn Rovers. It was three goals in eight games for the striker the following year and he established himself in the side in 1932-33, scoring 20 goals in 43 games as Leeds finished in eighth place in the First Division. The next season was even better for Hydes as despite only playing in 19 games he finished the side's top scorer with 16 goals. The best was yet to come for the Barnsley-born forward, as he scored 25 goals in 33 matches, including seven in three games (two away at Middlesbrough, three at home to Blackburn Rovers and a further brace at home to Bradford Park Avenue). Sixteen goals in his final 30 games soon followed before he joined Newport County in May 1938. Hydes died in his home town in June 1990.

BERT SPROTSON

Debut: Chelsea (A) 23 December 1933
Appearances: 140
Goals: 1

Sprotson, who was born in Elsworth near Sandbach in Cheshire, was rejected by Huddersfield Town following at trial and joined Leeds from Sandbach Ramblers in May 1933. He made his debut two days before Christmas in 1933 and made just five appearances as Leeds looked to cement themselves as an established First Division side as he deputised for the injured George Milburn. Another 28 appearances followed in season 1934-35, but his best return, in terms of games for Leeds, would be the following campaign as he missed just two games as the Whites finished 11th in Division One. He made his England debut aged 21 in a 2-1 away defeat against Wales in October 1936. His 11th and last cap for the country was in a friendly away to Norway in November 1938. As for his career at Elland Road, Sprotson made a further 63 appearances for the side, scoring his one and only goal in a 1-1 draw away at

Wolverhampton Wanderers in March 1938. From Elland Road, he moved down south to the bright lights of London when he joined Tottenham Hotspur in June 1938 for a fee of £9,500. He had further spells at Manchester City, Aldershot, Wrexham, Port Vale and as a war-time guest with Millwall, before ending his career with Ashton United. He died in Bolton on 27 January 2000.

ERIC STEPHENSON

Debut: Portsmouth (H) 2 March 1935
Appearances: 112
Goals: 22

Inside-left Stephenson, born in Bexleyheath in Kent, moved to Leeds with his parents after his father had got a job there. His debut came mid-way through the decade (after signing professional forms with the side in September 1934 on his 12th birthday) in a 3-1 home win against Portsmouth at the start of March 1935, and he made four appearances scoring two goals that season. It was ten games and one goal the following year, but he hit the 22 games in terms of appearances with six goals in season 1936-37 as Leeds finished 19th in the top flight. His six goals that campaign came in games away at Stoke City, home to Everton, home to Brentford, home to Manchester United, home to West Bromwich Albion and home to Derby County.

Stephenson's best return during his time at Elland Road was starting 40 games in season 1937-38 as Leeds finished in a respectable ninth place in the top flight. His most memorable moment in a Leeds shirt came in a 4-3 win over Sunderland when he hit his one and only hat-trick for the side. His last official appearance for the side was on the final day of the 1938-39 season but he also featured in all three games during the abandoned season of 1939-40. He was tragically killed in action on 8 September 1944.

BOBBY BROWNE

Debut: Aston Villa (H) 26 October 1935
Appearances: 111

Browne who was born in Londonderry in Northern Ireland and first came to prominence when he was a member of the Irish League side that made history by beating the English League at Bloomfield Road, with the English side containing such players as Frank Swift and future Leeds manager Raich Carter. At the time Browne was playing for Derry City and joined Leeds for a fee of £1,500 in October 1935. By the time he made his Leeds United debut on 26 October 1935 he had already made his debut for Northern Ireland. He made 29 appearances in his first season at the club, as Leeds finished mid-table in 1935-36. He went on to make a further 63 appearances before the start of the Second World War and he made seven wartime guest appearances for Leeds. He did join the police but then resigned and became an army PT instructor in Aldershot. He went onto guest for Aldershot as well as Tottenham Hotspur, Luton Town and Swansea Town. He was then demobbed and went to play a further 19 times for Leeds, which included his 100th appearance for the side in a 4-2 loss away at Arsenal on 16 November 1946. He swapped west Yorkshire for north Yorkshire and joined York City in August 1947. He had a spell managing Thorne Colliery and became coach of Halifax Town in August 1954 where he had a brief spell as manager. He passed away in 1994.

TOM HOLLEY

Debut: Stoke City (A) 5 September 1936
Appearances: 167
Goals: 1

Sunderland-born Holley had a 13-year association with the club either side of World War Two, making over 160 appearances for the side. He started his career with Wolverhampton Boys, but his father took him to the North East to join his home-town club in 1931. He never made a first-team appearance for the Mackems and subsequently joined Barnsley in September 1932.

From Oakwell, Holley joined Leeds for £3,750 in July 1936. He made his first-team debut at the start of September 1936, making seven appearances that season, and he went on to make a further 63 appearances for the side before the intervention of the World War Two. He captained the side during the 1938-39 campaign as Leeds finished 13th in Division One.

Following the resumption of the league programme in season 1946-47, Holley was named as permanent Leeds captain, missing just three games as Leeds were relegated to the Second Division, finishing rock bottom with just 18 points. Another 56 appearances followed over the next two seasons under Willis Edwards and Major Frank Buckley, and he made his last appearance for Leeds in a 1-0 loss away at West Bromwich Albion at the start of April 1949. He retired from football to forge a career in sports journalism, writing about Leeds in the *Yorkshire Evening Post* and the *Sunday People*. He passed away in the year that Leeds last won the top flight in 1992.

AUBREY POWELL

Debut: Middlesbrough (H) 25 December 1936
Appearances: 118
Goals: 25

Powell, an inside-forward, was born in Lower Cwmtwrch in Glamorgan in April 1918 and started with Cwm Wanderers before moving to Swansea Town. He was still on amateur forms when he was spotted by Leeds United scouts and he made the move to west Yorkshire in November 1935. He made his debut on Christmas Day 1936 at home to Middlesbrough and scored twice in defeats away at Middlesbrough in his third game for the club and in a 4-1 defeat away at Brentford, as Leeds finished 19th in Division One. Sadly for Powell, his first season was curtailed following a broken leg away at Preston and he was told he would never play again. He returned over 18 months later in a 3-0 loss in September 1938 and went on to make 31 appearances that season, scoring four goals as Leeds ended up in 13th position in the top flight.

45

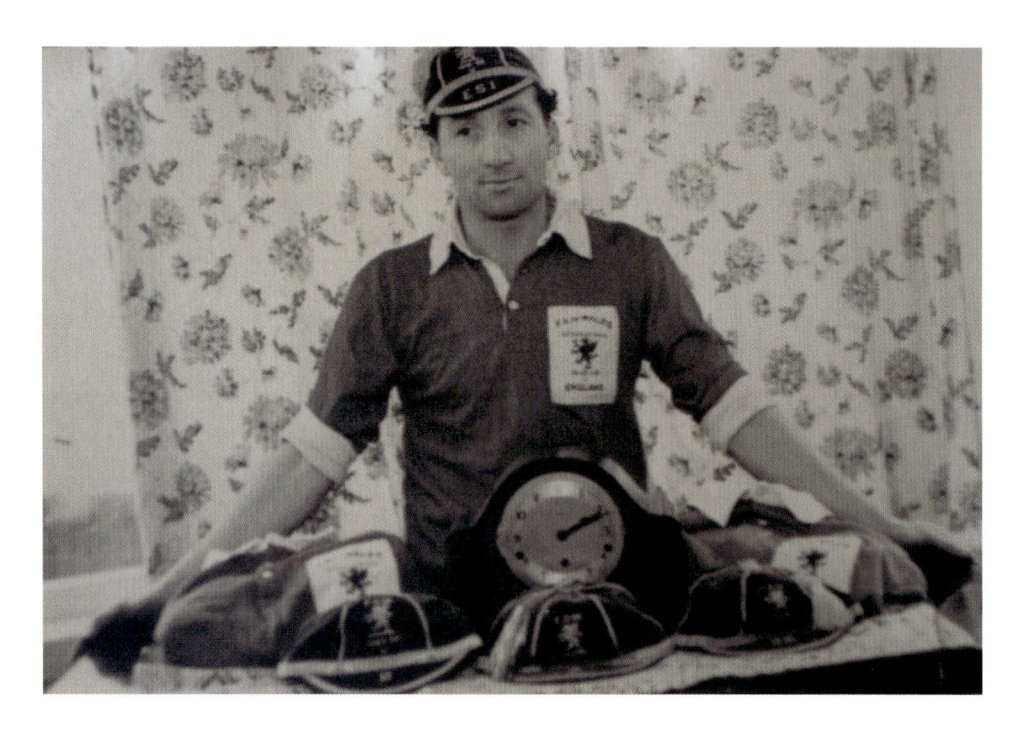

After the abandonment of league football following World War Two, Powell made 126 appearances in the war-time league and cup combined. The Welshman went on to feature a further 75 times, scoring 19 goals for the side. He was sold to Everton for £10,000 in June 1948. He did return to the city of Leeds as a confectionary rep until he retired aged 65. He died aged 90 in January 2009.

GORDON HODGSON

Debut: Everton (A) 3 March 1937
Appearances: 85
Goals: 53

Born in Johannesburg in South Africa in 1904, but an England international, Hodgson remains the only player in the club's history to score five goals in a game, achieving the feat in a record 8-2 win over Leicester City at the start of October 1938. Hodgson started his career back home in South Africa before heading to the United Kingdom to join Liverpool in November 1925. Incredibly, Hodgson scored 233 goals in 358 games for the reds before joining Aston Villa in January 1936 for £3,000. Compared to his stay at Anfield, his one at Villa Park was relatively short, joining Leeds in March 1937 for £1,500. In his first season in west Yorkshire, Hodgson hit six goals in 13 games, including one on his debut away at Everton. The following season saw Hodgson hit 26 goals in 38 games, including a four-goal salvo at home to Everton and a hat-trick at home to Brentford. His final year at Elland Road saw him break the Leeds United record for goals in a game at home to Leicester and he plundered a further 16 goals in 33 games under Billy Hampson. He retired from playing football following his spell in west Yorkshire and went on to become youth coach at Hartlepools United and later Port Vale manager in 1946. He passed away from cancer aged just 47 in 1951.

JIM TWOMEY

Debut: Blackpool (A) 19 March 1938
Appearances: 111

Northern Irishman Twomey had the honour of winning his first cap for his country whilst in the reserves at Elland Road. He started his career at Newry Town when he was just 15 years old and he was also a skilful boxer. He played on two occasions for the Irish League and it was a fantastic display against the Football League that brought him to the attention of Billy Hampson at Leeds. He joined the club in December 1937 and made his debut away at Blackpool on 19 March. Interestingly, he played against the same side seven days apart and between both games kept a clean sheet on his international debut against Wales. He played in the final ten games of the 1937-38 season, displacing Reg Savage and the following campaign played in 39 games. He played five times during war-time, and once the league campaign resumed in season 1946-47 Twomey featured 16 times, sharing number-one duties with

John Hodgson and Harry Fearnley. Another 46 games followed in the next two seasons and by January he was replaced by Harry Searson. He joined Halifax in August 1949, where he would later become trainer-coach. He did a great deal of charity work with the Leeds United ex-players Association before he passed away on 9 November 1984 aged 70.

DAVID COCHRANE

Debut: Derby County (H) 26 March 1938
Appearances: 183
Goals: 32

Born in Portadown in Northern Ireland in 1920, Cochrane started playing for Portadown Reserves aged 15 and turned professional five days later. He scored 14 goals in the league and cup and that alerted Leeds to him. They paid £2,000 to sign him in January 1937. He made his debut at home to Derby County in March 1938 (his only appearance that season), but it would be the last full season of the decade where he would establish himself in the Leeds side. He made 30 appearances, scoring five goals, including one in the famous 8-2 win over Leicester City where Gordon Hodgson scored five. His next two seasons following World War Two were exact replicas, scoring seven goals in 39 games as Leeds were first relegated to the Second Division and then finished in their lowest-ever league position of 18th.

The Northern Irishman went onto feature regularly under Major Frank Buckley over the next two seasons, playing in 72 games and scoring 13 goals, including playing in all the rounds of the FA Cup in season 1949-50 as Leeds bowed out to Arsenal in the last eight. He played in the opening two games of the 1950-51 season at home to Doncaster Rovers and away at Coventry City before somewhat surprisingly announcing his retirement from the game at the start of October 1950. He passed away in Leeds in June 2000, aged 79.

MANAGERS APPOINTED IN THE 1930s

BILLY HAMPSON

First game in charge: Everton (A) 6 March 1935
Last game in charge: Aston Villa (H) 19 April 1947
Games: 225
Won: 73
Drawn: 50
Lost: 102

Following Dick Ray's decision to resign at the start of March 1935, Hampson took charge and guided the side to safety, winning three of the side's last six games to finish in 18th place. Hamspon, who was born in Radcliffe, played for Rochdale, Bury and Norwich before moving to Newcastle United in January 1914. Sadly for Hampson, St James Park was closed during World War One and he had a lengthy spell as a guest at Leeds City before returning to Tyneside. He went on to become the oldest-ever FA Cup finalist at the age of 41 years and eight months when he appeared in the 1924 final when the Magpies defeated Aston Villa 2-0.

He left Newcastle for South Shields before taking over as manager at Carlisle United and is credited for discovering the great Bill Shankly. He had a short spell at Ashington before taking the reins at Elland Road. In his first full season at the club, and following a fight against the drop the previous year, Hampson consolidated the side to finish in 11th place, largely thanks to the goals of Jack Kelly and George Brown, the latter of whom had been signed the previous summer. The following term saw Leeds finish in 19th place, two points ahead of the dreaded relegation zone, but they improved massively the following year under Hampson's stewardship to finish in ninth place, with Gordon Hodgson finishing with 25 goals. The final season before World War Two again saw Leeds consolidate, finishing in 13th place, and Hodgson hit another 20 goals for the side.

League football was then postponed until the 1946-47 campaign (Leeds did play two FA Cup ties against Middlesbrough in 1945-46 and Hamspon did take the team during the war years), and it proved to be a disaster for both the manager and the club. Following a 1-1 draw at home to Aston Villa, Leeds were rock bottom, having won only six of 36 games, and were heading back to the Second Division. Hampson stepped down and was replaced by former player Willis Edwards. Hampson was made chief scout but only held the post for eight months. He passed away on 23 February 1966 in Congleton, Cheshire, aged 84. He had two brothers who also played football: Tom for Darlington and Walter for Charlton Athletic.

Billy Hampson's first line up: Everton (A) 6 March 1935: Savage, Sprotson, G. Milburn, Edwards, Hart, Hornby, Worsley, J. Kelly, Hydes, Stephenson, Cochrane.

Billy Hampson's last line up: Aston Villa (H) 19 April 1947: Twomey, Jim Milburn, Gadsby, Willingham, Holley, Browne, Cochrane, Powell, Clarke, Henry, Heaton.

DIVISION ONE

1930–31

Date	Opposition	Competition	Score
30/08/1930	**Portsmouth**	**Division One**	**2-2**
03/09/1930	Derby County	Division One	1-4
06/09/1930	Arsenal	Division One	1-3
08/09/1930	**Manchester City**	**Division One**	**4-2**
13/09/1930	**Blackburn Rovers**	**Division One**	**4-2**
17/09/1930	Manchester City	Division One	0-1
20/09/1930	Blackpool	Division One	7-3
27/09/1930	**Huddersfield Town**	**Division One**	**1-2**
04/10/1930	**Sunderland**	**Division One**	**0-3**
11/10/1930	Leicester City	Division One	0-4
18/10/1930	Liverpool	Division One	0-2
25/10/1930	**Middlesbrough**	**Division One**	**7-0**
01/11/1930	Newcastle United	Division One	1-4
08/11/1930	**Sheffield Wednesday**	**Division One**	**2-3**
15/11/1930	West Ham United	Division One	1-1
22/11/1930	**Chelsea**	**Division One**	**2-3**
29/11/1930	Grimsby Town	Division One	0-2
06/12/1930	**Bolton Wanderers**	**Division One**	**3-1**
13/12/1930	Aston Villa	Division One	3-4
20/12/1930	**Manchester United**	**Division One**	**5-0**
25/12/1930	Birmingham	Division One	1-0
26/12/1930	**Birmingham**	**Division One**	**3-1**
27/12/1930	Portsmouth	Division One	1-1
01/01/1931	Manchester United	Division One	0-0
10/01/1931	**Huddersfield Town**	**FA Cup 3rd Round**	**2-0**
17/01/1931	Blackburn Rovers	Division One	1-3
24/01/1931	**Newcastle United**	**FA Cup 4th Round**	**4-1**
28/01/1931	**Blackpool**	**Division One**	**2-2**
31/01/1931	Huddersfield Town	Division One	0-3
07/02/1931	Sunderland	Division One	0-4
14/02/1931	Exeter City	FA Cup 5th Round	1-3
18/02/1931	**Leicester City**	**Division One**	**1-3**
21/02/1931	**Liverpool**	**Division One**	**1-2**
28/02/1931	Middlesbrough	Division One	0-5
07/03/1931	**Newcastle United**	**Division One**	**1-0**
11/03/1931	**Arsenal**	**Division One**	**1-2**
14/03/1931	Sheffield Wednesday	Division One	1-2
21/03/1931	**West Ham United**	**Division One**	**3-0**
28/03/1931	Chelsea	Division One	0-1
04/04/1931	**Grimsby Town**	**Division One**	**0-0**
06/04/1931	Sheffield United	Division One	1-1
07/04/1931	**Sheffield United**	**Division One**	**4-0**
11/04/1931	Bolton Wanderers	Division One	0-2
18/04/1931	**Aston Villa**	**Division One**	**0-2**
02/05/1931	**Derby County**	**Division One**	**3-1**

Team	Pld	W	D	L	GF	GA	Pts
Arsenal	42	28	10	4	127	59	66
Aston Villa	42	25	9	8	128	78	59
Sheffield Wednesday	42	22	8	12	102	75	52
Portsmouth	42	18	13	11	84	67	49
Huddersfield Town	42	18	12	12	81	65	48
Derby County	42	18	10	14	94	79	46
Middlesbrough	42	19	8	15	98	90	46
Manchester City	42	18	10	14	75	70	46
Liverpool	42	15	12	15	86	85	42
Blackburn Rovers	42	17	8	17	83	84	42
Sunderland	42	16	9	17	89	85	41
Chelsea	42	15	10	17	64	67	40
Grimsby Town	42	17	5	20	82	87	39
Bolton Wanderers	42	15	9	18	68	81	39
Sheffield United	42	14	10	18	78	84	38
Leicester City	42	16	6	20	80	95	38
Newcastle United	42	15	6	21	78	87	36
West Ham United	42	14	8	20	79	94	36
Birmingham	42	13	10	19	55	70	36
Blackpool	42	11	10	21	71	125	32
Leeds United	42	12	7	23	68	81	31
Manchester United	42	7	8	27	53	115	22

Leeds were relegated to Division Two, despite the fact that Blackpool conceeded 125 goals and somehow survived.

Tom Jennings made his last appearance in a Leeds United shirt in a 2-1 home defeat to Liverpool. Jennings finished with 117 goals in 174 appearances.

Wilf Copping was the side's only ever-present during the campaign.

Leeds had three captains at the start of the decade, Willis Edwards did the job in 43 games, with Tom Townsley and Russell Wainscoat deputising.

The Whites used two goalkepers this campaign, Jimmy Potts played in 41 of the 45 games, with Bill Johnson playing in the other four.

1931–32

DIVISION TWO

Team	Pld	W	D	L	GF	GA	Pts
Wolverhampton W	42	24	8	10	115	49	56
Leeds United	42	22	10	10	78	54	54
Stoke City	42	19	14	9	69	48	52
Plymouth Argyle	42	20	9	13	100	66	49
Bury	42	21	7	14	70	58	49
Bradford Park Avenue	42	21	7	14	72	63	49
Bradford City	42	16	13	13	80	61	45
Tottenham Hotspur	42	16	11	15	87	78	43
Millwall	42	17	9	16	61	61	43
Charlton Athletic	42	17	9	16	61	66	43
Nottingham Forest	42	16	10	16	77	72	42
Manchester United	42	17	8	17	71	72	42
Preston North End	42	16	10	16	75	77	42
Southampton	42	17	7	18	66	77	41
Swansea Town	42	16	7	19	73	75	39
Notts County	42	13	12	17	75	75	38
Chesterfield	42	13	11	18	64	86	37
Oldham Athletic	42	13	10	19	62	84	36
Burnley	42	13	9	20	59	87	35
Port Vale	42	13	7	22	58	89	33
Barnsley	42	12	9	21	55	91	33
Bristol City	42	6	11	25	39	78	23

Date	Opposition	Competition	Score
29/08/1931	Swansea Town	Division Two	2-0
31/08/1931	Port Vale	Division Two	2-1
05/09/1931	Barnsley	Division Two	0-1
07/09/1931	Millwall	Division Two	0-1
12/09/1931	Notts County	Division Two	1-1
14/09/1931	Millwall	Division Two	3-2
19/09/1931	Plymouth Argyle	Division Two	0-0
26/09/1931	Bristol City	Division Two	2-0
03/10/1931	Oldham Athletic	Division Two	5-0
10/10/1931	Bury	Division Two	4-1
17/10/1931	Wolverhampton Wanderers	Division Two	2-1
24/10/1931	Charlton Athletic	Division Two	1-0
31/10/1931	Stoke City	Division Two	2-0
07/11/1931	Manchester United	Division Two	5-2
14/11/1931	Preston North End	Division Two	4-1
21/11/1931	Burnley	Division Two	5-0
28/11/1931	Chesterfield	Division Two	3-3
05/12/1931	Nottingham Forest	Division Two	3-3
12/12/1931	Tottenham Hotspur	Division Two	1-0
19/12/1931	Southampton	Division Two	1-2
25/12/1931	Bradford Park Avenue	Division Two	0-3
26/12/1931	Bradford Park Avenue	Division Two	3-2
02/01/1932	Swansea Town	Division Two	3-2
09/01/1932	Queens Park Rangers	FA Cup 3rd Round	1-3
16/01/1932	Barnsley	Division Two	2-0
23/01/1932	Notts County	Division Two	2-2
30/01/1932	Plymouth Argyle	Division Two	2-3
06/02/1932	Bristol City	Division Two	1-0
13/02/1932	Oldham Athletic	Division Two	1-2
20/02/1932	Bury	Division Two	1-0
27/02/1932	Wolverhampton Wanderers	Division Two	1-1
05/03/1932	Charlton Athletic	Division Two	2-0
12/03/1932	Stoke City	Division Two	4-3
19/03/1932	Manchester United	Division Two	1-4
26/03/1932	Preston North End	Division Two	0-0
28/03/1932	Bradford City	Division Two	1-4
29/03/1932	Bradford City	Division Two	1-1
02/04/1932	Burnley	Division Two	3-1
09/04/1932	Chesterfield	Division Two	1-1
16/04/1932	Nottingham Forest	Division Two	1-1
23/04/1932	Tottenham Hotspur	Division Two	1-3
30/04/1932	Southampton	Division Two	1-0
07/05/1932	Port Vale	Division Two	0-2

As the Whites returned to the top flight, Jack Miburn was the only ever-present in the side.

Russell Wainscoat started the first three games as captain, before moving on to pastures new, with Willis Edwards leading the team before Ernie Hart took over.

Like the previous season, Leeds used just two goalkeepers over 43 games, Jimmy Potts in 32 with Stan Morre playing in the other 11.

After beating Bristol City on 26 September 1931, Leeds went on a record nine-game winning run, which stood till October 1999!

Eric Clarke replaced Major Braithwaite as the chairman of the football club.

DIVISION ONE

1932–33

Date	Opposition	Competition	Score
27/08/1932	Derby County	Division One	0-2
29/08/1932	Blackpool	Division One	1-2
03/09/1932	Blackburn Rovers	Division One	1-1
05/09/1932	Blackpool	Division One	3-1
10/09/1932	Huddersfield Town	Division One	1-1
17/09/1932	Sheffield Wednesday	Division One	3-2
24/09/1932	West Bromwich Albion	Division One	1-0
01/10/1932	Birmingham	Division One	1-1
08/10/1932	Sunderland	Division One	0-0
15/10/1932	Manchester City	Division One	2-1
22/10/1932	Sheffield United	Division One	0-0
29/10/1932	Wolverhampton Wanderers	Division One	2-0
05/11/1932	Liverpool	Division One	1-0
12/11/1932	Leicester City	Division One	1-1
19/11/1932	Portsmouth	Division One	3-3
26/11/1932	Chelsea	Division One	2-0
03/12/1932	Newcastle United	Division One	1-3
10/12/1932	Aston Villa	Division One	1-1
17/12/1932	Middlesbrough	Division One	1-0
24/12/1932	Bolton Wanderers	Division One	4-3
26/12/1932	Arsenal	Division One	2-1
27/12/1932	Arsenal	Division One	0-0
31/12/1932	Derby County	Division One	1-5
07/01/1933	Blackburn Rovers	Division One	3-1
14/01/1933	Newcastle United	FA Cup 3rd Round	3-0
21/01/1933	Huddersfield Town	Division One	2-2
28/01/1933	Tranmere Rovers	FA Cup 4th Round	0-0
01/02/1933	Tranmere Rovers	FA Cup 4th Round Replay	4-0
04/02/1933	West Bromwich Albion	Division One	1-1
08/02/1933	Sheffield Wednesday	Division One	0-2
11/02/1933	Birmingham	Division One	1-2
18/02/1933	Everton	FA Cup 5th Round	0-2
22/02/1933	Sunderland	Division One	2-3
04/03/1933	Sheffield United	Division One	1-3
11/03/1933	Wolverhampton Wanderers	Division One	3-3
18/03/1933	Liverpool	Division One	5-0
25/03/1933	Leicester City	Division One	1-3
01/04/1933	Portsmouth	Division One	0-1
05/04/1933	Manchester City	Division One	0-0
08/04/1933	Chelsea	Division One	0-6
15/04/1933	Newcastle United	Division One	6-1
17/04/1933	Everton	Division One	1-0
18/04/1933	Everton	Division One	1-0
22/04/1933	Aston Villa	Division One	0-0
29/04/1933	Middlesbrough	Division One	0-1
06/05/1933	Bolton Wanderers	Division One	0-5

Team	Pld	W	D	L	GF	GA	Pts
Arsenal	42	25	8	9	118	61	58
Aston Villa	42	23	8	11	92	67	54
Sheffield Wednesday	42	21	9	12	80	68	51
West Bromwich Albion	42	20	9	13	83	70	49
Newcastle United	42	22	5	15	71	63	49
Huddersfield Town	42	18	11	13	66	53	47
Derby County	42	15	14	13	76	69	44
Leeds United	42	15	14	13	59	62	44
Portsmouth	42	18	7	17	74	76	43
Sheffield United	42	17	9	16	74	80	43
Everton	42	16	9	17	81	74	41
Sunderland	42	15	10	17	63	80	40
Birmingham	42	14	11	17	57	57	39
Liverpool	42	14	11	17	79	84	39
Blackburn Rovers	42	14	10	18	76	102	38
Manchester City	42	16	5	21	68	71	37
Middlesbrough	42	14	9	19	63	73	37
Chelsea	42	14	7	21	63	73	35
Leicester City	42	11	13	18	75	89	35
Wolverhampton W	42	13	9	20	80	96	35
Bolton Wanderers	42	12	9	21	78	92	33
Blackpool	42	14	5	23	69	85	33

Leeds had three ever-presents as they returned to the top tier, Jack and George Milburn played in all 46 games, as did Billy Furness.

The Whites has three debutants this term, Harry Roper, Harry O'Grady and Alan Fowler.

Ernie Hart was again skipper with Willis Edwards stepping in when needs be.

When Leeds defeated Liverpool at both Elland Road and Anfield, it was the first time of only three they have done the double over the Reds in the club's history.

On 27 December Leeds faced Arsenal at Elland Road in front of a record crowd of 56,796.

BACK ROW: HARRY O'GRADY, ALEX STACEY, GEORGE MILBURN, JIMMY POTTS, ERNIE HART, JACK MILBURN, WILF COPPING
FRONT ROW: HARRY DUGGAN, ARTHUR HYDES, CHARLIE KEETLEY, BILLY FURNESS, TOM COCHRANE

1933–34

DIVISION ONE

Team	Pld	W	D	L	GF	GA	Pts
Arsenal	42	25	9	8	75	47	59
Huddersfield Town	42	23	10	9	90	61	56
Tottenham Hotspur	42	21	7	14	79	56	49
Derby County	42	17	11	14	68	54	45
Manchester City	42	17	11	14	65	72	45
Sunderland	42	16	12	14	81	56	44
West Bromwich Albion	42	17	10	15	78	70	44
Blackburn Rovers	42	18	7	17	74	81	43
Leeds United	42	17	8	17	75	66	42
Portsmouth	42	15	12	15	52	55	42
Sheffield Wednesday	42	16	9	17	62	67	41
Stoke City	42	15	11	16	58	71	41
Aston Villa	42	14	12	16	78	75	40
Everton	42	12	16	14	62	63	40
Wolverhampton W	42	14	12	16	74	86	40
Middlesbrough	42	16	7	19	68	80	39
Leicester City	42	14	11	17	59	74	39
Liverpool	42	14	10	18	79	87	38
Chelsea	42	14	8	20	67	69	36
Birmingham	42	12	12	18	54	56	36
Newcastle United	42	10	14	18	68	77	34
Sheffield United	42	12	7	23	58	101	31

Date	Opposition	Competition	Score
26/08/1933	Blackburn Rovers	Division One	2-4
28/08/1933	Middlesbrough	Division One	5-2
02/09/1933	Newcastle United	Division One	3-0
09/09/1933	Huddersfield Town	Division One	0-0
16/09/1933	Derby County	Division One	1-3
23/09/1933	West Bromwich Albion	Division One	3-0
30/09/1933	Birmingham	Division One	0-4
07/10/1933	Sheffield Wednesday	Division One	2-1
14/10/1933	Manchester City	Division One	1-0
21/10/1933	Portsmouth	Division One	1-0
28/10/1933	Sunderland	Division One	2-4
04/11/1933	Aston Villa	Division One	2-4
11/11/1933	Liverpool	Division One	3-4
18/11/1933	Tottenham Hotspur	Division One	0-0
25/11/1933	Leicester City	Division One	2-2
02/12/1933	Stoke City	Division One	2-0
09/12/1933	Sheffield United	Division One	1-2
16/12/1933	Wolverhampton Wanderers	Division One	3-3
23/12/1933	Chelsea	Division One	1-1
25/12/1933	Arsenal	Division One	0-1
26/12/1933	Arsenal	Division One	0-2
30/12/1933	Blackburn Rovers	Division One	4-0
01/01/1934	Middlesbrough	Division One	1-2
06/01/1934	Newcastle United	Division One	0-2
13/01/1934	Preston North End	FA Cup 3rd Round	0-1
20/01/1934	Huddersfield Town	Division One	1-1
31/01/1934	Derby County	Division One	0-2
03/02/1934	West Bromwich Albion	Division One	3-0
10/02/1934	Birmingham	Division One	1-0
24/02/1934	Manchester City	Division One	3-1
26/02/1934	Sheffield Wednesday	Division One	2-0
07/03/1934	Portsmouth	Division One	1-2
10/03/1934	Sunderland	Division One	3-1
24/03/1934	Liverpool	Division One	5-1
30/03/1934	Everton	Division One	2-2
31/03/1934	Tottenham Hotspur	Division One	1-5
02/04/1934	Everton	Division One	0-2
07/04/1934	Leicester City	Division One	8-0
14/04/1934	Stoke City	Division One	2-1
21/04/1934	Sheffield United	Division One	1-1
28/04/1934	Wolverhampton Wanderers	Division One	0-2
30/04/1934	Aston Villa	Division One	0-3
05/05/1934	Chelsea	Division One	3-1

During the off season, Alf Masser took over the reins as chairman in place of Eric Clarke.

Goalkeeper Stan Moore was the side's only ever-present.

Leeds set a new scoreline record when they defeated Leicester City 8-0 at Elland Road on 7 April, a record that still stands today.

Manager Dick Ray was appointed the first manager of a Football League XI against a Scottish League XI.

Just the two debutants for the side this time round, Charlie Turner and Bert Sproston - the latter would go and play for England.

BACK ROW: CYRIL HORNBY, GEORGE MILBURN, STAN MOORE, FRED JONES, JACK MILBURN, WILF COPPING
FRONT ROW: JOHNNY MAHON, HARRY ROPER, ERNIE HART, CHARLIE KEETLEY, BILLY FURNESS, TOM COCHRANE

DIVISION ONE

1934–35

Date	Opposition	Competition	Score
25/08/1934	Middlesbrough	Division One	2-4
27/08/1934	Stoke City	Division One	1-8
01/09/1934	Blackburn Rovers	Division One	1-1
03/09/1934	Stoke City	Division One	4-2
08/09/1934	Arsenal	Division One	1-1
15/09/1934	Portsmouth	Division One	0-0
22/09/1934	Liverpool	Division One	0-3
29/09/1934	Huddersfield Town	Division One	2-0
06/10/1934	West Bromwich Albion	Division One	3-6
13/10/1934	Sheffield Wednesday	Division One	0-0
20/10/1934	Everton	Division One	2-0
27/10/1934	Grimsby Town	Division One	2-3
03/11/1934	Chelsea	Division One	5-2
10/11/1934	Wolverhampton Wanderers	Division One	2-1
17/11/1934	Sunderland	Division One	3-2
24/11/1934	Leicester City	Division One	0-1
01/12/1934	Derby County	Division One	4-2
08/12/1934	Aston Villa	Division One	1-1
15/12/1934	Preston North End	Division One	3-3
22/12/1934	Tottenham Hotspur	Division One	1-1
25/12/1934	Manchester City	Division One	1-2
26/12/1934	Manchester City	Division One	0-3
29/12/1934	Middlesbrough	Division One	3-3
05/01/1935	Blackburn Rovers	Division One	5-1
12/01/1935	Bradford Park Avenue	FA Cup 3rd Round	4-1
19/01/1935	Arsenal	Division One	0-3
26/01/1935	Norwich City	FA Cup 4th Round	3-3
30/01/1935	Norwich City	FA Cup 4th Round Replay	1-2
02/02/1935	Liverpool	Division One	2-4
09/02/1935	Huddersfield Town	Division One	1-3
20/02/1935	West Bromwich Albion	Division One	4-1
23/02/1935	Sheffield Wednesday	Division One	0-1
02/03/1935	Portsmouth	Division One	3-1
06/03/1935	Everton	Division One	4-4
09/03/1935	Grimsby Town	Division One	3-1
16/03/1935	Chelsea	Division One	1-7
23/03/1935	Wolverhampton Wanderers	Division One	1-1
30/03/1935	Sunderland	Division One	0-3
06/04/1935	Leicester City	Division One	0-2
13/04/1935	Derby County	Division One	2-1
19/04/1935	Birmingham	Division One	1-1
20/04/1935	Aston Villa	Division One	1-1
22/04/1935	Birmingham	Division One	1-3
27/04/1935	Preston North End	Division One	2-0
04/05/1935	Tottenham Hotspur	Division One	4-3

Team	Pld	W	D	L	GF	GA	Pts
Arsenal	42	23	12	7	115	46	58
Sunderland	42	19	16	7	90	51	54
Sheffield Wednesday	42	18	13	11	70	64	49
Manchester City	42	20	8	14	82	67	48
Grimsby Town	42	17	11	14	78	60	45
Derby County	42	18	9	15	81	66	45
Liverpool	42	19	7	16	85	88	45
Everton	42	16	12	14	89	88	44
West Bromwich Albion	42	17	10	15	83	83	44
Stoke City	42	18	6	18	71	70	42
Preston North End	42	15	12	15	62	67	42
Chelsea	42	16	9	17	73	82	41
Aston Villa	42	14	13	15	74	88	41
Portsmouth	42	15	10	17	71	72	40
Blackburn Rovers	42	14	11	17	66	78	39
Huddersfield Town	42	14	10	18	76	71	38
Wolverhampton W	42	15	8	19	88	94	38
Leeds United	42	13	12	17	75	92	38
Birmingham	42	13	10	19	63	81	36
Middlesbrough	42	10	14	18	70	90	34
Leicester City	42	12	9	21	61	86	33
Tottenham Hotspur	42	10	10	22	54	93	30

Wilf Copping left for Arsenal before the start of the season, playing 183 games and scoring four goals.

In their second game of the season, Leeds suffered a record-breaking 8-1 defeat at Stoke City.

Jack Milburn and Tom Cochrane were top of the appearance charts, misisng just one game each.

Manager Dick Ray resigned following a 7-1 defeat at Chelsea and a 3-0 defeat at Sunderland.

Leeds apppointed Billy Hampson who had played for Leeds City during World War One

1935–36

DIVISION ONE

Team	Pld	W	D	L	GF	GA	Pts
Sunderland	42	25	6	11	109	74	56
Derby County	42	18	12	12	61	52	48
Huddersfield Town	42	18	12	12	59	56	48
Stoke City	42	20	7	15	57	57	47
Brentford	42	17	12	13	81	60	46
Arsenal	42	15	15	12	78	48	45
Preston North End	42	18	8	16	67	64	44
Chelsea	42	15	13	14	65	72	43
Manchester City	42	17	8	17	68	60	42
Portsmouth	42	17	8	17	54	67	42
Leeds United	42	15	11	16	66	64	41
Birmingham	42	15	11	16	61	63	41
Bolton Wanderers	42	14	13	15	67	76	41
Middlesbrough	42	15	10	17	84	70	40
Wolverhampton W	42	15	10	17	77	76	40
Everton	42	13	13	16	89	89	39
Grimsby Town	42	17	5	20	65	73	39
West Bromwich Albion	42	16	6	20	89	88	38
Liverpool	42	13	12	17	60	64	38
Sheffield Wednesday	42	13	12	17	63	77	38
Aston Villa	42	13	9	20	81	110	35
Blackburn Rovers	42	12	9	21	55	96	33

Leeds had a new goalkeeper between the sticks with Albert McInroy joining from Sunderland.

Leeds equalled their best ever FA Cup run, reaching the fifth round for the third time.

Jack Milburn became the first player to score three spot kicks in successive matches, only Giles and Strachan have followed suit.

Albert McInory missed only one game with Reg Savage stepping in away at Birmingham City.

Leeds had four skippers, Ernie Hart, Jack McDougall, Jim Milburn and Willis Edwards.

Date	Opposition	Competition	Score
31/08/1935	Stoke City	Division One	1-3
04/09/1935	Birmingham	Division One	0-0
07/09/1935	Blackburn Rovers	Division One	1-4
11/09/1935	Birmingham	Division One	0-2
14/09/1935	Chelsea	Division One	0-1
18/09/1935	Arsenal	Division One	1-1
21/09/1935	Liverpool	Division One	1-0
28/09/1935	Grimsby Town	Division One	1-0
05/10/1935	Huddersfield Town	Division One	2-2
12/10/1935	West Bromwich Albion	Division One	1-1
19/10/1935	Middlesbrough	Division One	1-1
26/10/1935	Aston Villa	Division One	4-2
02/11/1935	Wolverhampton Wanderers	Division One	0-3
09/11/1935	Sheffield Wednesday	Division One	7-2
16/11/1935	Portsmouth	Division One	2-2
23/11/1935	Bolton Wanderers	Division One	5-2
30/11/1935	Brentford	Division One	2-2
07/12/1935	Derby County	Division One	1-0
14/12/1935	Everton	Division One	0-0
21/12/1935	Preston North End	Division One	0-1
26/12/1935	Sunderland	Division One	1-2
28/12/1935	Stoke City	Division One	4-1
04/01/1936	Blackburn Rovers	Division One	3-0
11/01/1936	Wolverhampton Wanderers	FA Cup 3rd Round	1-1
15/01/1936	Wolverhampton Wanderers	FA Cup 3rd Round Replay	3-1
18/01/1936	Chelsea	Division One	2-0
28/01/1936	Bury	FA Cup 4th Round	3-2
01/02/1936	Grimsby Town	Division One	1-2
08/02/1936	Huddersfield Town	Division One	2-1
15/02/1936	Sheffield United	FA Cup 5th Round	1-3
19/02/1936	West Bromwich Albion	Division One	2-3
22/02/1936	Middlesbrough	Division One	0-1
29/02/1936	Sheffield Wednesday	Division One	0-3
07/03/1936	Brentford	Division One	1-2
14/03/1936	Aston Villa	Division One	3-3
18/03/1936	Liverpool	Division One	1-2
21/03/1936	Portsmouth	Division One	1-0
28/03/1936	Bolton Wanderers	Division One	0-3
04/04/1936	Wolverhampton Wanderers	Division One	2-0
10/04/1936	Manchester City	Division One	3-1
11/04/1936	Derby County	Division One	1-2
13/04/1936	Manchester City	Division One	1-1
18/04/1936	Everton	Division One	3-1
22/04/1936	Sunderland	Division One	3-0
25/04/1936	Preston North End	Division One	0-5
02/05/1936	Arsenal	Division One	2-2

DIVISION ONE   1936–37

Date	Opposition	Competition	Score
29/08/1936	Chelsea	Division One	2-3
02/09/1936	Manchester City	Division One	0-4
05/09/1936	Stoke City	Division One	1-2
09/09/1936	Manchester City	Division One	1-1
12/09/1936	Charlton Athletic	Division One	2-0
16/09/1936	Portsmouth	Division One	0-3
19/09/1936	Grimsby Town	Division One	1-4
26/09/1936	Liverpool	Division One	2-0
03/10/1936	Huddersfield Town	Division One	0-3
10/10/1936	Birmingham	Division One	1-2
17/10/1936	Everton	Division One	3-0
24/10/1936	Bolton Wanderers	Division One	1-2
31/10/1936	Brentford	Division One	3-1
07/11/1936	Arsenal	Division One	1-4
14/11/1936	Preston North End	Division One	1-0
21/11/1936	Sheffield Wednesday	Division One	2-1
28/11/1936	Manchester United	Division One	2-1
05/12/1936	Derby County	Division One	3-5
19/12/1936	Sunderland	Division One	1-2
25/12/1936	Middlesbrough	Division One	5-0
26/12/1936	Chelsea	Division One	1-2
28/12/1936	Middlesbrough	Division One	2-4
02/01/1937	Stoke City	Division One	2-1
09/01/1937	Charlton Athletic	Division One	0-1
16/01/1937	Chelsea	FA Cup 3rd Round	0-4
23/01/1937	Grimsby Town	Division One	2-0
30/01/1937	Liverpool	Division One	0-3
06/02/1937	Huddersfield Town	Division One	2-1
13/02/1937	Birmingham	Division One	0-2
27/02/1937	Bolton Wanderers	Division One	2-2
03/03/1937	Everton	Division One	1-7
06/03/1937	Brentford	Division One	1-4
13/03/1937	Arsenal	Division One	3-4
20/03/1937	Preston North End	Division One	0-1
27/03/1937	Sheffield Wednesday	Division One	1-1
29/03/1937	West Bromwich Albion	Division One	0-3
30/03/1937	West Bromwich Albion	Division One	3-1
03/04/1937	Manchester United	Division One	0-0
10/04/1937	Derby County	Division One	2-0
17/04/1937	Wolverhampton Wanderers	Division One	0-3
21/04/1937	Wolverhampton Wanderers	Division One	0-1
24/04/1937	Sunderland	Division One	3-0
01/05/1937	Portsmouth	Division One	3-1

Team	Pld	W	D	L	GF	GA	Pts
Manchester City	42	22	13	7	107	61	57
Charlton Athletic	42	21	12	9	58	49	54
Arsenal	42	18	16	8	80	49	52
Derby County	42	21	7	14	96	90	49
Wolverhampton W	42	21	5	16	84	67	47
Brentford	42	18	10	14	82	78	46
Middlesbrough	42	19	8	15	74	71	46
Sunderland	42	19	6	17	89	87	44
Portsmouth	42	17	10	15	62	66	44
Stoke City	42	15	12	15	72	57	42
Birmingham	42	13	15	14	64	60	41
Grimsby Town	42	17	7	18	86	81	41
Chelsea	42	14	13	15	52	55	41
Preston North End	42	14	13	15	56	67	41
Huddersfield Town	42	12	15	15	62	64	39
West Bromwich Albion	42	16	6	20	77	98	38
Everton	42	14	9	19	81	78	37
Liverpool	42	12	11	19	62	84	35
Leeds United	42	15	4	23	60	80	34
Bolton Wanderers	42	10	14	18	43	66	34
Manchester United	42	10	12	20	55	78	32
Sheffield Wednesday	42	9	12	21	53	69	30

Arthur Hydes finished top scorer for the fourth time in five seasons, with 11 goals.

Billy Furness played his last and 257th game for Leeds, on the last day of season at home to Portsmouth.

Jack Milburn was top appearance maker with 38.

Captain wise, Jack McDougall, Willis Edwards, Jack Milburn and George Milburn all took the armband.

Important debutants of note this term were Tom Holley and Gordon Hodgson.

1937–38

DIVISION ONE

Team	Pld	W	D	L	GF	GA	Pts
Arsenal	42	21	10	11	77	44	52
Wolverhampton W	42	20	11	11	72	49	51
Preston North End	42	16	17	9	64	44	49
Charlton Athletic	42	16	14	12	65	51	46
Middlesbrough	42	19	8	15	72	65	46
Brentford	42	18	9	15	69	59	45
Bolton Wanderers	42	15	15	12	64	60	45
Sunderland	42	14	16	12	55	57	44
Leeds United	42	14	15	13	64	69	43
Chelsea	42	14	13	15	65	65	41
Liverpool	42	15	11	16	65	71	41
Blackpool	42	16	8	18	61	66	40
Derby County	42	15	10	17	66	87	40
Everton	42	16	7	19	79	75	39
Huddersfield Town	42	17	5	20	55	68	39
Leicester City	42	14	11	17	54	75	39
Stoke City	42	13	12	17	58	59	38
Birmingham	42	10	18	14	58	62	38
Portsmouth	42	13	12	17	62	68	38
Grimsby Town	42	13	12	17	51	68	38
Manchester City	42	14	8	20	80	77	36
West Bromwich Albion	42	14	8	20	74	91	36

Date	Opposition	Competition	Score
28/08/1937	Charlton Athletic	Division One	1-1
01/09/1937	Chelsea	Division One	2-0
04/09/1937	Preston North End	Division One	0-0
08/09/1937	Chelsea	Division One	1-4
11/09/1937	Grimsby Town	Division One	1-1
15/09/1937	Portsmouth	Division One	3-1
18/09/1937	Huddersfield Town	Division One	2-1
25/09/1937	Liverpool	Division One	2-0
02/10/1937	West Bromwich Albion	Division One	1-2
09/10/1937	Birmingham	Division One	1-0
16/10/1937	Everton	Division One	1-1
23/10/1937	Wolverhampton Wanderers	Division One	1-2
30/10/1937	Leicester City	Division One	4-2
06/11/1937	Blackpool	Division One	1-1
13/11/1937	Derby County	Division One	2-2
20/11/1937	Bolton Wanderers	Division One	1-1
27/11/1937	Arsenal	Division One	1-4
04/12/1937	Sunderland	Division One	4-3
11/12/1937	Brentford	Division One	1-1
18/12/1937	Manchester City	Division One	2-1
25/12/1937	Middlesbrough	Division One	5-3
27/12/1937	Middlesbrough	Division One	0-2
01/01/1938	Charlton Athletic	Division One	2-2
08/01/1938	Chester	FA Cup 3rd Round	3-1
15/01/1938	Preston North End	Division One	1-3
22/01/1938	Charlton Athletic	FA Cup 4th Round	1-2
26/01/1938	Grimsby Town	Division One	1-1
29/01/1938	Huddersfield Town	Division One	3-0
05/02/1938	Liverpool	Division One	1-1
12/02/1938	West Bromwich Albion	Division One	1-0
19/02/1938	Birmingham	Division One	2-3
26/02/1938	Everton	Division One	4-4
05/03/1938	Wolverhampton Wanderers	Division One	1-1
12/03/1938	Leicester City	Division One	0-2
19/03/1938	Blackpool	Division One	2-5
26/03/1938	Derby County	Division One	0-2
02/04/1938	Bolton Wanderers	Division One	0-0
09/04/1938	Arsenal	Division One	0-1
16/04/1938	Sunderland	Division One	0-0
18/04/1938	Stoke City	Division One	1-0
19/04/1938	Stoke City	Division One	2-1
23/04/1938	Brentford	Division One	4-0
30/04/1938	Manchester City	Division One	2-6
07/05/1938	Portsmouth	Division One	0-4

Manager Billy Hampson bought in teenagers Aubrey Powell, James Makinson and Ken Gadsby to last season's squad.

Again Jack Milburn was the side's only ever-present.

With nothing left to play for come mid-March, Jim Twomey replaced Reg Savage in goal.

Willis Edwards joined the coaching staff at Elland Road.

Ernest Pullan replaced Alf Masser as chairman of the side.

DIVISION ONE

1938–39

Date	Opposition	Competition	Score
27/08/1938	Preston North End	Division One	2-1
31/08/1938	Birmingham	Division One	2-0
03/09/1938	Charlton Athletic	Division One	0-2
05/09/1938	Stoke City	Division One	1-1
10/09/1938	Bolton Wanderers	Division One	1-2
17/09/1938	Huddersfield Town	Division One	1-0
24/09/1938	Liverpool	Division One	0-3
01/10/1938	Leicester City	Division One	8-2
08/10/1938	Middlesbrough	Division One	2-1
15/10/1938	Wolverhampton Wanderers	Division One	1-0
22/10/1938	Everton	Division One	0-4
29/10/1938	Portsmouth	Division One	2-2
05/11/1938	Arsenal	Division One	3-2
12/11/1938	Brentford	Division One	3-2
19/11/1938	Blackpool	Division One	2-1
26/11/1938	Derby County	Division One	1-4
03/12/1938	Grimsby Town	Division One	2-3
10/12/1938	Sunderland	Division One	3-3
17/12/1938	Aston Villa	Division One	1-2
24/12/1938	Preston North End	Division One	0-2
26/12/1938	Chelsea	Division One	1-1
27/12/1938	Chelsea	Division One	2-2
31/12/1938	Charlton Athletic	Division One	2-1
14/01/1939	Bolton Wanderers	Division One	2-2
17/01/1939	Bournemouth & Boscombe Athletic	FA Cup 3rd Round	3-1
21/01/1939	Huddersfield Town	FA Cup 4th Round	2-4
28/01/1939	Liverpool	Division One	1-1
04/02/1939	Leicester City	Division One	0-2
11/02/1939	Middlesbrough	Division One	0-1
18/02/1939	Wolverhampton Wanderers	Division One	1-4
25/02/1939	Everton	Division One	1-2
08/03/1939	Portsmouth	Division One	0-2
11/03/1939	Arsenal	Division One	4-2
18/03/1939	Brentford	Division One	1-0
25/03/1939	Blackpool	Division One	1-0
01/04/1939	Derby County	Division One	0-1
07/04/1939	Manchester United	Division One	0-0
08/04/1939	Grimsby Town	Division One	0-1
10/04/1939	Manchester United	Division One	3-1
15/04/1939	Sunderland	Division One	1-2
19/04/1939	Huddersfield Town	Division One	2-1
22/04/1939	Aston Villa	Division One	2-0
29/04/1939	Birmingham	Division One	0-4
06/05/1939	Stoke City	Division One	0-0

Team	Pld	W	D	L	GF	GA	Pts
Everton	42	27	5	10	88	52	59
Wolverhampton W	42	22	11	9	88	39	55
Charlton Athletic	42	22	6	14	75	59	50
Middlesbrough	42	20	9	13	93	74	49
Arsenal	42	19	9	14	55	41	47
Derby County	42	19	8	15	66	55	46
Stoke City	42	17	12	13	71	68	46
Bolton Wanderers	42	15	15	12	67	58	45
Preston North End	42	16	12	14	63	59	44
Grimsby Town	42	16	11	15	61	69	43
Liverpool	42	14	14	14	62	63	42
Aston Villa	42	16	9	17	71	60	41
Leeds United	42	16	9	17	59	67	41
Manchester United	42	11	16	15	57	65	38
Blackpool	42	12	14	16	56	68	38
Sunderland	42	13	12	17	54	67	38
Portsmouth	42	12	13	17	47	70	37
Brentford	42	14	8	20	53	74	36
Huddersfield Town	42	12	11	19	58	64	35
Chelsea	42	12	9	21	64	80	33
Birmingham	42	12	8	22	62	84	32
Leicester City	42	9	11	22	48	82	29

On 1 October 1938, Gordon Hodgson became the first and only Leeds player to date to score five goals in one game in the 8-2 win over Leicester City.

The only other player to score with Leeds connections is Billy McLeod for Leeds City vs Hull City in a 6-1 win at Hull on 16 January 1915.

Leeds played in a League Jubilee fund match at home to Huddersfield Town at Elland Road, the game finished 1-1.

Leeds had three skippers this term, Jack Milburn, Tom Holley and Eric Stephenson.

Keeper Jim Twomey was top of the appearance charts missing five games out of 44 with Reg Savage filling in.

THE 1940S
A TIME TO FORGET

The Football League campaign stopped during World War Two, with Leeds entering the FA Cup in season 1945-46 and losing 7-2 to Middlesbrough following a 4-3 draw at Elland Road.

The resumption of league football at Elland Road saw Billy Hampson still in charge and in came Con Martin from Glentoran and Harry Clarke from Darlington. Early season results saw Leeds lose 5-2 away at Stoke City, winning 4-0 at home to Bolton Wanderers and a 5-0 loss at Charlton Athletic. Following a 4-2 defeat away at Arsenal, Leeds were in 21st place and staring at relegation. A week later the side recovered to beat Blackpool 4-2 at Elland Road, but an eight-game win-less run saw the side deep in relegation trouble and bottom of the table. The FA Cup vanished in the blink of an eye with a 2-1 defeat at West Bromwich Albion, and league results were not much better. Willis Edwards replaced Hampson as manager but a run of no wins in the last 17 games saw Leeds finish rock bottom with only 18 points. They were 15 points from safety and lost 30 out of 42 games.

With Willis Edwards now at the helm, Leeds started their first campaign in 16 years in the second tier of English football looking to return at the first attempt. Despite five wins in

Leeds Utd 1944-45 team shot, Bob Roxborough, Frank Butterworth, Bob Shotton, Jim Twomey, Jack Milburn, Robson Campbell, Same Weaver, FR - Eddie Burbanks, Cyril Coyne, Gerry Henry, Tom Hindle, P. Pato.

their opening seven league games and Leeds up to fourth in the Second Division, hopes of a promotion campaign went astray when a run of only two wins in ten saw the side drop to 12th in the league ladder. A 6-1 defeat away at Luton Town saw the side in 16th place going into the new year. Like the previous season, the FA Cup lasted just one round, with Blackpool winning 4-0 at Bloomfield Road. Results proved to be extremely inconsistent, with Leeds only able to string back-to-back results together once in the second half of the campaign. They were never in danger of dropping into the third tier and a 5-1 win on the last day of the season over Bury saw Leeds finish in 18th place.

New chairman Sam Bolton replaced Edwards with Major Frank Buckley, who had enjoyed success at Wolverhampton Wanderers. His first game in charge was one to forget as Leicester City won 6-2 at Filbert Street, but the side did bounce back with three consecutive wins at the end of August and the start of September. A 3-1 win at home to Lincoln City in mid-September saw the Whites in fourth place and hopes were positive of a promotion challenge. But a run of two wins in 15 saw any hopes of that disappear and saw Leeds down in 18th place and Newport County added to the despair with a 3-1 win at Elland Road in the FA Cup third round. The side only won six of their remaining 18 league games and Buckley's first season in charge saw the side end up in 15th place.

The final season of the decade saw Harold Williams join the side from FA Cup conquerors Newport County and Frank Dudley joining in exchange with Albert Wakefield. Leeds only won one of their opening 11 league games and were in 20th place following a 1-0 defeat away at Luton Town. They proceeded to win their next three games, in which Dudley scored in all three, and following a 2-1 win over Swansea Town, Leeds were up to seventh. Five wins in their next seven league games saw the side up to fourth in the league, and cup results went hand in hand. A 5-2 win over Carlisle United in the third round was followed by a 3-2 replay win away at Bolton Wanderers, before Cardiff City were defeated 3-1 at Elland Road, which drew 53,000 fans. Leeds bowed out in the last eight away at Arsenal in front of over 62,000 supporters. They finished the season in fifth place with three wins out of the last five and Dudley finished top scorer with 16 goals.

DEBUTANTS IN 1940s

JIM MILBURN

Debut: Preston North End (A) 31 August 1946
Appearances: 219
Goals: 17

The third of the Milburn brothers to be featured, James, nicknamed the 'Iron Man', started his career at Ashington before joining Leeds in October 1935, but he did not make a first-team appearance until the start of the 1946-47 season. Milburn did actually play in the abandoned season of 1939-40 at home to Sheffield United before the World War Two. He did feature for the Whites in war-time football on 52 occasions and also served the Royal Artillery in India. He made several guest appearances for Darlington, Wrexham, Tranmere Rovers and Watford. His first competitive Leeds appearance came on the opening day of the 1946-47 away at Preston North End.

Despite Leeds having a disappointing campaign, finishing bottom of the pile and being relegated back to the Second Division, Milburn featured 37 times, scoring in a 3-3 draw away at Middlesbrough. The 1947-48 season saw Milburn make another 35 appearances for the side, as Leeds finished in a record low position of 18th in the second tier. The following season, 'Iron Man' made a further 43 starts for the side, scoring on four occasions, with goals coming against Brentford at Griffin Park from the penalty spot, Tottenham Hotspur at White Hart Lane, another penalty at home to Lincoln City and his third successful spot kick in a goal fest at home to Grimsby Town. The final season of the decade saw another 41 appearances as Leeds improved massively, finishing in fifth place and taking Arsenal all the way in the last eight of the FA Cup. Another four goals followed – at home to Queens Park Rangers on the opening day of the season from the penalty spot, in a 1-1 draw away at Barnsley, in a 3-1 win at home to Hull City and the winner from 12 yards at home to Grimsby Town. He also captained the side on five occasions. A further 63 appearances and eight goals followed at the start of the 1950s, and at the end of the 1951-52 season Milburn left for Bradford Park Avenue. He ended a 24-year link between Leeds and the family. However, this would be continued by their nephew, a certain Jack Charlton. Milburn passed away in Wakefield in January 1985.

LEN BROWNING

Debut: Charlton Athletic (A)
25 September 1946
Appearances: 105
Goals: 46

A home-town centre-forward, Browning started his career with Quarry Brae and Leeds Secondary Modern Schools before joining the then Whites feeder club Headingley Rangers. He joined the ranks at Elland Road initially as ground staff and hit a hat-trick for the reserves, and went on to make his first-team debut at the age of 18. He would make just one appearance that season and would have to wait for over two years for his next.

The spell in the reserves did Browning the world of good as he went on to hit 14 goals in 25 appearances in season 1948-49. He scored on his second start for the club in a 1-1 draw away at Barnsley and followed this up with goals at home to Grimsby Town, Fulham at Elland Road, Cardiff City away, West Ham United away a brace at home to Bradford Park Avenue and a brace in the return against Barnsley, to name but a few. Nine more goals in 34 games followed at the end of the decade as Leeds finished in fifth place under the stewardship of Major Frank Buckley and reached the last eight of the FA Cup. The first season in the 1950s saw Browning, for the second time in three seasons, finish as top scorer at Elland Road, this time reaching that magical 20 mark in 36 appearances as the Whites finished in fifth place. He scored his one and only hat-trick for the club, in a 5-3 win at home to Southampton in mid-January 1951. His last appearance in the colours of Leeds United came in a 3-1 loss away at Barnsley, before he was sold to Sheffield United for £12,000 in November 1951. Away from football, Browning worked as a technician at All Saints College in Horsforth. He passed away aged 80 in Leeds on 27 September 2008.

JIMMY DUNN

Debut: Cardiff City (A) 1 November 1947
Appearances: 443
Goals: 1

Born in Rutherglen in Scotland, the right-back served with the Royal Marines in World War Two, and even played in the Services Cup Final at Home Park, Plymouth. After taking on a job as a labourer and playing for Scottish side Rutherglen Glencairn, Dunn joined Leeds in

June 1947 for £200. He made his debut in a goalless draw away at Cardiff City at the start of November 1947 and would go on to make 15 appearances for the side in his first season at the club.

The next season saw him make 38 appearances, missing just six games, in which John Williams (one game) and Eddie Bannister (five games) deputised. He missed just two games the following season away at Leicester City and at home to Grimsby Town as Leeds ended the 1949-50 season in fifth place in Division Two. He scored his first and what would prove to be his only goal in a 2-1 home win against Blackburn Rovers on 26 April 1950. Dunn was making the number-two slot his own and very rarely missed any games. He helped Leeds finish in fifth place in season 1950-51 with 42 appearances and made a further 41 the following campaign. Dunn was an ever-present in season 1952-53 as the Whites finished in tenth place in the Second Division under Major Frank Buckley, and Dunn followed this up by missing just one game the next season. Another ever-present season in 1954-55, as the Whites ended up in fourth place, was followed by a third complete set of teamsheet entries, as the side finally ended their Second Division exile by finishing runners-up and gaining promotion back to the top flight. He had a fourth ever-present season in 1956-57, this time under Raich Carter as Leeds looked to cement themselves amongst the elite of the First Division, and Dunn started a further 36 games in 1957-58. His 443rd and final game in a Leeds United shirt took place on the last day of the 1958-59 season at home to West Ham United, as Leeds finished in 17th place in the First Division. Dunn left for Darlington in July 1959 and went on to play for Scarborough. He passed away in Leeds, on 24th January 2005, aged 82 after suffering a stroke.

JIM MCCABE

Debut: Bradford Park Avenue (A) 13 March 1948
Appearances: 161

Born in Draperstown, a village in Londonderry in Northern Ireland in 1918, McCabe's family moved to the South Bank area of Middlesbrough and he started his football career playing with South Bank, St Peters. He also played for Billingham Synthonia and South Bank East End before joining Middlesbrough in May 1937. Due to World War Two, McCabe had to wait to make his Boro debut, with his final game being at home to Chelsea at the start of March 1948. He moved to Elland Road for £10,000 in part exchange for goalkeeper John Hodgson. Having played for Chelsea the previous weekend, McCabe was thrust straight into action for Leeds seven days later in a 3-1 defeat away at Bradford Park Avenue. He played in the remaining ten games that season as Leeds finished in a disappointing 18th place in the Second Division.

The 1948-49 campaign saw the Northern Irishman play in 38 games for side, captaining the team on nine occasions in place of regular captain Tom Holley. McCabe started the next campaign as skipper, before it was handed over to Tom Burden and he made 32 appearances for the side. By this time McCabe had already been captained by his country, making his debut in a 3-2 defeat away to Scotland on 17 November 1948. He ended up playing six times for his national side. Another 54 appearances over the next two seasons at the start of the decade added to McCabe's total in a Leeds shirt, and this could have been more had it not been for an injury and the emergence of Eric Kerfoot, John Charles, Tom Burden and the debut of one Jack Charlton. He went on to make another 37 appearances before joining Peterborough United in May 1954. He never hit the back of the net for Leeds and scored only once for Posh. He passed away in Cleveland in July 1989.

TOMMY BURDEN

Debut: Sheffield Wednesday (A) 11 September 1948
Appearances: 259
Goals: 13

Born in Andover in Buckinghamshire, Burden played for Somerset County Boys before being recommended to Wolverhampton Wanderers by a certain Major Frank Buckley, who was his headmaster at the time. He then played for Chester during the last season of World War Two and was with the Third Division North side for two more seasons before Buckley bought him to Elland Road in July 1948. He made his debut away at Sheffield Wednesday in a 3-1 defeat and would go onto make 36 appearances in his first campaign at Elland Road, scoring a brace at home to Grimsby Town and one in the 2-1 defeat at home to Queens Park Rangers in mid-December 1948.

The 1949-50 campaign saw Burden became an ever-present in the side and he was handed the captaincy in October, a role that he would keep right through to the end of his Leeds United career. He scored once in season 1948-49 in a 1-1 draw away at Preston North End and ended up with 13 goals for the side. His best return for goals was the following year as he hit six in 41 games. The strikes came away at Brentford, away at Leicester City, at home to Birmingham City, at home to Southampton and a brace in the return game at home to Leicester City.

He missed just two games the following season, both away from home, at Coventry City and Brentford in consecutive weekend, but returned in the goalless draw at home to Doncaster Rovers the following week. Burden was an ever-present in season 1952-53, scoring in a 3-1 home win against Notts County and their bitter rivals Nottingham Forest at Elland Road towards the end of April. His last full season in west Yorkshire saw him miss just two games as Leeds finished in tenth place and his last game for the side came at the start of September in a 5-3 defeat away to Bury. As he was travelling up from Somerset, Burden asked for a move nearer home and he joined Bristol City for £3,000 in October 1954. After football, he worked as a senior executive with Clark's shoes in Somerset. He passed away in Taunton in 2001.

RAY IGGLEDEN

Debut: Luton Town (A) 1 January 1949
Appearances: 181
Goals: 50

Named as Horatio Iggleden, but always known as Ray, he was born in Hull. He was a former dock worker and started his career at Constable Street Old Boys before joining Leicester City as an amateur. He played for the Foxes during World War Two. He also played competitively for the side from the Midlands following the start of league football, and he joined Leeds in December 1948. The inside-forward made his debut at Luton Town on New Year's Day 1949 and went on to make 16 appearances for the side during his debut, scoring in a 4-2 home win against Bradford Park Avenue and a 1-0 home win against Nottingham Forest. The following season saw Iggleden make 19 appearances for the side, scoring on four occasions, against Tottenham Hotspur at Elland Road, Coventry City at Highfield Road, at home to Luton Town and Cardiff City in an FA

Cup fifth-round tie at Elland Road. Another 24 games followed for the inside-forward at the start of the new decade with only four goals, this time against Chesterfield at Elland Road, away at Luton Town, at home to Cardiff City and at home to Swansea City. So far, in all the games that he scored in, Iggleden was part of the winning side.

His best season in a Leeds United shirt came in 1951-52 when he missed just one game (a 2-1 home win against Leicester City), scoring 20 goals as Leeds finished in sixth position in the Second Division and reached the fifth round of the FA Cup, before losing against Chelsea in a second replay. Iggleden had a purple patch when he notched eight goals in six games between the end of September 1951 and the start of November 1951. He scored 20 goals in 72 appearances over the next two campaigns as Leeds battled in the Second Division, with his most memorable moment coming as he hit his one and only hat-trick for Leeds in a 7-1 thrashing of Leicester City at the start of February 1954. Iggleden hit his 50th and last goal for the club in a 5-2 home win against Lincoln City in mid-February 1954. His final game for Leeds was in a 2-0 loss away to Birmingham City at the start of March 1955 and he moved to Exeter City in July 1955. He passed away in Hull on 17 December 2003.

HARRY SEARSON

Debut: Coventry City (A) 15 January 1949
Appearances: 116

Goalkeeper Harry Searson was born in Mansfield in 1924 and was educated at High Oakham School. He went on to play for Mansfield and Nottinghamshire Schools and then Blisthorpe Colliery before serving with Fleet Air Arm in India. In 1942 he joined Sheffield Wednesday as an amateur and, due to the fact that the side had six keepers on their books, he returned to his home town and joined Mansfield Town in June 1947. He stayed with the Stags for a while, where he played 42 times before joining Leeds for £2,000 in mid-January 1949. Searson made his debut in a 4-1 loss at Coventry City. In his first campaign at Elland Road he made 18 appearances after taking over from Harry Fearnley between the sticks, keeping seven clean sheets in the process. Searson was an ever-present at the end of the decade, helping Leeds finish in fifth in the Second Division and taking First Division Arsenal all the way in the quarter-finals of the FA Cup. Searson started the first 14 games the following campaign before being displaced by John Scott. He did play a further 13 games as the Whites finished in fifth place in the Second Division, but he would go onto have a battle with Scott for the next 12 months. He made 24 appearances for the Whites in season 1951-52, which included his 100th in a 4-2 loss at Coventry in mid-December 1951, but he eventually lost his place to Scott for the final two months of the campaign and Searson went on to join York City in November 1952. He stayed in north Yorkshire until 1954 before joining Corby Town in June. He passed away on the 5 January 2013 after a battle with cancer.

JOHN CHARLES

First Debut: Blackburn Rovers (A) 23 April 1949
Second Debut: Stoke City (A) 18 August 1962
Appearances: 327
Goals: 157

Possibly one of the greatest-ever players to don the famous White shirt Charles, Il Gigante Bueno, the Gentle Giant, started at Cwymdy Junior School before moving onto Manselton Senior School and then Swansea Boys. In December 1947 Charles was spotted by United scout Jack Pickard whilst he was playing for a local junior side, going by the name of Gendros, and at the time he was on the groundstaff of Swansea Town. He had a trial at Leeds and signed for the club. The manager at the time, Major Frank Buckley, saw the potential in the Welshman and Charles played in the reserves before making his first-team bow in a friendly against Queen of the South towards the back end of the 1948-49 season.

He made his competitive debut in a 0-0 draw away at Blackburn Rovers and played in the last two games of that season as Leeds finished in 15th place in Division Two, and the rest, as they say, is history. He started as a centre-half and was an ever-present as Leeds ended the final season of the 1940s in fifth place, taking First Division Arsenal all the way in the final furlong of the FA Cup.

Charles scored his first goal for Leeds from the penalty spot in a 2-1 win away at Plymouth Arygle on 12 November 1949. In 1950 he became the country's youngest-ever international at the age of 18 years 71 days and would go on to win 38 caps for Wales. The 1950-51 season saw Charles still at centre-back, making 36 appearances and scoring on three occasions, and he missed a big part of the following campaign due to knee surgery. Buckley started him at centre-back ahead of the 1952-53 season, before debuting him as a number-nine in a 2-1 loss at Sheffield United, and he stayed there for the majority of his Leeds United record-breaking career after that. He hit 27 goals in 47 games that season, including three hat-tricks against Hull City, Brentford and Rotherham United all at Elland Road. The 1953-54 season would be a record-breaking one for the Welshman as he hit 43 goals in 41 games, despite the team finishing in tenth place. He started the season with eight goals in three games (four at home to Notts County and another hat-trick at home to Rotherham United) and broke the Leeds United record for most goals in a season. He hit another three hat-tricks against Bury at Gigg Lane, Rotherham for the third time, on this occasion away from Elland Road, and at home to Lincoln City.

The following season would be the only one, bar his last in the colours when he only featured 11 times, when he didn't hit 20 goals; this was due to him being moved back to centre-half by Raich Carter. He captained the side, making 42 appearances in total, still scoring 12 goals. The following year he missed just one game, scoring another 29 goals for the side, which included another hat-trick in a 6-1 win at home to Fulham. Amazingly, he hit another 39 goals in 41 games in 1956-57, which again included a pair of hat-tricks in both games against Sheffield Wednesday. He joined Italian giants Juventus for a British-record fee of £65,000 and he became a huge star over there.

In August 1962 then manager Don Revie, starting his second full season at the club, bought Charles back for £53,000, but he only featured in 11 games, scoring three goals. He joined Roma for £70,000 in October 1962 and would go on to have spells at Cardiff City, Hereford United, as player-manager, Merthyr Tydfil as manager and finally Swansea City as youth coach. Charles had a well-deserved testimonial with Bobby Collins in April 1988, in which the likes of Ian Rush, Kenny Dalglish and Michel Platini all played for Leeds. He passed away on 21 February 2004, with Leeds and Manchester United holding an impeccable minute's silence at Old Trafford. To commemorate his life, a bronze bust was commissioned by the club and unveiled at Elland Road in December 2006.

HAROLD WILLIAMS

Debut: Queens Park Rangers (H) 20 August 1949
Appearances: 227
Goals: 35

Born in Briton Ferry in Glamorgan, Williams was originally rejected by Swansea Town after trials and made guest appearances for Belfast Celtic and Cliftonville during World War Two.

He signed for Briton Ferry Athletic and would go on to join Newport County in January 1949. Williams then came to the attention of Leeds as he had a superb game at Elland Road as Newport pulled off a sensational 3-1 win in the FA Cup in January 1949. In the morning, Williams completed his milk round, before seeing off Leeds in the afternoon. Williams went on to stay at Somerton Park until June 1949, when he joined Leeds for £12,000. It proved to be an inspired signing as the Welshman hit 13 goals in 37 games in his first season at Elland Road. He made his debut on the opening day of that campaign and was a vital figure in the squad that finished in fifth place in the Second Division and took Arsenal to extra time in the final stages of the FA Cup. He hit five goals in 38 appearances at the start of the new decade, as Leeds again finished fifth and Williams would go on to have his best season in terms of games for the side. He played 42 times, scoring further goals as Leeds finished sixth and took Chelsea to two replays in the last 16 of the FA Cup.

Unfortunately for Williams, he broke a leg against Everton on 22 November 1952 and would be ruled out for about ten months. He marked his return with a goal in a 6-0 rout of Notts County on the opening day of the following season, and seven more goals in a further 37 appearances would soon follow. A further 33 games and two goals took place in season 1954-55 and he helped the side win promotion back to the top tier with 20 games and two goals in season 1955-56. His last game for Leeds was in a 2-1 win over Fulham at the end March 1956, and a year later he returned back to Newport. After retiring from football, he kept a pub near Elland Road and one in Gildersome.

ERIC KERFOOT

Debut: Queens Park Rangers (A) 17 December 1949
Appearances: 349
Goals: 10

Born in Ashton-Under-Lyne in Lancashire in 1924, Kerfoot played with Stenhousemuir during the war years, then he returned to Lancashire where he joined local side Ashton United. He then joined fellow Cheshire County League side Stalybridge Celtic, where he built up his reputation.

Leeds United soon realised his potential and bought him to Elland Road in December 1949. He made his debut away at Queens Park Rangers in a 1-1 draw and he went onto make nine appearances in his first season in west Yorkshire. His second campaign at Elland Road saw him make a further 31 appearances in the first full season of the decade, and this was improved 12 months later as Kerfoot played in 39 games, scoring three goals, away at Notts County, away at Coventry City and then at home to the Sky Blues, and Leeds finished in sixth position. He missed just three games the following campaign, scoring two goals. He had his first ever-present campaign in season 1953-54 as Leeds finished tenth in the Second Division. Another 41 games followed the next year and Kerfoot completed his second ever-present season as Leeds finally won promotion back to the top flight by finishing runners up to Sheffield Wednesday. He followed this up with back-to-back ever-present seasons in 1956-57 and 1957-58 as Leeds finished in eighth and 17th place in the First Division respectively. By this time Kerfoot had hit 300 appearances in his Leeds United career and was made captain at the start of the 1957-58 campaign. He made his last appearance in a Leeds shirt in the penultimate game of the 1958-59 season, away at Nottingham Forest, as Alan Shackleton's hat-trick saw off the side from the red half of Nottingham. Kerfoot left for Chesterfield in the summer of 1959 but only made nine appearances for the Spireites before being released. He returned home by rejoining Stalybridge Celtic and would later run a pub in Duckinfield. He died on 4 March 1980.

MANAGERS APPOINTED IN THE 1940s

WILLIS EDWARDS

First game in charge: Derby County (A) 26 April 1947
Last game in charge: Bury (H) 1 May 1948
Games: 49
Won: 14
Drawn: 8
Lost: 27

Following Hampson's decision to stand down, former player Willis Edwards, who had made 444 appearances for the side, took over. After retirement from the playing side of the game, he became assistant to trainer Bob Roxburgh, with his ethos based on the Central League after World War Two. He took over from Hampson with the side bottom of the pile and things couldn't have got any worse for the former England international as he lost all six games left in season 1946-47 for Leeds, though, the damage had already been done and they were relegated after eight seasons in the top flight. His job was to win promotion at the very first attempt, but the side went backwards, ending up in 18th place in the Second Division as they were haunted by consecutive relegations. After just 49 games as manager and just over 12 months at the club, the decision was taken to move Edwards back to assistant trainer. He remained on the backroom staff at the club for over a decade, and in fact he recommended Tommy Burden to new manager Major Frank Buckley. Following the departure of Bill Lambton, Edwards became assistant to caretaker manager Bob Roxburgh. He died aged 85 in Leeds on 27 September 1988, having spent the last years of his working life at a Moorhouse's jam factory.

WIllis Edwards's first line up: Derby County (A) 26 April 1947: Twomey, Jim Milburn, Gadsby, Willingham, Holley, Browne, Cochrane, Powell, Clarke, Henry, Heaton.

WIllis Edwards's last line up: Bury (H) 1 May 1948: Fearnley, Dunn, Milburn, Bullions, Holley, McCabe, Cochrane, Powell, Wakefield, Chisholm, Heaton.

MAJOR FRANK BUCKLEY

First game in charge: Leicester City (A) 21 August 1948
Last game in charge: Doncaster Rovers (A) 25 April 1953
Games: 224
Won: 87
Drawn: 63
Lost: 74

With Edwards moving back to assistant trainer and Leeds struggling at the wrong end of the Second Division, Leeds needed a pick me up in terms of their manager and they turned to one of the best-known names in football in Major Frank Buckley. Born in Urmston in Lancashire, Buckley played for Brighton & Hove Albion, Manchester United, Manchester City, Birmingham City, Derby County and Bradford City. He only played four league games for the Bantams before World War One and Buckley enlisted with the 17th Middlesex Regiment. He saw action and suffered lung and shoulder injuries in the Battle of the Somme where he rose to the rank of Major. He was appointed manager of non-league Norwich City in 1919 but left in July 1920 due to a financial dispute. Buckley was then appointed manager of Blackpool in October 1923 and stayed there for four years, and it was down to Buckley's clever thinking that the colours of the kit changed to the now famous tangerine. His next move would be the one that would change his career as he joined Wolverhampton Wanderers as manager in 1927 and would stay there until February 1944. Whilst at Molineux, he won the Division Two title in season 1931-32 and finished runners-up in the top flight in before 1937-38 as well as losing the FA Cup Final to Portsmouth the following season. He was also responsible for bringing through footballing greats such as Stan Cullis and Billy Wright.

In 1944 Buckley broke a contract for life that he had in the Black Country to join Notts County, where he was paid £4,000 a year. He resigned from there in January 1946 and joined Hull City within hours. Willis Edwards had been demoted from manager at the end of the 1947-48 season and Buckley took over at Elland Road after that.

Buckley was years ahead of his time, something that had never been seen at Leeds and he introduced dance sessions on the pitch, with the squad pairing up to strut their moves to music coming over the public address system. There was also the introduction of a mechanical kicking machine, which was installed to improve heading, trapping, volleying and goal kicking. His first game, and season, would be a forgettable one as the side lost 6-2 away to Leicester City and finished 15th in the Second Division, but Buckley was responsible for discovering one John Charles, who made his debut away at Blackburn Rovers on 23 April 1949. His second campaign at Elland Road saw the side finish in fifth place as well as taking top-flight Arsenal to extra-time in the last eight of the FA Cup at Highbury in a game played in front of over 62,000 supporters. There was another fifth place the following season and a sixth place in season 1951-52, but with the club expecting promotion in 1952-53 they finished in a disappointing tenth place. He resigned in April 1953 feeling that he had taken the club as far as he could go. His final job was at Walsall and he passed away in the Midlands aged 82 on 22 December 1964.

Major Frank Buckley's first line up: Leicester City (A) 21 August 1948: Twomey, Dunn, Milburn, Bullions, Holley, McCabe, Hindle, Short, Wakefield, Chisholm, Heaton.

Major Frank Buckley's last line up: Doncaster Rovers (H) 24 May 1953: Scott, Dunn, Hair, Kerfoot, Charlton, Burden, McCall, Nightingale, Charles, Iggleden, Meek.

1945–46

Following the Second World War, no League games were played between 1939 and 1946.

In season 1939-40, three games were played with Leeds drawing 0-0 at home to Preston North End and losing 1-0 at home to both Charlton Athletic and Sheffield United. Leeds were bottom of the league.

From season 1940-41 to 1945-46, Leeds played in the Regional League North-East Division, North Regional League and the Football League North Section. They also featured in the League War Cup.

Season 1939-40 - North East Division 5th.
Season 1940-41 - North East League 15th.
Season 1941-42 - Football League Northern Section 26th and 40th.
Season 1942-43 - Football League Northern Section 43rd and 47th.
Season 1943-44 - Football League Northern Section 27th and 35th.
Season 1944-45 - Football League Northern Section 22nd and 32nd.
Season 1945-46 - Football League Norterhn Section 22nd.

Date	Opposition	Competition	Score
05/01/1946	Middlesbrough	FA Cup 3rd Round 1st Leg	4-4
09/01/1946	Middlesbrough	FA Cup 3rd Round 2nd Leg	2-7

DIVISION ONE

1946–47

Date	Opposition	Competition	Score
31/08/1946	Preston North End	Division One	2-3
04/09/1946	Charlton Athletic	Division One	0-2
07/09/1946	Sheffield United	Division One	2-2
14/09/1946	Chelsea	Division One	0-3
16/09/1946	Stoke City	Division One	2-5
21/09/1946	Bolton Wanderers	Division One	4-0
25/09/1946	Charlton Athletic	Division One	0-5
28/09/1946	Liverpool	Division One	0-2
05/10/1946	Huddersfield Town	Division One	5-0
12/10/1946	Grimsby Town	Division One	1-0
19/10/1946	Wolverhampton Wanderers	Division One	0-1
26/10/1946	Blackburn Rovers	Division One	0-1
02/11/1946	Portsmouth	Division One	1-4
09/11/1946	Everton	Division One	2-1
16/11/1946	Arsenal	Division One	2-4
23/11/1946	Blackpool	Division One	4-2
30/11/1946	Brentford	Division One	1-1
07/12/1946	Sunderland	Division One	1-1
14/12/1946	Aston Villa	Division One	1-2
21/12/1946	Derby County	Division One	1-2
25/12/1946	Middlesbrough	Division One	3-3
26/12/1946	Middlesbrough	Division One	0-3
28/12/1946	Preston North End	Division One	0-3
04/01/1947	Sheffield United	Division One	2-6
11/01/1947	West Bromwich Albion	FA Cup 3rd Round	1-2
18/01/1947	Chelsea	Division One	2-1
01/02/1947	Liverpool	Division One	1-2
03/02/1947	Bolton Wanderers	Division One	0-2
22/02/1947	Wolverhampton Wanderers	Division One	0-1
01/03/1947	Blackburn Rovers	Division One	1-2
22/03/1947	Arsenal	Division One	1-1
29/03/1947	Blackpool	Division One	0-3
05/04/1947	Brentford	Division One	1-2
07/04/1947	Manchester United	Division One	1-3
08/04/1947	Manchester United	Division One	0-2
12/04/1947	Sunderland	Division One	0-1
19/04/1947	Aston Villa	Division One	1-1
26/04/1947	Derby County	Division One	1-2
03/05/1947	Stoke City	Division One	1-2
10/05/1947	Huddersfield Town	Division One	0-1
17/05/1947	Grimsby Town	Division One	1-4
24/05/1947	Portsmouth	Division One	0-1
26/05/1947	Everton	Division One	1-4

Team	Pld	W	D	L	GF	GA	Pts
Liverpool	42	25	7	10	84	52	57
Manchester United	42	22	12	8	95	54	56
Wolverhampton W	42	25	6	11	98	56	56
Stoke City	42	24	7	11	90	53	55
Blackpool	42	22	6	14	71	70	50
Sheffield United	42	21	7	14	89	75	49
Preston North End	42	18	11	13	76	74	47
Aston Villa	42	18	9	15	67	53	45
Sunderland	42	18	8	16	65	66	44
Everton	42	17	9	16	62	67	43
Middlesbrough	42	17	8	17	73	68	42
Portsmouth	42	16	9	17	66	60	41
Arsenal	42	16	9	17	72	70	41
Derby County	42	18	5	19	73	79	41
Chelsea	42	16	7	19	69	84	39
Grimsby Town	42	13	12	17	61	82	38
Blackburn Rovers	42	14	8	20	45	53	36
Bolton Wanderers	42	13	8	21	57	69	34
Charlton Athletic	42	11	12	19	57	71	34
Huddersfield Town	42	13	7	22	53	79	33
Brentford	42	9	7	26	45	88	25
Leeds United	42	6	6	30	45	90	18

It was a season of unwanted records for Leeds as they finished 15 points from safety.

They had the least points with 18, most defeats with 30 and least wins with six.

Tom Holley played in 40 out of the 43 games in season 1946-47.

Leeds had three captains this season, Tom Holley captained in 40 games, Aubrey Powell had one game and Gerry Henry the other two.

Between the sticks were John Hodgson, Harry Fearnley and Jim Twomey.

1947–48　　　　　　　　　　　　　　　　　　　　　DIVISION TWO

Team	Pld	W	D	L	GF	GA	Pts
Birmingham City	42	22	15	5	55	24	59
Newcastle United	42	24	8	10	72	41	56
Southampton	42	21	10	11	71	53	52
Sheffield Wednesday	42	20	11	11	66	53	51
Cardiff City	42	18	11	13	61	58	47
West Ham United	42	16	14	12	55	53	46
West Bromwich Albion	42	18	9	15	63	58	45
Tottenham Hotspur	42	15	14	13	56	43	44
Leicester City	42	16	11	15	60	57	43
Coventry City	42	14	13	15	59	52	41
Fulham	42	15	10	17	47	46	40
Barnsley	42	15	10	17	62	64	40
Luton Town	42	14	12	16	56	59	40
Bradford Park Avenue	42	16	8	18	68	72	40
Brentford	42	13	14	15	44	61	40
Chesterfield	42	16	7	19	54	55	39
Plymouth Argyle	42	9	20	13	40	58	38
Leeds United	42	14	8	20	62	72	36
Nottingham Forest	42	12	11	19	54	60	35
Bury	42	9	16	17	58	68	34
Doncaster Rovers	42	9	11	22	40	66	29
Millwall	42	9	11	22	44	74	29

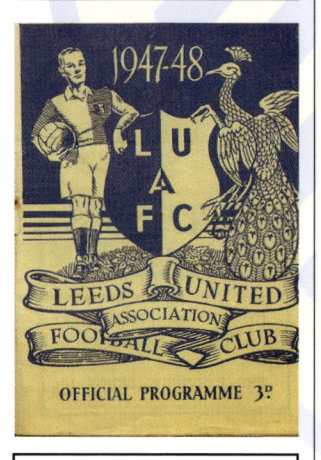

Date	Opposition	Competition	Score
23/08/1947	Leicester City	Division Two	3-1
27/08/1947	Barnsley	Division Two	0-3
30/08/1947	Southampton	Division Two	2-1
03/09/1947	Barnsley	Division Two	4-1
06/09/1947	Fulham	Division Two	2-3
10/09/1947	Plymouth Argyle	Division Two	5-0
13/09/1947	Coventry City	Division Two	2-1
17/09/1947	Plymouth Argyle	Division Two	0-1
20/09/1947	Newcastle United	Division Two	2-4
27/09/1947	Birmingham City	Division Two	0-1
04/10/1947	West Bromwich Albion	Division Two	2-3
11/10/1947	Doncaster Rovers	Division Two	0-0
18/10/1947	Nottingham Forest	Division Two	0-1
25/10/1947	Bradford Park Avenue	Division Two	2-0
01/11/1947	Cardiff City	Division Two	0-0
08/11/1947	Sheffield Wednesday	Division Two	2-2
15/11/1947	Tottenham Hotspur	Division Two	1-3
22/11/1947	Millwall	Division Two	2-1
29/11/1947	Chesterfield	Division Two	0-3
06/12/1947	West Ham United	Division Two	2-1
13/12/1947	Bury	Division Two	1-1
20/12/1947	Leicester City	Division Two	0-2
26/12/1947	Luton Town	Division Two	0-2
27/12/1947	Luton Town	Division Two	1-6
03/01/1948	Southampton	Division Two	0-0
10/01/1948	Blackpool	FA Cup 3rd Round	0-4
17/01/1948	Fulham	Division Two	0-1
24/01/1948	Newcastle United	Division Two	3-1
31/01/1948	Coventry City	Division Two	2-1
14/02/1948	Birmingham City	Division Two	1-5
21/02/1948	West Bromwich Albion	Division Two	3-1
28/02/1948	Doncaster Rovers	Division Two	0-3
06/03/1948	Nottingham Forest	Division Two	2-2
13/03/1948	Bradford Park Avenue	Division Two	1-3
20/03/1948	Cardiff City	Division Two	4-0
26/03/1948	Brentford	Division Two	0-3
27/03/1948	Sheffield Wednesday	Division Two	1-3
29/03/1948	Brentford	Division Two	1-1
03/04/1948	Tottenham Hotspur	Division Two	1-3
10/04/1948	Millwall	Division Two	1-1
17/04/1948	Chesterfield	Division Two	3-0
24/04/1948	West Ham United	Division Two	1-2
01/05/1948	Bury	Division Two	5-1

Aubrey Powell made the most appearances with 40.

During the campaign Sam Bolton had replaced Eric Clarke as chairman of the club.

Willis Edwards, who had taken over from Billy Hampson the previous season, was replaced by Major Frank Buckley at the end of the campaign.

By finishing 18th in the Second Division, Leeds recorded their lowest-ever League position since the club's formation back in 1919.

Tom Holley again captained the side, with Ken Willingham and Gerry Henry stepping in when called upon.

DIVISION TWO

1948–49

Date	Opposition	Competition	Score
21/08/1948	Leicester City	Division Two	2-6
25/08/1948	Brentford	Division Two	0-0
28/08/1948	Luton Town	Division Two	2-0
01/09/1948	Brentford	Division Two	3-1
04/09/1948	Coventry City	Division Two	4-1
08/09/1948	Tottenham Hotspur	Division Two	0-0
11/09/1948	Sheffield Wednesday	Division Two	1-3
13/09/1948	Tottenham Hotspur	Division Two	2-2
18/09/1948	Lincoln City	Division Two	3-1
25/09/1948	Chesterfield	Division Two	1-3
02/10/1948	West Bromwich Albion	Division Two	1-3
09/10/1948	Bradford Park Avenue	Division Two	1-1
16/10/1948	Southampton	Division Two	1-1
23/10/1948	Barnsley	Division Two	1-1
30/10/1948	Grimsby Town	Division Two	6-3
06/11/1948	Nottingham Forest	Division Two	0-0
13/11/1948	Fulham	Division Two	1-1
20/11/1948	Plymouth Argyle	Division Two	1-2
04/12/1948	Cardiff City	Division Two	1-2
11/12/1948	Queens Park Rangers	Division Two	1-2
18/12/1948	Leicester City	Division Two	3-1
25/12/1948	West Ham United	Division Two	2-3
26/12/1948	West Ham United	Division Two	1-3
01/01/1949	Luton Town	Division Two	0-0
08/01/1949	Newport County	FA Cup 3rd Round	1-3
15/01/1949	Coventry City	Division Two	1-4
22/01/1949	Sheffield Wednesday	Division Two	1-1
29/01/1949	Blackburn Rovers	Division Two	1-0
05/02/1949	Lincoln City	Division Two	0-0
12/02/1949	Bury	Division Two	0-1
19/02/1949	Chesterfield	Division Two	1-0
05/03/1949	Bradford Park Avenue	Division Two	4-2
12/03/1949	Southampton	Division Two	1-2
19/03/1949	Barnsley	Division Two	4-1
26/03/1949	Grimsby Town	Division Two	1-5
02/04/1949	Nottingham Forest	Division Two	1-0
06/04/1949	West Bromwich Albion	Division Two	0-1
09/04/1949	Fulham	Division Two	0-1
16/04/1949	Plymouth Argyle	Division Two	1-0
18/04/1949	Bury	Division Two	1-3
23/04/1949	Blackburn Rovers	Division Two	0-0
30/04/1949	Cardiff City	Division Two	0-0
07/05/1949	Queens Park Rangers	Division Two	0-2

Team	Pld	W	D	L	GF	GA	Pts
Fulham	42	24	9	9	77	37	57
West Bromwich Albion	42	24	8	10	69	39	56
Southampton	42	23	9	10	69	36	55
Cardiff City	42	19	13	10	62	47	51
Tottenham Hotspur	42	17	16	9	72	44	50
Chesterfield	42	15	17	10	51	45	47
West Ham United	42	18	10	14	56	58	46
Sheffield Wednesday	42	15	13	14	63	56	43
Barnsley	42	14	12	16	62	61	40
Luton Town	42	14	12	16	55	57	40
Grimsby Town	42	15	10	17	72	76	40
Bury	42	17	6	19	67	76	40
Queen's Park Rangers	42	14	11	17	44	62	39
Blackburn Rovers	42	15	8	19	53	63	38
Leeds United	42	12	13	17	55	63	37
Coventry City	42	15	7	20	55	64	37
Bradford Park Avenue	42	13	11	18	65	78	37
Brentford	42	11	14	17	42	53	36
Leicester City	42	10	16	16	62	79	36
Plymouth Argyle	42	12	12	18	49	64	36
Nottingham Forest	42	14	7	21	50	54	35
Lincoln City	42	8	12	22	53	91	28

Jim Milburn was the club's only ever-present playing in all 43 games during the season.

Captain Tom Holley made the last of 169 appearances for the club in the 1-0 away defeat at West Bromwich Albion.

23 April 1949 won't live long in the memory with it being a goalless draw at Blackburn Rovers, but it saw the debut of one John Charles.

Leeds used four goalkeepers this term, Jim Twomey, Albert Lomas, Harry Fearnley and Harry Searson.

Apart from Holley, the two Jims, Milburn and McCabe, captained the side.

1949–50

DIVISION TWO

Team	Pld	W	D	L	GF	GA	Pts
Tottenham Hotspur	42	27	7	8	81	35	61
Sheffield Wednesday	42	18	16	8	67	48	52
Sheffield United	42	19	14	9	68	49	52
Southampton	42	19	14	9	64	48	52
Leeds United	42	17	13	12	54	45	47
Preston North End	42	18	9	15	60	49	45
Hull City	42	17	11	14	64	72	45
Swansea Town	42	17	9	16	53	49	43
Brentford	42	15	13	14	44	49	43
Cardiff City	42	16	10	16	41	44	42
Grimsby Town	42	16	8	18	74	73	40
Coventry City	42	13	13	16	55	55	39
Barnsley	42	13	13	16	64	67	39
Chesterfield	42	15	9	18	43	47	39
Leicester City	42	12	15	15	55	65	39
Blackburn Rovers	42	14	10	18	55	60	38
Luton Town	42	10	18	14	41	51	38
Bury	42	14	9	19	60	65	37
West Ham United	42	12	12	18	53	61	36
Queen's Park Rangers	42	11	12	19	40	57	34
Plymouth Argyle	42	8	16	18	44	65	32
Bradford Park Avenue	42	10	11	21	51	77	31

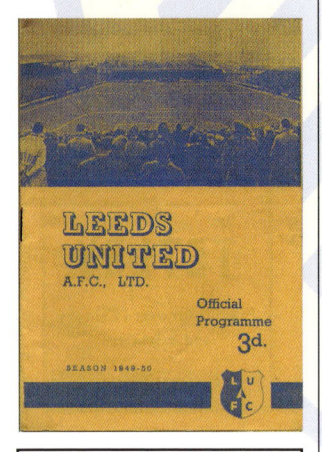

Date	Opposition	Competition	Score
20/08/1949	Queens Park Rangers	Division Two	1-1
22/08/1949	West Ham United	Division Two	1-3
27/08/1949	Preston North End	Division Two	1-1
31/08/1949	West Ham United	Division Two	2-2
03/09/1949	Swansea Town	Division Two	1-2
05/09/1949	Sheffield United	Division Two	1-0
10/09/1949	Tottenham Hotspur	Division Two	0-2
14/09/1949	Sheffield United	Division Two	0-1
17/09/1949	Southampton	Division Two	1-2
24/09/1949	Coventry City	Division Two	3-3
01/10/1949	Luton Town	Division Two	0-1
08/10/1949	Cardiff City	Division Two	2-0
15/10/1949	Blackburn Rovers	Division Two	1-0
22/10/1949	Brentford	Division Two	1-0
29/10/1949	Hull City	Division Two	0-1
05/11/1949	Sheffield Wednesday	Division Two	1-1
12/11/1949	Plymouth Argyle	Division Two	2-1
19/11/1949	Chesterfield	Division Two	0-0
26/11/1949	Bradford Park Avenue	Division Two	2-1
03/12/1949	Leicester City	Division Two	1-1
10/12/1949	Bury	Division Two	0-2
17/12/1949	Queens Park Rangers	Division Two	1-1
24/12/1949	Preston North End	Division Two	3-1
26/12/1949	Barnsley	Division Two	1-1
27/12/1949	Barnsley	Division Two	1-0
31/12/1949	Swansea Town	Division Two	2-1
07/01/1950	Carlisle United	FA Cup 3rd Round	5-2
14/01/1950	Tottenham Hotspur	Division Two	3-0
21/01/1950	Southampton	Division Two	1-0
28/01/1950	Bolton Wanderers	FA Cup 4th Round	1-1
01/02/1950	Bolton Wanderers	FA Cup 4th Round Replay	3-2
04/02/1950	Coventry City	Division Two	4-0
11/02/1950	Cardiff City	FA Cup 5th Round	3-1
18/02/1950	Luton Town	Division Two	2-1
25/02/1950	Cardiff City	Division Two	0-1
04/03/1950	Arsenal	FA Cup QF	0-1
11/03/1950	Brentford	Division Two	0-0
18/03/1950	Hull City	Division Two	3-0
25/03/1950	Sheffield Wednesday	Division Two	2-5
01/04/1950	Bradford Park Avenue	Division Two	0-0
07/04/1950	Grimsby Town	Division Two	0-2
08/04/1950	Leicester City	Division Two	1-1
10/04/1950	Grimsby Town	Division Two	1-0
15/04/1950	Plymouth Argyle	Division Two	1-1
22/04/1950	Chesterfield	Division Two	1-3
26/04/1950	Blackburn Rovers	Division Two	2-1
29/04/1950	Bury	Division Two	4-1

Leeds reached the last eight of the FA Cup for the first time in their history, bowing out 1-0 away at Arsenal.

The Whites had three ever-presents, John Charles, Harry Searson and Tommy Burden.

The season saw the debut of Eric Kerfoot who went on to make 349 appearances for the side.

Again the captaincy was shared out between Jim McCabe, Jim Milburn and Tommy Burden.

For the first time in their history, a game involving Leeds went into extra time, the FA Cup fourth-round replay away at Bolton Wanderers was won by Leeds after 120 minutes.

1950s
ARISE SIR JOHN

The 1950s started with Leeds as one of the favourites to win promotion. The season started in front of over 40,000 supporters and they were treated to a 3-1 win over Yorkshire rivals Doncaster Rovers thanks to a brace from Frank Dudley. The side only won two of the next eight away at Brentford and at home to Blackburn Rovers, and by mid-September they were in 16th place.

How the Daily Graphic *reported the 1950 Bolton Cup tie.*

Leeds Utd 1950s team shot, colour, from Soccer Bubble Gum Teams. E. Kerfoot, J. Overfield, K. Ripley, R. Wood, R. Forrest, G. Hair. Front row: G. Meek, J. Charlton, J. Charles, J. Dunn, H. Brook.

The next ten games, saw only four wins including a 5-1 win over Leicester City at Filbert Street. Form at the back of the year proved to be inconsistent, and going into the new year they were stuck in mid-table. Four consecutive wins pulled the side up to eighth place before a 2-1 defeat at Blackburn Rovers. The side responded with back-to-back wins at Luton Town (3-2) and Bury (1-0) respectively, which saw the team in sixth place. Despite a 4-1 defeat at Manchester City, Leeds won six of their last seven games to finish in fifth place. Len Browning top-scored with 20 goals.

The second season of the decade saw the team without John Charles, who was completing his National Service, and early-season results proved difficult, with Leeds as low down as 21st with no wins in the first six games. Consecutive home wins over Cardiff City and Sheffield Wednesday pushed the side up to 12th and by the start of December they were up to seventh following a 1-1 draw at home to Swansea Town. The festive football season saw Leeds win two out of three, and following a 3-0 win over Rotherham United at the start of February the Whites were up to fifth. The FA Cup saw Leeds defeat Rochdale (2-0) and Bradford Park Avenue (2-0), before setting up a tie with Chelsea. The first game finished 1-1 at Elland Road, before the replay ended with the same scoreline at Stamford Bridge in front of over 60,000 supporters. The third game played at Villa Park saw the Blues win 5-1. League form tailed off with only four wins in their last 11 to finish in sixth place. Ray Iggleden was top of the goalscoring charts with 20.

Season 1952-53 saw Leeds start with only one win in the opening six games, that coming in a 2-0 win at home to Bury. Leeds needed a change of fortune, especially up front, and that came with the decision to switch John Charles from centre-half to centre-forward. It had an immediate impact as the Welshman scored 11 in his first seven games playing as a number nine. Included in that were hat-tricks against Hull City and Brentford. Another hat-trick came for the Gentle Giant in a 4-0 win over Rotherham United in mid-January and he would finish the season with 27 goals. The FA Cup run was over before it even started as the side exited the competition in a 2-1 loss at Brentford as league form was inconsistent and the side struggled to put together a promotion run. The side finish in 11th position in what proved to be Major Frank Buckley's last in charge. One side note was the debut of Jack Charlton in the final game of the season at home to Doncaster Rovers.

The new man in charge would be Raich Carter and he started in emphatic style, with Charles scoring seven goals in the first two games. Notts County were demolished 6-0 at Elland Road, before Rotherham United went the same way in a 4-2 win. While Charles kept on scoring, Leeds slipped to 13th following a 2-1 defeat away at Brentford in mid-October. Results did improve, and following a 2-1 win over Oldham Athletic at Elland Road, they moved up to seventh in the Division Two table. Prior to the start of the FA Cup, Leeds demolished Leicester City at Elland Road with a hat-trick from Iggleden. Tottenham Hotspur made sure the FA Cup lasted no more than the third round, with Spurs winning a replay 1-0 at White Hart Lane. The side suffered three straight defeats but another Charles hat-trick came in a 5-2 win at home to Lincoln City. Despite the side finishing in tenth place, Charles finished with 43 goals which is a record that still stands today. It beat the record set by Tom Jennings in the 1926-27 season.

Carter's second season in charge saw him sign Harold Brook from Sheffield United and he made a goalscoring debut in a 2-0 win away at Hull City. Five straight defeats put paid to any early season optimism, but a 5-2 win at home to Swansea Town in early September did help matters. A run of ten

Goalkeeper Jack Scott is unable to stop Tottenham's Les Bennett netting the FA Cup replay winner in 1954.

wins out of 13, saw the Whites top the table and they stayed there following a Christmas Day win over Middlesbrough. Back-to-back defeats, away at Middlesbrough and Lincoln dropped the side to seventh, and worse was to follow as they crashed out of the FA Cup in a third-round replay defeat to Torquay United. Seven wins in 11 games looked to have helped Leeds to promotion but they missed out by a single point. Brook top-scored with 16 goals as attention turned to finally winning promotion and escaping the Second Division.

Having some success the previous season, hopes were finally high that Leeds could end their nine-year stay in the wilderness and gain promotion to the top flight. The side won three out of their opening six games, but results did prove hard to come by, and following a 5-2 loss at Leicester City at the end of November Leeds dropped as low as 11th. Promotion was as far away as possible.

Five wins in the next seven propelled Leeds up to third and hopes that the side could end their exile were back on. Cardiff City knocked the Whites out of the FA Cup in the third round, as they would do in the next two seasons, but it left the team to concentrate on promotion. A return of only one win in the next eight left Leeds in ninth place, but five wins in the next six saw Leeds up to second place. With Rotherham United defeated 2-0 at Elland Road thanks to a brace from Albert Nightingale, this meant a win over Hull City would secure promotion. Leeds won 4-1 thanks to a pair of braces from Charles and Brook, and they were back in the First Division. Charles again finished as top scorer with 29 as Leeds fans could finally look forward to top-tier football.

Leeds couldn't have started in better fashion as 30,000 fans turned up to watch the side destroy Everton 5-1 at Elland Road, with Brook scoring a hat-trick. A brace from Charles saw

Leeds United, 1956-57.

Leeds United, 1958-59.

off Charlton Athletic in the next game but reality set in as Tottenham Hotspur beat Leeds 5-1 at White Hart Lane in the next match. Leeds bounced back with a 4-0 win over Charlton Athletic at Elland Road, and they were in second place by the end of September. They stayed in and around the top five up to the new year, with Charles scoring for fun once again. Two wins in ten in the second half of the campaign put paid to any title hopes, but another hat-trick from Charles did see off Sheffield Wednesday at Hillsborough. Leeds ended the season in eighth place with Charles again top-scoring with 39 goals, but he was sold to Italian giants Juventus, which left a massive goalscoring problem at Elland Road.

Needing a striker, Carter spent £12,000 on Hugh Baird from Scottish side Airdrie and it would be prove to be an inspired move. He scored three in his first four games, including a brace in a 4-0 win at home to Aston Villa. However, three consecutive loses saw Leeds drop to 19th, but back-to-back wins over Bolton Wanderers and Sunderland saw the side up to tenth. That would be as good as it got for Carter's men as a run of five straight loses between the end of October and end of November saw the Whites drop to 20th. A 2-0 win over Portsmouth at Elland Road, thanks to a brace from Baird, moved Leeds up to 16th, but three more defeats dropped them to 21st. Back-to-back wins over Arsenal and Burnley at Elland Road soothed any nerves, as did a 1-0 win at Goodison Park over Everton. An unbeaten run of six games at the back end of the campaign kept Leeds above water as Baird finished top-scorer with 20 in his first season at the club.

At the end of the previous campaign, Carter's contract was not renewed as he was replaced by Bill Lambton. He first game was a disaster as Bolton Wanderers won 4-0 at Burnden Park and results were patchy, to the say the least. By mid-October, Leeds were in 21st and looked like facing another relegation battle. Leeds needed a boost and that came in the signing of one Don Revie, who joined from Sunderland in a £12,000 move. Their fortunes improved with four wins in the next five and they were up to 12th. Luton knocked the side out of the FA Cup with a 5-1 win at Kenilworth Road and a run of two wins in seven saw the end of Lambton as he was replaced by Bob Roxburgh in caretaker charge. Roxburgh led the side through the last ten games of the season, which saw the side win half of them and finish in 15th place. Alan Shackleton finished as top-scorer with 17.

Leeds needed a new manager and in came Jack Taylor ahead of the final season of the decade. Leeds started with back-to-back defeats at home to Burnley and away at Leicester City before a first win under Taylor came in a 1-0 match over Luton Town at Kenilworth Road thanks to a winner from Revie. A run of only one win in ten saw Leeds in 19th place, despite the signing of John McCole from Bradford City. Back-to-back wins in the new year over West Ham United (3-0) and Chelsea (3-1) at Stamford Bridge, in which a certain Billy Bremner made his debut, saw the Whites up to 17th, but four straight loses dropped them to 21st. McCole scored a brace in a 4-3 win over Manchester City at Elland Road, which raised hopes, but it proved to be in vain as defeats against Everton and Blackburn Rovers proved costly. Leeds would start the first full season of the 1960s back in the Second Division, but the new decade would see a change a fortunes.

Leeds United, 1959-60.

DEBUTANTS IN 1950s

GRENVILLE HAIR

Debut: Leicester City (H) 31 March 1951
Appearances: 474
Goals: 2

Born in Burton-Upon-Trent, Hair went to Burton Technical School and then manager Major Frank Buckley signed him from Burton & District League Club, Newhall United in November 1948. Hair completed National Service with the 12th Royal Lancers at Barnard Castle in north Yorkshire when they won the Northern Command Trophy. One piece of trivia relating to Hair is that he was signed on the same day as the great John Charles, but unlike the Welshman he had to wait to make his Leeds United debut. He broke into the first team towards the back end of the first full season of the new decade, making his debut in a 2-1 win over Leicester City as the Whites finished in fifth place in the Second Division. Hair started to establish himself the following campaign, making 32 appearances and taking over from Jim Milburn at full-back.

The next season Hair missed just two games and in seasons 1953-54 and 1954-55 he would become an ever-present for the side as Leeds finished in tenth and fourth place respectively. He featured on 35 occasions as the Whites ended their run in the Second Division by finishing as runners-up to Sheffield Wednesday. In 1955 he was rewarded with trips with the English FA touring teams to Bermuda, Jamaica, Trinidad and Curacao in the West Indies. Three years later he travelled to Nigeria and Ghana and then another three years later it was Malaysia, Singapore, Hong Kong, New Zealand and the USA.

At the start of the Whites campaign back in the First Division, Hair reached his 200th appearance in a 2-1 win away at Charlton and would be an ever-present as Leeds finished in eighth place under Raich Carter. He made a further 35 appearances in season 1957-58 and this was followed up by a further 38 the following year. As the Whites were relegated back to the Second Division under Jack Taylor, Hair made a further 33 appearances for the side, finishing the campaign on 347 games in total. Taylor was replaced by the great Don Revie in March 1961 and Hair missed just one game under both managers as Leeds finished in 14th place back in the second tier. He made his 400th appearance for the side in a 3-1 win at home to Stoke City on 16 September 1961 and in his 428th game for the club he finally hit the back of the net for the first time in a 2-0 win over Middlesbrough at Elland Road. He made 30 appearances in 1962-63 as the Whites finished in fifth place and he featured on ten occasions as Leeds returned to the top flight the following year. He became player-manager of Wellington Town in May 1964 and was granted a testimonial by the club on 15 November 1965. Wellington and Leeds also met on 8 March that year. He was appointed trainer at Bradford City in February 1967. Tragically, Hair collapsed and died on 7 March 1968. Leeds and Bradford played a testimonial for him on 30 July 1968 and the proceeds went to his widow.

GEORGE MEEK

Debut: Sheffield United (A) 11 October 1952
Appearances: 199
Goals: 19

Glaswegian-born Meek started his career at Thorniewood United before beginning his senior career at Hamilton Academical, scoring on his debut against Kilmarnock. He only played 15 league games for Hamilton, before swapping north of the border for south of the border as he joined Leeds for £500 in August 1952. He made his Leeds United debut away at Sheffield United in October 1952 and would go onto make 29 appearances in his first campaign at Elland Road, scoring away at Leicester City, a brace at home to Lincoln City and one each at home to Everton and in the 3-2 loss away at Swansea Town. He was then called up for National Service in 1954 with the Royal Armoured Corps as well as playing for the Army against a Scottish XI at Ibrox. He spent a season on loan at Walsall. Meek returned to feature in the final ten games of the 1954-55 season under Raich Carter as Leeds finished in fourth position in the second tier. The following season saw the Whites end their Second Division exile as they ended up runners-up to Sheffield Wednesday by three points, and Meek featured on 26 occasions, scoring in a 3-3 draw at home to West Ham United at the start of September 1955. Meek's next two campaigns under Carter's stewardship would be the best in terms of games played as he featured in 41 in each season. He missed just two games each season and hit the back of the net seven times. In season 1956-57, as Leeds adjusted to life back in the First Division, Meek scored against Manchester City at Elland Road, Bolton Wanderers at Burnden Park and in a 5-2 win over Portsmouth at Fratton Park. The following season he went one better with four strikes coming in games at home to Bolton Wanderers, in a 2-0 win at home to Arsenal, the winning goal at home to Burnley and in a 2-2 draw at home to Sheffield Wednesday. He proved the perfect winger for a certain John Charles, setting up the Welshman for many of his headed goals. Another 18 appearances followed in season 1958-59 and another 34 in 1959-60, as Leeds were relegated back to the Second Division. His 199th and final game in a Leeds shirt came under Jack Taylor in a 3-2 loss away at Blackburn Rovers in the penultimate game of season 1959-60, and he marked it with a goal. Meek then left for Leicester City in August 1960 for £7,000. Meek went onto play for the Leeds United ex-players, and did so until he reached the age of 60.

ALBERT NIGHTINGALE

Debut: Sheffield United (A) 11 October 1952
Appearances: 135
Goals: 48

Nightingale who was one of 14 children, born in Thrybergh near Rotherham in 1923, and he started in local football back home with Thurcroft before he moved to Sheffield United in June 1941. From playing for the Blades, he then joined Grimsby Town, Doncaster Rovers and back home to Rotherham United, where he featured as a guest during the war-time years. He also featured in war-time games for Chesterfield as well as Sheffield United. He joined Huddersfield Town in March 1947 and would stay with the Terriers until October 1951, with Leeds in a race to sign the inside-forward, but he chose to swap Yorkshire for Lancashire as he joined Blackburn Rovers. His stay at Ewood Park lasted only a year until he joined Leeds for £10,000. He made his Whites debut in the same game as George Meek and marked it with a goal as Leeds earned a point in a 1-1 draw against the Blades. His first season in west Yorkshire saw Nightingale feature on 27 occasions, scoring a total of eight goals. Other strikes came with a brace at home to Barnsley, one in the 5-1 hammering over Swansea Town at Elland Road, one in a 4-0 win over Rotherham United at Elland Road, one in the loss at Nottingham Forest and another brace in a 2-2 draw at Southampton. The following campaign was Nightingale's best in a Leeds shirt as he featured on 41 occasions, scoring 17 goals as the Whites finished in tenth place in the Second Division. Between 24 October 1953 and 21 November 1953, the Yorkshireman hit seven goals in five games, which included a hat-trick in a 3-1 win over one of his former clubs Doncaster Rovers at Elland Road. He followed this up with another 40 games for the club, plundering a further 13 goals with another hat-trick in a 5-2 win over Swansea Town at Elland Road. Despite only playing in 26 games as Leeds won promotion back to the top flight, Nightingale hit ten goals, including a pair of vital braces in a 6-1 win over Fulham at Elland Road and in a 2-0 away win at Rotherham United respectively. Sadly for Nightingale, his Leeds United and football career was cruelly cut short due to a bad knee injury received on the opening day of new First Division season in a 5-1 win at home to Everton. He passed away in Liverpool on Sunday, 26 February 2006.

BOBBY FORREST

Debut: Nottingham Forest (A) 4 April 1953
Appearances: 121
Goals: 37

Inside-forward Bobby Forest, born in Rossington, near Doncaster, started his career at Rossington Modern School before moving to Rossington Youth Club, then Rossington Colliery before joining Retford Town. The story goes that he went to watch Retford with a friend and the home side were two players short and asked both Forrest and his pal to play. After some stirring displays with the non-league side, he signed for Leeds for £500 in December 1952.

His debut came in a 2-1 defeat away at Nottingham Forest at the back end of the 1952-53 season and he played in six of the last seven league games that campaign, scoring in a 2-0 win at home to Everton and in a 2-1 win at home to Nottingham Forest. His strike rate the following season was almost one a game as he hit eight goals in ten games as Leeds finished tenth in the Second Division, which included a hat-trick in a six-goal thriller at home to Bristol Rovers and a brace in a 2-0 win over Derby County. His best return in terms of goals came the following season as he hit nine goals in 25 games as Leeds finished the season in fourth place in the second tier. He only played as a bit-part player as Leeds finally won promotion back to the promised land, but he did score a vital winner away at Ashton Gate and one in the 2-1 win over eventual champions Sheffield Wednesday at Elland Road.

As Leeds acclimatised to life back in the English top tier, Forrest featured on 28 occasions, scoring a brace in a 4-0 win at home to Charlton Athletic, Leeds's goal in the 4-1 loss at Cardiff City, one in a six-goal thriller at home to Arsenal, one away at Aston Villa and one in 3-0 win in the return against Cardiff City. He hit a further eight goals in 25 games as Leeds finished in 17th place and his last season in west Yorkshire saw him play in 15 games, scoring in a 1-1 draw at home to Burnley and in a 4-1 loss away at Birmingham City. His final game in the colours of Leeds United came in a 4-2 defeat at Blackburn Rovers before being transferred to Notts County in February 1959. He skippered the Magpies to promotion to Division Three before joining Weymouth. He died in Weymouth on 3 May 2005 after suffering a stroke.

JACK CHARLTON

Debut: Doncaster Rovers (H) 25 April 1953
Appearances: 773
Goals: 96

One of the greatest-ever centre-halves to play for the club, Charlton who was born in Ashington in 1935, started at Hurst Park Modern School, then moved on to East Northumberland School, Ashington YMCA and Ashington Welfare, before joining Leeds as an amateur in 1950. He turned professional in May 1952 and made his debut in April 1953. It was his uncle Jim Milburn who recommended him to Leeds, and after National Service with the Royal Horse Guards in 1957 he replaced John Charles, who had moved to the striking department, and he never looked back. He made his debut on the final day of the 1952-53 season at home to Blackburn Rovers and his next appearance was in 3-2 loss at home to Lincoln City in August 1954. He was a mainstay in the side that won promotion under Raich Carter in season 1955-56, making a total of 35 appearances for the side. Following his stint with the Royal Horse Guards, Charlton made 41 starts in season 1957-58, reaching his 100th game for Leeds in a 2-1 away win at Newcastle United on 26 April 1958. Charlton captained the club for the first time in a

2-1 defeat away at Manchester City as he made 40 appearances that season. He also scored his first of 96 goals for the side in a 2-1 win over Blackburn Rovers on 11 April 1959.

As the 1950s turned into the 1960s, Charlton missed just one game under Jack Taylor as the Whites tumbled out of the First Division, finishing in 21st place. By the following March, Taylor was gone and in came the greatest-ever manager in Leeds United's history, and a new era was set to begin under Don Revie. Charlton missed just one game in season 1960-61, scoring eight goals, which included braces away at Scunthorpe United and at home to Swansea Town. Season 1961-62, which was Revie's first full campaign at the club, saw Leeds escape relegation by finishing in 19th place, and Charlton played in 39 games in all competitions, scoring a career-best 12 goals, which included a brace in 4-1 win over Walsall. Another 42 games and three goals followed 12 months later as Leeds improved massively to finish in fifth place and even better was just around the corner for Revie's Leeds. The Whites won the Second Division in season 1963-64, with Charlton playing in 25 league games, scoring against Rotherham United at Millmoor, in a 2-2 draw at home to Derby County and in another draw at home to Charlton Athletic.

Charlton featured in 49 games in all competitions as Leeds returned to the top flight, with the Whites missing out on the League title on goal average, but the defender had the consolation of finishing in his first-ever FA Cup Final against Liverpool. During that season, even better was to follow for Charlton as he made his international debut in a British Home Championship game against Scotland.

The following summer would be the best in Charlton's playing career as on Saturday 30 July he was part of the England side that defeated West Germany to win the World Cup. Despite not winning any silverware with Leeds over the next two season's, the Ashington boy made exactly 100 appearances for the side, scoring 15 goals. By the end of the 1966-67 season he had made 483 appearances for the side, scoring 56 goals. It was during the previous campaign that he captained the side on a permanent basis but gave it up because of his superstition of coming onto the pitch last. Season 1967-68 saw Leeds win a cup double, winning the League Cup against Arsenal and the Inter-Cities Fairs Cup against Ferencvaros, and Charlton competed in a total of 54 games, scoring eight goals. The next season saw the holy grail finally land at Elland Road as Leeds won the top flight for the first time, with Charlton missing just one game, scoring three times. Season 1969-70 saw Leeds miss out on the honours board, but Charlton did score in the FA Cup Final against Chelsea at Wembley, before being part of the side that lost the replay at Old Trafford. Charlton played in ten out of the 12 games as Leeds won their second Inter-Cities Fairs Cup against Juventus in 1971 and in five out of seven games as Leeds won the FA Cup for the first time against Arsenal the following year. Charlton's last full season at Leeds before retirement as a player saw him feature on 25 occasions, with his last game coming on 28 April 1973 away at Southampton. At the end of that season, and two days after the side lost the FA Cup Final to Sunderland, Charlton had a well-deserved testimonial against Glasgow Celtic.

ROYDEN WOOD

Debut: Derby County (H) 24 October 1953
Appearances: 204

Born in Wallasey in Merseyside in 1930, Wood attended St George School before joining West Cheshire league side Harrowby. Wood then went on to join New Brighton as an amateur but left for Lancashire Combination side Clitheroe. It was from here that he signed for Leeds in May 1952 as a permanent successor to Jack Scott. He made his debut in a 3-1 win over Derby County towards the end of October 1953 and went on to make 11 appearances in his first season at Elland Road as Leeds finished tenth in Division Two.

Scott started the 1954-55 season between the sticks, but Wood took over from him in a 3-2 win over Plymouth Argyle and would never look back. He played in every game for the rest of that term as Leeds finished in fourth place, and the next campaign would be even better for both the team and Wood. He was an ever-present for the side as Leeds won promotion back to the First Division, finishing as runners-up to Sheffield Wednesday. The next 12 months saw

Wood yet again have an ever-present next to his name, along with Jimmy Dunn, Grenville Hair, Eric Kerfoot and Jackie Overfield, as Leeds finished in eighth place. The following season saw Wood just miss one game in a 2-0 win away at Bolton Wanderers as Willie Nimmo made his one and only appearance in a Leeds United shirt. Leeds finished in a disappointing 17th place in season 1957-58 and the side matched that the following year. As for Wood, he started the first 27 games of that campaign before losing his position to Ted Burgin under the stewardship of first Bill Lambton and then caretaker Bob Roxborough. By the start of the following season, Jack Taylor had taken the reins at Elland Road and preferred to start with Burgin so Wood did not feature until the end of September. In the end, he only made eight appearances but did reach his 200th game for Leeds in a 2-1 FA Cup loss away at Aston Villa. He took the decision to retire from the game despite not yet reaching his 30s and he became a betting shop manager. He turned to other sports and played as a wicket keeper in the Leeds and District League. Another string to his bow was the fact that he was a member of the PFA management committee that negotiated the abolition of the maximum wage for players.

HAROLD BROOK

Debut: Hull City (A) 21 August 1954
Appearances: 106
Goals: 47

A Yorkshireman born in Sheffield, Brook started with Sheffield Schools before joining Woodburn Alliance then Hallam and Fulwood, before joining Sheffield United in September 1940 and he turned professional in 1943. He featured for the Blades during World War Two and also played 16 times for Manchester United, scoring eight times. He also featured for Queens Park Rangers before returning to Sheffield United before the end of the war. He went on to score 89 goals in 229 league games for the red half of the city before swapping south Yorkshire for west Yorkshire and joining Leeds for £600 in the summer of 1954.

His debut couldn't have gone any better as he scored in a 2-0 home win against Hull City and he would end up as top scorer with

16 goals under the stewardship of Raich Carter. Other strikes included braces in a 4-2 win at Derby, in a 4-1 home win against Ipswich Town and a 2-0 win at home to Blackburn Rovers. The following season would be an exact replica for Brook, but an even better one for Leeds. The Sheffield-born forward scored the side's first goal of the season in a 2-1 loss at Barnsley and would go on to score another 15 goals in 32 games as Leeds ended their Division One exodus. He also scored the last two goals of that memorable season in a 4-1 win away at Hull City as Leeds bid farewell to second-tier football. Brook hit double figures for the third consecutive season as the Whites adjusted to life back in the top flight as he hit 11 goals in 26 games. He started the season like a house on fire, scoring his one and only hat-trick for the club in 5-1 opening-day demolition at home to Everton as Leeds roared back to First Division football. The following season (1957-58) would be his last in a Leeds United shirt, but he did make his 100th appearance in 2-0 loss at home to Luton Town on 11 September 1957, with his last strike for Leeds coming in a 2-1 win away at Portsmouth on 12 October 1957. He went on to join Lincoln City in March 1958 and this would be his final destination as a player. He became coach at Sheffield FC and ran a newsagent in Meadowcroft in his home city. He passed away in Sheffield in November 1998.

ARCHIE GIBSON

Debut: Birmingham City (A) 2 March 1955
Appearances: 174
Goals: 5

Scotsman Gibson who was born in Dailly, near Girvan, in Ayrshire and started at Girvan High School before going on to join Coylton Juveniles. He was first spotted by Leeds whilst playing in a Scottish Juvenile Cup semi-final at Falkirk in May 1951. He took up national service with RAC, where he was based in Catterick, and played for Northern Command.

After signing in May 1951, he made his Leeds United debut in a 2-0 loss away at Birmingham City at the start of March 1955. He featured in the remaining 12 games that campaign as Leeds finished in the top four of the Second Division. The promotion-winning season saw Gibson play in 28 games wearing the number-four shirt. The first season back in the top flight since 1948-49 would be Gibson's best in terms of games in a Leeds United shirt. He missed just two games – a 4-0 home win against Chelsea and 1-0 loss away at Manchester City – when Keith Ripley deputised as Leeds finished in a respectable eighth position. Gibson also reached the landmark of 100 games in Leeds colours in a 3-0 loss at Leicester City just after Christmas

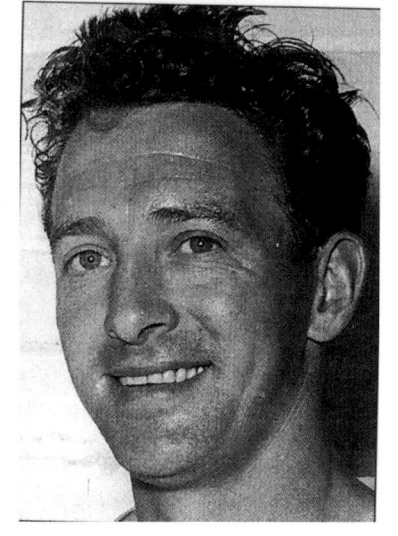

1957. The second season back in the top flight would be a lot tougher as the Whites ended up in 17th place and Gibson featured on 26 occasions, scoring the first of his five goals in a 2-1 win at home to Sunderland on 28 September 1957. The next season would see Gibson make the headlines for all the wrong reasons. On 27 December 1958 he became the first Leeds United player since Billy Poyntz (who was dismissed against Bury on 11 February 1922) to be sent off in a Football League match for fighting with Derek Hogg of West Bromwich Albion at Elland Road. Hogg was also subsequently shown the red card. Gibson ended up with 32 appearances that term, scoring in a thrilling 4-3 loss at home to Bolton Wanderers.

His final season at Elland Road, which saw the side finish in 21st place and relegation back to the second tier, saw Gibson play on 35 occasions, scoring three goals. His 174th and final game for Leeds was on the last day of the 1959-60 season and he was transferred to Scunthorpe United that summer. He ended his career at Barnsley but never made a Football League appearance for the Tykes. He suffered with Alzheimer's and died on 26 July 2012 at the age of 78.

JACK OVERFIELD

Debut: Nottingham Forest (H) 8 October 1955
Appearances: 163
Goals: 20

Leeds-born Jack Overfield went to Victoria Road School and played football for Ashley Road Methodists before being rejected by Sheffield United following a trial. To make matters worse, he was then turned away by Bolton Wanderers before initially finding solace at Yorkshire Amateurs, before making the move to Elland Road. He joined the side in May 1953, but before he could make his Leeds United debut he was on National Service, where he played in several representative games for the RAF. He made his Leeds United debut in a 3-0 win at home to Nottingham Forest wearing the number-11 shirt. He couldn't have picked a better first season in the colours of Leeds United as the home-town player featured on 31 occasions, scoring six goals as the Whites returned to the top division at long last. His goals came against Lincoln City in a 1-0 win at Elland Road, one in a 4-2 win at home to Liverpool, another in a 3-0 victory at home to Doncaster

Rovers, another in 3-2 win away at Blackburn Rovers, one in a 4-0 hammering of Leicester City and one in a vital 2-1 win at home to Bristol Rovers. Overfield had scored in six games and Leeds had won all six.

The winger was an ever-present with Leeds back in the First Division and scored in the opening day 5-1 win at home to Everton. Overfield hit a further four goals in 37 games the next campaign but the side struggled as they finished 17th in Division One. His record of scoring and being on the winning side ended in a 2-1 home defeat against Nottingham Forest on 14 September 1957. He marked his 100th appearance that season in a 2-0 win over Bolton Wanderers at Burden Park and the next season would be his best in a Leeds United shirt. Having played under only Raich Carter, Bill Lambton was now in charge. Overfield did request a transfer, but he scored eight goals in 36 games in the 1958-59 season. Lambton left with two months of the season to go, and Bob Roxborough took charge, before Jack Taylor took the role on ahead of the final season of the decade. Overfield made 16 appearances under Taylor, scoring his last goal in his last game for the Whites in a 1-0 win over Burnley in mid-December 1959. He left for Sunderland in August 1960 for £11,500.

WILBUR CUSH

Debut: Manchester City (H) 16 November 1957
Appearances: 90
Goals: 9

The Northern Irishman started his career at Carrish School and went on to join Lurgan Boys Club and Shankhill YMCA before signing for Glenavon in 1947. He spent over a decade there winning the Championship in 1951-52 and 1956-57, being runners-up in 1955-56, winning the Gold Cup twice in 1954 and 1956 and the Ulster Cup in 1955. He also featured in Glenavon's Irish Cup Final loss against Dundela in 1955. At the end of the 1956-57 season he was named Ulster's Footballer of the Year. He had been given the perfect tribute by one of football's greats in Sir Stanley Matthews as he once said, 'being tackled by Cush was like being hit by a tank'.

He swapped Northern Ireland for England in November 1957 when he joined Leeds for £7,000, and he made his debut in a 4-2 home loss against Manchester City. In his first season with the Whites

Cush made 22 appearances for the side, scoring three times, in a 1-1 draw at home to Birmingham City, in a 2-1 win at home to Blackpool and in a 2-0 win away at Bolton Wanderers. He was made captain at the start of the 1958-59 season and he featured on 37 occasions, scoring a further three goals, with the strikes coming in a 3-2 loss at Everton, a 3-2 win at Tottenham Hotspur and a 1-1 draw at home to Portsmouth at the end of February 1959. Under new manager Jack Taylor, the captaincy was handed to Don Revie for the start of the 1959-60, but Cush did take on the role when Revie wasn't involved. Cush went on to make a further 31 appearances as the side were relegated back to the second tier, finishing in the penultimate place in the league, four points off bottom-place Luton Town.

Just like in his previous two seasons with the club, Cush hit three goals in his final campaign, scoring from the spot against Burnley on the opening day of the 1959-60 term, another in a 3-2 loss at Leicester and one in the 2-2 draw at home to Manchester United. His 90th and last game for the side came in a 2-1 win at home to Preston North End in mid-April 1960. After finishing at Leeds, Cush returned home to join Portadown before rejoining Glenavon. He finished up with 26 international caps, featuring as a member of the Northern Ireland World Cup squad in 1958, scoring the winning goal against Czechoslovakia. He became a butcher after he retired and he passed away in Lurgen in July 1981 after a short illness.

MANAGERS APPOINTED IN THE 1950s

RAICH CARTER

First game in charge: Notts County (H) 19 August 1953
Last game in charge: Newcastle United (A) 26 April 1958
Games: 217
Won: 90
Drawn: 51
Lost: 76

Following Major Frank Buckley's decision to resign from the post, Raich Carter took over from him just like he had done at Hull City five years earlier. Carter, who was born in Hendon in Sunderland in 1913, was one of the greatest forwards ever produced. He managed to win every honour in the English game and helped Leeds United regain their First Division status in season 1955-56. Carter started his playing career at Sunderland after being offered amateur terms by his uncle and signed for the Mackems in the summer of 1931, turning down Huddersfield Town at the time. He led Sunderland to the holy grail of the First Division title in season 1935-36, becoming the youngest captain at that time to do so. A year later he followed it up with an FA Cup winner's medal, scoring in a 3-1 win over Preston North End at Wembley.

In November 1945 he was transfer-listed by the side after they refused his request for a new ten-year contract. He went on to join the Rams of Derby County, ironically making his league debut against his former side. He also had spells at Hull City and Cork Athletic. He was capped 13 times by England and also played cricket for Derbyshire. Carter's first crack of management when he joined Hull City was as player-assistant manager, on the proviso that he would learn under Buckley's tutelage. Buckley resigned on 23 April 1948 and Carter took over on Humberside. He led the club to the Third Division North Championship in 1949. He bought a certain Don Revie for the Tigers, but on 5 September 1951 he offered his resignation which was accepted by the club, though he did return as a player later that year.

Carter then moved to Ireland, where he took Cork Athletic to the 1953 FA of Ireland Cup Final, and he was appointed manager of Leeds United in May 1953. His first season in charge of the club saw the side finish in tenth place in the second tier, largely thanks to 42 league goals from the great John Charles. The following season saw an improvement as the side finished in fourth place and even better was to follow 12 months later. Season 1955-56 saw Carter's side finish in second place, with Charles top-scoring once again with 29 league goals and Leeds clinching promotion in a 4-1 at Hull City. Back in the First Division Leeds finished in eighth position with another 38 goals from the Welshman, but by the start of the following campaign Charles had been sold to Juventus for £65,000, with Carter and Leeds never recovering. They finished the 1957-58 campaign in 17th place and at the end of the season chairman Sam Bolton announced his contract would not be renewed.

Carter had further managerial spells at both Mansfield Town and Middlesbrough. His career in football ended after Boro had been relegated and Carter returned to Hull to run a sports department in a local store. He passed away in Willerby near Hull aged 80, on 9 October 1994. The opening game at the new KC Stadium in December 2002, between Hull and Sunderland, saw the winners carry off the Raich Carter Trophy.

Raich Carter's first line up: Notts County (H) 19 August 1953: Scott, Dunn, Hair, Kerfoot, McCabe, Williams, Nightingale, Charles, Iggleden, Burbanks.

Raich Carter's last line up: Newcastle United (A) 26 April 1958: Wood, Dunn, Hair, Gibson, Charlton, Kerfoot, Meek, Peyton, Baird, O'Brien, Overfield.

BILL LAMBTON

First game in charge: Bolton Wanderers (A) 23 August 1958
Last game in charge: Portsmouth (H) 28 February 1959
Games: 33
Won: 10
Drawn: 8
Lost: 15

Following the decision not to renew Carter's contract, Leeds then turned to lesser-known Bill Lambton at the start of the 1958-59 season. Lambton played in goal for Nottingham Forest, Exeter City and Doncaster Rovers, although his appearances were limited due to World War Two. His coaching career started with KB Copenhagen in Denmark and on his return to the United Kingdom he coached Scunthorpe United. Leeds manager Raich Carter then persuaded Lambton to join as a trainer-coach in November 1957 and once the board decided not to extended the contract of Carter, Lambton took over on a caretaker basis. His contribution may have been small as he lasted just over 30 games, but he did sign Don Revie and Billy Bremner. His first game as manager was a disaster as Leeds lost 4-0 to Bolton Wanderers, and by

8 November the Whites were third from bottom in the First Division with just 12 points from 16 games. Lambton dipped into the transfer window to sign Revie on 9 December 1958, and Sam Bolton offered Lambton the job on a permanent basis after he was unable to attract a bigger name. The decision to hire the Nottinghamshire-born Lambton didn't go down well, with stars Grenville Hair and Jack Overfield demanding transfers. He was sacked after 33 games, being replaced by Bob Roxburgh. He then spent three days as Scunthorpe United manager, although this was only a verbal agreement. He had one more managerial position at Chester in January 1962, but they finished bottom of the Football League and a season later they finished fourth from bottom and had to reapply for re-election to the League. Lambton had his contract cancelled in July 1963. He died in Nottingham on 16 September 1976, aged 61.

Bill Lambton's first line up: Bolton Wanderers (A) 23 August 1958: Wood, Dunn, Hair, Gibson, Charlton, Cush, Crowe, Peyton, Forrest, O'Brien, Overfield.

Bill Lambton's last line up: Portsmouth (H) 28 February 1959: Burgin, Ashall, Kilford, Revie, Charlton, Gibson, Humphries, Cush, Shackleton, O'Brien, Meek.

BOB ROXBURGH (CARETAKER)

First game in charge: Aston Villa (A) 7 March 1959
Last game in charge: West Ham United (H) 25 April 1959
Games: 10
Won: 5
Drawn: 1
Lost: 4

Roxburgh, who had been a trainer at the club since the mid-1930s, took on the role of caretaker-manager for the remaining ten games of the 1958-59 season with Leeds in 15th place. He presided over wins against Tottenham Hotspur 3-1 at Elland Road, Chelsea 4-0 at Elland Road, 2-1 at home to Blackburn Rovers, 3-0 away at Nottingham Forest and a 1-0 win on the final day of the campaign at home to West Ham United, thanks to an Alan Shackleton strike. He lost four of his ten games, away to Aston Villa (1-2), away at Manchester United (4-0), at home to Wolverhampton Wanderers (1-3) and away at Blackpool (0-3). Leeds ended up finishing in 15th place and Jack Taylor was then appointed in May 1959.

Bob Roxburgh's first line up: Aston Villa (A) 7 March 1959: Burgin, Dunn, Ashall, Kerfoot, Charlton, O'Brien, Meek, Crowe, Shackleton, Cush, Overfield.

Bob Roxburgh's last line up: West Ham United (H) 25 April 1959: Burgin, Dunn, Hair, McConnell, Charlton, Cush, Crowe, Revie, Shackleton, Revie, Meek.

JACK TAYLOR

First game in charge: Burnley (H) 22 August 1959
Last game in charge: Norwich City (H) 11 March 1961
Games: 81
Won: 27
Drawn: 17
Lost: 37

The final manager appointed in the 1950s was former Wolverhampton Wanderers, Norwich City and Hull City player Jack Taylor. Taylor, who was born in Barnsley, started his career in the Black Country with Wolves, staying at Molineux until the summer of 1938 when he joined Norwich City. His stay in East Anglia lasted nine years, either side of World War Two, and he finished his playing career at Hull City, who were at the time managed by a certain Raich Carter, and he was part of the side that won the Third Division North Championship in season 1948-49.

From Hull, Taylor dropped into non-league football to manage Weymouth but returned to league football with Queens Park Rangers. He suffered two humiliating FA Cup defeats whilst in west London, which included a 6-1 hammering by non-league Hereford United. At the time when Leeds were looking for a new manager, Arthur Turner, the Headington United boss and former Birmingham City supremo, had been red-hot favourite but decided to stay at Headington. Second choice was Tommy Burden, but he turned down the chance and the board turned to Taylor from QPR. His first full season at the club was an unmitigated disaster as the side were relegated from the top flight, finishing second from bottom with 34 points. The fans lost faith in Taylor following the sales of Jimmy Dunn and Eric Kerfoot with no replacements for them, and in September 1959 striker Alan Shackleton followed, joining Everton. He did replace him with Bradford City striker John McCole, but the rot had already set in. Mccole did score 23 goals in all competitions but Leeds were demoted back to the second tier. In the summer, Leeds lost Archie Gibson, George Meek and Wilbur Cush, though he did sign Eric Smith from Celtic, but he suffered a broken leg. Taylor resigned on 13 March 1961 and the job went to Don Revie, who took over as player-manager. Taylor passed away on 22 February 1978, aged 64.

Jack Taylor's first line up: Burnley (H) 22 August 1959: Burgin, Ashall, Hair, McConnell, Chartlon, Cush, Humphries, Revie, Shackleton, Crowe, Meek.

Jack Taylor's last line up: Norwich City (H) 11 March 1961: Humphreys, Jones, Kilford, Cameron, McConnell, Fitzgerald, Smith, McCole, Bremner, Francis.

DIVISION TWO

1950–51

Date	Opposition	Competition	Score
19/08/1950	Doncaster Rovers	Division Two	3-1
21/08/1950	Coventry City	Division Two	0-1
26/08/1950	Brentford	Division Two	2-1
30/08/1950	Coventry City	Division Two	1-0
02/09/1950	Blackburn Rovers	Division Two	0-1
07/09/1950	Swansea Town	Division Two	2-4
09/09/1950	Southampton	Division Two	0-2
16/09/1950	Barnsley	Division Two	2-2
23/09/1950	Sheffield United	Division Two	2-2
30/09/1950	Luton Town	Division Two	2-1
07/10/1950	Bury	Division Two	1-1
14/10/1950	Preston North End	Division Two	0-2
21/10/1950	Chesterfield	Division Two	2-0
28/10/1950	Queens Park Rangers	Division Two	0-3
04/11/1950	Manchester City	Division Two	1-1
11/11/1950	Leicester City	Division Two	5-1
18/11/1950	Notts County	Division Two	0-1
25/11/1950	Grimsby Town	Division Two	2-2
02/12/1960	Birmingham City	Division Two	3-0
09/12/1950	Cardiff City	Division Two	0-1
16/12/1950	Doncaster Rovers	Division Two	4-4
23/12/1950	Brentford	Division Two	1-0
25/12/1950	West Ham United	Division Two	1-3
26/12/1950	West Ham United	Division Two	2-0
06/01/1951	Middlesbrough	FA Cup 3rd Round	1-0
13/01/1951	Southampton	Division Two	5-3
20/01/1951	Barnsley	Division Two	2-1
27/01/1951	Manchester United	FA Cup 4th Round	0-4
03/02/1951	Sheffield United	Division Two	1-0
10/02/1951	Blackburn Rovers	Division Two	1-2
17/02/1951	Luton Town	Division Two	3-2
24/02/1951	Bury	Division Two	1-0
03/03/1951	Preston North End	Division Two	0-3
10/03/1951	Chesterfield	Division Two	0-1
17/03/1951	Queens Park Rangers	Division Two	2-2
23/03/1951	Hull City	Division Two	0-2
24/03/1951	Manchester City	Division Two	1-4
26/03/1951	Hull City	Division Two	3-0
31/03/1951	Leicester City	Division Two	2-1
07/04/1951	Notts County	Division Two	0-0
14/04/1951	Grimsby Town	Division Two	1-0
21/04/1951	Birmingham City	Division Two	1-0
28/04/1951	Cardiff City	Division Two	2-0
05/05/1951	Swansea Town	Division Two	2-0

Team	Pld	W	D	L	GF	GA	Pts
Preston North End	42	26	5	11	91	49	57
Manchester City	42	19	14	9	89	61	52
Cardiff City	42	17	16	9	53	45	50
Birmingham City	42	20	9	13	64	53	49
Leeds United	42	20	8	14	63	55	48
Blackburn Rovers	42	19	8	15	65	66	46
Coventry City	42	19	7	16	75	59	45
Sheffield United	42	16	12	14	72	62	44
Brentford	42	18	8	16	75	74	44
Hull City	42	16	11	15	74	70	43
Doncaster Rovers	42	15	13	14	64	68	43
Southampton	42	15	13	14	66	73	43
West Ham United	42	16	10	16	68	69	42
Leicester City	42	15	11	16	68	58	41
Barnsley	42	15	10	17	74	68	40
Queen's Park Rangers	42	15	10	17	71	82	40
Notts County	42	13	13	16	61	60	39
Swansea Town	42	16	4	22	54	77	36
Luton Town	42	9	14	19	57	70	32
Bury	42	12	8	22	60	86	32
Chesterfield	42	9	12	21	44	69	30
Grimsby Town	42	8	12	22	61	95	28

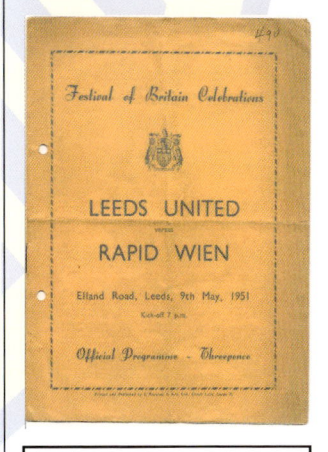

Leeds also played two Festival of Britain matches vs Rapid Vienna and Haarlem both at Elland Road.

Leeds were led by two captains in season 1950-51, Tom Burden and Jim McCabe.

The game at Maine Road on 24 March 1951 saw John Charles play at centre-forward for the first time in his career.

Defender Jim Milburn was the only ever-present in season 1950-51.

Leeds used two goalkeepers at the start of the decade, Harry Searson played in 27 games, with John Scott playing in the other 17.

1951–52

DIVISION TWO

Team	Pld	W	D	L	GF	GA	Pts
Sheffield Wednesday	42	21	11	10	100	66	53
Cardiff City	42	20	11	11	72	54	51
Birmingham City	42	21	9	12	67	56	51
Nottingham Forest	42	18	13	11	77	62	49
Leicester City	42	19	9	14	78	64	47
Leeds United	42	18	11	13	59	57	47
Everton	42	17	10	15	64	58	44
Luton Town	42	16	12	14	77	78	44
Rotherham United	42	17	8	17	73	71	42
Brentford	42	15	12	15	54	55	42
Sheffield United	42	18	5	19	90	76	41
West Ham United	42	15	11	16	67	77	41
Southampton	42	15	11	16	61	73	41
Blackburn Rovers	42	17	6	19	54	63	40
Notts County	42	16	7	19	71	68	39
Doncaster Rovers	42	13	12	17	55	60	38
Bury	42	15	7	20	67	69	37
Hull City	42	13	11	18	60	70	37
Swansea Town	42	12	12	18	72	76	36
Barnsley	42	11	14	17	59	72	36
Coventry City	42	14	6	22	59	82	34
Queen's Park Rangers	42	11	12	19	52	81	34

Date	Opposition	Competition	Score
18/08/1951	Brentford	Division Two	1-1
22/08/1951	Birmingham City	Division Two	1-1
25/08/1951	Doncaster Rovers	Division Two	0-2
29/08/1951	Birmingham City	Division Two	1-1
01/09/1951	Everton	Division Two	1-2
08/09/1951	Southampton	Division Two	0-0
12/09/1951	Cardiff City	Division Two	2-1
15/09/1951	Sheffield Wednesday	Division Two	3-2
22/09/1951	West Ham United	Division Two	0-2
29/09/1951	Rotherham United	Division Two	2-4
06/10/1951	Sheffield United	Division Two	3-1
13/10/1951	Barnsley	Division Two	1-3
20/10/1951	Hull City	Division Two	2-0
27/10/1951	Blackburn Rovers	Division Two	3-2
03/11/1951	Queens Park Rangers	Division Two	3-0
10/11/1951	Notts County	Division Two	2-1
17/11/1951	Luton Town	Division Two	1-1
24/11/1951	Bury	Division Two	2-1
01/12/1951	Swansea Town	Division Two	1-1
08/12/1951	Coventry City	Division Two	2-4
15/12/1951	Brentford	Division Two	1-2
22/12/1951	Doncaster Rovers	Division Two	0-0
25/12/1951	Leicester City	Division Two	2-1
26/12/1951	Leicester City	Division Two	2-1
29/12/1951	Everton	Division Two	0-2
05/01/1952	Southampton	Division Two	1-1
12/01/1952	Rochdale	FA Cup 3rd Round	2-0
19/01/1952	Sheffield Wednesday	Division Two	2-1
26/01/1952	West Ham United	Division Two	3-1
02/02/1952	Bradford Park Avenue	FA Cup 4th Round	2-0
09/02/1952	Rotherham United	Division Two	3-0
16/02/1952	Sheffield United	Division Two	0-3
23/02/1952	Chelsea	FA Cup 5th Round	1-1
27/02/1952	Chelsea	FA Cup 5th Round Replay	1-1
01/03/1952	Barnsley	Division Two	1-0
03/03/1952	Chelsea	FA Cup 5th Round 2nd Replay * at Villa Park	1-5
08/03/1952	Hull City	Division Two	2-3
15/03/1952	Blackburn Rovers	Division Two	1-0
22/03/1952	Queens Park Rangers	Division Two	0-0
29/03/1952	Notts County	Division Two	1-0
05/04/1952	Luton Town	Division Two	1-2
11/04/1952	Nottingham Forest	Division Two	1-1
12/04/1952	Bury	Division Two	2-1
14/04/1952	Nottingham Forest	Division Two	0-0
19/04/1952	Swansea Town	Division Two	1-4
26/04/1952	Coventry City	Division Two	3-1
03/05/1952	Cardiff City	Division Two	1-3

Leeds had three captains in season 1951-52, Tom Burden, Jim McCabe and John Charles.

Ray Iggeden was the top appearance maker, missing just one game on Boxing Day at home to Leicester City.

Leeds drew two 50,000-plus crowds at Elland Road, both in the FA Cup, 50,645 v Bradford Park Avenue and 52,328 v Chelsea.

Three goalkeepers were used this campaign, Brian Taylor, Harry Searson and John Scott.

Leeds had nine debutants, Brian Taylor, John Finlay, Ron Barritt, Ron Mollatt, Billy Hudson, Don Mills, Bobby Ross, Frank Fidler and Gordon Stewart.

DIVISION TWO

1952–53

Date	Opposition	Competition	Score
23/08/1952	Huddersfield Town	Division Two	0-1
28/08/1952	Bury	Division Two	2-2
30/08/1952	Plymouth Argyle	Division Two	1-1
03/09/1952	Bury	Division Two	2-0
06/09/1952	Rotherham United	Division Two	1-3
10/09/1952	Birmingham City	Division Two	0-1
13/09/1952	Fulham	Division Two	2-0
17/09/1952	Birmingham City	Division Two	2-2
20/09/1952	West Ham United	Division Two	2-2
24/09/1952	Southampton	Division Two	1-1
27/09/1952	Leicester City	Division Two	0-1
04/10/1952	Notts County	Division Two	2-3
11/10/1952	Sheffield United	Division Two	1-2
18/10/1952	Barnsley	Division Two	4-1
25/10/1952	Lincoln City	Division Two	1-1
01/11/1952	Hull City	Division Two	3-1
08/11/1952	Blackburn Rovers	Division Two	1-1
22/11/1952	Everton	Division Two	2-2
29/11/1952	Brentford	Division Two	3-2
06/12/1952	Doncaster Rovers	Division Two	0-0
13/12/1952	Swansea Town	Division Two	5-1
20/12/1952	Huddersfield Town	Division Two	2-1
26/12/1952	Luton Town	Division Two	0-2
27/12/1952	Luton Town	Division Two	2-2
03/01/1953	Plymouth Argyle	Division Two	1-0
10/01/1953	Brentford	FA Cup 3rd Round	1-2
17/01/1953	Rotherham United	Division Two	4-0
24/01/1953	Fulham	Division Two	1-2
07/02/1953	West Ham United	Division Two	3-2
14/02/1953	Leicester City	Division Two	3-3
21/02/1953	Notts County	Division Two	3-1
28/02/1953	Sheffield United	Division Two	0-3
07/03/1953	Barnsley	Division Two	2-2
14/03/1953	Lincoln City	Division Two	2-1
21/03/1953	Hull City	Division Two	0-1
28/03/1953	Blackburn Rovers	Division Two	0-3
04/04/1953	Nottingham Forest	Division Two	1-2
06/04/1953	Southampton	Division Two	2-2
11/04/1953	Everton	Division Two	2-0
16/04/1953	Swansea Town	Division Two	2-3
18/04/1953	Brentford	Division Two	3-3
22/04/1953	Nottingham Forest	Division Two	2-1
25/04/1953	Doncaster Rovers	Division Two	1-1

Team	Pld	W	D	L	GF	GA	Pts
Sheffield United	42	25	10	7	97	55	60
Huddersfield Town	42	24	10	8	84	33	58
Luton Town	42	22	8	12	84	49	52
Plymouth Argyle	42	20	9	13	65	60	49
Leicester City	42	18	12	12	89	74	48
Birmingham City	42	19	10	13	71	66	48
Nottingham Forest	42	18	8	16	77	67	44
Fulham	42	17	10	15	81	71	44
Blackburn Rovers	42	18	8	16	68	65	44
Leeds United	42	14	15	13	71	63	43
Swansea Town	42	15	12	15	78	81	42
Rotherham United	42	16	9	17	75	74	41
Doncaster Rovers	42	12	16	14	58	64	40
West Ham United	42	13	13	16	58	60	39
Lincoln City	42	11	17	14	64	71	39
Everton	42	12	14	16	71	75	38
Brentford	42	13	11	18	59	76	37
Hull City	42	14	8	20	57	69	36
Notts County	42	14	8	20	60	88	36
Bury	42	13	9	20	53	81	35
Southampton	42	10	13	19	68	85	33
Barnsley	42	5	8	29	47	108	18

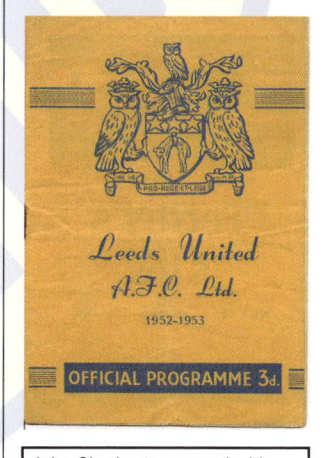

John Charles top scored with 27 goals, the highest since Tom Jennings struck 37 in 1926-27.

Captain Tom Burden, goalkeeper John Scott and defender Jimmy Dunn were ever-presents.

The end of the campaign saw the end of Major Frank Buckley's tenure at Elland Road.

The opening day of the season saw the debut of Andy McCall, the father of former Scunthorpe United manager and former Bradford City player and manager Stuart.

The last day of the season at home to Doncaster Rovers saw the debut of one Jack Charlton.

1953–54   DIVISION TWO

Team	Pld	W	D	L	GF	GA	Pts
Leicester City	42	23	10	9	97	60	56
Everton	42	20	16	6	92	58	56
Blackburn Rovers	42	23	9	10	86	50	55
Nottingham Forest	42	20	12	10	86	59	52
Rotherham United	42	21	7	14	80	67	49
Luton Town	42	18	12	12	64	59	48
Birmingham City	42	18	11	13	78	58	47
Fulham	42	17	10	15	98	85	44
Bristol Rovers	42	14	16	12	64	58	44
Leeds United	42	15	13	14	89	81	43
Stoke City	42	12	17	13	71	60	41
Doncaster Rovers	42	16	9	17	59	63	41
West Ham United	42	15	9	18	67	69	39
Notts County	42	13	13	16	54	74	39
Hull City	42	16	6	20	64	66	38
Lincoln City	42	14	9	19	65	83	37
Bury	42	11	14	17	54	72	36
Derby County	42	12	11	19	64	82	35
Plymouth Argyle	42	9	16	17	65	82	34
Swansea Town	42	13	8	21	58	82	34
Brentford	42	10	11	21	40	78	31
Oldham Athletic	42	8	9	25	40	89	25

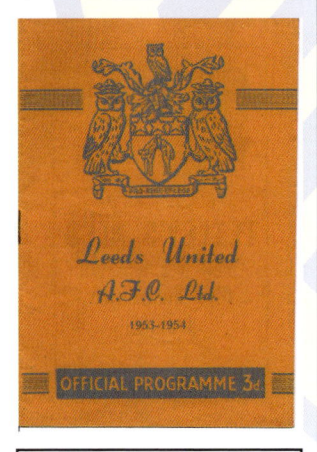

Date	Opposition	Competition	Score
19/08/1953	Notts County	Division Two	6-0
22/08/1953	Rotherham United	Division Two	4-2
27/08/1953	Swansea Town	Division Two	3-4
29/08/1953	Leicester City	Division Two	0-5
02/09/1953	Swansea Town	Division Two	3-2
05/09/1953	Stoke City	Division Two	1-1
07/09/1953	Plymouth Argyle	Division Two	1-1
12/09/1953	Fulham	Division Two	3-1
16/09/1953	Plymouth Argyle	Division Two	1-1
19/09/1953	West Ham United	Division Two	1-2
26/09/1953	Lincoln City	Division Two	0-2
03/10/1953	Birmingham City	Division Two	3-3
10/10/1953	Bristol Rovers	Division Two	3-3
17/10/1953	Brentford	Division Two	1-2
24/10/1953	Derby County	Division Two	3-1
31/10/1953	Blackburn Rovers	Division Two	2-2
07/11/1953	Doncaster Rovers	Division Two	3-1
14/11/1953	Bury	Division Two	4-4
21/11/1953	Oldham Athletic	Division Two	2-1
28/11/1953	Everton	Division Two	1-2
05/12/1953	Hull City	Division Two	0-0
12/12/1953	Notts County	Division Two	0-2
19/12/1953	Rotherham United	Division Two	4-2
25/12/1953	Nottingham Forest	Division Two	2-5
26/12/1953	Nottingham Forest	Division Two	0-2
02/01/1954	Leicester City	Division Two	7-1
09/01/1954	Tottenham Hotspur	FA Cup 3rd Round	3-3
13/01/1954	Tottenham Hotspur	FA Cup 3rd Round Replay	0-1
16/01/1954	Stoke City	Division Two	0-4
23/01/1954	Fulham	Division Two	1-2
06/02/1954	West Ham United	Division Two	2-5
13/02/1954	Lincoln City	Division Two	5-2
20/02/1954	Birmingham City	Division Two	1-1
27/02/1954	Bristol Rovers	Division Two	1-1
06/03/1954	Brentford	Division Two	4-0
13/03/1954	Derby County	Division Two	2-0
20/03/1954	Blackburn Rovers	Division Two	3-2
27/03/1954	Oldham Athletic	Division Two	2-4
03/04/1954	Everton	Division Two	3-1
10/04/1954	Doncaster Rovers	Division Two	0-0
16/04/1954	Luton Town	Division Two	1-1
17/04/1954	Bury	Division Two	3-4
19/04/1954	Luton Town	Division Two	2-1
24/04/1954	Hull City	Division Two	1-1

Leeds scored 89 goals, which was the highest in the league since 1927-28, when they won promotion with 98.

In the 1927-28 season, the team conceded only 49, this season they conceded 81.

John Charles scored five hat-tricks this season, (including four against Notts County) a record that still stands today.

Eric Kerfoot and Grenville Hair were ever-presents.

The club used three goalkeepers, John Scott, Royden Wood and Tom Wheatley

BACK ROW: ERIC KERFOOT, JIMMY DUNN, ROYDEN WOOD, GRENVILLE HAIR, JACK MARSDEN
FRONT ROW: HAROLD WILLIAMS, ALBERT NIGHTINGALE, JOHN CHARLES, TOM BURDEN, RAY IGGLEDEN, ARTHUR TYRER

DIVISION TWO

1954–55

Date	Opposition	Competition	Score
21/08/1954	Hull City	Division Two	2-0
25/08/1954	Rotherham United	Division Two	2-4
28/08/1954	Lincoln City	Division Two	2-3
30/08/1954	Rotherham United	Division Two	0-3
04/09/1954	Bury	Division Two	3-5
08/09/1954	Stoke City	Division Two	0-1
11/09/1954	Swansea Town	Division Two	5-2
13/09/1954	Stoke City	Division Two	1-0
18/09/1954	Nottingham Forest	Division Two	1-1
25/09/1954	Ipswich Town	Division Two	2-1
02/10/1954	Birmingham City	Division Two	1-0
09/10/1954	Derby County	Division Two	4-2
16/10/1954	West Ham United	Division Two	2-1
23/10/1954	Bristol Rovers	Division Two	1-5
30/10/1954	Plymouth Argyle	Division Two	3-2
06/11/1954	Port Vale	Division Two	1-0
13/11/1954	Doncaster Rovers	Division Two	1-0
20/11/1954	Notts County	Division Two	2-1
27/11/1954	Liverpool	Division Two	2-2
04/12/1954	Blackburn Rovers	Division Two	2-1
11/12/1954	Fulham	Division Two	1-1
18/12/1954	Hull City	Division Two	3-0
25/12/1954	Middlesbrough	Division Two	1-1
27/12/1954	Middlesbrough	Division Two	0-1
01/01/1955	Lincoln City	Division Two	0-2
08/01/1955	Torquay United	FA Cup 3rd Round	2-2
12/01/1955	Torquay United	FA Cup 3rd Round Replay	0-4
15/01/1955	Bury	Division Two	1-0
22/01/1955	Swansea Town	Division Two	0-2
05/02/1955	Nottingham Forest	Division Two	1-1
12/02/1955	Ipswich Town	Division Two	4-1
26/02/1955	Derby County	Division Two	1-0
02/03/1955	Birmingham City	Division Two	0-2
05/03/1955	West Ham United	Division Two	1-2
12/03/1955	Bristol Rovers	Division Two	2-0
19/03/1955	Plymouth Argyle	Division Two	1-3
26/03/1955	Port Vale	Division Two	3-0
02/04/1955	Doncaster Rovers	Division Two	1-0
08/04/1955	Luton Town	Division Two	0-0
09/04/1955	Notts County	Division Two	2-0
11/04/1955	Luton Town	Division Two	4-0
16/04/1955	Liverpool	Division Two	2-2
23/04/1955	Blackburn Rovers	Division Two	2-0
30/04/1955	Fulham	Division Two	3-1

Team	Pld	W	D	L	GF	GA	Pts
Birmingham City	42	22	10	10	92	47	54
Luton Town	42	23	8	11	88	53	54
Rotherham United	42	25	4	13	94	64	54
Leeds United	42	23	7	12	70	53	53
Stoke City	42	21	10	11	69	46	52
Blackburn Rovers	42	22	6	14	114	79	50
Notts County	42	21	6	15	74	71	48
West Ham United	42	18	10	14	74	70	46
Bristol Rovers	42	19	7	16	75	70	45
Swansea Town	42	17	9	16	86	83	43
Liverpool	42	16	10	16	92	96	42
Middlesbrough	42	18	6	18	73	82	42
Bury	42	15	11	16	77	72	41
Fulham	42	14	11	17	76	79	39
Nottingham Forest	42	16	7	19	58	62	39
Lincoln City	42	13	10	19	68	79	36
Port Vale	42	12	11	19	48	71	35
Doncaster Rovers	42	14	7	21	58	95	35
Hull City	42	12	10	20	44	69	34
Plymouth Argyle	42	12	7	23	57	82	31
Ipswich Town	42	11	6	25	57	92	28
Derby County	42	7	9	26	53	82	23

LEEDS UNITED A.F.C.

SEASON 1954-1955

OFFICIAL PROGRAMME 3d.

Harold Brook celebrated his debut season at Elland Road after signing from Sheffield United by becoming top scorer.

Leeds entertained Torquay for the first and only time in their competitive history, losing an FA Cup third-round replay 4-0.

Grenville Hair and Jimmy Dunn were again ever-presents, playing in all 44 games.

Royden Wood took over the number-one slot from John Scott in the home game against Plymouth Argyle.

Other debutants mid-way through the decade were Jimmy Toner, Keith Ripley, Micky Lydon, Archie Gibson and Jock Henderson.

1955–56

DIVISION TWO

Team	Pld	W	D	L	GF	GA	Pts
Sheffield Wednesday	42	21	13	8	101	62	55
Leeds United	42	23	6	13	80	60	52
Liverpool	42	21	6	15	85	63	48
Blackburn Rovers	42	21	6	15	84	65	48
Leicester City	42	21	6	15	94	78	48
Bristol Rovers	42	21	6	15	84	70	48
Nottingham Forest	42	19	9	14	68	63	47
Lincoln City	42	18	10	14	79	65	46
Fulham	42	20	6	16	89	79	46
Swansea Town	42	20	6	16	83	81	46
Bristol City	42	19	7	16	80	64	45
Port Vale	42	16	13	13	60	58	45
Stoke City	42	20	4	18	71	62	44
Middlesbrough	42	16	8	18	76	78	40
Bury	42	16	8	18	86	90	40
West Ham United	42	14	11	17	74	69	39
Doncaster Rovers	42	12	11	19	69	96	35
Barnsley	42	11	12	19	47	84	34
Rotherham United	42	12	9	21	56	75	33
Notts County	42	11	9	22	55	82	31
Plymouth Argyle	42	10	8	24	54	87	28
Hull City	42	10	6	26	53	97	26

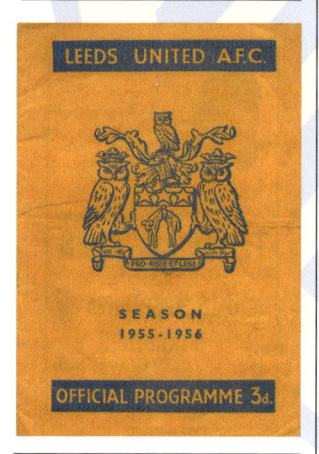

Date	Opposition	Competition	Score
20/08/1955	Barnsley	Division Two	1-2
22/08/1955	Bury	Division Two	1-0
27/08/1955	Middlesbrough	Division Two	2-0
30/08/1955	Bury	Division Two	0-1
03/09/1955	Bristol City	Division Two	1-0
05/09/1955	Hull City	Division Two	1-0
10/09/1955	West Ham United	Division Two	3-3
17/09/1955	Port Vale	Division Two	0-2
24/09/1955	Rotherham United	Division Two	4-1
01/10/1955	Swansea Town	Division Two	1-1
08/10/1955	Nottingham Forest	Division Two	3-0
15/10/1955	Sheffield Wednesday	Division Two	0-4
22/10/1955	Lincoln City	Division Two	1-0
29/10/1955	Bristol Rovers	Division Two	1-4
05/11/1955	Stoke City	Division Two	1-0
12/11/1955	Plymouth Argyle	Division Two	3-4
19/11/1955	Liverpool	Division Two	4-2
26/11/1955	Leicester City	Division Two	2-5
03/12/1955	Doncaster Rovers	Division Two	3-0
10/12/1955	Blackburn Rovers	Division Two	3-2
17/12/1955	Barnsley	Division Two	3-1
24/12/1955	Middlesbrough	Division Two	3-5
26/12/1955	Notts County	Division Two	1-0
27/12/1955	Notts County	Division Two	1-2
31/12/1955	Bristol City	Division Two	2-1
07/01/1956	Cardiff City	FA Cup 3rd Round	1-2
14/01/1956	West Ham United	Division Two	1-1
21/01/1956	Port Vale	Division Two	1-1
11/02/1956	Swansea Town	Division Two	2-2
25/02/1956	Sheffield Wednesday	Division Two	2-1
29/02/1956	Liverpool	Division Two	0-1
03/03/1956	Lincoln City	Division Two	1-1
10/03/1956	Blackburn Rovers	Division Two	1-2
17/03/1956	Stoke City	Division Two	1-2
24/03/1956	Plymouth Argyle	Division Two	4-2
30/03/1956	Fulham	Division Two	2-1
31/03/1956	Nottingham Forest	Division Two	0-2
02/04/1946	Fulham	Division Two	6-1
07/04/1956	Leicester City	Division Two	4-0
14/04/1956	Doncaster Rovers	Division Two	2-1
21/04/1956	Bristol Rovers	Division Two	2-1
23/04/1956	Rotherham United	Division Two	2-0
28/04/1956	Hull City	Division Two	4-1

Nine years after relegation, Leeds United secured a fourth promotion.

John Charles top scored with 29 goals, 28 came at centre-forward.

Roy Wood, Jimmy Dunn and Erik Kerfoot were ever-presents.

Charles captained the side all the way through, missing just one game away at Sheffield Wednesday when Eric Kerfoot stepped in.

Captain fantastic also finished third in the annual vote for the Footballer of the Year.

DIVISION ONE 1956–57

Date	Opposition	Competition	Score
18/08/1956	Everton	Division One	5-1
23/08/1956	Charlton Athletic	Division One	2-1
25/08/1956	Tottenham Hotspur	Division One	1-5
29/08/1956	Charlton Athletic	Division One	4-0
01/09/1956	Chelsea	Division One	0-0
05/09/1956	Manchester City	Division One	0-1
08/09/1956	Bolton Wanderers	Division One	3-2
12/09/1956	Manchester City	Division One	2-0
15/09/1956	Wolverhampton Wanderers	Division One	2-1
22/09/1956	Aston Villa	Division One	1-0
29/09/1956	Luton Town	Division One	2-2
06/10/1956	Cardiff City	Division One	1-4
13/10/1956	Birmingham City	Division One	1-1
20/10/1956	Burnley	Division One	0-0
27/10/1956	Preston North End	Division One	1-2
03/11/1956	Newcastle United	Division One	3-2
10/11/1956	Sheffield Wednesday	Division One	3-1
17/11/1956	Manchester United	Division One	2-3
24/11/1956	Arsenal	Division One	3-3
01/12/1956	West Bromwich Albion	Division One	0-0
08/12/1956	Portsmouth	Division One	4-1
15/12/1956	Everton	Division One	1-2
25/12/1956	Blackpool	Division One	1-1
26/12/1956	Blackpool	Division One	5-0
29/12/1956	Chelsea	Division One	1-1
05/01/1957	Cardiff City	FA Cup 3rd Round	1-2
12/01/1957	Bolton Wanderers	Division One	3-5
19/01/1957	Wolverhampton Wanderers	Division One	0-0
02/02/1957	Aston Villa	Division One	1-1
09/02/1957	Luton Town	Division One	1-2
16/02/1957	Cardiff City	Division One	3-0
23/02/1957	Preston North End	Division One	0-3
02/03/1957	Tottenham Hotspur	Division One	1-1
09/03/1957	Portsmouth	Division One	5-2
11/03/1957	Burnley	Division One	1-1
16/03/1957	Newcastle United	Division One	0-0
26/03/1957	Sheffield Wednesday	Division One	3-2
30/03/1957	Manchester United	Division One	1-2
06/04/1957	Arsenal	Division One	0-1
13/04/1957	West Bromwich Albion	Division One	0-0
19/04/1957	Sunderland	Division One	0-2
20/04/1957	Birmingham City	Division One	2-6
22/04/1957	Sunderland	Division One	3-1

Team	Pld	W	D	L	GF	GA	Pts
Manchester United	42	28	8	6	103	54	64
Tottenham Hotspur	42	22	12	8	104	56	56
Preston North End	42	23	10	9	84	56	56
Blackpool	42	22	9	11	93	65	53
Arsenal	42	21	8	13	85	69	50
Wolverhampton W	42	20	8	14	94	70	48
Burnley	42	18	10	14	56	50	46
Leeds United	42	15	14	13	72	63	44
Bolton Wanderers	42	16	12	14	65	65	44
Aston Villa	42	14	15	13	65	55	43
West Bromwich Albion	42	14	14	14	59	61	42
Chelsea	42	13	13	16	73	73	39
Birmingham City	42	15	9	18	69	69	39
Sheffield Wednesday	42	16	6	20	82	88	38
Everton	42	14	10	18	61	79	38
Luton Town	42	14	9	19	58	76	37
Newcastle United	42	14	8	20	67	87	36
Manchester City	42	13	9	20	78	88	35
Portsmouth	42	10	13	19	62	92	33
Sunderland	42	12	8	22	67	88	32
Cardiff City	42	10	9	23	53	88	29
Charlton Athletic	42	9	4	29	62	120	22

In finishing eighth in their first season back, it was the club's highest league position since season 1932-33 when they also finished eighth.

Leeds had five ever-presents, Royden Wood, Jimmy Dunn, Grenville Hair, Eric Kerfott and Jack Overfield.

The Whites had three debutants in their first season back in the top flight, Chris Crowe, Frank McKenna and George O'Brien.

Charles, who top scored with 39 goals, was sold to Juventus for at the time a world record of £65,000

The final game of the season at home to Sunderland saw the visitors captained by a certain Don Revie.

BACK ROW: ERIC KERFOOT, JACKIE OVERFIELD, KEITH RIPLEY, ROYDEN WOOD, BOB FORREST, GRENVILLE HAIR
FRONT ROW: GEORGE MEEK, JACK CHARLTON, JOHN CHARLES, JIMMY DUNN, HAROLD BROOK

1957–58

DIVISION ONE

Team	Pld	W	D	L	GF	GA	Pts
Wolverhampton W	42	28	8	6	103	47	64
Preston North End	42	26	7	9	100	51	59
Tottenham Hotspur	42	21	9	12	93	77	51
West Bromwich Albion	42	18	14	10	92	70	50
Manchester City	42	22	5	15	104	100	49
Burnley	42	21	5	16	80	74	47
Blackpool	42	19	6	17	80	67	44
Luton Town	42	19	6	17	69	63	44
Manchester United	42	16	11	15	85	75	43
Nottingham Forest	42	16	10	16	69	63	42
Chelsea	42	15	12	15	83	79	42
Arsenal	42	16	7	19	73	85	39
Birmingham City	42	14	11	17	76	89	39
Aston Villa	42	16	7	19	73	86	39
Bolton Wanderers	42	14	10	18	65	87	38
Everton	42	13	11	18	65	75	37
Leeds United	42	14	9	19	51	63	37
Leicester City	42	14	5	23	91	112	33
Newcastle United	42	12	8	22	73	81	32
Portsmouth	42	12	8	22	73	88	32
Sunderland	42	10	12	20	54	97	32
Sheffield Wednesday	42	12	7	23	69	92	31

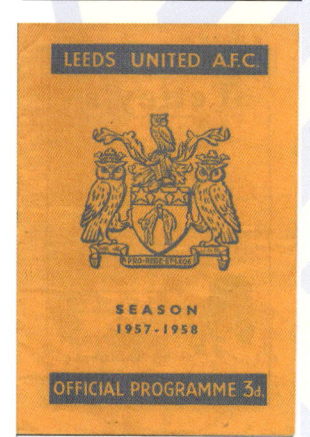

Date	Opposition	Competition	Score
24/08/1957	Blackpool	Division One	0-3
26/08/1957	Aston Villa	Division One	0-2
31/08/1957	Leicester City	Division One	2-1
04/09/1957	Aston Villa	Division One	4-0
07/09/1957	Manchester United	Division One	0-5
11/09/1957	Luton Town	Division One	0-2
14/09/1957	Nottingham Forest	Division One	1-2
18/09/1957	Luton Town	Division One	1-1
21/09/1957	Bolton Wanderers	Division One	2-1
25/09/1957	Sunderland	Division One	2-1
28/09/1957	Arsenal	Division One	1-2
05/10/1957	Wolverhampton Wanderers	Division One	1-1
12/10/1957	Portsmouth	Division One	2-1
19/10/1957	West Bromwich Albion	Division One	1-1
26/10/1957	Tottenham Hotspur	Division One	0-2
02/11/1957	Preston North End	Division One	2-3
09/11/1957	Sheffield Wednesday	Division One	2-3
16/11/1957	Manchester City	Division One	2-4
23/11/1957	Burnley	Division One	1-3
30/11/1957	Birmingham City	Division One	1-1
07/12/1957	Chelsea	Division One	1-2
14/12/1957	Newcastle United	Division One	3-0
21/12/1947	Blackpool	Division One	2-1
26/12/1957	Sunderland	Division One	1-2
28/12/1957	Leicester City	Division One	0-3
04/01/1958	Cardiff City	FA Cup 3rd Round	1-2
11/01/1958	Manchester United	Division One	1-1
18/01/1958	Nottingham Forest	Division One	1-1
01/02/1958	Bolton Wanderers	Division One	2-0
19/02/1958	Wolverhampton Wanderers	Division One	2-3
22/02/1958	Portsmouth	Division One	2-0
08/03/1958	Tottenham Hotspur	Division One	1-2
12/03/1958	West Bromwich Albion	Division One	0-1
15/03/1958	Preston North End	Division One	0-3
19/03/1958	Arsenal	Division One	2-0
22/03/1958	Burnley	Division One	1-0
29/03/1958	Manchester City	Division One	0-1
04/04/1958	Everton	Division One	1-0
05/04/1958	Sheffield Wednesday	Division One	2-2
07/04/1958	Everton	Division One	1-0
12/04/1958	Birmingham City	Division One	1-1
19/04/1958	Chelsea	Division One	0-0
26/04/1958	Newcastle United	Division One	2-1

Leeds were knocked out of the FA Cup by Cardiff City in the third round for the third successive season all by the same score.

Eric Kerfoot was the side's only ever-present.

Leeds used two goalkeepers in season 1957-58, Royden Wood played in 42 out of 43 games with Willie Nimmo stepping in away at Bolton Wanderers.

With captain Charles gone, Leeds needed a new skipper and Eric Kerfoot took over the mantle.

At the end of the season, Raich Carter's contract was not renewed with Bill Lambton taking over.

DIVISION ONE

1958–59

Date	Opposition	Competition	Score
23/08/1958	Bolton Wanderers	Division One	0-4
26/08/1958	Luton Town	Division One	1-1
30/08/1958	Burnley	Division One	1-1
03/09/1958	Luton Town	Division One	1-1
06/09/1958	Preston North End	Division One	2-1
10/09/1958	Birmingham City	Division One	0-0
13/09/1958	Leicester City	Division One	1-1
17/09/1958	Birmingham City	Division One	1-4
20/09/1958	Everton	Division One	2-3
27/09/1958	Arsenal	Division One	2-1
04/10/1958	Manchester City	Division One	1-2
11/10/1958	Portsmouth	Division One	0-2
18/10/1958	Aston Villa	Division One	0-0
25/10/1958	Tottenham Hotspur	Division One	3-2
01/11/1958	Manchester United	Division One	1-2
08/11/1958	Chelsea	Division One	0-2
15/11/1958	Blackpool	Division One	1-1
22/11/1958	Blackburn Rovers	Division One	4-2
29/11/1958	Newcastle United	Division One	3-2
06/12/1958	West Ham United	Division One	3-2
13/12/1958	Nottingham Forest	Division One	1-0
20/12/1958	Bolton Wanderers	Division One	3-4
26/12/1958	West Bromwich Albion	Division One	2-1
27/12/1958	West Bromwich Albion	Division One	0-1
03/01/1959	Burnley	Division One	1-3
10/01/1959	Luton Town	FA Cup 3rd Round	1-5
17/01/1959	Preston North End	Division One	1-3
31/01/1959	Leicester City	Division One	1-0
07/02/1959	Everton	Division One	1-0
14/02/1959	Wolverhampton Wanderers	Division One	2-6
21/02/1959	Manchester City	Division One	0-4
24/02/1959	Arsenal	Division One	0-1
28/02/1959	Portsmouth	Division One	1-1
07/03/1959	Aston Villa	Division One	1-2
14/03/1959	Tottenham Hotspur	Division One	3-1
21/03/1959	Manchester United	Division One	0-4
28/03/1959	Chelsea	Division One	4-0
31/03/1959	Wolverhampton Wanderers	Division One	1-3
04/04/1959	Blackpool	Division One	0-3
11/04/1959	Blackburn Rovers	Division One	2-1
18/04/1959	Newcastle United	Division One	2-2
22/04/1959	Nottingham Forest	Division One	3-0
25/04/1959	West Ham United	Division One	1-0

Team	Pld	W	D	L	GF	GA	Pts
Wolverhampton W	42	28	5	9	110	49	61
Manchester United	42	24	7	11	103	66	55
Arsenal	42	21	8	13	88	68	50
Bolton Wanderers	42	20	10	12	79	66	50
West Bromwich Albion	42	18	13	11	88	68	49
West Ham United	42	21	6	15	85	70	48
Burnley	42	19	10	13	81	70	48
Blackpool	42	18	11	13	66	49	47
Birmingham City	42	20	6	16	84	68	46
Blackburn Rovers	42	17	10	15	76	70	44
Newcastle United	42	17	7	18	80	80	41
Preston North End	42	17	7	18	70	77	41
Nottingham Forest	42	17	6	19	71	74	40
Chelsea	42	18	4	20	77	98	40
Leeds United	42	15	9	18	57	74	39
Everton	42	17	4	21	71	87	38
Luton Town	42	12	13	17	68	71	37
Tottenham Hotspur	42	13	10	19	85	95	36
Leicester City	42	11	10	21	67	98	32
Manchester City	42	11	9	22	64	95	31
Aston Villa	42	11	8	23	58	87	30
Portsmouth	42	6	9	27	64	112	21

LEEDS UNITED A.F.C.

SEASON 1958-1959

OFFICIAL PROGRAMME 3d.

29 November 1958 will go down as a red letter in the club's history as it saw the debut of one Don Revie following his move from Sunderland.

Leeds had four different captains, Wilbur Cush, Jack Charlton, Don Revie and Eric Kerfoot.

Bob Roxborough became the Whites first-ever caretaker-manager following Bill Lambton's resignation.

Jack Charlton was top of the appearance charts playing in 40 out of the 43 games.

Ted Burgin took over the goalkeeper's jersey from Royden Wood from the end of January 1959.

BACK ROW: PETER McCONNELL, JIMMY DUNN, TED BURGIN, JACK CHARLTON, WILBUR CUSH, GRENVILLE HAIR
FRONT ROW: CHRIS CROWE, GEORGE MEEK, HUGH BAIRD, NOEL PEYTON, JACKIE OVERFIELD

111

1959–60

DIVISION ONE

Team	Pld	W	D	L	GF	GA	Pts
Burnley	42	24	7	11	85	61	55
Wolverhampton W	42	24	6	12	106	67	54
Tottenham Hotspur	42	21	11	10	86	50	53
West Bromwich Albion	42	19	11	12	83	57	49
Sheffield Wednesday	42	19	11	12	80	59	49
Bolton Wanderers	42	20	8	14	59	51	48
Manchester United	42	19	7	16	102	80	45
Newcastle United	42	18	8	16	82	78	44
Preston North End	42	16	12	14	79	76	44
Fulham	42	17	10	15	73	80	44
Blackpool	42	15	10	17	59	71	40
Leicester City	42	13	13	16	66	75	39
Arsenal	42	15	9	18	68	80	39
West Ham United	42	16	6	20	75	91	38
Everton	42	13	11	18	73	78	37
Manchester City	42	17	3	22	78	84	37
Blackburn Rovers	42	16	5	21	60	70	37
Chelsea	42	14	9	19	76	91	37
Birmingham City	42	13	10	19	63	80	36
Nottingham Forest	42	13	9	20	50	74	35
Leeds United	42	12	10	20	65	92	34
Luton Town	42	9	12	21	50	73	30

Date	Opposition	Competition	Score
22/08/1959	Burnley	Division One	2-3
26/08/1959	Leicester City	Division One	2-3
29/08/1959	Luton Town	Division One	1-0
02/09/1959	Leicester City	Division One	1-1
05/09/1959	West Ham United	Division One	2-1
09/09/1959	Manchester United	Division One	0-6
12/09/1959	Chelsea	Division One	2-1
16/09/1959	Manchester United	Division One	2-2
19/09/1959	West Bromwich Albion	Division One	0-3
26/09/1959	Newcastle United	Division One	2-3
03/10/1959	Birmingham City	Division One	0-2
10/10/1959	Everton	Division One	3-3
17/10/1959	Blackpool	Division One	3-3
24/10/1959	Blackburn Rovers	Division One	0-1
31/10/1959	Bolton Wanderers	Division One	1-1
07/11/1959	Arsenal	Division One	3-2
14/11/1959	Wolverhampton Wanderers	Division One	2-4
21/11/1959	Sheffield Wednesday	Division One	1-3
28/11/1959	Nottingham Forest	Division One	1-4
05/12/1959	Fulham	Division One	1-4
12/12/1959	Manchester City	Division One	3-3
19/12/1959	Burnley	Division One	1-0
26/12/1959	Tottenham Hotspur	Division One	2-4
28/12/1959	Tottenham Hotspur	Division One	4-1
02/01/1960	Luton Town	Division One	1-1
09/01/1960	Aston Villa	FA Cup 3rd Round	1-2
16/01/1960	West Ham United	Division One	3-0
23/01/1960	Chelsea	Division One	3-1
06/02/1960	West Bromwich Albion	Division One	1-4
13/02/1960	Newcastle United	Division One	1-2
27/02/1960	Fulham	Division One	0-5
05/03/1960	Blackpool	Division One	2-4
09/03/1960	Birmingham City	Division One	3-3
19/03/1960	Manchester City	Division One	4-3
26/03/1960	Arsenal	Division One	1-1
02/04/1960	Wolverhampton Wanderers	Division One	0-3
09/04/1960	Sheffield Wednesday	Division One	0-1
16/04/1960	Bolton Wanderers	Division One	1-0
18/04/1960	Preston North End	Division One	1-1
19/04/1960	Preston North End	Division One	2-1
23/04/1960	Everton	Division One	0-1
27/04/1960	Blackburn Rovers	Division One	2-3
30/04/1960	Nottingham Forest	Division One	1-0

Jack Taylor became the White's fourth different manager of the decade (including caretakers).

Despite relegation back to Division Two, 23 January 1960 saw the debut of the White's greatest-ever captain Billy Bremner.

Other debutants at the back end of the decade included Bobby Cameron, John McCole, Terry Caldwell, Alan Humphreys and Freddie Goodwin.

Jack Charlton led the appearance charts missing just one game.

Leeds had three captains by the season's end, Don Revie, Wilbur Cush and Freddie Goodwin who captained the side on the last day of the campaign at home to Nottingham Forest.

THE 1960s
THE DON TAKES CHARGE

The first full season of the 1960s saw a wind of change at Elland Road, with the likes of Eric Smith from Celtic and Colin Grainger joining from Sunderland. The season didn't start in the greatest fashion for Leeds as they only won two of their first ten league games. Incredibly, among them were two 4-4 draws, away to Bristol Rovers and at home to Middlesbrough. The side found themselves in 13th place.

A new cup competition was in situ as Leeds entered the League Cup, drawing in their first game 0-0 against Blackpool at Elland Road. They won the replay 3-1 at Bloomfield Road, with Don Revie scoring the side's first-ever goal in the competition. League form again proved to be frustrating for the side, and by the time of the next round of the League Cup Leeds were stuck in 14th place following a 3-2 loss away at Swansea Town. Chesterfield were dispatched 4-0 in the third round of the League Cup, before Leeds were knocked out in a nine-goal thriller at Southampton. The FA Cup lasted just one round as Yorkshire rivals Sheffield Wednesday won 2-0 at Hillsborough, which left Leeds to concentrate on the league. For Taylor though, this proved a tough task and five losses in the next nine games, saw him depart the club, and Leeds were looking for a new manager.

Leeds United, 1960-61.

Revie, who had passed the captaincy to Freddie Goodwin, actually applied for the job at Bournemouth, before Leeds chairman Harry Reynolds realised that they needed Revie in charge at Elland Road, and in a move that his fellow directors agreed on, a new era at Leeds was born. Despite losing his first two games, Revie lead his side to a 7-0 hammering over Lincoln City in the penultimate home game of the campaign, and the side finished in 14th place. John McCole finished as top-scorer with 23 goals and hopes were now high that Leeds had a manager in charge who could propel them back into England's top flight.

In the summer of 1961, Derek Mayers joined from Preston North End and Revie added Syd Owen, Les Cocker and Maurice Lindley to the backroom staff. Bremner scored the winner on day one at home to Charlton Athletic, but by the start of September they were in 19th position. John McCole scored all four in a League Cup win over Brentford at Elland Road, but a 2-1 home defeat to Preston North End saw the side drop to 21st. Despite going through to the fourth round of the League Cup, Leeds were embroiled in a relegation scrap, and after a 4-1 home defeat to Scunthorpe United they were in 19th place. The first few weeks of January were a disaster as the side were eliminated from both cup competitions and Rotherham beat them 2-1 at Millmoor. Following a 3-2 loss at home to Plymouth Argyle, Leeds hit rock bottom and were staring at Third Division football for the first time in their history. Leeds needed a boost and in came Cliff Mason, Ian Lawson and a certain Bobby Collins from Everton for £25,000. Collins scored on his debut in a vital 2-1 home win over Swansea Town and two wins in the next four saw Leeds up a place to 21st. The side then went on an unbeaten run of six games (drawing five) and defeating Southampton 3-0 on the final day before saw the team finish in 19th place, which was the worst finish in the club's history. It proved to be a huge turning point in the club's history. Bremner and Jack Charlton finished as joint top-scorers with 12 goals a piece and Revie had changed the club's strip to all white to match that of European power house Real Madrid.

During the off season, Revie brought back John Charles from Juventus and also joining was striker Jim Storrie from Airdrie. Storrie scored the winner on his debut away at Stoke City, but yet again early season results proved inconsistent. Leeds were as low down as 15th following a goalless draw at Derby County in mid-October and worse was to follow as Blackburn Rovers knocked them out of the League Cup, winning 4-0 at the third-round stage. Leeds then went on an unbeaten run of five games, including a 6-1 hammering of Plymouth Argyle, in which Storrie scored a hat-trick and moved the side up to seventh. Another hat-trick from Don Weston in a 3-1 home win against Stoke City was proceeded

Jim Storrie

by a 2-1 loss at Sunderland on 22 December, which would be the last fixture Leeds played for just under three months. The big winter freeze of 1963 meant no games till March, and this seemed to help the side. Despite being knocked out of the FA Cup by Nottingham Forest in the last 16, Leeds went on a run of winning five of their next seven games which saw the side in eighth place. Three consecutive defeats in May saw any hopes of a promotion charge evaporate, but Leeds did end the season with a 5-0 hammering of Swansea Town at Elland Road. The side ended up in fifth, with Storrie top of the charts with 27 goals.

Leeds were one of the pre-season favourites going into the new campaign and one of the most important signings in the club's history as Johnny Giles joined from Manchester United. An opening-day win over Rotherham United was proceed by a 3-0 win over Bury, and a 2-2 draw at Rotherham saw the side in sixth place. However, a 3-2 defeat to Manchester City saw the team drop to 12th, but it proved to be the catalyst of a 20-game unbeaten run, which would propel the side to the top of the table. A 2-0 win over west Yorkshire rivals Huddersfield Town at Elland Road saw Leeds top the league for the first time in the season and they wouldn't be out of the top two for the remainder of the campaign. Manchester City followed their league win against Leeds with a League Cup win against the Whites at the end of November, but this failed to derail Revie's side. The side ended the year with only their

Leeds United in 1964.

second league defeat of the season away at Sunderland, but this would prove to be only the penultimate league defeat of a memorable season at Elland Road. Everton did knock Leeds out of the FA Cup, but this was a mere distraction as a run of one defeat in the final 15 games, saw Leeds finally return to the promised land of the First Division. Promotion was secured

THE CHALLENGE!

DON REVIE, manager of Leeds United—he took them to the First Division last season—discusses the challenge and the magic of that Division, the sternest test in football.

IN a few days time I shall be sitting in the stand at Villa Park waiting for the kick-off that will roll Leeds United into a new season, a new adventure and a challenge which makes these high and exciting days for all connected with the club.

A new adventure: seven of the probable team against the Villa have never played in the First Division before. The challenge will be to their temperament as much as their ability—because of the bigger crowds they will face.

Before a ball is kicked, it is thrilling to roll the names off your tongue . . . Aston Villa away . . . then home to Liverpool, the champions . . . home to Stan Cullis and his Wolves . . . up to Anfield and that terrific Liverpool crowd . . . then to my old stamping ground, Roker Park, and Sunderland, our great rivals last season.

That is the start, but my lads will find that it keeps on like this . . . Old Trafford, White Hart Lane and Highbury.

Always there is a bit of history, a touch of magic about such names because this is the First Division, the greatest test of them all.

United are back there after four years. Back to plan and fight to be as big as the biggest of our rivals. Our sights are high . . . very high.

It can be no other way now, we MUST go forward.

We had little to hope for

In the middle of this great anticipation I can't help looking back. This time three seasons ago we were wondering what a new season would bring.

Behind me was my first season as United manager. We had had to win our last match at Newcastle *to feel sure of staying in the Second Division.*

In those doldrum days we had averaged just over 13,000 for our home games; United did nothing but escape the drop by a fraction.

Why should the fans rush to see us? Nobody wants to cheer losers. United had been that for too long.

Apart from a bunch of people who had put in a lot of hard work inside the club there was little spirit, little enthusiasm.

And now . . . ?

Now you can feel the expectancy, the looking forward to exciting days. And there is the memory of that great backing our fans gave us last season.

The chanting of "Leeds, Leeds, Leeds"

DON REVIE

. . . the victory chorus of "Ilkley Moor" and the sight of cheering supporters even at faraway places like Plymouth.

And the most telling difference—a home average gate of 30,000, some 10,000 up on each home gate of the previous season.

We have been called a "hard" side, and worse. Last season it got to be "a thing" with some people who were always looking for something which I claim was not there.

Let me say here and now that I have no objections to my side being called a hard team. United DO play it hard because I expect all my players to work and fight hard.

But I would not tolerate or encourage a player who deliberately went in for foul play.

Hard tackling is not dirty play. In the Second Division we had to be hard.

I've played in both First and Second. We all aim, I hope, to play good football, but in the First a player is allowed more time in which to do that. Anticipation more than tackling is a factor. The Second is hard graft and bags of running.

I don't make forecasts. The boys who won promotion will get every chance. We shall have to wait and see how things work out. So much depends on a good start.

At Elland Road we preach that ability without effort is no good. Get the two together and you can go places. I've no doubt on the score of effort. Our ability in the higher grade is yet to be tested.

United have never been a big club. We have had great players but never won anything big. Now we have hope—and heart. We know that we shall have all the backing we need from our Board.

It is a football catch-phrase to talk of team-spirit "running down from the boardroom to the dressing-room". I make no apologies for trotting it out here. For we have that in abundance . . . and a great capacity for hard work.

All of which will soon be tested in some measure.

It is great to be at Elland Road—now that the First Division is so near!

in 3-0 win away at Swansea Town in which Alan Peacock scored a brace and the next target was the title. This was secured thanks to another brace from Peacock on the final day of the campaign at home to Charlton Athletic. Exactly 40 years since their last title, Leeds were back where they felt they belonged. They also broke some other records, including finishing with 63 points, which was the highest by a Second Division club since World War Two and they completed a full season at home unbeaten. Norman Hunter was the only ever-present, with Gary Sprake, Paul Reaney and Bobby Collins missing just one game. The next challenge was to consolidate in the First Division.

Back in the top flight, Leeds started the 1963-64 season with three consecutive wins over Aston Villa (2-1), Liverpool (4-2) and Wolverhampton Wanderers (3-2), which saw the Whites in third place. Following a 3-0 win over Blackpool, Leeds were up to second and hopes were high of a title challenge. Although Aston Villa did knock Leeds out of the League Cup, they did have success in the other domestic cup competition.

Before the FA Cup started in January, Leeds won their next six games – and one game stood out in that run – a 1-0 win over Everton at Goodison Park at the start of November, which saw Sandy Brown sent off for a foul on goalscorer Willie Bell, before the referee talked to both sides to make sure matters didn't boil over. A 2-1 victory over Sunderland, thanks to goals from Charlton and Hunter, took the Whites to the top of the pile and they

Leeds United 2 v West Ham United 1, 3 April 1965, Alan Peacock and Norman Hunter (Leeds) challenge Jim Standen (West Ham goalkeeper), Elland Road.

stayed there until the start of February. The FA Cup started with a 3-0 win over Southport at Elland Road and Everton were beaten in a replay at Goodison Park (2-1), before Shrewsbury Town went the same way in a 2-0 win in west Yorkshire. Crystal Palace were defeated 3-0 in a game watched by 45,000 fans at Elland Road, and suddenly Leeds were one game away from their first-ever Wembley visit. Three unbeaten games kept Leeds in second place and proceeded the side's first-ever semi-final. Manchester United were held 0-0 in the first game, before Bremner scored the winning goal in the replay at the City Ground. Three more wins took Leeds to the top of the pile, but back-to-back defeats at home to Manchester United and away at Sheffield Wednesday dampened spirits a bit, but the side responded well with wins over the Owls (2-0) at Elland Road and Sheffield United 3-0 at Bramall Lane, which took Leeds back to pole position. Then a 3-3 draw on the final day saw Leeds overtaken by 0.686 of a goal by Manchester United, as the Red Devils won the title on goal average. On 1 May Bobby Collins led Leeds out at Wembley for the cup final against Liverpool in front of 100,000 fans. Liverpool took the lead through Roger Hunt, but Bremner took the game to extra time before Ian St John won it for the Reds. Collins won the Football Writers' Player of the Year and Hunter made 51 appearances. It had been a remarkable return to the First Division and by finishing second they qualified for European football for the first time.

It was more of the same the following season as Leeds won four of their opening five league games and they topped the table by the start of September, but a run of no wins in the next four dropped the side to fifth. West Bromwich Albion knocked Leeds out of the League Cup at the third-round stage, but Leeds took to Europe like a duck to water. Torino were beaten 2-1 on aggregate in the first round of the Inter Cites Fairs Cup, which meant a second-round tie with German side SC Leipzig. In the league, Leeds were in third place heading into mid-November, and another 2-1 aggregate European win over SC Leipzing saw the Whites into the third round. League form was consistent going into the new year, and Bury were demolished 6-0 in the third round of the FA Cup.

Next up in Europe were Valencia. Leeds drew the first leg 1-1 at Elland Road, before a Mick O'Grady strike sent Leeds through to the last eight. Then a 3-2 win over Leicester City saw Leeds up to second in the league, but a 1-0 loss at Blackpool dropped them to third. Újpesti Dózsa were next up in Europe and a fantastic 4-1 win in the first leg ended the tie, before a Peter Lorimer strike ensured a 5-2 aggregate win. Back in the league, three consecutive wins at the end of April and start of May saw Leeds in second, and they would finish as runners up, six points away from Liverpool.

Real Zaragoza were next up in the semi-finals of the Inter-Cities Fairs Cup and the Spanish side won the first leg 1-0 at the La Romerada, before strikes from Albert Johanneson and Jack Charlton took the tie to a third game. In the end the Spanish side won through, winning 3-1 at Elland Road. Fifty-seven games later the season was over, as Lorimer top-scored with 19 goals.

Leeds United Team, 1966.

Season 1966-67 saw the departures of Ian Lawson, Alan Peacock and Jim Storrie and Leeds needed a striker. That came in the unlikely fashion of versatile Paul Madeley, who scored in the 3-1 win over Manchester United at the end of August. A title challenge never really happened, with only six wins in the side's first 15 games and worse was to follow as West Ham United destroyed Leeds 7-0 in the fourth-round League Cup tie at Upton Park. The European Campaign started with an 8-2 aggregate win over DWS Amsterdam and again Leeds would meet Valencia in European competition.

A 1-1 draw thanks to a Jimmy Greenhoff strike was then followed up by a 2-0 win in Spain, with goals coming from Giles and Lorimer. The FA Cup started with a 3-0 win over Crystal Palace, before West Bromwich Albion were destroyed 5-0 at Elland Road. The fifth round saw a 1-1 draw away at Sunderland, before a club-record crowd of 57,892 witnessed another 1-1 draw at Elland Road. A third match played at Boothferry Park saw Leeds go through to the last eight with the odd goal in three. In the Inter-Cities Fairs Cup, Leeds went through on the toss of a disc, following a 1-1 aggregate draw against Italian side Bologna, and this set up a battle against Scottish side Kilmarnock for a place in the final. Before that, Leeds had defeated Leicester City in the quarter-final of the FA Cup and this set up a last-four tie with Chelsea at Villa Park. Leeds lost 1-0 and Peter Lorimer's last-minute strike was disallowed. Leeds finished the league campaign in fourth place as attention turned to the tie against Kilmarnock. They won the first leg 4-2 at Elland Road with a hat-trick from Belfitt and a penalty from Giles, but the second leg was goalless and the Whites made it through to

Dynamo Zagreb 2 v Leeds United 0, 30 August 1967, Fairs Cup Final first leg.

their first-ever European final, where they would meet Dinamo Zagreb. Sadly for Leeds, they lost the first leg 2-0 at the Maksimir Stadium and they failed to overturn this at Elland Road. Leeds had played in 63 games, in which Hunter missed only three of them. Giles top-scored with 18 goals and Leeds had a new chairman, with Albert Morris replacing Harry Reynolds.

The exertions of the previous campaign showed as Leeds struggled in the opening month of the new season, winning only one of their first five league games, and they were down in 20th place. The League Cup run started with a 3-1 win over Luton Town thanks to Peter Lorimer, and this was followed up by 3-0 win over Bury in the next round. Leeds then smashed Spora Luxembourg 9-0 in the Inter-Cities Fairs Cup first-round, first-leg, before winning 7-0 in the second. In between this was another 7-0 league win over Chelsea at Elland Road, in which there were seven different goalscorers. Leeds were up to sixth, and in the next round of the League Cup Sunderland were defeated 2-0 with a brace from Jimmy Greenhoff.

Next up in Europe was a game against Partizan Belgrade in which Leeds won the first leg 2-1, with strikes from Lorimer and Belfitt, before drawing the second 1-1 at Elland Road. Stoke City were then defeated in the last eight of the League Cup before another Scottish side, Hibernian, travelled to Leeds for an Inter-Cities Fairs Cup tie. Leeds won the game thanks to a goal from Eddie Gray, and a Jack Charlton goal ensured a 1-1 draw at Easter Road. Leeds met Derby County in the semi-finals of the League Cup, and a Giles penalty saw the side 90 minutes away from Wembley. Leeds again met the Rams in the opening round of the FA Cup and again the result went the same way, with Leeds winning 2-0 this time at Elland Road. The second leg of the League Cup saw Leeds make a second trip to Wembley with a

3-2 win and a game against Arsenal at the start of March. In between times, Leeds defeated West Ham United in the league to move up to second, before a fourth-round win over Nottingham Forest in the FA Cup. Leeds travelled to Wembley and this time came away as winners with a goal from Terry Cooper. Bristol City were then knocked out of the FA Cup and Leeds were top of the pile in the First Division going into another Battle of Britain in Europe against Glasgow Rangers. A goalless draw at Ibrox put Leeds in the driving seat and goals from Giles and Lorimer sent the side through to the last four and a meeting with another Scottish side in the form of Dundee.

F.A. News, *October 1968, Leeds Utd players with the Inter Cities Fairs Cup.*

In between both legs against Rangers, Sheffield United were beaten in the last eight of the FA Cup, but a mistake from Gary Sprake saw Everton make to the trip to Wembley rather than Leeds. An exhausting campaign had still to reach its climax, with domestic and European glory still on the agenda. A Paul Madeley goal in the away game at Dundee was vital and an Eddie Gray goal in the second leg saw Leeds through to their second European final in two seasons. Three straight league defeats put paid to any title hopes and left Leeds to finish the season with a European final against Ferencvaros. Leeds won the first leg thanks to a goal from Mick Jones and a brilliant defensive display in Hungary in which Gary Sprake was magnificent. The Whites ended the season with two trophies, having played 66 games in which Paul Reaney played in 65 of them. The next task was to bring home the championship.

Leeds started the following season like a house on fire, winning their first four games of the season, which took them to the top of the pile, with Terry Hibbitt scoring in three of them. A 1-1 draw at home to Sunderland dropped them to second, and following their first loss of the season away at Manchester City, Leeds dropped to a season low of third. They bounced back with three consecutive wins: Newcastle United (1-0) at St James Park, Sunderland (1-0) at Roker Park and West Ham United 2-0 at Elland Road, which saw them back up to number one in the league ladder. Crystal Palace ended any hopes of retaining the League Cup and a shock 5-1 loss at Burnley, in which Bremner scored the White's lone

Leeds United team line-up, 1968-69, with the Division One Champions' Trophy.

goal, looked to have derailed Leeds, but it would prove to be the last league loss Revie's side would suffer all season.

By this stage, Standard Liege had been knocked out of the Inter-Cities Fairs Cup and a meeting with Napoli been set up. In the league, three goalless draws dropped Leeds to third, but consecutive wins over Coventry City at Highfield Road and Everton at Elland Road moved the side up a place. Incredibly Leeds went through to the third round of the Inter-Cities Fairs Cup on the toss of a disc once more, after the tie with Napoli had ended all square on aggregate. Next up were Hannover 96 and they were dispatched 7-2 on aggregate, setting up a tie with Újpesti Dózsa in the last eight.

The FA Cup was over before it began as Sheffield Wednesday won a third-round replay at Elland Road, but it left the side to concentrate on winning the league for the first time. Dosza ended any hopes of retaining the Inter-Cities Fairs Cup, but league form kept going and by mid-February they were top of the league. They wouldn't relinquish top spot for the remainder of the campaign. Following the 2-0 win at Ipswich, Leeds won their next four games, but back-to-back goalless draws at Wolverhampton Wanderers and Sheffield Wednesday kept Liverpool in the race. Leeds won three of the next five, which meant the side travelled to Anfield needing just a point to secure the dream of winning the championship. A point was achieved and the dream had been realised. Leeds broke numerous records, including the most points with 67, most home points with 39, most wins in total with 27, fewest league defeats

Allan Clarke (Leeds United) transfer from Leicester City, article from Goal Mag *48, 5 July 1969.*

£160,000 CLARKE GOES ON TRIAL...

ALLAN CLARKE joins his new Leeds United team mates in a few days knowing he is on trial for his football life—but fully aware that his reputation and price tag will neither help nor hinder him at Elland Road. Clarke's total cost move from Leicester brings his total cost in three years to £345,000—Walsall to Fulham (£35,000), Fulham to Leicester (£150,000) and now Leicester to Leeds.

But as Leeds skipper Billy Bremner said when told of the deal: "Transfer fees and the reputations that go with them mean nothing at Leeds. The only way to be successful here is to be conscious of the team's good."

DELIGHTED

Leicester manager Frank O'Farrell feels Clarke's move was inevitable — even if the team had stayed in the First Division. There can be no doubt that player and manager differed in their views on the role Clarke should play. But they have parted amicably.

Leeds boss Don Revie drove down the M1 early on Wednesday last week to clinch the transfer ... a move that caught Manchester United, favourites to buy Clarke, on the hop. Manager Sir Matt Busby was away in Bermuda.

Clarke was keen to join Leeds. He said: "I'm delighted. No player can ask for more than a place with the Football League champions, can they?

"I look forward to playing in Europe next season, and I hope I can be part of a successful Leeds run in the European Cup.

"The fee? Well, I've had to live with that for a year, so I can't let it worry me. The clubs pay the money, my job is to do my best to live up to it."

Clarke starts the season with Leeds knowing there are plenty of people who feel he has not yet proved he is worth the money spent on him.

But he has kept on scoring goals for two struggling teams—Fulham and Leicester. And the thought of what he can achieve with Leeds must be giving other First Division managers nightmares.

Clarke did not put in a written transfer request to the Football League are unlikely to stop him collecting five per cent of the fee—a bonus which brings his earnings from transfer deals to more than £17,000.

BRENTFORD PITCH

IN OUR issue of May 17, under the headline Brentford slump—but their pitch is tops, we named John Stepney as the person responsible for the pitch's conditions. In fact, Webb and Co. (Plants and Gardens) Ltd. are the contractors.

GOAL SPOTLIGHTS THE TRANSFER MARKET EXPLOSION THAT ROCKED FOOTBALL

■ SUDDENLY, it all happened. The transfer market exploded into life. First came the £160,000 transfer of Allan Clarke (above) from Leicester to Leeds. Then Colin Suggett joined West Bromwich from Sunderland for £100,000. Here, PETER BARNARD tells the inside stories behind the big moves.

But Clarke had made it clear he did not want to play Second Division football, and the League may well change the rules to cover future cases.

Indeed, I understand there is an ambiguity in the wording of a regulation which may yet leave Clarke on sticky ground regarding the bonus.

It seems there is a lot of arguing to be done before he can concentrate on playing again.

OTHER MOVES: Willie Bell, Scottish international full-back freed by Leicester, was snapped up by Brighton. Bell will also help with coaching.

Brian Greenhalgh, signed by Frank O'Farrell as forward cover last February, soon followed Clarke away from Leicester. He moved to Huddersfield in a £15,000 deal.

John Pratt, 25-year-old amateur goalkeeper with Wycombe Wanderers, has joined Reading as a professional.

...and Suggett moves for £100,000

IN A FRENZIED but typically stealthy eight weeks, West Bromwich Albion have splashed £258,000 on three players—and each deal successively broke Albion's record pay-out.

The final one was a £100,000 swoop for Sunderland striker Colin Suggett last week. Before that they paid Queen's Park Rangers £70,000 for Alan Glover and Ipswich £88,000 for Danny Hegan.

This spree by a club not previously ranked as big spenders means they could start next season with a glamour front line that reads: Glover, Hegan, Astle, Suggett.

Manager Alan Ashman has wanted to strengthen his strike force for a long time. Jeff Astle has too often been left to tread a lonely beat upfield. Now he'll have some pretty formidable company.

Another biggish move last week ... Huddersfield winger Brian Hill, unhappy with his role at Leeds Road, joined Blackburn for £30,000.

---

with two and fewest home goals conceded with nine. There were four ever-presents – Gary Sprake, Paul Reaney, Billy Bremner and Norman Hunter – and Mick Jones was top scorer with 14 goals.

Revie added fire power during the off season, bringing in Allan Clarke from Leicester City for a British record fee of £165,000, and he made his debut in the 2-1 Charity Shield win over Manchester City at Elland Road. Clarke then scored his first goal for his new side on the opening day of the new campaign in a 3-1 win over Tottenham Hotspur, but Leeds had their unbeaten league record ended at Everton at the end of September. Chelsea knocked the side out of the League Cup at the third-round stage, but the side had new targets in mind, with their first-ever foray into the European Cup. They made the most excellent start with a club-record 10-0 win at home to Lyn Oslo, in which Jones scored a hat-trick and they followed that up with a 6-0 win in the second leg in Norway. League form had seen the side in fifth place following a 1-1 draw at Crystal Palace, but come the start of November they were up to second. Old foes Ferencvaros were defeated 6-0 in the second round of the European Cup and by Christmas Day they were top of the table following a 4-1 demolition of West Ham United at Elland Road.

The road to Wembley in the FA Cup started with a 2-1 win over Swansea Town at Elland Road and that was followed up by a 6-0 hammering of non-league Sutton United, in which Clarke scored four. Leeds stayed top of the league come the end of January and stayed there until mid-March. Mansfield Town were defeated in round five of the FA Cup, in the only game in which the famous 11 played together, and Swindon Town went the same way in the last eight. The quarter-finals of the European Cup, saw Leeds drawn against Belgium side

Leeds United, 1969-70.

Standard Liege and goals from Peter Lorimer in the away leg and a penalty from Jonny Giles in the second leg saw Leeds through to a Battle of Britain with Glasgow Celtic.

It was back to the FA Cup and a trilogy of games against Manchester United in the last four. The first game was drawn 0-0 at Hillsborough, as was the replay at Villa Park, before a goal from Billy Bremner sent Leeds back to Wembley. By this time Leeds had dropped to second in the league, despite two wonder goals from Eddie Gray in a win over Burnley at Elland Road, but they still had high hopes in both the FA and European Cups. First up on April Fool's Day was Glasgow Celtic at Elland Road and the Scottish giants took a massive step to the final in a 1-0 win, and they won the second leg 2-1 at Hampden Park in front of over 130,000 fans. Before the second leg took place, Leeds had the small game of an FA Cup final against Chelsea at Wembley Stadium. In a game played on a Wembley pitch damaged by the Horse of the Year Show, Leeds drew 2-2, thanks to goals from Charlton and Jones and had to face the prospect of a replay at Old Trafford. After missing out on league glory and European glory, losing out in the semi-finals, this was one last chance of ending an unbelievable season with some silverware. Sadly for Leeds and despite opening the scoring through Jones, they ended an exhausting 63-game season with only the Charity Shield to show for it. A small consolation came in the form of Revie collecting his second consecutive Manager of the Year award and captain marvel Bremner the Football Writers' Player of the Year award. What would the 1970s bring?

DEBUTANTS IN 1960s

BILLY BREMNER

Debut: Chelsea (A) 23 January 1960
Appearances: 772 (1)
Goals: 115

The greatest captain the club have ever had, Bremner played for St Modan's High School and Gowanhill Juniors and joined Leeds in December 1959 after being rejected by Arsenal and Chelsea for being too small. Jack Taylor handed him his debut on 23 January 1960 in a 3-1 win away at Chelsea, where he played as an outside-right, aged just 17 years and 47 days. Yorkshire Evening Post writer Phil Brown commented that, 'he showed enthusiasm, guts, intelligence, most accurate use of the ball and unselfishness, despite poor weather conditions.' He made 11 appearances that season, scoring his first two goals for the club in a 3-3 draw at home to Birmingham City and ten days later in a 4-3 win at home to Manchester City.

Leeds were demoted to the second tier and Taylor was replaced by Don Revie the following March, and one of the greatest partnerships in the club's history was set to begin. Bremner started to establish himself in the side, playing in 34 games, scoring ten goals as Leeds finished in 14th place in the Second Division. Season 1961-62 was a lot tougher for the Whites as they finished fourth from bottom, staying up by three points, but for Bremner he made 45 appearances, scoring 12 goals. Season 1962-63 saw the Whites improve massively to finish in fifth place, with the Scotsman playing in 24 games, wearing the number-four shirt for the first time in a 2-1 loss away at Rotherham United on 28 August 1962.

By the start of the following season, he was handed the number-four shirt for good and would go on to wear it in every game bar ten for the rest of his Leeds United playing career. Season 1963-64 saw Bremner miss just three league games as Leeds won promotion and the Second Division title, scoring in a 3-1 win at home to Portsmouth, the winning goal away to Cardiff City in a FA Cup third-round tie

Bremner playing for Scotland

and in a 3-1 win at home to Grimsby Town. He hit 49 games in season 1964-65 as Leeds finished as runners-up to Manchester United in the league in their first term back in the top flight, and Bremner scored the White's first-ever goal at Wembley as they were unlucky to lose in the 1965 FA Cup Final to Liverpool. Two days prior to the prestigious event at Wembley,

Bremner was called up by his country and made his Scotland debut in a friendly game at home to Spain at Hampden Park wearing the number-four shirt. He achieved 54 caps for his country, playing in all three World Cup final games in 1974 in West Germany. Despite missing out on honours in season 1965-66, Bremner had the honour of captaining the side for the first time, with Jack Charlton missing in a 2-0 loss away at Sunderland. Leeds again missed out on league glory, finishing second, but had a brilliant first-ever European run as they made it all the way to the last four of the Inter-Cities Fairs Cup before losing out to Spanish side Real Zaragoza. Bremner played in all European games, scoring away to SC Leipzig and at home to Újpesti Dózsa. He again captained the side in four early games the following season (1966-67) due to the absence of both Bobby Collins and Jack Charlton, and he was handed the armband on a permanent basis later that season. He made a total of 57 appearances that campaign, coming off the bench for the one and only time in his Leeds United career for Eddie Gray on the final day of the season at home to Sheffield Wednesday. For the record, the captain that day was Alan Peacock.

Bremner lead the side to the Inter-Cities Fairs Cup Final against Dynamo Zagreb, only to lose 2-0 on aggregate, but he didn't have long to wait for his first silverware as skipper. The 1967-68 season saw Bremner lead the side to a cup double, lifting the League Cup in a 1-0 win at Wembley against Arsenal thanks to a Terry Cooper goal, and better was to come as on 11 September 1968, Billy lifted the Inter-Cities Fairs Cup thanks to a 1-0 aggregate win over Ferencvaros, in the main due to a brilliant defensive display in Hungary. Bremner played in a total of 58 games in all competitions, scoring four goals, which came against Spora Luxembourg in a 9-0 win on the way to winning the competition, a 7-0 win at home to Chelsea, a 2-0 Division One win at home to Stoke City and in a 1-1 draw at home to Nottingham Forest.

Bremner's greatest season to date would come the following year as he missed just one game – a League Cup loss to Crystal Palace, as he led the side to the First Division Championship, being an ever-present in the league campaign, scoring six vital goals. The Whites lost only two games that season and clinched the title at Anfield. Another 12 months later, a physically draining season, which had promised so much, saw Leeds end up with nothing, finishing second to Everton in the Championship, losing an FA Cup Final replay to Chelsea and a European Cup semi-final to Celtic. Bremner played in a total of 55 games, scoring eight goals, as the Whites missed out on honours. He was named the FWA Footballer of the Year as consolation for his magnificent displays in midfield.

The following season (1970-71), Bremner again lead his side to European glory as he lifted the Inter-Cities Fairs Cup for a second time when Leeds defeated Juventus, winning on away goals. Bremner featured in a total of 39 games and by the end of the campaign had made 522 appearances for his side. Bremner should have led the side to a famous double the following season after winning the FA Cup, but despite a goal from the captain away at Wolverhampton Wanderers two days after the final, Leeds were beaten to the title by Derby County. Bremner missed just one game as Revie put out a weakened side against Lierse in the second leg of the UEFA Cup tie at Elland Road.

Season 1972-73 saw Billy lead the side to the FA Cup Final, scoring the only goal in the semi-final win over Wolverhampton Wanderers at Maine Road, before suffering a shock loss to Sunderland at Wembley. Bremner missed the European Cup Winners' Cup Final to AC Milan through suspension. Just like in season 1968-69, Bremner would be an ever-present in a league campaign that saw the Whites clinch their second league title in season 1973-74. Bremner scored ten league goals, including the first of the season at home to Everton and vital goals in wins at home to Derby County and Ipswich Town towards the end of the campaign. He finished the campaign being named alongside Paul Madeley, Norman Hunter and Allan Clarke in the PFA First Division Team of the Year.

Following the departure of Don Revie in 1974, Bremner applied for the job but the board appointed self-made Leeds critic Brian Clough instead. In Clough's first competitive match in charge of Leeds, Bremner was sent off for fighting with Liverpool's Kevin Keegan in the Charity Shield and received an 11-game suspension. Clough lasted just 44 days and was replaced by Jimmy Armfield, who led the side all the way to European Cup Final. Bremner scored the vital goal away at Anderlecht in the quarter-final second leg and the opening goal in the semi-final first leg at home to Barcelona. The final against Bayern Munich in Paris would be the Scotsman's last chance of European silverware, but they lost the game in controversial circumstances. Peter Lorimer looked to have given Leeds the lead with a superb volley, but referee Kitabdjian, after being talked to by Franz Beckenbauer, disallowed the goal after he decided that Bremner was in an offside position.

Without European football, Bremner made a further 38 appearances the following year and his last and 773rd for the side came in a 2-2 draw at home to Newcastle United on 18 September 1976. He signed for Hull City as well as having a spell as manager of Doncaster Rovers and playing for the south Yorkshire side in emergencies. He returned to Elland Road as manager in October 1985 following the sacking of Eddie Gray. Tragically, he died from a heart attack on 7 December 1997, two days before his 55th birthday, and the world of football came together to celebrate his life. On 7 August 1999 a statue of Billy was unveiled outside the stadium to celebrate his career and supporters can now have 'dedication' bricks laid next to the statue on Bremner Square.

BOBBY COLLINS

Debut: Swansea Town (H) 10 March 1962
Appearances: 167
Goals: 26

Born in Goavanhill in Glasgow, Collins joined Celtic in 1948 after starting his career at Polmadie Street School, Polmadie Hawthorns and Glasgow Pollock. He joined the Scottish giants for a fee of £1,000 at the age of 17. He had a decade spell north of the border, winning the Scottish Cup in 1951 and the Scottish Cup double in 1954. By this time, he had made his international debut in a 3-1 win over Wales in which Collins set up a goal for Billy Liddell. Following his ten-year stay in Scotland, Collins moved to Everton for a fee of £25,000 in September 1958 but was subject to poison pen letters whilst at Goodison Park. In March 1962, with Leeds struggling to stay afloat in the Second Division, Revie paid Everton £25,000 for the Scotsman's services. His debut couldn't have gone any better, as he scored in a vital 2-1 win over Swansea Town and he played in the remaining 11 games that season as Leeds survived relegation by finishing in 19th place. Collins's first full campaign at Elland Road (season 1962-63) saw him miss just three games for the club, scoring nine goals as Leeds drastically improved to finish in fifth position. Goals came against Luton Town in a 2-2 draw at Kenilworth Road, in a 6-1 win at home to Plymouth Argyle, in a 3-3 draw at home to Portsmouth, one in an FA Cup home win against Stoke City, one in a 3-2 loss at Norwich City, a brace in a 3-0 win at home to Grimsby Town and strikes at home to Preston North End and Swansea Town respectively. The following campaign saw Revie hand Collins the captain's armband and it proved to be an inspired move. Collins missed just one league game (a 3-2 loss at Manchester City in September) as he led Leeds back to the promised land of First Division football in Revie's third full season at the club. Collins hit six goals as Leeds won the league from Sunderland by two points. The first term back in the top flight saw Leeds miss out on the league title by goal average to Manchester United. Collins did have personal glory to celebrate as he became the first-ever Leeds United captain to lead a side out at Wembley although the Whites were unlucky to lose the FA Cup Final to Liverpool. It did get better for Collins as he went away with the FWA Footballer of the Year having featured in 48 games and scored ten goals in all competitions. There was disappointment just round the corner, though; with Leeds now entering European competition for the first time, Collins broke a thigh bone in the second leg of the Inter-Cities Fairs Cup tie against Torino on 6 October 1965 and, despite making a brief comeback the following season, he struggled to find his form and his Leeds career came to a sad end. His final game in a Leeds United shirt came on 2 February 1967, before he joined Bury on a free transfer later that month. He was awarded a testimonial by Leeds (which was a joint one with John Charles) in April 1988 against his former club Everton, in which Ian Rush scored a hat-trick for Leeds. Collins was diagnosed with Alzheimer's in 2002 and he passed away on 13 January 2014.

PAUL REANEY

Debut: Swansea Town (A) 8 September 1962
Appearances: 736 (11)
Goals: 9

Born in Fulham in 1944, Reaney left the capital when he was only a few weeks old and moved north to start his education at Cross Green School and play for Middleton Parkside Juniors. He was an apprentice when he joined the Leeds groundstaff in 1961 and his debut followed in a 2-0 win away at Swansea Town on 8 September 1962. Reaney made 39 appearances in his first season, scoring one goal in the 3-1 FA Cup win at home to Stoke City. The following campaign would see Reaney miss just two games as Leeds won the Second Division and returned to the promised land of top-flight football, and a new era was on the cards at Elland Road. The following season saw Reaney miss just three games in all competitions as the Whites finished second behind Manchester United on goal average, and Reaney played in every game as Leeds reached their first-ever FA Cup Final, losing 2-1 to Liverpool after extra time. Reaney netted his second goal for the side on the final day of the league campaign in a 3-3 draw away at Birmingham City. The following year saw the right-back miss just two games in total as Leeds again finished in runners-up spot, this time to Liverpool by six points. Reaney featured in every European game as Leeds reached the semi-finals of the Inter-Cities Fairs Cup before losing in a replay to Real Zaragoza. He doubled his goal tally with strikes in a 6-0 FA Cup win against Bury at Elland Road, and for the second consecutive season he scored on the final day of the campaign, this time in a 1-1 draw away at Manchester United.

He played in 61 games in season 1966-67, missing just two – a 2-0 win over Valencia in Spain and a 3-0 win over Stoke City in which Paul Madeley deputised. He added another goal to his collection in an early season 3-1 win over Manchester United at Elland Road. Reaney featured in nine of the ten games as Leeds reached the final of the Inter-Cities Fairs Cup, only to lose 2-0 on aggregate to Dynamo Zagreb. Season 1967-68 would be a glorious one in the history of the football club as Reaney just missed one game all season on the final day away at Burnley, as Leeds celebrated glory domestically and abroad. He played in every cup game as the Whites won the League Cup against Arsenal at Wembley and the Inter-Cities Fairs Cup against Ferencvaros. On 23 September 1967 in a home game against Leicester City a rare occurrence happened as Reaney came off the bench for the first time in his Leeds United career. Reaney was an ever-present in a league campaign that finally saw the Whites win their first-ever top-flight title, defeating Liverpool by six points. Reaney's only goal of the season came in a 4-1 win over Queens Park Rangers in the second match of the term. In all he missed only game, which was the second leg of the Inter-Cities Fairs Cup quarter-final tie against Újpesti Dózsa in March. During that campaign he made his England debut in a 1-1 draw against Bulgaria in a friendly at Wembley, coming on as a late substitute for Keith Newton. He ended up with just three international caps to his name, with the others coming in another friendly against Portugal and in a European Championship qualifier away to Malta.

Season 1969-70 was disappointing for Reaney as he and Leeds missed out on glory in the League, FA Cup and in Europe. Worse was to follow as he broke a leg in an away game to West Ham United on 2 April 1970 and was ruled out not only for the rest of the season but also in representing England in the World Cup. It restricted him to just 32 appearances the following year as Leeds again finished second, but Reaney did have success as he played in both legs of the Inter-Cities Fairs Cup Final against Juventus. The following 12 months saw

Reaney take part in a total of 45 games, 40 starts and five off the bench, as Leeds won their first and to date only FA Cup against Arsenal. Reaney started in five of seven games during the cup run, coming off the bench for Terry Cooper in the quarter-final win over Tottenham Hotspur.

Both Reaney and Leeds lost out in the bid for an historic double as Derby County were crowned champions in 1972.

Another 47 games followed the next term, with Reaney featuring in the shock 1-0 loss in the FA Cup Final to Sunderland and he had the honour of leading the team out in the infamous European Cup Winners' Cup Final loss to AC Milan. Another goal came in a 1-0 win over Coventry City at the start of April 1973. He made 36 appearances as Leeds won the 1973-74 league title, missing just six games and by this stage had made over 500 appearances in a Leeds United shirt.

Reaney started 59 games under three different managers (Clough, Lindley and Armfield) as the Whites reached the 1975 European Cup Final against Bayern Munich. Despite missing the second leg of the semi-final against Barcelona, he started against the Germans, only to end up on the losing side, with former boss Don Revie watching on from the commentary box. He went on to make another 96 appearances for the side, with his last coming in a 2-1 loss away at West Ham United on 8 April 1978. He moved on to Bradford City on a free transfer and then joined Newcastle United in New South Wales, being named Australia's Player of the Year. He can still be seen at Elland Road as part of the matchday hospitality team.

NORMAN HUNTER

Debut: Swansea Town (A) 8 September 1962
Appearances: 724 (2)
Goals: 21

Nicknamed 'Bite Yer Legs', Norman Hunter started at Birtley Juniors in Chester-le-Street before joining the Leeds United groundstaff as a youngster in November 1960, turning professional in April 1961. He made his Leeds United on the same day as Paul Reaney and Rod Johnson in a 2-0 away win at Swansea Town in early September 1962. Hunter established himself in the Leeds side, making 41 appearances in all competitions in his first campaign, scoring in a 3-2 home loss against Middlesbrough and in a 2-1 win away at Charlton Athletic as the Whites finished the season in fifth place.

The following season (63-64) saw the County Durham-born defender play in every league game as Leeds returned to the top flight of English football after a four-year hiatus. The only game he missed was a league cup at home to Swansea Town. He popped up with two goals against Middlesbrough at Elland Road and Swindon Town at the County Ground. The following campaign saw him feature in 51 out of 52 games, missing a 3-1 win at home to Stoke City in which Jimmy Greenhoff took over. He hit three goals in games against Blackpool, Sunderland

and Huddersfield Town in a League Cup game, all at Elland Road. He played in all eight games as Leeds made it all the way to Wembley Stadium before losing out in extra time to Liverpool.

He only missed two games during the next term as Leeds again finished second in the league and made it all the way to the semi-finals of the Inter-Cities Fairs Cup before losing to

Real Zaragoza after a replay. Hunter had his best season as far as goals would go as he hit nap hand, with them all coming in the league, including a brace in a 5-0 win at home to West Ham United at the start of February. Prior to that he made his England debut in a friendly against Spain in Madrid, coming on as a substitute for Joe Baker, and he went on to gain 28 caps for his country, scoring two goals. He was part of the England squad that won the 1966 World Cup and he came on nine minutes from time in the 3-2 loss to West Germany four years later in Mexico.

In season 1966-67 he missed just three games as Leeds missed out in the FA Cup, losing to Chelsea in the semi-finals, and in the Inter-Cities Fairs Cup, losing to Dynamo Zagreb in the final. Leeds played in an astonishing 66 games the following season, with Hunter featuring in 60, claiming his first medals at the club as Leeds won both the League Cup against Arsenal and the Inter-Cities Fairs Cup against Ferencvaros. Hunter played in every cup game, missing just the last two league games of the season as Leeds finished in fourth place. Just like in season 1963-64, Hunter was an ever-present in the league campaign as he won his first ever domestic top-flight title. The only match he missed was a home League Cup tie against Bristol City. He hit another half-century of appearances for the Whites as Leeds missed out on honours, against Chelsea at Wembley, at Old Trafford as the Blues won the FA Cup and in the second leg of the European Cup semi-final against Glasgow Celtic in front of over 135,000 supporters. He missed only one game the following year as Leeds celebrated winning their second European trophy against Juventus, and even better was to come as he was the first-ever winner of the Leeds United Player of the Year award at the end of the campaign.

He started all but one game in season 1971-72 and for first the time in his Leeds United career he came on as a substitute for Jimmy Mann in a 4-0 loss at home to Lierse in the newly named UEFA Cup. He went away with his first-ever FA Cup medal in the 1-0 win over Arsenal and will best be remembered for going up to the royal box with an injury-stricken Mick Jones. By the end of that campaign he had reached 537 games for Leeds and there was still more to come. He made 53 starts for the side in season 1972-73, but he is best remembered for his red card against AC Milan in the infamous European Cup Winners' Cup Final loss in Greece when he retaliated after the referee missed a foul on Hunter. He followed this up with another ever-present league campaign as Leeds won their second top flight in season 1973-74, and he celebrated personal glory as he was named in the PFA First Division Team of the Year and won the first-ever PFA Players' Player of the Year.

He made another 42 appearances in season 1974-75, featuring in the controversial loss to Bayern Munich in the European Cup Final, and the following year he made 35 appearances, with the one that sticks in the memory being an away game to Derby County in which both he and Francis Lee traded punches, and both unsurprisingly were sent off. His last game in a Whites shirt was in a 3-1 win at West Ham United on 6 October 1976 before he joined

Bristol City. He went on to have spells as a player-coach at Barnsley, then as manager, before being sacked in February 1984. He was assistant manager to Johnny Giles at West Bromwich Albion before joining Rotherham United as their number one in June 1985. He was sacked in December 1987 before returning to Elland Road as part of the coaching staff in February 1988. He left following the appointment of Howard Wilkinson in October 1988 and then went on to become Terry Yorath's assistant at neighbours Bradford City. He was part of the BBC Radio Leeds commentary team for many a year and can still be seen at Elland Road on matchdays. The Norman Hunter suite in the West Stand has been named in his honour.

PETER LORIMER

Debut: Southampton (H) 29 September 1962
Appearances: 677 (28)
Goals: 238

The White's record goalscorer started his career at Eastern and Stobswell Schools, once scoring 167 goals in one season. Lorimer then went on to represent Dundee schools and Broughty YMCA before signing for Leeds as an amateur in May 1962. Rumour has it that Revie was so desperate to sign the Scotsman that he was stopped for speeding on the way to capture him. He turned professional in December 1963 and by that time had already made his Leeds United debut aged 15 years and 289 days, in a 1-1 draw at home to Southampton. He still holds the record for the club's youngest-ever player. He made two appearances that season before making his next towards the back end of the 1964-65 campaign as he recovered from a fractured leg.

Lorimer started to make a name for himself the following year, making 34 league appearances and scoring 13 league goals in the process. His first goal came in a 2-1 win over Nottingham Forest at Elland Road and his first hat-trick in a Leeds United shirt came in a resounding 6-0 FA Cup win over Bury at Elland Road. He also featured nine times, scoring three goals, as the Whites reached the semi-finals of the Inter-Cities Fairs Cup, only to lose out to Real Zaragoza in a replay.

The following season (1966-67) saw 'Lash' make a further 36 appearances as the side were beaten in the semi-finals of the FA Cup by Chelsea and the final of the Inter-Cities Fairs Cup by Dynamo Zagreb. But Lorimer did finish the season with another 14 goals under his belt. The following year saw the Scotsman hit the magic 30-goal mark and he finished the season with a League Cup winner's medal and a first European medal. Further memorable games came as he hit a hat-trick in a 3-1 League Cup win at home to Luton Town and a four-goal haul in a 9-0 away win against Spora Luxembourg in the Inter-Cities Fairs Cup.

The following 12 months saw Lorimer win his first top-flight title, scoring nine goals in 25 games as well as hitting further goals in other competitions. Another 19 goals followed in season 1969-70 as the Whites missed out in the league by finishing second to Everton and lose an FA Cup Final replay to Chelsea and a European Cup semi-final to Glasgow Celtic. Lorimer did hit another hat-trick in a 6-1 home drubbing against Nottingham Forest.

A further 19 goals followed in season 1970-71 and Lorimer was part of the side that won their second Inter-Cities Fairs Cup, this time against Juventus, winning on away goals after drawing both games, 2-2 away and 1-1 at Elland Road. He added another 28 goals in season 1971-72 and played in every round as Leeds won their first and only FA Cup thanks to an Allan Clarke header against Arsenal. He scored in the 4-1 win at home to Bristol Rovers in the third round and one as Leeds eased past Birmingham City in the last four to reach Wembley. He walked away with the Leeds United Player of the Year award and by the end of this season Lorimer was a Scottish international, having made his debut against Austria in November 1969. He went on to make 21 appearances, scoring four goals, one of which came in the World Cup Finals against Zaire. Season 1972-73 saw another 23 goals for Lorimer as again Leeds just missed on the honours, losing the FA Cup Final to Sunderland and the European Cup Winners' Cup to AC Milan. Lorimer then won his second championship title, scoring 13 league goals in 34 games, which included a hat-trick at home to Birmingham City, a vital brace away to Sheffield United and the opener in a crucial 3-2 win at home to Ipswich Town. Another 16 goals followed in 1974-75, but that campaign would be remembered for the one that got away as he had a perfect volley disallowed in the European Cup Final against Bayern Munich for an alleged offside.

The glory days were a thing of the past in 1975-76, but Lorimer still hit 11 goals as the Whites finished in fifth place under Jimmy Armfield. His last game in his first spell at the club came against West Bromwich Albion at Maine Road before spells at Toronto Blizzard in Canada, York City and as player-manager with Vancouver Whitecaps. He returned to Elland Road aged 37 in December 1983, then under player-manager Eddie Gray and he made his second debut in a 4-1 win over Middlesbrough on New Year's Eve 1983, coming on as a substitute for George McCluskey. He finished that season with a further five goals for the club and would take over the captaincy from David Harvey mid-way through the next season.

Season 1984-85 saw Lorimer miss just two games all season, scoring ten goals along the way. Following the sacking of Eddie Gray in October 1985 and the arrival of Billy Bremner, Lorimer ended his playing career at Elland Road. He made his last appearance for the Whites in Bremner's first game in charge (a 3-0 defeat at Barnsley) and he moved to Whitby Town in December 1985. His final stint was as a player-coach with Israeli side Hapoel Haifa before entering the hospitality business.

JOHNNY GILES

Debut: Bury (H) 31 August 1963
Appearances: 523 (4)
Goals: 115

Dublin-born Giles started his career at Brunswick Street School before moving on to St Colombus FC, Dublin and Republic of Ireland Schools, Dublin FC, The Leprechauns, Stella Maris and Home Farm, before joining Manchester United as an amateur in July 1956. He turned professional with the Red Devils in November 1957. He was given his Manchester United debut in 1958 and was part of the side that won the FA Cup against Leicester City in 1963. Giles had a hand in David Herd's vital goal as the side from the red half of Manchester won 3-1.

Following the cup final, he asked for a transfer and Don Revie paid the Red Devils £33,000 to secure his services.

By this time, Giles had made his international debut for the Republic of Ireland, which took place on 1 November 1959 in an international friendly against Sweden, and he marked it with a goal in a 3-2 win. He ended up winning 59 caps, scoring five goals along the way.

Back to his club career, Giles made his Leeds United debut in the second game of the season at home to Bury and he featured on 40 occasions in the league as the Whites returned to the top flight in Giles's first season at the club. He also hit seven goals as Leeds finished top of the pile, two points ahead of Sunderland. His first goal for the side came in a 2-0 win away at Huddersfield Town, and Giles hit vital strikes in a 4-1 win at Southampton, in a 2-2 draw at Swindon Town and in games against Middlesbrough (3-1), Newcastle United (1-0), Leyton Orient (2-1) and Swansea Town (3-0). With Leeds back at England's top table, Giles played in 46 games in all competitions, hitting eight goals from midfield. Season 1965-66 would be the Whites first playing European football, and the Irishman played in 54 games, scoring seven goals. The following term saw Giles hit 18 goals in 48 games as the Whites were denied in the penultimate hurdle in the FA Cup by Chelsea and in the final of the Inter-Cities Fairs Cup by Dynamo Zagreb. Giles captained the side in four games during that campaign.

A further 35 games (season 1967-68) and ten goals followed the next year and he returned to Wembley as a winner for the second time as Leeds defeated Arsenal thanks to Terry Cooper to secure the League Cup. It would be a case of double glory for Giles as he was part of the side that won their first-ever European trophy, defeating Ferencvaros over two legs, though Giles did miss the second leg. He then played an important role the following year as Leeds lost just two league games to secure their first-ever top-flight title, with Giles featuring 32 times in the league, scoring eight vital goals. He hit the half-century of appearances as Leeds looked for glory at home and abroad but would fall short on both targets. As for Giles, he did hit the back of the net 19 times (13 in the league, two in the FA Cup and four in Europe), with Leeds missing out to Chelsea in the FA Cup Final and to Glasgow Celtic in the last four of the European Cup.

Another 16 goals in 46 games followed in season 1970-71 as Giles played a vital part in the side that saw Leeds win the Inter-Cities Fairs Cup against Italian giants Juventus, but he missed out on his second league title by a single point to Arsenal. It would be another runners-up spot for Leeds and Giles in 1972, but he played in every game on the road to Wembley as the side won their first-ever FA Cup.

He hit double figures again the following campaign but suffered heartache as Leeds failed to retain the FA Cup, losing to Sunderland, though Giles did equal the pre-war mark of Arsenal and Huddersfield Town forward Joe Hulme of appearing in five finals. He missed the European Cup Winners' Cup Final against AC Milan due to an injury he picked up playing with Republic of Ireland. He made only 19 appearances as Leeds won their second top-flight title but controversy was just round the corner. With Don Revie taking up the England job, he recommended Giles to take over but the board opted for Brian Clough. Clough never got on with the players, who had also wanted Giles to take over, and he was relieved of his duties after 44 days. Again Giles was overlooked for Jimmy Armfield and Giles made 45 appearances in his last season with the club. His 527th and last game for the side was the infamous European Cup Final defeat to Bayern Munich. In June 1975 he joined West Bromwich Albion as player-manager, bringing down the curtain on a glorious career at Elland Road.

PAUL MADELEY

Debut: Manchester City (H) 11 January 1964
Appearances: 712 (13)
Goals: 34

Born in Beeston very close to Elland Road, Madeley attended Cross Flatts Park Junior School and then Parkside Secondary Modern School and played for Middleton Parkside Youth alongside Paul Reaney and Rod Johnson. He went on to play for Farsley Celtic in the Yorkshire League before signing on at Elland Road following trials with the side in May 1962. He would go on to play in every position for the Whites during an illustrious career in west Yorkshire.

He made his debut wearing the number-five shirt in a 1-0 win over Manchester City on 11 January 1964, then he went on to make a further five appearances for the side as Leeds won promotion back to the top flight. Another seven games the following year saw Madeley in the number-three, four and five shirt, and 12 months later he would make 20 appearances in all competitions as he wore the number three, five and even the number-nine shirt in games away at Chelsea in the FA Cup, away to Valencia in the Inter-Cities Fairs Cup, against Nottingham Forest at the City Ground and at home to Chelsea in the league. He also scored his first two goals for the side in a 3-3 draw at Leicester and in a 4-2 League Cup loss at home to West Bromwich Albion.

The 1966-67 season would be Madeley's breakthrough campaign at Elland Road as he featured in 45 games, though he did miss out on playing in the Inter-Cities Fairs Cup Final against Dynamo Zagreb. He nipped in with a further four goals, at home to Manchester United, at home to Arsenal, a 5-0 win at home to West Bromwich Albion in the FA Cup and in a 5-1 win at home to DWS Amsterdam in Europe. It would get even better for Madeley in season 1967-68 as he played in a total of 57 games, making 51 starts and six substitute appearances, scoring ten goals (the only season he hit double figures), as Leeds won the League Cup against Arsenal and the Inter-Cities Fairs Cup against Ferencvaros.

Madeley wore the number-nine shirt against the Gunners at Wembley, the same number against the Hungarians at Elland Road in the first leg and the number-ten shirt in the return.

Season 1968-69 saw 'The Rolls Royce' feature on 42 occasions, 31 in the league, as Revie's boys won their first-ever league title. Madeley hit four goals in all competitions, including three in the league against Leicester City, Coventry City and Newcastle United respectively. The end of the decade saw Madeley feature in 59 out of 63 games, wearing every outfield number as Leeds missed out on glory in the League, FA Cup and European Cup. Madeley wore the number-four shirt in both FA Cup Final games against Chelsea. It would be more of the same the following term as Madeley missed just one game all season as Leeds again finished second in the leg, but they did celebrate success against Juventus to claim the Inter-Cities Fairs Cup for a second time. This time Madeley wore the number-11 shirt for the Whites, and before the final took place he would make his debut for his country in a Home Championship game against Northern Ireland in Belfast. Season 1971-72 saw another 54 games for the side, with Madeley wearing the number-three shirt in the FA Cup Final win over Arsenal in place of the stricken Terry Cooper. Another half-century-plus games followed in 1972-73, and he wore the number-five shirt in both finals against Sunderland and AC Milan respectively. He missed only three league games as he claimed his second championship medal in 1974 and was named in the First Division PFA Team of the Year. He missed just five games as Leeds made it to the European Cup Final against Bayern Munich, in which Madeley again wore the number-five shirt. For the second consecutive campaign he was named in the PFA Team of the Year. By this time he had reached over 500 games for the club and another 200 would take place before retirement in 1980. With previous glories a thing of the past, Madeley's appearances just kept coming, with another 43 in season 1975-76 and yet again he was named in the Team of the Year.

He followed that up with 44 in season 1976-77, 45 in 1977-78, 49 in 1978-79, 29 in 1979-80 and eight in the season 1980-81. He played under Don Revie, Brian Clough, Maurice Lindley, Jimmy Armfield, Jock Stein, Jimmy Adamson and Allan Clarke, winning the Leeds United Player of the Year in season 1975-76. His final and 725th appearance for Leeds was on 8 November 1980 at home to Arsenal before retirement. After football he opened a sports shop in Leeds and kept an interest in the decor business. He passed away aged 73 in July 2018.

EDDIE GRAY MBE

Debut: Sheffield Wednesday (H) 1 January 1966
Appearances: 561 (18)
Goals: 69

Born in Glasgow, Gray signed professional forms with Leeds at the age of 16 in January 1965 and would go on to have a glorious career at Elland Road. He scored on his debut on New Year's Day 1966 against Sheffield Wednesday and featured on six occasions in his first season, scoring that one goal against the Owls.

EDDIE GRAY
Leeds and Scotland

The following campaign saw the Scotsman play in 36 games in all competitions, scoring four goals in games against Burnley at Turf Moor, Sunderland at Elland Road, Tottenham Hotspur at Elland Road and Sunderland in the return at Roker Park. Season 1967-68 saw Gray make a half-century of appearances, scoring nine goals, playing in every round as the

Whites won the League Cup for the first time. He featured in eight of the 11 games as Leeds followed that success with the European glory in the Inter-Cities Fairs Cup against Hungarian side Ferencvaros.

There would be more glory just round the corner for Gray both domestically and internationally as he won the First Division title with Leeds the following year, appearing 33 times, scoring five goals, and at the end of the season he made his full international debut in a 4-1 defeat against England in the British Championship at Wembley. Gray ended up with 12 caps, scoring three goals against Cyprus, Wales and Finland respectively.

The final season of the 1960s saw Gray appear on 43 occasions, scoring nine times, and despite losing the FA Cup Final to Chelsea he set up Jack Charlton for the first goal and he left David Webb for dead on many occasions. He was awarded the Man of the Match award as the game ended in a 2-2 draw. Gray's best day in a Leeds shirt came a week earlier as he scored two of the side's greatest-ever goals at Elland Road against Burnley in a 2-1 win over the Clarets. He went on a brilliant solo run, getting past six claret shirts before dropping his shoulder, rolling the ball back and finishing past Mellor in the away goal. He also scored a lob from 35 yards in front of 24,691 supporters. Gray went on to have further success the following year but due to injury he missed both legs of the Inter-Cities Fairs Cup win over Juventus.

Season 1971-72 saw Gray add another 31 appearances to his total as well as another six goals to his collection. He made up for the 1970 FA Cup Final loss as this time he was on the winning side against Arsenal. The following term saw only 24 appearances in the Whites side, scoring just the one goal, starting the FA Cup Final loss to Sunderland but missing out against AC Milan due to injury. Gray only played in nine games in all competitions as Leeds won the league for the second time in what proved to be Don Revie's last season in west Yorkshire after accepting the England job. To many people's surprise, the board appointed Brian Clough, who said about Gray, 'had he been a horse, he would have been shot long ago'. Clough lasted only 44 days before being replaced by Jimmy Armfield, and he led Leeds to the European Cup Final against Bayern Munich, but Gray had to settle for a place on the bench, coming on for Terry Yorath 11 minutes from the end, with the German side already a goal to the good. In the end Bayern went away with the trophy and Revie's side started to break up. In 1975-76, Gray made 30 appearances, scoring in a 5-2 win over Everton. It would be much better the following year as he featured 42 times, scoring six goals as Leeds finished in tenth place and making the last four of the FA Cup before losing to Manchester United at Hillsborough. Seven goals in 28 games saw Leeds finish in ninth place and again making the last four of a cup competition, losing to Nottingham Forest in the semi-finals of the League Cup 7-3 on aggregate. Another near miss took place the following year under the stewardship of first Jock Stein and then Jimmy Adamson, with Gray making 32 appearances in all competitions, scoring nine goals along the way as Leeds reached the last four of the League Cup once more, before losing to Southampton.

Adamson's first full season at the club saw Gray play in 31 games, scoring in a 1-1 draw against Bolton Wanderers and in a 3-1 loss at home to Bristol City. Adamson was sacked in September 1980 and replaced by Gray's former teammate Allan Clarke, and Gray missed just six games all season as Leeds finished in ninth place. Worse was to come for Leeds and Gray as the Whites were relegated the following year, with the winger playing in 36 games. Despite Leeds dropping out of the top flight, Gray did win the Whites' Player of the Year. Clarke was sacked and replaced by Gray, who took on the role of player-manager. His playing career lasted a further two seasons and he made his last appearance on the final day of the 1983-84 season at home to Charlton Athletic. Gray then had spells managing at Whitby Town, Rochdale and Hull City before returning to be part of the coaching staff in March 1995. He had a second spell as manager during the 2003-04 season and he is still very much part of the matchday team as co-commentator for LUTV.

MICK JONES

Debut: Leicester City (H) 23 September 1967
Appearances: 308 (5)
Goals: 111

Worksop-born Jones started his career at Priory Primary School where he once hit 14 goals in a game, and from there he went on to play for Worksop Boys, Rotherham Boys and Donnington Miners Welfare before his big move, as he was invited to train with Sheffield United Juniors and joined the ground staff in March 1961. He signed professional forms with the Blades in November 1962 and made his debut for the red half of the city against Manchester United in April 1963. He stayed at Bramall Lane until September 1967 and it was whilst he was in Sheffield that he made his England debut against West Germany in May 1965. He ended up with three international caps, all in friendly games.

He joined the ranks at Elland Road in September 1967 as he became the Whites' first-ever £100,000 player when he swapped South for west Yorkshire. He made his debut for the side in a 3-2 win over Leicester City and would score his first goal for the side two games later in a 9-0 win away at Spora Luxembourg in the Inter-Cities Fairs Cup.

In his first season at Elland Road, Jones featured 38 times, scoring 12 goals. He was handed the number-nine shirt by Don Revie and played a vital part of the side that were victorious against Ferencvaros in winning the Inter-Cities Fairs Cup for the first time. Jones scored the vital winning goal as Leeds won their first-ever European trophy. The following campaign would be even better for Jones as he ended up as top scorer with 17 goals in all competitions as Leeds won their first-ever top-flight title.

Season 1969-70 would be even better on a personal level for Jones, even if the side missed out on glory domestically and in Europe – Leeds finished runners-up to Everton, lost out in the FA Cup Final to Chelsea after a replay and lost a European Cup semi-final to Glasgow Celtic – Jones, hit 26 goals in 51 games, including in both cup final games against Chelsea at Wembley and in the replay at Old Trafford. The following season again saw Leeds miss out on domestic glory by finishing second once more, but Jones did feature in nine of the 12 games as Leeds won their second Inter-Cities Fairs Cup against Juventus.

The following 12 months were bittersweet for Jones, as he scored a brilliant 15-minute hat-trick against Manchester United in a sensational 5-0 win over the Red Devils and hit a fine cross for Allan Clarke to score the only goal in the 1972 FA Cup Final, but sadly he suffered a dislocated elbow in the last minute of the game in an accidental clash with Arsenal goalkeeper Geoff Barnett. He was unable to participate in match-winning celebrations and went up to the Royal Box with Norman Hunter. He recovered to feature in a total of 47 games the following year, scoring 16 goals and playing in both the FA Cup Final against Sunderland and the European Cup Winners' Cup Final against AC Milan.

The next campaign, in what proved to be Revie's last in charge at Elland Road, saw Leeds start the season like a house on fire going unbeaten in 29 league games before losing at Stoke City. Jones featured in 31 league games, hitting 14 goals, as Leeds became champions for the second time. He also walked away with the Leeds United Player of the Year award. His last appearance for the Whites came in the vital 3-2 win over Ipswich Town on 20 April 1974. Injuries proved to be a huge problem for Jones and he eventually called time on his career in October 1975.

ALLAN CLARKE

Debut: Manchester City (H) 2 August 1968
Appearances: 361 (5)
Goals: 151

The only Leeds United player to score a winning goal in an FA Cup, Clarke, who came from a football family represented Birmingham Schools and South East Staffordshire before moving on to Walsall as an apprentice in 1961. He signed professional forms with the Saddlers in August 1963 and won Walsall's Player of the Year, voted for by the supporters in 1964-65. He finished top scorer in both that season and 1965-66 before joining Fulham in March 1968. His stay at west London lasted just over two years and from there he joined Leicester City for a fee of £150,000 in June 1968. His stay at Filbert Street lasted only a year, but he did receive the Man of the Match award in the 1968-69 FA Cup Final loss to Manchester City. The following month Leeds paid £165,000, a British record transfer fee at the time. He made his debut in a 2-1 Charity Shield win over Manchester City, which was played at Elland Road, and by the end of his first campaign he had featured a total of 43 times, scoring 26 goals, which included braces against Lyn Oslo in a club-record 10-0 win, in a 2-0 win at home to Derby County, at home to Coventry City and a four-goal haul against non-league Sutton United in a 6-0 win in the FA Cup fourth round. The following campaign saw Clarke miss just one league game and three European games, scoring 23 goals, with the most vital clinching the Inter-Cities Fairs Cup against Juventus at Elland Road.

The Staffordshire-born striker hit his second four-goal salvo in a 4-0 win at home to Burnley as Leeds finished runners-up to Arsenal. He also scored in the infamous 2-1 loss at home to West Bromwich Albion. The 1971-72 season saw Clarke hit another 15 goals, with the most famous coming in the 53rd minute on Saturday 6 May 1972 as he headed in a Mick Jones cross to win the Whites their one and only FA Cup to date. Sadly for Leeds and Clarke, they were denied the double as they were forced to play Wolverhampton Wanderers just two days later and subsequently lost 2-1 at Molineux, handing the title to Derby County.

By this time Clarke had six international caps, scoring on his debut in the World Cup finals against Czechoslovakia in 1970. Clarke ended up with 19 caps, scoring ten goals. The 1972-73 season saw Clarke hit a further 26 goals as Leeds finished third in the League and lost both the FA Cup Final to Second Division Sunderland and the European Cup Winners' Cup Final controversially to AC Milan. 'Sniffer' then hit 13 crucial league goals in 1973-74 as Leeds won their second league title, scoring the final league goal of a memorable season away at Queens Park Rangers. By this point Clarke had clocked up 237 games in a Whites shirt, scoring 106 goals. The following season saw managerial upheaval at Elland Road, with Revie taking over at England. The board appointed Leeds's harshest critic in Brian Clough before replacing him with Jimmy Armfield. Armfield led Leeds to the European Cup Final against Bayern Munich, a game in which Clarke was denied a certain penalty and Leeds went on to lose 2-0. Clarke stayed at Elland Road until the end of the 1977-78 season, captaining the side in an FA Cup tie at home to Norwich City. He joined Barnsley as player-manager in May 1978 before returning as the Whites boss in October 1980.

MANAGERS APPOINTED IN THE 1960s

DON REVIE OBE

First game in charge: Portsmouth (A) 18 March 1961
Last game in charge: Queens Park Rangers (A) 27 April 1974
Games: 741
Won: 395
Drawn: 197
Lost: 149

Leeds needed someone to lift the spirits around the club following the end of Jack Taylor's rein, and Harry Reynolds turned to Don Revie, who had originally applied for the manager's post at Bournemouth before realising he was the person needed to take Leeds forward, despite his lack of managerial experience. Revie was born in Middlesbrough, started his playing career at Leicester City in 1944 and featured in an incredible four major transfer deals totalling nearly £80,000, which was a record at the time. He scored twice for the Foxes in their FA Cup semi-final against Portsmouth but missed the final against Wolverhampton Wanderers with broken blood vessels in his nose. He then moved to Hull City for £20,000 under a soon-to-be Leeds manager Raich Carter and then joined Manchester City in October 1951 for £25,000. He played in City's 1955 FA Cup Final loss to Newcastle United but returned as a winner a year later as City defeated Birmingham City 3-1. He also went away with the 1955 Footballer of the Year whilst at Maine Road.

In October 1956, he moved north to join Sunderland in a deal worth £22,000 but suffered relegation from the First Division at the end of the 1957-58 season. In November 1958 Revie joined Leeds, and by the time he was made player-manager he had made 73 appearances for the Whites, scoring 11 goals. He started his managerial career with a 3-1 loss at Portsmouth and would win only one of his first eight games, which was a 7-0 hammering of Lincoln City. The Whites finished season 1960-61 in 14th place.

Revie's first full season at the helm saw Derek Mayers join from Preston North End and he added Syd Owen, Les Cocker and Maurice Lindley to his backroom team. His team survived relegation to the third tier of English football thanks to a 3-0 win away at Newcastle United and the side finished in 19th place. One piece of important transfer news that did take place was the purchase of Bobby Collins from Everton for £25,000. The following year saw Revie start to blood some of the youngsters and the likes of Paul Reaney, Norman Hunter and Rod Johnson all made their debuts in a 2-0 win away at Swansea Town. It was also the second appearance in goal for Gary Sprake.

Next in line to make his debut was 15-year-old Peter Lorimer, who did so in a 1-1 draw at home to Southampton. Leeds improved from the previous season's 19th-place finish to end up in fifth and hopes were high that Revie could deliver a promotion push in season 1963-64.

At the start of the new campaign, Revie again dipped into the transfer market, bringing in Irish international Johnny Giles from Manchester United. Leeds had a brilliant season, winning promotion with a 3-0 away win at Swansea Town and clinched the title on the final day courtesy of a brace from Alan Peacock. Revie had been at the helm for over three seasons and had delivered First Division football, as a new era domestically and in Europe was set to begin at Elland Road. During the off season, the FA News printed a list of clubs with the worst disciplinary record from the previous season and Leeds topped it after accusations of 'dirty play' and 'over professionalism'. As for the football, Leeds took to top-flight football like a duck to water, going second after a 3-0 win at home to Blackpool with a brace from Bobby Collins. After a 2-1 win over Sunderland on 2 January 1965, Leeds topped the table, with Norman Hunter on the scoresheet. Leeds started their FA Cup run with a 3-0 win over Southport and followed it up with a fourth-round replay win over Everton, before Shrewsbury Town were beaten 2-0 at Elland Road in the last 16. Crystal Palace were brushed aside in the last eight before a meeting with eventual champions Manchester United at Hillsborough. The game ended in a 0-0 draw, before a Billy Bremner goal in the replay at Burden Park took Leeds to Wembley. The Red Devils got their revenge, winning the title on goal average from Leeds as the Whites then concentrated on the 1965 FA Cup Final. Revie led his team to Wembley, but it was Liverpool who went away with the glory. Revie, in his first season in the top flight as Leeds manager, ensured European football for the first time in the club's history.

Season 1965-66, saw Leeds challenge both domestically and in Europe, but they missed out in the league again, finishing second this time six points behind champions Liverpool, but they were never out of the top four all season. Just as they did back in the top flight, Leeds took to European football like they had never been away from it, defeating Torino 2-1 on aggregate, SC Leipzig by the same scoreline, Valencia again by the same scoreline, and Újpesti Dózsa 5-2 on aggregate, which set up a last-four meeting with Real Zaragoza. Leeds lost the first tie 1-0 before goals from Albert Johanneson and Jack Charlton took the tie to a replay, also at Elland Road, which the Spanish side won 3-1 to reach the final; not a bad first season in Europe and there was more to come in the years that followed. Season 1966-67 saw Leeds finish in fourth place, concentrating on the FA and Inter-Cities Fairs Cup. In the FA Cup, Revie's side defeated Crystal Palace, West Bromwich Albion, Sunderland after two replays and Manchester City to reach the semi-finals, playing against Chelsea at Villa Park. Leeds lost the game after having Peter Lorimer's last-minute strike disallowed.

In Europe, Revie took Leeds a step further than they had in the previous year, reaching the final having disposed of DWS Amsterdam, Valencia (again), Bologna and Kilmarnock before meeting Dynamo Zagreb. Zagreb won the tie 2-0 on aggregate as the manager's focus turned to strengthening the attack. He did this by signing Sheffield United forward Mick Jones for a club-record fee of £100,000.

Leeds started the season poorly following two defeats in their first league games but got stronger as the season went on. Following a 2-0 win over Manchester City they then went top of the pile but ended in fourth place with four consecutive defeats. They again turned their attention to the cups and this time Revie was successful. Leeds made it to their first ever League Cup Final, having beaten Luton Town, Bury, Sunderland and Derby County, before a Terry Cooper winner at Wembley saw off Arsenal and Revie had his first major silverware at Elland Road. He followed it up with a double as he led Leeds to their first-ever European trophy. Having seen off Spora Luxembourg (16-0 on aggregate), Partizan Belgrade and a treble of Scottish sides in Hibernian, Rangers and Dundee, they met Ferencvaros in the two-leg final. A Mick Jones goal settled the first and a brilliant defensive display in the second gave Revie his first success in Europe. Revie then set his sights on winning his first top-flight title the following year, and they did so in record-breaking fashion. They had the most points with 67, most home points with 39, most wins with 27, most home wins with 18, fewest defeats with two, fewest goals conceded with 26 and fewest home goals conceded with nine. Leeds again looked to improve with the signing of Leicester City striker Allan Clarke, but season 1969-70 would be one of heartbreak on three fronts: they again finished second, nine points behind Everton, lost the FA Cup Final after a replay to Chelsea and lost a European Cup semi-final to Glasgow Celtic, with the second leg being played in front of over 135,000 fans at Hampden Park. Season 1970-71 again saw silverware with the Inter-Cities Fairs Cup but another second-place finish in the league. They were top of the league going into a home game with West Bromwich Albion, but a controversial goal from Jeff Astle helped the Baggies to a 2-1 win. Barry Davies commentating on *Match of the Day* said, 'Don Revie will go mad.'

Arsenal ended up winning the title and Leeds were handed a four-match home ban following a pitch invasion in that game. They were better times in Europe for Leeds. They had disposed of Sarpsborg, Dynamo Dresden, Sparta Prague, Vitoria Setubal and Liverpool before meeting Juventus in their second Inter-Cities Fairs Cup Final. Goals from Paul Madeley and

Mick Bates meant Leeds had the upper hand going into the second leg at Elland Road, and an Allan Clarke strike handed Leeds the trophy on away goals.

Leeds started the 1971-72 campaign playing their home games at Leeds Road, Boothferry Park and Hillsborough, and looked set to win their first-ever league and cup double. In the FA Cup, Bristol Rovers were beaten 4-1 at Elland Road, Liverpool 2-0 after a replay at Elland Road, Cardiff City 2-0 at Ninian Park, Tottenham Hotspur 2-1 in the last eight and Birmingham City 3-0 at Hillsborough before another final showdown with Arsenal. Revie had won the FA Cup as a player and now did it as a manager in the competition's centenary

DON REVIE SAYS...

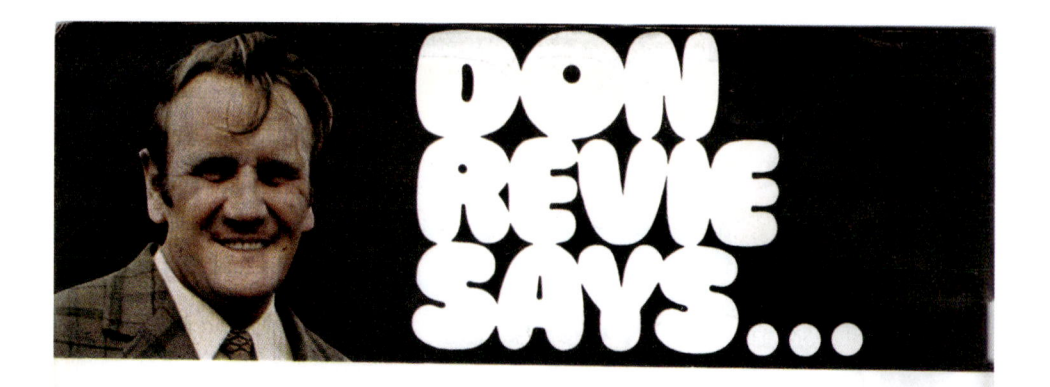

The name of Leeds United has once again been sullied; blackened by critics and writers even before the new season has started. Once more we have been branded by sour tongues; mercilessly lashed by others. We begin our latest quest for success cast in the roles of music hall villains. Not unnaturally, we are somewhat exasperated by this latest critical broadside. The guns have all been trained on Elland Road. We have become the butt of everyone's bad feeling. At a time when we felt we had at last thrown off that cliched old tag of being a 'dirty' side; bang, off go the guns again and we have to run for cover.

But then our critics—and what club has had more criticism than us in the last decade?—have always been quick to regularly point out that our slip is showing. This hoary old chestnut has been roasted and re-roasted so much that we have grown an extra layer of thick skin to combat it. Indeed, every year we answered each and every one of our critics in a way which you would have thought was impossible to criticise—we brought success to Elland Road.

And, as 1973-74 gets off to a start, we hope to keep in that same vein.

We want to be able to maintain interest right up to the very last kick of the season as we have in the past nine years. Last year, it is true, was a tremendous disappointment—but only in terms of not adding more silver to our trophy cupboard. We appeared in two cup finals and finished third in the First Division. And yet people still criticise us! It is a body blow when you work so hard for such a long time and don't finish with tangible rewards—particularly for you supporters. By now it probably sounds like just another managerial cliche but believe me, without your fanatical support there would be no Leeds United. **Without you we are nothing—but with you we can scale the tallest heights of human achievement.**

Which brings us back to that criticism. Not only is it hard for we at the club to take—but it must be even more galling for you fans. The close season has been full of criticism about the way our players play the game. But I will say here and now that in 1973-74 we will be doing everything in our power to improve our conduct record. The situation is not helped by the fact that ahead of us lie nine months of highly personalised limbo. **We live under threat of suspended sentence—a nice situation to be in indeed for the club who have become a household name for soccer success.**

Despite what people say about us, I believe that we have a tremendously skilful side. Our record proves that, because, make no mistake, however physical a team is, trophies are only won in football by sides with skill, flair and artistry. So many of the things that have been said about us during the close season are so far from the truth that we must treat them with the contempt they so obviously deserve.

What the critics don't realise is that their attacks have nothing like the effect on us they think. With every critical word or story we'll work twice as hard to try and prove all these 'knockers' wrong. We hope you will continue to back us with your fantastic support as we try to right one of football's wrongs.

I accept it as a fact of British life that there will always be sympathy for the underdog. When a team plays as consistently well as Leeds United have in the last nine seasons, it is a natural defence mechanism to look for flaws, to criticise even the slightest failing which ordinarily would go completely unnoticed. It has been said to me that we have achieved so much and produced so many astonishingly flawless performances that the writers have run out of epithets, of praises, of powers of description.

But, surely, that does not mean that we should then be criticised for things which, as I have said, go unseen at other grounds? And by that, I mean that each time a Leeds United performance does not reach its ultimate peak we are slandered as being 'below form' or even 'sub-standard.'

When such high standards of perfection have been set it is only natural that Everest cannot be climbed every week. Football, you see, is a game of human assets and failings. The secret of a good team and of good management is to establish an easily repeated pattern in which the player who might be slightly off peak is not noticed because of the all-round teamwork of the others. This is what we have always tried to do at Leeds United—and I think our record shows that we have achieved it.

year, thanks to an Allan Clarke flying header. Amazingly, just two days later, they travelled to Wolverhampton Wanderers knowing a point would secure the double. Sadly goals from Munro and Dougan put Wolves 2-0 up and, despite one back from captain marvel Bremner, the home side held on and the title went to Derby County.

Revie responded by adding Trevor Cherry from Huddersfield Town for £100,000 and Gordon McQueen from St Mirren for £30,000. Leeds finished in third place, seven points

Elation and disappointment have gone hand in hand in the last few years—but each has been on a consistently high level. In football, it does not do to dwell too much upon the past. Yet our immediate past is the undeniable answer to all those who criticise and damn with faint praise.

Leeds United can never repay the debt we owe to you and your unfailing support. That is why this season we are aiming to give you even more for your money at Elland Road. As you will have read, soccer watching at Leeds will be somewhat unique this season. Not only will you have England's premier team to cheer but also a carefully formulated programme to give you increased creature comforts.

Saturday afternoon at Elland Road will no longer be just a case of clicking through the turnstiles, watching the match and going home again.

Not just for Leeds United, but for all the 92 clubs who make up The Football League, 1973-74 promises to be a milestone. For the first time, promotion and relegation in the First and Second Divisions affects three teams, not just two. This can only be for the good of the game. Stimulus in the methods of promotion and relegation has long been needed because for all too many clubs, the season is as good as over by the end of January every year.

With Football League attendances showing a drastic fall last season, it was obvious that the fans were missing something in the way of competitiveness. It is my belief that three-up, three-down will restore this missing piece of the jigsaw puzzle. By the end of the season, more teams than ever before will be jostling for a place in the game's honours' stakes.

It certainly promises to be a season to remember—and particularly for you priceless fans here at Elland Road.

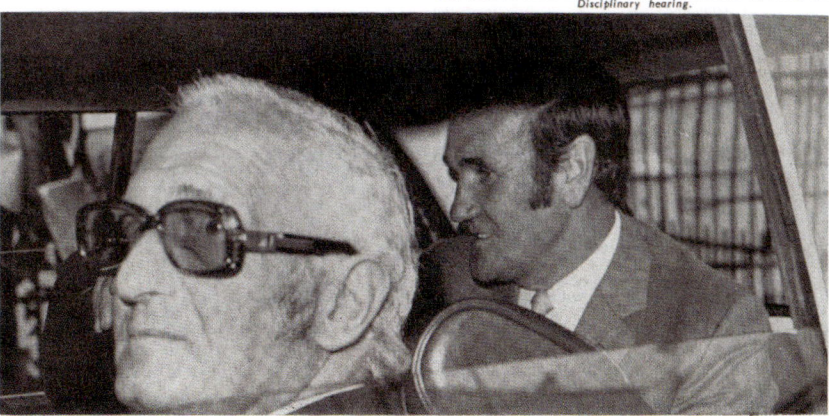

United in trouble . . . Chairman Mr. Manny Cussins and Manager Don Revie are driven away from Lancaster Gate after the recent F.A. Disciplinary hearing.

3

behind champions Liverpool, and looked set for glory in both the FA Cup and the European Cup Winners' Cup. For the second consecutive campaign they reached the FA Cup Final, this time against Second Division Sunderland, with Leeds being odds-on favourites. Thanks to a goal from Ian Porterfield and an incredible point-blank save from Jim Montgomery, the Mackems went home with the cup. Worse was to follow for Revie's men as they made it through to the European Cup Winners' Cup Final against AC Milan in Greece. Missing Billy Bremner, Johnny

Giles and Allan Clarke, Leeds lost 1-0, with the goal coming from Luciano Chairugi. It didn't help the Whites that they were on the end of some dreadful referring decisions from Christos Michas, who was then banned for life following a UEFA investigation.

After deciding against joining Everton and following discussions with chairman Manny Cussins, Revie set about another tilt at the title. They got off to a brilliant start, winning their first seven games and topping the league table after the third game away at Tottenham Hotspur – and they wouldn't surrender top spot all season, despite some hiccups along the way. They set a new record of being unbeaten 29 games into a league season before losing a 2-0 lead at Stoke City, and all of a sudden the doubts started to creep in. Leeds were out of all cup competitions, losing to Ipswich Town in the League Cup, Bristol City in the FA Cup and Vitoria Setubal in the UEFA Cup. It left the side to concentrate on winning the league for the second time, and, following vital wins away at Sheffield United (2-0) and at home to Ipswich Town (3-2), nearest rivals Liverpool chocked, losing at home to Arsenal, and handed Leeds the championship. In July 1974 Revie ended his glorious time at Elland Road by accepting the England job. The most wonderful period in Leeds United's history was coming to an end. As for Revie, after England he managed the United Arab Emirates as well as club sides Al Nasir and Al Ahy. The greatest manager in Leeds United's history passed away in a Murrayfield hospital on 26 May 1989, aged 61. He was cremated in Edinburgh four days later. Football legends such as Brian Moore, Kevin Keegan and Denis Law all attended his funeral. Even today, 30 years after his death, his presence is still felt at Elland Road and at the start of the 1994-95 season the North Stand Kop was renamed the Revie Stand. A statue of Revie was unveiled in front of the Family Stand in May 2012 to commemorate his career at Elland Road.

Don Revie's first line up: Portsmouth (A) 18 March 1961: Humphreys, Jones, Kilford, Cameron, Goodwin, McConnell, Francis, Fitzgerald, Charlton, Bremner, Grainger.

Don Revie's last line up: Queens Park Rangers (A) 27 April 1974: Harvey, Reaney (Yorath), Cherry, Bremner, McQueen, Hunter, Lorimer, Clarke, Jordan, Giles, Madeley.

DIVISION TWO
1960–61

Date	Opposition	Competition	Score
20/08/1960	Liverpool	Division Two	0-2
24/08/1960	**Bristol Rovers**	**Division Two**	**1-1**
27/08/1960	**Rotherham United**	**Division Two**	**2-0**
29/08/1960	Bristol Rovers	Division Two	4-4
03/09/1960	Southampton	Division Two	4-2
07/09/1960	**Leyton Orient**	**Division Two**	**1-3**
10/09/1960	**Huddersfield Town**	**Division Two**	**1-4**
14/09/1960	Leyton Orient	Division Two	1-0
17/09/1960	**Middlesbrough**	**Division Two**	**4-4**
24/09/1960	Brighton & Hove Albion	Division Two	1-2
28/09/1960	**Blackpool**	**League Cup 2nd Round**	**0-0**
01/10/1960	**Ipswich Town**	**Division Two**	**2-5**
05/10/1960	Blackpool	League Cup 2nd Round Replay	3-1
08/10/1960	Sunderland	Division Two	3-2
15/10/1960	**Plymouth Argyle**	**Division Two**	**2-1**
22/10/1960	Norwich City	Division Two	2-3
29/10/1960	**Charlton Athletic**	**Division Two**	**1-0**
05/11/1960	Sheffield United	Division Two	2-3
12/11/1960	**Stoke City**	**Division Two**	**0-1**
19/11/1960	Swansea Town	Division Two	2-3
23/11/1960	Chesterfield	League Cup 3rd Round	4-0
03/12/1960	Lincoln City	Division Two	3-2
05/12/1960	Southampton	League Cup 4th Round	4-5
10/12/1960	**Portsmouth**	**Division Two**	**0-0**
17/12/1960	**Liverpool**	**Division Two**	**2-2**
24/12/1960	Derby County	Division Two	3-2
27/12/1960	**Derby County**	**Division Two**	**3-3**
31/12/1960	Rotherham United	Division Two	3-1
07/01/1961	Sheffield Wednesday	FA Cup 3rd Round	0-2
14/01/1961	**Southampton**	**Division Two**	**3-0**
21/01/1961	Huddersfield Town	Division Two	1-0
04/02/1961	Middlesbrough	Division Two	0-3
10/02/1961	**Brighton & Hove Albion**	**Division Two**	**3-2**
18/02/1961	Ipswich Town	Division Two	0-4
25/02/1961	**Sunderland**	**Division Two**	**2-4**
04/03/1961	Plymouth Argyle	Division Two	1-3
08/03/1961	**Luton Town**	**Division Two**	**1-2**
11/03/1961	**Norwich City**	**Division Two**	**1-0**
18/03/1961	Portsmouth	Division Two	1-3
25/03/1961	**Sheffield United**	**Division Two**	**1-2**
01/04/1961	Luton Town	Division Two	1-1
03/04/1961	Scunthorpe United	Division Two	2-3
08/04/1961	**Swansea Town**	**Division Two**	**2-2**
15/04/1961	Stoke City	Division Two	0-0
22/04/1961	**Lincoln City**	**Division Two**	**7-0**
25/04/1961	**Scunthorpe United**	**Division Two**	**2-2**
29/04/1961	Charlton Athletic	Division Two	0-2

Team	Pld	W	D	L	GF	GA	Pts
Ipswich Town	42	26	7	9	100	55	59
Sheffield United	42	26	6	10	81	51	58
Liverpool	42	21	10	11	87	58	52
Norwich City	42	20	9	13	70	53	49
Middlesbrough	42	18	12	12	83	74	48
Sunderland	42	17	13	12	75	60	47
Swansea Town	42	18	11	13	77	73	47
Southampton	42	18	8	16	84	81	44
Scunthorpe United	42	14	15	13	69	64	43
Charlton Athletic	42	16	11	15	97	91	43
Plymouth Argyle	42	17	8	17	81	82	42
Derby County	42	15	10	17	80	80	40
Luton Town	42	15	9	18	71	79	39
Leeds United	42	14	10	18	75	83	38
Rotherham United	42	12	13	17	65	64	37
Brighton & Hove Albion	42	14	9	19	61	75	37
Bristol Rovers	42	15	7	20	73	92	37
Stoke City	42	12	12	18	51	59	36
Leyton Orient	42	14	8	20	55	78	36
Huddersfield Town	42	13	9	20	62	71	35
Portsmouth	42	11	11	20	64	91	33
Lincoln City	42	8	8	26	48	95	24

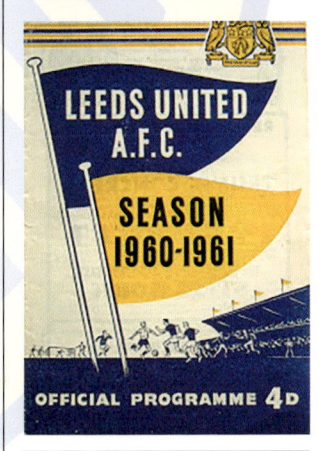

Don Revie started the season leading the side out at Anfield and ended up as manager, taking over from Jack Taylor.

Revie also went down in history as he became Leeds's first-ever scorer in the newly formed League Cup in a replay away at Blackpool.

Aside from Revie being captain, Freddie Goodwin was handed the armband, as was Jack Charlton for five games.

The Whites 7-0 win at home to Lincoln City was the side's biggest victory for seven years, a 7-1 win at home to Leicester in January 1954.

The side used three different goalkeepers in season 1960-61, Ted Burgin (11 games), Alan Humphreys (31 games) and Terry Carling (5 games).

1961–62

DIVISION TWO

Team	Pld	W	D	L	GF	GA	Pts
Liverpool	42	27	8	7	99	43	62
Leyton Orient	42	22	10	10	69	40	54
Sunderland	42	22	9	11	85	50	53
Scunthorpe United	42	21	7	14	86	71	49
Plymouth Argyle	42	19	8	15	75	75	46
Southampton	42	18	9	15	77	62	45
Huddersfield Town	42	16	12	14	67	59	44
Stoke City	42	17	8	17	55	57	42
Rotherham United	42	16	9	17	70	76	41
Preston North End	42	15	10	17	55	57	40
Newcastle United	42	15	9	18	64	58	39
Middlesbrough	42	16	7	19	76	72	39
Luton Town	42	17	5	20	69	71	39
Walsall	42	14	11	17	70	75	39
Charlton Athletic	42	15	9	18	69	75	39
Derby County	42	14	11	17	68	75	39
Norwich City	42	14	11	17	61	70	39
Bury	42	17	5	20	52	76	39
Leeds United	42	12	12	18	50	61	36
Swansea Town	42	12	12	18	61	83	36
Bristol Rovers	42	13	7	22	53	81	33
Brighton & Hove Albion	42	10	11	21	42	86	31

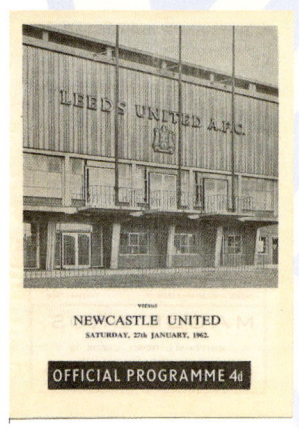

Date	Opposition	Competition	Score
19/08/1961	Charlton Athletic	Division Two	1-0
22/08/1961	Brighton & Hove Albion	Division Two	3-1
26/08/1961	Liverpool	Division Two	0-5
30/08/1961	Brighton & Hove Albion	Division Two	1-1
02/09/1961	Rotherham United	Division Two	1-3
06/09/1961	Norwich City	Division Two	0-2
09/09/1961	Sunderland	Division Two	1-2
13/09/1961	Brentford	League Cup 2nd Round	4-1
16/09/1961	Stoke City	Division Two	3-1
20/09/1961	Norwich City	Division Two	0-1
23/09/1961	Bristol Rovers	Division Two	0-4
30/09/1961	Preston North End	Division Two	1-2
04/10/1961	Huddersfield Town	League Cup 3rd Round	3-2
07/10/1961	Plymouth Argyle	Division Two	1-1
14/10/1961	Huddersfield Town	Division Two	1-0
21/10/1961	Swansea Town	Division Two	1-2
28/10/1961	Southampton	Division Two	1-1
04/11/1961	Luton Town	Division Two	2-3
11/11/1961	Leyton Orient	Division Two	0-0
18/11/1961	Middlesbrough	Division Two	3-1
25/11/1961	Walsall	Division Two	4-1
02/12/1961	Derby County	Division Two	3-3
12/12/1961	Rotherham United	League Cup 4th Round	1-1
16/12/1961	Charlton Athletic	Division Two	1-3
23/12/1961	Liverpool	Division Two	1-0
26/12/1961	Scunthorpe United	Division Two	1-4
06/01/1962	Derby County	FA Cup 3rd Round	2-2
10/01/1962	Derby County	FA Cup 3rd Round Replay	1-3
12/01/1962	Rotherham United	Division Two	1-2
15/01/1962	Rotherham United	League Cup 4th Round Replay	1-2
20/01/1962	Sunderland	Division Two	1-0
27/01/1962	Newcastle United	Division Two	0-1
03/02/1962	Stoke City	Division Two	1-2
10/02/1962	Bristol Rovers	Division Two	0-0
20/02/1962	Scunthorpe United	Division Two	1-2
24/02/1962	Plymouth Argyle	Division Two	2-3
03/03/1962	Huddersfield Town	Division Two	1-2
10/03/1962	Swansea Town	Division Two	2-1
17/03/1962	Southampton	Division Two	1-4
24/03/1962	Luton Town	Division Two	2-1
31/03/1962	Leyton Orient	Division Two	0-0
07/04/1962	Middlesbrough	Division Two	2-0
09/04/1962	Preston North End	Division Two	1-1
14/04/1992	Walsall	Division Two	1-1
20/04/1992	Bury	Division Two	1-1
21/04/1962	Derby County	Division Two	0-0
24/04/1962	Bury	Division Two	0-0
28/04/1962	Newcastle United	Division Two	3-0

Skipper Freddie Goodwin topped the appearances charts with 47, missing just one game away at Preston North End.

Grenville Hair took the armband for the away trip to Deepdale in place of Goodwin.

The home game to Swansea Town was a red letter in the White's history as it saw the debut of Bobby Collins following his move from Everton.

The away game at Southampton on 17 March 1962 saw the debut of Gary Sprake following Tommy Younger's illness.

The season also saw the retirement of Don Revie as a player, to enable him to concentrate on managerial duties and getting Leeds back to Division One.

DIVISION TWO

1962–63

Date	Opposition	Competition	Score
18/08/1962	Stoke City	Division Two	1-0
22/08/1962	**Rotherham United**	**Division Two**	**3-4**
25/08/1962	**Sunderland**	**Division Two**	**1-0**
28/08/1962	Rotherham United	Division Two	1-2
01/09/1962	Huddersfield Town	Division Two	1-1
05/09/1962	**Bury**	**Division Two**	**1-2**
08/09/1962	Swansea Town	Division Two	2-0
15/09/1962	**Chelsea**	**Division Two**	**2-0**
18/09/1962	Bury	Division Two	1-3
22/09/1962	Luton Town	Division Two	2-2
26/09/1962	**Crystal Palace**	**League Cup 2nd Round**	**2-1**
29/09/1962	**Southampton**	**Division Two**	**1-1**
06/10/1962	**Middlesbrough**	**Division Two**	**2-3**
13/10/1962	Derby County	Division Two	0-0
17/10/1962	Blackburn Rovers	League Cup 3rd Round	0-4
20/10/1962	Newcastle United	Division Two	1-0
27/10/1962	Walsall	Division Two	1-1
03/11/1962	**Norwich City**	**Division Two**	**3-0**
10/11/1962	Grimsby Town	Division Two	1-1
17/11/1962	**Plymouth Argyle**	**Division Two**	**6-1**
24/11/1962	Preston North End	Division Two	1-4
01/12/1962	**Portsmouth**	**Division Two**	**3-3**
08/12/1962	Cardiff City	Division Two	0-0
15/12/1962	**Stoke City**	**Division Two**	**3-1**
22/12/1962	Sunderland	Division Two	1-2
02/03/1963	**Derby County**	**Division Two**	**3-1**
06/03/1963	**Stoke City**	**FA Cup 3rd Round**	**3-1**
09/03/1963	Newcastle United	Division Two	1-1
13/03/1963	**Walsall**	**Division Two**	**3-0**
16/03/1963	Middlesbrough	FA Cup 4th Round	2-0
19/03/1963	Nottingham Forest	FA Cup 5th Round	0-3
23/03/1963	Norwich City	Division Two	2-3
30/03/1963	**Grimsby Town**	**Division Two**	**3-0**
03/04/1963	**Scunthorpe United**	**Division Two**	**1-0**
06/04/1963	Plymouth Argyle	Division Two	1-3
13/04/1963	**Preston North End**	**Division Two**	**4-1**
15/04/1963	Charlton Athletic	Division Two	2-1
16/04/1963	**Charlton Athletic**	**Division Two**	**4-1**
20/04/1963	Portsmouth	Division Two	0-3
23/04/1963	Scunthorpe United	Division Two	2-0
27/04/1963	**Cardiff City**	**Division Two**	**3-0**
30/04/1963	Chelsea	Division Two	2-2
04/05/1963	**Luton Town**	**Division Two**	**3-0**
06/05/1963	Middlesbrough	Division Two	1-2
11/05/1963	**Huddersfield Town**	**Division Two**	**0-1**
15/05/1963	Southampton	Division Two	1-3
18/05/1963	**Swansea Town**	**Division Two**	**5-0**

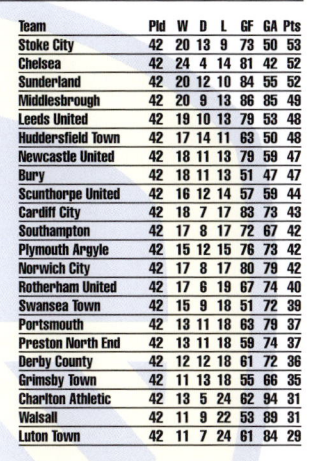

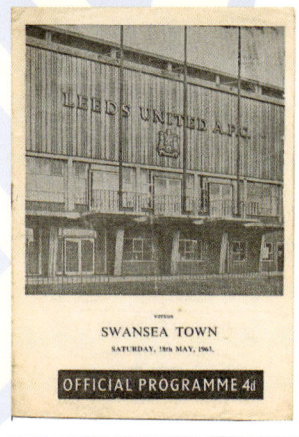

Team	Pld	W	D	L	GF	GA	Pts
Stoke City	42	20	13	9	73	50	53
Chelsea	42	24	4	14	81	42	52
Sunderland	42	20	12	10	84	55	52
Middlesbrough	42	20	9	13	86	85	49
Leeds United	42	19	10	13	79	53	48
Huddersfield Town	42	17	14	11	63	50	48
Newcastle United	42	18	11	13	79	59	47
Bury	42	18	11	13	51	47	47
Scunthorpe United	42	16	12	14	57	59	44
Cardiff City	42	18	7	17	83	73	43
Southampton	42	17	8	17	72	67	42
Plymouth Argyle	42	15	12	15	76	73	42
Norwich City	42	17	8	17	80	79	42
Rotherham United	42	17	6	19	67	74	40
Swansea Town	42	15	9	18	51	72	39
Portsmouth	42	13	11	18	63	79	37
Preston North End	42	13	11	18	59	74	37
Derby County	42	12	12	18	61	72	36
Grimsby Town	42	11	13	18	55	66	35
Charlton Athletic	42	13	5	24	62	94	31
Walsall	42	11	9	22	53	89	31
Luton Town	42	11	7	24	61	84	29

SWANSEA TOWN
SATURDAY, 18th MAY, 1963.
OFFICIAL PROGRAMME 4d

Jim Storrie marked his debut after signing from Airdrie with the winner on the opening day away at Stoke City.

Paul Reaney made his Leeds United debut on 8 September 1962 in the 2-0 away win at Swansea Town.

29 September 1962 saw the Leeds United debut of one Peter Lorimer in the home fixture against Southampton.

Leeds had four captains, Freddie Goodwin, Grenville Hair, Cliff Mason and Jack Charlton.

Leeds used three goalkeepers, Gary Sprake, Tommy Younger and Brian Williamson.

1963–64

DIVISION TWO

Team	Pld	W	D	L	GF	GA	Pts
Leeds United	42	24	15	3	71	34	63
Sunderland	42	25	11	6	81	37	61
Preston North End	42	23	10	9	79	54	56
Charlton Athletic	42	19	10	13	76	70	48
Southampton	42	19	9	14	100	73	47
Manchester City	42	18	10	14	84	66	46
Rotherham United	42	19	7	16	90	78	45
Newcastle United	42	20	5	17	74	69	45
Portsmouth	42	16	11	15	79	70	43
Middlesbrough	42	15	11	16	67	52	41
Northampton Town	42	16	9	17	58	60	41
Huddersfield Town	42	15	10	17	57	64	40
Derby County	42	14	11	17	56	67	39
Swindon Town	42	14	10	18	57	69	38
Cardiff City	42	14	10	18	56	81	38
Leyton Orient	42	13	10	19	54	72	36
Norwich City	42	11	13	18	64	80	35
Bury	42	13	9	20	57	73	35
Swansea Town	42	12	9	21	63	74	33
Plymouth Argyle	42	8	16	18	45	67	32
Grimsby Town	42	9	14	19	47	75	32
Scunthorpe United	42	10	10	22	52	82	30

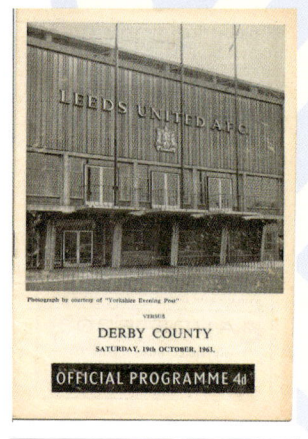

Date	Opposition	Competition	Score
28/03/1963	Rotherham United	Division Two	1-0
31/08/1963	Bury	Division Two	3-0
03/09/1963	Rotherham United	Division Two	2-2
07/09/1963	Manchester City	Division Two	2-3
11/09/1963	Portsmouth	Division Two	3-1
14/09/1963	Swindon Town	Division Two	0-0
18/09/1963	Portsmouth	Division Two	1-1
21/09/1963	Cardiff City	Division Two	0-0
25/09/1963	Mansfield Town	League Cup 2nd Round	5-1
28/09/1963	Norwich City	Division Two	4-2
01/10/1963	Northampton Town	Division Two	3-0
05/10/1963	Scunthorpe United	Division Two	1-0
09/10/1963	Middlesbrough	Division Two	2-0
12/10/1963	Huddersfield Town	Division Two	2-0
19/10/1963	Derby County	Division Two	2-2
22/10/1963	Swansea Town	League Cup 3rd Round	2-0
26/10/1963	Southampton	Division Two	4-1
02/11/1963	Charlton Athletic	Division Two	1-1
09/11/1963	Grimsby Town	Division Two	2-0
16/11/1963	Preston North End	Division Two	1-1
23/11/1963	Leyton Orient	Division Two	2-0
27/11/1963	Manchester City	League Cup 4th Round	1-3
30/11/1963	Swansea Town	Division Two	2-1
07/12/1963	Plymouth Argyle	Division Two	1-0
14/12/1963	Northampton Town	Division Two	0-0
21/12/1963	Bury	Division Two	2-1
26/12/1963	Sunderland	Division Two	1-1
28/12/1963	Sunderland	Division Two	0-2
04/01/1964	Cardiff City	FA Cup 3rd Round	1-0
11/01/1964	Manchester City	Division Two	1-0
18/01/1964	Swindon Town	Division Two	2-2
25/01/1964	Everton	FA Cup 4th Round	1-1
28/01/1964	Everton	FA Cup 4th Round Replay	0-2
01/02/1964	Cardiff City	Division Two	1-1
08/02/1964	Norwich City	Division Two	2-2
15/02/1964	Scunthorpe United	Division Two	1-0
22/02/1964	Huddersfield Town	Division Two	1-1
03/03/1964	Preston North End	Division Two	0-2
07/03/1964	Southampton	Division Two	3-1
14/03/1964	Middlesbrough	Division Two	3-1
21/03/1964	Grimsby Town	Division Two	3-1
27/03/1964	Newcastle United	Division Two	1-0
28/03/1964	Derby County	Division Two	1-1
30/03/1964	Newcastle United	Division Two	2-1
04/04/1964	Leyton Orient	Division Two	2-1
11/04/1964	Swansea Town	Division Two	3-0
18/04/1964	Plymouth Argyle	Division Two	1-1
25/04/1964	Charlton Athletic	Division Two	2-0

Leeds started the new season with a new captain with Bobby Collins taking the armband on.

When Collins was missing, Jack Charlton, Grenville Hair and Freddie Goodwin all took over.

New signing from Manchester United Johnny Giles made his debut in a 3-0 home win against Bury.

Norman Hunter played in 47 out of 48 games, missing a League Cup tie at home to Swansea Town.

Following a 3-2 league defeat away at Manchester City, Leeds went on a 20 match unbeaten run, their best since season 1927-28.

DIVISION ONE

1964–65

Date	Opposition	Competition	Score
22/08/1964	Aston Villa	Division One	2-1
26/08/1964	Liverpool	Division One	4-2
29/08/1964	Wolverhampton Wanderers	Division One	3-2
02/09/1964	Liverpool	Division One	1-2
05/09/1964	Sunderland	Division One	3-3
07/09/1964	Blackpool	Division One	0-4
12/09/1964	Leicester City	Division One	3-2
16/09/1964	Blackpool	Division One	3-0
19/09/1964	Chelsea	Division One	0-2
23/09/1964	Huddersfield Town	League Cup 2nd Round	3-2
26/09/1964	Nottingham Forest	Division One	1-2
30/09/1964	Fulham	Division One	2-2
10/10/1964	Stoke City	Division One	3-2
14/10/1964	Aston Villa	League Cup 3rd Round	2-3
17/10/1964	Tottenham Hotspur	Division One	3-1
24/10/1964	Burnley	Division One	1-0
31/10/1964	Sheffield United	Division One	4-1
07/11/1964	Everton	Division One	1-0
11/11/1964	Arsenal	Division One	3-1
14/11/1964	Birmingham City	Division One	4-1
21/11/1964	West Ham United	Division One	1-3
28/11/1964	West Bromwich Albion	Division One	1-0
05/12/1964	Manchester United	Division One	1-0
12/12/1964	Aston Villa	Division One	1-0
19/12/1964	Wolverhampton Wanderers	Division One	1-0
26/12/1964	Blackburn Rovers	Division One	1-1
28/12/1964	Blackburn Rovers	Division One	2-0
02/01/1965	Sunderland	Division One	2-1
09/01/1965	Southport	FA Cup 3rd Round	3-0
16/01/1965	Leicester City	Division One	2-2
23/01/1965	Chelsea	Division One	2-2
30/01/1965	Everton	FA Cup 4th Round	1-1
02/02/1965	Everton	FA Cup 4th Round Replay	2-1
06/02/1965	Nottingham Forest	Division One	0-0
13/02/1965	Arsenal	Division One	2-1
20/02/1965	Shrewsbury Town	FA Cup 5th Round	2-0
27/02/1965	Tottenham Hotspur	Division One	0-0
10/03/1965	Crystal Palace	FA Cup QF	3-0
13/03/1965	Fulham	Division One	2-2
15/03/1965	Burnley	Division One	5-1
20/03/1965	Everton	Division One	4-1
27/03/1965	Manchester United	FA Cup SF at Hillsborough	0-0
31/03/1965	Manchester United	FA Cup SF Replay at City Ground	1-0
03/04/1965	West Ham United	Division One	2-1
05/04/1965	Stoke City	Division One	3-1
12/04/1965	West Bromwich Albion	Division One	2-1
17/04/1965	Manchester United	Division One	0-1
19/04/1965	Sheffield Wednesday	Division One	0-3
20/04/1965	Sheffield Wednesday	Division One	2-0
24/04/1965	Sheffield United	Division One	3-0
26/04/1965	Birmingham City	Division One	3-3
01/05/1965	Liverpool	FA Cup Final at Wembley	1-2

Team	Pld	W	D	L	GF	GA	Pts
Manchester United	42	26	9	7	89	39	61
Leeds United	42	26	9	7	83	52	61
Chelsea	42	24	8	10	89	54	56
Everton	42	17	15	10	69	60	49
Nottingham Forest	42	17	13	12	71	67	47
Tottenham Hotspur	42	19	7	16	87	71	45
Liverpool	42	17	10	15	67	73	44
Sheffield Wednesday	42	16	11	15	57	55	43
West Ham United	42	19	4	19	82	71	42
Blackburn Rovers	42	16	10	16	83	79	42
Stoke City	42	16	10	16	67	66	42
Burnley	42	16	10	16	70	70	42
Arsenal	42	17	7	18	69	75	41
West Bromwich Albion	42	13	13	16	70	65	39
Sunderland	42	14	9	19	64	74	37
Aston Villa	42	16	5	21	57	82	37
Blackpool	42	12	11	19	67	78	35
Leicester City	42	11	13	18	69	85	35
Sheffield United	42	12	11	19	50	64	35
Fulham	42	11	12	19	60	78	34
Wolverhampton W	42	13	4	25	59	89	30
Birmingham City	42	8	11	23	64	96	27

Leeds had just one debutant in season 1964-65, Rod Belfitt at home to Huddersfield Town on 23 September 1964.

Norman Hunter made 51 out of 52 appearances, missing just one league game at home to Stoke City.

Bobby Collins became the club's first player to win the Football Writers' Player of the Year award.

By finishing second in Division One, it was the club's highest-ever league position since being formed in 1919.

Leeds reached the FA Cup Final for the first time with Billy Bremner becoming the first Leeds player to score at the old Wembley stadium.

1965–66

DIVISION ONE

Team	Pld	W	D	L	GF	GA	Pts
Liverpool	42	26	9	7	79	34	61
Leeds United	42	23	9	10	79	38	55
Burnley	42	24	7	11	79	47	55
Manchester United	42	18	15	9	84	59	51
Chelsea	42	22	7	13	65	53	51
West Bromwich Albion	42	19	12	11	91	69	50
Leicester City	42	21	7	14	80	65	49
Tottenham Hotspur	42	16	12	14	75	66	44
Sheffield United	42	16	11	15	56	59	43
Stoke City	42	15	12	15	65	64	42
Everton	42	15	11	16	56	62	41
West Ham United	42	15	9	18	70	83	39
Blackpool	42	14	9	19	55	65	37
Arsenal	42	12	13	17	62	75	37
Newcastle United	42	14	9	19	50	63	37
Aston Villa	42	15	6	21	69	80	36
Sheffield Wednesday	42	14	8	20	56	66	36
Nottingham Forest	42	14	8	20	56	72	36
Sunderland	42	14	8	20	51	72	36
Fulham	42	14	7	21	67	85	35
Northampton Town	42	10	13	19	55	92	33
Blackburn Rovers	42	8	4	30	57	88	20

Date	Opposition	Competition	Score
21/08/1965	**Sunderland**	**Division One**	**1-0**
23/08/1965	Aston Villa	Division One	2-0
28/08/1965	**West Ham United**	**Division One**	**1-2**
01/09/1965	**Aston Villa**	**Division One**	**2-0**
04/09/1965	**Nottingham Forest**	**Division One**	**2-1**
08/09/1965	Tottenham Hotspur	Division One	2-3
11/09/1965	**Sheffield United**	**Division One**	**2-2**
15/09/1965	**Tottenham Hotspur**	**Division One**	**2-0**
18/09/1965	Leicester City	Division One	3-3
22/09/1965	**Hartlepools United**	**League Cup 2nd Round**	**4-2**
25/09/1965	**Blackburn Rovers**	**Division One**	**3-0**
29/09/1965	**Torino**	**Inter Cities Fairs Cup 1st Round 1st Leg**	**2-1**
06/10/1965	Torino	Inter Cities Fairs Cup 1st Round 2nd Leg	0-0
09/10/1965	Sheffield Wednesday	Division One	0-0
13/10/1965	**West Bromwich Albion**	**League Cup 3rd Round**	**2-4**
16/10/1965	**Northampton Town**	**Division One**	**6-1**
23/10/1965	Stoke City	Division One	2-1
30/10/1965	**Burnley**	**Division One**	**1-1**
06/11/1965	Chelsea	Division One	0-1
13/11/1965	**Arsenal**	**Division One**	**2-0**
20/11/1965	Everton	Division One	0-0
24/11/1965	SC Leipzig	Inter Cities Fairs Cup 2nd Round 1st Leg	2-1
01/12/1965	**SC Leipzig**	**Inter Cities Fairs Cup 2nd Round 2nd Leg**	**0-0**
11/12/1965	**West Bromwich Albion**	**Division One**	**4-0**
27/12/1965	Liverpool	Division One	1-0
28/12/1965	**Liverpool**	**Division One**	**0-1**
01/01/1966	**Sheffield Wednesday**	**Division One**	**3-0**
08/01/1965	West Bromwich Albion	Division One	2-1
12/01/1966	**Manchester United**	**Division One**	**1-1**
15/01/1966	**Stoke City**	**Division One**	**2-2**
22/01/1966	**Bury**	**FA Cup 3rd Round**	**6-0**
29/01/1966	Sunderland	Division One	0-2
02/02/1966	**Valencia**	**Inter Cities Fairs Cup 3rd Round 1st Leg**	**1-1**
05/02/1966	**West Ham United**	**Division One**	**5-0**
12/02/1966	Chelsea	FA Cup 4th Round	0-1
16/02/1966	Valencia	Inter Cities Fairs Cup 3rd Round 2nd Leg	1-0
19/02/1966	Nottingham Forest	Division One	4-0
26/02/1966	Sheffield United	Division One	1-1
02/03/1966	**Ujpesti Dózsa**	**Inter Cities Fairs Cup 4th Round 1st Leg**	**4-1**
05/03/1966	Northampton Town	Division One	1-2
09/03/1966	Ujpesti Dózsa	Inter Cities Fairs Cup 4th Round 2nd Leg	1-1
12/03/1966	**Leicester City**	**Division One**	**3-2**
19/03/1966	Blackburn Rovers	Division One	3-2
26/03/1966	**Blackpool**	**Division One**	**1-2**
28/03/1966	Blackpool	Division One	0-1
04/04/1966	Chelsea	Division One	2-0
08/04/1966	Fulham	Division One	3-1
12/04/1966	**Fulham**	**Division One**	**0-1**
16/04/1966	**Everton**	**Division One**	**4-1**
20/04/1966	Real Zaragoza	Inter Cities Cup SF 1st Leg	0-1
27/04/1966	**Real Zaragoza**	**Inter Cities Cup SF 2nd Leg**	**2-1**
30/04/1966	**Newcastle United**	**Division One**	**3-0**
05/05/1966	Arsenal	Division One	3-0
07/05/1966	Burnley	Division One	1-0
11/05/1966	**Real Zaragoza**	**Inter Cities Cup SF Replay**	**1-3**
16/05/1966	Newcastle United	Division One	0-2
19/05/1966	Manchester United	Division One	1-1

Rod Johnson created history when he became the club's first-ever used substitute at home to Aston Villa on 1 September 1965.

Peter Lorimer scored his first-ever goal for the Whites in the 2-1 win over Nottingham Forest at Elland Road on 4 September 1965.

Billy Bremner captained the side for the first time on 29 January 1966 with Jack Charlton missing.

Bremner also became the first-ever Leeds player to score in European competition with the opening goal at home to Torino.

Paul Reaney and Norman Hunter made 55 appearances, just missing two games each.

DIVISION ONE
1966–67

Date	Opposition	Competition	Score
20/08/1966	Tottenham Hotspur	Division One	1-3
24/08/1966	West Bromwich Albion	Division One	2-1
27/08/1966	Manchester United	Division One	3-1
31/08/1966	West Bromwich Albion	Division One	0-2
03/09/1966	Burnley	Division One	1-1
07/09/1966	Sunderland	Division One	2-1
10/09/1966	Nottingham Forest	Division One	1-1
13/09/1966	Newcastle United	League Cup 2nd Round	1-0
17/09/1966	Fulham	Division One	2-2
24/09/1966	Everton	Division One	1-1
01/10/1966	Stoke City	Division One	0-0
04/10/1966	Preston North End	League Cup 3rd Round	1-1
08/10/1966	Aston Villa	Division One	0-3
12/10/1966	Preston North End	League Cup 3rd Round Replay	3-0
15/10/1996	Arsenal	Division One	3-1
18/10/1966	DWS Amsterdam	Inter Cities Fairs Cup 2nd Round 2nd 1st Leg	3-1
26/10/1966	DWS Amsterdam	Inter Cities Fairs Cup 2nd Round 2nd Leg	5-1
29/10/1966	Southampton	Division One	0-1
05/11/1966	Arsenal	Division One	1-0
07/11/1966	West Ham United	League Cup 4th Round	0-7
12/11/1966	Leicester City	Division One	3-1
19/11/1966	Liverpool	Division One	0-5
26/11/1966	West Ham United	Division One	2-1
03/12/1966	Sheffield Wednesday	Division One	0-0
10/12/1966	Blackpool	Division One	1-1
17/12/1966	Tottenham Hotspur	Division One	3-2
24/12/1966	Newcastle United	Division One	2-1
26/12/1996	Newcastle United	Division One	5-0
31/12/1966	Manchester United	Division One	0-0
07/01/1967	Burnley	Division One	3-1
14/01/1967	Nottingham Forest	Division One	0-1
18/01/1967	Valencia	Inter Cities Fairs Cup 3rd Round 1st Leg	1-1
21/01/1967	Fulham	Division One	3-1
28/01/1967	Crystal Palace	FA Cup 3rd Round	3-0
04/02/1967	Everton	Division One	0-2
08/02/1967	Valencia	Inter Cities Fairs Cup 3rd Round 2nd Leg	2-0
11/02/1967	Stoke City	Division One	3-0
18/02/1967	West Bromwich Albion	FA Cup 4th Round	5-0
25/02/1967	Aston Villa	Division One	0-2
04/03/1967	Southampton	Division One	2-0
11/03/1967	Sunderland	FA Cup 5th Round	1-1
15/03/1967	Sunderland	FA Cup 5th Round Replay	1-1
18/03/1967	Manchester City	Division One	0-0
20/03/1967	Sunderland	FA Cup 5th Round 2nd Replay at Boothferry Park	2-1
22/03/1967	Bologna	Inter Cities Fairs Cup 4th Round 1st Leg	0-1
25/03/1967	Blackpool	Division One	2-0
27/03/1967	Sheffield United	Division One	4-1
28/03/1967	Sheffield United	Division One	2-0
01/04/1967	Chelsea	Division One	1-0
08/04/1967	Manchester City	FA Cup QF	1-0
10/04/1967	Leicester City	Division One	0-0
19/04/1967	Bologna	Inter Cities Fairs Cup 4th Round 2nd Leg	1-0
22/04/1967	West Ham United	Division One	1-0
29/04/1967	Chelsea	FA Cup SF at Villa Park	0-1
03/05/1967	Liverpool	Division One	2-1
06/05/1967	Chelsea	Division One	2-2
08/05/1967	Manchester City	Division One	1-2
13/05/1967	Sunderland	Division One	2-0
15/05/1967	Sheffield Wednesday	Division One	1-0
19/05/1967	Kilmarnock	Inter Cities Fairs Cup SF 1st Leg	4-2
24/05/1967	Kilmarnock	Inter Cities Fairs Cup SF 2nd Leg	0-0
30/08/1967	Dinamo Zagreb	Inter Cities Fairs Cup Final 1st Leg	0-2
06/09/1967	Dinamo Zagreb	Inter Cities Fairs Cup Final 1st Leg	0-0

Team	Pld	W	D	L	GF	GA	Pts
Manchester United	42	24	12	6	84	45	60
Nottingham Forest	42	23	10	9	64	41	56
Tottenham Hotspur	42	24	8	10	71	48	56
Leeds United	42	22	11	9	62	42	55
Liverpool	42	19	13	10	64	47	51
Everton	42	19	10	13	65	46	48
Arsenal	42	16	14	12	58	47	46
Leicester City	42	18	8	16	78	71	44
Chelsea	42	15	14	13	67	62	44
Sheffield United	42	16	10	16	52	59	42
Sheffield Wednesday	42	14	13	15	56	47	41
Stoke City	42	17	7	18	63	58	41
West Bromwich Albion	42	16	7	19	77	73	39
Burnley	42	15	9	18	66	76	39
Manchester City	42	12	15	15	43	52	39
West Ham United	42	14	8	20	80	84	36
Sunderland	42	14	8	20	58	72	36
Fulham	42	11	12	19	71	83	34
Southampton	42	14	6	22	74	92	34
Newcastle United	42	12	9	21	39	81	33
Aston Villa	42	11	7	24	54	85	29
Blackpool	42	6	9	27	41	76	21

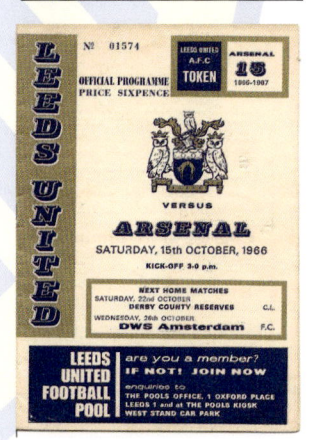

Five captains took the armband, Bobby Collins, Billy Bremner, Jack Charlton, Johnny Giles and Alan Peacock.

The Whites had just two debutants this season, Bobby Sibbald and Jimmy Lumsden.

Paul Reaney was top of the appearances charts starting 61 of the 63 games in season 1966/67.

Jack Charlton won the Football Writers' Player of the Year award.

Albert Morris took over the reins as chairman from Harry Reynolds.

1967–68

DIVISION ONE

Team	Pld	W	D	L	GF	GA	Pts
Manchester City	42	26	6	10	86	43	58
Manchester United	42	24	8	10	89	55	56
Liverpool	42	22	11	9	71	40	55
Leeds United	42	22	9	11	71	41	53
Everton	42	23	6	13	67	40	52
Chelsea	42	18	12	12	62	68	48
Tottenham Hotspur	42	19	9	14	70	59	47
West Bromwich Albion	42	17	12	13	75	62	46
Arsenal	42	17	10	15	60	56	44
Newcastle United	42	13	15	14	54	67	41
Nottingham Forest	42	14	11	17	52	64	39
West Ham United	42	14	10	18	73	69	38
Leicester City	42	13	12	17	64	69	38
Burnley	42	14	10	18	64	71	38
Sunderland	42	13	11	18	51	61	37
Southampton	42	13	11	18	66	83	37
Wolverhampton W	42	14	8	20	66	75	36
Stoke City	42	14	7	21	50	73	35
Sheffield Wednesday	42	11	12	19	51	63	34
Coventry City	42	9	15	18	51	71	33
Sheffield United	42	11	10	21	49	70	32
Fulham	42	10	7	25	56	98	27

Date	Opposition	Competition	Score
19/08/1967	Sunderland	Division One	1-1
23/08/1967	Manchester United	Division One	0-1
26/08/1967	Wolverhampton Wanderers	Division One	0-2
02/09/1967	Fulham	Division One	2-0
09/09/1967	Southampton	Division One	1-1
13/09/1967	Luton Town	League Cup 2nd Round	3-1
16/09/1967	Everton	Division One	1-0
20/09/1967	Burnley	Division One	2-1
23/09/1967	Leicester City	Division One	3-2
30/09/1967	West Ham United	Division One	0-0
03/10/1967	Spora Luxembourg	Inter Cities Fairs Cup 1st Round 1st Leg	9-0
07/10/1967	Chelsea	Division One	7-0
11/10/1967	Bury	League Cup 3rd Round	3-0
14/10/1967	West Bromwich Albion	Division One	0-2
17/10/1967	Spora Luxembourg	Inter Cities Fairs Cup 1st Round 2nd Leg	7-0
25/10/1967	Newcastle United	Division One	2-0
28/10/1967	Manchester City	Division One	0-1
04/11/1967	Arsenal	Division One	3-1
08/11/1967	Manchester United	Division One	1-0
11/11/1967	Sheffield United	Division One	0-1
15/11/1967	Sunderland	League Cup 4th Round	2-0
18/11/1967	Coventry City	Division One	1-1
25/11/1967	Nottingham Forest	Division One	2-0
29/11/1967	Partizan Belgrade	Inter Cities Fairs Cup 2nd Round 1st Leg	2-1
02/12/1967	Stoke City	Division One	2-0
06/12/1967	Partizan Belgrade	Inter Cities Fairs Cup 2nd Round 2nd Leg	1-1
09/12/1967	Liverpool	Division One	0-2
13/12/1967	Stoke City	League Cup 5th Round	2-0
16/12/1967	Sunderland	Division One	2-2
20/12/1967	Hibernian	Inter Cities Fairs Cup 3rd Round 1st Leg	1-0
23/12/1967	Wolverhampton Wanderers	Division One	2-1
26/12/1967	Sheffield Wednesday	Division One	1-0
30/12/1967	Sheffield Wednesday	Division One	3-2
06/01/1968	Fulham	Division One	5-0
10/01/1968	Hibernian	Inter Cities Fairs Cup 3rd Round 2nd Leg	1-1
13/01/1968	Southampton	Division One	5-0
17/01/1968	Derby County	League Cup SF 1st Leg	1-0
20/01/1968	Everton	Division One	2-0
27/01/1968	Derby County	FA Cup 3rd Round	2-0
03/02/1968	Leicester City	Division One	2-2
07/02/1968	Derby County	League Cup SF 2nd Leg	3-2
10/02/1968	West Ham United	Division One	2-1
17/02/1968	Nottingham Forest	FA Cup 4th Round	2-1
02/03/1968	Arsenal	League Cup Final at Wembley	1-0
09/03/1968	Bristol City	FA Cup 5th Round	2-0
13/03/1968	Nottingham Forest	Division One	1-1
16/03/1968	Newcastle United	Division One	1-1
20/03/1968	Chelsea	Division One	0-0
23/03/1968	Manchester City	Division One	2-0
26/03/1968	Glasgow Rangers	Inter Cities Fairs Cup 4th Round 1st Leg	0-0
30/03/1968	Sheffield United	FA Cup QF	1-0
06/04/1968	Sheffield United	Division One	3-0
09/04/1968	Glasgow Rangers	Inter Cities Fairs Cup 4th Round 2nd Leg	2-0
12/04/1968	Tottenham Hotspur	Division One	1-2
13/04/1968	Coventry City	Division One	1-0
17/04/1968	Tottenham Hotspur	Division One	1-0
20/04/1968	West Bromwich Albion	Division One	3-1
23/04/1968	Stoke City	Division One	2-3
27/04/1968	Everton	FA Cup SF at Old Trafford	0-1
01/05/1968	Dundee	Inter Cities Fairs Cup SF 1st Leg	1-1
04/05/1968	Liverpool	Division One	1-2
07/05/1968	Arsenal	Division One	3-4
11/05/1968	Burnley	Division One	0-3
15/05/1968	Dundee	Inter Cities Fairs Cup SF 2nd Leg	1-0
07/08/1968	Ferencvaros	Inter Cities Fairs Cup Final 1st Leg	1-0
11/09/1968	Ferencvaros	Inter Cities Fairs Cup Final 2nd Leg	0-0

On 20 March 1968, when Leeds drew 0-0 at Chelsea, Paul Madeley became the first-ever Leeds United player to wear every outfield shirt as he wore number 11.

Yet again Mr Dependable Paul Reaney was top of the appearances tables featuring in 65 out of 66 games, missing a 3-0 League defeat at Burnley on 11 May.

The Whites only had two debutants, but they would go on to play an important part in the side's future, Mick Jones at home to Leicester City and Terry Yorath at Burnley.

Four weeks after Leeds won their first trophy, a 1-0 League Cup Final win over Arsenal, Albert Morris passed away and Percy Woodward became chairman.

Peter Lorimer hit 30 goals, becoming only the third Leeds player to do so after Tom Jennings and John Charles.

DIVISION ONE

1968–69

Date	Opposition	Competition	Score
10/08/1968	Southampton	Division One	3-1
14/08/1968	Queens Park Rangers	Division One	4-1
17/08/1968	Stoke City	Division One	2-0
20/08/1968	Ipswich Town	Division One	3-2
28/08/1968	Sunderland	Division One	1-1
31/08/1968	Liverpool	Division One	1-0
04/09/1968	Charlton Athletic	League Cup 2nd Round	1-0
07/09/1968	Wolverhampton Wanderers	Division One	2-1
14/09/1968	Leicester City	Division One	1-1
18/09/1968	Standard Liege	Inter Cities Fairs Cup 1st Round 1st Leg	0-0
21/09/1968	Arsenal	Division One	2-0
25/09/1968	Bristol City	League Cup 3rd Round	2-1
28/09/1968	Manchester City	Division One	1-3
05/10/1968	Newcastle United	Division One	1-0
09/10/1968	Sunderland	Division One	1-0
12/10/1968	West Ham United	Division One	2-0
16/10/1968	Crystal Palace	League Cup 4th Round	1-2
19/10/1968	Burnley	Division One	1-5
23/10/1968	Standard Liege	Inter Cities Fairs Cup 1st Round 2nd Leg	3-2
26/10/1968	West Bromwich Albion	Division One	0-0
02/11/1968	Manchester United	Division One	0-0
09/11/1968	Tottenham Hotspur	Division One	0-0
13/11/1968	Napoli	Inter Cities Fairs Cup 2nd Round 1st Leg	2-0
16/11/1968	Coventry City	Division One	1-0
23/11/1968	Everton	Division One	2-1
27/11/1968	Napoli	Inter Cities Fairs Cup 2nd Round 1st Leg	0-2
30/11/1968	Chelsea	Division One	1-1
07/12/1968	Sheffield Wednesday	Division One	2-0
14/12/1968	West Ham United	Division One	1-1
18/12/1968	Hannover 96	Inter Cities Fairs Cup 3rd Round 1st Leg	5-1
21/12/1968	Burnley	Division One	6-1
26/12/1968	Newcastle United	Division One	2-1
04/01/1969	Sheffield Wednesday	FA Cup 3rd Round	1-1
08/01/1969	Sheffield Wednesday	FA Cup 3rd Round Replay	1-3
11/01/1969	Manchester United	Division One	2-1
18/01/1969	Tottenham Hotspur	Division One	0-0
24/01/1969	Queens Park Rangers	Division One	1-1
01/02/1969	Coventry City	Division One	3-0
04/02/1969	Hannover 96	Inter Cities Fairs Cup 3rd Round 2nd Leg	2-1
12/02/1969	Ipswich Town	Division One	2-0
15/02/1969	Chelsea	Division One	1-0
25/02/1969	Nottingham Forest	Division One	2-0
01/03/1969	Southampton	Division One	3-2
05/03/1969	Ujpest Dozsa	Inter Cities Fairs Cup QF 1st Leg	0-1
08/03/1969	Stoke City	Division One	5-1
19/03/1969	Ujpest Dozsa	Inter Cities Fairs Cup QF 2nd Leg	0-2
29/03/1969	Wolverhampton Wanderers	Division One	0-0
01/04/1969	Sheffield Wednesday	Division One	0-0
05/04/1969	Manchester City	Division One	1-0
09/04/1969	West Bromwich Albion	Division One	1-1
12/04/1969	Arsenal	Division One	2-1
19/04/1969	Leicester City	Division One	2-0
22/04/1969	Everton	Division One	0-0
28/04/1969	Liverpool	Division One	0-0
30/04/1969	Nottingham Forest	Division One	1-0

Team	Pld	W	D	L	GF	GA	Pts
Leeds United	42	27	13	2	66	26	67
Liverpool	42	25	11	6	63	24	61
Everton	42	21	15	6	77	36	57
Arsenal	42	22	12	8	56	27	56
Chelsea	42	20	10	12	73	53	50
Tottenham Hotspur	42	14	17	11	61	51	45
Southampton	42	16	13	13	57	48	45
West Ham United	42	13	18	11	66	50	44
Newcastle United	42	15	14	13	61	55	44
West Bromwich Albion	42	16	11	15	64	67	43
Manchester United	42	15	12	15	57	53	42
Ipswich Town	42	15	11	16	59	60	41
Manchester City	42	15	10	17	64	55	40
Burnley	42	15	9	18	55	82	39
Sheffield Wednesday	42	10	16	16	41	54	36
Wolverhampton W	42	10	15	17	41	58	35
Sunderland	42	11	12	19	43	67	34
Nottingham Forest	42	10	13	19	45	57	33
Stoke City	42	9	15	18	40	63	33
Coventry City	42	10	11	21	46	64	31
Leicester City	42	9	12	21	39	68	30
Queen's Park Rangers	42	4	10	28	39	95	18

For the first time in the club's history, Leeds didn't have a single debutant in a season.

When Leeds defeated Nottingham Forest it created a lot of new records, most points (67), most home points (39) and most wins (27).

Other records that were broken were most home wins (18), fewest defeats (2), fewest away defeats (3), goals conceded (26) and goals conceded at home (9).

Leeds had four ever-presents as they won their first-ever league title, Gary Sprake, Paul Reaney, Billy Bremner and Norman Hunter.

Overall Gary Sprake didn't miss a minute of action, playing in all 55 games for the Whites.

1969–70

DIVISION ONE

Team	Pld	W	D	L	GF	GA	Pts
Everton	42	29	8	5	72	34	66
Leeds United	42	21	15	6	84	49	57
Chelsea	42	21	13	8	70	50	55
Derby County	42	22	9	11	64	37	53
Liverpool	42	20	11	11	65	42	51
Coventry City	42	19	11	12	58	48	49
Newcastle United	42	17	13	12	57	35	47
Manchester United	42	14	17	11	66	61	45
Stoke City	42	15	15	12	56	52	45
Manchester City	42	16	11	15	55	48	43
Tottenham Hotspur	42	17	9	16	54	55	43
Arsenal	42	12	18	12	51	49	42
Wolverhampton W	42	12	16	14	55	57	40
Burnley	42	12	15	15	56	61	39
Nottingham Forest	42	10	18	14	50	71	38
West Bromwich Albion	42	14	9	19	58	66	37
West Ham United	42	12	12	18	51	60	36
Ipswich Town	42	10	11	21	40	63	31
Southampton	42	6	17	19	46	67	29
Crystal Palace	42	6	15	21	34	68	27
Sunderland	42	6	14	22	30	68	26
Sheffield Wednesday	42	8	9	25	40	71	25

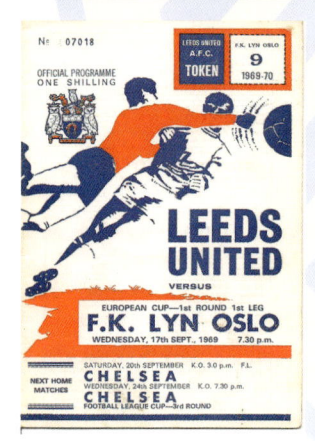

Date	Opposition	Competition	Score
02/08/1969	Manchester City	Charity Shield	2-1
09/08/1969	Tottenham Hotspur	Division One	3-1
13/08/1969	Arsenal	Division One	0-0
16/08/1969	Nottingham Forest	Division One	4-1
19/08/1969	Arsenal	Division One	1-1
23/08/1969	Newcastle United	Division One	1-1
26/08/1969	Burnley	Division One	1-1
30/08/1969	Everton	Division One	2-3
03/09/1969	Fulham	League Cup 2nd Round	1-0
06/09/1969	Manchester United	Division One	2-2
13/09/1969	Sheffield Wednesday	Division One	2-1
17/09/1969	Lyn Oslo	European Cup 1st Round 1st Leg	10-0
20/09/1969	Chelsea	Division One	2-0
24/09/1969	Chelsea	League Cup 3rd Round	1-1
27/09/1969	Coventry City	Division One	2-1
01/10/1969	Lyn Oslo	European Cup 1st Round 2nd Leg	6-0
04/10/1969	Stoke City	Division One	2-1
06/10/1969	Chelsea	League Cup 3rd Round Replay	0-2
11/10/1969	West Bromwich Albion	Division One	1-1
18/10/1969	Crystal Palace	Division One	1-1
25/10/1969	Derby County	Division One	2-0
29/10/1969	Nottingham Forest	Division One	6-1
01/11/1969	Sunderland	Division One	0-0
08/11/1969	Ipswich Town	Division One	4-0
12/11/1969	Ferencvaros	European Cup 2nd Round 1st Leg	3-0
15/11/1969	Southampton	Division One	1-1
19/11/1969	Sunderland	Division One	2-0
22/11/1969	Liverpool	Division One	1-1
26/11/1969	Ferencvaros	European Cup 2nd Round 2nd Leg	3-0
29/11/1969	Manchester City	Division One	2-1
06/12/1969	Wolverhampton Wanderers	Division One	3-1
13/12/1969	Sheffield Wednesday	Division One	2-0
17/12/1969	West Ham United	Division One	4-1
26/12/1969	Newcastle United	Division One	1-2
27/12/1969	Everton	Division One	2-1
03/01/1970	Swansea Town	FA Cup 3rd Round	2-1
10/01/1970	Chelsea	Division One	5-2
17/01/1970	Coventry City	Division One	3-1
24/01/1970	Sutton United	FA Cup 4th Round	6-0
26/01/1970	Manchester United	Division One	2-2
31/01/1970	Stoke City	Division One	1-1
07/02/1970	Mansfield Town	FA Cup 5th Round	2-0
10/02/1970	West Bromwich Albion	Division One	5-1
14/02/1970	Tottenham Hotspur	Division One	1-1
21/02/1970	Swindon Town	FA Cup QF	2-0
28/02/1970	Crystal Palace	Division One	2-0
04/03/1970	Standard Liege	European Cup QF 1st Leg	1-0
07/03/1970	Liverpool	Division One	0-0
14/03/1970	Manchester United	FA Cup SF at Hillsborough	0-0
18/03/1970	Standard Liege	European Cup QF 2nd Leg	1-0
21/03/1970	Wolverhampton Wanderers	Division One	2-1
23/03/1970	Manchester United	FA Cup SF Replay at Villa Park	0-0
26/03/1970	Manchester United	FA Cup SF 2nd Replay at Burnden Park	1-0
28/03/1970	Southampton	Division One	1-3
30/03/1970	Derby County	Division One	1-4
01/04/1970	Glasgow Celtic	European Cup SF 1st Leg	0-1
02/04/1970	West Ham United	Division One	2-2
04/04/1970	Burnley	Division One	2-1
11/04/1970	Chelsea	FA Cup Final at Wembley	2-2
15/04/1970	Glasgow Celtic	European Cup SF 2nd Leg	1-2
18/04/1970	Manchester City	Division One	1-3
21/04/1970	Ipswich Town	Division One	2-3
29/04/1970	Chelsea	FA Cup Final Replay at Old Trafford	1-2

Leeds had six captains, Billy Bremner, Paul Reaney, Johnny Giles, Paul Madeley, Jimmy Lumsden and Peter Lorimer.

Paul Madeley featured in 59 out of 63 games, missing just four games.

Captain fantastic Billy Bremner collected the Football Writers' Player of the Year.

Don Revie collected his second Manager of the Year trophy in a row after winning it the previous season.

When Leeds faced Glasgow Celtic at Hampden Park they did so in front of a record crowd of 136,505.

THE 1970s
FROM REVIE TO CLOUGH TO ARMFIELD TO ADAMSON TO STEIN

The first full campaign of a new decade saw Leeds set off like a house on fire, winning their first five games of the season and topping the league table going into September. The League Cup lasted just one round, with Sheffield United winning 1-0 at Bramall Lane, but there were better fortunes in Europe. The Inter-Cities campaign kicked off with a 1-0 win away at Sarpsborg thanks to a Peter Lorimer strike and the side eased through to the second round with a 5-0 win at Elland Road. Leeds stayed top of the league going into 1971 and hopes were extremely high that they could claim their second championship. By the new year, Leeds had disposed of Dynamo Dresden and Sparta Prague to reach the last eight of the Inter-Cities Fairs Cup and a meeting with Vitoria Setubal in March. The FA Cup saw Leeds defeat Rotherham United in the third round and Swindon Town in the fourth round, before coming a cropper to Fourth Division side Colchester United at Layer Road. It left Leeds to focus on winning both the league and the Inter-Cities Fairs Cup. By the time they faced Setubal, they were still looking good and still in pole position. The side from Portugal were beaten 3-2 and it set up a mouth-watering semi-final with Liverpool. Leeds won the first leg thanks to a strike from Bremner, which set up the second leg perfectly. The 17 April 1971 was a day that will go down in history for all the wrong reasons. Leeds faced West Bromwich Albion, still in the hunt for the title, but a controversial goal from Baggies striker Jeff Astle saw the away side win the game 2-1. Referee Ray Tinkler required a police escort and to no surprise he never refereed at Elland Road again. It was a result that cost Leeds the title.

After that, Leeds had to get their minds switched back on, which they did, and made it through to the final of the Inter-Cities Fairs Cup with a 0-0 draw at Elland Road and a meeting with Italian giants Juventus. A terrific away performance at the Comunale Stadium saw two crucial away goals from Paul Madeley and Mick Bates as the tie ended 2-2. The second leg five days later saw Leeds finish the job with a goal from Allan Clarke as Leeds won the Cup when the tie ended 3-3 on aggregate but the two away goals proved vital. Clarke was top scorer with 23 goals.

Following the West Bromwich Albion incident, Leeds were forced to play their opening four home league games away from Elland Road. These were played at Leeds Road, Boothferry Park and Hillsborough respectively. It didn't seem to affect matters too much though, as Leeds were second in the table after the first batch of seven games. The European campaign lasted one round as Lierse surprisingly won 6-0 on aggregate and league form from there on was up and down.

Leeds United v Juventus, 2 June 1971, Inter-Cities Fairs Cup Final second Leg, Elland Road.

By the end of 1971, the side were in third place, having been knocked out of the Inter-Cities Fairs Cup and the League Cup by West Ham United. It left Leeds to concentrate on the league and FA Cup only. The second domestic cup competition started with a 4-1 win over Bristol Rovers at Elland Road before a meeting with Liverpool. The first game ended

Leeds United 1971-72.

goalless on Merseyside before a brace from Allan Clarke sent Leeds through to the last 16. Before the tie away at Cardiff City, Leeds produced one of their best-ever performances, demolishing arch rivals Manchester United 5-1 at Elland Road. They then defeated the Bluebirds at Ninian Park to make it through to the last eight. After the Manchester United game, no one could imagine what would happen in the next home league fixture against Southampton. The Saints were demolished in a performance that eclipsed the Red Devils one, with Leeds winning 7-0, thanks to a hat-trick from Lorimer. Attention then turned to the FA Cup, with a place in the last four at stake. Leeds made it through to a tie with Birmingham City thanks to goals from Clarke and Charlton.

League form continued apace but the side lost a vital game away at Derby County. However, Leeds bounced back with consecutive wins over Huddersfield Town (3-1) and Stoke City (3-0). The Stoke win was tinged with sadness as League Cup Final hero Terry Cooper broke his leg just a week before the FA Cup semi-final.

Birmingham City were beaten with ease, thanks to a brace from Jones and one from Lorimer. It set up another final against Arsenal. Leeds still had eyes on the title and won two out of the next three leading up to the cup final. After coming so close in 1965 and 1970, Leeds finally lifted the country's most prestigious cup competition in the cup's centenary year with a winning goal from Allan Clarke after a Mick Jones cross. Amazingly, Leeds had little time to celebrate as they had to travel to Molineux just two days later knowing a point would secure an historic double.

FA Cup Final at Wembley, which ended 1-0. Allan Clarke celebrates with the trophy.

Leeds United players celebrate their 1-0 win for Leeds over Arsenal in the FA Cup Final at Wembley.

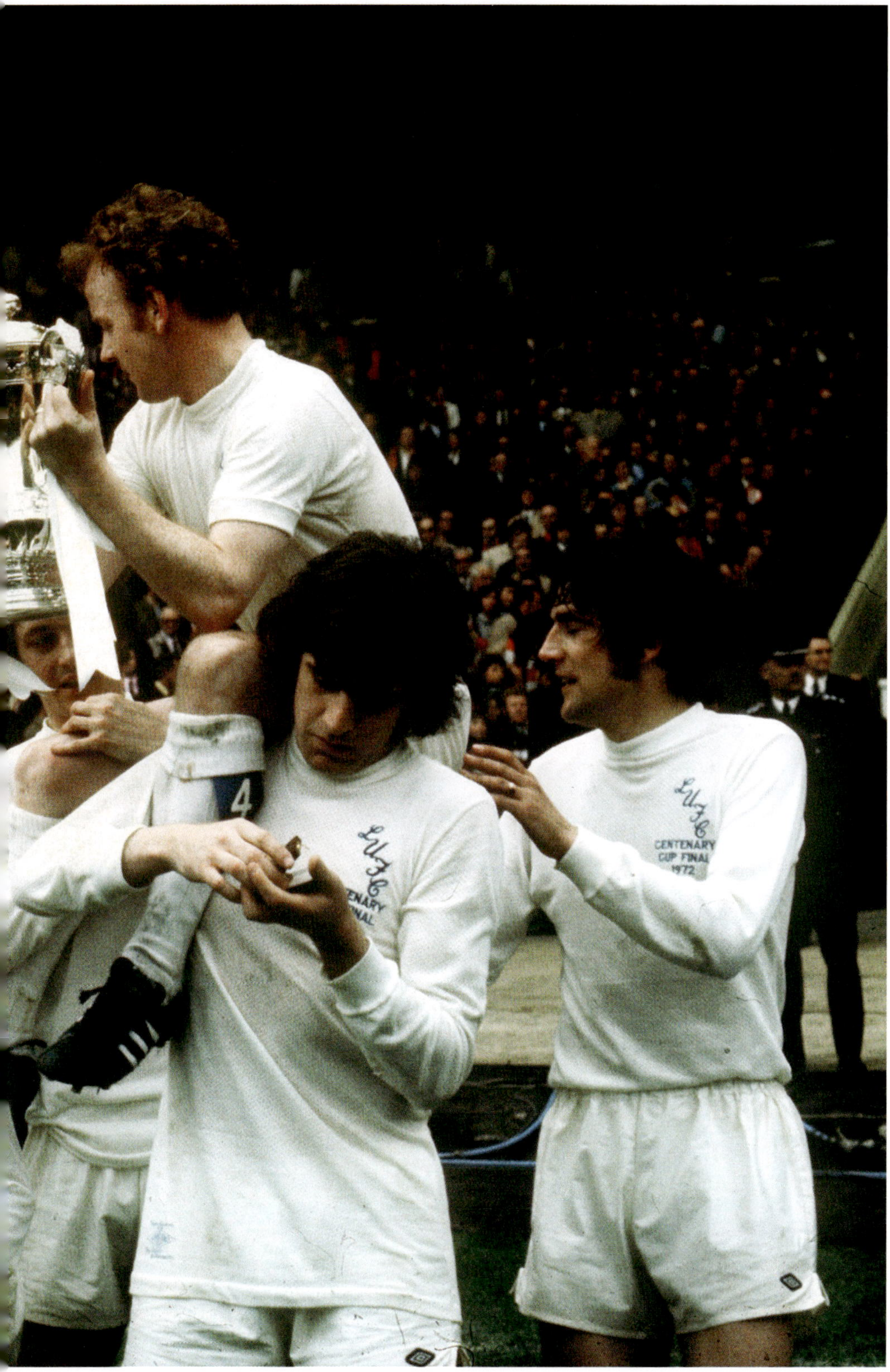
CENTENARY
CUP FINAL
1972

Sadly for Leeds and despite a goal back from Bremner, they fell short losing 2-1, meaning the title went to Derby County. They had finished runners-up for a third consecutive season, with Lorimer top scoring with 29 goals and Revie winning his third Manager of the Year award. One other game took place during the season, with Barcelona winning an Inter-Cities Fairs Cup play-off 2-1, with reserve striker Joe Jordan scoring White's goal.

In the summer Revie freshened up his squad with Trevor Cherry from Huddersfield Town and Gordon McQueen from St Mirren. Leeds lost their opening-day game 4-0 at Chelsea, in which Peter Lorimer ended up replacing David Harvey in goal, but they bounced back with an unbeaten run of six games. Following their victory in the FA Cup Final, Leeds entered the Cup Winners' Cup for the first time and first up was Turkish side MKE Ankaragugu. They were defeated 2-1 on aggregate and it set up a tie with Carl Zeiss Jena. Leeds made it through to the fourth round of the League Cup before being knocked out by Liverpool, but they made it through to the quarter-finals of the Cup Winners' Cup with a 2-0 aggregate win.

The Whites were third in the First Division going into the new year where they would remain for the rest of the season. The defence of the FA Cup started with a game against Norwich City. The first game was drawn at Carrow Road, as was the first replay at Elland Road. The third game, played at Villa Park, saw Leeds breeze through 5-0 with a hat-trick from Clarke. Plymouth Argyle were beaten in round four and West Bromwich Albion in round five.

After that, the focus switched back to Europe and Rapid Bucharest were beaten 5-0 at Elland Road in the first leg. Derby County were then beaten in the quarter-finals of the FA Cup, with Leeds playing in all red. The second against Rapid was a formality as Leeds won 3-1 and set up a semi-final with Hadjuk Split. But before they could think about that they had the small matter of reaching the FA Cup Final again. A winner from Billy Bremner secured this and the possibility of retaining the FA Cup. The first leg of the Cup Winners' Cup last-four tie against Split saw Leeds win 1-0, with Clarke scoring, and a goalless draw in the return leg secured a place in another final. The only black spot was a yellow card for Bremner, meaning he would miss the prestigious event.

First up was the FA Cup Final against Second Division Sunderland. In what should have been a formality, it proved to be anything but as an Ian Porterfield goal and a point-blank save from Jim Montgomery ensured the Mackems pulled off one of the biggest Cup Final shocks in its history. Leeds had to lift themselves for the final against AC Milan in Salonika nine days later, but sadly for Leeds, after some unfavourable refereeing decisions, the Italian side won 1-0 and the Whites ended the season empty handed. To make matters worse, Norman Hunter also saw red. What had started with such high hopes ended up in heartache.

Just before the Cup Winners' Cup Final, there were newspaper stories appearing suggesting that Revie could be joining Everton. Thankfully, after discussions with chairman Manny

Cussins he decided to stay and set about winning back the title. Jack Charlton had retired at the end of the previous campaign and was replaced by Gordon McQueen.

Leeds made an historic start to the season, winning their first seven games, and they never looked back. The UEFA Cup run started with a 1-1 draw away at Stromsgodset before a 6-1 win in the second leg at Elland Road. The 100 per cent winning start to the season ended in a goalless draw against Manchester United, but Leeds just continued their relentless form with five wins out of their next nine. However, the League Cup lasted just one round, with Ipswich Town winning 2-0 at Portman Road.

The European journey continued with a penalty shoot-out win over Scottish side Hibernian then a meeting with Vitoria Setubal, who they had played before. Following a 1-1 draw at Birmingham City, in which Joe Jordan salvaged a late equaliser four minutes from time, the bookies stopped taking bets on the Whites winning the title. By that time, the European adventure was over as Setubal overturned a 1-0 deficit to win the second leg 3-1.

The unbeaten run kept on going heading into 1974, and it reached 23 February before Leeds were defeated in the league, setting a club record of 29 games unbeaten from the start of a campaign. By then, and despite beating Wolverhampton Wanderers in round three and Peterborough United in round four, they had been knocked out of the FA Cup by lower league Bristol City.

The defeat at Stoke saw doubts creep in, and a run of three straight defeats against Liverpool, Burnley and West Ham United enhanced this. But Leeds got back to winning

BACK ROW: Trevor Cherry, Paul Madeley, Mick Jones, Roy Ellam, Joe Jordan, Jack Charlton
CENTRE ROW: Paul Reaney, Chris Galvin, David Harvey, Gary Sprake, Norman Hunter, Allan Clarke
FRONT ROW: Peter Lorimer, John Giles, Billy Bremner, Mick Bates, Eddie Gray, Terry Yorath

ways with a vital 2-0 win over Derby County, thanks to goals from Lorimer and Bremner. However, successive goalless draws at Coventry City and at home to Sheffield United meant Leeds had no room for error. A day later they defeated Sheffield United at Bramall Lane with a brace from Lorimer. An Allan Clarke winner in a nervy game at home to Ipswich Town kept Liverpool under pressure. In the end they cracked when they lost at home to Arsenal, and Leeds had finally secured their second championship. Clarke finished the season with a winner at Queens Park Rangers as Revie bowed out at Elland Road as a winner and he became England manager. For the first time since March 1961, Leeds had to find a new manager.

So who would be the new man at the helm at Elland Road? The answer would be one of the club's harshest critics – Brian Clough. Everyone from players to supporters were stunned. Clough started with a penalty shoot-out loss to Liverpool in the Charity Shield, in which Billy Bremner and Kevin Keegan saw red and things were only to get worse for Clough. One win in the side's first six games left the champions in 19th place and following a 1-1 League Cup draw away at Huddersfield Town, Clough was gone. He lasted just 44 days and was initially replaced by Maurice Lindley on a caretaker basis. Lindley oversaw a safe passage through to the second round of the European Cup with a 5-3 win over FC Zurich as well as a 5-1 league win over Yorkshire rivals Sheffield United.

The new man at the helm would be Jimmy Armfield, assisted by Don Howe as the first-team coach. Armfield started with a 2-0 win over Arsenal thanks to a pair from Duncan McKenzie and he then guided Leeds through to the fourth round of the League Cup with a

Leeds United, 1975-76.

replay win over Huddersfield Town and a third-round win over Bury. League form was still a concern for Armfield as they dropped to 19th place by the start of November, but come the new year they were up to tenth. Leeds defeated Újpesti Dózsa 5-1 on aggregate to reach the quarter-finals of the European Cup, which would resume in the new year, but League Cup hopes were put out by a shock defeat at Chester City.

The FA Cup run started with a 4-1 win over Cardiff City, before a Dickie Guy penalty save ensured a shock draw for non-league Wimbledon at Elland Road. Leeds won the replay thanks to a Dave Bassett own goal, before another own goal from David Nish saw off Derby County at the Baseball Ground.

By the time Anderlecht visited Elland Road for a quarter-final tie in the European Cup, Leeds were up to sixth as league results had steadily improved. The Belgian side were easily beaten 3-0, with goals from Jordan, McQueen and Lorimer, and Leeds had one foot in the semi-finals. Before the second leg took place, Leeds met Ipswich Town for a place in the last four of the FA Cup, but two games couldn't settle matters. Anderlecht were beaten in the second leg thanks to a winner from Bremner, and a meeting with Spanish giants Barcelona was set up.

Ipswich finally defeated Leeds after four games and it left Leeds to concentrate on European glory. The first leg saw Leeds take a 2-1 lead to the Nou Camp, with strikes from Bremner and Clarke and they finished the job off two weeks later, with Peter Lorimer striking in the Nou Camp. The only sour note was the red card of Gordon McQueen, who would miss the final against Bayern Munich. A month after the league season had finished, in which the Whites had finished ninth, Leeds travelled to Paris to face the German side to attempt to win the biggest trophy in European football. Just as they had in 1973 against AC Milan, Leeds were on the end of some questionable refereeing decisions, with the side being denied what

Billy Bremner and Franz Beckenbauer exchange pennants as Leeds take on Bayern Munich in the final of the European Cup on 28 May 1975.

Peter Lorimer scores but Bill Bremner is deemed to be offside in the 1975 European Cup Final in Paris.

looked like a clear penalty for a foul by Beckenbauer on Clarke and they had a Lorimer volley ruled out when Bremner was harshly ruled to be offside. Bayern went up the other end to win the cup and left Leeds to reflect on what looked to be the end of the club's greatest-ever era.

Having missed out on European glory, Armfield knew he had a task on to lift sprits and attempt to bring back the days of success to Elland Road. The problem was that the side that Revie had built started to break up, with Johnny Giles moving on to West Brom as player-manager. For the first time since 1965-66 there would be no European football at Elland Road as Armfield was left to concentrate on domestic matters.

The 1975-76 season started in a positive manner and the team found themselves in third spot after an encouraging start to the campaign. Lower league side Notts County dampened spirits with a 1-0 win in the League Cup at Elland Road and league results proved to be too inconsistent to mount a serious title tilt. There were some highs, including a 5-2 win over Everton at Elland Road and they did reach third after a brace from Duncan McKenzie saw off Arsenal at Highbury. A 4-0 win over Leicester City, with another brace from McKenzie, kept them in the top three going into 1976. Leeds avenged the League Cup defeat against Notts County by defeating them in the third round of the FA Cup, but another shock was in store as Crystal Palace defeated Leeds in the fourth round. Leeds did reach a season high of second place after a 2-0 win over Stoke City in January, but a run of one win in eight saw the side drop to fifth. They won four of the next five, but only two wins in the last five games of the season saw them finish in fifth palace. McKenzie finished as top scorer with 17, but the season was overshadowed by the retirement of Mick Jones.

Leeds spent big in the summer, bringing in Tony Currie from Sheffield United for £240,000, but the start to the season was inauspicious to say the least. By the start of October the side were in 19th place and the glory days of the previous years were gone. The greatest-ever captain in the club's history, Billy Bremner, was gone, as was Norman Hunter. The challenge now for Armfield was to rebuild a new squad to fight for honours. Stoke City knocked Leeds out of the League Cup at the second-round stage. A 3-1 win at West Ham United set Leeds on a run of eight games unbeaten and took them up seventh, but a run of one win in the next four dropped them to 12th. The FA Cup started with a 5-2 hammering of Norwich City at Elland Road and Birmingham City (2-1) and Manchester City (1-0) went the same way. It set up a last-eight tie with Wolverhampton Wanderers, which Leeds won thanks to a strike from Eddie Gray, but in the last four of the competition Manchester United made it through to Wembley, winning by the odd goal in three. League form trailed as the side finished in a disappointing tenth place, but there was a new name at the top of the scoring charts in Joe Jordan with 12 and Frank Gray and Trevor Cherry, who had now been appointed new club captain, played in 47 out of 48 games.

In the close season Armfield bought in Arthur Graham from Aberdeen and Ray Hankin started his first full season at the club, having been brought in during the previous campaign.

Frank Gray (Leeds) and Sammy McIlroy (Manchester United) in action on 6 October 1976 at Elland Road.

The start of the season (1977-78) proved to be unwelcoming as a run of two wins in the opening 14 games saw Leeds entrenched in mid-table. Armfield did return to the transfer window with Brian Flynn joining from Burnley, and results did improve with an unbeaten run of eight games, which included five wins. By this point, the side had seen off Rochdale, Colchester United and Bolton Wanderers to reach the last eight of the League Cup, and Everton went the same way in a 4-1 win at Elland Road. Manchester City knocked Leeds out of the FA Cup to gain revenge for their defeat last season in a game where David Harvey and Gordon McQueen exchanged punches. There were also disgraceful crowd scenes which saw fences being erected around the ground and the club banned from staging home ties for three years, but this was later rescinded.

McQueen was sold to Manchester United, and with it results did improve. Leeds were up to sixth following an Allan Clarke winner at Old Trafford and stayed there following a 5-0 win over Middlesbrough at Elland Road. Former manager Brian Clough ended Leeds' hopes in the League Cup with 7-3 aggregate win for Nottingham Forest in the last four and the league form was up and down towards the end of the campaign. They did defeat Leicester City 5-1 thanks to a hat-trick from Eddie Gray, but two wins from the last seven saw Leeds end in ninth place. Hankin was top scorer with 21 goals.

Despite having the tough job of rebuilding Revie's squad and leading the side to the European Cup Final in his first season at the club, Armfield was dismissed in the summer as Leeds looked for a new boss. More bad news was to follow with the departures of Allan

Leeds United v QPR, 3 December 1977, Elland Road. Bryan Flynn scores in the 3-0 win.

Leeds United, 1978-79.

Clarke and Paul Reaney, although John Hawley did join from Hull City to partner Hankin. Leeds didn't have a manager by the time the new season kicked off away at Arsenal, and yet again Maurice Lindley stepped into the breach. A 2-2 draw with a brilliant goal from Currie was encouraging and by the time rivals Manchester United arrived four days later, Leeds had a new boss.

Jock Stein had joined the side, and despite a 3-2 defeat, the Scotsman only had to wait three days for his first win, a 3-0 victory over Wolverhampton Wanderers at Elland Road. However, it did not have the desired impact and, despite a 3-0 win over Birmingham City at Elland Road, Leeds were in 11th place. After a 1-0 win in the League Cup second round, second replay over West Bromwich Albion, thanks to a Paul Hart winner, Stein was gone, having accepted the Scottish national job, and Leeds were again on the lookout for another new manager. Once again Lindley took charge of team affairs and oversaw a League Cup win over Sheffield United and three games without a win in the league. Burnley boss Jimmy Adamson was appointed the new manager and he had a start to remember in a 4-1 win over Derby County at Elland Road. The new manager oversaw a brilliant run in both the league and the League Cup, as by mid-January Leeds were up to fifth and into the last four of the first cup competition of the season, for the second time in two seasons. Amazingly the side met West Bromwich Albion on seven occasions during the season, and the Baggies gained some sort of revenge as they knocked Leeds out of the FA Cup after a fourth-round replay. Just like 12 months previously, Leeds fell at the final hurdle before Wembley, as Southampton knocked them out of the League Cup, winning 3-2 on aggregate, but league form was consistent as the side finished in fifth and qualified for the UEFA Cup. Frank Gray and Brian Flynn missed only one game all season and new signing Hawley finished as top scorer with 17 goals.

The final full season of the decade, saw Leeds back in Europe and plenty of transfer activity. Frank Gray was sold to Nottingham Forest and Tony Currie to Queens Park Rangers, while

Leeds United, 1979-80.

other players departed included John Hawley, David Stewart and the great Peter Lorimer. Adamson needed new blood and that came in the form of Alan Curtis from Swansea City, Gary Hamson and Brian Greenhoff. Curtis scored a brace on his debut in a 2-2 draw at Bristol City, but early league form was inconsistent, winning only three of their first 12 games. Arsenal defeated Leeds 8-1 on aggregate in the League Cup second round, but the European campaign did start in much better fashion. An Arthur Graham hat-trick saw off Valletta before a 3-0 win in the second leg at Elland Road. The second tie saw the debut of John Lukic, who would go on to have a distinguished career between the sticks at Elland Road. Romanian side Universitate Craiova ended any European hopes, winning 4-0 on aggregate, and the fans were getting restless. The result had a detrimental impact and Leeds fell as low as 19th following a shocking 5-1 defeat at Everton, but the introduction of local lad Terry Connor sparked a renaissance. Connor scored the winner on his debut at home to West Bromwich Albion and was on the scoresheet in a draw away at Old Trafford and wins at home to Wolverhampton Wanderers and away at Stoke City. Like the League Cup before it, the FA Cup lasted one round, with Nottingham Forest easing to a 4-1 win at Elland Road. Another new signing came in the form of Derek Parlane from Rangers, and he marked his debut with a goal in a 2-0 home win against Southampton. Despite finishing in 11th place, Leeds did deny old foes Manchester United the league championship, winning 2-0 at Elland Road, with strikes from Parlane and a penalty from Kevin Hird. The 70s had been a mixed decade, starting on a high, ending on a low. What would the 1980s serve up?

DEBUTANTS IN 1970s

JOE JORDAN

Debut: Vitoria Setubal (H) 10 March 1971
Appearances: 183 (38)
Goals: 48

Born in Cleland in North Lanarkshire in Scotland, Jordan started his career at Scottish side Morton where he played 12 games, scoring twice, before being recommended to Leeds by former player Bobby Collins. He signed for the Whites in the autumn of 1970 for a bargain fee of £15,000 and an initial bonus of £5,000 if he played 20 games for the club. He made his Leeds United debut in an Inter-Cities Fairs Cup tie at home to Vitoria Setubal in March 1971, coming off the bench for Mick Jones. His other appearance that season came in a 3-0 win away at Southampton at the end of April where he again came off the bench, this time replacing Allan Clarke. He scored his first goal for the Whites in an Inter-Cities play-off tie away at Barcelona to decide who would keep the trophy.

The 1972-73 season would be his most productive in a Leeds United shirt as they fought for domestic and European glory. Jordan started 23 games, playing in another 13 after coming off the bench, and he scored 12 goals. His goals included a brace in a 3-3 draw at home to Ipswich Town, one against their rivals Norwich City, a vital away goal against Ankaragugu in the European Cup Winners' Cup, as well as nine further strikes. Sadly for the Whites, they missed out on glory, losing the FA Cup Final to Sunderland and the European Cup Winners' Cup Final to AC Milan. As for

Jordan though, he would go on to play an important part the following season, featuring in 42 games and scoring nine important goals, as Leeds finally won the prestigious league championship. League strikes included one in the 3-0 win at home to Coventry City, one in the 2-1 win away at Chelsea, a late equaliser away at Birmingham City, which kept the unbeaten run going and one in the win at Manchester United. Having won the league, it meant qualification for the European Cup, and under the guidance of Jimmy Armfield (who had replaced Brian Clough), Leeds made it all the way through to the final, in which Jordan started against Bayern Munich in Paris. Unfortunately for Leeds a series of decisions went against them as the German side walked away with the trophy. Jordan went on to play for Leeds until January 1978 when he joined arch-rivals Manchester United and his former teammate Gordon McQueen soon followed suit.

TREVOR CHERRY

Debut: Chelsea (A) 12 August 1972
Appearances: 478 (8)
Goals: 32

A west Yorkshire man through and through, Cherry played professional football for only three clubs, all in west Yorkshire – Huddersfield Town, Leeds and Bradford City – before heading into management with the Bantams as a player-manager.

Starting his career at Leeds Road with Huddersfield Town where he joined as part of the groundstaff in July in 1963 as a 15-year-old, Cherry would go onto captain the Terriers to the Second Division title in 1969-70. He then swapped the colours of Huddersfield for the Whites of Leeds in June 1972 for £100,000 and he made his debut in a 4-0 loss away to Chelsea at the start of the 1972-73 campaign. He made 60 appearances at Elland

Road, wearing the number-three shirt in both the FA Cup Final against Sunderland and the European Cup Winners' Cup Final against AC Milan, scoring three goals. In the 1973-74 season, he started 37 out of the 42 league games as Leeds ended five years of hurt by winning the old First Division, and he played in all of the domestic and UEFA Cup games.

Cherry went down in history the following season by scoring the first goal under new boss Brian Clough but had to settle for a place on the bench under Jimmy Armfield in the European Cup Final against Bayern Munich, despite marking Dutch legend Johan Cruyff out of the semi-final, second leg in Barcelona.

The 1975-76 season saw Cherry miss just two games as Leeds finished in fifth place, but they were knocked out of both domestic competitions by lower league sides. He started the new season captaining the side in the opening two games at home to West Bromwich Albion and away at Birmingham City. He was then handed the job on a permanent basis following Bremner's move to Hull City. He missed only one game (a 5-2 win over Norwich City in the FA Cup) as Leeds finished tenth and reached the FA Cup semi-finals. Cherry kept going at Elland Road and the following campaign he missed just one game, a 2-1 home loss against West Ham United in April, when Peter Lorimer filled in as skipper. Cherry stayed with the club when they were relegated from the top flight in 1982, making over 470 appearances, but the 1982-83 season would be his last. He played in his final game for the club in a 1-0 loss at home to Queens Park Rangers at the start of December 1982 in front of just over 11,000 fans. He then joined Bradford City as player-manager.

FRANK GRAY

First Debut: Leicester City (A) 10 February 1973
Second Debut: Swansea City (A) 29 August 1981
Appearances: 397(10)
Goals: 35

Frank, the younger brother of Leeds United legend Eddie, joined the ranks at Elland Road in the summer of 1971 and would go on to have two spells in west Yorkshire. He turned professional in November 1971 and had to wait until February 1973 to make his Leeds United debut, coming on as a substitute for Mick Bates in a 2-0 loss at Leicester City. He made six appearances that season, scoring on his full debut in a 4-0 win at home to Crystal Palace at the end of April. One of his six appearances was a start in the infamous European Cup Winners' Cup Final loss against AC Milan.

As Leeds won the First Division in 1973-74, he started just nine times (with five further appearances from the bench) with three of them coming in the league, five in the UEFA Cup, where he scored in a 6-1 home win against Stromsgodset, and the other in a League Cup defeat to Ipswich Town. The 1974-75 season saw Gray start 32 games and come off the bench in three others. He displaced Trevor Cherry in the European Cup Final against Bayern Munich. He was an ever-present the following season, scoring the winner away at Coventry City and a penalty in the 1-1 draw at home to Derby County. The 1976-77 saw Leeds miss out on FA Cup glory at the penultimate round, losing the semi-final against Manchester United, but for Gray it was almost a faultless season in terms of games, missing just one, a 1-1 home draw against West Ham United. He would stay for two more full seasons at Elland Road, missing just two games (2-0 at home to West Bromwich Albion on 24 August 1977 and Bristol City at Elland Road on 9 December 1978), before making the move to Nottingham Forest in July 1979. He appeared in the 1980 European Cup Final for Forest, making him the first player to appear in a final for two different sides, this time being on the winning side against Hamburg. He returned to Elland Road for £300,000 but, despite him featuring in 40 games, Leeds were relegated finishing in 20th place in the old First Division. Gray did have the honour of captaining the side on seven occasions, though he led them to just one win, a famous 4-1 win over European Cup finalists Aston Villa at the end of April. He missed one game in 1982-83, made 30 appearances in 1983-84 and the following season, when he made 43 appearances, would be his last at the club as he left for Sunderland.

CARL HARRIS

Debut: Újpesti Dózsa (H) 6 November 1974
Appearances: 136 (40)
Goals: 29

Born in Neath in Wales, Harris attended Cwrtsart Secondary School and looked likely to join fellow Welshman Brian Flynn at Burnley, but it was Jack Pritchard who persuaded Harris to join Leeds for a trial. Harris became homesick but Leeds had a trick up their sleeves, sending the great John Charles to Wales to talk to Harris, and he eventually signed as a professional in November 1973 under Don Revie when he was just 17. He didn't make his first-team debut until the arrival of new manager Jimmy Armfield when he came on

as a 70th-minute substitute in a 3-0 win over Újpesti Dózsa for Peter Lorimer in a UEFA Cup tie at Elland Road. He had to wait over five months before his first league game, but the wait was worthwhile as he marked it with the winning goal coming off the bench in a 2-1 win over Ipswich Town. He featured a couple more times that season in away games at Wolverhampton Wanderers and Tottenham Hotspur respectively. He was being nurtured into first-team action and he started the final nine games the following season, scoring in a 3-1 away win at Everton, a 3-2 win at Newcastle United and a 2-1 home win against Manchester City. The 1976-77 season saw Harris start eight games with a further nine off the bench, scoring another three goals.

Nineteen appearances and three goals followed as Leeds reached the final four of the League Cup before losing out to Nottingham Forest in 1977-78. The season later he scored five goals in 36 games as again, Leeds missed out on a trip to Wembley in the last four of the League Cup, this time losing out over two legs to Southampton.

The Welshman featured just 15 times in the 1979-80 season, hitting the back of the net four times, including a brace in the 3-0 home win against Stoke City as Leeds finished in 11th place. Harris's best season in the colours of Leeds came the following year as he reached double scoring figures for the side and he finished as top scorer. Another 18 appearances followed in his last season at the club as Leeds were relegated to the Second Division, and he joined Charlton for £100,000 in July 1982. He had a trial back at Leeds in 1985, which proved unsuccessful as Eddie Gray had been sacked and the Welshman subsequently joined Bury.

TONY CURRIE

Debut: West Bromwich Albion (H) 21 August 1976
Appearances: 124
Goals: 16

Born in Edgware in Middlesex, Currie joined Queens Park Rangers as an amateur and was rejected by Chelsea before moving to Watford in 1967. On his debut for the Hornets he scored a brace at home to Bristol Rovers, but his stay at Vicarage Road was a short one as he joined Sheffield United in February 1968 for £26,500. Just as he had done at Watford, Currie scored on his debut for the Blades but was ruled out of the next game as he was getting married. He stayed in south Yorkshire until the summer of 1976, when west Yorkshire and Leeds United came calling.

Currie joined Leeds in June 1976 for a fee of around £240,000 and, despite only staying for three seasons, he proved to be an inspired

Tony Currie scores for Leeds United in their 3-1 defeat at Elland Road by Arsenal on 22 April 1978 as Willie Young tries to block.

signing. He made his Leeds debut in a 2-2 draw at home to West Bromwich Albion on the opening day of the season and went on to make 41 appearances that campaign, scoring in losses away at Coventry City and Stoke City in the League Cup. He helped Leeds to the last four of the FA Cup, only for Manchester United to end Leeds's and Currie's hopes of playing in their first final in four years. The 1977-78 season saw Currie feature on 41 occasions, scoring four goals, at home to Queens Park Rangers in a 3-0 win, one in a resounding 4-1 League Cup win at home to Everton, one in the 2-0 home win over Chelsea and one in a 3-1 loss to Arsenal. Despite the side only finishing in ninth place, Currie did walk away with one personal accolade, winning the Leeds United Player of the Year at the end of the season. The following season, his final in the colours of Leeds United, would be his best yet. He started with a quite brilliant goal away at Arsenal and kept the form going all the way through the season. He also captained the side for the majority, making 42 appearances in all competitions and hitting double figures for the one and only time in his Leeds career.

There is one goal that will always stand out for Currie, which came at home to Southampton, with a fantastic curling shot in a memorable 4-0 win for Leeds. It was voted as the Big Match Goal of the Season on ITV. His final award in a Leeds shirt came as he was voted in the 1978-79 PFA First Division Team of the Year. He was sold to Queens Park Rangers in August 1979.

ARTHUR GRAHAM

Debut: Newcastle United (A) 20 August 1977
Appearances: 259 (1)
Goals: 47

Graham, of Glaswegian descendant was at first approached by Celtic before signing for Aberdeen. Despite being young, he started in the Scottish Cup Final as the Dons defeated Celtic, with the 17-year-old assisting in two goals. He remained north of the border before moving to Elland Road for £15,000 in July 1977.

In his first season at Elland Road, Graham featured in a total of 47 games, scoring on 12 occasions. He made his debut away at Newcastle United at the start of the 1977-78 season, making the number-11 shirt his own. His 12 goals included a hat-trick in a 3-2 win away at Birmingham City in mid-January 1978 as Leeds finished in ninth place and reached the last four of the League Cup.

The following season proved to be another success for Graham as he started 49 games for the side, again reaching double figures as Leeds qualified for the UEFA Cup and again reached the semi-finals of the League Cup under new manager Jimmy Adamson. Graham's European debut for the club couldn't have gone any better, as he scored his second hat-trick for the club away in Valletta as Leeds eased to a 4-0 win over the Maltese side. Sadly for Graham and Leeds, the European adventure ended in the second round against Universitate Craiova and their league form slumped as they finished in 11th place and were knocked out of both domestic competitions early on. Graham did finish that campaign with six goals, with his other strikes coming at home to Wolverhampton Wanderers, at home to Bolton Wanderers and away at Manchester City.

Despite the sacking of Jimmy Adamson and the arrival of former player Allan Clarke as manager, Graham was all but an ever-present, starting 44 games and scoring another four goals for the side as Clarke's men finished in ninth place. The 1981-82 season would go down in the almanacs for the all wrong reasons, as Leeds were relegated to the old Second Division, but Graham did finish as joint top scorer with Frank Worthington both scoring nine, including his third hat-trick for the club in the early season win over Wolverhampton Wanderers. The Scotsman stayed with the side, despite demotion to the second tier in 1982-83 and made 46 appearances, scoring a final six goals for the club. In the summer of 1983 he was sold to Manchester United form £50,000 to play First Division football.

BRIAN FLYNN

Debut: Norwich City (H) 5 November 1977
Appearances: 174 (3)
Goals: 11

Born in Port Talbot in Glamorgan, Flynn joined Burnley in 1970 and signed professional forms in October 1972. He stayed at Turf Moor for five years before making the trip across the motorway from Lancashire to Yorkshire to join Leeds in November 1977, as the Whites shelled out £175,000 to the Clarets for his services. He made his debut in a 2-2 draw at Elland Road against Norwich City in the autumn of 1977 and he became one of the smallest players to play for the club, at 5ft 3.5 inches.

In his first season at the club, Flynn made 30 appearances in total, 29 starts and one from the bench, scoring just the once in a 3-0 home win over Queens Park Rangers at the start of December 1977. The following season saw him an almost ever-present, missing just one game in all competitions as he made the famous number-four shirt his own. The only game he missed was a goalless draw away at Bristol City at the back end of the season. He popped up with three goals from midfield, at home to Birmingham City, at home to Derby County and at home to Bristol City as Leeds finished in fifth place and reached the last four of the League Cup.

From playing in 52 games the previous season, Flynn only featured on 30 occasions at the start of the new decade, again scoring three goals as Leeds failed to pull up any trees, finishing in 11th place and being knocked out of all of the cup competitions early on, but he did pop up with three more goals to his name. The 1980-81 season may not have been one to remember as a whole, but for Flynn, who made 45 appearances, one moment stood out. On 28 February 1981 Leeds travelled across the Pennines to face Manchester United in 15th place in the league table, but in the 85th minute up stepped the Welshman to score the only goal of the game. It would be the Whites' last win at Old Trafford until 3 January 2010 (albeit they didn't play there between the end of February 2004 and the start of 2010). After that season Flynn only featured 18 more times for the Whites before re-joining Burnley, originally on loan in March 1982, before joining them permanently eight months later for a fee of £60,000. He would go on to manage Wrexham, Swansea City, Wales (as caretaker) and Doncaster Rovers in 2013.

PAUL HART

Debut: Liverpool (A) 11 March 1978
Appearances: 223
Goals: 20

Born in Manchester, Hart made his professional debut at Stockport County in September 1970 before he moved to Blackpool for £25,000 in June 1973. It was from Blackpool where he would make the move to west Yorkshire and join Leeds for £300,000 in March 1978 as they looked for a direct replacement for Gordon McQueen. He couldn't have picked a more daunting place to make his Leeds United debut, a 1-0 loss away at Anfield. He went on to play in the rest of the games that season as Leeds finished in ninth position. The following campaign, which saw Hart play under three different managers (Maurice Lindley, Jock Stein and Jimmy Adamson), he hit the half-century of appearances, chipping in with seven goals along the way as the Whites qualified for the UEFA Cup. He scored the first goal under Stein in a 3-2 loss at home to Manchester United and other strikes included in the League Cup against West Bromwich Albion, in a 4-1 win over Derby County, which was Jimmy Adamson's first game in charge and in the 6-2 demolition of Hartlepool United in the FA Cup.

Another 37 appearances and two goals followed in seaosn 1979-80 and he also captained the side at home to Southampton, away at Crystal Palace and at home to Aston Villa in the absence of Trevor Cherry. It would be more of the same over the next three terms as he made 124 appearances, scoring eight more goals before joining Nottingham Forest in the summer of 1983. Hart's career took him full circle as he returned to Elland Road in the summer of 1992 (after Leeds had won the old First Division title) to look after the youth development and what an appointment it proved to be. In May 1993 he won the FA Youth Cup as Leeds defeated a star-studded Manchester United side 4-1 on aggregate. In the Whites side were the likes of Noel Whelan, Jamie Forrester, Mark Tinkler and Mark Ford, who would all go on to play for the first team. Four seasons later he did it again as the side defeated Crystal Palace 3-1 on aggregate, with players such as Paul Robinson, Jonathan Woodgate, Alan Maybury, Stephen McPhail and Harry Kewell, who all went on to play for the Whites at the very highest level, including the Champions League in 2001 as Leeds made it through to the semi-finals.

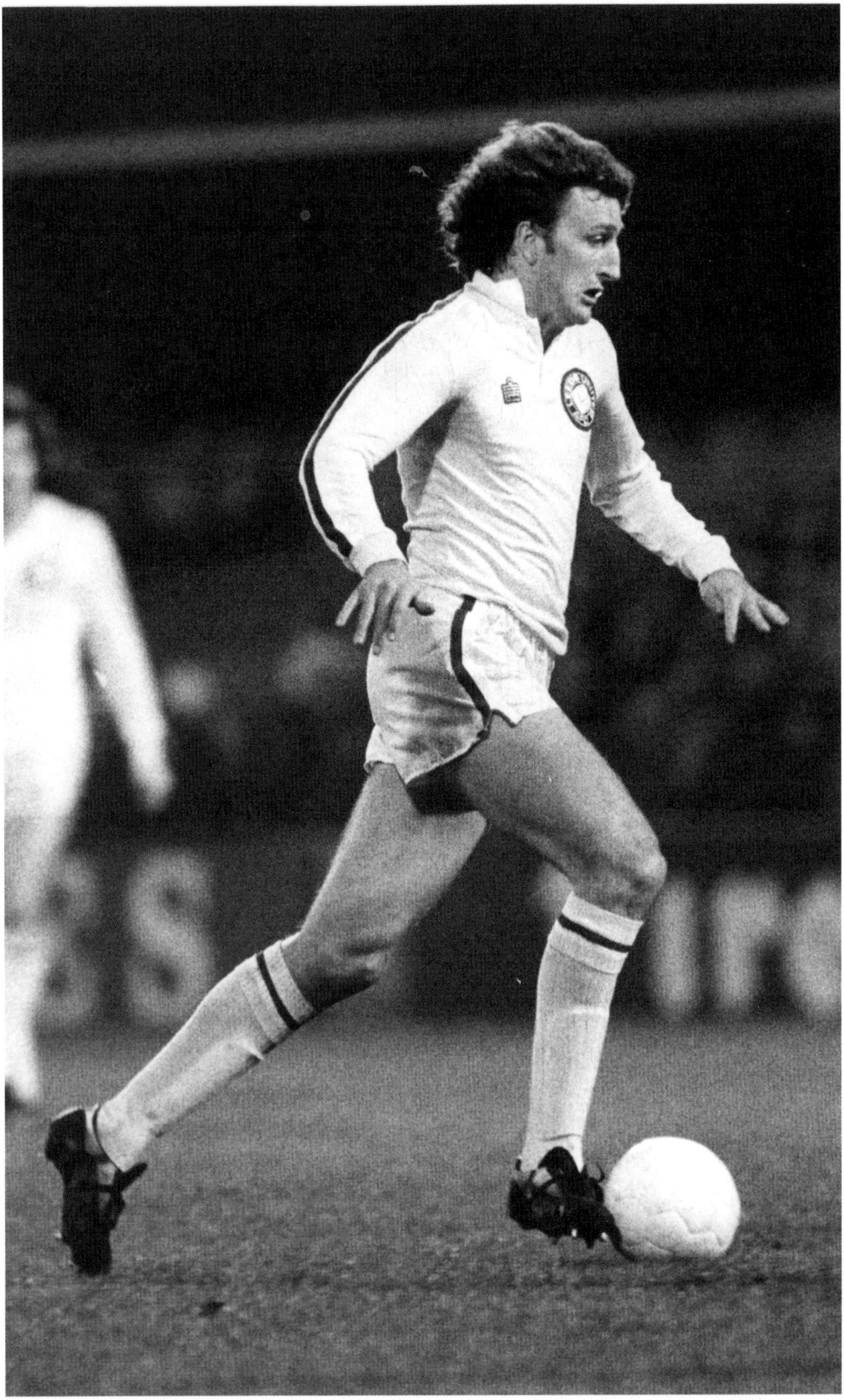

GARY HAMSON

Debut: Valletta (H) 3 October 1979
Appearances: 142 (10)
Goals: 4

Hamson, born in Nottingham, had trials with their rivals Derby County, but started his career at Sheffield United and turned professional with the Blades in November 1976. He made over 100 appearances in the red half of Sheffield, before swapping south Yorkshire with west Yorkshire as he joined Leeds United in July 1979 when Jimmy Adamson paid the Blades £140,000 for his services. In his first season at Elland Road he made 22 appearances in the colours of Leeds United, scoring his first goal for the club in an impressive 3-0 win over Wolverhampton Wanderers as the Whites finished in a disappointing 11th place.

The next season saw Hamson make a total of only 14 appearances. He had disciplinary issues at the club as he was hit with a nine-game ban, which at the time was a record under the penalty system. The following campaign saw him play 21 times for the side, mostly in the number ten shirt, scoring three goals, a 2-1 win away at Stoke City, a 3-1 FA Cup win at Wolverhampton Wanderers and what seemed at the time to be a vital 2-1 win at home to Brighton & Hove Albion as Leeds battled to stay afloat in the First Division. Sadly for Leeds the battle was lost, and even worse for Hamson was that he picked up an injury in the 2-0 loss away at West Bromwich Albion, which all but ended Leeds United's hopes of staying in the top flight. It also kept Hamson out of all but one of their games the following season. By this time Allan Clarke had been sacked and replaced by another of Revie's former players, Eddie Gray, and Hamson made his return in a FA Cup tie away at Arsenal in January but failed to last the full game and was substituted. He didn't feature again that season and made his second return at home to Brighton the following August.

Hamson made a total of 28 appearances in 1983-84, but it would get better over the next two seasons. Season 1984-85 saw him start 32 games as Leeds finished seventh in the Second Division and the following campaign, under both Eddie Gray and Billy Bremner, saw him start on 34 occasions. He left Elland Road in the summer of 1986 and moved to the south west, where he joined Bristol City on a free transfer.

JOHN LUKIC

First Debut: Valletta (H) 3 October 1979
Second Debut: Everton (A) 25 August 1990
Appearances: 431

The Derbyshire-born goalkeeper first signed professional forms at Elland Road in December 1978 and battled with other young goalkeepers such as David Seaman and Henry Smith. He made his first Leeds United debut in the UEFA Cup second-leg tie against Valletta at Elland Road with the Whites being 4-0 up from the first leg. He kept a clean sheet and although David Harvey returned for the next game at home to Ipswich Town, Lukic was back between the sticks away at Brighton and would go on to start every game until March 1983. He then handed in a transfer request and subsequently joined First Division Arsenal for a fee of £125,000 as the Gunners looked for a long-term replacement for Pat Jennings. Lukic re-joined the club in the summer of 1990 following promotion back to the top flight and would go on to be a massive part of the future over the next six seasons.

In his first season back, Lukic played in every league game, missing just two cup games at home to Leicester City in the Rumbelows Cup and away at Wolverhampton Wanderers in the Zenith Data Systems Cup. The following season he was an ever-present in all league and cup games and produced an inspired performance away at Liverpool as Leeds held on for a vital point in the run to the First Division Championship. He had a magnificent season and became a rare member of the goalkeepers' union, playing in the top flight with two different clubs following his success with Arsenal in 1989. The introduction of the back-pass rule saw Lukic struggle a season later, and he is best remembered for the own goal in the European Cup tie away at Glasgow Rangers. He missed four games in total, replaced in three by Mervyn Day and on the final day of the season away at Coventry City, when new signing

Mark Beeney made his debut. The following season was his most frustrating as he shared goalkeeping duties with Beeney, but he bounced back with another ever-present campaign in 1994-95 as Leeds qualified for the UEFA Cup. The 1995-96 season saw Lukic dropped after a 6-2 loss at Sheffield Wednesday, but he reclaimed his place in the Coca Cola Cup semi-final, first leg away at Birmingham City and he missed just two games after that. He re-joined the Gunners for his second spell in north London ahead of the 1996-97 campaign.

MANAGERS APPOINTED IN THE 1970s

BRIAN CLOUGH

First game in charge: Liverpool (Wembley) 10 August 1974
Last game in charge: Huddersfield Town (A) 10 September 1974
Games: 8
Won: 1
Drawn: 4
Lost: 3

When Revie left for England, he recommended that the board appoint Johnny Giles as the next manager, but to the surprise of everyone in football, they dismissed that idea and appointed one of the White's harshest critics in Brian Howard Clough.

Born in Middlesbrough, Clough played for only two sides, his home-town club and Sunderland, where on 26 December 1962 he collided with Bury goalkeeper Chris Harker and tore his medial and cruciate ligaments in his knee. He did return two years later but was forced to retire at the age of 29. Clough's management career started at Hartlepools United in October 1965, and he asked Peter Taylor, who was at the time managing Burton Albion, to be his assistant. He was initially dismissed just over a year later, but was reinstated after then chairman Ernest Ord was ousted.

In May 1967 Clough joined Derby County, where he would make his name in the game. At the Baseball Ground he won promotion back to the top flight, winning the Second Division title in 1968 and three years later, at the expense of Leeds, won the top-flight title. He originally resigned from the Rams in April 1972, before changing his mind, when then chairman Sam Longson offered Clough and Taylor more money.

On 15 October 1973 he did resign and moved to Brighton & Hove Albion who were in the Third Division. Clough left the Seagulls and joined Leeds United and one of the most tumultuous period's in the club history was about to begin. The first problem was that Taylor did not join him and he had publicly shamed Revie's side, calling them dirty. He also called for Leeds to be relegated due to their poor disciplinary record. Former Derby players John McGovern and John O'Hare joined, along with Duncan McKenzie, but Clough got off to a bad start, losing the Charity Shield on penalties to Liverpool, which saw captain Billy Bremner sent off for fighting with Kevin Keegan and he was banned for 11 games. Things

Brian Clough talking

Champions of England . . . England's hopes for the European Cup . . . a club with a record over the last decade unsurpassed by any other in the history of the game. Leeds United are the most successful club in the country—a club absolutely steeped in that word success.

And that, in a nutshell, is the reason why I simply had to join Leeds United. There were those who said that anyone following in Don Revie's footsteps was on a hiding to nothing. Needless to say I don't look at it that way . . . quite the opposite in fact. It was Leeds' own Chairman who said the day I was appointed manager "Who else could replace Don Revie?"

Don has gone to England and we wish him every possible success. In the archives of the game, he will be remembered for all he did for Leeds United. But now the club has to look to the future—just as England have to look to theirs. And it's the future, not the past, of this great club that directly concerns me.

The day I arrived at Elland Road I stepped onto the pitch and savoured the magnificent ground the club's directors have built over the last ten years. Not only in my opinion but in most other people's this is the finest stadium in the country. Leeds United have overtaken Arsenal—for so long an institution in football—and Manchester United and now have everything the game has to offer—

two

a side at the top of the First Division and a ground fit to match.

Quite obviously, people have asked me just what I'm going to have to do to improve on all this. Improve? I'll have my hands full just maintaining existing playing standards to think about improving them! But if I do want one thing above all for Leeds United it's this . . . I do not think that Leeds United have ever received their just reward both in terms of image and public success that the standards of their ability deserves.

I want to change that. For the first time ever, I want them to be fully accepted for the skill, ability and brilliance they so obviously have. To be the best side in the country is not enough.

Whenever Leeds United have won a trophy or challenged to the last gasp for a competition in the last ten years whether they've been successful or not people have begrudged them their success. For certain reasons they have been criticised and condemned. In my opinion, they have not been a thoroughly popular team.

Now I want supporters everywhere not to have grudging admiration but true admiration. Liverpool, Arsenal and Derby fans, Newcastle, Birmingham and Tottenham fans

would get worse as Leeds lost their first game as champions – 3-0 at Stoke City – and Queens Park Rangers went away with all three points four days later in a 1-0 win at Elland Road. He did achieve his first win thanks to an Allan Clarke winner against Birmingham City but that would prove to be his only league win in charge at Elland Road. After a 1-1 league cup draw away at Huddersfield Town, chairman Manny Cussins called a board meeting and Clough

have all got to accept that Leeds United are the country's best team.

I don't want anyone turning round and 'knocking' us in the future. The next time we win something I want everyone to say that we deserved that win. If we can continue to be successful in style everyone will be delighted. I have already won one First Division Championship with Derby . . . and Derby's win two years ago was a breath of fresh air for the game. Everyone was delighted because we had done it in style and the 'right' way.

For the last decade Leeds have had a team to be proud of . . . but are people really proud deep down? The Leeds team and the Leeds club has had to be sold to the public because what they achieved on the field was not enough to win over the public's hearts. This should not have been necessary. Leeds United should be a British institution like that other great Yorkshire export, roast beef and Yorkshire pudding.

I want us to be recognised for being dour, sincere and honest— with honesty the main factor. I want to embody in Leeds United the characteristics of Yorkshire people . . . dourness with humour, flair and honesty.

I want to be convinced by you, the supporting public that our image is just right—and that means that when we continue to win League Championships the supporters will be turning up in vast numbers to justify our efforts and this great stadium that has been built for you.

The justification for my idealism will come not this season but next season. If at the end of that season I can look back after winning something with a full complement of players I will be able to say that I have succeeded in my efforts to improve our image. I want to be able to fully justify everything we do in that season. I want to be able to say that we didn't have players like Norman Hunter, Allan Clarke and Billy Bremner out of action due to suspensions.

Yes, of course I have my ideas about how this great game of ours should be played. And it is my intention to turn idealism into fact and make Leeds United a truly great club accepted by everyone for the really wonderful side they are.

LEEDS UNITED AFC LTD

President: The Rt. Hon. The Earl of HAREWOOD
Life Vice-Presidents: JOHN H. BROMLEY STANLEY L. BLENKINSOP HARRY L. REYNOLDS
Chairman: MANNY CUSSINS   Vice-Chairman: PERCY A. WOODWARD
Directors: SAM BOLTON ROBERT R. ROBERTS SIDNEY G. SIMON
Team Manager: BRIAN CLOUGH   General Manager/Secretary: KEITH ARCHER
Public Relations Officer: PETER FAY, ELLAND ROAD, LEEDS LS11 0ES tel 715037
Leeds United Information Service: tel 702621/5
Leeds United Magazine and Match Day Programme produced by Charles Harrold Promotions Ltd
Edited by Peter Fay.   Designed by Tony Cieciala.   Photography by Peter Robinson.
Printed by L. M. Lee (Printers) Ltd, Leeds LS6 2TD

three

was gone after just 44 days in charge. The chairman stated 'it was for the good of football,' and Clough responded, 'I think it's a very sad day for football.' Clough later went on Yorkshire Television's *Calendar* programme, where he had a frank and open discussion with presenter Austin Mitchell and former Leeds boss Revie.

He later joined Nottingham Forest, where he won numerous trophies, including the First Division title in 1977-78, the League Cup on four occasions and back-to-back European Cups in 1979 and 1980.

He passed away on 20 September 2004 from cancer. After his death, novelist David Peace wrote about Clough's time at Elland Road in a book titled *The Damned United*. This was turned into a film, in 2009 with Michael Sheen playing Clough.

Brian Clough's first line up: Liverpool (Wembley) 10 August 1974: Harvey, Reaney, Cherry, Bremner, McQueen, Hunter, Lorimer, Clarke (McKenzie), Jordan, Giles, E Gray. Subs not used: Stewart, Yorath, Bates, Cooper.

Brian Clough's last line up: Huddersfield Town (A) 10 September 1974: Harvey, Reaney, Cherry, Bates, Hunter, Lorimer, Clarke, Jordan, Giles, Madeley. Sub not used: McKenzie.

MAURICE LINDLEY (CARETAKER)

First game in charge: Burnley (A) 14 September 1974
Last game in charge: FC Zurich (A) 2 October 1974
Games: 6
Won: 2
Drawn: 1
Lost: 3

Whilst the club searched for a new manager, Maurice Lindley took over on a caretaker basis. Lindley played at Everton as a wing-half before joining Swindon Town as a coach in 1951. He took over as manager when current boss Louis Page was sacked. The Robins finished in 20th in season 1953-54 and he left the club in April 1955. He reappeared as manager at Crewe Alexandra in 1955, but the Railwaymen finished bottom of Division Three North in three consecutive campaigns and he was soon to be sacked. He then teamed up with the great Don Revie and would be caretaker of the club on four occasions (five if you count the time Leeds were looking for a new manager after Revie) when the Whites were looking for a new number one. His first stint in charge

Maurice Lindley talking...

Anyone who believes these are not difficult times for Leeds United is deluding himself. I doubt whether any club has had such internal upheaval at a time when things needed to be as placid and uninterrupted as possible. With not only the domestic competitions to think about but also the highly prestigious European Cup, the club needed to be settled . . . I hope that in the next few weeks we can get back to how things were until the start of this season.

Until the club find a new manager, myself and Syd Owen are handling the team. Obviously the onus is on us to make sure the players are not only superbly fit, but in exactly the right frame of mind to pick up the traces once again . . . and we hope that we will have got back to something like the form of last year by the time the next manager is appointed.

Syd is responsible for the training —myself for the administration. We have to work closely together in an effort to recapture the necessary cohesion—and if the players have managed to throw off the tensions and pressures of the last few weeks then there is no reason why we shouldn't get back on the right lines; lines that brought the club an incredible amount of success.

It is true to say that we have reverted to the methods and detailed planning that proved so successful in the past. These are tried and tested methods and

two

they're based on hard work, dedication and application.

There is no doubt that in the first few weeks of the season, the missing ingredient in Leeds United's play was the arrogance which makes men into Champions. Over the years, these players have built up a supreme belief in their capabilities. They truly believed before every game that it was not possible for them to be beaten. They believed that their team spirit and brilliant individual skills were more than a match for anything the other team could throw at them.

Leeds United have been so successful because the players had these beliefs. What we have got to do is reinstate those beliefs into every player. Difficult ? Well, it can be done. There is no reason why not. The critics would have it that Leeds United have gone back, are no longer the side that won so many honours.

How can that be true ? No team of Champions can lose everything that took them to the Championship in the space of a few months—and forget it ever existed. How can a side that went an unbelieveable 29 games without defeat—a feat that will never be equalled in the future—suddenly go back ?

Take it from me, Leeds United still have that ability. The confidence which helped to engender the form of last season has not really been evident in recent weeks . . . but I see no reason why it should not return quickly.

Given a little time, these players will soon recapture their old arrogance and supreme belief in their ability. They have been subject to pressures, anxieties and tensions in recent weeks and, at the best of times, those sort of pressures are not good. Coming at the time they did, it was not surprising we have not seen the true Leeds United this season. Now is the time to get the recent events out of their systems. To recapture the freedom of open minds which should see them re-emerge as the country's leading club.

And, of course, I have no doubt that they will re-emerge. Never have I known a team of players with such character and dedication —quite apart from very special skills. These qualities will start to show again as the pressures blow away.

But we all know that it is going to take dedication and effort from everyone in the club to overcome the traumas of recent weeks. All our players and all our staff will be working hard to re-establish a new platform for success with the full support of the board of directors.

We are, of course, a little short staffed behind the scenes now. Syd Owen, apart from his duties with me, has to run the coaching side not only for the first team

of the side came when the club dispensed of Clough and he had a mixed spell, winning two – 4-1 at home to FC Zurich in the European Cup, 5-1 at home to Sheffield United – drawing a League Cup replay at home to Huddersfield Town and losing the other three away to Burnley (1-2), away to Everton (2-3) and away to FC Zurich. 'Gentleman' Jimmy Armfield was then appointed the next Leeds United manager.

but for the two other teams as well. But Cyril Partridge has been a tower of support and without his help we could have been in difficulties.

Bob English is the only qualified 'medico' on the staff... so he's not only had to treat injuries and run a busy treatment room but also be with the first team on match days. He, too, has had a very busy time and again, has been doing a truly invaluable job.

Through Chief Scout Tony Collins we've also kept our scouting system ticking over nicely. So all the backroom staff are pulling together and showing a team spirit of their own to help us through until the new manager arrives.

And talking of team spirit, the players have shown new depths of loyalty and dedication. I would not be telling the truth if I said that the team spirit did not take a knock during the last few weeks through the uncertainty that was caused by the various internal and external pressures.

But the signs are encouraging. I can already see a return to the sort of attitude we showed last season. At Burnley last week, against Zurich and against Sheffield United the signs were obvious that things are beginning to slot together again.

The players only need a little more self confidence to put the whole pattern right.

So until the new manager arrives, we're keeping things going in the way they always have—a way that has brought the club untold success. I see it as my task to carry things through and re-establish a sound basis which the new manager will find necessary. With your continued support, we can forget the early days of this season and once again hold our heads high. I, for one, am sure it can be done.

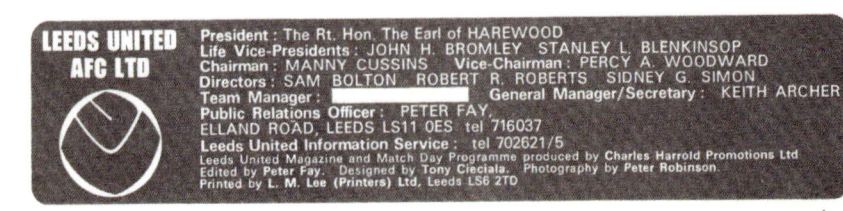

LEEDS UNITED AFC LTD
President: The Rt. Hon. The Earl of HAREWOOD
Life Vice-Presidents: JOHN H. BROMLEY STANLEY L. BLENKINSOP
Chairman: MANNY CUSSINS Vice-Chairman: PERCY A. WOODWARD
Directors: SAM BOLTON ROBERT R. ROBERTS SIDNEY G. SIMON
Team Manager: General Manager/Secretary: KEITH ARCHER
Public Relations Officer: PETER FAY,
ELLAND ROAD, LEEDS LS11 0ES tel 716037
Leeds United Information Service: tel 702621/5
Leeds United Magazine and Match Day Programme produced by Charles Harrold Promotions Ltd
Edited by Peter Fay. Designed by Tony Cieciala. Photography by Peter Robinson.
Printed by L. M. Lee (Printers) Ltd, Leeds LS6 2TD

three

Maurice Lindley's first line up: Burnley (A) 14 September 1974: Harvey, Reaney, Cherry, Yorath, McQueen, Hunter, Lorimer, Clarke, Jordan, Giles, Madeley. Sub not used: Cooper.

Maurice Lindley's last line up: FC Zurich (A) 2 October 1974: Harvey, Reaney, Cherry, Yorath, Madeley, Hunter, Lorimer, Clarke, Jordan, Bates, F. Gray (Hampton). Subs not used: Stewart, Stevenson, Giles, McKenzie.

JIMMY ARMFIELD

First game in charge: Arsenal (H) 2 October 1978
Last game in charge: Queens Park Rangers (A) 29 April 1978
Games: 194
Won: 88
Drawn: 47
Lost: 59

Following the Brian Clough experiment, Leeds turned to former Blackpool hero Jimmy Armfield. Born in Denton in Lancashire, his family moved to the seaside town during World War Two. He was spotted in a practice match by then Blackpool manager Joe Smith and he made his league debut for the Tangerines on 27 December 1954 away at Portsmouth. He would go on to establish himself as the club's first-choice right-back and his stint at Bloomfield Road would see Armfield become the club's record appearance holder. He was voted the Young Player of the Year in 1959. Seven years later he only just lost out to Bobby Charlton for the prestigious Footballer of the Year award, but did win the Blackpool Player of the Year award. He was rewarded for his excellent displays with 43 England caps and was called up to the victorious World Cup squad, but he missed the tournament through injury.

His first steps into management came at Lancashire rivals Bolton Wanderers, leading them to promotion to the Second Division as Third Division champions. He then joined Leeds and, following an atrocious start to the 1974-75 campaign, results started to improve, and by the end of February, following a 3-1 win over Carlisle United at Elland Road, Leeds were up to sixth place.

Jimmy Armfield talking...

A fortnight ago, while Leeds United were carrying England's flag in the European Cup in Switzerland, I was pacing the rooms of my home in Blackpool trying to decide whether or not to become the next manager at Elland Road. It was one of the most difficult weeks of my life. Decisions of such a nature are always hard to make.

You see, I was very happy at Bolton Wanderers. We had a good staff, a great bunch of players, good directors and a good club. Things were just starting to move on the right lines at Burnden Park. I had been approached before for other vacant managerial seats with top clubs and had turned them down because I thought there was just as bright a future at Bolton.

This time it was different. To say I felt flattered that Leeds United had approached me would be an understatement. This club's record of success over the last decade has been staggering. They are one of the biggest names not only in England but in Europe and possibly even the world. This was what I had to try and emulate.

So while United were playing Zurich, I thought over everything ... and the day after they returned I was ready to give my decision. How could I possibly refuse ? You might think that most managers would bite the hand off anyone who offered them one of the game's top jobs. But I was not going to be rushed into deciding. To make any decision, let alone an on-the-spot one, is one of the hardest things in life when the job two

concerned is so major and prestigious.

Money had nothing to do with it for I was quite content with life at Bolton. Ambition would be a better word. So why did I accept the job ? Mainly because of United's astonishingly successful record over the last ten years—coupled with the fact that this is such a good club.

Of course I'd heard stories about 'player power' and dressing room unrest and the advice going round that the Elland Road dressing room was no place for any outsider. But if you listen to all the stories you hear going the rounds in football and believe them, you'd go mad.

In any case, I certainly found some of the tales I heard hard to take. How could players who had been so loyal, so dedicated, so successful, suddenly be talked about in the light of left wing reactionaries ? My attitude is this —every man unto himself. All we managers are different—we all have our different ideas. Our job is to pass on these ideas and do the things we are there to do—after all, that's why we're in the job in the first place. It's an old managerial cliche that we stand or fall by results—but it's true.

The first few days at Elland Road seemed to be a blur. I met the players for the first time over lunch before the Arsenal game a fortnight ago, officially took over the following Monday, then sat down to try and absorb everything that goes to make up this great club. Syd Owen and Maurice Lindley did a wonderful job in the period between managers and, together with our Chief Scout Tony Collins, they've been telling me all there is to know about the set-up.

I see the club's priority as winning League points. After the difficult start to the season your priorities have got to be that—but if we can stay clear of injuries we'll be going out to try and capture a bit of the icing on soccer's cake too. We're still in the European and League Cups—and the FA Cup is still to come.

I'm very aware that the eyes of the British Isles will be on us when we travel to Hungary on Tuesday in an effort to go a step further in the European Cup. It is important for British football—particularly now Celtic are out—that we do well. But it would be wrong to classify our priorities. Priorities come along every week. We must

They finished the season in ninth place, but Armfield achieved something that his predecessor Revie had not done, by reaching the European Cup Final against Bayern Munich, the pinnacle of the European game. Sadly for Armfield and the club, the Germans won 2-0 in a controversial game in Paris, in which former boss Don Revie watched on from the BBC commentary box. Sadly for Leeds, the game would be remembered for the rioting of the Leeds fans in the aftermath.

With no European football to look forward to, Revie's side started to break up, with the sales of Cooper, Giles, Bremner, Hunter and Yorath. Armfield did bring in Brian Flynn

take each game as it comes on its merits.

This is a taxing period for us. In the next five weeks we have to play nine games—mostly in the First Division but two in Europe and a League Cup tie. We must think in terms of doing our best at all times no matter who we're playing or what competition. But a swollen fixture schedule like that puts everyone—particularly the players and manager—under great pressure.

The sort of pressure I'm talking about is new to me—but these players have seen it all before and know better than anyone what to expect. I am sure they are capable of doing good things again just as they have in the past decade.

I've been very impressed with the set-up at Elland Road. It was a talking point throughout football that Don Revie and his staff had done a first class job here. Even things like having the training ground so close are important.

But with a long hard winter ahead, our hope is to stay clear of serious injury problems. Leeds United, even in their Second Division days, have always had an immensely strong first team squad. If these players can remain free from injury they can start to take us out of the woods into the sunlight.

Is it a problem inheriting such a set-up? When standards have been set so high it is bound to be a problem in just living up to them. As manager here, I will tackle things with honesty and integrity. Doing the right things will be important.

And by that I mean this... we must present the right image to the people not only of Leeds but of England. They are very much part of this club—without them there would have been no successful Leeds United, no flow of trophies to our cabinets. I've been very well received by the players and it's now up to us all to go on from there.

The critics who seem to delight in taking a swipe at Leeds United can take a rest. The most important thing is that people are talking about us. Only when you're a club who no one ever mentions do you start to worry. Publicity and talk is good for the club—that's why the right sort of relationship with the public and the press is so important.

These are relationships we intend to foster and cultivate in the months and years to come. Take it from me, there's still a lot more to be won at Leeds United—and we're going to try and win it.

LEEDS UNITED AFC LTD
President: The Rt. Hon. The Earl of HAREWOOD
Life Vice-Presidents: JOHN H. BROMLEY   STANLEY L. BLENKINSOP
Chairman: MANNY CUSSINS   Vice-Chairman: PERCY A. WOODWARD
Directors: SAM BOLTON   ROBERT R. ROBERTS   SIDNEY G. SIMON
Team Manager: JIMMY ARMFIELD   General Manager/Secretary: KEITH ARCHER
Public Relations Officer: PETER FAY,
ELLAND ROAD, LEEDS LS11 0ES   tel 716037
Leeds United Information Service: tel 702621/5
Leeds United Magazine and Match Day Programme produced by Charles Harrold Promotions Ltd
Edited by Peter Fay.   Designed by Tony Cieciala.   Photography by Peter Robinson.
Printed by L. M. Lee (Printers) Ltd, Leeds LS6 2TD

three

and Ray Hankin from Burnley, Tony Currie from Sheffield United and Arthur Graham from Aberdeen. Leeds finished the 1975-76 season in a respectable fifth position, though did suffer shock defeats in both cup competitions to Notts County in the League Cup and Crystal Palace in the FA Cup. The following campaign saw the Whites finish in tenth place, their lowest placing since winning the Second Division in 1964, though the side did reach the last four of the FA Cup. In front of 55,000 fans at Hillsborough, Manchester United reached Wembley thanks to goals from Steve Coppell and former Leeds United player Jimmy

Greenhoff. Allan Clarke did pull one back for the Whites, but it was the Red Devils who reached the final.

The following year saw Leeds finish in ninth place and again reach the last four of a cup competition. This time it would be the League Cup and a certain Brian Clough. Forest won the first leg 3-1 at Elland Road, Eddie Gray scoring for the home side and Forest reached Wembley following a 4-2 win at the City Ground two weeks later. Armfield was dismissed at the end of that campaign and worked in the media, first as a journalist at the *Daily Express* and as an expert summariser for BBC Radio Five Live. He sadly passed away at the age of 82 on 22 January 2018 following a battle with cancer.

Jimmy Armfield's first line up: Arsenal (H) 5 October 1974: Harvey, Reaney, Cooper (Bates), Yorath, McQueen, Hunter, Lorimer, McKenzie, Jordan, Giles, Madeley.

Jimmy Armfield's last line up: Queens Park Rangers (A) 29 April 1978: Harvey, Madeley, F. Gray, Flynn, Hart, Cherry, E. Gray, Hankin, Clarke, Currie, Graham. Sub not used: Stevenson.

MAURICE LINDLEY (CARETAKER)

First game in charge: Arsenal (A) 19 August 1978
Last game in charge: Arsenal (A) 19 August 1978
Games: 1
Won: 0
Drawn: 1
Lost: 0

Lindley took the role as caretaker for a second time at the start of the 1978-79 before the arrival of Jock Stein, though he did pick the team against Manchester United four days later.

Maurice Lindley's first line up: Arsenal (A) 19 August 1978: Harvey, Madeley, F. Gray, Flynn, Madeley, Harris, Hankin, E. Gray, Currie, Graham. Sub not used: Stevenson.

Maurice Lindley's last line up: Arsenal (A) 19 August 1978: Harvey, Madeley, F. Gray, Flynn, Madeley, Harris, Hankin, E. Gray, Currie, Graham. Sub not used: Stevenson.

JOCK STEIN OBE

First game in charge: Manchester United (H) 23 August 1978
Last game in charge: West Bromwich Albion (Maine Road) 2 October 1978
Games: 10
Won: 4
Drawn: 3
Lost: 3

After the dismissal of the likeable Armfield, Leeds turned to one of football's greats as their next manager in Scotsman Jock Stein. Stein who was born in Burnbank, Lanarkshire, started work as a coalminer and played part time for Blantrye Victoria and then Albion Rovers.

He then moved to Llanelli Town in Wales before joining Celtic in 1951. He retired from playing in 1957 and rejoined the Glasgow side as manager of the reserve side. His first job managing a first team would be at Dunfermline Athletic in March 1960, where Stein led them to Scottish Cup glory in 1961.

He joined Hibernian in March 1964, but he left for a return to Celtic as the main man. He became the club's fourth-ever manager and would win ten championships (nine in consecutive years), eight Scottish Cups and six Scottish League Cups. He led Celtic to the European Cup Final in 1967 and defeated Italian giants Inter Milan in Lisbon, thanks to goals from Tommy Gemmell and Stevie Chalmers. He did it again with Celtic in 1970, beating Leeds in the semi-finals, but lost to Feyenoord in the final.

He was nearly killed in a car crash in 1975 but returned to management at the start of the 1976-77 season. After Celtic struggled in season 1977-78, Stein was persuaded to stand down. He nominated his successor, Billy McNeil and in August 1978 was appointed manager of Leeds United, succeeding Jimmy Armfield. Stein had been a long-time friend of Don Revie. His first game in charge was a 3-2 defeat at home to Manchester United, but he recorded his first win three days later in a 3-0 home win against Wolverhampton Wanderers. Stein backed this up with another 3-0 win, this time away at Chelsea thanks to a brace from new arrival John Hawley, but then took only one point from the next six available, losing 3-0 at Manchester City, 2-1 at home to Tottenham Hotspur (in a game featured on *Match of the Day*) and a 0-0 draw at Coventry City. His side did bounce back with a 3-0 win over Birmingham City and a 1-0 League Cup replay win over West Bromwich Albion, but after 44 days just like Clough, he was gone accepting the Scotland job and Leeds were looking for another manager. Tragedy struck Stein on 10 September 1985 when he suffered from a heart attack at the end of a World Cup qualifier against Wales at Ninian Park and he died shortly afterwards in the stadium's medical room. He was 62 years old.

THE JOCK STEIN COLUMN

"I am a man who likes challenges and with the co-operation of all concerned I am sure we can re-establish United as the major power in League football again."

I have always looked on Leeds United as one of the big clubs in Britain and Europe. That was one of the main reasons that I made the decision to leave another club in the same category — Celtic — to take on the manager's job at Elland Road and I am delighted to have this early opportunity of setting out some of my aims this evening.

In the past few seasons I have been a fairly frequent visitor to Elland Road and I remember, of course, the epic games Celtic had against United in the European Cup a few years ago so I do not think I am a complete stranger to Leeds.

I have always been an admirer of the way United play and my immediate target is to maintain this pattern. There will be no sudden or dramatic changes. I want to get the feel of things here as quickly as possible and any changes will be carried out gradually rather than in a matter of a few days. Without setting out any targets that cannot be reached, my aim is to build up to the success level that United are associated with and if I did not think that this was possible then I would not have taken on the job.

It will be a challenge but I am a man who likes challenges and I am sure that, with the co-operation and backing of all concerned, we can re-establish Leeds United as the major power in League football once again.

I took the opportunity of watching the side at Arsenal on Saturday and I liked what I saw. I was also at the reserves match at Bramall Lane last night and I want to get to know everyone on the staff just as quickly as possible.

I have always demanded a hundred per cent effort and dedication from all the players I have worked with and I am sure that I will receive this at Elland Road. But I also want to establish a close contact with you, the supporters of Leeds United because you have a very important part to play in the future. I intend to go out of my way to meet as many of you as I can and I am sure that we can all work together to get United back where I believe they belong — at the forefront of British football.

I could not have wished for a better game than tonight's against Manchester United with which to start my career at Elland Road. I know all the lads can count on your full backing this evening and in the future.

LEEDS UNITED AFC
Elland Road
Leeds LS11 0ES
Tel: Leeds 716037
Information Service:
Leeds 702621/5

President:
The Rt. Hon. The Earl of Harewood
Chairman: Manny Cussins
Directors:
Rayner Barker, M.C.I.T., M.B.I.M.,
Jack Marjason,
R. Brian Roberts, J.P., F.I.O.B.,
Robert R. Roberts,
Sidney G. Simon,
Brian Woodward
Assistant Manager: Maurice Lindley
General Manager/Secretary:
Keith Archer
Commercial Manager: Mike Lockwood

Manny Cussins *Chairman*

Rayner Barker — Jack Marjason
R. Brian Roberts — Robert R. Roberts
Sidney G. Simon — Brian Woodward

Leeds United Match Day Programme
Published by Leeds United A.F.C.
Edited by Bob Baldwin
Printed by Hemmings, Ireton Avenue, Leicester
Cover Man... United's 'Flying Scot' Arthur Graham in action against Nottingham Forest. Barrett is the Forest man trying to stop Graham.

Jock Stein's first line up: Manchester United (H) 23 August 1978: Harvey, Stevenson, F. Gray, Flynn, Hart, Madeley, Harris, Hankin, E. Gray, Currie, Graham. Sub not used: Hampton.

Jock Stein's last line up: West Bromwich Albion (N★) 2 October 1978: Harvey, Stevenson, Cherry, Flynn, Hart, Madeley, Thomas (Lorimer), Hankin, E. Gray, F. Gray, Graham.

(N★) – Played at Maine Road

MAURICE LINDLEY (CARETAKER)

First game in charge: Bolton Wanderers (A) 7 October 1978
Last game in charge: Norwich City (A) 21 October 1978
Games: 4
Won: 1
Drawn: 1
Lost: 2

Following Stein's decision to accept the Scottish national job, Lindley was asked to take the role for a third time that season. His tenure lasted four games, in which the side lost 3-1 at Bolton Wanderers, beat Sheffield United 4-1 in a League Cup tie at Elland Road, lost 3-1 at home to West Bromwich Albion and drew 2-2 away at Norwich City.

Maurice Lindley's first line up: Bolton Wanderers (A) 7 October 1978: Harvey, Stevenson, F. Gray, Flynn, Hart, Madeley, Harris, Hankin, E. Gray, Cherry, Graham. Sub not used: Thomas.

Maurice Lindley's last line up: Norwich City (A) 21 October 1978: Harvey, Cherry, F. Gray, Flynn, Hart, Madeley, E. Gray, Hankin, Hawley, Currie, Graham: Subs not used: Parker.

"It's important that we start improving our results at home beginning this afternoon against Derby."

It is difficult to explain why we have been struggling for consistency at home this season and I don't think anyone can put a finger on one reason in particular. We may have become too anxious in some games and against West Bromwich Albion a fortnight ago we pushed so many players forward from midfield later on that we left ourselves open for the counter attack and suffered in the end.

It's important that we start improving our results at Elland Road and we can only do this by applying ourselves to the job at hand beginning this afternoon against Derby.

Our attitude at Norwich last Saturday was right and although the game overall did not rise to any great heights and was very fierce at times, I thought that we certainly did enough to take a point.

We had the edge in the first half but after half time the game evened itself out and Norwich threw everything at us towards the end.

Our second goal was a little bit freakish but I think John Hawley must be given full credit for being on the spot and alert when other players might have been slow to react.

It was unfortunate that we then got caught by a free kick. I think we thought it was safe but Martin Peters put it away at the far post from a position where he has always been a danger with his ability to ghost in almost unnoticed.

The Norwich game was Tony Currie's first League match as skipper after taking over from Trevor Cherry but I don't think we will see Tony's full influence as captain until he is completely a hundred per cent fit.

A MESSAGE FROM JIMMY ADAMSON

"I am delighted to have been appointed manager at Elland Road for Leeds United are one of the big clubs in football. I don't believe in setting targets but my aim has always been to try to produce a side that plays skilful football, one I believe that is attractive for spectators.

"Supporters are important to every club and I have always believed in a close relationship with fans. I look forward to this at Elland Road and I ask you to give the players your full backing beginning this afternoon."

JIMMY ADAMSON

First game in charge: Derby County (H) 28 October 1978
Last game in charge: Stoke City (A) 6 September 1980
Games: 94
Won: 34
Drawn: 28
Lost: 32

Following Stein's decision to take the Scotland job and Lindley yet again taking the job on an interim period, Leeds turned to a man who was once offered the England job before Sir Alf Ramsey, appointing Ashington-born Jimmy Adamson. He turned professional with Burnley on New Year's Day 1947 and went on to became one of the Clarets' all-time greats. He was an ever-present as the side won the First Division title in season 1959-60 and captained the side in the 1962 FA Cup Final against Tottenham Hotspur, which they lost 3-1. He did have personal glory to celebrate as he was named Footballer of the Year that same year. He retired from the playing side of the game in 1964 and joined the coaching staff at Turf Moor. He was

JIMMY ADAMSON

LEEDS UNITED AFC
Elland Road
Leeds LS11 0ES
Tel: Leeds 716037
Information Service:
Leeds 702621/5

President:
The Rt. Hon. The Earl of Harewood
Chairman: Manny Cussins
Directors:
Rayner Barker, M.C.I.T., M.B.I.M.,
Jack Marjason,
R. Brian Roberts, J.P., F.I.O.B.,
Robert R. Roberts,
Sidney G. Simon,
Brian Woodward

Team Manager: Jimmy Adamson
Assistant Manager: Maurice Lindley
General Manager/Secretary: Keith Archer
Commercial Manager: Mike Lockwood

Manny Cussins
Chairman

Rayner Barker   Jack Marjason

R. Brian Roberts   Robert R. Roberts

Sidney G. Simon   Brian Woodward

Leeds United Match Day Programme
Published by Leeds United A.F.C.
Edited by Bob Baldwin
Printed by Hemmings, Ireton Avenue, Leicester
Designed by Bernard Gallagher
Cover Man . . . Paul Madeley, one of United's stars in last week's outstanding performance at Liverpool.

"From what I've seen so far, the club has the right quality of players to challenge for honours . . ."

United supporters have been used to seeing the side challenging for honours over the years and from what I have seen since coming to Elland Road, the club has the right quality of players to be there or thereabouts at the end of the season.

I was especially pleased with the way the side performed at Anfield last week. They showed a lot of character and played without any sign of fear against a Liverpool side that had a hundred per cent home record in the League before our visit.

We were unfortunate in my view not to take both points and those who claimed that Liverpool did not play particularly well were being a little unfair on United's performance.

Referees seem to have been very much in the news again recently. Some people have advocated League referees going full-time but this is something I have never believed in. All the men on the League list know the Laws of the Game inside out and are physically fit, otherwise they would not be on the list.

There's a lot of pressure on them though and the presence of an assessor sitting in the stands at every League game only adds to this pressure in my opinion.

The relationship that exists between referees, managers and players is at its lowest ebb since I have been in football and I do not think some of my fellow managers help by commenting publicly on a referee's performance after a game as this can only inflame the situation.

David Stewart left Elland Road recently and moved on to West Bromwich Albion and on behalf of everyone at the club I would wish David well with Albion, apart from when they play United of course!

In saying goodbye and good luck to David I would also like to welcome Henry Smith, a young 'keeper who joined United last week. We all hope that Henry has a successful career at Elland Road.

We were delighted with the good result in the League Cup at Queens Park Rangers on Tuesday. The League Cup is an important competition with a place in next year's UEFA Cup for the winners and on a personal note I have always fancied leading a side out at Wembley as manager. There is still some way to go before we can think in terms of a Wembley appearance next March and our main priority this afternoon must be a win against Arsenal to help our climb up the table.

Walter Winterbottom's assistant in the 1962 World Cup and was offered the job but turned it down to stay as part of the backroom staff at Burnley.

When Harry Potts was made general manager, Adamson became the new manager, and despite being relegated in his first season they won the Second Division in 1973. He left in January 1976 before being appointed manager of Dutch side Sparta Rotterdam. He left the following month and took over at Sunderland in November 1976, but he couldn't stop the Mackems being relegated to the Second Division. He left Sunderland to take over at Elland Road and his first game couldn't have gone any better as his new side defeated Derby County 4-1, with goals coming from Brian Flynn, Paul Hart, Ray Hankin and John Hawley. In his first season at the club, Adamson led the club to a League Cup semi-final, but following a 2-2 draw in the first leg against Southampton at Elland Road, a goal from Terry Curran took the Saints to Wembley. Leeds had missed out on a trip to Wembley in each of the last three seasons. Adamson did, however, lead the club back into Europe following a fifth-place finish, but the likes of Frank Gray, John Hawley and Tony Currie were all sold. Although he did bring in Alan Curtis, who scored a brace on his debut against Bristol City, Brian Greenhoff from Manchester United and Derek Parlane from Rangers.

The 1979-80 season proved to be a disaster for both Leeds and Adamson, and following a 5-1 loss at Everton the team found themselves in 19th place in the First Division. They did recover to finish in 11th place and end Manchester United's title challenge with a 2-0 win over the Red Devils on the final day. Crowds suffered and after a 0-0 draw against Coventry City, played in front of only 16,967, the lowest in 17 years, demonstrations ensued. Adamson saw it out but the pressure was on from the off ahead of the new season, and despite the signing of Alex Sabella from Sheffield United, Adamson was gone following a 3-0 loss at Stoke City which saw Leeds in last place in the First Division.

He subsequently retired from football and lived back in Burnley. He died aged 82 on 8 November 2011.

Jimmy Adamson's first line up: Derby County (H) 28 October 1978: Harvey, Cherry, F. Gray, Flynn, Hart, Madeley, E. Gray, Hankin, Hawley, Currie, Graham. Sub not used: Stevenson.

Jimmy Adamson's line up: Stoke City (A) 6 September 1980: Lukic, Cherry, Greenhoff, Flynn, Hart, Madeley (Harris), Parlane, Hamson, Connor, Sabella, Graham.

DIVISION ONE   **1970–71**

Date	Opposition	Competition	Score
15/08/1970	Manchester United	Division One	1-0
19/08/1970	Tottenham Hotspur	Division One	2-0
22/08/1970	Everton	Division One	3-2
26/08/1970	West Ham United	Division One	3-0
29/08/1970	Burnley	Division One	3-0
01/09/1970	Arsenal	Division One	0-0
05/09/1970	Chelsea	Division One	1-0
08/09/1970	Sheffield United	League Cup 2nd Round	0-1
12/09/1970	Stoke City	Division One	0-3
15/09/1970	Sarpsborg	Inter Cities Fairs Cup 1st Round 1st Leg	1-0
19/09/1970	Southampton	Division One	1-0
26/09/1970	Nottingham Forest	Division One	0-0
29/09/1970	Sarpsborg	Inter Cities Fairs Cup 1st Round 2nd Leg	5-0
03/10/1970	Huddersfield Town	Division One	2-0
10/10/1970	West Bromwich Albion	Division One	2-2
17/10/1970	Manchester United	Division One	2-2
21/10/1970	Dynamo Dresden	Inter Cities Fairs Cup 2nd Round 1st Leg	1-0
24/10/1970	Derby County	Division One	2-0
31/10/1970	Coventry City	Division One	2-0
04/11/1970	Dynamo Dresden	Inter Cities Fairs Cup 2nd Round 2nd Leg	1-2
07/11/1970	Crystal Palace	Division One	1-1
14/11/1970	Blackpool	Division One	3-1
18/11/1970	Stoke City	Division One	4-1
21/11/1970	Wolverhamtpon Wanderers	Division One	3-2
28/11/1970	Manchester City	Division One	1-0
02/12/1970	Sparta Prague	Inter Cities Fairs Cup 3rd Round 1st Leg	6-0
05/12/1970	Liverpool	Division One	1-1
09/12/1970	Sparta Prague	Inter Cities Fairs Cup 3rd Round 2nd Leg	3-2
12/12/1970	Ipswich Town	Division One	0-0
19/12/1970	Everton	Division One	1-0
26/12/1970	Newcastle United	Division One	3-0
09/01/1971	Tottenham Hotspur	Division One	1-2
11/01/1971	Rotherham United	FA Cup 3rd Round	0-0
16/01/1971	West Ham United	Division One	3-2
18/01/1971	Rotherham United	FA Cup 3rd Round Replay	3-2
23/01/1971	Swindon Town	FA Cup 4th Round	4-0
30/01/1971	Manchester City	Division One	2-0
06/02/1971	Liverpool	Division One	0-1
13/02/1971	Colchester United	FA Cup 5th Round	2-3
20/02/1971	Wolverhamtpon Wanderers	Division One	3-0
23/02/1971	Ipswich Town	Division One	4-2
26/02/1971	Coventry City	Division One	1-0
06/03/1971	Derby County	Division One	1-0
10/03/1971	Vitoria Setubal	Inter Cities Fairs Cup QF 1st Leg	2-1
13/03/1971	Blackpool	Division One	1-1
20/03/1971	Crystal Palace	Division One	2-1
24/03/1971	Vitoria Setubal	Inter Cities Fairs Cup QF 2nd Leg	1-1
27/03/1971	Chelsea	Division One	1-3
03/04/1971	Burnley	Division One	4-0
10/04/1971	Newcastle United	Division One	1-1
12/04/1971	Huddersfield Town	Division One	0-0
14/04/1971	Liverpool	Inter Cities Fairs Cup SF 1st Leg	1-0
17/04/1971	West Bromwich Albion	Division One	1-2
24/04/1971	Southampton	Division One	3-0
26/04/1971	Arsenal	Division One	1-0
28/04/1971	Liverpool	Inter Cities Fairs Cup SF 2nd Leg	0-0
01/05/1971	Nottingham Forest	Division One	2-0
28/05/1971	Juventus	Inter Cities Fairs Cup Final 1st Leg	2-2
03/06/1971	Juventus	Inter Cities Fairs Cup Final 2nd Leg	1-1

Team	Pld	W	D	L	GF	GA	Pts
Arsenal	42	29	7	6	71	29	65
Leeds United	42	27	10	5	72	30	64
Tottenham Hotspur	42	19	14	9	54	33	52
Wolverhampton W	42	22	8	12	64	54	52
Liverpool	42	17	17	8	42	24	51
Chelsea	42	18	15	9	52	42	51
Southampton	42	17	12	13	56	44	46
Manchester United	42	16	11	15	65	66	43
Derby County	42	16	10	16	56	54	42
Coventry City	42	16	10	16	37	38	42
Manchester City	42	12	17	13	47	42	41
Newcastle United	42	14	13	15	44	46	41
Stoke City	42	12	13	17	44	48	37
Everton	42	12	13	17	54	60	37
Huddersfield Town	42	11	14	17	40	49	36
Nottingham Forest	42	14	8	20	42	61	36
West Bromwich Albion	42	10	15	17	58	75	35
Crystal Palace	42	12	11	19	39	57	35
Ipswich Town	42	12	10	20	42	48	34
West Ham United	42	10	14	18	47	60	34
Burnley	42	7	13	22	29	63	27
Blackpool	42	4	15	23	34	66	23

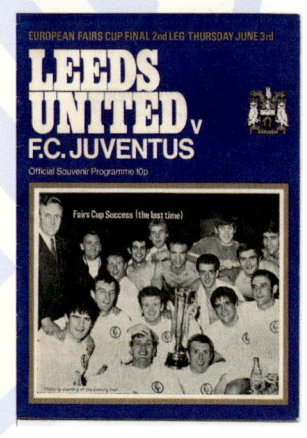

Just the one debutant in season 1970-71, Joe Jordan who was signed from Morton.

Billy Bremner and Johnny Giles shared the captaincy, with Giles taking over when Bremner missed out.

The first leg of the Inter Cities Fairs Cup tie at home to Sarpsborg saw unused sub appearances for Paul Peterson, Bobby Rutherford and Keith M. Edwards.

Norman Hunter and Paul Madeley topped the appearance charts with 58 each.

When Allan Clarke scored four goals at home to Burnley, he became the first Leeds player to do so in a league game since John Charles at home to Notts County on 19 August 1953.

1971–72

DIVISION ONE

Team	Pld	W	D	L	GF	GA	Pts
Derby County	42	24	10	8	69	33	58
Leeds United	42	24	9	9	73	31	57
Liverpool	42	24	9	9	64	30	57
Manchester City	42	23	11	8	77	45	57
Arsenal	42	22	8	12	58	40	52
Tottenham Hotspur	42	19	13	10	63	42	51
Chelsea	42	18	12	12	58	49	48
Manchester United	42	19	10	13	69	61	48
Wolverhampton W	42	18	11	13	65	57	47
Sheffield United	42	17	12	13	61	60	46
Newcastle United	42	15	11	16	49	52	41
Leicester City	42	13	13	16	41	46	39
Ipswich Town	42	11	16	15	39	53	38
West Ham United	42	12	12	18	47	51	36
Everton	42	9	18	15	37	48	36
West Bromwich Albion	42	12	11	19	42	54	35
Stoke City	42	10	15	17	39	56	35
Coventry City	42	9	15	18	44	67	33
Southampton	42	12	7	23	52	80	31
Crystal Palace	42	8	13	21	39	65	29
Nottingham Forest	42	8	9	25	47	81	25
Huddersfield Town	42	6	13	23	27	59	25

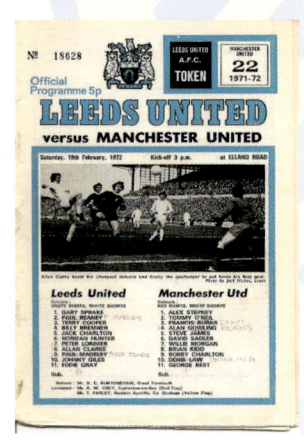

Date	Opposition	Competition	Score
14/08/1971	Manchester City	Division One	1-0
17/08/1971	Sheffield United	Division One	0-3
21/08/1971	Wolverhampton Wanderers	Division One at Leeds Road	0-0
25/08/1971	Tottenham Hotspur	Division One at Boothferry Park	1-1
28/08/1971	Ipswich Town	Division One	2-0
01/09/1971	Newcastle United	Division One at Hillsborough	5-1
04/09/1971	Crystal Palace	Division One at Leeds Road	2-0
08/09/1971	Derby County	League Cup 2nd Round	0-0
11/09/1971	Arsenal	Division One	0-2
15/09/1971	Lierse	UEFA Cup 1st Round 1st Leg	2-0
18/09/1971	Liverpool	Division One	1-0
22/09/1971	Barcelona	Inter Cities Fairs Cup Play Off	1-2
25/09/1971	Huddersfield Town	Division One	1-2
27/09/1971	Derby County	League Cup 2nd Round Replay	2-0
29/09/1971	Lierse	UEFA Cup 1st Round 2nd Leg	0-4
02/10/1971	West Ham United	Division One	0-0
06/10/1971	West Ham United	League Cup 3rd Round	0-0
09/10/1971	Coventry City	Division One	1-3
16/10/1971	Manchester City	Division One	3-0
20/10/1971	West Ham United	League Cup 3rd Round Replay	0-1
23/10/1971	Everton	Division One	3-2
30/10/1971	Manchester United	Division One	1-0
06/11/1971	Leicester City	Division One	2-1
13/11/1971	Southampton	Division One	1-2
20/11/1971	Stoke City	Division One	1-0
27/11/1971	Nottingham Forest	Division One	2-0
04/12/1971	West Bromwich Albion	Division One	3-0
11/12/1971	Chelsea	Division One	0-0
18/12/1971	Crystal Palace	Division One	1-1
27/12/1971	Derby County	Division One	3-0
01/01/1972	Liverpool	Division One	2-0
08/01/1972	Ipswich Town	Division One	2-2
15/01/1972	Bristol Rovers	FA Cup 3rd Round	4-1
22/01/1972	Sheffield United	Division One	1-0
29/01/1972	Tottenham Hotspur	Division One	0-1
05/02/1972	Liverpool	FA Cup 4th Round	0-0
09/02/1972	Liverpool	FA Cup 4th Round Replay	2-0
12/02/1972	Everton	Division One	0-0
19/02/1972	Manchester United	Division One	5-1
26/02/1972	Cardiff City	FA Cup 5th Round	2-0
04/03/1972	Southampton	Division One	7-0
11/03/1972	Coventry City	Division One	1-0
18/03/1972	Tottenham Hotspur	FA Cup QF	2-1
22/03/1972	Leicester City	Division One	0-0
25/03/1972	Arsenal	Division One	3-0
27/03/1972	Nottingham Forest	Division One	6-1
31/03/1972	West Ham United	Division One	2-2
01/04/1972	Derby County	Division One	0-2
05/04/1972	Huddersfield Town	Division One	3-1
08/04/1972	Stoke City	Division One	3-0
15/04/1972	Birmingham City	FA Cup SF at Hillsborough	3-0
19/04/1972	Newcastle United	Division One	0-1
22/04/1972	West Bromwich Albion	Division One	1-0
01/05/1972	Chelsea	Division One	2-0
06/05/1972	Arsenal	FA Cup Final at Wembley	1-0
08/05/1972	Wolverhampton Wanderers	Division One	1-2

Top appearances makers in 1971-72 went to both Norman Hunter and Peter Lorimer who both made 56.

Three players made their debuts this season, Keith M. Edwards, Jon Shaw and Jimmy Mann.

Chris Galvin scored his one and only goal for the club in the 2-0 win away at Lierse.

Sean O'Neill and John Saunders featured on the bench for the first time in the Inter-Cities Cup play-off tie v Barcelona.

Manny Cussins replaced Percy Woodward as chairman of the football club.

DIVISION ONE
1972–73

Date	Opposition	Competition	Score
12/08/1972	Chelsea	Division One	0-4
15/08/1972	Sheffield United	Division One	2-0
19/08/1972	West Bromwich Albion	Division One	2-0
23/08/1972	Ipswich Town	Division One	3-3
26/08/1972	Tottenham Hotspur	Division One	0-0
30/08/1972	Southampton	Division One	1-0
02/09/1972	Norwich City	Division One	2-0
06/09/1972	Burnley	League Cup 2nd Round	4-0
09/09/1972	Stoke City	Division One	2-2
13/09/1972	MKE Ankaragucu	European Cup Winners Cup 1st Round 1st Leg	1-1
16/09/1972	Leicester City	Division One	3-1
23/09/1972	Newcastle United	Division One	2-3
27/09/1972	MKE Ankaragucu	European Cup Winners Cup 1st Round 2nd Leg	1-0
30/09/1972	Liverpool	Division One	1-2
04/10/1972	Aston Villa	League Cup 3rd Round	1-1
07/10/1972	Derby County	Division One	5-0
11/10/1972	Aston Villa	League Cup 3rd Round Replay	2-0
14/10/1972	Everton	Division One	2-1
21/10/1972	Coventry City	Division One	1-1
25/10/1972	Carl Zeiss Jena	European Cup Winners Cup 2nd Round 1st Leg	0-0
28/10/1972	Wolverhampton Wanderers	Division One	2-0
31/10/1972	Liverpool	League Cup 4th Round	2-2
04/11/1972	Ipswich Town	Division One	2-2
08/11/1972	Carl Zeiss Jena	European Cup Winners Cup 2nd Round 2nd Leg	2-0
11/11/1972	Sheffield United	Division One	2-1
18/11/1972	Crystal Palace	Division One	2-2
22/11/1972	Liverpool	League Cup 4th Round Replay	0-1
25/11/1972	Manchester City	Division One	3-0
02/12/1972	Arsenal	Division One	1-2
09/12/1972	West Ham United	Division One	1-0
16/12/1972	Birmingham City	Division One	4-0
23/12/1972	Manchester United	Division One	1-1
26/12/1972	Newcastle United	Division One	1-0
06/01/1973	Tottenham Hotspur	Division One	3-1
13/01/1973	Norwich City	FA Cup 3rd Round	1-1
17/01/1973	Norwich City	FA Cup 3rd Round Replay	1-1
20/01/1973	Norwich City	Division One	2-1
27/01/1973	Stoke City	Division One	1-0
29/01/1973	Norwich City	FA Cup 3rd Round 2nd Replay at Villa Park	5-0
03/02/1973	Plymouth Argyle	FA Cup 4th Round	2-1
10/02/1973	Leicester City	Division One	0-2
17/02/1973	Chelsea	Division One	1-1
24/02/1973	West Bromwich Albion	FA Cup 5th Round	2-0
03/03/1973	Derby County	Division One	3-2
07/03/1973	Rapid Bucharest	European Cup Winners Cup QF 1st Leg	5-0
10/03/1973	Everton	Division One	2-1
17/03/1973	Derby County	FA Cup QF	1-0
21/03/1973	Rapid Bucharest	European Cup Winners Cup QF 2nd Leg	3-1
24/03/1973	Wolverhampton Wanderers	Division One	0-0
28/03/1973	West Bromwich Albion	Division One	1-1
31/03/1973	Manchester City	Division One	0-1
02/04/1973	Coventry City	Division One	1-0
07/04/1973	Wolverhampton Wanderers	FA Cup SF at Maine Road	1-0
11/04/1973	Hadjuk Split	European Cup Winners Cup SF 1st Leg	1-0
14/04/1973	West Ham United	Division One	1-1
18/04/1973	Manchester United	Division One	0-1
21/04/1973	Crystal Palace	Division One	4-0
23/04/1973	Liverpool	Division One	0-2
25/04/1973	Hadjuk Split	European Cup Winners Cup SF 2nd Leg	0-0
28/04/1973	Southampton	Division One	1-3
30/04/1973	Birmingham City	Division One	1-2
05/05/1973	Sunderland	FA Cup Final at Wembley	0-1
09/05/1973	Arsenal	Division One	6-1
16/05/1973	AC Milan	European Cup Winners Final at the Kaftantzoglio Stadium	0-1

Team	Pld	W	D	L	GF	GA	Pts
Liverpool	42	25	10	7	72	42	60
Arsenal	42	23	11	8	57	43	57
Leeds United	42	21	11	10	71	45	53
Ipswich Town	42	17	14	11	55	45	48
Wolverhampton W	42	18	11	13	66	54	47
West Ham United	42	17	12	13	67	53	46
Derby County	42	19	8	15	56	54	46
Tottenham Hotspur	42	16	13	13	58	48	45
Newcastle United	42	16	13	13	60	51	45
Birmingham City	42	15	12	15	53	54	42
Manchester City	42	15	11	16	57	60	41
Chelsea	42	13	14	15	49	51	40
Southampton	42	11	18	13	47	52	40
Sheffield United	42	15	10	17	51	59	40
Stoke City	42	14	10	18	61	56	38
Leicester City	42	10	17	15	40	46	37
Everton	42	13	11	18	41	49	37
Manchester United	42	12	13	17	44	60	37
Coventry City	42	13	9	20	40	55	35
Norwich City	42	11	10	21	36	63	32
Crystal Palace	42	9	12	21	41	58	30
West Bromwich Albion	42	9	10	23	38	62	28

Leeds declined the offer of playing in the Charity Shield having won the FA Cup the previous season.

When David Harvey was injured on the opening day at Chelsea, Peter Lorimer took over in goal.

David Harvey and Peter Lorimer topped the appearances charts with 63, missing just one game each.

Season 1972-73 saw the debut of Frank Gray in a 2-0 away defeat at Leicester City,

With no Billy Bremner and Johnny Giles, Paul Reaney led the side in the Cup Winners' Cup Final v AC Milan.

1973–74

DIVISION ONE

Team	Pld	W	D	L	GF	GA	Pts
Leeds United	42	24	14	4	66	31	62
Liverpool	42	22	13	7	52	31	57
Derby County	42	17	14	11	52	42	48
Ipswich Town	42	18	11	13	67	58	47
Stoke City	42	15	16	11	54	42	46
Burnley	42	16	14	12	56	53	46
Everton	42	16	12	14	50	48	44
Queen's Park Rangers	42	13	17	12	56	52	43
Leicester City	42	13	16	13	51	41	42
Arsenal	42	14	14	14	49	51	42
Tottenham Hotspur	42	14	14	14	45	50	42
Wolverhampton W	42	13	15	14	49	49	41
Sheffield United	42	14	12	16	44	49	40
Manchester City	42	14	12	16	39	46	40
Newcastle United	42	13	12	17	49	48	38
Coventry City	42	14	10	18	43	54	38
Chelsea	42	12	13	17	56	60	37
West Ham United	42	11	15	16	55	60	37
Birmingham City	42	12	13	17	52	64	37
Southampton	42	11	14	17	47	68	36
Manchester United	42	10	12	20	38	48	32
Norwich City	42	7	15	20	37	62	29

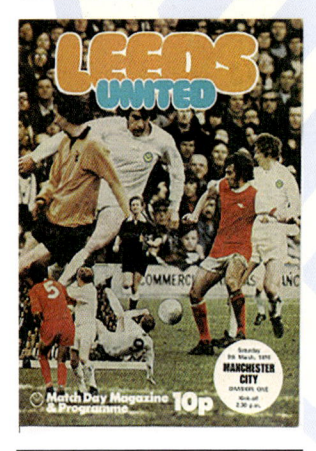

Date	Opposition	Competition	Score
25/08/1973	Everton	Division One	3-1
28/08/1993	Arsenal	Division One	2-1
01/09/1973	Tottenham Hotspur	Division One	3-0
05/09/1973	Wolverhampton Wanderers	Division One	4-1
08/09/1973	Birmingham City	Division One	3-0
11/09/1973	Wolverhampton Wanderers	Division One	2-0
15/09/1973	Southampton	Division One	2-1
19/09/1973	Stromsgodset	UEFA Cup 1st Round 1st Leg	1-1
22/09/1973	Manchester United	Division One	0-0
29/09/1973	Norwich City	Division One	1-0
03/10/1973	Stromsgodset	UEFA Cup 1st Round 2nd Leg	6-1
06/10/1973	Stoke City	Division One	1-1
08/10/1973	Ipswich Town	League Cup 2nd Round	0-2
13/10/1973	Leicester City	Division One	2-2
20/10/1973	Liverpool	Division One	1-0
24/10/1973	Hibernian	UEFA Cup 2nd Round 1st Leg	0-0
27/10/1973	Manchester City	Division One	1-0
03/11/1973	West Ham United	Division One	4-1
07/11/1973	Hibernian	UEFA Cup 2nd Round 2nd Leg	0-0 (5-4 On Pens)
10/11/1973	Burnley	Division One	0-0
17/11/1973	Coventry City	Division One	3-0
24/11/1973	Derby County	Division One	0-0
28/11/1973	Vitoria Setubal	UEFA Cup 3rd Round 1st Leg	1-0
01/12/1973	Queens Park Rangers	Division One	2-2
08/12/1973	Ipswich Town	Division One	3-0
12/12/1973	Vitoria Setubal	UEFA Cup 3rd Round 2nd Leg	1-3
15/12/1973	Chelsea	Division One	2-1
22/12/1973	Norwich City	Division One	1-0
26/12/1973	Newcastle United	Division One	1-0
29/12/1973	Birmingham City	Division One	1-1
01/01/1974	Tottenham Hotspur	Division One	1-1
05/01/1974	Wolverhampton Wanderers	FA Cup 3rd Round	1-1
09/01/1974	Wolverhampton Wanderers	FA Cup 3rd Round Replay	1-0
12/01/1974	Southampton	Division One	2-1
19/01/1974	Everton	Division One	0-0
26/01/1974	Peterborough United	FA Cup 4th Round	4-1
02/02/1974	Chelsea	Division One	1-1
05/02/1974	Arsenal	Division One	3-1
09/02/1974	Manchester United	Division One	2-0
16/02/1974	Bristol City	FA Cup 5th Round	1-1
19/02/1974	Bristol City	FA Cup 5th Round Replay	0-1
23/02/1974	Stoke City	Division One	2-3
26/02/1974	Leicester City	Division One	1-1
02/03/1974	Newcastle United	Division One	1-1
09/03/1994	Manchester City	Division One	1-0
16/03/1974	Liverpool	Division One	0-1
23/03/1974	Burnley	Division One	1-4
30/03/1974	West Ham United	Division One	1-3
06/04/1974	Derby County	Division One	2-0
13/04/1974	Coventry City	Division One	0-0
15/04/1974	Sheffield United	Division One	0-0
16/04/1974	Sheffield United	Division One	2-0
20/04/1974	Ipswich Town	Division One	3-2
27/04/1974	Queens Park Rangers	Division One	1-0

Leeds made their best-ever start to a league campaign winning their first seven games; this wouldn't be equalled until the 2007-08 season.

Captain fantastic Billy Bremner made 52 appearances, missing just two European away games at Stromsgodset and Vitoria Setubal respectivley.

Leeds featured in their first ever penalty shoot-out when they played Hibernian in the UEFA Cup second round.

Leeds used five goalkeepers in this season with two in one game, David Harvey, Gary Sprake, David Stewart, Glen Letheran, and Jon Shaw.

Les Cocker was in charge for the UEFA Cup third-round first leg at Elland Road with Vitoria Setubal as Don Revie was suspended by UEFA.

DIVISION ONE
1974–75

Date	Opposition	Competition	Score
10/08/1974	Liverpool	Charity Shield at Wembley	1-1 (5-6 On Pens)
17/08/1974	Stoke City	Division One	0-3
21/08/1974	**Queens Park Rangers**	**Division One**	**0-1**
24/08/1974	**Birmingham City**	**Division One**	**1-0**
27/08/1974	Queens Park Rangers	Division One	1-1
31/08/1974	Manchester City	Division One	1-2
07/09/1974	**Luton Town**	**Division One**	**1-1**
10/09/1974	Huddersfield Town	League Cup 2nd Round	1-1
14/09/1974	Burnley	Division One	1-2
18/09/1974	**FC Zurich**	**European Cup 1st Round 1st Leg**	**4-1**
21/09/1974	**Sheffield United**	**Division One**	**5-1**
24/09/1974	**Huddersfield Town**	**League Cup 2nd Round Replay**	**1-1**
28/09/1974	Everton	Division One	2-3
02/10/1974	**FC Zurich**	**European Cup 1st Round 2nd Leg**	**1-2**
05/10/1974	**Arsenal**	**Division One**	**2-0**
07/10/1974	**Huddersfield Town**	**League Cup 2nd Round 2nd Replay**	**2-1**
09/10/1974	Bury	League Cup 3rd Round	2-1
12/10/1974	Ipswich Town	Division One	0-0
15/10/1974	Birmingham City	Division One	0-1
19/10/1974	**Wolverhampton Wanderers**	**Division One**	**2-0**
23/10/1974	Újpesti Dózsa	European Cup 2nd Round 1st Leg	2-1
26/10/1974	Liverpool	Division One	0-1
02/11/1974	**Derby County**	**Division One**	**0-1**
06/11/1974	**Újpesti Dózsa**	**European Cup 2nd Round 2nd Leg**	**3-0**
09/11/1974	Coventry City	Division One	3-1
13/11/1974	Chester City	League Cup 4th Round	0-3
16/11/1974	**Middlesbrough**	**Division One**	**2-2**
23/11/1974	Carlisle United	Division One	2-1
30/11/1974	**Chelsea**	**Division One**	**2-0**
04/12/1974	**Tottenham Hotspur**	**Division One**	**2-1**
07/12/1974	West Ham United	Division One	1-2
14/12/1974	**Stoke City**	**Division One**	**3-1**
21/12/1974	Newcastle United	Division One	0-3
26/12/1974	**Burnley**	**Division One**	**2-2**
28/12/1974	Leicester City	Division One	2-0
04/01/1975	**Cardiff City**	**FA Cup 3rd Round**	**4-1**
11/01/1975	**West Ham United**	**Division One**	**2-1**
118/01/1975	Chelsea	Division One	2-0
25/01/1975	**Wimbledon**	**FA Cup 4th Round**	**0-0**
01/02/1975	**Coventry City**	**Division One**	**0-0**
08/02/1975	Derby County	Division One	0-0
10/02/1975	Wimbledon	FA Cup 4th Round Replay at Selhurst Park	1-0
18/02/1975	Derby County	FA Cup 5th Round	1-0
22/02/1975	Middlesbrough	Division One	1-0
25/02/1975	**Carlisle United**	**Division One**	**3-1**
01/03/1975	**Manchester City**	**Division One**	**2-2**
05/03/1975	**Anderlecht**	**European Cup 3rd Round 1st Leg**	**3-0**
08/03/1975	Ipswich Town	FA Cup QF	0-0
11/03/1975	**Ipswich Town**	**FA Cup QF Replay**	**1-1**
15/03/1975	**Everton**	**Division One**	**0-0**
19/03/1975	Anderlecht	European Cup 3rd Round 2nd Leg	1-0
22/03/1975	Luton Town	Division One	1-2
25/03/1975	Ipswich Town	FA Cup QF 2nd Replay at Filbert Street	0-0
27/03/1975	Ipswich Town	FA Cup QF 3rd Replay at Filbert Street	2-3
29/03/1975	**Newcastle United**	**Division One**	**1-1**
31/03/1975	**Leicester City**	**Division One**	**2-2**
01/04/1975	Sheffield United	Division One	1-1
05/04/1975	**Liverpool**	**Division One**	**0-2**
09/04/1975	**Barcelona**	**European Cup SF 1st Leg**	**2-1**
12/04/1975	Arsenal	Division One	2-1
19/04/1975	**Ipswich Town**	**Division One**	**2-1**
23/04/1975	Barcelona	European Cup SF 2nd Lg	1-1
26/04/1975	**Wolverhampton Wanderers**	**Division One**	**1-1**
28/04/1975	Tottenham Hotspur	Division One	2-4
28/05/1975	Bayern Munich	European Cup Final	0-2
		at the Parc Des Princes	

Team	Pld	W	D	L	GF	GA	Pts
Derby County	42	21	11	10	67	49	53
Liverpool	42	20	11	11	60	39	51
Ipswich Town	42	23	5	14	66	44	51
Everton	42	16	18	8	56	42	50
Stoke City	42	17	15	10	64	48	49
Sheffield United	42	18	13	11	58	51	49
Middlesbrough	42	18	12	12	54	40	48
Manchester City	42	18	10	14	54	54	46
Leeds United	42	16	13	13	57	49	45
Burnley	42	17	11	14	68	67	45
Queen's Park Rangers	42	16	10	16	54	54	42
Wolverhampton W	42	14	11	17	57	54	39
West Ham United	42	13	13	16	58	59	39
Coventry City	42	12	15	15	51	62	39
Newcastle United	42	15	9	18	59	72	39
Arsenal	42	13	11	18	47	49	37
Birmingham City	42	14	9	19	53	61	37
Leicester City	42	12	12	18	46	60	36
Tottenham Hotspur	42	13	8	21	52	63	34
Luton Town	42	11	11	20	47	65	33
Chelsea	42	9	15	18	42	72	33
Carlisle United	42	12	5	25	43	59	29

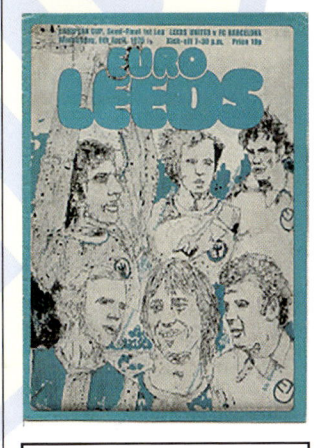

Leeds had six debutants, Duncan McKenzie, John McGovern, John O'Hare, Carl Harris, Byron Stevenson and Gwyn Thomas.

Jimmy Armfield became the first Leeds United manager to win his first three games. It was a record that stood until August 2018.

Paul Madeley was top of the appearance table, making 60 of 65 appearances for the club.

Terry Cooper made the last of his 351 appearances for the Whites in the 1-0 away win at Middlesbrough on 22 February 1975.

The FA Cup tie with Ipswich Town took four games to settle, with Ipswich finally winning after a third replay at Filbert Street.

1975–76

DIVISION ONE

Team	Pld	W	D	L	GF	GA	Pts
Liverpool	42	23	14	5	66	31	60
Queen's Park Rangers	42	24	11	7	67	33	59
Manchester United	42	23	10	9	68	42	56
Derby County	42	21	11	10	75	58	53
Leeds United	42	21	9	12	65	46	51
Ipswich Town	42	16	14	12	54	48	46
Leicester City	42	13	19	10	48	51	45
Manchester City	42	16	11	15	64	46	43
Tottenham Hotspur	42	14	15	13	63	63	43
Norwich City	42	16	10	16	58	58	42
Everton	42	15	12	15	60	66	42
Stoke City	42	15	11	16	48	50	41
Middlesbrough	42	15	10	17	46	45	40
Coventry City	42	13	14	15	47	57	40
Newcastle United	42	15	9	18	71	62	39
Aston Villa	42	11	17	14	51	59	39
Arsenal	42	13	10	19	47	53	36
West Ham United	42	13	10	19	48	71	36
Birmingham City	42	13	7	22	57	75	33
Wolverhampton W	42	10	10	22	51	68	30
Burnley	42	9	10	23	43	66	28
Sheffield United	42	6	10	26	33	82	22

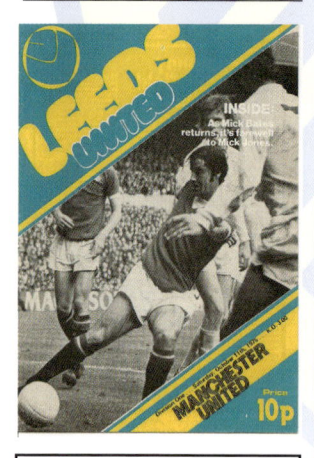

Date	Opposition	Competition	Score
16/08/1975	Aston Villa	Division One	2-1
20/08/1975	Norwich City	Division One	1-1
23/08/1975	**Ipswich Town**	**Division One**	**1-0**
26/08/1975	**Liverpool**	**Division One**	**0-3**
30/08/1975	Sheffield United	Division One	2-0
06/09/1975	**Wolverhampton Wanderers**	**Division One**	**3-0**
09/09/1975	**Ipswich Town**	**League Cup 2nd Round**	**3-2**
13/09/1975	Stoke City	Division One	2-3
20/09/1975	**Tottenham Hotspur**	**Division One**	**1-1**
27/09/1975	Burnley	Division One	1-0
04/10/1975	**Queens Park Rangers**	**Division One**	**2-1**
08/10/1975	**Notts County**	**League Cup 3rd Round**	**0-1**
11/10/1975	**Manchester United**	**Division One**	**1-2**
18/10/1975	Birmingham City	Division One	2-2
25/10/1975	**Coventry City**	**Division One**	**2-0**
01/11/1975	Derby County	Division One	2-3
08/11/1975	**Newcastle United**	**Division One**	**3-0**
15/11/1975	Middlesbrough	Division One	0-0
22/11/1975	**Birmingham City**	**Division One**	**3-0**
29/11/1975	**Everton**	**Division One**	**5-2**
06/12/1975	Arsenal	Division One	2-1
13/12/1975	Ipswich Town	Division One	1-2
20/12/1975	**Aston Villa**	**Division One**	**1-0**
26/12/1975	Manchester City	Division One	1-0
27/12/1975	Leicester City	Division One	4-0
03/01/1976	Notts County	FA Cup 3rd Round	1-0
10/01/1976	**Stoke City**	**Division One**	**2-0**
17/01/1976	Wolverhampton Wanderers	Division One	1-1
24/01/1976	**Crystal Palace**	**FA Cup 4th Round**	**0-1**
31/01/1976	**Norwich City**	**Division One**	**0-3**
07/02/1976	Liverpool	Division One	0-2
21/02/1976	**Middlesbrough**	**Division One**	**0-2**
23/02/1976	West Ham United	Division One	1-1
28/02/1976	Coventry City	Division One	1-0
02/03/1976	**Derby County**	**Division One**	**1-1**
09/03/1976	**West Ham United**	**Division One**	**1-1**
13/03/1976	Manchester United	Division One	2-3
20/03/1976	Everton	Division One	3-1
27/03/1976	**Arsenal**	**Division One**	**3-0**
31/03/1976	Newcastle United	Division One	3-2
03/04/1976	**Burnley**	**Division One**	**2-1**
10/04/1976	Tottenham Hotspur	Division One	0-0
14/04/1976	**Sheffield United**	**Division One**	**0-1**
17/04/1976	**Manchester City**	**Division One**	**2-1**
20/04/1976	Leicester City	Division One	1-2
24/04/1976	Queens Park Rangers	Division One	0-2

Jimmy Armfield handed out debuts to just two players, David McNiven at home to Notts County and Keith Parkinson at home to Middlesbrough.

The break up of Don Revie's side continued with luckless Mick Jones retiring after 312 games for the Whites.

Frank Gray was the club's only ever-present, starting all 46 games for the side.

When Allan Clarke scored the winner at home to Aston Villa, it was his 100th league goal for the side.

Another title winner, this time Mick Bates left the club at the end of the campaign for Walsall.

DIVISION ONE

1976–77

Date	Opposition	Competition	Score
21/08/1976	West Bromwich Albion	Division One	2-2
24/08/1976	Birmingham City	Division One	0-0
28/08/1976	Coventry City	Division One	2-4
01/09/1976	Stoke City	League Cup 2nd Round	1-2
04/09/1976	Derby County	Division One	2-0
11/09/1976	Tottenham Hotspur	Division One	0-1
18/09/1976	Newcastle United	Division One	2-2
25/09/1976	Middlesbrough	Division One	0-1
02/10/1976	Manchester United	Division One	0-2
06/10/1976	West Ham United	Division One	3-1
16/10/1976	Norwich City	Division One	2-1
23/10/1976	Liverpool	Division One	1-1
30/10/1976	Arsenal	Division One	2-1
06/11/1976	Everton	Division One	2-0
10/11/1976	Stoke City	Division One	1-1
20/11/1976	Ipswich Town	Division One	1-1
27/11/1976	Leicester City	Division One	2-2
11/12/1976	Aston Villa	Division One	1-3
27/12/1976	Manchester City	Division One	0-2
29/12/1976	Sunderland	Division One	1-0
03/01/1977	Arsenal	Division One	1-1
08/01/1977	Norwich City	FA Cup 3rd Round	5-2
22/01/1977	West Bromwich Albion	Division One	2-1
29/01/1977	Birmingham City	FA Cup 4th Round	2-1
02/02/1977	Birmingham City	Division One	1-0
05/02/1977	Coventry City	Division One	1-2
12/02/1977	Derby County	Division One	1-0
19/02/1977	Tottenham Hotspur	Division One	2-1
26/02/1977	Manchester City	FA Cup 5th Round	1-0
02/03/1977	Newcastle United	Division One	0-3
05/03/1977	Middlesbrough	Division One	2-1
08/03/1977	Queens Park Rangers	Division One	0-0
12/03/1977	Manchester United	Division One	0-1
19/03/1977	Wolverhampton Wanderers	FA Cup QF	1-0
23/03/1977	Norwich City	Division One	3-0
02/04/1977	Liverpool	Division One	1-3
08/04/1977	Manchester City	Division One	1-2
09/04/1977	Sunderland	Division One	1-1
12/04/1977	Stoke City	Division One	1-2
16/04/1977	Ipswich Town	Division One	2-1
23/04/1977	Manchester United	FA Cup SF at Hillsborough	1-2
26/04/1977	West Ham United	Division One	1-1
30/04/1977	Bristol City	Division One	2-0
04/05/1977	Everton	Division One	0-0
07/05/1977	Aston Villa	Division One	1-2
10/05/1977	Bristol City	Division One	0-1
14/05/1977	Queens Park Rangers	Division One	0-1
26/05/1977	Leicester City	Division One	1-0

Team	Pld	W	D	L	GF	GA	Pts
Liverpool	42	23	11	8	62	33	57
Manchester City	42	21	14	7	60	34	56
Ipswich Town	42	22	8	12	66	39	52
Aston Villa	42	22	7	13	76	50	51
Newcastle United	42	18	13	11	64	49	49
Manchester United	42	18	11	13	71	62	47
West Bromwich Albion	42	16	13	13	62	56	45
Arsenal	42	16	11	15	64	59	43
Everton	42	14	14	14	62	64	42
Leeds United	42	15	12	15	48	51	42
Leicester City	42	12	18	12	47	60	42
Middlesbrough	42	14	13	15	40	45	41
Birmingham City	42	13	12	17	63	61	38
Queen's Park Rangers	42	13	12	17	47	52	38
Derby County	42	9	19	14	50	55	37
Norwich City	42	14	9	19	47	64	37
West Ham United	42	11	14	17	46	65	36
Bristol City	42	11	13	18	38	48	35
Coventry City	42	10	15	17	48	59	35
Sunderland	42	11	12	19	46	54	34
Stoke City	42	10	14	18	28	51	34
Tottenham Hotspur	42	12	9	21	48	72	33

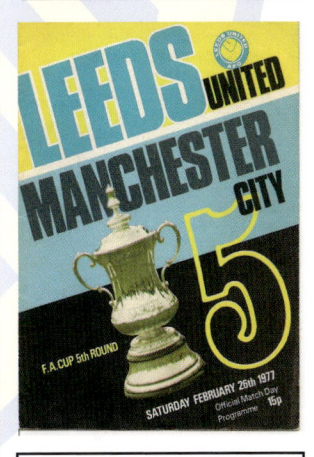

18 September 1976, saw the last appearance for the White's greatest-ever captain, Billy Bremner, following 773 games.

With Bremner now at Hull City, Leeds needed a new captain and Armfield chose Trevor Cherry.

The Whites had four debutants, Tony Currie, Ray Hankin, Billy McGhie and David Whyte.

Cherry made 47 appearances missing an FA Cup tie at home to Norwich City in which Allan Clarke took on the role of skipper.

In finishing tenth it was the Whites' lowest league positioning since winning promotion back in 1964.

215

1977–78

DIVISION ONE

Team	Pld	W	D	L	GF	GA	Pts
Nottingham Forest	42	25	14	3	69	24	64
Liverpool	42	24	9	9	65	34	57
Everton	42	22	11	9	76	45	55
Manchester City	42	20	12	10	74	51	52
Arsenal	42	21	10	11	60	37	52
West Bromwich Albion	42	18	14	10	62	53	50
Coventry City	42	18	12	12	75	62	48
Aston Villa	42	18	10	14	57	42	46
Leeds United	42	18	10	14	63	53	46
Manchester United	42	16	10	16	67	63	42
Birmingham City	42	16	9	17	55	60	41
Derby County	42	14	13	15	54	59	41
Norwich City	42	11	18	13	52	66	40
Middlesbrough	42	12	15	15	42	54	39
Wolverhampton W	42	12	12	18	51	64	36
Chelsea	42	11	14	17	46	69	36
Bristol City	42	11	13	18	49	53	35
Ipswich Town	42	11	13	18	47	61	35
Queen's Park Rangers	42	9	15	18	47	64	33
West Ham United	42	12	8	22	52	69	32
Newcastle United	42	6	10	26	42	78	22
Leicester City	42	5	12	25	26	70	22

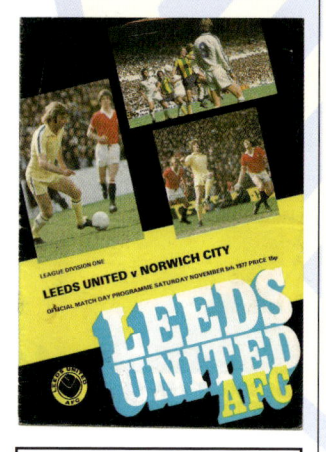

Date	Opposition	Competition	Score
20/08/1977	Newcastle United	Division One	2-3
24/08/1977	West Bromwich Albion	Division One	2-2
27/08/1977	Birmingham City	Division One	1-0
31/08/1977	Rochdale	League Cup 2nd Round	3-0
03/09/1977	Coventry City	Division One	2-2
10/09/1977	Ipswich Town	Division One	2-1
17/09/1977	Derby County	Division One	2-2
24/09/1977	Manchester United	Division One	1-1
01/10/1977	Chelsea	Division One	2-1
05/10/1977	Aston Villa	Division One	1-1
08/10/1977	Bristol City	Division One	2-3
15/10/1977	Liverpool	Division One	1-2
22/10/1977	Middlesbrough	Division One	1-2
26/10/1977	Colchester United	League Cup 3rd Round	4-0
29/10/1977	Leicester City	Division One	0-0
05/11/1977	Norwich City	Division One	2-2
12/11/1977	Manchester City	Division One	3-2
19/11/1977	Nottingham Forest	Division One	1-0
26/11/1977	West Ham United	Division One	1-0
30/11/1977	Bolton Wanderers	League Cup 4th Round	3-1
03/12/1977	Queens Park Rangers	Division One	3-0
10/12/1977	Arsenal	Division One	1-1
17/12/1977	Manchester City	Division One	2-0
26/12/1977	Wolverhampton Wanderers	Division One	1-3
27/12/1977	Everton	Division One	3-1
31/12/1977	West Bromwich Albion	Division One	0-1
02/01/1978	Newcastle United	Division One	0-2
07/01/1978	Manchester City	FA Cup 3rd Round	1-2
14/01/1978	Birmingham City	Division One	3-2
18/01/1978	Everton	League Cup 5th Round	4-1
21/01/1978	Coventry City	Division One	2-0
04/02/1978	Ipswich Town	Division One	1-0
08/02/1978	Nottingham Forest	League Cup SF 1st Leg	1-3
22/02/1978	Nottingham Forest	League Cup SF 2nd Leg	2-4
25/02/1978	Chelsea	Division One	2-0
01/03/1978	Manchester United	Division One	1-0
04/03/1978	Bristol City	Division One	0-2
11/03/1978	Liverpool	Division One	0-1
18/03/1978	Middlesbrough	Division One	5-0
25/03/1978	Everton	Division One	0-2
27/03/1978	Wolverhampton Wanderers	Division One	2-1
28/03/1978	Leicester City	Division One	5-1
01/04/1978	Norwich City	Division One	0-3
08/04/1978	West Ham United	Division One	1-2
12/04/1978	Derby County	Division One	2-0
15/04/1978	Nottingham Forest	Division One	1-1
22/04/1978	Arsenal	Division One	1-3
26/04/1978	Aston Villa	Division One	1-3
29/04/1978	Queens Park Rangers	Division One	0-0

Trevor Cherry and Frank Gray both made 48 appearances, missing just one game each.

Peter Lorimer took over the captaincy in the West Ham United game at Elland Road.

Jimmy Armfield handed debuts to Arthur Graham, Brian Flynn, Paul Hart and Neil Parker.

Both Joe Jordan and Gordon McQueen crossed the Pennines to join arch rivals Manchester United.

FA Cup-winning hero Allan Clarke made his last appearance for the club in the 0-0 draw at QPR on the last day of the season.

DIVISION ONE

1978–79

Date	Opposition	Competition	Score
19/08/1978	Arsenal	Division One	2-2
23/08/1978	Manchester United	Division One	2-3
26/08/1978	Wolverhampton Wanderers	Division One	3-0
29/08/1978	West Bromwich Albion	League Cup 2nd Round	0-0
02/09/1978	Chelsea	Division One	3-0
06/09/1978	West Bromwich Albion	League Cup 2nd Round Replay	0-0
09/09/1978	Manchester City	Division One	0-3
16/09/1978	Tottenham Hotspur	Division One	1-2
23/09/1978	Coventry City	Division One	0-0
30/09/1978	Birmingham City	Division One	3-0
02/10/1978	West Bromwich Albion	League Cup 2nd Round 2nd Replay at Maine Road	1-0
07/10/1978	Bolton Wanderers	Division One	1-3
10/10/1978	Sheffield United	League Cup 3rd Round	4-1
14/10/1978	West Bromwich Albion	Division One	1-3
21/10/1978	Norwich City	Division One	2-2
28/10/1978	Derby County	Division One	4-0
04/11/1978	Liverpool	Division One	1-1
07/11/1978	Queens Park Rangers	League Cup 4th Round	2-0
11/11/1978	Arsenal	Division One	0-1
18/11/1978	Wolverhampton Wanderers	Division One	1-1
22/11/1978	Chelsea	Division One	2-1
25/11/1978	Southampton	Division One	4-0
02/12/1978	Ipswich Town	Division One	3-2
09/12/1978	Bristol City	Division One	1-1
13/12/1978	Luton Town	League Cup 5th Round	4-1
16/12/1978	Everton	Division One	1-1
23/12/1978	Middlesbrough	Division One	3-1
26/12/1978	Aston Villa	Division One	2-2
30/12/1978	Queens Park Rangers	Division One	4-1
13/01/1979	Manchester City	Division One	1-1
18/01/1979	Hartlepool United	FA Cup 3rd Round	6-2
20/01/1979	Tottenham Hotspur	Division One	2-1
24/01/1979	Southampton	League Cup SF 1st Leg	2-2
30/01/1979	Southampton	League Cup SF 2nd Leg	0-1
03/02/1979	Coventry City	Division One	1-0
10/02/1979	Birmingham City	Division One	1-0
24/02/1979	West Bromwich Albion	Division One	2-1
26/02/1979	West Bromwich Albion	FA Cup 4th Round	3-3
01/03/1979	West Bromwich Albion	FA Cup 4th Round Replay	0-2
03/03/1979	Norwich City	Division One	2-2
10/03/1979	Derby County	Division One	1-0
24/03/1979	Manchester United	Division One	1-4
31/03/1979	Southampton	Division One	2-2
07/04/1979	Ipswich Town	Division One	1-1
10/04/1979	Middlesbrough	Division One	0-1
14/04/1979	Aston Villa	Division One	1-0
16/04/1979	Nottingham Forest	Division One	0-0
21/04/1979	Everton	Division One	1-0
25/04/1979	Bolton Wanderers	Division One	5-1
28/04/1979	Bristol City	Division One	0-0
04/05/1979	Queens Park Rangers	Division One	4-3
15/05/1979	Nottingham Forest	Division One	1-2
17/05/1979	Liverpool	Division One	0-3

Team	Pld	W	D	L	GF	GA	Pts
Liverpool	42	30	8	4	85	16	68
Nottingham Forest	42	21	18	3	61	26	60
West Bromwich Albion	42	24	11	7	72	35	59
Everton	42	17	17	8	52	40	51
Leeds United	42	18	14	10	70	52	50
Ipswich Town	42	20	9	13	63	49	49
Arsenal	42	17	14	11	61	48	48
Aston Villa	42	15	16	11	59	49	46
Manchester United	42	15	15	12	60	63	45
Coventry City	42	14	16	12	58	68	44
Tottenham Hotspur	42	13	15	14	48	61	41
Middlesbrough	42	15	10	17	57	50	40
Bristol City	42	15	10	17	47	51	40
Southampton	42	12	16	14	47	53	40
Manchester City	42	13	13	16	58	56	39
Norwich City	42	7	23	12	51	57	37
Bolton Wanderers	42	12	11	19	54	75	35
Wolverhampton W	42	13	8	21	44	68	34
Derby County	42	10	11	21	44	71	31
Queen's Park Rangers	42	6	13	23	45	73	25
Birmingham City	42	6	10	26	37	64	22
Chelsea	42	5	10	27	44	92	20

Maurice Lindley took the role of caretaker for the opening game of the season at Arsenal as the club pondered on a new manager.

Tony Currie captained the Whites in 40 of the 53 games whilst Trevor Cherry skippered the side in the other 13.

Maurice Lindley stepped up again for the third time since September 1974 when new manager Jock Stein decided to take the Scotland job.

Frank Gray and Brian Flynn were joint top of the appearance table, starting 52 of the 53 games the side played.

Leeds finished in the highest position since winning the league in 1974 under new boss Jimmy Adamson as they secured UEFA Cup qualification.

217

1979–80

DIVISION ONE

Team	Pld	W	D	L	GF	GA	Pts
Liverpool	42	25	10	7	81	30	60
Manchester United	42	24	10	8	65	35	58
Ipswich Town	42	22	9	11	68	39	53
Arsenal	42	18	16	8	52	36	52
Nottingham Forest	42	20	8	14	63	43	48
Wolverhampton W	42	19	9	14	58	47	47
Aston Villa	42	16	14	12	51	50	46
Southampton	42	18	9	15	65	53	45
Middlesbrough	42	16	12	14	50	44	44
West Bromwich Albion	42	11	19	12	54	50	41
Leeds United	42	13	14	15	46	50	40
Norwich City	42	13	14	15	58	66	40
Crystal Palace	42	12	16	14	41	50	40
Tottenham Hotspur	42	15	10	17	52	62	40
Coventry City	42	16	7	19	56	66	39
Brighton & Hove Albion	42	11	15	16	47	57	37
Manchester City	42	12	13	17	43	66	37
Stoke City	42	13	10	19	44	58	36
Everton	42	9	17	16	43	51	35
Bristol City	42	9	13	20	37	66	31
Derby County	42	11	8	23	47	67	30
Bolton Wanderers	42	5	15	22	38	73	25

Date	Opposition	Competition	Score
18/08/1979	Bristol City	Division One	2-2
22/08/1979	**Everton**	**Division One**	**2-0**
25/08/1979	Norwich City	Division One	1-2
29/08/1979	**Arsenal**	**League Cup 2nd Round 1st Leg**	**1-1**
01/09/1979	**Arsenal**	**Division One**	**1-1**
04/09/1979	Arsenal	League Cup 2nd Round 2nd Leg	0-7
08/09/1979	Nottingham Forest	Division One	0-0
15/09/1979	**Liverpool**	**Division One**	**1-1**
19/09/1979	Valletta	UEFA Cup 1st Round 1st Leg	4-0
22/09/1979	Bolton Wanderers	Division One	1-1
29/09/1979	**Manchester City**	**Division One**	**1-2**
03/10/1979	Valletta	UEFA Cup 1st Round 2nd Leg	3-0
06/10/1979	**Ipswich Town**	**Division One**	**2-1**
13/10/1979	Brighton & Hove Albion	Division One	0-0
20/10/1979	**Tottenham Hotspur**	**Division One**	**1-2**
24/10/1979	Universitate Craiova	UEFA Cup 2nd Round 1st Leg	0-2
27/10/1979	Southampton	Division One	2-1
03/11/1979	**Bristol City**	**Division One**	**1-3**
07/11/1979	**Universitate Craiova**	**UEFA Cup 2nd Round 2nd Leg**	**0-2**
10/11/1979	Coventry City	Division One	0-3
13/11/1979	Everton	Division One	1-5
17/11/1979	**West Bromwich Albion**	**Division One**	**1-0**
24/11/1979	Aston Villa	Division One	0-0
01/12/1979	**Crystal Palace**	**Division One**	**1-0**
08/12/1979	Manchester United	Division One	1-1
15/12/1979	**Wolverhampton Wanderers**	**Division One**	**3-0**
21/12/1979	Stoke City	Division One	2-0
26/12/1979	Middlesbrough	Division One	1-3
29/12/1979	**Norwich City**	**Division One**	**2-2**
01/01/1980	**Derby County**	**Division One**	**1-0**
05/01/1980	Nottingham Forest	FA Cup 3rd Round	1-4
12/01/1980	Arsenal	Division One	1-0
19/01/1980	**Nottingham Forest**	**Division One**	**1-2**
09/02/1980	**Bolton Wanderers**	**Division One**	**2-2**
16/02/1980	Manchester City	Division One	1-1
23/02/1980	**Brighton & Hove Albion**	**Division One**	**1-1**
01/03/1980	Tottenham Hotspur	Division One	1-2
08/03/1980	**Southampton**	**Division One**	**2-0**
14/03/1980	Ipswich Town	Division One	0-1
19/03/1980	Liverpool	Division One	0-3
22/03/1980	**Coventry City**	**Division One**	**0-0**
29/03/1980	West Bromwich Albion	Division One	1-2
02/04/1980	**Middlesbrough**	**Division One**	**2-0**
05/04/1980	Derby County	Division One	0-2
08/04/1980	**Stoke City**	**Division One**	**3-0**
12/04/1980	Crystal Palace	Division One	0-1
19/04/1980	**Aston Villa**	**Division One**	**0-0**
26/04/1980	Wolverhampton Wanderers	Division One	1-3
03/05/1980	**Manchester United**	**Division One**	**2-0**

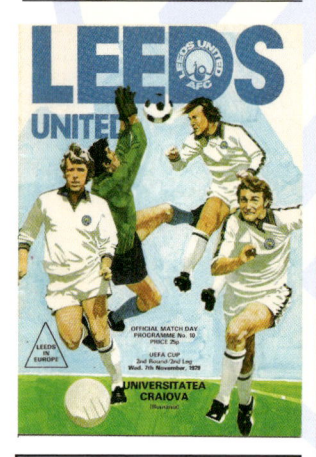

John Lukic made his first debut in goal for Leeds United in the home UEFA Cup tie v Valletta.

Goalkeepers Henry Smith away at Valletta and Kevin Seggie at home to Valetta and in both legs against Universitate Craiova were unused subs for the first time.

Also, the home game against Valletta saw the only unused sub appearance of Brian Bennett.

Kevin Hird finished top scorer with eight goals which was a record low for a top scorer in Leeds United's history.

On the last day of the season, Leeds denied Manchester United the title thanks to a 2-0 win at Elland Road.

THE 1980s
DOWN DOWN DEEPER AND DOWN AND BACK UP AGAIN

With the glory days of the 1970s a thing of the past going into the first season of a new decade, pressure was growing on Jimmy Adamson. He was sacked following a 3-0 defeat away at Stoke City, which left Leeds bottom of the pile. Maurice Lindley, as he had done in the 1970s, took caretaker charge for a goalless draw at home to Tottenham Hotspur before FA Cup-winning goalscorer Allan Clarke was named as the manager. His first game was another goalless draw, this time at home to arch rivals Manchester United before a dismal 4-1 defeat away at Sunderland. Slowly, results did start to improve, with Leeds taking five points from their next six, with a 1-1 draw away at Ipswich Town and 1-0 home wins against Manchester City and Everton respectively. A 5-0 home defeat to Arsenal reminded Clarke that things wouldn't be easy and results proved to be inconsistent. Leeds were also knocked out in the third round of the FA Cup following a 1-0 defeat in a replay away at Coventry City.

Following the turn of the year, results improved as Leeds dragged themselves away from 18th position to tenth in the space of two months. The last day of February 1981 would be a red letter for the side as a Brian Flynn winner saw off Manchester United at Old Trafford. They did not win another game at Old Trafford until 2010. Three straight victories – 1-0 at Crystal Palace (Derek Parlane scoring the winner), 3-0 at home to Ipswich Town, with goals from Kevin Hird, Carl Harris and Paul Hart, and another 3-0 home win against Coventry City with Bryon Stevenson, Derek Parlane and Brian Flynn getting on the scoresheet – helped matters and Leeds ended up in ninth place.

Leeds United, 1980-81.

Peter Barnes, training in Leeds United tracksuit, 1980s.

During the off season, Peter Barnes joined from Manchester City and Frank Gray returned from Nottingham Forest. The opening day was one to forget as newly promoted Swansea City routed Leeds 5-1 at the Vetch Field, which set the alarm bells ringing early on. Leeds did respond with a 1-1 draw at home to Everton, and an Arthur Graham hat-trick saw off

Leeds United, 1981-82.

Wolverhampton Wanderers at Elland Road. However, by the end of September Leeds were rock bottom and facing a relegation battle. Kenny Burns joined the club from Nottingham Forest and was made the new captain. It had the desired effect as Leeds defeated West Bromwich Albion 3-1 at Elland Road in front of the *Match of the Day* cameras. An Eddie Gray winner at home to Sunderland saw Leeds up to 18th, but a 4-0 defeat at Southampton put Leeds in to 20th place. Leeds exited the FA Cup in the fourth round away at Tottenham Hotspur and, following a run of four straight defeats, Leeds were in 19th place and short of goals. Allan Clarke bought in Frank Worthington and he scored the winner at Sunderland in his second game for the club. They didn't win for another month, 1-0 away at Birmingham City, before three games without a win set them back to 21st place. A 4-1 win over European Cup finalists Aston Villa at Villa Park gave Leeds hope, as did a 2-1 win over Brighton & Hove Albion, but a 2-0 defeat at West Bromwich Albion and Stoke City's 3-0 win over the Baggies sent Leeds crashing down to the Second Division.

Aidan Butterworth (Leeds United) and Graham Roberts (Tottenham Hotspur), 12 December 1981.

Aidan Butterworth scores (Leeds United) against Arsenal at Elland Road in the FA Cup on 2 February 1983.

Clarke was sacked and replaced by another player from the Revie era in Eddie Gray and his task was to gain promotion. Leeds started slowly and it took until game four to record their first win, a 3-2 Yorkshire derby win away at Sheffield Wednesday. Derby County were then beaten 2-1 at Elland Road, before a 3-2 defeat at Fulham. A win over Cambridge United sent Leeds into sixth place, but they couldn't quite get the consistency to manage a promotion charge at the first attempt. A high point was a 4-1 win away at Newcastle United in the Milk Cup second round, second leg and the Magpies was beaten 3-1 at Elland Road in the next match. A Mark Gavin goal saw Leeds victorious in another Yorkshire derby, this time away at Rotherham two weeks before Christmas, but a series of draws kept Leeds away from the top end of the league. Following a 3-0 defeat away at Wolverhampton Wanderers, it left the side in ninth position. An FA Cup marathon with First Division Arsenal dominated the last week of January and the first of February. Leeds looked like they were heading to the fifth round thanks to a late goal from Arthur Graham, but an even later goal from Graham Rix meant a second replay, which Arsenal went on to win 2-1. Back-to-back victories over Crystal Palace 2-1 at Elland Road and 2-1 away at Bolton Wanderers sent Leeds up to fifth place, but in the end the side finished in eighth place. The one big positive was the emergence of youngsters such as Neil Aspin, Tommy Wright, John Sheridan and Scott Sellars.

During the summer, George McCluskey joined from Celtic, as did Andy Watson from Aberdeen. Leeds lost six of their opening nine league games, including an embarrassing 5-1

Leeds United, 1984-85.

defeat at Shrewsbury Town, which left Leeds in 19th position. Sheridan broke his leg in a 3-1 win at home to Cambridge United and, like the previous campaign, too many draws meant Leeds were unable to mount a promotion challenge. Leeds produced a season's best in a 4-1 win at home to Middlesbrough with goals from Sellars, a brace from McCluskey and one from Wright, which left Leeds in 17th place going into the new year.

Scunthorpe United knocked the Whites out of the FA Cup following a second replay at the Old Showground, but league form did pick up with five straight wins, which included a 1-0 win away at Cardiff City thanks to a winner from McCluskey. A 2-1 win at home to Grimsby Town sent Leeds to a season high of ninth, although they ended up in tenth place. Eddie Gray made his last appearance in a Leeds shirt on the final day at home to Charlton Athletic, which left him to concentrate on moulding a side ready for promotion.

In came Andy Linighan from Hartlepool United in the summer. The emphasis was on youth and things couldn't have started better, winning their opening four games and hopes were high of a promotion challenge. Sadly for the Whites, spirits were soon dampened with three straight defeats, but a 6-0 hammering of Oldham Athletic, in which Andy Ritchie scored a hat-trick, lifted Leeds back into fourth place. From there on in, results went from the ridiculous to the sublime. Leeds were beaten 5-2 away at Oxford United, a game in which Peter Lorimer saw red, but they bounced back the following week with the same scoreline at home to newly promoted Wimbledon. Mervyn Day joined from Aston Villa and would play a prominent role over the next five years as did Ian Baird who also joined from Southampton. Leeds's journey in the FA Cup lasted one round as current holders Everton knocked them out in a televised game at Elland Road. Following that defeat Notts County were beaten 5-0, with Tommy Wright grabbing three, but the side failed to gain any consistency and finished

England v Germany squads from the 1966 final play in July 1985 in memory of the Bradford fire disaster victims at Elland Road

in seventh place. The season ended in tragedy when a teenager died following the collapse of a wall in the away game at Birmingham City. This was on the same day that football mourned the victims of the Bradford City fire.

During the close season, Frank Gray left to join Sunderland and Ian Snodin arrived from Doncaster Rovers. The opening month saw Leeds fail to win any of its first five league games

Leeds United, 1985-86.

including a 6-3 defeat away at Stoke City. (It would get worse a season later). The side did pick up a 3-1 win away at Shrewsbury Town and a 2-1 home win against west Yorkshire rivals Bradford City. However, following a 3-0 away win in the Milk Cup second round, second leg tie away at Walsall, Gray was sacked, much to the shock of the Leeds United fans. Peter Gunby was placed in the caretaker role before a third of Revie's old boys, Billy Bremner, took over. His first job was to appoint Snodin as captain, which saw the end of Peter Lorimer's illustrious career at Elland Road.

Just as previous seasons, the results were inconsistent to say the least and the highest Leeds achieved in the league was 11th place, following a 2-1 win over Portsmouth at Elland Road in which Lyndon Simmonds scored both goals. A rare high point was a 3-0 win at Plough Lane in which Snodin, Baird and Martin Dickinson scored the goals. The Whites were knocked out of the FA Cup at the third-round stage yet again, this time to lower league side Peterborough United. This game which saw Scott Sellars dismissed and the league form taking a nose dive, with the side finishing in 14th position, their lowest since the 1961-62 season.

Changes were made in the summer with the signings of Keith Edwards from Sheffield United, Peter Haddock from Newcastle United and Jack Ashurst from Carlisle United. The early signs were good and with the introduction of a new play-off system at the season's end, the club knew a top-four finish would mean a chance at promotion. By the end of September and following a 3-0 win at Elland Road over Hull City, with goals from Ritchie, Baird and skipper Brendan Ormsby, Leeds were in fourth place and set for a tilt at promotion. Results got even better with back-to-back home wins against Crystal Palace (3-0) and Portsmouth

Leeds United, 1986-87.

Micky Adams is congratulated on his goal against Wigan Athletic in the FA Cup quarter-final on 15 March 1987.

(3-1), which took the Whites to second in the league. However, come the festive season, which included a 7-2 reverse at Stoke City, Leeds slipped back down to eighth place going into 1987. The FA Cup started with no real hopes, but once Leeds beat non-league Telford United 2-1 at The Hawthorns and 2-1 away at Swindon, they were suddenly three steps from Wembley. Queens Park Rangers were defeated in front of a packed house at Elland

Road with a late winning goal from captain Ormsby. The last-eight draw favoured Leeds with a trip to lower league side Wigan Athletic and in swirling conditions they booked a place in the semi-finals, with goals from John Stiles and Micky Adams, who had signed from Coventry City. Ironically, it would be the Sky Blues who would face Leeds next, with a place at Wembley at stake. Leeds took the lead through David Rennie, then Coventry levelled through Micky Gynn. Keith Houchen then gave the side from the First Division the lead before Edwards levelled for the ecstatic Whites. However, in the end Dave Bennett won it late on for Coventry and the only consolation for Leeds was there was still the chance they would meet the Sky Blues in the First Division the following season.

Despite making the last four of the FA Cup, league form never waned and a 3-2 win at home to West Bromwich Albion secured a play-off place. First up were Oldham Athletic at Elland Road in which Edwards scored a last-minute winner and in the return leg he notched a last-gasp leveller which took Leeds through on away goals and a tie with First Division side Charlton Athletic. The Addicks won the first game 1-0 at Selhurst Park, before Brendan Ormsby tapped home the winner at Elland Road two days later. This meant a third game at St Andrews and more heartbreak for the Whites. John Sheridan scored with a brilliant free kick in the first half of stoppage time, before a brace from Peter Shirtliff meant another season in England's second tier. It really was a case of so near, so far.

Coming so close the previous season, Leeds were installed as strong favourites to finally make a return to the promised land of the First Division. However, the opposite couldn't have been more true as the side struggled for goals, with only three in its opening nine league

Leeds United, 1989-90.

Ian Baird scores in a 2-1 win for Leeds United v Hull City on 29 October 1988.

games, which left the side in 16th place. Unlike the previous season, Leeds never looked like a promotion-winning side, losing 6-3 away at Plymouth Argyle as wins were all too hard to come by. The signing of Bobby Davison from Derby County proved to be an inspired one, and he marked his debut with a goal in a 4-2 home win against Swindon Town. The game was also memorable for the debut of one David Batty. Leeds failed to make any headway in the FA Cup, as Aston Villa dispatched them, winning 2-1 at Elland Road. Results did improve from January onwards, including a 4-1 win at West Bromwich Albion and an impressive 5-0 win at home to Sheffield United in which John Pearson scored a hat-trick. Leeds finished the campaign in seventh, which considering the start they had was a decent finish, but the bigger picture was that they were about to start their seventh campaign in football's wilderness.

Bremner didn't make too many changes in the off season, with the arrivals of Noel Blake and Vince Hilaire both from Portsmouth. The start of the campaign was dreadful to say the least, winning just one of their opening six games. Despite a morale-boosting 2-1 win away at Peterborough United in the Littlewoods Cup, Bremner was sacked and the hunt was on for another manager. Peter Gunby again took caretaker charge and watched over three straight defeats, before Sheffield Wednesday manager Howard Wilkinson was appointed the new boss. Wilkinson's first job was to install confidence into a fragile squad and move them away from the relegation zone. He got off to a winning start, a 3-1 low key victory in the second leg against Peterborough United at Elland Road. Ian Baird, who had returned from

Portsmouth the previous season, scored in home wins against Hull City and West Bromwich Albion as Wilkinson's arrival started to have the desired effect. A 4-0 home win against Stoke City and a 3-0 away win at Walsall took Leeds into 11th place and a run of three consecutive wins over Christmas and New Year kept them there. Former manager Brian Clough's team knocked them out of the FA Cup at the fourth-round stage, but league form steadily kept improving following a 2-1 win over Leicester City sent them into sixth place and possible a tilt at promotion. Unfortunately for Leeds, it did not occur.

One day in March 1989 would change the club's history as Scotsman Gordon Strachan joined from Manchester United in a £300,000 move. It was a transfer that would shape the following 12 months. Leeds finished in a respectable 10th place, but all eyes were now on the following season in the hope that the Whites could end eight years out of England's top flight.

There was a real sense of expectancy that Wilkinson could deliver in his first full season and he added Vinnie Jones, Mel Sterland, John Hendrie and John McClelland to strengthen the squad, but his most important move was to make Strachan captain. Despite a shock 5-2 loss away at Newcastle United, in which Mick Quinn scored four, Leeds went on a 15-game unbeaten league win, which started thanks to a late own goal from Gary Parkinson at home to Middlesbrough. Other results of note were a 4-0 home win against Swindon Town in which Strachan scored his first hat-trick for the club and a 1-0 away win at West Ham United in which Jones scored the only goal. Bobby Davison then scored in six straight league games, and, following a 2-1 win away at Middlesbrough, Leeds topped the table for the first time all season. They stayed there after a 3-0 win at home to Brighton & Hove Albion just before Christmas and despite a rocky patch over the festive period, in which they picked up just two points from a possible nine, Lee Chapman joined from Nottingham Forest to strengthen the promotion push. His arrival was immediately effective as he scored in the 2-1 win away at Blackburn Rovers.

February was a sticky month for Leeds, with only one win coming from it in a crazy game at home to Hull City in which Strachan scored the winner in injury time as Leeds won 4-3. Other signings were made including Imre Varadi and Chris Kamara and they would play a vital part in the chase for promotion. Many point to the second half away at Oxford United as season defining. The side found themselves 2-0 down at the interval, but whatever was said in the dressing room seemed to work as goals from Chapman (2), Varadi and Chris Fairclough ensured a vital 4-2 win. Three more wins followed, including a 1-0 win away at Sunderland thanks to a Mel Sterland header.

Every season, Easter can be vital to a club's fortunes, and for Leeds this season it was no different. It started in disastrous fashion, following a 3-1 defeat on Good Friday away at Oldham Athletic. Three days later, though Leeds turned in a performance that had First Division class written all over it. Promotion rivals Sheffield United were destroyed 4-0 at

Lee Chapman scores the only goal for Leeds United to guarantee becoming champions of Division Two against Bournemouth on 5 May 1990.

Leeds United the Division Two Championship Trophy, 1989-90.

The civic reception for the promotion-winning Leeds United team, 13 May 1990.

Elland Road, in which youngster Gary Speed scored a brilliant fourth goal. Leeds were closing in on promotion, but their nerve failed them in a shock 2-1 home defeat to Barnsley. The club had two games left to seal the deal and a late wonder goal from captain marvel at home to Leicester City looked to have delivered promotion. However, results went against them, so they travelled to Bournemouth knowing they would need a win to secure a return to the Promised Land. A tense game was settled by a header from Lee Chapman and the celebrations could finally begin. Wilkinson had brought the Second Divison title in his first full season at the club; next up on the agenda was the First Divison.

DEBUTANTS IN THE 1980s

JOHN SHERIDAN

Debut: Middlesbrough (H) 20 November 1982
Appearances: 261 (6)
Goals: 52

Born in Manchester and discarded by Manchester City after signing schoolboy forms with them in August 1981, he joined Leeds in March 1982 and made his debut on the 20th November in a 0-0 draw at home to Middlesbrough. His first goal for the side came on Boxing Day 1982 away at Oldham Athletic and he would finish his first season as a professional with three goals in 29 games, with his other goals coming in a 3-0 FA Cup win over Preston North End and a 1-0 win over Charlton Athletic at the Valley.

He started the next season as a first-team regular but disaster struck for Sheridan when he suffered a broken leg in October that ruled him out for the rest campaign. He made 11 appearances that season, scoring in a 3-2 away win at Brighton & Hove Albion. The following season, he bounced back to became an ever-present in the side, scoring six goals, with goals coming against Oldham Athletic at Elland Road, another strike away at Charlton Athletic, a 5-0 win at home to Notts County, one in the loss at Portsmouth and a brace at home to Crystal Palace.

The following season, saw Sheridan captain the side for two games in the absence of newly appointed skipper Ian Snodin and he played in 38 games, scoring four goals. The 1986-87 season would be Sheridan's most productive in a Leeds shirt, scoring 16 goals in 53 appearances, with his most memorable strike coming in the play-off final replay against Charlton Athletic when he scored a fantastic free kick in the first half of extra time at St Andrews. Sheridan finished the season with the Leeds United Player of the Year award and was named in the 1986-87 PFA Second Division Team of the Year.

It would be more of the same over the next two campaigns as he featured 90 times, scoring 22 goals. Like in the 1986-87 season, Sheridan was named in the PFA Second Division Team of the Year. By this time, manager Billy Bremner, who led Leeds into the play-offs and FA Cup semi-finals in 1987 was replaced by Howard Wilkinson and although Sheridan played a huge part in Wilkinson's first season, by the 3 August 1989, after seven years, the Republic of Ireland international had joined Nottingham Forest for £650,000. It was the end of a glorious career at Elland Road.

DENIS IRWIN

Debut: Scunthorpe United (A) 16 January 1984
Appearances: 82
Goals: 1

The Cork-born player joined the ranks at Elland Road in February 1982 and would go on to captain the side at both Northern Intermediate League level and Central league level before signing professional ranks at Elland Road at the start of November 1983. By the time Irwin was 18, he made his Leeds United debut in an FA Cup tie away at Scunthorpe United at the Old Showground, having come through the youth and reserve-team ranks. By the end of the 1983-84 season, Leeds had finished tenth in the old Second Division, but for the Irishman he had made his breakthrough at first-team level. The start of the following campaign saw Irwin feature in the opening four games, which saw Leeds top the table with wins over Notts County (2-1), Fulham (2-0), Wolverhampton Wanderers (3-2) and Grimsby Town (2-0) at Blundell Park.

It looked at one point, like Irwin would be part of a promotion-winning squad under the stewardship of Eddie Gray, but the promotion dream faded out and Leeds ended up finishing seventh. As for Irwin, he only missed one game – a 3-2 away win at Charlton Athletic at the start of November – and scored his one and only goal in a 5-0 win over Notts County in mid-January 1985. Having missed out on promotion the previous season, there were hopes that Leeds could go one better the following campaign, but following the appointment of Billy Bremner, Eddie Gray's young squad was broken up and Irwin, who had started every game under the Scotsman and all three under caretaker Peter Gunby (when Gray was relieved of his duties) rarely featured, with the last of his 82 appearances in the colours of Leeds United coming in a 4-0 loss away at Charlton Athletic on 18 January 1986. He moved across the Pennines to join Oldham Athletic at the end of the season, where he became part of the Latics who would battle with Leeds over the next three seasons. He scored for Oldham against the Whites in a League Cup tie at Boundary Park, which featured on *Sportsnight* on the BBC. From Oldham he went on to join Manchester United, who would battle with Leeds for the First Division title in 1992. It was a battle Leeds ended up winning and Irwin went on to play a further 32 times in the red of Manchester United against Leeds only scoring once, in a 3-0 win at the back end of the 1997-98 season.

MERVYN DAY

Debut: Oldham Athletic (A) 2 February 1985
Appearances: 268

The Chelmsford-born stopper had an extinguished career in the English game, which started way back in 1973 at West Ham United. At the age of 19, Day became the youngest goalkeeper to play in an FA Cup Final in 1975 in the Hammers' 2-0 win over London rivals Fulham.

In 1979 he joined another London club in Leyton Orient and stayed at Brisbane Road until 1983, when he moved to the Midlands to join Aston Villa in August. With Eddie Gray in charge of rebuilding things at Elland Road, the Scotsman spent £30,000 on the goalkeeper, and Day made his debut in a 1-1 draw away at Oldham Athletic at the start of February 1985. He played in the remaining 18 games that season as the Whites finished in seventh place, in the days before the end-of-season play-offs. The 1985-86 season saw a change of manager, with Billy Bremner replacing Eddie Gray, with Day missing just two games all season, a 1-1 draw at home to Grimsby Town and a 2-0 home loss against eventual champions Norwich City on a gloomy November day. One game that will live long in the memory for all the wrong reasons was the 6-3 loss away at Stoke City, but it would get even worse the following season!

The 1986-87 season saw Day play a vital part as Leeds reached the FA Cup semi-finals and missed out on promotion, losing a play-off replay against Charlton Athletic at St Andrews. Day had missed the first eight games, when he was replaced by new signing Ronnie Sinclair, but he didn't look back after starting at home to Hull City in mid-September. As for Stoke City, Day conceded seven!

Over the next two campaigns, Day was almost an ever-present, missing just one game – a 0-0 draw at Crystal Palace in mid-December 1988 when he was replaced by Ian Andrews. The 1989-90 season saw Day finally help Leeds back to the Promised Land of the First Division, and he missed only three games due to an injury picked up in the 4-3 loss away at Leicester City. As Leeds returned to the First Division, John Lukic rejoined the side from Arsenal and Day only featured in a League Cup tie at home to Leicester City and a Zenith Data Systems Cup tie away at Wolverhampton Wanderers over the next two seasons. In his final season at the club, Day started in games away at Manchester City, Charlton Athletic and Everton before joining Carlisle United as an assistant coach.

BRENDAN ORMSBY

Debut: Huddersfield Town (H) 8 March 1986
Appearances: 57
Goals: 7

The Birmingham-born centre-half joined Aston Villa from Ladywood Comprehensive School and signed full professional forms in October 1978. Sadly for Ormsby, as would be the story throughout his career, injuries took their toll and he missed the whole of the claret-and-blue title win in 1981, but he did feature on three occasions as they won the European Cup for the first time in 1981-82. He stayed at Villa Park until March 1986, from where he joined up with Billy Bremner at Elland Road.

In his first season in west Yorkshire he played in the last 12 games of that campaign and captained the club on the final day of the season away at Norwich City, with current skipper Ian Snodin ruled out. The 1986-87 campaign would be the one to remember for Ormsby as, not only did he take on the captaincy duties full time following the sale of Snodin to Everton, but he scored some memorable goals along the way.

Leeds started the season in decent form, and Ormsby marked his first game as stand-in captain that season (before Snodin's sale) with a goal in a 3-0 derby-day win over Hull City at Elland Road. He followed this strike up with league goals against Crystal Palace, Ipswich Town and West Bromwich Albion as Leeds reached the end-of-season play-offs. Ormsby's greatest day in a Leeds shirt came when they had reached the FA Cup fifth round and were paired with First Division Queens Park Rangers at Elland Road. With the tie evenly balanced with five minutes to go (Leeds had taken the lead through Ian Baird only for a David Rennie own goal to restore parity), up popped Ormsby with a header at the Kop end to send Leeds into the quarter-finals of the competition for the first time in ten years. They eventually beat Wigan Athletic, a game Ormsby missed through injury, before losing to Coventry City in an emotionally draining game at Hillsborough. Having qualified for the play-offs, Leeds saw off Oldham Athletic in the semi-finals, before meeting First Division side Charlton Athletic in the final. The Addicks won the first leg at Selhurst Park, before an Ormsby goal sent the tie into a replay at St Andrews. Sadly for Ormsby, he severely damaged his cartilage, an injury that would keep him out for just under two years. He made his last appearance in a Leeds shirt in the 3-3 draw away at Shrewsbury Town on 13 May 1989.

PETER HADDOCK

Debut: Blackburn Rovers (A) 23 August 1986
Appearances: 130(17)
Goals: 1

Born and bred in Newcastle, Haddock, or 'the Fish' as he was affectively known, joined his home-town club as an apprentice in 1978 before making his football league debut in a 3-0 win over Queens Park Rangers at the start of September 1981. It was whilst he was as St James Park that he had a brief loan spell at Burnley before returning north. At this time he had lost his place at Newcastle United and subsequently joined Leeds United for a fee of £45,000 in July 1986.

Sadly for Haddock, his first season was blighted by injury, featuring in total only 13 times as the Whites reached both the FA Cup semi-final and the play-off final before losing out in both. The following season though would be a completely different kettle of fish, as Haddock had battled back from his Achilles' injury, and, following his first appearance in a 1-0 win over Leicester City in mid-August 1987, he never looked back. He started 44 games and came off the bench in two others, scoring his one and only goal for the side in a 4-2 win over Swindon Town in which a certain David Batty made his debut. To add to the plaudits, Haddock walked away with the Leeds United Player of the Year award at the end of the campaign. Injury struck once more the following season, and he only started eight times, with a further seven off the bench. His best season came in 1989-90 as he forged a centre-half partnership with Chris Fairclough as Leeds won promotion back to the top flight following eight years away. He made 47 appearances in total and became a huge fans' favourite.

With Leeds back in the big time, they splashed the cash and bought in Chris Whyte to partner Fairclough, and Haddock would start the 1990-91 season at left-back. Sadly for the Fish, he sustained a serious knee injury in a Rumbelows Cup semi-final tie at Elland Road against Manchester United and would never kick another ball in the colours of Leeds United. He was awarded a deserved testimonial by the club three years later at home to Bradford City, with the likes of Chris Kamara, Vinnie Jones and Bobby Davison all featuring for the Whites. For the record, Leeds won the game 3-2 with goals coming from Colin Hoyle (og), Jamie Forrester and Rod Wallace in front of a crowd of just over 6,000.

DAVID BATTY

First Debut: Swindon Town (H) 21 November 1987
Second Debut: Coventry City (H) 14 December 1998
Appearances: 350 (23)
Goals: 4

Born in Leeds and educated at Allerton Grange, Batty signed apprentice forms at Elland Road in the summer of 1985 when he joined from Tingley Athletic. He made his debut on 21 November 1987 in a 4-2 win over Swindon Town, and he would go on to make 26 appearances in his first season as a professional, scoring in a 2-1 win away at Manchester City on Boxing Day 1987. The 1988-89 season saw a change of manager at Elland Road, as Howard Wilkinson replaced Billy Bremner. Batty still became an important part of the side under 'Sgt Wilko' as he featured 35 times as Leeds finished in tenth position in the old Second Division. The 1989-90 season saw Batty play a huge role as Leeds finally ended their eight-year exile from England's top flight when he started in 39 league games and came off the bench in three others. With Leeds back in the First Division, Batty would play a starring role as he missed just two games all season, as the Whites looked for glory on four fronts. He missed one league game – a goalless draw away at Tottenham Hotspur – and the first leg of the Rumbelows Cup semi-final away at Manchester United. At the end of the season he was voted Leeds United Player of the Year and also celebrated his first England cap against the USSR in May 1991.

The 1991-92 season not only saw Leeds finally end 18 years of hurt as they beat arch rivals Manchester United to the First Division title, but it also saw Batty handed the captaincy when Gordon Strachan was out injured. He led the side seven times, losing only twice, a last-minute defeat away at Crystal Palace and a Zenith Data Systems Cup defeat at home to Nottingham Forest, when Leeds played an under-strength team. Batty also hit the back of the net amongst jubilant scenes at Elland Road at home to Manchester City on a glorious sunny day at the start of September and at home to Notts County in February 1992. He featured a further 40 times in 1992-93, scoring the second at home to Middlesbrough and a further nine times in 1993-94 before he was surprisingly sold to Blackburn Rovers, where he would go on to win the Premier League title in 1995.

When David O'Leary was appointed manager of the Whites in October 1998, his first signing was to bring back Batty from his exile at Newcastle United. He picked up a rib injury in his second debut at home to Coventry City which ruled him out for three months, before he returned at home to Tottenham Hotspur. He started the millennium season in fine form before picking up another injury, this time away at Leicester City, which kept him out for over a year. He returned in December 2000 at home to Sunderland and he would became a vital cog under David O'Leary. Sadly for Batty, once O'Leary was gone, new boss Terry Venables never picked him. Peter Reid used him on eight occasions at the start of the 2003-04 season, but he would play his last and 373rd game for Leeds under Eddie Gray away at his old Newcastle United in January 2004 when he was substituted after half an hour.

CHRIS FAIRCLOUGH

Debut: Portsmouth (H) 25 March 1989
Appearances: 232 (9)
Goals: 23

The Nottingham-born defender joined his hometown club in 1981, where he stayed at the City Ground until June 1987 when he moved down south to join Tottenham Hotspur. It was from here that he joined Leeds, originally on loan in March 1989, before making the move permanent and he played in the last 11 games of the 1988-89 campaign. He became

an integral part of what manager Howard Wilkinson was attempting to achieve at Elland Road. He featured 48 times when Leeds won promotion to the old First Division after an eight-year hiatus. He also hit the back of the net with nine vital goals, including strikes at home to Blackburn Rovers, Sunderland, AFC Bournemouth, Watford and Barnsley, with the latter coming despite having stitches for a wound above his eye. He was rewarded for his excellent displays in his first full season at Elland Road with a place in the 1989-90 Second Division Team of the Year and also being named the Leeds United Player of the Year. He went down in history the following season by scoring the Whites' first goal back in the top flight in a memorable 3-2 win away at Everton, and he followed this up with four further strikes in 51 appearances from centre-back. With club captain Gordon Strachan missing due to injury away at Southampton at the start of March 1991, Wilkinson threw Fairclough the armband and he would deputise at home to Aston Villa and away against Sheffield United. Having forged a brilliant centre-half partnership with Chris Whyte, Fairclough continued his excellent form in season 1991-92 as Leeds ended 18 years of hurt by winning the First Division title. Fairclough scored the vital first goal on Easter Monday at home to Coventry City as Leeds went on to win the game 2-0. The following two seasons saw Fairclough feature on 86 occasions, scoring seven times, with goals coming in the 1992-93 season at home to Coventry City, Arsenal, Middlesbrough and the following campaign away at Sheffield Wednesday, Newcastle United, at home to the Magpies and away at Swindon Town, which was the 100th Premier League goal that the Robins would concede as they were relegated out of the top flight. With the signings of Carlton Palmer, John Pemberton, Lucas Radebe and the emergence of David Wetherall, Fairclough found chances difficult to come by the following campaign, and in the summer of 1995 the title winner joined newly promoted Bolton Wanderers for £500,000.

GORDON STRACHAN OBE

Debut: Portsmouth (H) 25 March 1989
Appearances: 235 (10)
Goals: 45

Born in Edinburgh, Strachan began his career with Dundee north of the border and was a regular in the 1975-76 season. He stayed in Tayside until November 1977 when he joined Aberdeen. It was at Pittodrie where Strachan would go on to win the European Cup Winners' Cup when Aberdeen defeated Real Madrid in 1983. He moved south of border when he joined Manchester United in August 1984 and would go on to win the 1985 FA Cup Final with the Red Devils against Everton.

Fast forward to March 1989, and Howard Wilkinson would pay Manchester United £300,000 to take Strachan across the Pennines as a new era was about to begin at Elland Road. Strachan played in the last 11 games of that season, scoring three goals, and by the start of the 1989-90 season he was made club captain as Wilkinson chose his new leader. It proved to be an inspirational choice as Strachan was an ever-present in all competitions, only being substituted in two games, at home to Wolves when he came off after 64 minutes and at home to Portsmouth when he came off six minutes from time. The Scotsman scored 18 vital goals, with him becoming the team's penalty taker, but one goal would really stand out. With Leeds needing a win in the penultimate game at home to Leicester City, the game was evenly poised with five minutes to go and up stepped Captain Marvel to fire in from 25 yards, and commentator John Helm uttered the famous words, 'have you ever seen a better goal, have you ever seen one better timed?' In the end, Leeds needed a win at AFC Bournemouth on the final day to secure the Second Division title, and that is exactly what transpired thanks to a Lee Chapman winner. Strachan was also named in the PFA Second Division Team of the Year. As well as leading Leeds out of the wilderness, he went on to get even better over the next 24 months. He made 52 appearances and scored ten goals in the first season back, which saw him win the Football Writers' award of Footballer of the Year, as well as being named in the First Division PFA Team of the Year.

What transpired the following season took everyone's breath away as Strachan led the side to First Division glory after a titanic battle with his former club Manchester United. He scored four goals along the way, all penalties, as Leeds won the title. The following season saw Leeds fail to set the world alight both domestically and in Europe, though Strachan was in majestic form in the games at home to Stuttgart, the replay in Barcelona and away at Rangers, and he was awarded with the Leeds United Player of the Year award in 1993. Another 38 appearances were added in season 1993-94 as Leeds finished in fifth place and Strachan nipped in with four goals. The 1994-95 campaign would be his last at Elland Road and with only seven games to his name and a back injury, he joined the coaching staff at Coventry City, where he would go on to manage the side until September 2001.

GARY SPEED

Debut: Oldham Athletic (H) 6 May 1989
Appearances: 291 (20)
Goals: 57

The late, great Gary Speed became a Leeds United trainee in April 1986 and he signed fully at the start of June 1988. He made his name in the Northern Intermediate League, scoring in 12 consecutive games, and he made his Leeds United debut in a goalless draw at home to Oldham Athletic at the start of May 1989, with Leeds having little to play for. The following season, Speed made 12 starts and 14 substitute appearances as Leeds ended their eight-year stay in the Second Division. The Welshman scored three goals and is best remembered for his strike in the 4-0 derby win over Sheffield United on Easter Monday, when club commentator John Boyd proudly announced, 'go on Gary Speed, go get one yourself,' and he did! His other goals came at home to Bradford City in a 1-1 draw and a 2-2 draw away at Brighton & Hove Albion.

Speed's real breakthrough year came the following season with the Whites back in the big time and the side needing a permanent number 11. Speed, who had started ten of the last 11 games the previous season, fitted the bill perfectly and featured in a total of 56 games, starting 51 of them. He chipped in with double goalscoring figures with notable strikes coming on the opening day of the season away at his boyhood side Everton, a half volley in a 3-0 win at home to Derby County and a double in the 5-0 drubbing over Sunderland and by this time he had already been capped by Wales.

Season 1991-92 would be one that would stick in the memory as Speed missed just one league game, a 4-1 drubbing of Aston Villa at Villa Park, as Leeds defeated arch rivals Manchester United to the First Division title. It was this season that the Welshman took a liking to the League Cup, scoring a brace against Everton and one at home to Manchester United in the fifth round. He would end his Leeds United career with 11 goals in that competition. However, the

1992-93 season proved to be disappointing for all concerned at Elland Road as the side failed to build on the previous season's success, but Speed played a starring role in the demolition of Stuttgart in the European Cup, scoring the opening goal as Leeds looked to overturn a 3-0 deficit. Speed featured 52 times that season, missing just three games, and was voted into the 1992-93 FA Premier League Team of the Year along with Tony Dorigo.

It would be more of the same over the next three seasons, when he appeared 130 times, scoring 22 goals. He had the honour of captaining the Whites in the 3-0 loss at home to Arsenal, with Gary McAllister ruled out. He joined his boyhood club Everton in the summer of 1996 and would go on to represent Newcastle United, Bolton Wanderers and Sheffield United before managing the Blades and his own country.

Tragically, it was announced on 27 November 2011 that Speed had passed away and the pouring of grief could be seen up and down the country. His former midfield teammates, Gary McAllister, Gordon Strachan and David Batty, all returned to Elland Road for the home game against Millwall at the start of December 2011 as the club paid a wonderful tribute to its former title winner and there wasn't a dry eye in the house. There is now a Gary Speed suite in the Family Stand named in his honour.

MEL STERLAND

Debut: Newcastle United (A) 19 August 1989
Appearances: 143 (3)
Goals: 20

The Sheffield-born right-back started his career in the blue half of the city, making his debut at Hillsborough under one former Leeds United icon Jack Charlton, and he went on to play under another, a certain Howard Wilkinson. It was at Sheffield Wednesday where Sterland would win his one and only England cap in a friendly against Saudi Arabia.

After ten years in the north of England he decided to travel further north and joined Glasgow Rangers, but he only stayed at Ibrox for one season, before linking up with Howard Wilkinson once again when he joined Leeds for a fee of £600,000. His first season couldn't have gone any better as he featured 48 times, scoring five goals as Leeds battled with the other half of Sheffield for promotion to the First Division. When the goals came they were special, a fine free kick at home to Oxford United, another away at Portsmouth in a crazy 3-3 draw on the south coast, an even better free kick from around 35 yards at Bramall Lane, a vital headed winner away at Sunderland and the opener in the nerve-wracking 2-1 win over Leicester City at the back end of April. In the end both sides from Yorkshire would go on to win promotion on the final day of an emotionally draining campaign.

Back in the top flight, Leeds battled on four fronts, the First Division, the Rumbelows Cup, the FA Cup and the Zenith Data Systems Cup, and Sterland, or 'Zico' as he was nicknamed, started in 55 of 56 games, only missing a league cup win at home to Oldham Athletic. He nipped in with a further eight goals from right-back, including strikes away at Manchester United, another winner away at Sunderland, the opener in the Boxing Day win at home to Chelsea and another free kick, this time at home to Sheffield United at the back end of the season. The following season would go down as one of Leeds United's greatest as they battled for First Division supremacy with arch rivals Manchester United and Sterland was at the forefront of it, scoring a further seven goals in 38 games. He scored a brace at home to Sheffield United (he took a real liking to them), a free kick at home to Queens Park Rangers, a fantastic diving header away at Aston Villa and a vital penalty kick at home to Manchester United. Sadly for Zico, an injury away at Tottenham Hotspur ended his season, but he picked up a deserved Championship medal at home to Norwich City at the start of May 1992. He made his return from injury the following January but he announced his retirement from the game in January 1994.

MANAGERS APPOINTED IN THE 1980s

MAURICE LINDLEY (CARETAKER)

Only game in charge: Tottenham Hotspur (H) 13 September 1980
Games: 1
Won: 0
Drawn: 1
Lost: 0

MAURICE LINDLEY

It's probably more important now than at any time since the early 'sixties — when we were struggling in the Second Division — that the true supporters of Leeds United rally round the club.

A lot of things have happened in the last few weeks that I hope will never occur again. Without making excuses in any way for our poor results, I think that some of the feeling generated by sections of our supporters has got through to the players and had an effect on them.

All that, I hope, is in the past. We are now in a position where we need all the support we can muster. To those who have stayed away in the last weeks I would say . . . give us your backing again. To those who have stuck by the club all I can say is thanks a million and keep it up. Now is the time for all of us to pull together and for the players to show their true professionalism.

There have been times this season when we have put ourselves into situations on the pitch that should never have occured. I am sure the players realise what's needed and with the support of all concerned, I am sure things will improve.

I believe we are probably short of two or three players of a certain type who would provide the kind of stability we have been lacking. I don't think that it is any secret that we need a central midfield player who can command situations in the way that Graeme Souness does for Liverpool. Having said that, this type of player is in short supply but it is a key role, preventing opposing players from breaking through and getting at our back four, an area of the game we seem to have slipped up in this season.

As acting manager until a permanent appointment is made, I do not see myself in a position to make signings. Every manager has his own ideas and I certainly would not want to clutter up the place with new players whom the new manager might not feel were required.

Whoever is appointed will not be able to sweep away the cobwebs overnight but it needs an appointment to be made reasonably quickly and then the backing of everyone connected with the club to get things moving.

LEEDS UNITED AFC
Elland Road
Leeds LS11 0ES
Telephone:
Leeds (0532) 716037
Information Service:
Leeds (0532) 702621/5
Pools Office:
Leeds 713403
Sports & Souvenir
Shop: Leeds 706844
Lottery Office:
Leeds 771170
Programme
Editorial/Advertising:
Leeds 706344

President:
The Right Honourable
The Earl of Harewood, LL.D.
Chairman: Manny Cussins
Vice-Chairman:
Rayner Barker, M.C.I.T., M.B.I.M.
Directors:
Jack Marjason
Sidney G. Simon
Brian Woodward.

Deputy Manager: Dave Merrington
Assistant Managers: Dave Blakey,
Maurice Lindley
General Manager/Secretary:
Keith Archer
Commercial Manager: Mike Lockwood

Leeds United Match Day Programme
Published by Leeds United A.F.C.
Edited by Bob Baldwin
Designed and Printed by Hemmings & Capey (Leicester) Ltd., Ireton Avenue, Leicester
Colour photography by Andrew Varley (Cover) and Neville Chadwick Photography, Leicester (Centre Pages)

Following the sacking of Adamson, Lindley again took control on a caretaker basis, overseeing a goalless draw at home to Tottenham Hotspur before the arrival of former striker Allan Clarke in the managerial hot seat.

Maurice Lindley's only line up: Tottenham Hotspur (H) 13 September 1980: Lukic, Hird, Stevenson, Cherry, Hart, Firm, Chandler, Parlane, Connor (Hamson), Sabella, Graham.

ALLAN CLARKE

First game in charge: Manchester United (H) 20 September 1980
Last game in charge: West Bromwich Albion (A) 18 May 1982
Games: 84
Won: 27
Drawn: 22
Lost: 35

The first of Don Revie's disciples, Allan Clarke took on the role as manager when he replaced Jimmy Adamson as the new Leeds United boss in September 1980. Clarke, who to this day goes down in the history of the football club as the only player to score a winning goal in an FA Cup Final, started his managerial career down the road at Barnsley as player-manager and won promotion with the Tykes to the old Third Division in May 1979. He then finished the following season in 11th place before the lure of his old club came knocking. He left the Barnsley job to another former Leeds stalwart in Norman Hunter as he moved to Elland Road.

He was given a standing ovation ahead of his first game against Manchester United, which ended in a 0-0 draw, and he achieved his first win as manager at Leeds thanks to a Carl Harris strike at home to Manchester City. The defensive frailties were still an issue though, as the side embarrassingly lost 5-0 at home to Arsenal, but by the start of December 1980 Leeds were slowly improving, winning three in a row – at home to Brighton & Hove Albion (1-0), away at West

ALLAN CLARKE

The two most important sets of people in football are players and supporters and while I shall do everything possible to ensure that every player gives 110 per cent for Leeds United, it is just as important that we get the backing of all supporters.

My first priority is obviously to get the team away from the wrong end of the table. Leeds United are a big club only in name at the moment not performances and while I do not want to make too many predictions or lay down too many targets I shall regard myself as a failure if we have not won a major trophy over the next three years.

I have told the players that they will all be given the opportunity in the next few weeks to show me what they can do and I think they realise what I expect from them in terms of attitude, not only on Saturday afternoons but throughout the week in training.

As soon as I have settled in at Elland Road I want to get out and about as much as possible to meet our supporters and in the two years I have had in management I have learned that the public relations side of the business is very important.

So far as my backroom staff goes, I have brought with me from Barnsley Martin Wilkinson who will work as my number two and Barry Murphy who will be first team coach.

We shall be working very closely with Maurice Lindley who has almost a lifetime's experience in the game and I hope to make further appointments in the next few weeks.

We shall work very much as a team off the pitch and I hope that this team spirit will spread to our supporters and you will give us your support in every possible way.

LEEDS UNITED AFC
Elland Road
Leeds LS11 0ES
Telephone:
Leeds (0532) 716037
Information Service:
Leeds (0532) 702621/5
Pools Office:
Leeds 713403
Sports & Souvenir
Shop: Leeds 706844
Lottery Office:
Leeds 771170
Programme
Editorial/Advertising:
Leeds 706344

President:
The Right Honourable
The Earl of Harewood, LL.D.
Chairman: Manny Cussins
Vice-Chairman:
Rayner Barker, M.C.I.T., M.B.I.M.
Directors:
Jack Marjason
Sidney G. Simon
Brian Woodward.
Team Manager: Allan Clarke
Deputy Manager: Martin Wilkinson
Assistant Manager: Maurice Lindley
First Team Coach: Barry Murphy
General Manager/Secretary:
Keith Archer
Commercial Manager: Mike Lockwood
Leeds United Match Day Programme
Published by Leeds United A.F.C.
Edited by Bob Baldwin
Designed and Printed by Hemmings & Capey
(Leicester) Ltd., Ireton Avenue, Leicester
Colour photography by
Neville Chadwick Photography, Leicester

Bromwich Albion (2-1) and at home to Nottingham Forest (1-0), thanks to a rare strike from Brian Greenhoff. The second half of the season under Clarke saw results improve massively, and Leeds went on a run of winning eight in 11 league games, which included a memorable 1-0 win at Old Trafford thanks to a late Brian Flynn goal five minutes from time. Clarke finished his first season in a respectable ninth position, but goals had been an issue with only

39 in 42 league games. To help with this, Clarke splashed the cash on West Bromwich Albion winger Peter Barnes for £930,000, but it didn't work out and he bought back his old teammate Frank Gray from Nottingham Forest. The season started awfully for Clarke and Leeds as former player Alan Curtis scored in a 5-1 win for newly promoted Swansea City at the Vetch Field in front of the *Match of the Day* cameras. Results didn't get much better in the early months of the season. Clarke did bring in Kenny Burns from Nottingham Forest and immediately made him captain ahead of Trevor Cherry. It had the desired impact at first, as Leeds defeated West Bromwich Albion 3-1 at Elland Road with a brilliant third goal from Terry Connor, and they recorded back-to-back wins thanks to an Eddie Gray winner a week later at home to Sunderland. However, results were inconsistent and again Clarke turned to the transfer window, this time bringing in Frank Worthington from Birmingham City in exchange for Byron Stevenson. Worthington scored the winner in his second game away at Sunderland and would go on to score a further eight goals as Leeds battled against the drop. Despite an excellent 4-1 win at Aston Villa and a nail-biting victory over Brighton & Hove Albion in the penultimate game of the campaign, Leeds were relegated to the Second Division for the first time since 1964 and Clarke and his assistant Martin Wilkinson paid the price with their jobs. 'Sniffer' did go onto manage Scunthorpe United, defeating Leeds in the FA Cup in season 1983-84. He had a second spell at Oakwell and a brief time at Lincoln City.

Allan Clarke's first line up: Manchester United (H) 20 September 1980: Lukic, Hird, Stevenson, Flynn, Hart, Firm, Cherry, Connor, Parlane, Gray, Graham. Sub not used: Greenhoff.

Allan Clarke's last line up: West Bromwich Albion (A) 18 May 1982: Lukic, Hird, Burns, Thomas, Hart, Cherry, E. Gray, Hamson (F. Gray), Connor, Barnes.

EDDIE GRAY MBE

First game in charge: Grimsby Town (A) 28 August 1982
Last game in charge: Walsall (A) 8 October 1985
Games: 157
Won: 57
Drawn: 55
Lost: 45

With no money available to spend, Leeds turned to another of Don Revie's former players in winger Eddie Gray. Gray continued to carry on playing for another two seasons whilst managing the side. Gray was not only manager on the opening day of the 1982-83 season, but he captained them as well as the side drew 1-1 away at Grimsby Town and by the end of Derby County's visit to Elland Road in mid-September, Leeds were in fifth position after three consecutive victories.

Gray led the side to a magnificent 4-1 League Cup win at Newcastle United when the side were 2-0 down on aggregate (the game was also featured on the BBC's *Sportsnight* programme) and following a pre-Christmas win at Rotherham United, thanks to a goal from youngster Mark Gavin, they were handily placed in the top five.

Gray again captained the side as they took First-Division Arsenal all the way in an FA Cup tie in which Aidan Butterworth looked to have won it in the 118th minute, only for a Graham Rix free kick to take the tie to a third game. A promotion bid failed to materialise, with the side finishing in eighth place at the end of Gray's first season in charge. Season two for the Scottish winger saw George McCluskey join from Celtic and Andy Watson from Aberdeen. The first half of the season turned into a disaster, with Leeds suffering a series of defeats that saw them in 19th place following a 3-2 loss away at Oldham Athletic on 27 December 1983. Towards the back end of the previous campaign, Gray put his emphasis on youth, handing debuts to John Sheridan, Tommy Wright and Scott Sellars, and the 1983-84 season saw another youngster in Denis Irwin make his debut for the side. A run of six wins in seven games propelled the side into a comfortable mid-table position and a Tommy Wright winner on the final day of the season saw the side finish in tenth place. In the game at home to Charlton Athletic, Gray wore the famous number 11 shirt for the last time as he retired as a player from the game.

His first season as a full on manager saw his young side get off to a brilliant start, winning their first four games of the campaign, and they topped the table after a 2-0 win away at Grimsby Town. There were some impressive displays, including a 6-0 demolition of Oldham Athletic in which Ritchie scored a hat-trick and Leeds were in a promising position of fifth heading into the Christmas period. The BBC cameras were in situ as the cup holders were

EDDIE GRAY'S POINT OF VIEW...

This afternoon sees the start of our home programme of matches and on behalf of everyone connected with the club I would like to welcome you to Elland Road and wish you all a good season.

We hope it will be an enjoyable and successful one. The players and my backroom staff have worked hard in the pre-season period to build up for the start of the season and I thought we were a little unfortunate not to start the new campaign in the best possible way with a win at Grimsby last week.

Had we taken all the chances we created, particularly in the first half at Blundell Park last Saturday, then I think we would have ended comfortable winners. But a draw was a useful result from our first match and hopefully we can go on from there against Wolves this afternoon.

For many of our side, last Saturday was our first experience of Second Division football. Although I joined the club in their last spell in Division Two, I never actually played in the Second Division until last week and one of the factors that pleased me about our performance was that we were able to dictate the pace of the game for long periods.

We have a number of players with a good turn of speed and if we can continue to play to this strength like we did for a good part of the Grimsby game then I am sure we will reap the benefits.

Some people have said how tight it will be in the Second Division this season and we certainly do not expect there to be any easy games over the course of the next nine months. All we can do is take one match at a time and hope to get the results that will see us there or thereabouts by the end of the season.

I would like to welcome Jimmy Lumsden back to Elland Road this afternoon. Jimmy who was here as a junior when I started my career at Leeds linked up with me again during the close-season and will work closely with myself and the other members of our coaching and backroom staff.

The younger players we currently have at the club have a tremendous chance to progress this season and I have made it clear to all of them that age and experience does not matter. If they show me they have what it takes then they can expect to come into consideration for a first team place this season.

Wolves fielded sides containing a large number of youngsters last Saturday when they beat Blackburn and in midweek when they drew at Chelsea and we are expecting a close game with them this afternoon.

I mentioned earlier on that I am hoping for an enjoyable season and I think it is important that we enjoy our football in the coming months and that you, our supporters, enjoy watching the side in action.

If we can hit this target then I am sure we will all be happy.

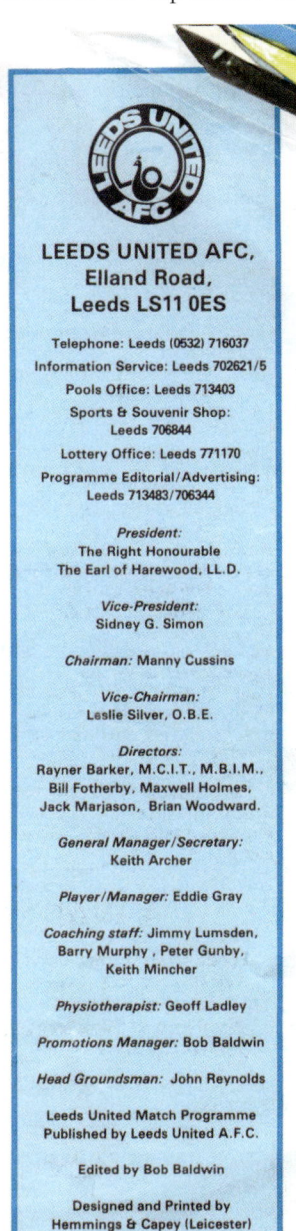

**LEEDS UNITED AFC,
Elland Road,
Leeds LS11 0ES**

Telephone: Leeds (0532) 716037
Information Service: Leeds 702621/5
Pools Office: Leeds 713403
Sports & Souvenir Shop:
Leeds 706844
Lottery Office: Leeds 771170
Programme Editorial/Advertising:
Leeds 713483/706344

President:
The Right Honourable
The Earl of Harewood, LL.D.

Vice-President:
Sidney G. Simon

Chairman: Manny Cussins

Vice-Chairman:
Leslie Silver, O.B.E.

Directors:
Rayner Barker, M.C.I.T., M.B.I.M.,
Bill Fotherby, Maxwell Holmes,
Jack Marjason, Brian Woodward.

General Manager/Secretary:
Keith Archer

Player/Manager: Eddie Gray

Coaching staff: Jimmy Lumsden,
Barry Murphy, Peter Gunby,
Keith Mincher

Physiotherapist: Geoff Ladley

Promotions Manager: Bob Baldwin

Head Groundsman: John Reynolds

Leeds United Match Programme
Published by Leeds United A.F.C.

Edited by Bob Baldwin

Designed and Printed by
Hemmings & Capey (Leicester)
Ltd., Ireton Avenue, Leicester

Colour photography by:
Andrew Varley

victorious in an FA Cup third-round tie at Elland Road played on a Friday night and despite some promising performances, which included a 5-0 win over Notts County at Elland Road and a 4-1 win over Crystal Palace, Leeds missed out on promotion by five points, finishing in seventh place.

The Whites made an awful start to the following campaign, which included a 6-2 loss away at Stoke City, and despite a 3-0 League Cup win over Walsall, Gray, along with his assistant Jimmy Lumsden, were sacked on 11 October. Director Brian Woodward resigned and the players were upset following the decision. Coach Peter Gunby was put in caretaker charge as Leeds looked for another new manager. As for Gray, he played for a brief spell at Whitby Town before coaching Middlesbrough reserve and youth sides. He was appointed manager of Rochdale in December 1986 and had a year as manager of Hull City. His second spell with Leeds commenced ahead of the 1995-96 season and he would go on to manage the side for a second time during the ill-fated 2003-04 season.

Eddie Gray's first line up: Grimsby Town (A) 28 August 1982: Lukic, Hird, E. Gray, Dickinson, Hart, Thomas, Connor, Butterworth, Worthington, F. Gray, Graham. Sub not used: Flynn.

Eddie Gray's last line up: Walsall (A) 8 October 1985: Day, Irwin, Phelan, Snodin, Linighan, Dickinson (McCluskey), Ritchie, Sheridan, Baird, Lorimer, Hamson.

PETER GUNBY (CARETAKER) OBE

First game in charge: Middlesbrough (H) 12 October 1985
Last game in charge: Grimsby Town (H) 19 October 1985
Games: 4
Won: 1
Drawn: 2
Lost: 1

Following the sacking of Gray, Leeds turned to Peter Gunby in the interim as they looked for a new manager. Gunby who was born in Leeds, made three appearances for Bradford City in the Football League. He also managed at Harrogate Town. His four games in caretaker charge saw Leeds defeat Middlesbrough thanks to a Peter Lorimer penalty, be on the end of a 6-1 hammering in the newly formed Full Members Cup, draw 1-1 to Sheffield United in the same competition and also draw 1-1 at home to Grimsby Town in a league game at Elland Road.

Peter Gunby's first line up: Middlesbrough (H) 12 October 1985: Day, Irwin, Phelan, Hamson, Linighan, Aspin, McCluskey, Sheridan, Baird, Lorimer, Ritchie (Wright)

Peter Gunby's last line up: Grimsby Town (H) 19 October 1985: Swinburne, Irwin, Phelan, Hamson, Linighan, Aspin, McCluskey, Dickinson, Baird, Lorimer, Ritchie. Sub not used: Sellars.

BILLY BREMNER

First game in charge: Barnsley (A) 27 October 1985
Last game in charge: Peterborough United (A) 27 September 1988
Games: 144
Won: 59
Drawn: 31
Lost: 54

Leeds again turned to another former player, this time the greatest captain the side has ever had, as Billy Bremner was appointed manager in October 1985. Bremner had been appointed manager of then Fourth Division side Doncaster Rovers and his stay at Belle Vue saw him win the Manager of the Month award in Division Four and in Division Three. He led Doncaster to promotion to the third tier of English football, finishing in third place, but they were relegated two seasons later. They were promoted back immediately finishing as runners-up, and ahead of the 1984-85 season Bremner returned to his old club to sign Aiden Butterworth. He also sold midfielder Ian Snodin to Leeds in May 1985 for £200,000. They ended up being part of the same team just a few months later.

Despite losing his first game in charge away at Barnsley, one of his moves was to hand the captaincy to Snodin, taking it away from Peter Lorimer. His first season at Elland Road saw a raft of players leave the club, allowing Bremner the opportunity to stamp his own authority on the side. Before the end of the 1985-86, in came David Harle from Doncaster Rovers,

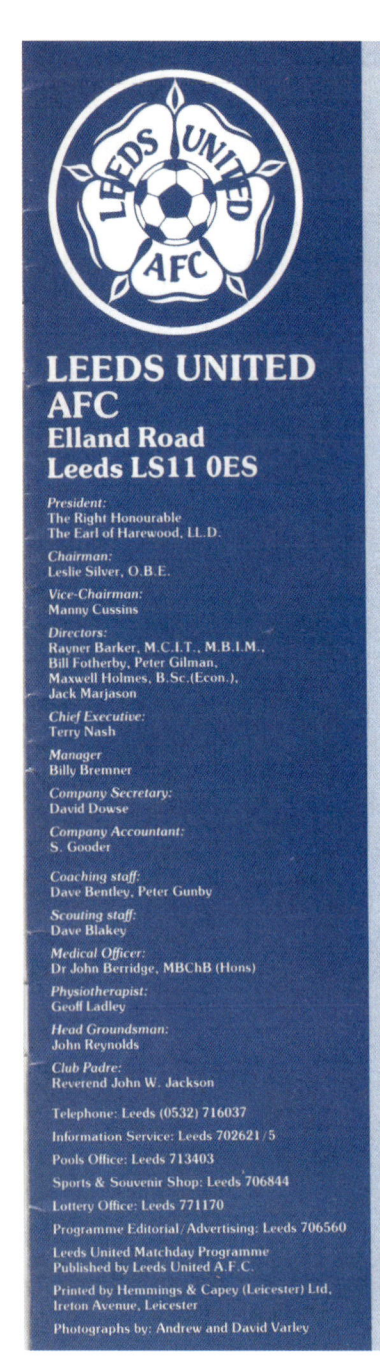

BILLY BREMNER

WELCOME TO THE MATCH

LEEDS UNITED AFC
**Elland Road
Leeds LS11 0ES**

President:
The Right Honourable
The Earl of Harewood, LL.D.

Chairman:
Leslie Silver, O.B.E.

Vice-Chairman:
Manny Cussins

Directors:
Rayner Barker, M.C.I.T., M.B.I.M.,
Bill Fotherby, Peter Gilman,
Maxwell Holmes, B.Sc.(Econ.),
Jack Marjason

Chief Executive:
Terry Nash

Manager:
Billy Bremner

Company Secretary:
David Dowse

Company Accountant:
S. Gooder

Coaching staff:
Dave Bentley, Peter Gunby

Scouting staff:
Dave Blakey

Medical Officer:
Dr John Berridge, MBChB (Hons)

Physiotherapist:
Geoff Ladley

Head Groundsman:
John Reynolds

Club Padre:
Reverend John W. Jackson

Telephone: Leeds (0532) 716297
Information Service: Leeds 702621/5
Pools Office: Leeds 713403
Sports & Souvenir Shop: Leeds 706844
Lottery Office: Leeds 771170
Programme Editorial/Advertising: Leeds 706560

Leeds United Matchday Programme
Published by Leeds United A.F.C.

Printed by Hemmings & Capey (Leicester) Ltd,
Ireton Avenue, Leicester

Photographs by: Andrew and David Varley

The last two weeks have been particularly difficult for the club following the departure of Eddie Gray.

Eddie was both a valued friend and a respected fellow manager, for whom everyone connected with Elland Road held a warm regard. His loss has therefore been keenly felt by fans and players alike, all of whom I know will join me in wishing him well in what we know will be a highly successful future.

For United, however, it must be business as usual as we play host tonight to First Division Aston Villa in the third round of the Milk Cup. Everyone in the game knows that we have the players at the club with the skill needed to make an impact in the Cup competitions and, more importantly, challenge for promotion. All too often, however, the performance of the whole team has not equalled the sum of the parts and some vital ingredient has appeared to be missing.

My task, quite simply therefore, is to identify that ingredient so that the team as a whole can realise its full potential.

Needless-to-say, this is a role which I both relish and value; to lead a top club like Leeds United is every manager's ambition and for me to return to a ground I know so well is doubly welcome.

I therefore look forward in the coming months to renewing old friendships and acquaintances, and to restoring United to its rightful position as one of the country's leading teams.

LEEDS UNITED AFC — GROUND REGULATIONS

1. All matches are played in accordance with the Rules and Regulations of the Football Association and The Football League and all persons entering this ground are admitted subject to the above Regulations and to the Regulations contained herein.
2. The Club reserves the right to remove or ban from the Ground any person who does not comply with the Regulations or whose presence is in the unfettered discretion of the Club a source of danger or annoyance to other persons or to the property of the Club.
3. The Club reserves the right to make changes to its advertised fixtures without notice and cannot guarantee play on any day.
4. There will be no refund of cash admission charges paid at the turnstiles under any circumstances.
5. A refund will be made in respect of seats booked in advance in the event of the match being postponed subject to a request being made within a reasonable time. No refund will be made when a match has been commenced or, in the case of season tickets, once the season has commenced.
6. No person is entitled to enter upon the field of play.
7. Taking video film, photographs or cine photographs is prohibited without permission.
8. No person may without the express authority of the Club in writing offer for sale any newspapers, periodicals or any other articles in the Ground or in the area surrounding the Ground.
9. Radio sets must be used in such a way as to cause no unnecessary noise or inconvenience to any other persons in the ground.
10. No person shall bring into the Ground any bottles, glasses or dangerous flags and banners; the consumption of intoxicating liquor is permitted only in bars or other places licensed or authorised by the Licensing Justices for the City of Leeds.
11. Any person entering onto the Ground must behave so as not to cause any annoyance to any other person on the ground and must not damage or intend to damage any property of the Club, must not use foul or abusive language, or throw missiles on to the pitch or elsewhere.
12. A willingness to submit to search by a Police Officer is a condition of entry and the Club will refuse admission to, or eject any person who refuses to be so searched.

Brendan Ormsby from Aston Villa, David Rennie from Leicester City and Bob Taylor, a striker from non-league Horden Colliery. Leeds finished in 14th place and further changes were needed. More signings arrived, with Ronnie Sinclair, Peter Haddock, Keith Edwards, Jack Ashurst and John Buckley all joining. Following a 3-0 win over Hull City at the end of September, Leeds were in fourth position and even hit the heights of second following impressive home wins against Crystal Palace (3-0) and Portsmouth (3-1). Leeds's results fluctuated from the sublime to the ridiculous (a 7-2 loss at Stoke City was proof of this), but the side finished in fourth place and qualified for the newly formed play-off competition. As well as their impressive league form, Leeds quietly made their way through the last four of the FA Cup, beating Telford United (2-1), Swindon Town (2-1), Queens Park Rangers (2-1) and Wigan Athletic (2-0), before a meeting with First Division Coventry City at Hillsborough. Despite taking the lead through a David Rennie header and equalising six minutes from time through another header from Keith Edwards, Leeds lost out thanks to a goal from Dave Bennett eight minutes into extra time. As for the play-offs, Leeds defeated Oldham on away goals and would meet First Division Charlton Athletic for a place back in the top flight. Charlton won the first leg thanks to a goal from Jim Melrose, but a tap-in from captain Ormsby took the tie to a replay at St Andrews. When John Sheridan scored a brilliant free kick in the 100th minute, Leeds looked set for promotion, but two goals from Peter Shirtliff earned the Addicks another crack at First Division football and left Leeds to lick their wounds.

They were installed as favourites the following season but finished in seventh place, missing out on the play-offs altogether, but Bremner did hand youngster David Batty his debut in a 4-2 win over Swindon Town. Following a poor start the 1988-89 season, which saw Leeds down in 18th place, Bremner was sacked, ending his second association with the club. Peter Gunby again took on the role and Billy returned to Doncaster in the summer of 1989, staying in south Yorkshire until November 1991. He tragically passed away on 7 December 1997.

Billy Bremner's first line up: Barnsley (A) 27 October 1985: Day, Dickinson, Phelan, I. Snodin, Linighan, Aspin, McCluskey, Hamson, Baird, Lorimer, Ritchie. Sub not used: Sellars.

Billy Bremner's last line up: Peterborough United (A) 27 September 1988: Day, G. Williams (Haddock), Adams, Aizlewood, Blake, Rennie, Batty, G. Snodin, Baird, Pearson, Hillaire. Sub not used: Davison.

PETER GUNBY (CARETAKER) OBE

First game in charge: Brighton & Hove Albion (A) 1 October 1988
Last game in charge: Watford (H) 8 October 1988
Games: 3
Won: 0
Drawn: 0
Lost: 3

Gunby again took on the role of caretaker boss before the arrival of Sheffield Wednesday manager Howard Wilkinson and Leeds were to lose all three games. Despite taking the lead away at Brighton & Hove Albion thanks to an Ian Baird goal, Leeds lost 2-1 and three days later, in what was the same scoreline, away at Sunderland, with Bobby Davison equalising a

NOTICEBOARD

PETER GUMBY'S LOOK BACK AT UNITED'S LAST TWO GAMES

LEEDS UNITED A.F.C.
ELLAND ROAD
LEEDS LS11 0ES

PRESIDENT
The Right Honourable
The Earl of Harewood, K.B.E., LL.D

Chairman:
Leslie Silver, O.B.E.

Managing Director: Bill Fotherby

Directors:
Rayner Barker, M.C.I.T., M.B.I.M.,
Peter Gilman,
Maxwell Holmes B.Sc (Econ),
Jack Marjason (Deputy Chairman),
Peter Ridsdale, Malcolm J. Bedford,
Eric Carlile, Ronald D. Feldman,
Alec Hudson

Manager:
Assistant Manager:
Chief Scout:
Coaches:
Norman Hunter, Peter Gunby
Physiotherapist: Alan Sutton
Medical Officers:
Dr John Berridge, M.BCh.B(Hons),
Dr Stewart Manning, M.B.B.S.
Company Secretary: David Dowse
Administration Manager: Alan Roberts
Commercial Manager: Bob Baldwin
Promotions Manager:
Maurice Bamford
Pools Manager: Arnie Todd
Company Accountant: Steve Gooder
Head Groundsman: John Reynolds
Club Padre:
Reverend John W. Jackson
Telephone: (0532) 716037
Fax: (0532) 706560
Leeds United Ticket Call 0898 12 16 80
Sports & Souvenir Shop (0532) 706844
Cashline/Lottery Office (0532) 771170
Leeds United Club Call 0898 12 11 80
Accounts Office (0532) 718538

Matchday programme
Published by Leeds United AFC
Printed by Printstream Ltd
33 Ashville Way, Whetstone,
LEICESTER
Tel: 0533 750057
Photographs by: Andrew Varley

HONOURS
League Champions: 1968-69, 1973-74
Runners-Up: 1964-65, 1965-66,
1969-70, 1970-71, 1971-72
Division Two Champions:
1923-24, 1963-64
Division Two Runners-Up: 1927-28,
1931-32, 1955-56
F.A. Cup Winners: 1972
Finalists: 1965, 1970, 1973
League Cup Winners: 1968
European Cup Finalists: 1974-75
European Cup Winners Cup Finalists:
1972-73
Fairs Cup Winners: 1970-71
Fairs Cup Finalists: 1966-67

"Our games at Brighton and Sunderland brought us two disappointing results but there was a vast improvement on our attitude at Sunderland on Tuesday compared with the Brighton game.

I can't fault any of the lads for the spirit they showed at Roker. At Brighton we looked lethargic and our concentration let us down in the second half. Really we did not deserve anything from the match.

We're not getting any run of the ball at the moment and I certainly thought we were worth something against Sunderland. The spirit was superb, all the lads worked hard and I thought we played the only decent football on the night. But we were caught out by their second goal and that's the way things are going against us at the moment.

The team spirit in the club is good and and we'll be looking to do well today against a Watford side that has made a good start to the season. A win this afternoon would do a world of good for our confidence and that's really all we need at the moment."

CUP DRAW
United have been drawn at home to Shrewsbury Town in the first round of the Simod Cup. The match will be played at Elland Road on Wednesday, 9th November, kick off 7.30 p.m. and will see the likely return to Leeds of striker Jim Melrose who was with us briefly last season before moving to Shrewsbury.

IRISH VISITORS
Elland Road staged a Gaelic Football match last Sunday when two leading exponents of the Irish game put on a special exhibition game. Galway and Mayo gave a stunning example of a game that is a cross between soccer, rugby, hockey... and a few other bodily contact sports as well. Honours ended even at 16 all.

DOUBLE CENTURY
John Sheridan made his 200th first team appearance for United in Tuesday's match at Sunderland, a double century that started off almost five years ago when he made his debut at home to Middlesbrough.

IN TODAY'S MATCH PROGRAMME
Page 5 ..... Chairman Leslie Silver's message for all supporters
Page 12 ... Brendan Ormsby recalls his debut days
Page 14 ... All the news from the Panini Family Stand
Page 16 ..... Question Time with Gary Williams
Pages 18/19.. Form check on today's visitors from Watford
Pages 24/25 ..... Up to date statistics and tables
Page 32 ...... Today's teams and match day officials.

12 16 80... TICKET CALL 0898 12 16 80... KEEP IN TO

Marco Gabbiadini goal. To complete the week to forget, Leeds lost 1-0 at home to Watford thanks to a Glyn Hodges goal and were in 21st place and in need of new pair of managerial hands.

Peter Gunby's first line up: Brighton & Hove Albion (A) 1 October 1988: Day, G. Williams, Adams, Aizlewood (Sheridan), Blake, Rennie, Batty, G Snodin, Baird, Pearson, Hillaire. Sub not used: Haddock.

258

Peter Gunby's last line up: Watford (H) 8 October 1988: Day, Aspin, Adams, Stiles (Snodin), Blake, Rennie, Batty, Sheridan, Baird, Davison (Pearson), Hillaire.

HOWARD WILKINSON

First game in charge: Peterborough United (H) 12 October 1988
Last game in charge: Manchester United (H) 7 September 1996
Games: 412
Won: 179
Drawn: 117
Lost: 116

After the experiment of using Don Revie's former players, Leeds then turned to a man who had been there and done it, in terms of winning promotion from the Second Division. Step forward Sheffield Wednesday boss Howard Wilkinson. Born in Sheffield, Wilkinson signed as an amateur with Sheffield United before moving across the city to join Sheffield Wednesday in June 1962. After four years at Hillsborough he joined Brighton & Hove Albion in the summer of 1966. He left the Seagulls in 1971 before joining his final club in Boston United. He joined them as player-coach and then player-manager, leading the Pilgrims to consecutive Northern Premier League titles. From Boston he joined Mossley as player-manager once more, before managing the England C Team. Wilkinson then began his first full-time coaching career at Notts County after legendary boss Jimmy Sirrell became general manager. He took control of the side from Meadow Lane before leaving for Sheffield Wednesday in June 1983.

In his first full season with the Owls, he led them to promotion to the top flight, finishing in second place behind champions Chelsea. In Wednesday's second season back in the top flight they finished fifth and would have qualified for Europe had there not been a ban in place on English sides following the Heysel disaster.

Following a lack of spending power in SW6, Wilkinson moved up the M1 and on 10 October 1988 was appointed manager of Leeds United. His first job was to move the Whites away from the relegation zone, having been in 21st place when he first took over. Slowly but surely, performances and results improved and following a 3-0 win away at Walsall, where one of Wilko's new signings Mike Whitlow was on the mark, Leeds moved up to 11th place. The crowds started to flock back to Elland Road and on Boxing Day 1988, 31,622 supporters saw the Whites dispose of Blackburn Rovers thanks to goals from Ian Baird and Bobby Davison. After a 1-0 win over Birmingham City in mid-January, Leeds were up to seventh, and instead of nervously looking over their shoulders, they were now looking up. The 23 March 1989 would be a red letter day in Wilkinson's short tenure as he paid Manchester United £300,000 for the services of Gordon Strachan, and Wilko had his new leader. Also joining that day but originally on loan was Chris Fairclough from Tottenham Hotspur.

Wilkinson already had eyes on promotion in season 1989-90. Leeds finished in a respectable tenth place in 1988-89 but attention quickly turned to the following season. In came Vinnie Jones, John McClelland, Jim Beglin, Mel Sterland, Chris O'Donnell, Michael Thomas and John Hendrie, nicknamed the 'magnificent seven'. Despite getting off to a forgettable start, losing 5-2 at Newcastle United, Leeds went on a brilliant unbeaten run and by the start of November, following a 3-0 win at home to AFC Bournemouth, were up to second. They reached the summit after a 2-0 win at Middlesbrough, which was marred by crowd issues and they wouldn't be replaced in top spot all season. With things never straight forward and Leeds seeming to like doing things the hard way, they hit a rocky patch at the end of March and going into April, where they failed to win in four games. By this time Wilkinson had dipped back into the transfer window, bringing in Lee Chapman from Nottingham Forest, Chris Kamara from Stoke City and Imre Varadi from Sheffield Wednesday. His side were involved in a fascinating battle for promotion with near-neighbours Sheffield United. Writing in the programme ahead of the battle with the Blades, he said, 'What can I say about today's game that has not already been said or appeared in print. Including this afternoon's encounter, we have five matches to go in what can turn out to be Leeds United's most important season for a decade. So let's get on with it.'

The players did get on with the job in hand, winning 4-0, led by captain marvel Strachan, but yet again they made it hard for themselves, drawing 2-2 at Brighton & Hove Albion and losing at home for the first time in the league all season to Barnsley. The pressure was on at home to Leicester City but up stepped Strachan with a fantastic goal and the fans celebrated

Wilkinson in caretaker charge of the England National Side.

as if promotion was won. Results meant it would go to the final day and Leeds visited AFC Bournemouth knowing a win would secure promotion and the championship after an eight-year stay in the wilderness. Lee Chapman headed the winning goal and fans celebrated long into the night. Wilkinson had done what was asked of him, returning the side back to where it belonged and now the challenge was on to consolidate the side in the First Division.

Again, Wilkinson splashed the cash, bringing in Gary McAllister from Leicester City, Chris Whyte from West Bromwich Albion and John Lukic back from Arsenal for his second stint at Elland Road. Writing in his programme column ahead of the first home game against Manchester United, Wilkinson said, 'Tonight is without question the biggest occasion in our club's recent history, our first game back in the First Division has seemed a long time coming.'

The first season back went better than anyone could have imagined, with the side finishing in fourth position with Lee Chapman top-scoring with 31 goals in all competitions. Leeds took champions Arsenal all the way in four epic FA Cup battles and reached the last four of both the Rumbelows League Cup and the Zenith Data Systems Cup. Wilkinson didn't rest on his laurels though, and in came Tony Dorigo from Chelsea, Rod and Ray Wallace from Southampton, David Wetherall and Jon Newsome from Sheffield Wednesday and Steve Hodge from Nottingham Forest.

Then what occurred in season 1991-92 would go down in the history of the football club. Leeds were unbeaten in their first ten league games before losing to a last-minute Mark Bright header away at Crystal Palace. They bounced back with two four goal salvos against Sheffield United (4-3) and Notts County (4-2), before topping the table for the first time since 1974 thanks to a 1-0 win at home to Oldham Athletic. Wilkinson told the *Yorkshire Evening Post* after the game, 'I have never been at the top of the First Division, so it is something entirely new to me, but sometimes when a team gets to the top people ask if they can stay the course. It is vital we keep getting good results until Christmas, because we have played enough games now to be able to say to ourselves, given a fair run of the ball, we can have a say in this title race.'

Leeds produced some fantastic performances, especially the 4-1 televised win away to Aston Villa at the end of November that kept them in pole position. They hit a brief rocky spell over the festive period, drawing four consecutive games, but again bounced back in style with a New Year's Day win at West Ham United and a phenomenal 6-1 win at Sheffield Wednesday, which was achieved without both Strachan and Batty. With top-scorer Lee Chapman ruled out following an injury in an FA Cup tie against Manchester United, Wilkinson turned to Frenchman Eric Cantona, signed on loan from Nimes. Cantona scored his first goal on leap year day at home to Luton Town, but again Leeds hit a rocky spell, losing 4-1 at Queens Park Rangers and 4-0 at Manchester City at the start of April. The title pendulum looked to have swung back to rivals Manchester United, but, following defeats at home to Nottingham Forest and West Ham United, Leeds knew two wins from their last two games at Sheffield United and at home to Norwich City would make them champions.

A crazy game at Bramall Lane saw Leeds win 3-2 thanks to a spectacular own goal from Blades Skipper Brian Gayle and hours later a 2-0 win for Liverpool over Manchester United meant the title would be heading to Elland Road. Wilkinson told the *Daily Express*, 'Career-

TEAMTALK

WITH HOWARD WILKINSON

Today's game is my first League match in front of the Elland Road fans and only my second game in the Second Division in the last five years so in a sense we are all breaking new ground today.

I want to get one thing right from the start. My reference in the press to Leeds United's illustrious past and glory years did not reflect my full view. One of the reasons I came to Leeds was that I thought the successes this club achieved were near enough to the present time for it to happen again and in that respect the past can prove a useful part of our history for the future.

I have been here for just under a fortnight and it has seemed like two days with everything we have crammed in. I have learnt a lot, mostly about the players because that is where I have concentrated everything to date. Wholesale changes at this time are not the answer but if I feel they are, then they will come after I have had a chance to size up the situation. What we need is a group of people committed totally to re-establishing Leeds United as a respectable force.

Ideally, I would like to have cancelled our games over the next five weeks and done purely pre-season work. This obviously is not possible so I have to try to balance what I think needs doing. We have to inch our way forward initially and I've tried to stress to the players that I don't expect them to give me anything more than they are capable of giving. No one should expect to see a startling overnight change but rest assured that steps are being taken to bring about a change.

I am well aware of the tremendous reputation Leeds fans have supporting their team and I saw this for myself at Swindon. The game there was a match of guts. It was spirit, commitment and attitude that saw us through against an effective team.

I have taken over a similar situation to the one David Pleat inherited at Leicester last season and after an understandably unspectacular start, it is easy to see why Leicester are now being considered as promotion contenders. We watched City beat Stoke last week and we can expect nothing less than a very tough match today.

I hope we'll win through today and that the game represents all that's good in football on and off the field.

OUCH... PHONE UNITED CLUBCALL 0898 12 11 80... TICKET CALL 0898 12

wise this is the most fantastic day of my life, one of those days when dreams come true.' Leeds were now back in the European Cup and another drama was set to start. Having beaten German side Stuttgart 4-1 in a memorable second-leg tie at Elland Road, the side thought they were out of the competition, losing on away goals, but were given a reprieve following the German's overuse of foreign players. A third game at the Nou Camp saw super-sub Carl Shutt send Leeds through to a Battle of Britain with Glasgow Rangers. Wilkinson said after, 'I am proud of the them and over the three games I felt we were the better side and improved with each game.'

Following Rangers' win in the next round, the wheels came off that season. Cantona was sold to Manchester United (who went on to win the first-ever Premier League title) and Leeds finished in 17th place a year after winning the title. There was a small consolation as Paul Hart saw his youth side win the FA Youth Cup against the Red Devils for the first time, and the likes of Jamie Forrester, Noel Whelan, Rob Bowman, Mark Tinkler and Kevin Sharp all made their first-team debuts that season. Leeds improved massively in 1993-94 to finish in fifth place, despite the sale of home-grown David Batty to Blackburn Rovers, and qualified for the UEFA Cup thanks to the goals of mid-season signing Anthony Yeboah from Eintracht Frankfurt.

Leeds won their first three league games of season 1995-96 but became more of a cup side as they made their way through the last eight of the FA Cup and their first League Cup Final since 1968. It all started to go wrong for Wilkinson and Leeds as his side were booed off at Wembley following Aston Villa's 3-0 win. Leeds finished in 13th place and Wilkinson responded by bringing in Lee Bowyer from Charlton Athletic, Nigel Martyn from Crystal Palace, Lee Sharpe from Manchester United and Ian Rush on a free transfer from Liverpool. After a 4-0 loss at home to Alex Ferguson's Manchester United, in which Cantona missed a penalty, Wilkinson was sacked on the Monday and a glorious period in the Whites' history was over. He had two caretaker spells managing the England international side before a brief spell at Sunderland in 2002-03. He had two months in China managing Shanghai Shenhua and is currently the chairman of the League Managers' Association.

Howard Wilkinson's first line up: Peterborough United (H) 12 October 1988: Day, Aspin, G. Snodin, Aizlewood, Blake, Rennie, Batty, Sheridan, Davison (Pearson), Hillaire. Sub not used: Stiles.

Howard Wilkinson's last line up: Manchester United (H) 7 September 1996: Martyn, Kelly, Jobson, Wetherall, Harte, Palmer, Bowyer (Radebe), Ford (Gray), Sharpe, Rush, Wallace (Hateley). Subs not used: Beeney, Couzens.

DIVISION ONE   **1980–81**

Date	Opposition	Competition	Score
16/08/1980	**Aston Villa**	**Division One**	**1-2**
19/08/1980	Middlesbrough	Division One	0-3
23/08/1980	Norwich City	Division One	3-2
27/08/1980	Aston Villa	League Cup 2nd Round 1st Leg	0-1
30/08/1980	**Leicester City**	**Division One**	**1-2**
03/09/1980	**Aston Villa**	**League Cup 2nd Round 2nd Leg**	**1-3**
06/09/1980	Stoke City	Division One	0-3
13/09/1980	**Tottenham Hotspur**	**Division One**	**0-0**
20/09/1980	**Manchester United**	**Division One**	**0-0**
27/09/1980	Sunderland	Division One	1-4
04/10/1980	Ipswich Town	Division One	1-1
08/10/1980	**Manchester City**	**Division One**	**1-0**
11/10/1980	**Everton**	**Division One**	**1-0**
18/10/1980	Wolverhampton Wanderers	Division One	1-2
22/10/1980	Nottingham Forest	Division One	1-2
25/10/1980	**Crystal Palace**	**Division One**	**1-0**
01/11/1980	Coventry City	Division One	1-2
08/11/1980	**Arsenal**	**Division One**	**0-5**
12/11/1980	**Middlesbrough**	**Division One**	**2-1**
15/11/1980	Aston Villa	Division One	1-1
22/11/1980	Southampton	Division One	1-2
29/11/1980	**Brighton & Hove Albion**	**Division One**	**1-0**
06/12/1980	West Bromwich Albion	Division One	2-1
13/12/1980	**Nottingham Forest**	**Division One**	**1-0**
20/12/1980	Manchester City	Division One	0-1
26/12/1980	**Birmingham City**	**Division One**	**0-0**
27/12/1980	Liverpool	Division One	0-0
03/01/1981	**Coventry City**	**FA Cup 3rd Round**	**1-1**
06/01/1981	Coventry City	FA Cup 3rd Round Replay	0-1
10/01/1981	**Southampton**	**Division One**	**0-3**
17/01/1981	Leicester City	Division One	1-0
31/01/1981	**Norwich City**	**Division One**	**1-0**
07/02/1981	Tottenham Hotspur	Division One	1-1
14/02/1981	**Stoke City**	**Division One**	**1-3**
21/02/1981	**Sunderland**	**Division One**	**1-0**
28/02/1981	Manchester United	Division One	1-0
14/03/1981	Everton	Division One	2-1
21/03/1981	**Wolverhampton Wanderers**	**Division One**	**1-3**
28/03/1981	Crystal Palace	Division One	1-0
31/03/1981	**Ipswich Town**	**Division One**	**3-0**
04/04/1981	**Coventry City**	**Division One**	**3-0**
11/04/1981	Arsenal	Division One	0-0
18/04/1981	**Liverpool**	**Division One**	**0-0**
21/04/1981	Birmingham City	Division One	2-0
02/05/1981	Brighton & Hove Albion	Division One	0-2
06/05/1981	**West Bromwich Albion**	**Division One**	**0-0**

Team	Pld	W	D	L	GF	GA	Pts
Aston Villa	42	26	8	8	72	40	60
Ipswich Town	42	23	10	9	77	43	56
Arsenal	42	19	15	8	61	45	53
West Bromwich Albion	42	20	12	10	60	42	52
Liverpool	42	17	17	8	62	42	51
Southampton	42	20	10	12	76	56	50
Nottingham Forest	42	19	12	11	62	44	50
Manchester United	42	15	18	9	51	36	48
Leeds United	42	17	10	15	39	47	44
Tottenham Hotspur	42	14	15	13	70	68	43
Stoke City	42	12	18	12	51	60	42
Manchester City	42	14	11	17	56	59	39
Birmingham City	42	13	12	17	50	61	38
Middlesbrough	42	16	5	21	53	61	37
Everton	42	13	10	19	55	58	36
Coventry City	42	13	10	19	48	68	36
Sunderland	42	14	7	21	52	53	35
Wolverhampton W	42	13	9	20	43	55	35
Brighton & Hove Albion	42	14	7	21	54	67	35
Norwich City	42	13	7	22	49	73	33
Leicester City	42	13	6	23	40	67	32
Crystal Palace	42	6	7	29	47	83	19

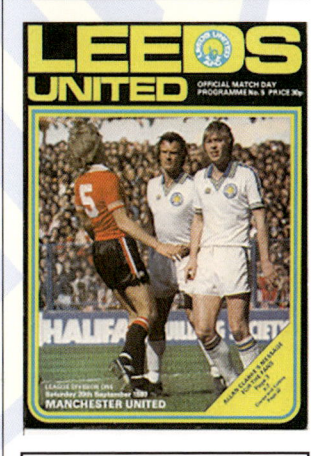

Season 1980-81 saw the debuts of Alex Sabella against Aston Villa and Aidan Butterworth at home to Coventry City.

Maurice Lindley stepped into the breach for the fourth time following the sacking of Jimmy Adamson.

The late great Paul Madeley made his last apearance in a Leeds United shirt in the 5-0 defeat at home to Arsenal on 8 November.

Paul Hart took over as captain when Trevor Cherry missed the 3-0 home win against Coventry City in April 1981.

It was three doubles for Leeds, Norwich City (3-2) and (1-0), Everton (1-0) and (2-1) and Crystal Palace (1-0 on both occasions).

1981-82

DIVISION ONE

Team	Pld	W	D	L	GF	GA	Pts
Liverpool	42	26	9	7	80	32	87
Ipswich Town	42	26	5	11	75	53	83
Manchester United	42	22	12	8	59	29	78
Tottenham Hotspur	42	20	11	11	67	48	71
Arsenal	42	20	11	11	48	37	71
Swansea City	42	21	6	15	58	51	69
Southampton	42	19	9	14	72	67	66
Everton	42	17	13	12	56	50	64
West Ham United	42	14	16	12	66	57	58
Manchester City	42	15	13	14	49	50	58
Aston Villa	42	15	12	15	55	53	57
Nottingham Forest	42	15	12	15	42	48	57
Brighton & Hove Albion	42	13	13	16	43	52	52
Coventry City	42	13	11	18	56	62	50
Notts County	42	13	8	21	61	69	47
Birmingham City	42	10	14	18	53	61	44
West Bromwich Albion	42	11	11	20	46	57	44
Stoke City	42	12	8	22	44	63	44
Sunderland	42	11	11	20	38	58	44
Leeds United	42	10	12	20	39	61	42
Wolverhampton W	42	10	10	22	32	63	40
Middlesbrough	42	8	15	19	34	52	39

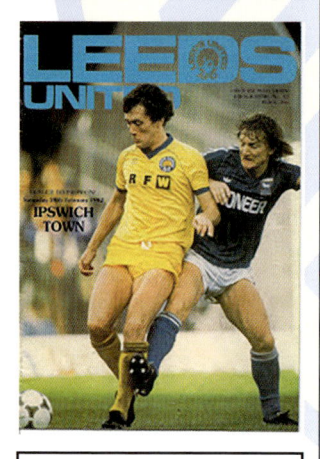

Date	Opposition	Competition	Score
29/08/1981	Swansea City	Division One	1-5
02/09/1981	**Everton**	**Division One**	**1-1**
05/09/1981	**Wolverhampton Wanderers**	**Division One**	**3-0**
12/09/1981	Coventry City	Division One	0-4
19/09/1981	**Arsenal**	**Division One**	**0-0**
23/09/1981	Manchester City	Division One	0-4
26/09/1981	Ipswich Town	Division One	1-2
30/09/1981	Manchester United	Division One	0-1
03/10/1981	**Aston Villa**	**Division One**	**1-1**
07/10/1981	**Ipswich Town**	**League Cup 2nd Round 1st Leg**	**0-1**
10/10/1981	Liverpool	Division One	0-3
17/10/1981	**West Bromwich Albion**	**Division One**	**3-1**
24/10/1981	**Sunderland**	**Division One**	**1-0**
27/10/1981	Ipswich Town	League Cup 2nd Round 2nd Leg	0-3
31/10/1981	Nottingham Forest	Division One	1-2
07/11/1981	**Notts County**	**Division One**	**1-0**
21/11/1981	Southampton	Division One	0-4
28/11/1981	**West Ham United**	**Division One**	**3-3**
05/12/1981	Stoke City	Division One	2-1
12/12/1981	**Tottenham Hotspur**	**Division One**	**0-0**
02/01/1982	Wolverhampton Wanderers	FA Cup 3rd Round	3-1
16/01/1982	**Swansea City**	**Division One**	**2-0**
23/01/1982	Tottenham Hotspur	FA Cup 4th Round	0-1
30/01/1982	Arsenal	Division One	0-1
06/02/1982	**Coventry City**	**Division One**	**0-0**
20/02/1982	**Ipswich Town**	**Division One**	**0-2**
27/02/1982	**Liverpool**	**Division One**	**0-2**
02/03/1982	Brighton & Hove Albion	Division One	0-1
10/03/1982	**Manchester City**	**Division One**	**0-1**
13/03/1982	Sunderland	Division One	1-0
16/03/1982	Wolverhampton Wanderers	Division One	0-1
20/03/1982	**Nottingham Forest**	**Division One**	**1-1**
27/03/1982	Notts County	Division One	1-2
03/04/1982	**Manchester United**	**Division One**	**0-0**
06/04/1982	Middlesbrough	Division One	0-0
10/04/1982	Birmingham City	Division One	1-0
13/04/1982	**Middlesbrough**	**Division One**	**1-1**
17/04/1982	**Southampton**	**Division One**	**1-3**
24/04/1982	West Ham United	Division One	3-4
28/04/1982	Aston Villa	Division One	4-1
01/05/1982	**Stoke City**	**Division One**	**0-0**
04/05/1982	Everton	Division One	0-1
08/05/1982	Tottenham Hotspur	Division One	1-2
12/05/1982	**Birmingham City**	**Division One**	**3-3**
15/05/1982	**Brighton & Hove Albion**	**Division One**	**2-1**
18/05/1982	West Bromwich Albion	Division One	0-2

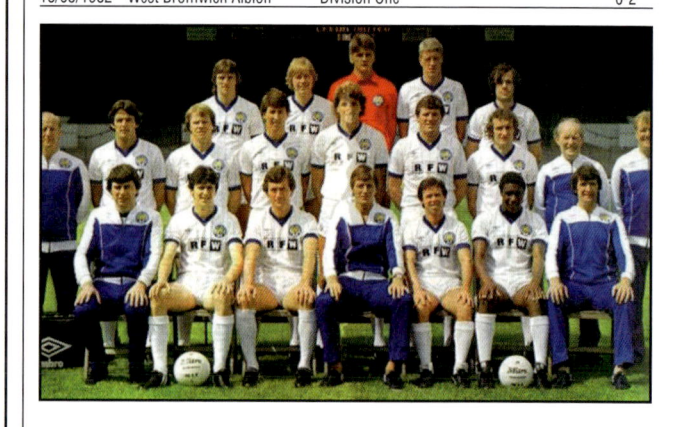

Arthur Graham finished joint top scorer with nine, scoring three in the third game of the season at home to Wolves.

Frank Worthington was signed from Birmingham City and ended up as joint top scorer with nine goals in 17 games.

John Lukic was the only ever-present, featuring in all 46 games for the side.

Just the one double for Leeds as they slipped out of the First Division, defeating Sunderland 1-0 at Elland Road and 1-0 at Roker Park.

Steve Balcombe made an instant impact in a Leeds shirt, scoring on his debut in the 1-1 home draw against Aston Villa.

DIVISION TWO

1982–83

Date	Opposition	Competition	Score
28/08/1982	Grimsby Town	Division Two	1-1
04/09/1982	Wolverhampton Wanderers	Division Two	0-0
08/09/1982	Leicester City	Division Two	1-0
11/09/1982	Sheffield Wednesday	Division Two	3-2
18/09/1982	Derby County	Division Two	2-1
25/09/1982	Fulham	Division Two	2-3
02/10/1982	Cambridge United	Division Two	2-1
06/10/1982	Newcastle United	Milk Cup 2nd Round 1st Leg	0-1
09/10/1982	Chelsea	Division Two	0-0
16/10/1982	Carlisle United	Division Two	1-1
20/10/1982	Burnley	Division Two	3-1
23/10/1982	Blackburn Rovers	Division Two	0-0
27/10/1982	Newcastle United	Milk Cup 2nd Round 2nd Leg	4-1
30/10/1982	Newcastle United	Division Two	3-1
06/11/1982	Charlton Athletic	Division Two	1-2
10/11/1982	Huddersfield Town	Milk Cup 3rd Round	0-1
13/11/1982	Crystal Palace	Division Two	1-1
20/11/1982	Middlesbrough	Division Two	0-0
27/11/1982	Barnsley	Division Two	1-2
04/12/1982	Queens Park Rangers	Division Two	0-1
11/12/1982	Rotherham United	Division Two	1-0
18/12/1982	Shrewsbury Town	Division Two	1-1
26/12/1982	Oldham Athletic	Division Two	2-2
28/12/1982	Bolton Wanderers	Division Two	1-1
01/01/1983	Middlesbrough	Division Two	0-0
03/01/1983	Wolverhampton Wanderers	Division Two	0-3
08/01/1983	Preston North End	FA Cup 3rd Round	3-0
15/01/1983	Grimsby Town	Division Two	1-0
22/01/1983	Derby County	Division Two	3-3
29/01/1983	Arsenal	FA Cup 4th Round	1-1
02/02/1983	Arsenal	FA Cup 4th Round Replay	1-1
09/02/1983	Arsenal	FA Cup 4th Round 2nd Replay	1-2
12/02/1983	Cambridge United	Division Two	0-0
19/02/1983	Chelsea	Division Two	3-3
26/02/1983	Carlisle United	Division Two	2-2
05/03/1983	Blackburn Rovers	Division Two	2-1
12/03/1983	Newcastle United	Division Two	1-2
19/03/1983	Charlton Athletic	Division Two	1-0
26/03/1983	Crystal Palace	Division Two	2-1
02/04/1983	Bolton Wanderers	Division Two	2-1
05/04/1983	Oldham Athletic	Division Two	0-0
09/04/1983	Burnley	Division Two	2-1
16/04/1983	Fulham	Division Two	1-1
23/04/1983	Queens Park Rangers	Division Two	0-1
27/04/1983	Sheffield Wednesday	Division Two	1-2
30/04/1983	Barnsley	Division Two	0-0
02/05/1983	Leicester City	Division Two	2-2
07/05/1983	Shrewsbury Town	Division Two	0-0
14/05/1983	Rotherham United	Division Two	2-2

Team	Pld	W	D	L	GF	GA	Pts
Queen's Park Rangers	42	26	7	9	77	36	85
Wolverhampton W	42	20	15	7	68	44	75
Leicester City	42	20	10	12	72	44	70
Fulham	42	20	9	13	64	47	69
Newcastle United	42	18	13	11	75	53	67
Sheffield Wednesday	42	16	15	11	60	47	63
Oldham Athletic	42	14	19	9	64	47	61
Leeds United	42	13	21	8	51	46	60
Shrewsbury Town	42	15	14	13	48	48	59
Barnsley	42	14	15	13	57	55	57
Blackburn Rovers	42	15	12	15	58	58	57
Cambridge United	42	13	12	17	42	60	51
Derby County	42	10	19	13	49	58	49
Carlisle United	42	12	12	18	68	70	48
Crystal Palace	42	12	12	18	43	52	48
Middlesbrough	42	11	15	16	46	67	48
Charlton Athletic	42	13	9	20	63	86	48
Chelsea	42	11	14	17	51	61	47
Grimsby Town	42	12	11	19	45	70	47
Rotherham United	42	10	15	17	45	68	45
Burnley	42	12	8	22	56	66	44
Bolton Wanderers	42	11	11	20	42	61	44

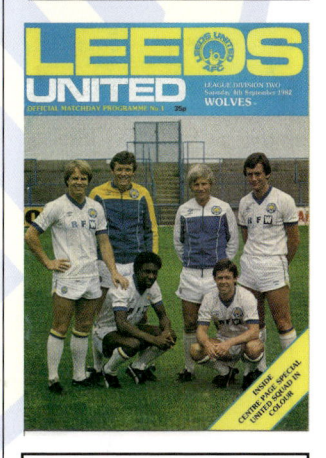

Leeds had five captains this season, Eddie Gray, Trevor Cherry, Kenny Burns, Paul Hart and David Harvey.

John Lukic played his final game in his first spell at Elland Road in the 2-1 over Blackburn Rovers at Elland Road.

Loan signing Neil McNab featured in six games whilst on loan from Manchester City.

Frank Gray was the top appearance maker, featuring in 48 out of the 49 games, missing the FA Cup third-round tie at home to Preston North End.

Youngsters Tommy Wright at home to Fulham and Scott Sellars away at Shrewsbury Town made their Leeds United debuts in season 1982-83.

267

1983–84

DIVISION TWO

Team	Pld	W	D	L	GF	GA	Pts
Chelsea	42	25	13	4	90	40	88
Sheffield Wednesday	42	26	10	6	72	34	88
Newcastle United	42	24	8	10	85	53	80
Manchester City	42	20	10	12	66	48	70
Grimsby Town	42	19	13	10	60	47	70
Blackburn Rovers	42	17	16	9	57	46	67
Carlisle United	42	16	16	10	48	41	64
Shrewsbury Town	42	17	10	15	49	53	61
Brighton & Hove Albion	42	17	9	16	69	60	60
Leeds United	42	16	12	14	55	56	60
Fulham	42	15	12	15	60	53	57
Huddersfield Town	42	14	15	13	56	49	57
Charlton Athletic	42	16	9	17	53	64	57
Barnsley	42	15	7	20	57	53	52
Cardiff City	42	15	6	21	53	66	51
Portsmouth	42	14	7	21	73	64	49
Middlesbrough	42	12	13	17	41	47	49
Crystal Palace	42	12	11	19	42	52	47
Oldham Athletic	42	13	8	21	47	73	47
Derby County	42	11	9	22	36	72	42
Swansea City	42	7	8	27	36	85	29
Cambridge United	42	4	12	26	28	77	24

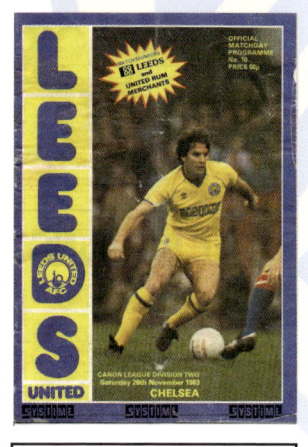

Date	Opposition	Competition	Score
27/08/1983	Newcastle United	Division Two	0-1
29/08/1983	Brighton & Hove Albion	Division Two	3-2
03/09/1983	Middlesbrough	Division Two	2-2
06/09/1983	Grimsby Town	Division Two	0-2
10/09/1983	Cardiff City	Division Two	1-0
17/09/1983	Fulham	Division Two	1-2
24/09/1983	Manchester City	Division Two	1-2
01/10/1983	Shrewsbury Town	Division Two	1-5
05/10/1983	Chester City	Milk Cup 2nd Round 1st Leg	0-1
08/10/1983	Sheffield Wednesday	Division Two	1-3
14/10/1983	Cambridge United	Division Two	3-1
22/10/1983	Barnsley	Division Two	2-0
26/10/1983	Chester City	Milk Cup 2nd Round 2nd Leg	4-1
29/10/1983	Portsmouth	Division Two	2-1
05/11/1983	Crystal Palace	Division Two	1-1
09/11/1983	Oxford United	Milk Cup 3rd Round	1-1
12/11/1983	Blackburn Rovers	Division Two	1-1
19/11/1983	Derby County	Division Two	1-1
23/11/1983	Oxford United	Milk Cup 3rd Round Replay	1-4
26/11/1983	Chelsea	Division Two	1-1
03/12/1983	Carlisle United	Division Two	0-1
15/12/1983	Charlton Athletic	Division Two	0-2
26/12/1983	Huddersfield Town	Division Two	1-2
27/12/1983	Oldham Athletic	Division Two	2-3
31/12/1983	Middlesbrough	Division Two	4-1
02/01/1984	Manchester City	Division Two	1-1
07/01/1984	Scunthorpe United	FA Cup 3rd Round	1-1
10/01/1994	Scunthorpe United	FA Cup 3rd Round Replay	1-1
16/01/1984	Scunthorpe United	FA Cup 3rd Round 2nd Replay	2-4
21/01/1984	Fulham	Division Two	1-0
04/02/1984	Shrewsbury Town	Division Two	3-0
11/02/1984	Cardiff City	Division Two	1-0
15/02/1984	Swansea City	Division Two	1-0
18/02/1984	Portsmouth	Division Two	3-2
25/02/1984	Barnsley	Division Two	1-2
03/03/1984	Crystal Palace	Division Two	0-0
10/03/1984	Blackburn Rovers	Division Two	1-0
17/03/1984	Grimsby Town	Division Two	2-1
24/03/1984	Brighton & Hove Albion	Division Two	0-3
28/03/1984	Newcastle United	Division Two	0-1
31/03/1984	Sheffield Wednesday	Division Two	1-1
07/04/1984	Cambridge United	Division Two	2-2
14/04/1984	Derby County	Division Two	0-0
21/04/1984	Huddersfield Town	Division Two	2-2
24/04/1984	Oldham Athletic	Division Two	2-0
28/04/1984	Chelsea	Division Two	0-5
05/05/1984	Carlisle United	Division Two	3-0
07/05/1984	Swansea City	Division Two	2-2
12/05/1984	Charlton Athletic	Division Two	1-0

Just the two skippers for Leeds in season 1983-84, David Harvey and Gwyn Thomas.

When Peter Lorimer scored in the away game at Swansea City it took him past John Charles's all-time league goalscoring mark.

Eddie Gray made his last appearance in a Leeds United shirt on the final day of the season at home to Charlton Athletic.

Just the two doubles for Leeds, Cardiff City 1-0 on both occasions and Portsmouth 2-1 and 3-2.

Leslie Silver replaced Manny Cussins as chairman.

DIVISION TWO

1984–85

Date	Opposition	Competition	Score
25/08/1984	Notts County	Division Two	2-1
27/08/1984	Fulham	Division Two	2-0
01/09/1984	Wolverhampton Wanderers	Division Two	3-2
08/09/1984	Grimsby Town	Division Two	2-0
12/09/1994	Cardiff City	Division Two	1-2
15/09/1984	Portsmouth	Division Two	0-1
22/09/1984	Crystal Palace	Division Two	1-3
25/09/1984	Gillingham	Milk Cup 2nd Round 1st Leg	2-1
29/09/1984	Oldham Athletic	Division Two	6-0
06/10/1984	Sheffield United	Division Two	1-1
10/10/1984	Gillingham	Milk Cup 2nd Round 2nd Leg	3-2
13/10/1984	Barnsley	Division Two	0-1
20/10/1984	Huddersfield Town	Division Two	0-1
27/10/1984	Middlesbrough	Division Two	2-0
31/10/1994	Watford	Milk Cup 3rd Round	0-4
03/11/1984	Charlton Athletic	Division Two	3-2
10/11/1984	Carlisle United	Division Two	1-1
17/11/1984	Brighton & Hove Albion	Division Two	1-0
24/11/1984	Oxford United	Division Two	2-5
01/12/1984	Wimbledon	Division Two	5-2
08/12/1984	Shrewsbury Town	Division Two	3-2
15/12/1984	Birmingham City	Division Two	0-1
22/12/1994	Wolverhampton Wanderers	Division Two	2-0
26/12/1994	Blackburn Rovers	Division Two	1-2
29/12/1994	Cardiff City	Division Two	1-1
01/01/1985	Manchester City	Division Two	1-1
04/01/1985	Everton	FA Cup 3rd Round	0-2
19/01/1985	Notts County	Division Two	5-0
02/02/1985	Oldham Athletic	Division Two	1-1
09/02/1985	Grimsby Town	Division Two	0-0
23/02/1985	Charlton Athletic	Division Two	1-0
26/02/1985	Carlisle United	Division Two	2-2
02/03/1985	Middlesbrough	Division Two	0-0
09/03/1985	Huddersfield Town	Division Two	0-0
12/03/1985	Portsmouth	Division Two	1-3
16/03/1985	Barnsley	Division Two	2-0
23/03/1985	Sheffield United	Division Two	1-2
30/03/1985	Fulham	Division Two	2-0
06/04/1985	Blackburn Rovers	Division Two	0-0
08/04/1985	Manchester City	Division Two	2-1
13/04/1985	Crystal Palace	Division Two	4-1
20/04/1985	Brighton & Hove Albion	Division Two	1-1
27/04/1985	Oxford United	Division Two	1-0
04/05/1985	Wimbledon	Division Two	2-2
06/05/1985	Shrewsbury Town	Division Two	1-0
11/05/1985	Birmingham City	Division Two	0-1

Team	Pld	W	D	L	GF	GA	Pts
Oxford United	42	25	9	8	84	36	84
Birmingham City	42	25	7	10	59	33	82
Manchester City	42	21	11	10	66	40	74
Portsmouth	42	20	14	8	69	50	74
Blackburn Rovers	42	21	10	11	66	41	73
Brighton & Hove Albion	42	20	12	10	54	34	72
Leeds United	42	19	12	11	66	43	69
Shrewsbury Town	42	18	11	13	66	53	65
Fulham	42	19	8	15	68	64	65
Grimsby Town	42	18	8	16	72	64	62
Barnsley	42	14	16	12	42	42	58
Wimbledon	42	16	10	16	71	75	58
Huddersfield Town	42	15	10	17	52	64	55
Oldham Athletic	42	15	8	19	49	67	53
Crystal Palace	42	12	12	18	46	65	48
Carlisle United	42	13	8	21	50	67	47
Charlton Athletic	42	11	12	19	51	63	45
Sheffield United	42	10	14	18	54	66	44
Middlesbrough	42	10	10	22	41	57	40
Notts County	42	10	7	25	45	73	37
Cardiff City	42	9	8	25	47	79	35
Wolverhampton W	42	8	9	25	37	79	33

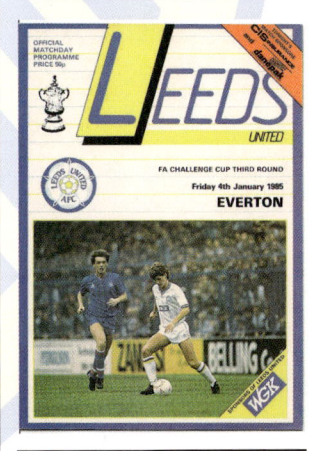

Mervyn Day was signed from Aston Villa in the middle of the season and replaced David Harvey as Leeds United's number 1.

Denis Irwin scored his one and only goal in a White's shirt in the 5-0 home win against Notts County in January 1985.

The FA Cup third-round tie at home to Everton was the first time that Leeds appeared live on the BBC at Elland Road.

Roger Eli made his Leeds United debut coming off the bench in the 5-2 win over Wimbledon. He went on to make only one more appearance for the side.

Leeds had three ever-presents Andy Linighan, Tommy Wright and John Sheridan.

1985-86

DIVISION TWO

Team	Pld	W	D	L	GF	GA	Pts
Norwich City	42	25	9	8	84	37	84
Charlton Athletic	42	22	11	9	78	45	77
Wimbledon	42	21	13	8	58	37	76
Portsmouth	42	22	7	13	69	41	73
Crystal Palace	42	19	9	14	57	52	66
Hull City	42	17	13	12	65	55	64
Sheffield United	42	17	11	14	64	63	62
Oldham Athletic	42	17	9	16	62	61	60
Millwall	42	17	8	17	64	65	59
Stoke City	42	14	15	13	48	50	57
Brighton & Hove Albion	42	16	8	18	64	64	56
Barnsley	42	14	14	14	47	50	56
Bradford City	42	16	6	20	51	63	54
Leeds United	42	15	8	19	56	72	53
Grimsby Town	42	14	10	18	58	62	52
Huddersfield Town	42	14	10	18	51	67	52
Shrewsbury Town	42	14	9	19	52	64	51
Sunderland	42	13	11	18	47	61	50
Blackburn Rovers	42	12	13	17	53	62	49
Carlisle United	42	13	7	22	47	71	46
Middlesbrough	42	12	9	21	44	53	45
Fulham	42	10	6	26	45	69	36

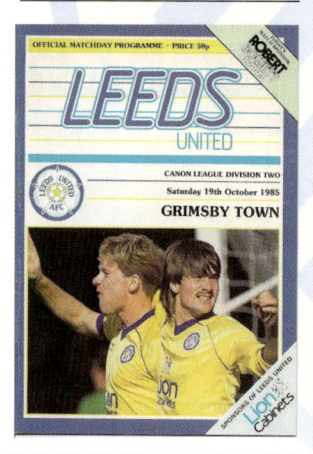

Date	Opposition	Competition	Score
17/08/1985	Fulham	Division Two	1-3
21/08/1985	Wimbledon	Division Two	0-0
24/08/1985	Hull City	Division Two	1-1
26/08/1985	Stoke City	Division Two	2-6
31/08/1985	Charlton Athletic	Division Two	1-2
04/08/1985	Brighton & Hove Albion	Division Two	1-0
07/09/1985	Shrewsbury Town	Division Two	3-1
14/09/1985	Sunderland	Division Two	1-1
21/09/1985	Bradford City	Division Two	2-1
25/09/1985	Walsall	Milk Cup 2nd Round 1st Leg	0-0
28/09/1985	Sheffield United	Division Two	1-1
05/10/1985	Huddersfield Town	Division Two	1-3
08/10/1985	Walsall	Milk Cup 2nd Round 2nd Leg	3-0
12/10/1985	Middlesbrough	Division Two	1-0
14/10/1985	Manchester City	Full Members Cup Northern Section Group1	1-6
16/10/1985	Sheffield United	Full Members Cup Northern Section Group1	1-1
19/10/1985	Grimsby Town	Division Two	1-1
27/10/1985	Barnsley	Division Two	0-3
30/10/1985	Aston Villa	Milk Cup 3rd Round	0-3
02/11/1985	Portsmouth	Division Two	2-1
09/11/1985	Millwall	Division Two	1-3
16/11/1985	Crystal Palace	Division Two	1-3
23/11/1985	Carlisle United	Division Two	2-1
30/11/1985	Norwich City	Division Two	0-2
07/12/1985	Wimbledon	Division Two	3-0
14/12/1985	Fulham	Division Two	1-0
22/12/1985	Hull City	Division Two	1-2
26/12/1985	Blackburn Rovers	Division Two	0-2
28/12/1985	Brighton & Hove Albion	Division Two	2-3
01/01/1986	Oldham Athletic	Division Two	3-1
04/01/1986	Peterborough United	FA Cup 3rd Round	0-1
11/01/1986	Sunderland	Division Two	2-4
18/01/1986	Charlton Athletic	Division Two	0-4
01/02/1986	Stoke City	Division Two	4-0
08/02/1996	Grimsby Town	Division Two	0-1
15/02/1986	Barnsley	Division Two	0-2
08/03/1986	Huddersfield Town	Division Two	2-0
15/03/1986	Middlesbrough	Division Two	2-2
22/03/1986	Shrewsbury Town	Division Two	1-1
28/03/1986	Oldham Athletic	Division Two	1-3
31/03/1986	Blackburn Rovers	Division Two	1-1
05/04/1986	Portsmouth	Division Two	3-2
09/04/1986	Bradford City	Division Two	1-0
12/04/1986	Millwall	Division Two	3-1
19/04/1986	Crystal Palace	Division Two	0-3
22/04/1986	Sheffield United	Division Two	2-3
26/04/1986	Carlisle United	Division Two	2-0
03/05/1986	Norwich City	Division Two	0-4

Season 1985-86 saw the debut of Terry Phelan in a Leeds United shirt. The Manchester-born defender made 19 appearances for the club.

Peter Lorimer made his last-ever appearance in a Leeds shirt in Billy Bremner's first game in charge away at Barnsley.

Following Lorimer's departure Ian Snodin was appointed new club captain for the Whites.

Trevor Swinburne made his only two appearances for Leeds United in this season, at home to Grimsby Town and at home to Norwich City.

The Whites managed three doubles, Portsmouth (2-1 and 3-2), Bradford City (2-1 and 1-0) and Carlisle United (2-1 and 2-0).

DIVISION TWO

1986–87

Date	Opposition	Competition	Score
23/08/1986	Blackburn Rovers	Division Two	1-2
25/08/1986	Stoke City	Division Two	2-1
30/08/1986	Sheffield United	Division Two	0-1
02/09/1986	Barnsley	Division Two	1-0
06/09/1986	Huddersfield Town	Division Two	1-1
13/09/1986	Reading	Division Two	3-2
20/09/1986	Bradford City	Division Two	0-2
23/09/1986	Oldham Athletic	Littlewoods Cup 2nd Round 1st Leg	2-3
27/09/1996	Hull City	Division Two	3-0
01/10/1986	Bradford City	Full Members Cup 1st Round	0-1
04/10/1986	Plymouth Argyle	Division Two	1-1
08/10/1986	Oldham Athletic	Littlewoods Cup 2nd Round 2nd Leg	0-1
11/10/1986	Crystal Palace	Division Two	3-0
18/10/1986	Portsmouth	Division Two	3-1
25/10/1986	Grimsby Town	Division Two	0-0
01/11/1986	Shrewsbury Town	Division Two	1-0
08/11/1986	Millwall	Division Two	0-1
15/11/1986	Oldham Athletic	Division Two	0-2
21/11/1986	Birmingham City	Division Two	1-2
29/11/1986	Derby County	Division Two	2-0
06/12/1986	West Bromwich Albion	Division Two	0-3
13/12/1986	Brighton & Hove Albion	Division Two	3-1
21/12/1986	Stoke City	Division Two	2-7
26/12/1986	Sunderland	Division Two	1-1
27/12/1986	Oldham Athletic	Division Two	1-0
01/01/1987	Ipswich Town	Division Two	0-2
03/01/1987	Huddersfield Town	Division Two	1-1
11/01/1987	Telford United	FA Cup 3rd Round at the Hawthorns	2-1
24/01/1987	Blackburn Rovers	Division Two	0-0
03/02/1987	Swindon Town	FA Cup 4th Round	2-1
07/02/1987	Sheffield United	Division Two	0-0
14/02/1987	Barnsley	Division Two	2-2
21/02/1987	Queens Park Rangers	FA Cup 5th Round	2-1
28/02/1987	Bradford City	Division Two	1-0
07/03/1987	Grimsby Town	Division Two	2-0
10/03/1987	Portsmouth	Division Two	1-1
15/03/1987	Wigan Athletic	FA Cup QF	2-0
21/03/1987	Crystal Palace	Division Two	0-1
28/03/1987	Plymouth Argyle	Division Two	4-0
04/04/1987	Millwall	Division Two	2-0
08/04/1987	Hull City	Division Two	0-0
12/04/1987	Coventry City	FA Cup SF at Hillsborough	2-3
14/04/1987	Shrewsbury Town	Division Two	2-0
18/04/1987	Ipswich Town	Division Two	3-2
20/04/1987	Sunderland	Division Two	1-1
22/04/1987	Reading	Division Two	1-2
25/04/1987	Birmingham City	Division Two	4-0
02/05/1987	Derby County	Division Two	1-2
04/05/1987	West Bromwich Albion	Division Two	3-2
09/05/1987	Brighton & Hove Albion	Division Two	1-0
14/05/1987	Oldham Athletic	Division Two Play Off SF 1st Leg	1-0
17/05/1987	Oldham Athletic	Division Two Play Off SF 2nd Leg	1-2
23/05/1987	Charlton Athletic	Division Two Play Off Final 1st Leg	0-1
25/05/1987	Charlton Athletic	Division Two Play Off Final 2nd Leg	1-0
29/05/1987	Charlton Athletic	Division Two Play Off Final Replay at St Andrews	1-2

Team	Pld	W	D	L	GF	GA	Pts
Derby County	42	25	9	8	64	38	84
Portsmouth	42	23	9	10	53	28	78
Oldham Athletic	42	22	9	11	65	44	75
Leeds United	42	19	11	12	58	44	68
Ipswich Town	42	17	13	12	59	43	64
Crystal Palace	42	19	5	18	51	53	62
Plymouth Argyle	42	16	13	13	62	57	61
Stoke City	42	16	10	16	63	53	58
Sheffield United	42	15	13	14	50	49	58
Bradford City	42	15	10	17	62	62	55
Barnsley	42	14	13	15	49	52	55
Blackburn Rovers	42	15	10	17	45	55	55
Reading	42	14	11	17	52	59	53
Hull City	42	13	14	15	41	55	53
West Bromwich Albion	42	13	12	17	51	49	51
Millwall	42	14	9	19	39	45	51
Huddersfield Town	42	13	12	17	54	61	51
Shrewsbury Town	42	15	6	21	41	53	51
Birmingham City	42	11	17	14	47	59	50
Sunderland	42	12	12	18	49	59	48
Grimsby Town	42	10	14	18	39	59	44
Brighton & Hove Albion	42	9	12	21	37	54	39

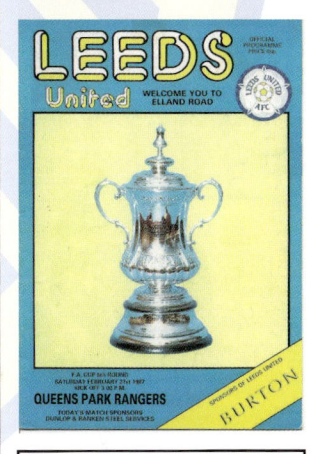

Leeds played Oldham Athletic six times in this season, winning one in the League at Elland Road and the play-off semi-final first leg also at Elland Road.

The Whites were led out by three different players, Ian Snodin, Brendan Ormsby and Jack Ashurst.

Leeds reached the last eight of the FA Cup for the first time in ten years.

Leeds used two goalkeepers this season, with Ronnie Sinclair playing in nine and Mervyn Day in 46.

Leeds had four red cards as they came within moments of reaching the First Division, Ian Snodin twice at Blackburn Rovers and West Bromwich Albion, Ian Baird at Barnsley and John Stiles also at West Bromwich Albion.

1987–88

DIVISION TWO

Team	Pld	W	D	L	GF	GA	Pts
Millwall	44	25	7	12	72	52	82
Aston Villa	44	22	12	10	68	41	78
Middlesbrough	44	22	12	10	63	36	78
Bradford City	44	22	11	11	74	54	77
Blackburn Rovers	44	21	14	9	68	52	77
Crystal Palace	44	22	9	13	86	59	75
Leeds United	44	19	12	13	61	51	69
Ipswich Town	44	19	9	16	61	52	66
Manchester City	44	19	8	17	80	60	65
Oldham Athletic	44	18	11	15	72	64	65
Stoke City	44	17	11	16	50	57	62
Swindon Town	44	16	11	17	73	60	59
Leicester City	44	16	11	17	62	61	59
Barnsley	44	15	12	17	61	62	57
Hull City	44	14	15	15	54	60	57
Plymouth Argyle	44	16	8	20	65	67	56
Bournemouth	44	13	10	21	56	68	49
Shrewsbury Town	44	11	16	17	42	54	49
Birmingham City	44	11	15	18	41	66	48
West Bromwich Albion	44	12	11	21	50	69	47
Sheffield United	44	13	7	24	45	74	46
Reading	44	10	12	22	44	70	42
Huddersfield Town	44	6	10	28	41	100	28

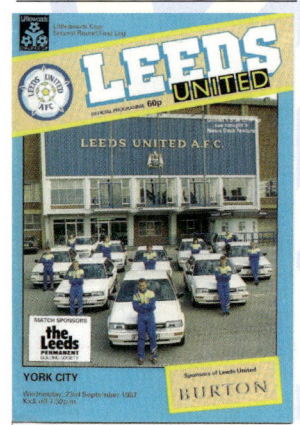

Date	Opposition	Competition	Score
16/08/1987	Barnsley	Division Two	1-1
19/08/1997	Leicester City	Division Two	1-0
22/08/1987	Reading	Division Two	0-0
29/08/1987	Bradford City	Division Two	0-0
31/08/1987	West Bromwich Albion	Division Two	1-0
05/09/1987	Ipswich Town	Division Two	0-1
12/09/1987	Hull City	Division Two	0-2
15/09/1987	Huddersfield Town	Division Two	0-0
19/09/1987	Middlesbrough	Division Two	0-2
23/09/1987	York City	Littlewoods Cup 2nd Round 1st Leg	1-1
26/09/1997	Manchester City	Division Two	2-0
30/09/1987	Stoke City	Division Two	0-0
03/10/1987	Blackburn Rovers	Division Two	1-1
06/10/1987	York City	Littlewoods Cup 2nd Round 2nd Leg	4-0
10/10/1987	Aston Villa	Division Two	1-3
17/10/1987	Plymouth Argyle	Division Two	3-6
20/10/1987	Oldham Athletic	Division Two	1-1
24/10/1987	AFC Bournemouth	Division Two	3-2
28/10/1987	Oldham Athletic	Littlewoods Cup 3rd Round	2-2
31/10/1987	Sheffield United	Division Two	2-2
04/11/1987	Oldham Athletic	Littlewoods Cup 3rd Round Replay	2-4
07/11/1987	Shrewsbury Town	Division Two	2-1
14/11/1987	Millwall	Division Two	1-3
21/11/1987	Swindon Town	Division Two	4-2
25/11/1987	Sheffield United	Simod Cup 1st Round	3-0
28/11/1987	Crystal Palace	Division Two	0-3
05/12/1987	Birmingham City	Division Two	4-1
08/12/1987	Millwall	Simod Cup 2nd Round	0-2
12/12/1987	Reading	Division Two	1-0
19/12/1987	Huddersfield Town	Division Two	3-0
26/12/1987	Manchester City	Division Two	2-1
28/12/1987	Middlesbrough	Division Two	2-0
01/01/1988	Bradford City	Division Two	2-0
03/01/1988	Hull City	Division Two	1-3
09/01/1988	Aston Villa	FA Cup 3rd Round	1-2
16/01/1988	Barnsley	Division Two	0-2
30/01/1988	West Bromwich Albion	Division Two	4-1
06/02/1988	Ipswich Town	Division Two	1-0
13/02/1988	Leicester City	Division Two	2-3
23/02/1988	Stoke City	Division Two	1-2
27/02/1988	Blackburn Rovers	Division Two	2-2
05/03/1988	Plymouth Argyle	Division Two	1-0
12/03/1988	Aston Villa	Division Two	2-1
19/03/1988	Sheffield United	Division Two	5-0
26/03/1988	AFC Bournemouth	Division Two	0-0
02/04/1988	Shrewsbury Town	Division Two	0-1
06/04/1988	Millwall	Division Two	1-2
23/04/1988	Oldham Athletic	Division Two	1-1
30/04/1988	Swindon Town	Division Two	2-1
02/05/1988	Crystal Palace	Division Two	1-0
06/05/1988	Birmingham City	Division Two	0-0

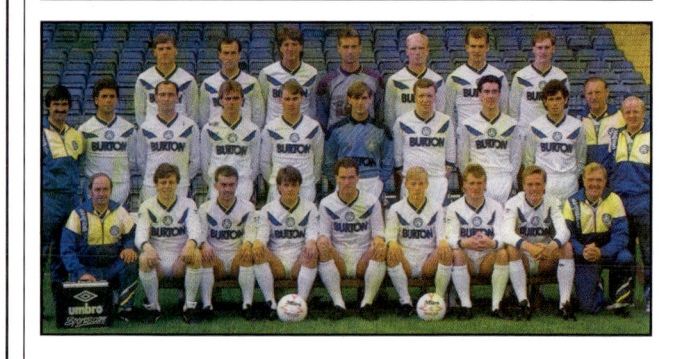

Ken De Mange made a goalscoring debut for the Whites, signing on loan from Liverpool and scoring at home to Manchester City in a 2-0 win.

Glyn Snodin was the only player to see red in season 1987-88 in a 2-0 win at home to Middlesbrough at the end of 1987.

Youngsters Simon Grayson, Vince Brockie and Peter Maguire were all handed their debuts by manager Billy Bremner in season 1987-88.

Mark Aizlewood and Jack Ashurst shared the captain's armband during the season.

Peter Haddock scored his one and only goal for the club in the 4-2 win over Swindon Town at Elland Road in November 1987.

272

DIVISION TWO

1988–89

Date	Opposition	Competition	Score
27/08/1988	**Oxford United**	**Division Two**	**1-1**
03/09/1988	Portsmouth	Division Two	0-4
10/09/1988	**Manchester City**	**Division Two**	**1-1**
17/09/1988	AFC Bournemouth	Division Two	0-0
21/09/1988	**Barnsley**	**Division Two**	**2-0**
24/09/1988	**Chelsea**	**Division Two**	**0-2**
27/09/1988	Peterborough United	Littlewoods Cup 2nd Round 1st Leg	2-1
01/10/1988	Brighton & Hove Albion	Division Two	1-2
04/10/1988	Sunderland	Division Two	1-2
08/10/1988	**Watford**	**Division Two**	**0-1**
12/10/1988	**Peterborough United**	**Littlewoods Cup 2nd Round 2nd Leg**	**3-1**
16/10/1988	Swindon Town	Division Two	0-0
22/10/1988	**Leicester City**	**Division Two**	**1-1**
26/10/1988	Bradford City	Division Two	1-1
29/10/1988	**Hull City**	**Division Two**	**2-1**
02/11/1988	**Luton Town**	**Littlewoods Cup 3rd Round**	**0-2**
05/11/1988	Ipswich Town	Division Two	1-0
09/11/1988	**Shrewsbury Town**	**Simod Cup 1st Round**	**3-1**
12/11/1988	**West Bromwich Albion**	**Division Two**	**2-1**
19/11/1988	Oldham Athletic	Division Two	2-2
22/11/1988	Birmingham City	Division Two	0-0
26/11/1988	**Stoke City**	**Division Two**	**4-0**
29/11/1988	**Millwall**	**Simod Cup 2nd Round**	**0-2**
03/12/1988	Walsall	Division Two	3-0
10/12/1988	**Shrewsbury Town**	**Division Two**	**2-3**
17/12/1988	Crystal Palace	Division Two	0-0
26/12/1988	**Blackburn Rovers**	**Division Two**	**2-0**
31/12/1988	**Plymouth Argyle**	**Division Two**	**2-0**
02/01/1989	Manchester City	Division Two	0-0
07/01/1989	Brighton & Hove Albion	FA Cup 3rd Round	2-1
14/01/1989	**Birmingham City**	**Division Two**	**1-0**
21/01/1989	Oxford United	Division Two	2-3
28/01/1989	Nottingham Forest	FA Cup 4th Round	0-2
04/02/1989	**Sunderland**	**Division Two**	**2-0**
11/02/1989	Watford	Division Two	1-1
18/02/1989	Leicester City	Division Two	2-1
25/02/1989	**Swindon Town**	**Division Two**	**0-0**
01/03/1999	**Bradford City**	**Division Two**	**3-3**
05/03/1989	West Bromwich Albion	Division Two	1-2
11/03/1989	**Ipswich Town**	**Division Two**	**2-4**
14/03/1989	Hull City	Division Two	2-1
19/03/1989	Barnsley	Division Two	2-2
25/03/1989	**Portsmouth**	**Division Two**	**1-0**
27/03/1989	Blackburn Rovers	Division Two	0-2
01/04/1989	**AFC Bournemouth**	**Division Two**	**3-0**
05/04/1989	**Crystal Palace**	**Division Two**	**1-2**
09/04/1989	Plymouth Argyle	Division Two	0-1
15/04/1989	**Brighton & Hove Albion**	**Division Two**	**1-0**
22/04/1989	Chelsea	Division Two	0-1
29/04/1989	Stoke City	Division Two	3-2
01/05/1989	**Walsall**	**Division Two**	**1-0**
06/05/1989	**Oldham Athletic**	**Division Two**	**0-0**
13/05/1989	Shrewsbury Town	Division Two	3-3

Team	Pld	W	D	L	GF	GA	Pts
Chelsea	46	29	12	5	96	50	99
Manchester City	46	23	13	10	77	53	82
Crystal Palace	46	23	12	11	71	49	81
Watford	46	22	12	12	74	48	78
Blackburn Rovers	46	22	11	13	74	59	77
Swindon Town	46	20	16	10	68	53	76
Barnsley	46	20	14	12	66	58	74
Ipswich Town	46	22	7	17	71	61	73
West Bromwich Albion	46	18	18	10	65	41	72
Leeds United	46	17	16	13	59	50	67
Sunderland	46	16	15	15	60	60	63
Bournemouth	46	18	8	20	53	62	62
Stoke City	46	15	14	17	57	72	59
Bradford City	46	13	17	16	52	59	56
Leicester City	46	13	16	17	56	63	55
Oldham Athletic	46	11	21	14	75	72	54
Oxford United	46	14	12	20	62	70	54
Plymouth Argyle	46	14	12	20	55	66	54
Brighton & Hove Albion	46	14	9	23	57	66	51
Portsmouth	46	13	12	21	53	62	51
Hull City	46	11	14	21	52	68	47
Shrewsbury Town	46	8	18	20	40	67	42
Birmingham City	46	8	11	27	31	76	35
Walsall	46	5	16	25	41	80	31

Leeds had three captains during the 1988-89 season, Mark Aizlewood, Micky Adams and Noel Blake.

Leeds had just two red cards this season, Ian Baird away at Portsmouth and Noel Blake away at Barnsley.

Carl Shutt had a debut to remember following his move from Bristol City scoring a hat-trick against AFC Bournemouth.

The late great Gary Speed made his Leeds United debut in a 0-0 draw at home to Oldham Athletic on 6 May 1989.

Former skipper Brendan Ormsby made his first Leeds United appearance in almost two years, on the last day of the season away at Shrewsbury Town.

273

1989–90

DIVISION TWO

Team	Pld	W	D	L	GF	GA	Pts
Leeds United	46	24	13	9	79	52	85
Sheffield United	46	24	13	9	78	58	85
Newcastle United	46	22	14	10	80	55	80
Swindon Town	46	20	14	12	79	59	74
Blackburn Rovers	46	19	17	10	74	59	74
Sunderland	46	20	14	12	70	64	74
West Ham United	46	20	12	14	80	57	72
Oldham Athletic	46	19	14	13	70	57	71
Ipswich Town	46	19	12	15	67	66	69
Wolverhampton W	46	18	13	15	67	60	67
Port Vale	46	15	16	15	62	57	61
Portsmouth	46	15	16	15	62	65	61
Leicester City	46	15	14	17	67	79	59
Hull City	46	14	16	16	58	65	58
Watford	46	14	15	17	58	60	57
Plymouth Argyle	46	14	13	19	58	63	55
Oxford United	46	15	9	22	57	66	54
Brighton & Hove Albion	46	15	9	22	56	72	54
Barnsley	46	13	15	18	49	71	54
West Bromwich Albion	46	12	15	19	67	71	51
Middlesbrough	46	13	11	22	52	63	50
Bournemouth	46	12	12	22	57	76	48
Bradford City	46	9	14	23	44	68	41
Stoke City	46	6	19	21	35	63	37

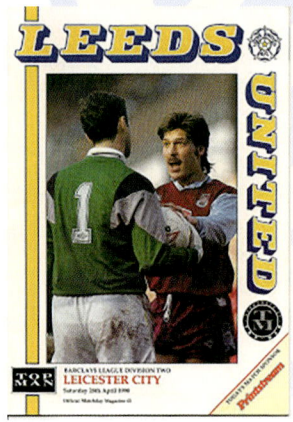

Date	Opposition	Competition	Score
19/08/1989	Newcastle United	Division Two	2-5
23/08/1989	Middlesbrough	Division Two	2-1
26/08/1989	Blackburn Rovers	Division Two	1-1
02/09/1989	Stoke City	Division Two	1-1
09/09/1989	Ipswich Town	Division Two	1-1
16/09/1989	Hull City	Division Two	1-0
19/09/1990	Oldham Athletic	Littlewoods Cup 2nd Round 1st Leg	1-2
23/09/1989	Swindon Town	Division Two	4-0
27/09/1989	Oxford United	Division Two	2-1
30/09/1989	Port Vale	Division Two	0-0
03/10/1989	Oldham Athletic	Littlewoods Cup 2nd Round 2nd Leg	1-2
07/10/1989	West Ham United	Division Two	1-0
14/10/1989	Sunderland	Division Two	2-0
17/10/1989	Portsmouth	Division Two	3-3
21/10/1989	Wolverhampton Wanderers	Division Two	1-0
28/10/1989	Bradford City	Division Two	1-0
01/11/1989	Plymouth Argyle	Division Two	2-1
04/11/1989	AFC Bournemouth	Division Two	3-0
07/11/1989	Blackburn Rovers	ZDS Cup Northern Section 1st Round	1-0
11/11/1989	Leicester City	Division Two	3-4
18/11/1989	Watford	Division Two	2-1
25/11/1989	West Bromwich Albion	Division Two	1-2
28/11/1989	Barnsley	ZDS Cup Northern Section 2nd Round	2-1
02/12/1989	Newcastle United	Division Two	1-0
09/12/1989	Middlesbrough	Division Two	2-0
16/12/1989	Brighton & Hove Albion	Division Two	3-0
19/12/1989	Stoke City	ZDS Cup Northern Section 3rd Round 2-2 (5-4 on pens)	
26/12/1989	Sheffield United	Division Two	2-2
30/12/1989	Barnsley	Division Two	0-1
01/01/1990	Oldham Athletic	Division Two	1-1
06/01/1990	Ipswich Town	FA Cup 3rd Round	0-1
13/01/1990	Blackburn Rovers	Division Two	2-1
17/01/1990	Aston Villa	ZDS Cup Northern Section SF	0-2
20/01/1990	Stoke City	Division Two	2-0
04/02/1990	Swindon Town	Division Two	2-3
10/02/1990	Hull City	Division Two	4-3
17/02/1990	Ipswich Town	Division Two	2-2
24/02/1990	West Bromwich Albion	Division Two	2-2
03/03/1990	Watford	Division Two	0-1
07/03/1990	Port Vale	Division Two	0-0
10/03/1990	Oxford United	Division Two	4-2
17/03/1990	West Ham United	Division Two	3-2
20/03/1990	Sunderland	Division Two	1-0
24/03/1990	Portsmouth	Division Two	2-0
31/03/1990	Wolverhampton Wanderers	Division Two	0-1
07/04/1990	Bradford City	Division Two	1-1
10/04/1990	Plymouth Argyle	Division Two	1-1
13/04/1990	Oldham Athletic	Division Two	1-3
16/04/1990	Sheffield United	Division Two	4-0
21/04/1990	Brighton & Hove Albion	Division Two	2-2
25/04/1990	Barnsley	Division Two	1-2
28/04/1990	Leicester City	Division Two	2-1
05/05/1990	AFC Bournemouth	Division Two	1-0

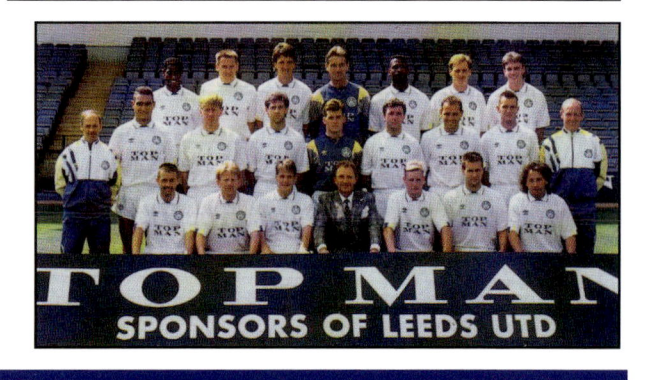

Only one side managed to do the double over the champions, Barnsley, winning 1-0 at Oakwell and 2-1 at Elland Road.

Neil Edwards and Chris O'Donnell joined the one appearance club, playing at home in the Zenith Data Systems Cup against Barnsley and Hull City respectively.

Leeds were awarded nine penalties, with the captain Gordon Strachan scoring eight of them, missing at home to Portsmouth.

Carl Shutt was forced in goal when Mervyn Day went off injured in the 4-3 defeat away at Leicester City in November 1989.

Vinnie Jones only received three yellow cards in a Leeds shirt following his move from Wimbledon in the summer of 1989.

THE 1990s
TIME FLIES WHEN YOU'RE HAVING FUN

Following promotion back to the top flight for the first time in eight years, manager Howard Wilkinson set his sights on the bigger prize of mounting a side ready to go for the First Division title. Gary McAllister from Leicester City, Chris Whyte from West Bromwich Albion and John Lukic, returning for a second spell from Arsenal, joined the side ahead of the 1990-91 campaign. The first season back in England's top table saw the side finish fourth with some memorable games, including a 5-4 home defeat to Liverpool, despite being 4-0 down at half time. They went on an unbeaten league run of 11 games that took them to a season finish of third place. The cup competitions saw Leeds reach the semi-finals of the Rumbelows Cup, losing 3-1 to Manchester United on aggregate, the Northern Area Final of the Zenith Data Systems Cup, losing 6-4 to Everton on aggregate, and taking eventual champions Arsenal to four games in the FA Cup before losing 2-1 in the replay at Elland Road.

The seeds had been sown, and with the addition of Rod Wallace from Southampton, Steve Hodge from Nottingham Forest, Tony Dorigo from Chelsea and Jon Newsome from Sheffield Wednesday, the side were ready for a tilt at the title. The side started on a unbeaten run of 10 games, which included a famous 1-0 victory at home to Liverpool, thanks to a Steve Hodge winner, and saw the Whites cemented in the top two for the rest of campaign. Despite a 1-0 defeat away at Crystal Palace, Leeds bounced back with three straight victories, and for the first time since winning the league in 1974 they were top of the table. A swashbuckling

Leeds United, 1990-91.

Lee Chapman (9) scores one of his brace for Leeds United v Norwich City in a 3-0 win on 1 September 1990.

performance away at Aston Villa, thanks to a brilliant goal from Lee Chapman, kept Leeds top of the league, and they stayed top until a run of three draws over Christmas. A 3-1 win at West Ham United, coupled with a shock 4-1 home loss for Manchester United against Queens Park Rangers, sent the Whites back to the top of the pile and set them up for a double header against the Red Devils in both the Rumbelows Cup and FA Cup. The side from Old Trafford got the better of Leeds in both games, but Leeds bounced back with a fantastic 6-1 win away at Sheffield Wednesday. David Batty scored a memorable goal in a 3-0 home win against Notts County, but defeat at Oldham Athletic (2-0), a game in which Eric Cantona made his debut after signing on loan from Nimes, sent Leeds back to second place. Cantona scored his first goal for Leeds in a 2-0 win at home to Luton Town on leap year day, but it would be nip and tuck between Leeds United and Manchester United come the end of the season. Going into the vital Easter period, Leeds drew at Anfield (0-0) and beat Coventry City (2-0) at Elland Road, whilst Manchester United slipped up with a 1-1 draw at Luton Town and a shock 2-1 home defeat to Nottingham Forest. When the side from Old Trafford lost their game in hand at bottom of the table West Ham United, Leeds knew that they were two games away from the Championship for the first time since 1974. Leeds kicked off early at Sheffield United and won a crazy game 3-2, thanks to an own goal from Brian Gayle. Two hours later they were crowned champions following Liverpool's 2-0 win over Manchester United at Anfield. Leeds lifted the trophy at home to Norwich City a week later and wild celebrations soon followed.

Leeds United celebrate being 1992 Division One Champions on a open-top bus tour of Leeds.

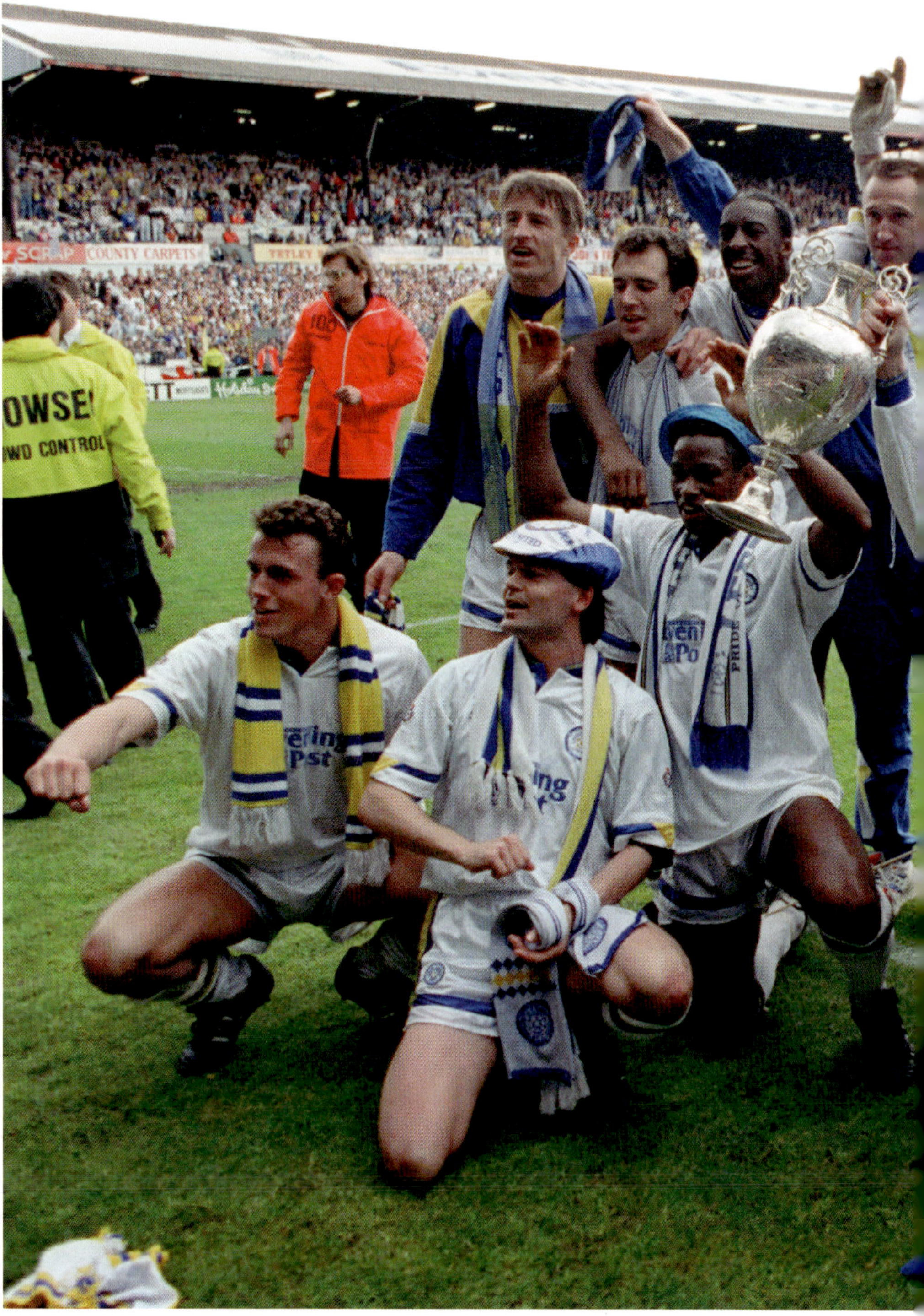
COUNTY CARPETS

Leeds United celebrate their 1992 title-winning season following the 1-0 win over Norwich at Elland Road.

The next task for Sergeant Wilko was to build on this success and with Eric Cantona joining permanently the early signs were good. Cantona scored a hat-trick in a thrilling 4-3 Charity Shield win over Liverpool and a brace from Lee Chapman at home to Wimbledon on day one looked to have set the tone. However, following a 4-1 defeat away at Middlesbrough the alarm bells were ringing. Leeds failed to win an away league game all season and were in real danger of being sucked into a relegation scrap. Thankfully, the home form was much better, with only Nottingham Forest winning at Elland Road all season. In the end the side finished 17th, but it was a league season to forget. Winning the league the previous season meant qualification to the European Cup, and despite losing the first leg to Stuttgart 3-0 they

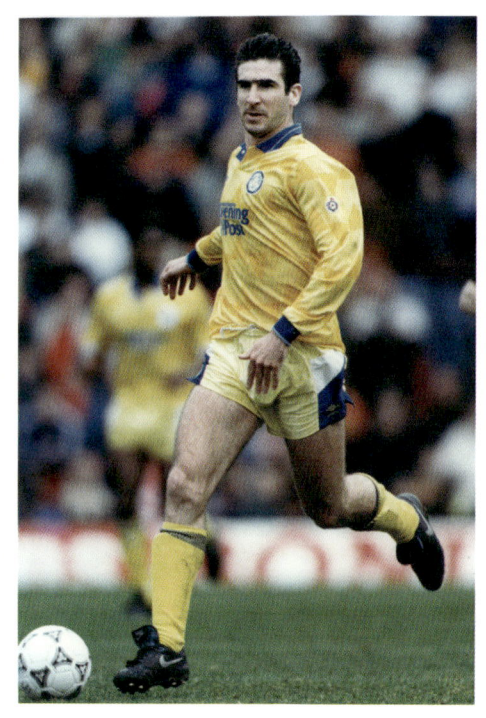

Eric Cantona, Leeds United, 22 March 1992.

Eric Cantona (Leeds United) scores the third goal against VfB Stuttgart in the 4-1 win at Elland Road in the European Cup first round, 30 September 1992.

produced their best performance in years, winning 4-1 at Elland Road. Sadly for the Whites, it looked like they would be heading out, but thanks to the Germans fielding an ineligible player, they were handed a reprieve and won a third game at the Nou Camp courtesy of a late goal from super sub Carl Shutt. It set up a Battle of Britain against Glasgow Rangers, and, despite taking the lead through Gary McAllister early on, an own goal from John Lukic got the Scottish Champions going and they went through on aggregate. Cantona was sold soon after to arch rivals Manchester United, and the season suffered. The cups came and went, with Watford knocking them out of the Coca Cola Cup, and eventually winners Arsenal knocked them out of the FA Cup. The only bright spot was the success of the youth side, who won the FA Youth Cup thanks to a brilliant 4-1 aggregate win over former winners Manchester United.

Leeds had to improve the following season and changes were made; out went title winners Lee Chapman and Chris Whyte and in came Brian Deane from Sheffield United and David O'Leary from Arsenal. Early season results were up and down, but a 1-0 win over Oldham Athletic, thanks to a winning goal from Gordon Strachan, set Leeds on an unbeaten run that would last all the way to start of December. They finally won on the road away at Southampton and the side found themselves in second place. The bad news was the sale of David Batty to Blackburn Rovers and the second half of the campaign saw league form stutter and a shock home defeat to lower league Oxford United in the FA Cup didn't help matters. Leeds rallied themselves and finished the season in fifth place but just missed on a European qualification. After the previous season's disaster this was a massive improvement and things were to get better the following campaign.

Season 1994-95 kicked off with four new signings, Phil Masinga and Lucas Radebe joined from Mamelodi Sundowns and Kasier Chiefs respectively and from Sheffield Wednesday

Leeds United, 1994-95.

in came Carlton Palmer and Nigel Worthington. Early season form was patchy despite a first league win over Manchester United in 13 years at Elland Road. A shock Coca Cola Cup defeat to Mansfield Town didn't help matters. Leading up to the New Year Leeds were in seventh position. Goals had dried up but fans need not worry, with the signing of Ghanian Anthony Yeboah from Eintracht Frankfurt proving to be the missing piece of the jigsaw. Yeboah scored his first goal for the side as they exited the FA Cup at Manchester United. His goals would prove vital in the race to UEFA Cup qualification. Going into the last day of the campaign, they needed a point away at Tottenham Hotspur to secure European football at Elland Road. Despite falling behind to a Teddy Sheringham volley a wonderful individual goal from Brian Deane saw the Whites finish in fifth place and that meant a place in the UEFA Cup.

Phil Masinga in action in the 0-0 draw with Wimbledon on 4 February 1995.

Leeds had high hopes going into the following season and topped the table after three games that included a magnificent volley from Yeboah in a 1-0 win at home to Liverpool. That was as good as it got as the league form was extremely inconsistent and the side ended up in 13th place. A Yeboah hat-trick in the first leg of the UEFA Cup first round away at Moncao was a high point, as was his goal in a 4-2 win away at Wimbledon in mid-September. European football was ended thanks to an 8-3 aggregate defeat to Dutch side PSV Eindhoven, but Leeds did fare better in the domestic cup competitions. In the FA Cup, they made it through to the last eight before being beaten at Anfield 3-0 in a replay. In the Coca Cola Cup they made it all the way through to Wembley and a game against Aston Villa. Sadly for the Whites, they were well beaten (3-0) and the writing was on wall for Wilkinson. One bright spot was the emergence of youngsters Ian Harte and Andy Gray, and even new signing Tomas Brolin, who was bought in from Parma in mid-November flopped, which just summed the season up.

Wilkinson knew he had to make changes and out went Gary McAllister to Coventry, Gary Speed to Everton and John Lukic back to Arsenal. In came Ian Rush from Liverpool,

Ian Rush in action against Coventry City on 14 September 1996.

Lee Bowyer from Charlton Athletic, Nigel Martyn from Crystal Palace and Lee Sharpe from Manchester United. The side won two of their first four games, but a 4-0 defeat at home to champions Manchester United signalled the end of the Wilkinson era. He had bought success to a side that many supporters had never seen, but changes were needed and former Arsenal manager George Graham was brought in to steady the ship. It took Graham till his fourth league game in charge to achieve a league victory (2-0) at home to Nottingham Forest, but he knew he had a task on his hands. Aston Villa, like they had done the previous season, knocked Leeds out of the Coca Cola Cup, but league form did pick up, and going into the Christmas period Leeds were in 12th position. A fantastic 1-0 win over Arsenal in the FA Cup fourth round set Leeds up for a tie against Portsmouth from the First Division. Sadly for the Whites, Pompey knocked Leeds out 3-2 at Elland Road and they were left to rue a missed opportunity. In the end Leeds finished the season in 11th place and Graham's first objective had been met, though goalscoring had been a problem all season.

Jimmy Floyd Hasselbaink playing for Leeds against Aston Villa on 30 August 1997.

Changes were made, with the likes of Rush, Palmer, Dorigo and even Yeboah all surplus to requirements. They were replaced by Jimmy Floyd Hasselbaink, Bruno Ribeiro, Alfie Haaland, David Robertson and David Hopkin. Graham knew it would take time for his side to gel and early season results were inconsistent. A frenetic 4-3 over Blackburn Rovers at Ewood Park, in which all seven goals were scored in the first half, got the season going, as did a famous 1-0 win over Manchester United in which David Wetherall scored the winner. November 1997 proved to be a month no Leeds fan would ever forget. The 1-0 win over Tottenham Hotspur at White Hart Lane was routine, but when the side were 3-0 down at home to Derby County after 33 minutes, no one could imagine what would happen next. Fast forward to just over an hour and four goals later, Leeds had achieved the impossible and won the game 4-3. They then became the come-back kings after winning 3-1 at home to West Ham United from 1-0 down and 3-2 at Barnsley after being 2-0 down. The only blot on the copybook was a disappointing 3-2 home Coca Cola Cup defeat to First Division Reading. The following month saw the passing of Billy Bremner, the greatest captain in Leeds United's history and the club paid tribute to him in the away game at Chelsea and the home game against Bolton Wanderers. The aim at the start of

Gary Kelly (Leeds United) challenges Gary Rowett (Derby County) in the 4-3 win over Derby County at Elland Road having been 3-0 down, 8 November 1997.

the season had been European football and this was achieved, as it had been in 1994-95 as the side finished in fifth place. As in the Coca Cola Cup, Leeds were knocked out by lower league opposition in the FA Cup as well by Wolverhampton Wanderers, just as Leeds had looked like they were on the way to Wembley.

David Batty re-signs in 1998 with David O'Leary.

The following season saw Clyde Wijnhard and Danny Granville join and early season form was good following an early September win over Southampton that saw Leeds top the table for 24 hours. With the news of Tottenham Hotspur axing Christian Gross, George Graham was made favourite for the job. Talks were on going and ironically, on the last Saturday of September, Leeds made the trip to the capital to face managerless Spurs. In an entertaining game the points were shared (3-3), but all at Leeds knew the writing was on the wall in that Graham would join Tottenham. Despite going through the second round of the UEFA Cup with a penalty shoot-out win over Maritimo, 24 hours later Graham was gone and David O'Leary was appointed caretaker manager, whilst chairman Peter Ridsdale decided on his next move. O'Leary impressed and was handed the reins on 25 October. Slowly but surely, the Irishman stamped his authority on the side and this was evident following an impressive 3-1 win at Anfield, in which youngster Alan Smith scored with his first touch at the Kop end. The football on show was a pleasure to watch and West Ham United were dispatched 4-0 as Leeds made it up to third place in the Premiership. Better news was to follow as O'Leary's first signing was to bring back David Batty, a move that pleased all supporters. Come the new year, hopes were high that Leeds could qualify for European football again, and despite back-to-back defeats to Southampton (3-0) and Newcastle United (1-0), Leeds then went on a seven-game winning run, their best since season 1973-74, to propel themselves into Champions League contention. In the end, O'Leary's youngsters finished in fourth place and UEFA Cup qualification for the second consecutive campaign, the first time since season

Harry Kewell, Leeds Utd.

1974-75. The influence of youngsters such as Alan Smith, Harry Kewell, Ian Harte, Paul Robinson and Stephen Mcphail was there for all to see.

During the off season, Michael Bridges (Sunderland), Michael Duberry (Chelsea), Danny Mills (Charlton Athletic) and Eirik Bakke (Songdal) all joined, but then on the eve of the new campaign Jimmy Floyd Hasselbaink, top scorer for the last two seasons, joined Athletico Madrid. No supporter will ever forget the events of season 1990-2000 both on and off the pitch. Following an early defeat to Liverpool, Leeds dropped to seventh. What followed was a ten-match winning run in all competitions, which took Leeds to the top of the table and a place in the second round of the UEFA Cup. Partizan Belgrade were dispatched 4-1 on aggregate, Lokomotiv Moscow were then seen off 7-1 on aggregate, before a tricky trip to Spartak Moscow. The winning run ended in a thrilling 4-4 draw away at Goodison Park. Leeds stayed top until a 2-0 defeat at Wimbledon. The side returned to the top with a last-gasp victory over Southampton thanks to a brilliant goal from Michael Bridges. Spartak won the first leg 2-1, played in Bulgaria after the original tie was postponed. In front of a sell-out crowd at Elland Road, Lucas Radebe headed the winning goal six minutes before the end and earned Leeds a tie against Roma in the fourth round. Leeds stayed top of the pile until the end of January, when events off the field took a turn for the worse. Despite a wonderful FA Cup win (5-2) at Manchester City, league form was affected and despite a 1-0 win over Tottenham Hotspur, a 1-0 defeat to champions Manchester United ended all hopes of a title challenge. Leeds made it through to the last eight of the UEFA Cup, thanks to a wonderful goal from Harry Kewell, and a week later defeated Slavia Prague 3-0 at Elland Road to all but book a place in the last four. Despite the Czech side winning 2-1, Leeds made it through to a tie with Galatasaray. Tragically the tie was overshadowed by the deaths of two Leeds United supporters, Kevin Speight and Christopher Loftus and the players' mentality was certainly not on the game. Leeds lost the game 2-0, which paled into insignificance and tributes were paid to the two supporters at the next home game against Arsenal. Leeds lost the tie 4-2 on aggregate, but somehow the players regrouped for the last four league games of an arduous campaign and took eight points from the last 12, earning a place in the coveted Champions League qualifiers, which was achievement in itself in O'Leary's first full season at the helm.

DEBUTANTS OF THE 90s

LEE CHAPMAN

Debut: Blackburn Rovers (A) 13 January 1990
Appearances: 171 (4)
Goals: 80

Lee Chapman joined the Whites from Nottingham Forest in January 1990. After saying 'I had played under Howard Wilkinson at Sheffield Wednesday, and he trained hard and I joined Leeds for all the right reasons,' Chappy had a dream debut in the Whites of Leeds United. With the side trailing at half-time against Blackburn Rovers, he popped up with an equaliser in the second period followed by a winner from Gordon Strachan, which proved vital for the side. The Lincolnshire-born striker went on to score one of the most important goals in the club's history, away at AFC Bournemouth, as Leeds clinched promotion on a sweltering hot day on the south coast. 'I knew there was a lot of expectation, it was one of the biggest games I've played in. Chris Kamara crossed the ball in and I headed it in, we knew we were back!'

In their first season back on top, there was little expected at Elland Road, but Wilkinson's side ended up finishing fourth, taking champions Arsenal to four games in the FA Cup and reaching the semi-final of the Rumbelows Cup and the Northern Area final of the Zenith Data System Cup. Chapman finished top scorer with 31 that season, but two games in particular stand out. Tottenham Hotspur away, where he landed on the hoardings, off the pitch following a collision with Steve Sedgley. Chapman recalls: 'I went for a header on the touchline and he kicked my chin; I swallowed my tongue, had plastic surgery and the surgeons put glue on top of all my stitches.' The other game was the 5-4 home defeat against Liverpool, in which he scored a hat-trick and had a fourth goal disallowed for a foul on the Reds goalkeeper Mike Hooper. Chapman said of the game, 'When you score a hat-trick, you don't expect to be on the losing side.'

The following season he exceeded all expectations as Leeds won their first Championship in 18 years. 'We had settled in, we were a great danger, we went from strength to strength. The manager never mentioned winning the title and his ambition was to finish runners-up. The wins at Aston Villa (4-1) and Sheffield Wednesday (6-1) were magnificent.' Following the league success, there were hopes that Leeds would push on, but this failed to materialise as Leeds ended the season in 17th place, just about clear from relegation. Chapman left Elland Road to join Portsmouth that summer, but he did return to west Yorkshire in January 1996 following an injury crisis. His second debut was remembered for all the wrong reasons, as he was sent off for a challenge on Mark Rieper against his former club West Ham United. He would feature only one more time for Leeds in a 5-0 loss at Anfield before returning to Ipswich Town.

GARY McALLISTER MBE

Debut: Everton (A) 25 August 1990
Appearances: 294 (1)
Goals: 45

Following promotion to the old First Division, McAllister joined the Whites from Leicester City just before the World Cup of 1990 in Italy. The Scotsman looked set to join Brian Clough at Nottingham Forest, but chose to join Leeds instead. In the previous season before with the Foxes, the former Motherwell player was influential in a 4-3 win for Leicester over Leeds and scored a brilliant goal at Elland Road for the Foxes in the Whites' vital 2-1 win in April 1990.

McAllister proved to be one of the side's most important and inspiring signings in recent times. In his first season at Elland Road, he played in 55 games, scoring six goals, his first coming ironically at home to Nottingham Forest as Leeds finished fourth in the First Division. It also helped that by the time he had arrived he had his international partner Gordon Strachan as club captain, a role that would soon be his.

The following campaign saw McAllister start 41 of the club's 42 league games (he came on as a substitute in the 4-2 win over Notts County) as Leeds won their first League Championship in 18 long years. McAllister kicked-off the season with the winning goal at home to Nottingham Forest and went on to score a further four goals including vital ones away at West Ham United, Tottenham Hotspur and his first penalty in a Leeds shirt in the Easter Monday win at home to Coventry City.

With the championship in the bag, it meant a trip to Wembley to face FA Cup winners Liverpool on a glorious sunny August weekend. With Strachan on the bench, McAllister took over captaincy duties, a role he would keep for the next four seasons, and he led the side out at Wembley. McAllister also took on the role as penalty taker with Strachan out of the team. The 1992-93 season was a disappointing one, but McAllister did have the honour of scoring at Ibrox in the European Cup second-round, first-leg tie, in a game that Leeds fans were banned from attending. The next three seasons saw the Scotsman miss only three games and he led the side to reach the UEFA Cup in 1994-95. For the second time in a Leeds shirt he led them out at Wembley in the Coca Cola Cup Final against Aston Villa in March 1996. At the end of that season, McAllister joined up with Strachan at Coventry City before returning to the Elland Road hot seat in February 2008, which you can read about in the managers' section in the following decade.

TONY DORIGO

Debut: Nottingham Forest (H) 20 August 1991
Appearances: 205 (4)
Goals: 6

Dorigo joined the Elland Road revolution in the summer of 1991 and explains how the move came about from Chelsea: 'I was definitely leaving Chelsea, with my contract waiting to run out. I had one or two options: Rangers were sniffing, but Leeds came in and I went to see Howard Wilkinson, talks went well and the club were looking to build something and wanted

Eric Cantona and Tony Dorigo, scorers in the 4-3 win against Liverpool in the 1992 Charity Shield at Wembley, with the trophy, 8 August 1992.

to be the best.' Dorigo described his debut as incredible, which was at home to Nottingham Forest, with the noise being just nuts! His first goal came in a 3-0 win over Manchester City, with a half volley from the edge of the area: 'When you catch them right, you catch them right, the noise was deafening, then Batts scored and it was fantastic.' Dorigo felt that Leeds had a chance of winning the title: 'We felt we had a chance, we kept doing our thing, you don't realise until you hit March, the target was two points per game. The wins at Aston Villa and Sheffield Wednesday just seemed very easy, everything just seemed to click.'

Dorigo then picks out two vital wins towards the back end of the season that helped Leeds clinch the title: 'Chelsea at home, Eric [Cantona] produced something we needed, it was his time to shine.' As for the Sheffield United game, 'it was the weirdest game I've ever played in, with the wind, the rubbish on the pitch, the game itself was one we felt we could win and when Gayle scored the own goal it was just nuts!'

The following season saw Leeds fail to win a single away game in the league and finish in 17th position: 'We found it difficult to adapt to the back-pass rule, but the home form was brilliant, it was a crazy situation.' Dorigo scored a vital winner from the spot at home to Ipswich Town. With McAllister out injured and Strachan struggling, Dorigo took on penalty taking duties.

Sadly for the former Chelsea man, he missed the Coca Cola Cup Final against Aston Villa in 1996. 'In the second leg against Birmingham City my hamstring went, I had to get fit for the final, I trained at Bisham Abbey but in my last sprint, it went again.' Dorigo had one more season at Elland Road before leaving the club to join Italian side Torino in the summer of 1997, who were in Seria B at the time.

GARY KELLY

Debut: Scunthorpe United (H) 8 October 1991
Appearances: 516 (15)
Goals: 4

The Drogheda-born full back joined the Whites from Home Farm in July 1991 and no one could have imagined the impact he would go on to have as he became a one club player.

The Irishman featured on three occasions in season 1991-92, all as a substitute, before an injury to Mel Sterland meant manager Howard Wilkinson had an issue at right-back at the start of the 1993-94 season. Kelly made the position his own and was an ever-present from August 1993 right through to December 1995, when a play-off game for the Republic of Ireland meant that he had to miss the home game with Wimbledon. During the 1995-96 campaign, he was part of the side that reached the Coca Cola Cup Final against Aston Villa. The same season saw the debut of his nephew Ian Harte. In his 166th game for the side, Kelly found the back of the net with a brilliant volley away at Southampton and followed it up with a free kick in a televised win over West Ham United in January 1997.

At the back end of the 1997-98 season, then manager George Graham handed him the captaincy for the remaining nine games of the campaign and he led the side out under numerous managers before retirement in 2007.

He missed the whole of the 1998-99 season due to shin splints but played a massive part the following season as Leeds finished third and reached the UEFA Cup semi-finals under David O'Leary. Kelly was a vital part of the team that reached the second group stage of the

Champions League, but an injury in the FA Cup tie at home to Liverpool saw the emergence of Danny Mills in a Leeds shirt, with Kelly only starting two more games that season. Kelly played under Howard Wilkinson, George Graham, David O'Leary, Terry Venables, Peter Reid, Eddie Gray, Kevin Blackwell, John Carver and Dennis Wise. Following relegation to the third tier and at the age of 32, he retired from the game, scoring a further two goals, both in FA Cup ties away at Crystal Palace and at home to Wigan Athletic. In 2002 he was awarded a well-deserved testimonial at home to Glasgow Celtic and he donated all the money raised to cancer charities following the death of his sister. He also represented his country at the 1994 and 2002 World Cups.

LUCAS RADEBE

Debut: Mansfield Town (H) 21 September 1994
Appearances: 235 (27)
Goals: 3

Lucas Radebe was the second South African to join Leeds United in the summer of 1994. Following the signing of Phil Masinga from Mamelodi Sundowns, Radebe joined from the Kasier Chiefs in August 1994. He featured only 15 times in his first season at Elland Road, with injury keeping him sidelined for over nine months. But it was in his second season at Elland Road that fans started to take to him as he took over in goal in the 1-0 home defeat against Middlesbrough, when John Lukic went off injured. It wasn't just on one occasion, he also did it again when Mark Beeney was sent off in the 1-0 loss at Old Trafford.

It was the arrival of new manager George Graham that turned Radebe into a top-notch centre-half. He scored his first goal in a 4-0 FA Cup win over Oxford United in January 1998, but an even bigger honour was to follow as Graham awarded him with the club captaincy at the start of the 1998-99 season.

The South African blossomed even further under David O'Leary as Leeds reached the semi-finals of the UEFA Cup and finished third in the Premier League. The South African chipped in with a couple of vital goals along the way – in the away game against Partizan Belgrade, when he was on his back, and the vital winner at home to Spartak Moscow on a wonderful European night as Leeds made it through to the last 16 of the UEFA Cup.

The Chief played a massive part in the 2000-01 campaign, but he missed the final stages of the season through injury, when new signing Rio Ferdinand took his place. The 2001-02 was a wipeout for Radebe as he missed the entire campaign, only playing in Gary Kelly's testimonial. He bounced back in seasons 2002-03 and 2003-04 and stayed on following relegation from the Premier League, only for another injury in the third game of the season away at Wolverhampton Wanderers to keep him out until the final minutes of the last game of the season, against Rotherham United in May. He was awarded a deserved testimonial in which players such as Gary McAllister, Gordon Strachan, Gary Speed and David Batty played for Leeds and football legends such as Jay Jay Okocha, Bruce Grobbelaar and John Carew played for the Rest of the World side. The Leeds based band The Kaiser Chiefs took the name from Radebe's old club.

ANTHONY YEBOAH

Debut: Queens Park Rangers (H) 24 January 1994
Appearances: 61 (5)
Goals: 32

With goals in short supply at Elland Road during the festive period of 1994 and into the new year of 1995, manager Howard Wilkinson needed a striker. The club paid Eintracht Frankfurt £3.4 million for the services of the Ghanaian and what a signing he proved to be.

His debut came on a cold midweek night at home to Queens Park Rangers, coming on as a substitute for Phil Masinga with his first goal coming away at Manchester United in an FA Cup fifth round defeat in February 1995. He then followed this up with a late winner at home to Everton and scored five in three consecutive games away at Leicester City and Chelsea and at home to Coventry City as Leeds looked for points to reach the UEFA Cup.

His first hat-trick for the club came in a 4-0 win at home to Ipswich Town, and Yeboah scored vital goals in the wins at Newcastle United and a brace at home to Crystal Palace as Leeds assured themselves of a European place for season 1995-96. The following season couldn't have started any better for Yeboah, a brace away at West Ham United was followed up with a goal-of-the-season contender against Liverpool live on Sky Sports and he then scored a fantastic hat-trick in a wonderful 3-0 away win at Monaco in the first-round, first-leg tie in Monte Carlo. The Ghanaian followed this up with another three-goal haul away at Wimbledon, which included another goal-of-the-season contender! Sadly for Yeboah, the

goals did start to dry up, but he was on the scoresheet on Christmas Eve with a brilliant solo goal in a 3-1 win over arch rivals Manchester United at Elland Road. He helped Leeds through to the Coca Cola Cup Final, scoring in both legs against Birmingham City, but his brace away at Queens Park Rangers at the start of March 1996 would prove to be his last goals for the club as injury ruled him out of the last two months of that season. With the departure of Wilkinson, Leeds saw the arrival of George Graham and Yeboah spent too much time on the sidelines. He did reappear on Boxing Day 1996 at home to Coventry City, but made only a handful of appearances that season. His last action in a Leeds shirt came away at Tottenham Hotspur when he was substituted and he threw his shirt at the bench; he would never play for Leeds again.

NIGEL MARTYN

Debut: Derby County (A) 17 August 1996
Appearances: 273

With the departure of title-winning goalkeeper John Lukic at the end of the 1995-96 campaign, Leeds were on the lookout for a new number one and Nigel Martyn fitted the bill perfectly. The Cornishman looked set to join Everton, but instead chose to join Leeds in the summer of 1996 for £2.25m instead.

He had an instant impact with some wonderful displays in his first season and missed only one game through injury, a goalless draw at home to Derby County in which Mark Beeney deputised. During his first season, he went seven league games without conceding at Elland Road before a deflected strike from Middlesbrough's Juninho beat him on the last day of the season. He finished his first season in west Yorkshire as the Leeds United Player of the Year.

The following term he produced another string of superb performances and missed just one game after a sending off at home to Oxford United in the FA Cup third round in January 1998. At the end of that campaign he was voted in to the 1997-98 FA Premier League Team of the Year.

Season 1998-99 would be another memorable one for the former Bristol Rovers stopper, as he helped Leeds to finish fourth in the Premier League and qualify for the UEFA Cup. Just like the previous season, he was voted in the Premier League Team of the Year.

The millennium campaign proved to be one of the best in Martyn's career at Elland Road, and the stand-out fixture was the first-leg tie away at AS Roma in the UEFA Cup last 16, when Martyn produced save after save to keep the Italian side out. *Yorkshire Evening Post* reporter Phil Rostron gave Martyn ten out of ten for his display, and for the third successive season he was named the Premier League Team of the Year. Martyn started the following season in fine fettle but an injury at home to Charlton Athletic saw him ruled out for three months and young Paul Robinson deputised. He made his return at home to Liverpool in the FA Cup and helped Leeds reach the last four of the Champions League. He was an ever-present the following season, but following the arrival of Terry Venables Martyn sat the whole season on the bench. He would go on to join Everton in August 2003, when Robinson started the new campaign as number one.

LEE BOWYER

Debut: Derby County (A) 17 August 1996
Appearances: 257 (8)
Goals: 55

In July 1996 Bowyer left the bright lights of London and swapped it for the North of England as he joined the Whites for a fee of £2.8 million.

His career at Elland Road was a bit of a slow burner, but he will be remembered for scoring the winning goal in the memorable 4-3 comeback win over Derby County in the last minute at the start of November 1997.

It was during the following season that Bowyer's Leeds United career really took off under the stewardship of David O'Leary. He started in 45 games, scoring nine goals from midfield, most notably a brace in the 4-0 home win against his boyhood club West Ham United and in victories at home to Coventry City, away at Newcastle United and at home to Middlesbrough and Derby County. He was named the Leeds United Player of the Year for his all action displays as the Whites finished the season in fourth place and qualified for the UEFA Cup.

The following season would go down as a campaign of two halves for the London-born midfielder. He was a vital part as Leeds topped the league going into the new millennium and scored some crucial goals, especially in European competition. He scored a brace away at Partizan Belgrade and another pair in the home leg against Lokomotiv Moscow as Leeds made it through to the third round of the UEFA Cup.

Sadly for Bowyer, he made the headlines for all the wrong reasons in the second half of the season but bounced back in fantastic fashion the following year as Leeds reached the Champions League last four in their first season in the competition. Bowyer produced some memorable performances and scored the winner at home to AC Milan, a brace at home to Besiktas, a free kick against Barcelona, a vital late winner against Anderlecht in front of a jubilant Elland Road crowd and a fine chip against Lazio. Just like two years before, he was named the Leeds United Player of the Year as the side took all before them in the second half of that season. Season 2001-02 was disappointing in contrast as he only hit the back of the net on seven occasions, one of them being a last-ditch win away at Southampton at the back end of 2001. At the end of that season it looked like he was on the way to Liverpool, but the Reds pulled out of the deal. However, Bowyer did leave Leeds in the first January transfer window to join his boyhood heroes at Upton Park.

ALAN SMITH

Debut: Liverpool (A) 14 November 1998
Appearances: 191 (37)
Goals: 56

'Smudger' signed professional forms with the club in March 1998 and his debut away at Liverpool was Roy of the Rovers stuff. Having come off the bench for Clyde Wijnhard, with the side losing 1-0 thanks to a Robbie Fowler penalty, Smith scored with his first touch in front of the kop end and helped Leeds to a rare away victory on Merseyside. He followed this up with another goal off the bench at home to Charlton Athletic, and in the second half of the campaign he became the regular striking partner with Jimmy Floyd Hasselbaink. He ended his first season at Elland Road with nine goals in 26 games as the club finished in fourth position. He added six more goals to his collection the following season, including a brace in the Yorkshire derby at home to Sheffield Wednesday and one in the 4-1 win over Lokomotiv Moscow at Elland Road.

Smith scored the vital goals in both legs of the Champions League qualifier against 1860 Munich and it earned him a place in Kevin Keegan's England squad. His most memorable moment in a Leeds United shirt came in a 1-0 win away at Lazio, as Smith scored the only goal in the Stadio Olimpico to see off the Italian side.

With the signing of Robbie Keane on loan from Inter Milan, Smith was in and out of the side, but with Keane unable to play in the Champions League, Smith took his chance, scoring a brilliant brace away at Anderlecht, the opener away at Real Madrid and the second at home to Deportivo La Coruna as Leeds demolished the then Spanish champions. He hit the back of the net a further five times in 2001-02 but was pushed back into an unfamiliar right midfield position as injuries took their toll at Elland Road.

Under Terry Venables, Smith started 43 games and again had happy memories of playing in European competition as he hit a four-goal haul in the second leg against Hapoel Tel Aviv to defeat the side from Israel. Sadly for the Whites, the squad that had reached the last four of Europe's premier competition was broken up and exactly three years to the day that they faced Valencia in the first leg of the semi-finals, Leeds were relegated to the second tier of English football for the first time in 14 years. Smith was made captain in his last appearance at Elland Road against Charlton Athletic and marked the occasion by scoring from the spot. He left for rivals Manchester United for £6 million, with Smith waiving the transfer fee owed to him by the club.

EIRIK BAKKE

Debut: Southampton (A) 11 August 1999
Appearances: 164 (32)
Goals: 21

The Norwegian joined Leeds in the summer of 1999 as the Whites paid £1.75 million to sign him from Sogndal as one for the future, but following an impressive first start in a 3-2 win over Newcastle United he forced himself into the Whites starting eleven under manager David O'Leary.

In his first season he had a liking for scoring in the FA Cup, as he hit a brace against Port Vale, one against Manchester City and one away at Aston Villa. He also scored a pair at home to Wimbledon in the Premier League and in the second leg of the emotional return against Galatasaray. He was awarded with the Young Player of the Year award in his first season and he also represented Norway at Euro 2000.

The following season saw Bakke became a vital part in the Leeds midfield as he started 37 games and came off the bench in seven others. He hit the back of the net on three occasions, in the 6-0 win over Besiktas, in a 4-0 win at Manchester City and in a 6-1 hammering of local rivals Bradford City.

For the next two campaigns (2001-02 and 2002-03), Bakke featured on 80 occasions, scoring eight times. The 2003- 04 season, proved to be a nightmare as he missed virtually the whole campaign, making his first appearance off the bench at home to David O'Leary's Aston Villa on Boxing Day 2003. The following campaign was even worse for the Norwegian as his campaign lasted a mere two minutes (he had suffered a cruciate ligament injury in a pre-season game), coming off the bench at home to Brighton & Hove Albion before the injury jinx struck again. Season 2005-06 saw Bakke start the season fit and raring to go and he started the first three games of the season, at home to Millwall and away to both Cardiff City and Luton Town. He was then loaned out to Aston Villa in August 2005 before returning to the club the following January. He went on to make a further nine appearances and replaced Sean Gregan in the 2006 Championship play-off final against Watford. He started the first two league games the following season and scored the last of his 21 goals in a 1-0 win over Chester City in the Carling Cup. He left the club after seven years in August 2006 and returned to Norway to join SK Brann on a free transfer.

MANAGERS APPOINTED IN THE 1990s

GEORGE GRAHAM

First game in charge: Coventry City (A) 14 September 1996
Last game in charge: Maritimo (A) 29 September 1998
Games: 95
Won: 37
Drawn: 27
Lost: 31

Following the sacking of Leeds's most successful manager, the Whites turned to former Arsenal boss George Graham, who had been out of the game since 1995 when he was banned by the FA for his involvement in the transfers of John Jensen and Pal Lydersen, whilst manager at the Gunners.

Graham started his career at Aston Villa and played in a League Cup Final loss to neighbours Birmingham City. He then joined Chelsea, winning a League Cup medal in 1965, but joined rivals Arsenal in 1966. He was part of the side that won a glorious double in 1971 and made his international debut later that year. He went on to join Manchester United before seeing out his footballing career at Portsmouth, Crystal Palace and California Surf in America. His managerial career started in London at Millwall, where he won promotion to the Old Second Division in season 1984-85. He was appointed manager of Arsenal in May 1986 and went on to success at Highbury, winning the top-flight title twice (most memorably thanks to a Michael Thomas goal against Liverpool in May 1989), the League Cup twice, the FA Cup in 1993 and the European Cup Winners' Cup, defeating Parma in Copenhagen in 1994.

He returned to management in September 1996, replacing Wilkinson and his first job was to stop a leaky defence sinking goals. His first game couldn't have got off to a better start, with Andy Couzens scoring in the first minute away to Coventry City, but goals from John Salako and former Leeds youngster Noel Whelan ensured a losing start. Performances were improving under Graham, but he had to wait till his fourth league game for a win, which came courtesy of a Rod Wallace double at home to Nottingham Forest. Slowly but surely, results and performances improved, with three wins in four in November and December and a 3-0 win at home to Leicester City which saw the club up to 12th place. He even managed to get Ian Rush scoring. An FA Cup run looked possible, following wins over Crystal Palace after a replay and at his old club Arsenal thanks to a brilliant display by goalkeeper Nigel Martyn, but a third old club, Portsmouth, knocked the side out in the last 16.

By the end of his first campaign, Graham had resolved the defensive inabilities that had dogged the team, but goalscoring was still a problem. This would be answered during the summer as Leeds spent money to bring in Jimmy Floyd Hasselbaink from Boavista, Bruno Ribeiro from Vitoria Setubal, midfielders Alfie Haaland and David Hopkin from Nottingham Forest and Crystal Palace respectively and left-back David Robertson from Glasgow Rangers. In May 1997 Graham oversaw his youth team, managed by Paul Hart, win the FA Youth Cup for a second time, defeating Crystal Palace 3-1 on aggregate. The likes of Harry Kewell, Stephen McPhail, Matthew Jones and Paul Robinson would be involved in the first-team squad the following campaign. Hasselbaink got off to a dream debut, scoring the equaliser at home to Arsenal, but early results were disappointing. A 4-3 win at Blackburn Rovers in which all seven goals were scored in the first half at a sun drenched Ewood Park kick started the season, and 13 days later a David Wetherall header defeated Manchester United at Elland Road. Graham's side then became known as the comeback kings, coming from 3-0 down to defeat Derby County 4-3 at Elland Road, beating West Ham United 3-1 after being 1-0 down and toppling Barnsley 3-2 after being 2-0 down at Oakwell. Again, there were hopes of a cup run after wins over Oxford United (4-0), Grimsby Town (2-0) and Birmingham City (3-

By George

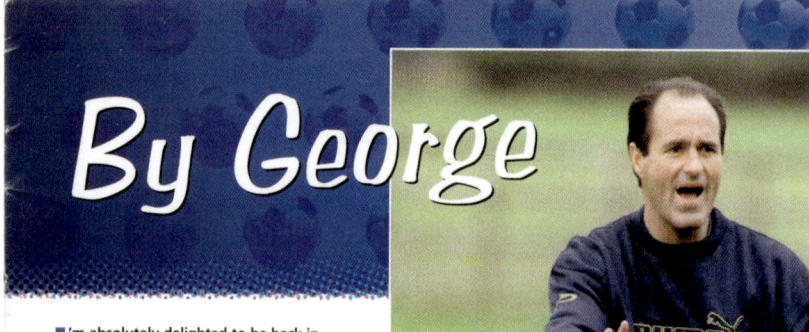

I'm absolutely delighted to be back in management and I'm even more delighted to come back with such a big club as Leeds United.

I have fond memories of coming to Elland Road both as a player and a manager and I was a big fan of the club, especially in the Don Revie era.

I thought he created one of the best teams I have ever seen.

I was also impressed with the side that won the championship under Howard Wilkinson.

Those two periods showed me what a big

> "I will give 100 percent, and I shall make sure that the staff and players also give 100 percent and if we do that I know it will please you."

club this can be when you have got a settled team - it's a one club city and has enormous support, not only from Leeds but from far afield as well.

Now my objective is to get Leeds United back up there with the big boys.

I never promise that I will win the championship or win cups - you can't guarantee that. But what I do promise you, the Leeds United fans, is that if we can get the right squad together we shall have a realistic chance of challenging for those trophies along with the best of them.

After all, I'm a passionate Scot and we passionate Scots have got a habit of winning things here in England!

My first job is to assess the present playing staff and then make decisions. If I have to go into the market I want quality players but I have to say that is easier said than done. There are not many managers I know who are keen to sell their best players.

I will give 100 percent, and I shall make sure that the staff and players also give 100 percent and if we do that I know it will please you.

If we can then play quality football allied to the commitment, we shall be on the right road.

You fans can play your part as well.

When you have had good sides, you have been unbelievable - I used to be frightened to come here as a player and as a manager because it was always going to be such a tough match. I want to make Elland Road a place clubs fear coming once more.

We are building here at present. Please get behind us because you are such an asset when you are cheering Leeds on.

Leeds United Club Call 0891 12 11 80 3

---

2), but a late goal from Don Goodman of Wolverhampton Wanderers and a Hans Segars penalty save from Hasselbaink put paid to that. Leeds responded brilliantly with back-to-back wins over Blackburn Rovers (4-0) and away at Derby County (5-0), in which McPhail played a peach of a pass for Hasselbaink to score Leeds's fifth and the Whites ended the season qualifying for Europe for the first time since season 1995-96. Striker Rod Wallace left the club on a free transfer to join Glasgow Rangers and was replaced by Clyde Wijnhard from Dutch side Willem II. Leeds got off to a decent start, topping the league after a 3-0 home win against Southampton. Following the sacking of Christian Gross at Tottenham Hotspur, rumours started that Graham would head back down to north London. Following a 3-3 draw with Spurs, compensation was agreed and after a penalty shoot-out win over Maritimo in the UEFA Cup first round, Graham was gone and his assistant David O'Leary was put in caretaker charge of the side.

George Graham's first line up: Coventry City (A) 14 September 1996: Martyn, Kelly, Jobson, Wetherall, Harte, Palmer, Couzens (Ford), Gray (Blunt), Hateley, Rush, Wallace, Beeney, Radebe, Jackson.

George Graham's last line up: Maritimo (A) 29 September 1998: Martyn, Hiden, Harte, Radebe, Molenaar, Haaland, Hopkin (Granville), Bowyer (Wijnhard), Halle, Kewell (Sharpe), Hasselbaink. Subs not used: Robinson, Wetherall, Woodgate, Lilley.

DAVID O'LEARY

First game in charge: Leicester City (H) 3 October 1998 (as caretaker)
First game in charge: Bradford City (H) 28 October 1998 (as permanent manager)
Last game in charge: Middlesbrough (H) 11 May 2002
Games: 203
Won: 101
Drawn: 47
Lost: 55

Many expected Graham's assistant David O'Leary to follow suit and join him at White Hart Lane, but the Irishman stayed put, taking over the side on a caretaker basis.

O'Leary only played for two club sides during his distinguished career, signing on at Arsenal as an apprentice in 1973. He made his debut for the Gunners against Burnley in August 1975 and never looked back. He would make at least 40 appearances per season for the next ten years (bar season 1980-81, when he made only 27 due to injury) and went on to win two Division One titles (both under George Graham), the FA Cup in 1979 defeating Manchester United 3-2, and in 1993, thanks to a late injury-time goal from former Leeds defender Andy Linighan As well as the League Cup in both 1987 and 1993. He holds the record for the Gunners' all-time appearance record with 722 and moved to Leeds on a free transfer in the summer of 1993. Sadly, injury restricted him to just ten games at Elland Road, and he retired from the game at the age of 37. He re-joined Leeds as Graham's assistant in September 1996 and took on the role of caretaker manager following the Scot's move back to north London.

In his role of caretaker he handed debuts to youngsters Jonathan Woodgate away at Nottingham Forest and Paul Robinson at home to Chelsea. He had four games in charge at first, a 1-0 loss at home to Leicester City, where favourite for the job Martin O'Neill was in the opposite dugout, a 1-1 draw away at Nottingham Forest, an inspired display away at Roma, which resulted in a 1-0 loss and a goalless draw at home to star-studded Chelsea in which Jimmy Floyd Hasselbaink missed a penalty.

The Leeds board offered the job to O'Neill but Leicester City refused and the Whites turned to O'Leary and an era that no one would forget was about to begin. He started with 1-0 win over Bradford City in the League Cup but what lay ahead took everyone's breath away inside Elland Road. O'Leary had emphasis on youth and handed Alan Smith his debut away at Anfield on 14 November 1998 and with his first touch he scored at the Kop end. Leeds won the game 3-1 and moved up to fifth place in the league. They took eventual treble winners Manchester United all the way in an exciting game at Old Trafford and destroyed Newcastle United 3-0 in their own backyard on Boxing Day. He also bought back fans' favourite David Batty from Newcastle United as his first signing and in the new year Middlesbrough were beaten thanks to goals from Alan Smith and Lee Bowyer in front of then England coach Glenn Hoddle. A week later, Portsmouth were demolished 5-1 in a brilliant display of attacking football in the fourth round of the FA Cup. After losing back-to-back league games for the first time, O'Leary's side bounced back with seven straight league wins that propelled the side to third in the league and a real possibility of Champions League football. Leeds went on to have a huge say in the destination of the title, drawing at home to Manchester United on a sweltering hot day at the end of April, then defeating his old side Arsenal in a brilliant display to all but hand the title to their arch rivals. Leeds finished in fourth position and qualified for the newly structured UEFA Cup. In the summer, Hasselbaink left for Athletico Madrid and Leeds brought in Michael Bridges from Sunderland, Michael Duberry from Chelsea, Danny Mills from Charlton Athletic, Eirik Bakke from Songdal and Darren Huckerby from Coventry City. Leeds made a reasonable start to the millennium campaign, but after winning 2-1 at Tottenham and against his former manger, Leeds won their next nine games in all competitions to top the Premier League and reach the next stages of both the Worthington Cup and UEFA Cup. O'Leary, after the tenth win against Lokomotiv Moscow, said, 'Winning ten games in a row takes some doing but it hasn't won us a trophy. My aim here is to win trophies, though maybe in years to come it will be nice to look back on the record and say, yes, that was quite an achievement, and not least because of the way we went about breaking the record.'

Leeds stayed in the title race until March when Manchester United pulled away, but the Whites still had the UEFA Cup to go for. They had beaten Partizan Belgrade, Locomotiv Moscow and Spartak Moscow before being drawn for the second time in two years against Italian side Roma. A magnificent defensive display saw a 0-0 draw and a Harry Kewell strike was enough to book a place in the last eight. They defeated Slavia Prague in the quarter-finals before tragedy struck the night before the side met Galatasaray in the last four. Kevin Speight and Christopher Loftus were murdered and Leeds felt the game should never have been played as grief poured in from the football community. For the record, Leeds lost the tie 4-2 on aggregate. The players regrouped and qualified for the Champions League following a 0-0 draw away at West Ham United and a header from former player David Wetherall for Bradford City that kept the Bantams up and saw off Liverpool's challenge.

That summer, Mark Viduka from Glasgow Celtic, Olivier Dacourt from Lens and Dominic Matteo from Liverpool joined the ranks and Leeds won their opening two league games, and, despite having an injury-ravaged squad, defeated German side 1860 Munich to make it through to the Champions League group stage. Europe's Premier competition started with a stark warning for Leeds as Barcelona won 4-0 in the Nou Camp, after which O'Leary commented, 'We were up against some of the best players in the world and we were well and truly beaten.' They bounced back in style, beating AC Milan thanks to a late Lee Bowyer goal, and even better was to come the following week as Turkish side Besiktas were demolished 6-0 in a game that saw Mark Viduka break his duck. League form was inconsistent at times, but there were some superb performances

David's Dialogue

It's a great feeling to be writing my first notes as the Leeds United manager. I am thrilled to have the job. It's a great honour and privilege. I played all my career at top level and now I have the chance to start my managerial career at at the top as well.

As you know, I finally agreed to take over on Sunday night after the Chelsea game. With that match to prepare for and Bradford City to watch on Saturday afternoon, there was no time for the chairman and I to get round a table before then. When we did get together it didn't take long to reach agreement.

Dressing room side

There was no need for me to go home and sleep on it. I knew what I wanted to do, made the decision and went for it.

I know that some people have questioned that I might be 'too nice' to be a manager but I can assure you I am perfectly happy to make the difficult and unpopular decisions when necessary.

I've never felt the need to give off a macho image and I'm not impressed by people who do. But I do have another side that I keep in the dressing room and if I've got to make decisions that upset people, then I'm willing to do that.

It's inevitable that some people will be upset by what you do as a manager - you can only pick 11 players each game, and the rest are bound to think you've made a mistake.

I think as long as you are fair with players, they might not like all your decisions but they will at least respect them.

Families

There has been a lot of rubbish talked about the players going out and playing for me against Forest and again against Roma.

I don't believe in all that and I told the players before the match in Rome to go out and play, not for me, but for themselves and their families. They had to be able to step off the plane when

2 BECOMES 1:
David O'Leary has taken the big step into full management

4

Leeds United FC on the Internet: www.lufc.co.uk

in defeating Tottenham Hotspur 4–3 at Elland Road, and the same score line saw off Liverpool, a game in which Viduka scored all four in one of the best displays ever seen at Elland Road.

Back to Europe and Leeds were moments away from beating Barcelona in the return and qualifying for the second group stage, but did the job in Milan two weeks later as a Dominic

Official Matchday Magazine of **Leeds United AFC**

I'm proud to be your manager

they got back to England having made their families proud of them. Anything else was just a bonus.

I'm delighted that Eddie Gray has agreed to be my number two.

Eddie has a passion for Leeds United that this club needs. He has lots of experience, has been a manager and he wants to play the game the same way I do, which is an aggressive passing game.

I was pleased with the way we did that against Chelsea. The pitch was perfect for passing and I thought we knocked the ball around very well at times.

I'm not a great believer in passing for the sake of it, 20 passes that go nowhere. I want an end result.

We were playing against a World XI out there and should have won the game. You have to take your chances, especially when you get a penalty, but overall I was very pleased with the performance.

We know we have still got to improve. Over the last two years we have come a long way under George Graham but we still have a long way to go.

Lads will get their chance.

We have a young side here and I am not afraid to throw youngsters in if I think they are good enough. I was given my chance when I was 17 years old, so I've no nerves about giving our lads their opportunity.

I have been wanting to play Stephen McPhail for some time and one of the

"I've never felt the need to give off a macho image and I'm not impressed by people who do. But I do have another side that I keep in the dressing room and if I've got to make decisions that upset people, then I'm willing to do that."

great things about being the manager is you get to pick the team. I think he is a very good passer of the ball who has the knack of picking out his team-mates. I also believe Jonathon Woodgate is going to be a tremendous player and has deserved his chance.

Having said that, I admit I felt nervous for Paul Robinson making his debut against Chelsea. It's always harder for a young keeper and with the conditions and against a team like that, the circumstances were not ideal for his first game.

Impressed with Paul

I've been very impressed with Paul in training over the last two years and believe he is going to be a fine goalkeeper, but I admit I was scared that he might have a bad time and go backwards for a bit.

But he did very well and I hope he can go on and build from that.

Tonight we face a tough test against a Bradford City side which is playing very well at the moment and if we are not at the top of our game we could be on the end of another cup upset.

I went to watch them on Saturday but didn't get much chance to assess them because the conditions became so bad, I only saw how well they can slip about and the game was called off at half-time!

Thanks to the fans

It will be how we play on the night that matters. They have nothing to lose and we are on a hiding to nothing. It's sure to be a full-blooded Yorkshire derby and the players and I know we will be completely tested.

Finally I want to thank you, the fans, for your fantastic support over the last few weeks while I have been caretaker manager. It has been greatly appreciated.

I know how much you love this club and I'm sure you will carry on giving us your superb support.

In return you can be assured that Eddie and I, and all the players and staff, will always give it our best shot.

Leeds United Travel Company - Call Freephone **0500 225 151**

Matteo header was enough to qualify for the last 16 at the expense of the Spanish giants. Leeds then splashed out £18 million on Rio Ferdinand, and although his debut was a disaster, he proved to be an excellent buy. In the second group stage of the Champions League, Leeds lost to current champions Real Madrid, but they were celebrating a fortnight later thanks to

311

a fantastic goal from Alan Smith against Lazio. Back in the league, form had to improve, with the side in the bottom half of the table in the new year, but they would go on to lose only two more league games.

They qualified for the last eight of the Champions League after back-to-back wins over Anderlect and in the quarter-finals against Spanish champions Deportivo La Coruna, which produced one of the best-ever European displays in which Leeds won 3-0, with Ferdinand scoring his first goal for the side. Leeds made it through to the last four, but another Spanish side Valencia ended hopes of a first European final since 1975 with a 3-0 win in the second leg. Leeds failed to qualify for the competition at the end of that season and that would have serious consequences for the club's future.

Leeds started the new 2001-02 season as one of the favourites for the Championship, but despite being top on New Year's Day after a 3-0 win over West Ham United, the wheels fell off spectacularly (injuries and suspensions didn't help) and the side, despite the signings of Robbie's, Keane and Fowler finished in fifth place and outside the Champions League places for the second consecutive season. O'Leary paid the price with his job. He went on to manage Aston Villa and United Arab Emirates side Al-Ahli.

David O'Leary's first line up (as caretaker): Leicester City (H) 3 October 1998: Martyn, Hiden, Harte (Granville), Wetherall, Molenaar, Halle, Haaland, Bowyer (McPhail), Sharpe, Wijnhard (Kewell), Hasselbaink. Subs not used: Robinson, Woodgate.

David O'Leary's first line up (as manager): Bradford City (H) 28 October 1998: Robinson, Halle, Granville, Woodgate, Radebe, Molenaar, Hopkin, McPhail, Bowyer, Hasselbaink, Kewell. Subs not used: Santos, Wetherall, Harte, Haaland, Wijnhard.

David O'Leary's last line up: Middlesbrough (H) 11 May 2002: Martyn, Kelly, Harte, Matteo, Ferdinand, Johnson, Bakke, Bowyer, Kewell (Wilcox), Keane, Smith: Subs not used: Robinson, Duberry, McPhail, Batty.

DIVISION ONE

1990–91

Date	Opposition	Competition	Score
25/08/1990	Everton	Division One	3-2
29/08/1990	Manchester United	Division One	0-0
01/09/1990	Norwich City	Division One	3-0
08/08/1990	Luton Town	Division One	0-1
15/09/1990	Tottenham Hotspur	Division One	0-2
23/09/1990	Sheffield United	Division One	2-0
26/09/1990	Leicester City	Rumbelows Cup 2nd Round 1st Leg	0-1
29/09/1990	Arsenal	Division One	2-2
06/10/1990	Crystal Palace	Division One	1-1
10/10/1990	Leicester City	Rumbelows Cup 2nd Round 2nd Leg	3-0
20/10/1990	Queens Park Rangers	Division One	2-3
27/10/1990	Aston Villa	Division One	0-0
31/10/1990	Oldham Athletic	Rumbelows Cup 3rd Round	2-0
03/11/1990	Nottingham Forest	Division One	3-1
11/11/1990	Manchester City	Division One	3-2
17/11/1990	Derby County	Division One	3-0
24/11/1990	Coventry City	Division One	1-1
27/11/1990	Queens Park Rangers	Rumbelows Cup 4th Round	3-0
01/12/1990	Southampton	Division One	2-1
08/12/1990	Manchester United	Division One	1-1
16/12/1990	Everton	Division One	2-0
19/12/1990	Wolverhampton Wanderers	ZDS Cup Northern Section 2nd Round	2-1
23/12/1990	Sunderland	Division One	1-0
26/12/1990	Chelsea	Division One	4-1
29/12/1990	Wimbledon	Division One	3-0
01/01/1991	Liverpool	Division One	0-3
06/01/1991	Barnsley	FA Cup 3rd Round	1-1
09/01/1991	Barnsley	FA Cup 3rd Round Replay	4-0
12/01/1991	Norwich City	Division One	0-2
16/01/1991	Aston Villa	Rumbelows Cup 5th Round	4-1
19/01/1991	Luton Town	Division One	2-1
22/01/1991	Derby County	ZDS Cup Northern Section 3rd Round	2-1
27/01/1991	Arsenal	FA Cup 4th Round	0-0
30/01/1991	Arsenal	FA Cup 4th Round Replay	1-1
02/02/1991	Tottenham Hotspur	Division One	0-0
10/02/1991	Manchester United	Rumbelows Cup SF 1st Leg	1-2
13/02/1991	Arsenal	FA Cup 4th Round 2nd Replay	0-0
16/02/1991	Arsenal	FA Cup 4th Round 3rd Replay	1-2
20/02/1991	Manchester City	ZDS Cup Northern Area SF	2-0
24/02/1991	Manchester United	Rumbelows Cup SF 2nd Leg	0-1
02/03/1991	Southampton	Division One	0-2
09/03/1991	Coventry City	Division One	2-0
17/03/1991	Arsenal	Division One	0-2
19/03/1991	Everton	ZDS Cup Northern Area Final 1st Leg	3-3
21/03/1991	Everton	ZDS Cup Northern Area Final 2nd Leg	1-3
23/03/1991	Crystal Palace	Division One	1-2
30/03/1991	Chelsea	Division One	2-1
02/04/1991	Sunderland	Division One	5-0
06/04/1991	Wimbledon	Division One	1-0
10/04/1991	Manchester City	Division One	1-2
13/04/1991	Liverpool	Division One	4-5
17/04/1991	Queens Park Rangers	Division One	0-2
23/04/1991	Derby County	Division One	1-0
04/05/1991	Aston Villa	Division One	5-2
08/05/1991	Sheffield United	Division One	2-1
11/05/1991	Nottingham Forest	Division One	3-4

Team	Pld	W	D	L	GF	GA	Pts
Arsenal	38	24	13	1	74	18	83
Liverpool	38	23	7	8	77	40	76
Crystal Palace	38	20	9	9	50	41	69
Leeds United	38	19	7	12	65	47	64
Manchester City	38	17	11	10	64	53	62
Manchester United	38	16	12	10	58	45	59
Wimbledon	38	14	14	10	53	46	56
Nottingham Forest	38	14	12	12	65	50	54
Everton	38	13	12	13	50	46	51
Tottenham Hotspur	38	11	16	11	51	50	49
Chelsea	38	13	10	15	58	69	49
Queen's Park Rangers	38	12	10	16	44	53	46
Sheffield United	38	13	7	18	36	55	46
Southampton	38	12	9	17	58	69	45
Norwich City	38	13	6	19	41	64	45
Coventry City	38	11	11	16	42	49	44
Aston Villa	38	9	14	15	46	58	41
Luton Town	38	10	7	21	42	61	37
Sunderland	38	8	10	20	38	60	34
Derby County	38	5	9	24	37	75	24

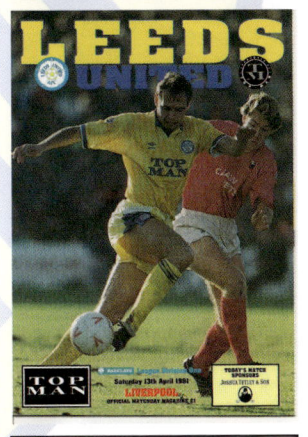

Chris Fairclough scored the Whites first top-flight goal since May 1982 in the 3-2 opening day win at Everton.

Leeds featured live on national TV when they faced Manchester City in November 1990 for the first time since January 1985.

In the days before penalty shoot-outs, Leeds ended up facing eventual Champions Arsenal, four times in the FA Cup fourth round.

Leeds failed at the final hurdle to reach Wembley in both the Rumbelows Cup and Zenith Data Systems Cup, losing to Manchester United and Everton respectively.

Lee Chapman became the first Leeds player to reach 30 goals in a season since Peter Lorimer in season 1967-68.

1991–92

DIVISION ONE

Team	Pld	W	D	L	GF	GA	Pts
Leeds United	42	22	16	4	74	37	82
Manchester United	42	21	15	6	63	33	78
Sheffield Wednesday	42	21	12	9	62	49	75
Arsenal	42	19	15	8	81	46	72
Manchester City	42	20	10	12	61	48	70
Liverpool	42	16	16	10	47	40	64
Aston Villa	42	17	9	16	48	44	60
Nottingham Forest	42	16	11	15	60	58	59
Sheffield United	42	16	9	17	65	63	57
Crystal Palace	42	14	15	13	53	61	57
Queen's Park Rangers	42	12	18	12	48	47	54
Everton	42	13	14	15	52	51	53
Wimbledon	42	13	14	15	53	53	53
Chelsea	42	13	14	15	50	60	53
Tottenham Hotspur	42	15	7	20	58	63	52
Southampton	42	14	10	18	39	55	52
Oldham Athletic	42	14	9	19	63	67	51
Norwich City	42	11	12	19	47	63	45
Coventry City	42	11	11	20	35	44	44
Luton Town	42	10	12	20	38	71	42
Notts County	42	10	10	22	40	62	40
West Ham United	42	9	11	22	37	59	38

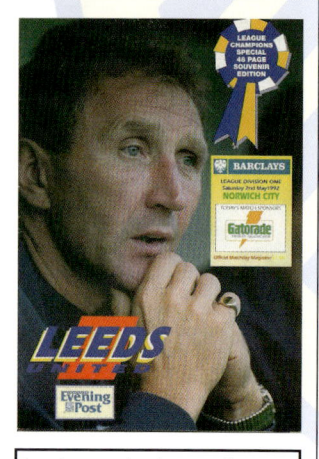

Date	Opposition	Competition	Score
20/08/1991	**Nottingham Forest**	**Division One**	**1-0**
24/08/1991	**Sheffield Wednesday**	**Division One**	**1-1**
28/08/1991	Southampton	Division One	4-0
31/08/1991	Manchester United	Division One	1-1
03/09/1991	**Arsenal**	**Division One**	**2-2**
07/09/1991	**Manchester City**	**Division One**	**3-0**
14/09/1991	Chelsea	Division One	1-0
18/09/1991	Coventry City	Division One	0-0
21/09/1991	**Liverpool**	**Division One**	**1-0**
24/09/1991	Scunthorpe United	Rumbelows Cup 2nd Round 1st Leg	0-0
28/09/1991	Norwich City	Division One	2-2
01/10/1991	Crystal Palace	Division One	0-1
05/10/1991	**Sheffield United**	**Division One**	**4-3**
08/10/1991	Scunthorpe United	Rumbelows Cup 2nd Round 2nd Leg	3-0
19/10/1991	Notts County	Division One	4-2
22/10/1991	Nottingham Forest	ZDS Cup Northern Area 2nd Round	1-3
26/10/1991	**Oldham Athletic**	**Division One**	**1-0**
29/10/1991	Tranmere Rovers	Rumbelows Cup 3rd Round	3-1
02/11/1991	Wimbledon	Division One	0-0
16/11/1991	**Queens Park Rangers**	**Division One**	**2-0**
24/11/1991	Aston Villa	Division One	4-1
30/11/1991	**Everton**	**Division One**	**1-0**
04/12/1991	Everton	Rumbelows Cup 4th Round	4-1
07/12/1991	Luton Town	Division One	2-0
14/12/1991	**Tottenham Hotspur**	**Division One**	**1-1**
22/12/1991	Nottingham Forest	Division One	0-0
26/12/1991	**Southampton**	**Division One**	**3-3**
29/12/1991	**Manchester United**	**Division One**	**1-1**
01/01/1992	West Ham United	Division One	3-1
08/01/1992	**Manchester United**	Rumbelows Cup 5th Round	**1-3**
12/01/1992	Sheffield Wednesday	Division One	6-1
15/01/1992	**Manchester United**	FA Cup 3rd Round	**0-1**
18/01/1992	**Crystal Palace**	**Division One**	**1-1**
01/02/1992	**Notts County**	**Division One**	**3-0**
08/08/1992	Oldham Athletic	Division One	0-2
23/02/1992	Everton	Division One	1-1
29/02/1992	**Luton Town**	**Division One**	**2-0**
03/03/1992	**Aston Villa**	**Division One**	**0-0**
07/03/1992	Tottenham Hotspur	Division One	3-1
11/03/1992	Queens Park Rangers	Division One	1-4
14/03/1992	**Wimbledon**	**Division One**	**5-1**
22/03/1992	Arsenal	Division One	1-1
28/03/1992	**West Ham United**	**Division One**	**0-0**
04/04/1992	Manchester City	Division One	0-4
11/04/1992	**Chelsea**	**Division One**	**3-0**
18/04/1992	Liverpool	Division One	0-0
20/04/1992	**Coventry City**	**Division One**	**2-0**
26/04/1992	Sheffield United	Division One	3-2
02/05/1992	**Norwich City**	**Division One**	**1-0**

Leeds were due to open the season at Crystal Palace but it was called off due to building work at Selhurst Park.

Gary Kelly made his Leeds United debut in the Rumbelows Cup 2nd Round tie at Elland Road v Scunthorpe United.

When Leeds defeated Oldham Atheltic on 26 October, they hit top spot of Division One for the first time since April 1974.

Leeds had three different captains when they won the league, Gordon Strachan, David Batty and Chris Fairclough.

John Lukic was the only ever-present, featuring in every game with 49 appearances.

PREMIER LEAGUE

1992–93

Date	Opposition	Competition	Score
08/08/1992	Liverpool	Charity Shield at Wembley	4-3
15/08/1992	Wimbledon	Premier League	2-1
19/08/1992	Aston Villa	Premier League	1-1
22/08/1992	Middlesbrough	Premier League	1-4
25/08/1992	Tottenham Hotspur	Premier League	5-0
29/08/1992	Liverpool	Premier League	2-2
01/09/1992	Oldham Athletic	Premier League	2-2
06/09/1992	Manchester United	Premier League	0-2
13/09/1992	Aston Villa	Premier League	1-1
16/09/1992	Stuttgart	European Cup 1st Round 1st Leg	0-3
19/09/1992	Southampton	Premier League	1-1
22/09/1992	Scunthorpe United	Coca Cola Cup 2nd Round 1st Leg	4-1
26/09/1992	Everton	Premier League	2-0
30/09/1992	Stuttgart	European Cup 1st Round 2nd Leg	4-1
03/10/1992	Ipswich Town	Premier League	2-4
09/10/2012	Stuttgart	European Cup 1st Round Play Off at the Nou Camp	2-1
17/10/1992	Sheffield United	Premier League	3-1
21/10/1992	Glasgow Rangers	European Cup 2nd Round 1st Leg	1-2
24/10/1992	Queens Park Rangers	Premier League	1-2
27/10/1992	Scunthorpe United	Coca Cola Cup 2nd Round 2nd Leg	2-2
31/10/1992	Coventry City	Premier League	2-2
04/11/1992	Glasgow Rangers	European Cup 2nd Round 2nd Leg	1-2
07/11/1992	Manchester City	Premier League	0-4
10/11/1992	Watford	Coca Cola Cup 3rd Round	1-2
21/11/1992	Arsenal	Premier League	3-0
29/11/1992	Chelsea	Premier League	0-1
05/12/1992	Nottingham Forest	Premier League	1-4
12/12/1992	Sheffield Wednesday	Premier League	3-1
20/12/1992	Crystal Palace	Premier League	0-1
26/12/1992	Blackburn Rovers	Premier League	1-3
28/12/1992	Norwich City	Premier League	0-0
02/01/1993	Charlton Athletic	FA Cup 3rd Round	1-1
09/01/1993	Southampton	Premier League	2-1
13/01/1993	Charlton Athletic	FA Cup 3rd Round Replay	3-1
16/01/1993	Everton	Premier League	0-2
25/01/1993	Arsenal	FA Cup 4th Round	2-2
30/01/1993	Middlesbrough	Premier League	3-0
03/02/1993	Arsenal	FA Cup 4th Round Replay	2-3
06/02/1993	Wimbledon	Premier League	0-1
08/02/1993	Manchester United	Premier League	0-0
13/02/1993	Oldham Athletic	Premier League	2-0
20/02/1993	Tottenham Hotspur	Premier League	0-4
24/02/1993	Arsenal	Premier League	0-0
27/02/1993	Ipswich Town	Premier League	1-0
13/03/1993	Manchester City	Premier League	1-0
21/03/1993	Nottingham Forest	Premier League	1-1
24/03/1993	Chelsea	Premier League	1-1
06/04/1993	Sheffield United	Premier League	1-2
10/04/1993	Blackburn Rovers	Premier League	5-2
14/04/1993	Norwich City	Premier League	2-4
17/04/1993	Crystal Palace	Premier League	0-0
21/04/1993	Liverpool	Premier League	0-2
01/05/1993	Queens Park Rangers	Premier League	1-1
04/05/1993	Sheffield Wednesday	Premier League	1-1
08/05/1993	Coventry City	Premier League	3-3

Team	Pld	W	D	L	GF	GA	Pts
Manchester United	42	24	12	6	67	31	84
Aston Villa	42	21	11	10	57	40	74
Norwich City	42	21	9	12	61	65	72
Blackburn Rovers	42	20	11	11	68	46	71
Queen's Park Rangers	42	17	12	13	63	55	63
Liverpool	42	16	11	15	62	55	59
Sheffield Wednesday	42	15	14	13	55	51	59
Tottenham Hotspur	42	16	11	15	60	66	59
Manchester City	42	15	12	15	56	51	57
Arsenal	42	15	11	16	40	38	56
Chelsea	42	14	14	14	51	54	56
Wimbledon	42	14	12	16	56	55	54
Everton	42	15	8	19	53	55	53
Sheffield United	42	14	10	18	54	53	52
Coventry City	42	13	13	16	52	57	52
Ipswich Town	42	12	16	14	50	55	52
Leeds United	42	12	15	15	57	62	51
Southampton	42	13	11	18	54	61	50
Oldham Athletic	42	13	10	19	63	74	49
Crystal Palace	42	11	16	15	48	61	49
Middlesbrough	42	11	11	20	54	75	44
Nottingham Forest	42	10	10	22	41	62	40

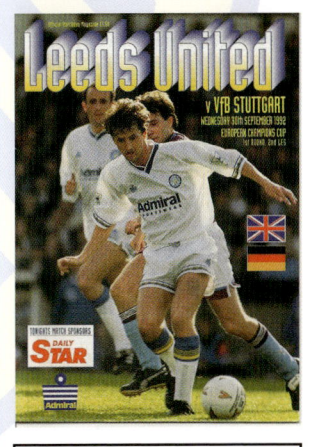

Leeds ended up playing Liverpool three times in the month of August, first at Wembley in the Charity Shield, then in Jim Beglin's testimonial, then in the Premier League.

Eric Cantona scored the first ever Premier League hat-trick in the 5-0 home win against Tottenham Hotspur on 25 August 1992.

Mervyn Day made his first Leeds United appearance away at Manchester City for the first time since December 1990.

Noel Whelan, Jamie Forrester, Kevin Sharp, Robert Bowman and Mark Tinkler all made their debuts for the club in season 1992-93.

Leeds won the Youth Cup for the first time in their history, defeating defending Champions Manchester United 4-1 on aggregate.

1993-94

PREMIERSHIP

Team	Pld	W	D	L	GF	GA	Pts
Manchester United	42	27	11	4	80	38	92
Blackburn Rovers	42	25	9	8	63	36	84
Newcastle United	42	23	8	11	82	41	77
Arsenal	42	18	17	7	53	28	71
Leeds United	42	18	16	8	65	39	70
Wimbledon	42	18	11	13	56	53	65
Sheffield Wednesday	42	16	16	10	76	54	64
Liverpool	42	17	9	16	59	55	60
Queen's Park Rangers	42	16	12	14	62	61	60
Aston Villa	42	15	12	15	46	50	57
Coventry City	42	14	14	14	43	45	56
Norwich City	42	12	17	13	65	61	53
West Ham United	42	13	13	16	47	58	52
Chelsea	42	13	12	17	49	53	51
Tottenham Hotspur	42	11	12	19	54	59	45
Manchester City	42	9	18	15	38	49	45
Everton	42	12	8	22	42	63	44
Southampton	42	12	7	23	49	66	43
Ipswich Town	42	9	16	17	35	58	43
Sheffield United	42	8	18	16	42	60	42
Oldham Athletic	42	9	13	20	42	68	40
Swindon Town	42	5	15	22	47	100	30

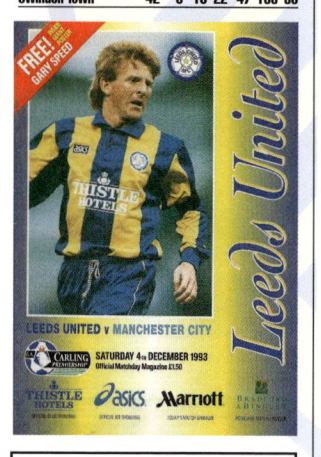

Date	Opposition	Competition	Score
14/08/1993	Manchester City	Premiership	1-1
17/08/1993	**West Ham United**	**Premiership**	**1-0**
21/08/1993	**Norwich City**	**Premiership**	**0-4**
24/08/1993	Arsenal	Premiership	1-2
28/08/1993	Liverpool	Premiership	0-2
30/08/1993	**Oldham Athletic**	**Premiership**	**1-0**
11/09/1993	Southampton	Premiership	2-0
18/09/1993	**Sheffield United**	**Premiership**	**2-1**
21/09/1993	Sunderland	Coca Cola Cup 2nd Round 1st Leg	1-2
25/09/1993	Coventry City	Premiership	2-0
02/10/1993	**Wimbledon**	**Premiership**	**4-0**
06/10/1993	Sunderland	Coca Cola Cup 2nd Round 2nd Leg	1-2
17/10/1993	Ipswich Town	Premiership	0-0
23/10/1993	**Blackburn Rovers**	**Premiership**	**3-3**
30/10/1993	Sheffield Wednesday	Premiership	3-3
06/11/1993	**Chelsea**	**Premiership**	**4-1**
20/11/1993	Tottenham Hotspur	Premiership	1-1
23/11/1993	Everton	Premiership	1-1
27/11/1993	**Swindon Town**	**Premiership**	**3-0**
04/12/1993	**Manchester City**	**Premiership**	**3-2**
08/12/1993	West Ham United	Premiership	1-0
13/12/1993	Norwich City	Premiership	1-2
18/12/1993	**Arsenal**	**Premiership**	**2-1**
22/12/1993	Newcastle United	Premiership	1-1
29/12/1993	**Queens Park Rangers**	**Premiership**	**1-1**
01/01/1994	Manchester United	Premiership	0-0
08/01/1994	**Crewe Alexandra**	**FA Cup 3rd Round**	**3-1**
15/01/1994	**Ipswich Town**	**Premiership**	**0-0**
23/01/1994	Blackburn Rovers	Premiership	1-2
29/01/1994	Oxford United	FA Cup 4th Round	2-2
06/02/1994	Aston Villa	Premiership	0-1
09/02/1994	**Oxford United**	**FA Cup 4th Round Replay**	**2-3**
19/02/1994	**Liverpool**	**Premiership**	**2-0**
28/02/1994	Oldham Athletic	Premiership	1-1
05/03/1994	**Southampton**	**Premiership**	**0-0**
13/03/1994	Sheffield United	Premiership	2-2
16/03/1994	**Aston Villa**	**Premiership**	**2-0**
19/03/1994	**Coventry City**	**Premiership**	**1-0**
26/03/1994	Wimbledon	Premiership	0-1
01/04/1994	**Newcastle United**	**Premiership**	**1-1**
04/04/1994	Queens Park Rangers	Premiership	4-0
17/04/1994	**Tottenham Hotspur**	**Premiership**	**2-0**
23/03/1994	Chelsea	Premiership	1-1
27/04/1994	**Manchester United**	**Premiership**	**0-2**
30/04/1994	**Everton**	**Premiership**	**3-0**
03/05/1994	**Sheffield Wednesday**	**Premiership**	**2-2**
07/05/1994	Swindon Town	Premiership	5-0

When Leeds entertained West Ham United at Elland Road, it was the first game at Elland Road in front of the new 17,000 all-seater East Stand.

When the Whites beat Southampton on the south coast on 11 September, it was the club's first away league win since 26 April 1992.

Leeds entertained Crewe Alexandra for the first time in their history in the FA Cup third round when they won 3-1.

Rod Wallace won BBC *Match of the Day's* goal of the season for his first strike at home to Tottenham Hotspur on 17 April 1994.

On 3 May 1994, Leeds played Sheffield Wednesday in front of an all-standing kop for the final time at Elland Road.

316

PREMIERSHIP

1994–95

Date	Opposition	Competition	Score
20/08/1994	West Ham United	Premiership	0-0
23/08/1994	Arsenal	Premiership	1-0
27/08/1994	Chelsea	Premiership	2-3
30/08/1994	Crystal Palace	Premiership	2-1
11/09/1994	Manchester United	Premiership	2-1
17/09/1994	Coventry City	Premiership	1-2
21/09/1994	Mansfield Town	Coca Cola Cup 2nd Round 1st Leg	0-1
26/09/1994	Sheffield Wednesday	Premiership	1-1
01/10/1994	Manchester City	Premiership	2-0
04/10/1994	Mansfield Town	Coca Cola Cup 2nd Round 2nd Leg	0-0
08/10/1994	Norwich City	Premiership	1-2
15/10/1994	Tottenham Hotspur	Premiership	1-1
24/10/1994	Leicester City	Premiership	2-1
29/10/1994	Southampton	Premiership	3-1
01/11/1994	Ipswich Town	Premiership	0-2
05/11/1994	Wimbledon	Premiership	3-1
19/11/1994	Queens Park Rangers	Premiership	2-3
26/11/1994	Nottingham Forest	Premiership	1-0
05/12/1994	Everton	Premiership	0-3
10/12/1994	West Ham United	Premiership	2-2
17/12/1994	Arsenal	Premiership	3-1
26/12/1994	Newcastle United	Premiership	0-0
31/12/1994	Liverpool	Premiership	0-2
02/01/1995	Aston Villa	Premiership	0-0
07/01/1995	Walsall	FA Cup 3rd Round	1-1
14/01/1995	Southampton	Premiership	0-0
17/01/1995	Walsall	FA Cup 3rd Round Replay	5-2
24/01/1995	Queens Park Rangers	Premiership	4-0
28/01/1995	Oldham Athletic	FA Cup 4th Round	3-2
01/02/1995	Blackburn Rovers	Premiership	1-1
04/02/1985	Wimbledon	Premiership	0-0
19/02/1995	Manchester United	FA Cup 5th Round	1-3
22/02/1995	Everton	Premiership	1-0
25/02/1995	Manchester City	Premiership	0-0
04/03/1995	Sheffield Wednesday	Premiership	0-1
11/03/1995	Chelsea	Premiership	3-0
15/03/1995	Leicester City	Premiership	3-1
18/03/1995	Coventry City	Premiership	3-0
22/03/1995	Nottingham Forest	Premiership	0-3
02/04/1995	Manchester United	Premiership	0-0
05/04/1995	Ipswich Town	Premiership	4-0
09/04/1995	Liverpool	Premiership	1-0
15/04/1995	Blackburn Rovers	Premiership	1-1
17/04/1995	Newcastle United	Premiership	2-1
29/04/1995	Aston Villa	Premiership	1-0
06/05/1995	Norwich City	Premiership	2-1
09/05/1995	Crystal Palace	Premiership	3-1
14/05/1995	Tottenham Hotspur	Premiership	1-1

Team	Pld	W	D	L	GF	GA	Pts
Blackburn Rovers	42	27	8	7	80	39	89
Manchester United	42	26	10	6	77	28	88
Nottingham Forest	42	22	11	9	72	43	77
Liverpool	42	21	11	10	65	37	74
Leeds United	42	20	13	9	59	38	73
Newcastle United	42	20	12	10	67	47	72
Tottenham Hotspur	42	16	14	12	66	58	62
Queen's Park Rangers	42	17	9	16	61	59	60
Wimbledon	42	15	11	16	48	65	56
Southampton	42	12	18	12	61	63	54
Chelsea	42	13	15	14	50	55	54
Arsenal	42	13	12	17	52	49	51
Sheffield Wednesday	42	13	12	17	49	57	51
West Ham United	42	13	11	18	44	48	50
Everton	42	11	17	14	44	51	50
Coventry City	42	12	14	16	44	62	50
Manchester City	42	12	13	17	53	64	49
Aston Villa	42	11	15	16	51	56	48
Crystal Palace	42	11	12	19	34	49	45
Norwich City	42	10	13	19	37	54	43
Leicester City	42	6	11	25	45	80	29
Ipswich Town	42	7	6	29	36	93	27

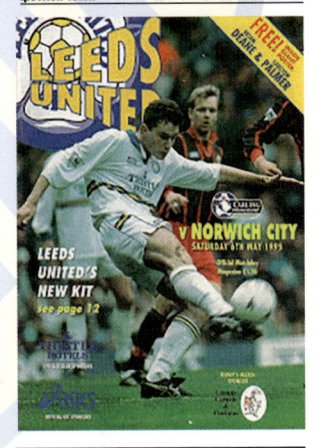

Philemon Masinga and Lucas Radebe became the first South African players to play in the Premier League for Leeds United.

11 September 1994, will be a date no Leeds fan will forget as it was the White's first victory over Manchester United since February 1981.

Leeds recorded their first League win at Anfield on 9 April for the first time since 1 January 1972.

Leeds had two captains that led the side in season 1994-95, Gary McAllister for 47 games and Carlton Palmer away at Arsenal.

Both John Lukic and Gary Kelly were ever-presents, playing in all 48 games this season.

1995–96

PREMIERSHIP

Team	Pld	W	D	L	GF	GA	Pts
Manchester United	38	25	7	6	73	35	82
Newcastle United	38	24	6	8	66	37	78
Liverpool	38	20	11	7	70	34	71
Aston Villa	38	18	9	11	52	35	63
Arsenal	38	17	12	9	49	32	63
Everton	38	17	10	11	64	44	61
Blackburn Rovers	38	18	7	13	61	47	61
Tottenham Hotspur	38	16	13	9	50	38	61
Nottingham Forest	38	15	13	10	50	54	58
West Ham United	38	14	9	15	43	52	51
Chelsea	38	12	14	12	46	44	50
Middlesbrough	38	11	10	17	35	50	43
Leeds United	38	12	7	19	40	57	43
Wimbledon	38	10	11	17	55	70	41
Sheffield Wednesday	38	10	10	18	48	61	40
Coventry City	38	8	14	16	42	60	38
Southampton	38	9	11	18	34	52	38
Manchester City	38	9	11	18	33	58	38
Queen's Park Rangers	38	9	6	23	38	57	33
Bolton Wanderers	38	8	5	25	39	71	29

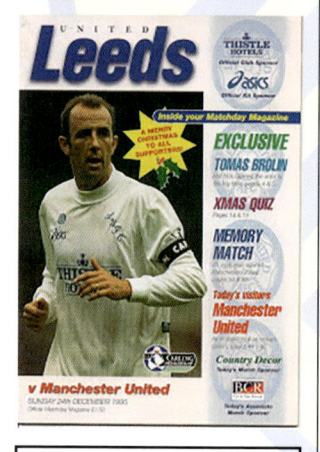

Date	Opposition	Competition	Score
19/08/1995	West Ham United	Premiership	2-1
21/08/1995	**Liverpool**	**Premiership**	**1-0**
26/08/1995	**Aston Villa**	**Premiership**	**2-0**
30/08/1995	Southampton	Premiership	1-1
09/09/1995	Tottenham Hotspur	Premiership	1-2
12/09/1995	Monaco	UEFA Cup 1st Round 1st Leg	3-0
16/09/1995	**Queens Park Rangers**	**Premiership**	**1-3**
19/09/1995	**Notts County**	**Coca Cola Cup 2nd Round 1st Leg**	**0-0**
23/09/1995	Wimbledon	Premiership	4-2
26/09/1995	**Monaco**	**UEFA Cup 1st Round 2nd Leg**	**0-1**
30/09/1995	**Sheffield Wednesday**	**Premiership**	**2-0**
03/10/1995	Notts County	Coca Cola Cup 2nd Round 2nd Leg	3-2
14/10/1995	**Arsenal**	**Premiership**	**0-3**
17/10/1995	PSV Eindhoven	UEFA Cup 2nd Round 1st Leg	3-5
21/10/1995	Manchester City	Premiership	0-0
25/10/1995	Derby County	Coca Cola Cup 3rd Round	1-0
28/10/1995	**Coventry City**	**Premiership**	**3-1**
31/10/1995	PSV Eindhoven	UEFA Cup 2nd Round 2nd Leg	0-3
04/11/1995	Middlesbrough	Premiership	1-1
18/11/1995	**Chelsea**	**Premiership**	**1-0**
25/11/1995	Newcastle United	Premiership	1-2
29/11/1995	**Blackburn Rovers**	**Coca Cola Cup 4th Round**	**2-1**
02/12/1995	**Manchester City**	**Premiership**	**0-1**
09/12/1995	**Wimbledon**	**Premiership**	**1-1**
16/12/1995	Sheffield Wednesday	Premiership	2-6
24/12/1995	**Manchester United**	**Premiership**	**3-1**
27/12/1995	Bolton Wanderers	Premiership	2-0
30/12/1995	Everton	Premiership	0-2
01/01/1996	**Blackburn Rovers**	**Premiership**	**0-0**
07/01/1996	Derby County	FA Cup 3rd Round	4-2
10/01/1996	**Reading**	**Coca Cola Cup 5th Round**	**2-1**
13/01/1996	**West Ham United**	**Premiership**	**2-0**
20/01/1996	Liverpool	Premiership	0-5
31/01/1996	Nottingham Forest	Premiership	1-2
03/02/1996	**Aston Villa**	**Premiership**	**0-3**
11/02/1996	Birmingham City	Coca Cola Cup SF 1st Leg	2-1
14/02/1996	Bolton Wanderers	FA Cup 4th Round	1-0
21/02/1996	**Port Vale**	**FA Cup 5th Round**	**0-0**
25/02/1996	**Birmingham City**	**Coca Cola Cup SF 2nd Leg**	**3-0**
27/02/1996	Port Vale	FA Cup 5th Round Replay	2-1
02/03/1996	**Bolton Wanderers**	**Premiership**	**0-1**
06/03/1996	Queens Park Rangers	Premiership	2-1
10/03/1996	**Liverpool**	**FA Cup QF**	**0-0**
13/03/1996	Blackburn Rovers	Premiership	0-1
17/03/1996	**Everton**	**Premiership**	**2-2**
20/03/1996	Liverpool	FA Cup QF Replay	0-3
24/03/1996	Aston Villa	Coca Cola Cup Final at Wembley	0-3
30/03/1996	**Middlesbrough**	**Premiership**	**0-1**
03/04/1996	**Southampton**	**Premiership**	**1-0**
06/04/1996	Arsenal	Premiership	1-2
08/04/1996	**Nottingham Forest**	**Premiership**	**1-3**
13/04/1996	Chelsea	Premiership	1-4
17/04/1996	Manchester United	Premiership	0-1
29/04/1996	**Newcastle United**	**Premiership**	**0-1**
02/05/1996	**Tottenham Hotspur**	**Premiership**	**1-3**
05/05/1996	Coventry City	Premiership	0-0

Leeds won their opening three League games for the first time since season 1984-85.

Tony Dorigo scored his first goal for the club since February 1993, in the 1-1 draw at Southampton.

Lee Chapman made his second debut for the club in a 2-0 home win against West Ham but ended up having an early bath.

Jason Blunt, Mark Jackson, Harry Kewell, Alan Maybury, Ian Harte and Andy Gray were the next batch of youngsters to make their Leeds United debuts.

In the FA Cup fifth-round replay at Port Vale, Leeds introduced a new all-yellow kit, as the players couldn't see each other in the green/navy blue shirts at Bolton.

PREMIERSHIP

1996–97

Date	Opposition	Competition	Score
17/08/1996	Derby County	Premiership	3-3
20/08/1996	**Sheffield Wednesday**	**Premiership**	**0-2**
26/08/1996	**Wimbledon**	**Premiership**	**1-0**
04/09/1996	Blackburn Rovers	Premiership	1-0
07/09/1996	**Manchester United**	**Premiership**	**0-4**
14/09/1996	Coventry City	Premiership	1-2
18/09/1996	**Darlington**	**Coca Cola Cup 2nd Round 1st Leg**	**2-2**
21/09/1996	**Newcastle United**	**Premiership**	**0-1**
24/09/1996	Darlington	Coca Cola Cup 2nd Round 2nd Leg	2-0
28/09/1996	Leicester City	Premiership	0-1
12/10/1996	**Nottingham Forest**	**Premiership**	**2-0**
19/10/1996	Aston Villa	Premiership	0-2
23/10/1996	**Aston Villa**	**Coca Cola Cup 3rd Round**	**1-2**
26/10/1996	Arsenal	Premiership	0-3
02/11/1996	**Sunderland**	**Premiership**	**3-0**
16/11/1996	**Liverpool**	**Premiership**	**0-2**
23/11/1996	Southampton	Premiership	2-0
01/12/1996	**Chelsea**	**Premiership**	**2-0**
07/12/1996	Middlesbrough	Premiership	0-0
14/12/1996	**Tottenham Hotspur**	**Premiership**	**0-0**
21/12/1996	Everton	Premiership	0-0
26/12/1996	**Coventry City**	**Premiership**	**1-3**
28/12/1996	Manchester United	Premiership	0-1
01/01/1997	Newcastle United	Premiership	0-3
11/01/1997	**Leicester City**	**Premiership**	**3-0**
14/01/1997	Crystal Palace	FA Cup 3rd Round	2-2
20/01/1997	West Ham United	Premiership	2-0
25/01/1997	**Crystal Palace**	**FA Cup 3rd Round Replay**	**1-0**
29/01/1997	**Derby County**	**Premiership**	**0-0**
01/02/1997	**Arsenal**	**Premiership**	**0-0**
04/02/1997	Arsenal	FA Cup 4th Round	1-0
15/02/1997	**Portsmouth**	**FA Cup 5th Round**	**2-3**
19/02/1997	Liverpool	Premiership	0-4
22/02/1997	Sunderland	Premiership	1-0
01/03/1997	**West Ham United**	**Premiership**	**1-0**
08/03/1997	**Everton**	**Premiership**	**1-0**
12/03/1997	**Southampton**	**Premiership**	**0-0**
15/03/1997	Tottenham Hotspur	Premiership	0-1
22/03/1997	Sheffield Wednesday	Premiership	2-2
07/04/1997	**Blackburn Rovers**	**Premiership**	**0-0**
16/04/1997	Wimbledon	Premiership	0-2
19/04/1997	Nottingham Forest	Premiership	1-1
22/04/1997	**Aston Villa**	**Premiership**	**0-0**
03/05/1997	Chelsea	Premiership	0-0
11/05/1997	**Middlesbrough**	**Premiership**	**1-1**

Team	Pld	W	D	L	GF	GA	Pts
Manchester United	38	21	12	5	76	44	75
Newcastle United	38	19	11	8	73	40	68
Arsenal	38	19	11	8	62	32	68
Liverpool	38	19	11	8	62	37	68
Aston Villa	38	17	10	11	47	34	61
Chelsea	38	16	11	11	58	55	59
Sheffield Wednesday	38	14	15	9	50	51	57
Wimbledon	38	15	11	12	49	46	56
Leicester City	38	12	11	15	46	54	47
Tottenham Hotspur	38	13	7	18	44	51	46
Leeds United	38	11	13	14	28	38	46
Derby County	38	11	13	14	45	58	46
Blackburn Rovers	38	9	15	14	42	43	42
West Ham United	38	10	12	16	39	48	42
Everton	38	10	12	16	44	57	42
Southampton	38	10	11	17	50	56	41
Coventry City	38	9	14	15	38	54	41
Sunderland	38	10	10	18	35	53	40
Middlesbrough	38	10	12	16	51	60	39
Nottingham Forest	38	6	16	16	31	59	34

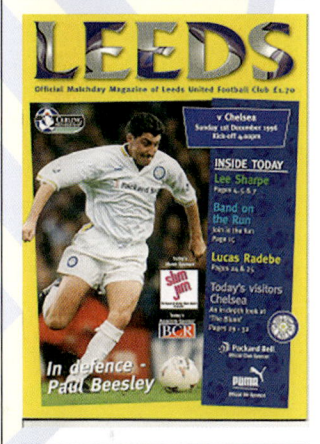

Leeds started with a new goalkeeper for the first time since season 1989-90 when Nigel Martyn made his debut on day one away at Derby County.

Paul Shepherd joined the one appearance club with the 3-0 defeat away at Arsenal on 26 October 1996.

Following Gary McAllister's penalty on Boxing Day for Coventry City, Leeds didn't concede a league goal at home until the last of the season against Middlesbrough.

Leeds were only awarded one penalty all season, which Gary Kelly missed at home to Coventry City.

For the second time in five seasons, Paul Hart led the Whites to FA Youth Cup glory defeating Crystal Palace 3-1 on aggregate.

1997–98

PREMIERSHIP

Team	Pld	W	D	L	GF	GA	Pts
Arsenal	38	23	9	6	68	33	78
Manchester United	38	23	8	7	73	26	77
Liverpool	38	18	11	9	68	42	65
Chelsea	38	20	3	15	71	43	63
Leeds United	38	17	8	13	57	46	59
Blackburn Rovers	38	16	10	12	57	52	58
Aston Villa	38	17	6	15	49	48	57
West Ham United	38	16	8	14	56	57	56
Derby County	38	16	7	15	52	49	55
Leicester City	38	13	14	11	51	41	53
Coventry City	38	12	16	10	46	44	52
Southampton	38	14	6	18	50	55	48
Newcastle United	38	11	11	16	35	44	44
Tottenham Hotspur	38	11	11	16	44	56	44
Wimbledon	38	10	14	14	34	46	44
Sheffield Wednesday	38	12	8	18	52	67	44
Everton	38	9	13	16	41	56	40
Bolton Wanderers	38	9	13	16	41	61	40
Barnsley	38	10	5	23	37	82	35
Crystal Palace	38	8	9	21	37	71	33

Date	Opposition	Competition	Score
09/08/1997	Arsenal	Premiership	1-1
13/08/1997	Sheffield Wednesday	Premiership	3-1
23/08/1997	Crystal Palace	Premiership	0-2
26/08/1997	Liverpool	Premiership	0-2
30/08/1997	Aston Villa	Premiership	0-1
14/09/1997	Blackburn Rovers	Premiership	4-3
17/09/1997	Bristol City	Coca Cola Cup 2nd Round 1st Leg	3-1
20/09/1997	Leicester City	Premiership	0-1
24/09/1997	Southampton	Premiership	2-0
27/09/1997	Manchester United	Premiership	1-0
30/09/1997	Bristol City	Coca Cola Cup 2nd Round 2nd Leg	1-2
04/10/1997	Coventry City	Premiership	0-0
15/10/1997	Stoke City	Coca Cola Cup 3rd Round	3-1
18/10/1997	Newcastle United	Premiership	4-1
25/10/1997	Wimbledon	Premiership	0-1
01/11/1997	Tottenham Hotspur	Premiership	1-0
08/11/1997	Derby County	Premiership	4-3
18/11/1997	Reading	Coca Cola Cup 4th Round	2-3
23/11/1997	West Ham United	Premiership	3-1
29/11/1997	Barnsley	Premiership	3-2
06/12/1997	Everton	Premiership	0-0
13/12/1997	Chelsea	Premiership	0-0
20/12/1997	Bolton Wanderers	Premiership	2-0
26/12/1997	Liverpool	Premiership	1-3
28/12/1997	Aston Villa	Premiership	1-1
03/01/1998	Oxford United	FA Cup 3rd Round	4-0
10/01/1998	Arsenal	Premiership	1-2
17/01/1998	Sheffield Wednesday	Premiership	1-2
24/01/1998	Grimsby Town	FA Cup 4th Round	2-0
31/01/1998	Crystal Palace	Premiership	2-0
07/02/1998	Leicester City	Premiership	0-1
14/02/1998	Birmingham City	FA Cup 5th Round	3-2
22/02/1998	Newcastle United	Premiership	1-1
28/02/1998	Southampton	Premiership	0-1
04/03/1998	Tottenham Hotspur	Premiership	1-0
07/03/1998	Wolverhampton Wanderers	FA Cup QF	0-1
11/03/1998	Blackburn Rovers	Premiership	4-0
15/03/1998	Derby County	Premiership	5-0
30/03/1998	West Ham United	Premiership	0-3
04/04/1998	Barnsley	Premiership	2-1
08/04/1998	Chelsea	Premiership	3-1
11/04/1998	Everton	Premiership	0-2
18/04/1998	Bolton Wanderers	Premiership	3-2
25/04/1998	Coventry City	Premiership	3-3
04/05/1998	Manchester United	Premiership	0-3
09/05/1998	Wimbledon	Premiership	1-1

Leeds came from 3-0 to beat Derby 4-3, 1-0 down to beat West Ham 3-1 and 2-0 down to beat Barnsley 3-2 in three successive league games.

Derek Lilley scored his one and only goal for the Whites in a dramatic 3-2 win over Barnsley at Oakwell.

Lucas Radebe finally broke his duck for the Whites in a routine 4-0 win over Oxford United in the FA Cup third-round win.

Mark Beeney made his last appearance in a Leeds United shirt in the 2-1 home defeat to Sheffeld Wednesday on 17 January 1998.

Goalkeeper Paul Robinson made his first appearance on the Leeds United bench in the 3-1 win over West Ham United on 23 November 1997.

PREMIERSHIP

1998–99

Date	Opposition	Competition	Score
15/08/1998	Middlesbrough	Premiership	0-0
24/08/1998	Blackburn Rovers	Premiership	1-0
29/08/1998	Wimbledon	Premiership	1-1
08/09/1998	Southampton	Premiership	3-0
12/09/1998	Everton	Premiership	0-0
15/09/1998	Maritimo	UEFA Cup 1st Round 1st Leg	1-0
19/09/1998	Aston Villa	Premiership	0-0
26/09/1998	Tottenham Hotspur	Premiership	3-3
29/09/1998	Maritimo	UEFA Cup 1st Round 2nd Leg	0-1 (4-1 on pens)
03/10/1998	Leicester City	Premiership	0-1
17/10/1998	Nottingham Forest	Premiership	1-1
20/10/1998	Roma	UEFA Cup 2nd Round 1st Leg	0-1
25/10/1998	Chelsea	Premiership	0-0
28/10/1998	Bradford City	Worthington Cup 3rd Round	1-0
31/10/1998	Derby County	Premiership	2-2
03/11/1998	Roma	UEFA Cup 2nd Round 2nd Leg	0-0
08/11/1998	Sheffield Wednesday	Premiership	2-1
11/11/1998	Leicester City	Worthington Cup 4th Round	1-2
14/11/1998	Liverpool	Premiership	3-1
21/11/1998	Charlton Athletic	Premiership	4-1
29/11/1998	Manchester United	Premiership	2-3
05/12/1998	West Ham United	Premiership	4-0
14/12/1998	Coventry City	Premiership	2-0
20/12/1998	Arsenal	Premiership	1-3
26/12/1998	Newcastle United	Premiership	3-0
29/12/1998	Wimbledon	Premiership	2-2
02/01/1999	Rushden & Diamonds	FA Cup 3rd Round	0-0
09/01/1999	Blackburn Rovers	Premiership	0-1
13/01/1999	Rushden & Diamonds	FA Cup 3rd Round Replay	3-1
16/01/1999	Middlesbrough	Premiership	2-0
23/01/1999	Portsmouth	FA Cup 4th Round	5-1
30/01/1999	Southampton	Premiership	0-3
06/02/1999	Newcastle United	Premiership	0-1
13/02/1999	Tottenham Hotspur	FA Cup 5th Round	1-1
17/02/1999	Aston Villa	Premiership	2-1
20/02/1999	Everton	Premiership	1-0
24/02/1999	Tottenham Hotspur	FA Cup 5th Round Replay	0-2
01/03/1999	Leicester City	Premiership	2-1
10/03/1999	Tottenham Hotspur	Premiership	2-0
13/03/1999	Sheffield Wednesday	Premiership	2-0
20/03/1999	Derby County	Premiership	4-1
03/04/1999	Nottingham Forest	Premiership	3-1
12/04/1999	Liverpool	Premiership	0-0
17/04/1999	Charlton Athletic	Premiership	1-1
25/04/1999	Manchester United	Premiership	1-1
01/05/1999	West Ham United	Premiership	5-1
05/05/1999	Chelsea	Premiership	0-1
11/05/1999	Arsenal	Premiership	1-0
16/05/1999	Coventry City	Premiership	2-2

Team	Pld	W	D	L	GF	GA	Pts
Manchester United	38	22	13	3	80	37	79
Arsenal	38	22	12	4	59	17	78
Chelsea	38	20	15	3	57	30	75
Leeds United	38	18	13	7	62	34	67
West Ham United	38	16	9	13	46	53	57
Aston Villa	38	15	10	13	51	46	55
Liverpool	38	15	9	14	68	49	54
Derby County	38	13	13	12	40	45	52
Middlesbrough	38	12	15	11	48	54	51
Leicester City	38	12	13	13	40	46	49
Tottenham Hotspur	38	11	14	13	47	50	47
Sheffield Wednesday	38	13	7	18	41	42	46
Newcastle United	38	11	13	14	48	54	46
Everton	38	11	10	17	42	47	43
Coventry City	38	11	9	18	39	51	42
Wimbledon	38	10	12	16	40	63	42
Southampton	38	11	8	19	37	64	41
Charlton Athletic	38	8	12	18	41	56	36
Blackburn Rovers	38	7	14	17	38	52	35
Nottingham Forest	38	7	9	22	35	69	30

Leeds were involved in a penalty shoot-out for the first time since the Charity Shield in 1974 when they faced Maritimo in the UEFA Cup first round.

The above mentioned UEFA Cup tie at Maritimo finished at around 11:45pm UK time due to the 9pm kick-off.

When Mark Beeney was injured in a reserve-team game, Leeds moved quickly to sign Portuguese keeper Nuno Santos on a three-month trial.

Tommy Knarvik had one of the shortest career's in the history of the club, coming on for just four minutes in the FA Cup fourth-round win at Portsmouth.

Harry Kewell was the only Leeds United player to feature in every game for the side.

1999–2000

PREMIERSHIP

Team	Pld	W	D	L	GF	GA	Pts
Manchester United	38	28	7	3	97	45	91
Arsenal	38	22	7	9	73	43	73
Leeds United	38	21	6	11	58	43	69
Liverpool	38	19	10	9	51	30	67
Chelsea	38	18	11	9	53	34	65
Aston Villa	38	15	13	10	46	35	58
Sunderland	38	16	10	12	57	56	58
Leicester City	38	16	7	15	55	55	55
West Ham United	38	15	10	13	52	53	55
Tottenham Hotspur	38	15	8	15	57	49	53
Newcastle United	38	14	10	14	63	54	52
Middlesbrough	38	14	10	14	46	52	52
Everton	38	12	14	12	59	49	50
Coventry City	38	12	8	18	47	54	44
Southampton	38	12	8	18	45	62	44
Derby County	38	9	11	18	44	57	38
Bradford City	38	9	9	20	38	68	36
Wimbledon	38	7	12	19	46	74	33
Sheffield Wednesday	38	8	7	23	38	70	31
Watford	38	6	6	26	35	77	24

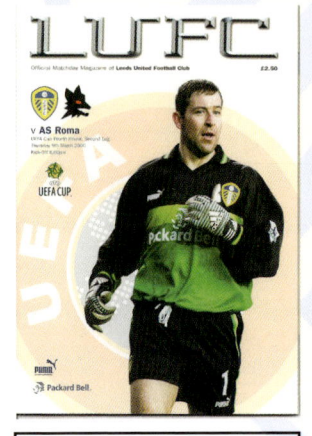

Date	Opposition	Competition	Score
07/08/1999	Derby County	Premiership	0-0
11/08/1999	Southampton	Premiership	3-0
14/08/1999	Manchester United	Premiership	0-2
21/08/1999	Sunderland	Premiership	2-1
23/08/1999	Liverpool	Premiership	1-2
28/08/1999	Tottenham Hotspur	Premiership	2-1
11/09/1999	Coventry City	Premiership	4-3
14/09/1999	Partizan Belgrade	UEFA Cup 1st Round 1st Leg at the Abe Lenstra Stadion	3-1
19/09/1999	Middlesbrough	Premiership	2-0
25/09/1999	Newcastle United	Premiership	3-2
30/09/1999	Partizan Belgrade	UEFA Cup 1st Round 2nd Leg	1-0
03/10/1999	Watford	Premiership	2-1
13/10/1999	Blackburn Rovers	Worthington Cup 3rd Round	1-0
16/10/1999	Sheffield Wednesday	Premiership	2-0
21/10/1999	Lokomotiv Moscow	UEFA Cup 2nd Round 1st Leg	4-1
24/10/1999	Everton	Premiership	4-4
30/10/1999	West Ham United	Premiership	1-0
04/11/1999	Lokomotiv Moscow	UEFA Cup 2nd Round 2nd Leg	3-0
07/11/1999	Wimbledon	Premiership	0-2
20/11/1999	Bradford City	Premiership	2-1
28/11/1999	Southampton	Premiership	1-0
02/12/1999	Spartak Moscow	UEFA Cup 3rd Round 1st Leg at the Georgi Asparuchov Stadium	1-2
05/12/1999	Derby County	Premiership	1-0
09/12/1999	Spartak Moscow	UEFA Cup 3rd Round 2nd Leg	1-0
12/12/1999	Port Vale	FA Cup 3rd Round	2-0
15/12/1999	Leicester City	Worthington Cup 4th Round	0-0 (2-4 on pens)
19/12/1999	Chelsea	Premiership	2-0
26/12/1999	Leicester City	Premiership	2-1
28/12/1999	Arsenal	Premiership	0-2
03/01/2000	Aston Villa	Premiership	1-2
09/01/2000	Manchester City	FA Cup 4th Round	5-2
23/01/2000	Sunderland	Premiership	2-1
30/01/2000	Aston Villa	FA Cup 5th Round	2-3
05/02/2000	Liverpool	Premiership	1-3
12/02/2000	Tottenham Hotspur	Premiership	1-0
20/02/2000	Manchester United	Premiership	0-1
26/02/2000	Middlesbrough	Premiership	0-0
02/03/2000	Roma	UEFA Cup 4th Round 1st Leg	0-0
05/03/2000	Coventry City	Premiership	3-0
09/03/2000	Roma	UEFA Cup 4th Round 2nd Leg	1-0
12/03/2000	Bradford City	Premiership	2-1
16/03/2000	Slavia Prague	UEFA Cup QF 1st Leg	3-0
19/03/2000	Wimbledon	Premiership	4-1
23/03/2000	Slavia Prague	UEFA Cup QF 2nd Leg	1-2
26/03/2000	Leicester City	Premiership	1-2
01/04/2000	Chelsea	Premiership	0-1
06/04/2000	Galatasaray	UEFA Cup SF 1st Leg	0-2
09/04/2000	Aston Villa	Premiership	0-1
16/04/2000	Arsenal	Premiership	0-4
20/04/2000	Galatasaray	UEFA Cup SF 2nd Leg	2-2
23/04/2000	Newcastle United	Premiership	2-2
30/04/2000	Sheffield Wednesday	Premiership	3-0
03/05/2000	Watford	Premiership	3-1
08/05/2000	Everton	Premiership	1-1
14/05/2000	West Ham United	Premiership	0-0

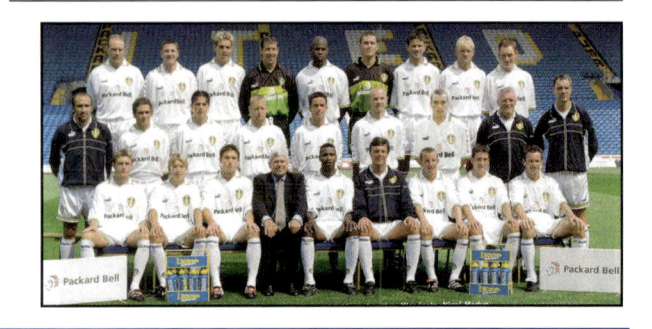

Michael Bridges scored the White's first Premier League hat-trick at Southampton since Gary McAllister did against Coventry City in October 1995.

When Leeds defeated Lokomotiv Moscow at Elland Road, it broke a record of ten straight wins in all competitions.

Leeds had two of their UEFA Cup away ties moved, Partizan Belgrade to Heerenveen and Spartak Moscow to Sofia.

Nigel Martyn was the only ever-present, featuring in all 55 games.

Leeds did the double over all three promoted sides, Bradford City 2-1 and 2-1, Watford 2-1 and 3-1 and Sunderland 2-1 and 2-1.

THE 2000s
FROM THE SUBLIME TO THE RIDICULOUS

Leeds United headed into the new millennium in rosy fashion, into the Champions League for the first time in their history and players such as Rio Ferdinand and Robbie Keane joined the club with Ferdinand moving from West Ham United for a club record fee of £18 million. Having seen off the likes of Barcelona and Lazio in both group stages, Leeds demolished Deportivo La Coruna 3-0 at Elland Road in the first leg of the quarter-finals before edging through to the last four with a 2-0 defeat over in Galicia, which meant a meeting with another Spanish side Valencia in the semi-finals. Sadly for the Whites they were beaten 3-0 in the second leg, having drawn the first 0-0 at Elland Road and then finished fourth and missed out on the competition for the following campaign.

The following season saw the club follow a similar pattern when the Whites topped the league on New Year's Day following a 3-0 home win over West Ham United. A 2-1 FA Cup third-round defeat at Cardiff City also saw the club's league form deteriorate and for the second consecutive season finish just outside the Champions League places, despite the signing of Robbie Fowler from Liverpool. David O'Leary paid with his job and the then Chairman Peter Ridsdale brought in former England manager Terry Venables.

At first it looked like it may have had the desired effect as Leeds topped the table early on following a 1-0 lunchtime win over Manchester United. Soon the rot set in which was difficult to get out of. A 2-1 Worthington Cup defeat at Sheffield United, when leading into the last few minutes, didn't help matters and neither did a 2-1 aggregate defeat to Malaga in the third round of the UEFA Cup. Leeds's form did pick up over Christmas with the emergence of James Milner, but another cup defeat at Sheffield United in the FA Cup all but signalled the end of Venables's tenure at Elland Road. The defeat at home to Middlesbrough

Leeds United, 2000-01.

that followed was the final straw as Peter Reid was handed the reins and given the task of keeping Leeds in the top flight. He oversaw a 6-1 hammering away at the Valley in which Mark Viduka was outstanding in scoring a hat-trick and a famous 3-2 win at Arsenal kept Leeds afloat for another season, but the problems had already set in.

With Harry Kewell sold to Liverpool, Reid knew he had little money to spend and relied on loans such as Zoumana Camara, Didier Domi and Jermaine Pennant. Following a 6-1 defeat away at Portsmouth in November, Reid was sacked and Leeds United legend Eddie Gray was given the task of keeping the Whites in the Premier League. Victories over Charlton Athletic (1-0) and Fulham (3-2), saw a brief upturn in results, but the club were always fighting against the odds. A six-match losing streak was ended in emphatic fashion at home to Wolves (4-1). The results were inconsistent and despite the club being taken over by Gerald Krasner, a 4-1 defeat away at Bolton Wanderers saw the end of 14 years in the top flight. The squad that reached the Champions League semi-finals just three years earlier would find themselves playing in the second tier of English football for the first time since season 1989-90.

Most of the high earners were sold to balance the books and Kevin Blackwell, who was assistant to Peter Reid and Eddie Gray, was given the manager's job. Paul Butler replaced Dominic Matteo as skipper, but everyone around the club knew it would be a difficult task to return to the Premier League at the first attempt. Results went from the sublime to the ridiculous, a 6-1 win over Queens Park Rangers in which returning hero Brian Deane

Eddie Gray, Leeds United, 2003.

Kevin Blackwell, Leeds United, 2004.

scored four, to an embarrassing 1-0 defeat in front of the Sky Sports cameras at Rotherham United summed up the first half of the campaign. In mid-January the club was sold to former Chelsea Chairman Ken Bates and results steadily improved. Rob Hulse was bought in on loan from West Bromwich Albion and marked his debut with a brace against Reading, and the side finished in a respectable 14th position.

The following season hopes were high of at least a play-off position, with the likes of Richard Cresswell, Eddie Lewis and Robbie Blake all joining the club. The side never really looked like challenging for a top-two place, but a four-game winning run in November and December, which included a magnificent comeback away at Southampton (4-3) in which the side were 3-0 down at the interval, showed the fans what the side could produce. After a victory in early March away to Crystal Palace, Leeds didn't win another league game until the penultimate weekend at home to already relegated Crewe Alexandra and ended up in fifth place and a two-leg play-off against Preston North End. The first leg was drawn 1-1 at Elland Road, and despite having Stephen Crainey and Cresswell sent off at Deepdale, Leeds won through to the Play Off Final thanks to goals from Rob Hulse and Frazer Richardson. Sadly for the Whites that was a good as it got as Watford demolished them in a very one-sided final at the Millennium Stadium and Leeds had to prepare for a third season in the Championship.

Season 2006-07 was one that went down in history for all the wrong reasons. After only two wins in their opening eight games, Blackwell was sacked and initially replaced by John Carver, only for him to be sacked following a shocking 5-1 defeat away at Luton Town in mid-October. Former Chelsea captain Dennis Wise was appointed as the new manager and

Leeds United, 2006-07.

won his first game in charge 2-0 at home to Southend United thanks to goals from Ian Moore and Robbie Blake. Results were inconsistent and going into the new year Leeds were in 23rd place. They hit rock bottom at the end of January, despite winning at Hull City. Easter proved pivotal as a win over Plymouth Argyle saw the Whites escape from the bottom three, but two days later, two late goals away at Colchester United saw them plummet back in and it was a blow that the club would never recover that season. A 1-1 draw at home to Ipswich Town meant the club would be in the third tier of English football for the first time in their history.

The summer of 2007 was perhaps one of the most bizarre, with the club not able to sign any players until just before the start of the campaign. A week before the League One campaign started, the EFL deducted Leeds 15 points for failing to comply with rules on insolvency. It meant the side were playing catch up from day one. Amazingly, Wise got on with the job and oversaw seven straight wins at the start of a campaign for the first time since season 1973-74 and by 3pm on Boxing Day they were actually top of the league table. Problems were soon afloat for Leeds though, with Wise leaving for a new role at Newcastle United. A former title winner, Gary McAllister, was asked to take the reins and see Leeds back in the Championship. The likeable Scotsman had to wait till his fifth game in charge to experience his first win, 1-0 away at Swindon and the play-offs were achieved with a 1-0 win away at Yeovil Town in the penultimate game of the season. Despite losing the first leg at home to Carlisle United (2-1), a goal five minutes into stoppage time from Dougie Freedman kept the tie alive and a brace from Jonny Howson, the second in the 90th minute, took Leeds back to Wembley. That was a good as it got as Yorkshire rivals Doncaster Rovers proved too good for Leeds and the Whites were faced with a second consecutive season in League One.

Leeds had to shrug off the disappointment and pick themselves up and were installed as one of the favourites to return to the Championship. They started the season well with a 2-1 win away at Scunthorpe United, and a four-match winning run in September saw the side end the month in third place. The away form proved to be a nuisance, with defeats at Peterborough United (2-0), Millwall (3-1) and Southend United (1-0), which set the Whites back, but not as much as an embarrassing 1-0 away defeat to non-league Histon in the FA Cup second round, played in atrocious conditions at the Glassword Stadium. That proved to be the beginning of the end for McAllister as Leeds kept conceding from set pieces and a 3-1 defeat away at Milton Keynes Dons was the final straw as he was sacked the next day. Bates looked to another former Leeds United player Simon Grayson as the next throw of the dice, and he looked like an inspired appointment at first as results steadily improved. The nadir for the season was a dreadful 2-0 defeat away at Hereford in which words were exchanged in the dressing room afterwards. Leeds went on to lose only one of their remaining 15 league games which was at eventual champions Leicester City on Easter Monday. Leeds finished fourth, which set up a two-leg play-off semi-final with Millwall. The Lions won the first leg 1-0

Jonny Howson celebrates scoring the equaliser in the 2-1 win at Elland Road to seal promotion, 8 May 2010.

thanks to a goal from Neil Harris and they went through to Wembley thanks to a 1-1 draw at Elland Road, in which Jermaine Beckford missed a penalty in the second half.

Onto a third season in League One, Leeds knew they had to get it right from the off. They started the campaign like a house on fire and won their opening six league games. They were never out of the top two up until Easter, and a famous 1-0 win over Premier League Champions Manchester United in the FA Cup third round, thanks to a Jermaine Beckford goal, looked to have helped things along the way. Leeds being Leeds, though who like to do things the hard way and following the famous win at Old Trafford, league form suffered and set the alarm bells ringing. Despite a 4-1 win over relegation haunted Tranmere Rovers at the start of March, four straight defeats saw Leeds drop to fourth and it looked like a third consecutive season in the play-offs. Three straight victories, 2-1 at Yeovil Town on Easter Monday, 2-0 at home to Southend United and 3-1 at Carlisle United, saw the Whites bounce back to second place and despite losing at Gillingham (3-2) and Charlton Athletic (1-0), it was in the Whites' hands on the last day of the campaign at home to Bristol Rovers. All they had to do was beat the Gasheads at Elland Road. As simple as it sounds, Leeds made it difficult with the sending off of Max Gradel in the first half and once Daryl Duffy scored for the visitors it looked like Leeds would have to settle for the play-offs. Thankfully for the Whites, they dug deep into their reserve and found an equaliser from local Jonny Howson and a winner from star striker Jermaine Beckford who took Leeds back to the Championship at the third attempt and wild celebrations ensued at Elland Road.

Jermaine Beckford celebrates scoring the winner in the 2-1 win at Elland Road to seal promotion.

DEBUTANTS IN THE 2000s

MARK VIDUKA

Debut: 1860 Munich (H) 9 August 2000
Appearances: 163 (4)
Goals: 72

The Melbourne-born striker was signed from Scottish side Glasgow Celtic in the summer of 2000 and what a signing he proved to be. At first he struggled for fitness and goals and it wouldn't be until he returned from the Olympic Games with Australia that things really started to click for Viduka. He scored his first goal for the club in the 6-0 win over Besiktas at Elland Road and followed it up with a brace against both Tottenham Hotspur and Charlton Athletic respectively. Saturday, 4 November 2000 would go down as a day Viduka would never forget as he hit all four goals in one of the most memorable individual performances Elland Road had ever seen in a 4-3 win over Liverpool. By the time Christmas had hit, Viduka had scored 13 goals and he hit a hot streak in the month of March, scoring in every game. He hit 22 goals in his first season and became a firm fans' favourite. The following season saw him score a brilliant winner at Highbury in the second game of the season, as well as goals in a 6-0 win at Leicester City and away in a 1-1 draw at Old Trafford. He didn't quite hit the heights of the first season, but Viduka still finished as top scorer with 14.

The 2002-03 campaign started with goals in back-to-back games against Manchester City and West Bromwich Albion, but the striker struggled as did the side in the first half of the season. Following the sacking of Terry Venables and the arrival of Peter Reid, Viduka took it upon himself to lead the Whites to Premier League safety and he scored a wonderful hat-trick in Reid's second game in charge in a 6-1 hammering of Charlton Athletic at the Valley. Seven more goals followed, including a vital late winner at Arsenal that kept Leeds afloat for a further 12 months. Despite scoring on the opening day of the new season at home to Newcastle United and in a 3-2 win at Middlesbrough, the goals dried up and Peter Reid was sacked following a 6-1 loss at Portsmouth. Viduka found his form under interim manager Eddie Gary as Leeds battled against the drop for a second consecutive season, but a red card in the 3-2 home win against Leicester City would prove costly. Viduka saw red again in the 4-1 loss at Bolton Wanderers on 2 May 2004 and Leeds were relegated from the top flight. The Aussie left the club to join Middlesbrough after four successful seasons at Elland Road.

DOMINIC MATTEO

Debut: AC Milan (H) 19 September 2000
Appearances: 146
Goals: 4

Matteo joined Leeds from Liverpool in the summer of 2000, but he didn't make his debut until mid-September. 'Playing pre-season, I didn't even know I had an injury; there was a tear on the knee, Dave Hancock [physio] found an injury. It was frustrating to miss the opening day, but it gave me a chance to settle in the city.' He made his debut in the 1-0 win over AC Milan on a rain-trodden night at Elland Road. 'I had not trained for six weeks, but we were struggling for players and I couldn't say no!' By the time the return to the San Siro came round at the start of November, Leeds needed a point to make it through the second group stage, and Matteo stepped up with a vital header from Lee Bowyer as Leeds got the point they needed. 'When you play against AC Milan, with my family Italian, for me it was always going to be a good night, the atmosphere was going to be amazing. To get the goal and the support was immense, I don't think it will ever be replicated, it felt like we were all together that night! It was an amazing thing, that goal was very memorable, one of the best away days of my life.'

Matteo would become an integral part of the side that reached the semi-finals of the competition and built up a rapport with Rio Ferdinand in the centre of defence. The second leg away to Valencia brought the end to the Champions League fun and Matteo felt that experience cost them in the end. 'We were naive in experience at that level, we ran out of steam tactically, Valencia had more experience.'

Things would get better for Matteo as he captained the side the following season when Ferdinand was out injured, and he was made club captain after Rio left for Manchester United in the summer of 2002. He proved a vital leader as Leeds pulled clear from relegation under Peter Reid, and he set up Mark Viduka for the vital goal away at Arsenal.

Sadly for Matteo and the club, the financial rot had set in and players were sold to balance the books with the side relegated to the Championship. 'I think about relegation every day! On and off the field it was a mess, possibly bought too many players. We out battled teams, we lost that ethic.' Matteo joined Blackburn Rovers following the Whites' relegation, but no one will ever forget that goal in the San Siro.

RIO FERDINAND

Debut: Leicester City (A) 2 December 2000
Appearances: 74
Goals: 3

When Leeds United broke the British transfer record when they signed Rio Ferdinand for £18 million from West Ham United in November 2000 (his last appearance in a West Ham United shirt was in the Hammers' 1-0 win at Elland Road, in which he excelled), there were plenty of eyebrows raised, but he would have an enormous impact at Elland Road. He had a debut to forget away at Leicester City, as he was the only centre-back to finish the game as Lucas Radebe was sent off and Jonathan Woodgate was taken off as Leeds were 3-0 down at the interval.

Slowly but surely Ferdinand found his feet up north and despite missing the game away at Lazio, he would go on to play a massive part of Leeds reaching the last four of the Champions League. He captained the side in the absence of Radebe in away games at both Tottenham Hotspur and Charlton Athletic and led the side to two wins. With Radebe ruled out for the remainder of the 2000-01 season, manager David O'Leary handed the armband over to the Peckham-born defender. He responded with a magnificent display at home to Deportivo La Coruna in the quarter-final, first leg at Elland Road and even followed it up with the vital third goal as Leeds took a three-goal lead to the Riazor.

Nine days later, Leeds travelled to Anfield for a vital showdown with Liverpool in the race for Champions League football in the 2001-02 season. Ferdinand scored the first goal as Leeds won the game 2-1. He scored his third goal in five games away at his old club West Ham United but refused to celebrate in front of his old adoring public. With Radebe ruled out for the 2001-02 season, Ferdinand was awarded the captaincy on a permanent basis and a string of fine performances earned him the coveted Leeds United Player of the Year at the end of that season. With the vultures starting to circle as Leeds had missed out on Champions League qualification for a second consecutive season, the Whites knew they had to balance the books and following a fantastic showing at the 2002 World Cup in Japan and South Korea, Ferdinand joined arch rivals Manchester United for a fee of £30 million. He was roundly booed on his return to Elland Road the following season as a Harry Kewell header settled matters in favour of the Whites.

JAMES MILNER

Debut: West Ham United (A) 10 November 2002
Appearances: 30 (24)
Goals: 5

Milner, who had always been a Leeds United supporter growing up with his parents being season-ticket holders, joined the Leeds United Academy at the age of ten after being spotted by a scout whilst playing for Westbrook Juniors in Horsforth. He was taken on as a trainee as well as attending college once a week. Milner was part of the England Under 17s squad that won the Nationwide summer tournament against Italy, Czech Republic and Brazil respectively.

He made his Leeds United debut coming on as a late substitute for Jason Wilcox in a 4-3 win over West Ham United in early November 2002. When he came off the bench for an injured Alan Smith on Boxing Day 2002 away at Sunderland, it took the Wortley-born player just 11 minutes to level matters and he thus became the youngest ever player to score in the Premier League at the time. Two days later at home to Chelsea, he came off the bench to replace Harry Kewell after Leeds had taken the lead, and he repeated the act, leaving Chelsea captain Marcel Desailly flat on his back before curling past Ed De Goey, giving Leeds an unassailable 2-0 win.

Despite not scoring again that season, Milner had already made his mark at Elland Road. At the start of his second season, he was loaned out to Swindon Town to gain first-team experience, where he scored two goals in six league games. He returned to Elland Road in October 2003 and would feature heavily as Leeds battled against the drop. He scored the vital winner away at Charlton Athletic, in what was Eddie Gray's first win back at Elland Road and he followed it up with the third goal in the side's best performance of the season, a 4-1 win over Wolverhampton Wanderers at Elland Road. His fifth and final strike came in a 1-1 draw at home to Everton, in which former Leeds goalkeeper Nigel Martyn excelled and kept Leeds at bay time and time again. Despite Milner's performances, it wasn't enough to see them over the line and the side were relegated to the Championship. It was hoped that Milner may be kept on at Elland Road and he appeared on the front of the club's official magazine Leeds Leeds Leeds, but he was sold to Newcastle United for an initial fee of £3.6 million. He went on to win the Premier League with Manchester City in 2012 and 2014. He also won the Champions League with Liverpool in 2019.

DAVID HEALY

Debut: Wigan Athletic (H) 31 October 2004
Appearances: 89 (32)
Goals: 31

Healy who was born and bred in Killyleagh in Northern Ireland, came to the Whites' attention following relegation from the Premier League in 2004. Ironically for Leeds, when they met Healy's current club at the time Preston North End in October 2004, the Northern Irishman gave the Whites fans a wave when he was substituted in the side's 1-0 win. By the time the sides met again in November 2004, Healy was a Leeds United player after the two clubs agreed on a reported fee of £650,000.

Despite not hitting the back of the net in his first two games for the club, it was written in the script that he would return to haunt his former employees on 6 November 2004, he did exactly that by scoring a brace in a 4-2 win. He ended his first season at Elland Road with seven goals, including a chip in the memorable 6-1 win over Queens Park Rangers and a fine lob at home to Plymouth Argyle on 28 December. His season ended prematurely after an injury in the 2-1 win at Watford at the start of April, but he was raring to go on day one of the new campaign at home to Millwall. He marked it with a brace and weeks later he was on the front pages back home as he scored the winning goal for Northern Ireland in their famous 1-0 win over Sven Goran Eriksson's England side.

He hit 14 goals in his second campaign as Leeds reached the play-off final, but had to settle for a place on the bench as Leeds lost to Watford in Cardiff. Just like on day one of the previous campaign, Healy hit the winner, this time at home to Norwich City and for the second successive season he hit double goalscoring figures, including vital goals away at Southend United, a late, late winner against his former club Preston North End and the equaliser at home to Plymouth Argyle on Easter Saturday.

Sadly for Leeds, they lost the battle against relegation, but Healy was awarded the captain's armband for the games at home to Burnley, Ipswich and away at Southampton, following the suspension of Jonathan Douglas. In his three seasons at the club, he finished either joint or top scorer in all of them and joined up with his former Northern Ireland manager Lawrie Sanchez at Fulham for the 2007-08 season.

JERMAINE BECKFORD

Debut: Crystal Palace (H) 21 March 2006
Appearances: 134 (18)
Goals: 85

Not many people know that Beckford was in fact a former Chelsea Junior and he came through the ranks at the same time as Carlton Cole. However, he was rejected by Chelsea and joined non-league side Wealdstone. It was from there that he caught the eye of Leeds United.

Originally he had a trial at south London-club Crystal Palace, but joined Leeds for an undisclosed fee in March 2006, describing it as 'a clean break from London' and he said he will 'never forget the roar' on his debut against Crystal Palace.

Beckford admitted he needed to go out on loan to gain first team experience and he had loan spells at both Carlisle United and Scunthorpe United during the 2006-07 campaign. The loan moves proved to be exactly what he needed, as he started the 2007-08 season on fire as

Leeds looked to get out of League One at the first attempt. He finished top scorer with 20 goals, which included some fantastic strikes at home to Hartlepool United, away at Bristol Rovers and away at Swansea City. Only a terrific goalkeeping display from Carlisle United stopper Kieran Westwood kept him at bay in the first leg of the play-off semi-final at Elland Road. Despite missing out on promotion after losing the final to Doncaster Rovers, Beckford was straight back at it the following season, scoring the winner on the opening day at Scunthorpe United, before a brilliant hat-trick away at Chester City in the first round of the Carling Cup, broadcast live on Sky Sports. He ended the season with 34 goals, including two further hat-tricks, away at Northampton Town in the FA Cup and at home to Yeovil Town in a 4-0 drubbing at Elland Road. The only thing that was missing was that promotion back to the Championship.

It was more of the same for Beckford as he opened the season with a brace at home to Exeter City, and with the team flying at the top of the League One table the goals flowed. 3 January 2010 will always go down as very special day in the hearts of all Leeds United supporters as they beat arch rivals Manchester United in the FA Cup third round, with Beckford scoring the winning goal at the Stretford End. He described it as 'a surreal day'.

On the final day of the season, at home to Bristol Rovers, Leeds needed a win to secure promotion back to the Championship at the third attempt, and Beckford was made captain for the day – 'I thought Glyn Snodin (assistant manager) was messing about!' Beckford stepped up to the plate and amongst jubilant scenes he scored the last of his 85 goals as Leeds ended their three-year exile from League One. He went onto join Everton at the end of his contract in the summer of 2010.

JONNY HOWSON

Debut: Barnet (H) 19 September 2006
Appearances: 193 (32)
Goals: 27

The Morley-born youngster joined the club at the start of July 2005 and became a regular part of the reserve side that season. He was an unused substitute against Chester City the following season, wearing squad-number 33 (as was Danny Rose) and made his Leeds United debut in the next round at home to Barnet, coming on for Steve Stone with 14 minutes to play. He made his first start for his hometown club at Elland Road against Hull City on 23 December and would go on to feature 11 times in total in his first season at the club. His first goal for the side came as he gave them the lead away at Norwich City at the start of February, but it proved to be in vain as the Canaries battled back to win 2-1.

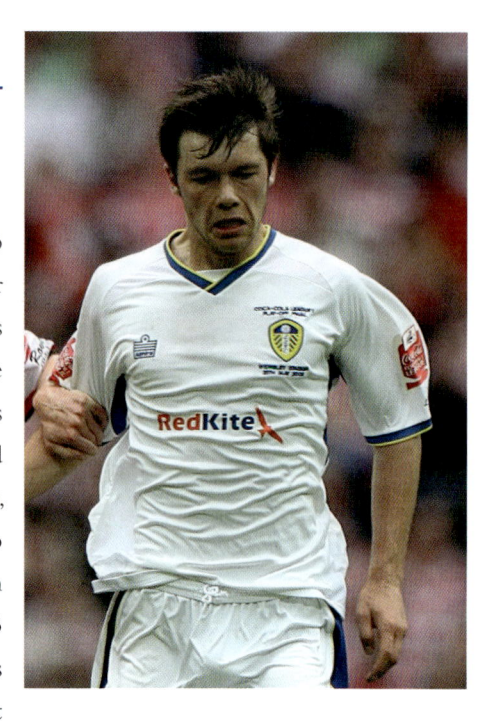

The 2007-08 season would be Howson's breakthrough campaign at Elland Road, when he would feature on 35 occasions under both Dennis Wise and Gary McAllister as Leeds looked to return to the Championship at the first attempt. Howson scored four goals that season, away at Northampton Town in a 1-1 draw, one in the dramatic 3-2 win over Carlisle United in the League at Elland Road and famously a brace away against the same opponents in the second leg of the play-off semi-final as Leeds reached Wembley. To top Howson's season off, he was made captain in the 2-0 win away at Millwall in April 2008 and was voted the Young Player of the Year at the club's end of season awards function.

It would be more of the same for Howson, as he made a further 51 appearances in the 2008-09 season, scoring five goals and he went on to be part of the furniture at Elland Road. The following season would be one that Howson would never forget as he created the winning goal for Jermaine Beckford at Old Trafford and scored the vital equaliser off the bench against Bristol Rovers on the promotion winning day. He also captained the side on various occasions when Richard Naylor was out. He was an ever-present back in the Championship and scored 11 goals from midfield, including a perfect hat-trick away at Scunthorpe United, the winner away at Burnley when the side were 2-0 down and a brace in the 5-2 win at home to Doncaster Rovers in March 2011. He was made club captain at the start of the 2011-12 season, but to the surprise of many he was sold to Norwich City in January 2012.

ROBERT SNODGRASS

Debut: Scunthorpe United (A) 9 August 2008
Appearances: 166 (26)
Goals: 41

Snodgrass, who was born in Glasgow and was offered an apprenticeship with Clyde and Livingston, chose to join Livi in 2003. He turned down a trial at Barcelona to stay at the Scottish side and this was where he made his breakthrough.

In the summer of 2008, Leeds United came calling and he proved to be one of the club's most inspired signings. He made his debut in the 2-1 win at Scunthorpe United and scored his first goal for the club in only his second appearance in a 5-2 League Cup win at Chester City. He featured 51 times in his first season, scoring a total of 11 goals, which included scoring the first goal under new boss Simon Grayson at home to Leicester City on Boxing Day 2008.

The following season saw the Scotsman start 52 games and he came off the bench in five others. He hit double goalscoring figures again, including a last-minute winner away at Milton Keynes Dons and brilliant goals away at Brighton & Hove Albion and Stockport Count respectively. He came off the bench as a late substitute for Jermaine Beckford in the promotion winning game against Bristol Rovers and was named in the PFA Team of the Year. An injury in a pre-season game in Norway kept him out of the early games the following season, but he went on to feature a further 40 times, scoring seven goals. Funnily enough all of his seven goals came away from Elland Road, with his most memorable strikes coming in a 2-2 draw at Leicester City and in the 1-1 FA Cup third-round draw at Arsenal. The following season, which proved to be his last in Leeds United colours, saw the former Livingston man play 44 times with his best run of goals – 13. He will best be remembered for his brace at home to Millwall when Leeds mourned the death of former title-winner Gary Speed; some say it was written in the stars that a player in Speed's position would grab the headlines. The first one was a brilliant free kick and the second was Speed's trademark, a fine header from a cross from the right. Following the sale of Jonny Howson, Snodgrass was awarded the captaincy under new boss Neil Warnock and he was named the Leeds United Supporters' and Players' Player of the Year. He joined former Leeds players Bradley Johnson and Jonny Howson at Norwich City that summer.

LUCIANO BECCHIO

Debut: Scunthorpe United (A) 9 August 2008
Appearances: 177 (44)
Goals: 86

Becchio started his footballing career with Boca Juniors in Argentina but moved to Europe in 2003, signing for Mallorca B. Further spells at Terrassa, Barcelona B and Merida took place, before Gary McAllister and Leeds United came calling in the off season of 2008. He was originally signed on trial by the Scotsman and he impressed in games against Shelbourne and Barnet and he signed a three-year contract at the end of July. He made his debut as a substitute for goalscorer Enoch Shouwnmi in the 2-1 win at Scunthorpe on day one of the new campaign and he scored his first goal for the club inside a minute, away at Yeovil Town two weeks later. In his first season at the club, the Argentinean featured on 58 occasions, scoring 19 goals, with the most memorable of his 19 strikes being in the play-off semi-final, second leg at home to Millwall, when the roof lifted off Elland Road. Despite missing out on promotion in his first season in English football, it would be more of the same for Becchio the following campaign as he hit 17 goals in 47 games as Leeds ended their three-year stay in the third tier. He scored vital goals towards the back end of the season, with a brace away at Carlisle United and one in the 4-1 home win against Milton Keynes Dons. Becchio scored the first goal back in the Championship at home to Derby County and hit the 20 mark in the Whites' first season back in the second tier. He hit a hat-trick at home to Bristol City, coming off the bench for Davide Somma, but an injury against Watford in mid-April curtailed his season. He marked his return the following season with a vital goal in the 3-2 win over Crystal Palace and finished the campaign with 11 goals, with one to remember in the late, late winner over Doncaster Rovers as new boss Neil Warnock watched on. The following season was even better as he hit 19 goals in the first half of the season, including giving Leeds the lead in their last-eight League Cup tie at home to Chelsea. His 86th and final goal came in the 1-1 FA Cup third-round draw at home to Birmingham City and his last appearance came two weeks later at home to Bristol City. He joined Norwich City in exchange for Steve Morison and £200,000 but still remains a firm favourite with all Leeds United supporters.

MAX GRADEL

Debut: Norwich City (H) 19 October 2009
Appearances: 58 (26)
Goals: 25

The Ivorian who signed his first professional contract at Leicester City in May 2007 made his breakthrough at AFC Bournemouth during the following campaign before returning to the Walkers Stadium. It was from there where Gradel joined Leeds, originally on loan in October 2009, making his debut as substitute in the dramatic 2-1 win at home to Norwich City. In that season he quickly established himself as a fans' favourite and by the time the January transfer window came around he signed a two and a half year contract at Elland Road. By the end of that campaign he would feature 35 times, scoring six vital goals, with strikes against Carlisle United and Milton Keynes Dons.

Gradel played a huge part as Leeds looked to clinch promotion against Bristol Rovers. Sadly for him, he was sent off in the first half of that game for an alleged stamp on Daniel Jones. Leeds bounced back to win the game thanks to goals from Jonny Howson and Jermaine Beckford, with Gradel sitting in the dressing room.

He played his first game back in a League Cup tie at home to Leicester City and scored his first goal in the 4-1 win away at Scunthorpe United at the end of October. He would be a vital part of the squad that just missed out on the play-offs, playing in 44 games and scoring 18 goals. He scored a brace of goals in home games against Queens Park Rangers

(2-0), Barnsley (3-3), Doncaster Rovers (5-2) and Nottingham Forest (4-1), the latter being broadcast live on the BBC. He finished the campaign winning the prestigious Leeds United Player of the Year award as well as the Players' Player of the Year award. During the summer, he was linked with several clubs including German side Hamburg, but Gradel confirmed he would like to stay at Elland Road.

He started the 2011-12 season scoring the Whites' consolation goal away at Southampton, but he was sent off for a second bookable offence in the 1-0 loss at home to Middlesbrough. It would be the last time he would feature in a Leeds shirt at Elland Road. His last appearance in Leeds colours came in a 2-1 loss at Ipswich Town at the end of August and by the end of month it was announced that he had joined French club Saint-Etienne for an undisclosed fee.

MANAGERS APPOINTED IN THE 00s

TERRY VENABLES

First game in charge: Manchester City (H) 17 August 2002
Last game in charge: Middlesbrough (H) 15 March 2003
Games: 42
Won: 16
Drawn: 7
Lost: 19

Following the departure of O'Leary, rumours were abound as to who would take over. Yet again Martin O'Neill was installed as the bookmakers' favourite but Leeds turned to former England boss Terry Venables.

El Tel started his playing career with Chelsea in 1960, winning promotion from the Second Division with the Blues in 1962-63 and the 1965 League Cup against Chelsea, in which he scored one of the Londoners' three goals. He moved from west to north London in 1966 joining Tottenham Hotspur, making his debut in a derby against Arsenal. He added the FA Cup to his honours as Tottenham defeated his former club at Wembley. He made it a hat-trick of London clubs, joining Queens Park Rangers and winning promotion back to the top flight in 1973. It was a quadruple of clubs in the capital when he joined Crystal Palace in 1974 before being appointed manager of the Selhurst Park club ahead of the 1976-77 season. He won two promotions at Palace and then rejoined another of his former clubs as manager. At QPR, he was a runner-up in the FA Cup against Tottenham and again won promotion to the top flight in 1983. Venables then moved to Spain and joined Barcelona, where he won the La Liga title once in 1985, the Copa de la Liga in 1986 and was runner-up in the European Cup in 1986. He returned to England with Tottenham Hotspur and won the FA Cup once more thanks to a Des Walker own goal against Nottingham Forest and he was then appointed as the new national coach following the dismissal of Graham Taylor. Venables led England to the last four in Euro 96, before losing on penalties to Germany, and made way for Glenn Hoddle ahead of the 1996-

97 campaign. He had a spell as manager of Australia before returning to Crystal Palace for a second stint, before saving Middlesbrough from the drop in 2001.

Hopes were high when he joined Leeds United, but he was up against it from the off with the sale of club captain Rio Ferdinand for £30 million to arch rivals Manchester United

TERRYVENABLES

LET'S GET THE SHOW ON THE ROAD

THE FIRST GAME IN A NEW CAMPAIGN IS ALWAYS A SPECIAL OCCASION AND AS YOU CAN IMAGINE IT'S PARTICULARLY EXCITING FOR ME AT A NEW CLUB WITH NEW CHALLENGES.

I'm delighted with the welcome I've received from the fans and the club, and I'm really looking forward to working here.

It's all been very hectic since Peter Ridsdale flew out to Spain for lunch with me and I agreed to take the job, but I've been pleased with the way things have gone so far.

We've worked hard and the players have been very receptive to what I've been trying to do. Now I'm just looking forward to getting on with it.

"WHAT HAS PLEASED ME IS THAT THE PLAYERS HAVE SHOWN A DESIRE TO LEARN AND A WILLINGNESS TO TRY THINGS."

There's nothing players and coaches like more than the build up to games and putting the work on the training ground into practice on match day. When it's going well, especially at this time of year, there is no better job.

But we were reminded this summer of how dreadful things can be when the dreams are snatched away. At 18 years old, Peter Mitchell should have been looking forward to his third season at our Academy. A Northern Ireland youth international, he seemed to have a bright future in the game, but a terrible car accident has left him unable to play again.

Everyone at Leeds United, and I'm sure I include our supporters in this, wish Peter a speedy recovery and hope things work out well for him in the future.

FITNESS

As you know the club were committed to a tour of the Far East and Australia, and I was tied into a TV contract and joined up with them in Melbourne.

We had a couple of good, hard games on that trip then came back and faced Glasgow Rangers where I thought our fitness looked good.

With so much travelling we haven't been able to spend as much time as we might have liked on the training ground, working on things like team pattern, but I don't like to change too many things too quickly anyway.

I'm going to creep up on the thing slowly rather than try and do lots and lots straight away and find none of it sticks.

What has pleased me is that the players have shown a desire to learn and a willingness to try things.

And while I might have liked a little longer working at Thorp Arch, it's much better than when I went into Middlesbrough and we had a game the next day!

4

and there would be a financial crisis that gripped the club, which also saw Robbie Keane join Tottenham. Leeds actually got off to a decent start, topping the table for a few hours at least after four wins in their first six games, which included a famous 1-0 win over the Red Devils at Elland Road. Venables described the performance in the second half as 'outstanding'.

LEEDS v MAN CITY 17.08.02

LEEDS UNITED on the internet: www.leedsunited.com

SIGNINGS

The introduction of the transfer restrictions whereby you can only sign players at certain times, means you don't know what problems you are going to come up against. This will mean we may have to shift players around at times and get them to do something different.

With that in mind I was very pleased to be able to sign Nicky Barmby and Paul Okon, and I'm sure they will prove good additions to our squad.

I know Nicky Barmby very well from my time at Spurs and England. He's a very intelligent player, very quick to pick things up and he knows what I want.

He's a good team player. His passes are simple, he's got good movement and he's always making runs and threatening the opposition.

Nicky can play right across midfield and up front, while Paul Okon can play midfield or at the back so they provide us with a lot of possibilities.

When you look at the Premiership this season, it's hard to see beyond Arsenal, Manchester United and Liverpool again if you are looking for a favourite.

DARK HORSES

I think Newcastle have acquired some good players, and Middlesbrough have also bought well and could be dark horses. The kept their finances right last year and that's allowed them to bring in some good players this time.

I thought Juninho was one of the best signings of the summer and it is a terrible blow for them that he's picked up an injury before the season has got under way. He's an exceptional player and I was looking forward to seeing his skills – except against us, of course.

"I'VE BEEN IMPRESSED BY THE GREAT DESIRE THERE IS IN OUR SQUAD TO DO WELL AND THE PASSION THEY HAVE TO PLAY FOR LEEDS UNITED."

I think another great signing this close season was when Kevin Keegan snapped up Nicolas Anelka.

He's a tremendously dangerous player with great pace and shooting ability. He knows what he's doing and times his runs extremely well. And in the tapes I've seen of him recently, he looks as though he's enjoying himself.

This is going to be a difficult first game for us. As well as Anelka, City have skilled players like Ali Benarbia and Eyal Berkovic, who can be a real threat.

Benarbia and Anelka have played together before and they have good understanding, so we shall have to be very careful of that.

PASSION

What do I think of our chances this season? I'm not going to make a sackful of promises but we'll be trying to play some good football and hopefully it will be winning football.

I've been impressed by the great desire there is in our squad to do well and the passion they have to play for Leeds United.

I always say you have to aim for the top. At the end of the season you can assess what you did with what you had and I'm always fairly tough on myself in that. But at the beginning we've got to think of one thing only and that's to win.

Enjoy the game **TERRY**
© leedsunited 2002

• Paul Okon will give us new options

Sadly for Leeds and the charismatic manager, that was as good as it would get, as following a 2-1 home defeat to Charlton Athletic Leeds found themselves in 16th place. They had been knocked out of the Worthington Cup to Sheffield United and Malaga would then knock them out of the UEFA Cup on a sobering night at Elland Road.

Results did pick up over the Christmas and new year period due to the emergence of youngster James Milner, but disaster was to come in the newly formed January transfer window as Lee Bowyer, Jonathan Woodgate and Robbie Fowler were sold to West Ham United, Newcastle United and Manchester City respectively. Unfortunately, the relationship between chairman, Peter Ridsdale and Venables was strained to say the least. Venables galvanised the squad and they made it through to the last eight of the FA Cup before a weak surrender to Sheffield United once more. Following a defeat at home to Middlesbrough, Venables was gone, to be replaced by former Sunderland boss Peter Reid.

Terry Venables's first line up: Manchester City (H) 17 August 2002: Robinson, Mills, Harte, Matteo, Radebe, Bakke, Barmby (Seth Johnson), Bowyer, Kewell, Smith, Viduka (Keane). Subs not used: Martyn, Kelly, Dacourt.

Terry Venables's last line up: Middlesbrough (H) 15 March 2003: Robinson, Mills, Bravo, Lucic, Radebe, Bakke, Okon, Barmby (Milner), Wilcox, Smith, Viduka. Subs not used: Martyn, Harte, Kilgallon, McMaster.

PETER REID

First game in charge: Liverpool (A) 23 March 2003 (interim manager)
First game in charge: Newcastle United (H) 17 August 2003 (manager)
Last game in charge: Portsmouth (A) 8 November 2003
Games: 22
Won: 6
Drawn: 4
Lost: 12

With Leeds nervously looking over their shoulder and staring down the barrel of relegation, they turned to former Manchester City and Sunderland boss Peter Reid, who had been out of the game since the previous October following his sacking at the Stadium of Light.

Born in Huyton in Lancashire, Reid started his playing career at Bolton Wanderers, winning the Second Division title in season 1977-78. He joined Everton in 1982, winning the top flight twice in 1985 and 1987, the FA Cup in 1984 and the European Cup Winners' Cup in 1985. He could have been part of an historic treble in 1985 but lost the FA Cup Final to ten-men Manchester United. He had a spell at Queens Park Rangers before joining Manchester City in 1990. He was made caretaker-manager in November of that year following the departure of Howard Kendall back to Everton and took the role on a permanent contract later that month. He was sacked by City early on in season 1993-94 and joined Southampton as a player. He made his return to management with Sunderland in March 1995 and within 14 months had won promotion to the top flight with the Mackems.

Despite relegation in season 1996-97, they lost an enthralling play-off final to Charlton Athletic the following season, before winning the second tier with 105 points. He led the Black Cats to two top seven finishes before struggling in 2001-02 and finishing in 17th place. Reid was sacked after a 3-1 loss at Arsenal and joined Leeds in March 2003 as interim manager.

He saw the problems first hand in a 3-1 defeat at Anfield, but two weeks later Leeds returned to the form that had seen them reach the Champions League semi-finals with a magnificent 6-1 win away at Charlton Athletic in which Reid commented after the game, 'We looked like a decent side'. Results were still inconsistent and the spectre of relegation loomed large over the club. Despite a win over Fulham, thanks to a brace from Mark Viduka, results over the penultimate weekend of the season meant Leeds travelled to Highbury knowing only a win would secure safety. Leeds produced arguably their best performance in years to win 3-2 thanks to a late Viduka goal which meant they would see another season in the top flight.

He was handed the job on a permanent basis ahead of the 2003-04 season, but again money was tight and Harry Kewell was sold to Liverpool, so Reid had to rely on loans and free transfers. In came the likes of Jody Morris, Jermaine Pennant, Zoumana Camara, Didier Domi and Lamine Sakho. Leeds started the season in reasonable form, and after a 3-2 win at Middlesbrough Reid commented, 'Everybody wants to win a game, especially us. We hadn't a win in pre-season, this is our first win in a long time and it makes you feel good.' That was about as good as it got for Reid as Leeds lost all their league games in September without scoring and the high point

THE MANAGER

IT'S GOOD TO HAVE YOU ON

I'VE BEEN LOOKING FORWARD TO THIS AFTERNOON EVER SINCE I GOT THE PHONE CALL ASKING ME TO TAKE OVER AS MANAGER.

It has already been a hectic but enjoyable three weeks, topped by last Saturday's fantastic win at Charlton, but there is always something special about your first home game.

I've been aware of the Elland Road atmosphere as an opposing player and manager. Now I'm looking forward to having you on my side!

The fans were terrific at Anfield, where we didn't play well, and again at Charlton, and we need that support. We need your help. We need you to get behind every player and I'm sure they will respond to that.

ATTITUDE

I was delighted by the performance at Charlton. People always look at the goals - and there were some great goals and some good football - but I was more pleased by the attitude of the whole team.

From the very first minute we were in their faces making tackles. We didn't let them settle into their game at all.

For the first 15 minutes Charlton didn't get out of their half. And make no mistake that's a very good Charlton side, especially at home. The Valley is a very difficult place to go.

Alan Curbishley was disappointed with their performance but I think that was mainly because we didn't let them play.

What topped the lot for me was that in the last minute, when we were 6-1 up, our players were still

The management team lead the celebrations during the rout of Charlton

hunting the ball. That says it all. They never took the finger off the pulse for the 90 minutes and they got their reward.

BRIGHTNESS

People have asked me what we did to bring about such a dramatic change, but there's no magic wand. The players have done really well in training. We've been working hard, but everything has been short and sharp.

After the Liverpool game I said I thought they were feeling a bit sorry for themselves but to be fair to them, the training since then has been bright and breezy.

They don't get paid for doing it on the training ground; they get paid for what they do on a Saturday – or Sunday or Monday these days.

> **I WAS DELIGHTED BY THE PERFORMANCE AT CHARLTON. PEOPLE ALWAYS LOOK AT THE GOALS - AND THERE WERE SOME GREAT GOALS AND SOME GOOD FOOTBALL - BUT I WAS MORE PLEASED BY THE ATTITUDE OF THE WHOLE TEAM.**

I wanted them to take that brightness into the game and they did.

We worked hard from front to back and all the players helped each other out.

But we haven't done anything yet. We've won one game very well

8

---

would be goalkeeper Paul Robinson scoring a late equaliser in a League Cup tie at home to Swindon Town. Reid survived a vote of confidence and achieved his first home win against Blackburn thanks to a double from Seth Johnson, but the damage had been done. Following a 6-1 hammering at newly promoted Portsmouth, Reid was gone. He had further managerial

LEEDS v TOTTENHAM HOTSPUR 12.04.03

MY SIDE FOR A CHANGE!

but we need to do that for the next six, starting today.

It's important we tackle Tottenham in the same way. I watched them against Bolton and they've got a lot of quality in the

THE FANS WERE TERRIFIC AT ANFIELD, WHERE WE DIDN'T PLAY WELL, AND AGAIN AT CHARLTON, AND WE NEED THAT SUPPORT. WE NEED YOUR HELP. WE NEED YOU TO GET BEHIND EVERY PLAYER AND I'M SURE THEY WILL RESPOND TO THAT.

side. Everyone here knows how good Robbie Keane can be but they've also got people like Teddy Sheringham, Gus Poyet, and Darren Anderton who can influence a game.

LONG TERM

It will be good to see Glenn Hoddle and John Gorman again today but we know they will be doing everything they can to stop us in our tracks and we've got to make sure we have a great attitude again.

Another question I've been asked since I came here is what it is like to be manager for just eight games. The answer is that I'm not thinking about it like that.

I'm managing Leeds United the way I would if I'd been appointed for eight years.

I'm doing the job the way I see it. If it doesn't happen, then it doesn't happen, but

I'm going about the job as though it were a long-term appointment.

It's important that certain decisions are made, that plans are put in place for pre-season training, and I will be making my recommendations to the board on squad strengthening and things like that.

If someone else comes in, so be it, but until then I will do things the way I think they should be done for the good of the club.

Finally, I would like to thank everyone for the way they have made me so welcome.

Enjoy the game,

LEEDS UNITED on the internet: www.leedsunited.com

9

spells at Coventry City, the Thailand national side, Plymouth Argyle and Mumbai City.

Peter Reid's first line up (as interim manager): Liverpool (A) 23 March 2003: Robinson, Mills, Bravo (Harte), Lucic, Radebe, Bakke, Okon (McMaster), Barmby (Milner), Wilcox, Smith, Viduka. Subs not used: Martyn, Batty.

Peter Reid's first line up (as manager): Newcastle United (H) 17 August 2003: Robinson, Kelly, Matteo, Camara, Radebe, Morris, Seth Johnson, Wilcox (Batty), Smith, Viduka, Sakho. Subs not used: Martyn, Milner, Lennon.

Peter Reid's last line up: Portsmouth (A) 8 November 2003: Robinson, Kelly, Olembe, Matteo, Dubbery, Roque Junior (Bridges), Seth Johnson, Morris, Pennant (Sakho), Milner, Smith. Subs not used: Carson, Camara, Harte.

EDDIE GRAY MBE

First game in charge: Bolton Wanderers (H) 22 November 2003
Last game in charge: Charlton Athletic (H) 8 May 2004
Games: 26
Won: 6
Drawn: 7
Lost: 13

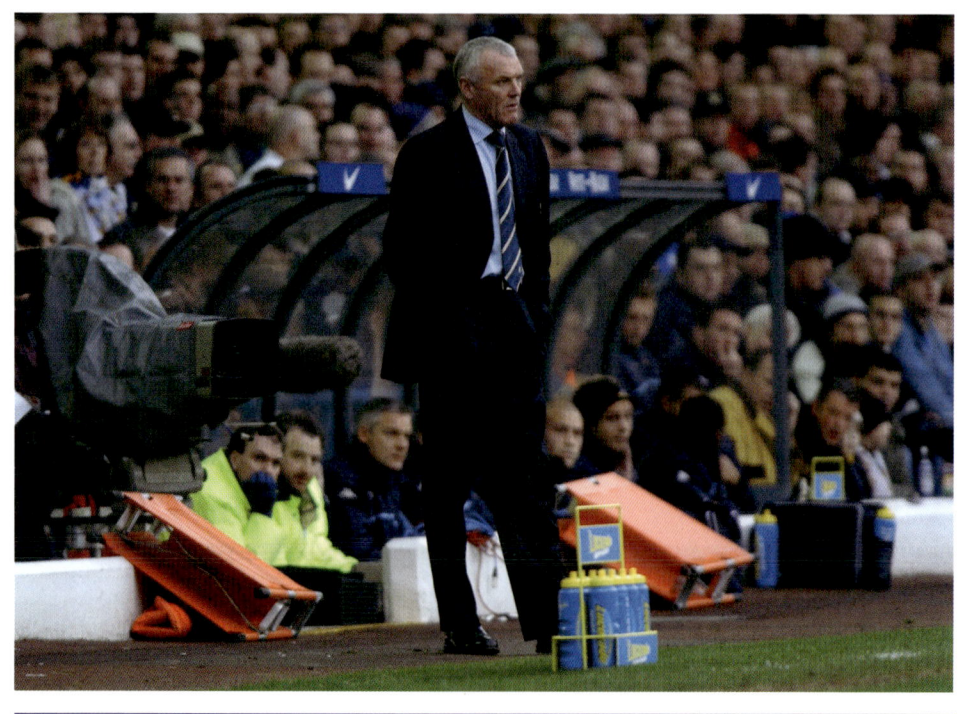

With the Whites starring down at Nationwide football for the first time since season 1989-90, they turned to a man who knew the club inside out and had seen all the ups and down in his first stint as a player and manager – step forward Eddie Gray. The Scotsman knew he was battling against the odds and he witnessed the problems the club had first hand following a dismal 2-0 home defeat against Bolton Wanderers the day England won the rugby union World Cup. After the game he said, 'I expected a better performance from them, but it didn't materialise. I didn't expect them to get beaten 2-0 at home.' Whatever Gray said and did on the training field that week, it had the desired impact and a James Milner goal away at Charlton Athletic earned the side only their third win of the season. A week later they took "moneybags" Chelsea all the way in an exciting 1-1 draw at Elland Road and eight days later,

THE MANAGER

Delighted to be back at this great club

I'M LOOKING FORWARD TO THIS AFTERNOON MORE THAN I'VE LOOKED FORWARD TO ANYTHING FOR SOME TIME.

Some people thought I was crazy agreeing to take over when Peter Reid left, but as I said to the players, I'm delighted to be back here because it's a great club. I've always liked the day-to-day business of being on the training ground and even though we have a lot of problems at the moment, I am just enjoying being back involved.

You can never tell what is going to happen in football, but however long I'm here as manager I am going to do what I think is right to get the team picking up points.

None of us has any illusions. Forget any problems off the pitch; you only have to look at the league table to know that we are not in a healthy situation.

I think the supporters have recognised that and have decided they will give everything they can.

Now it's up to the players to give them something back, to show them they are going to work their socks off to make sure Leeds United stay in the Premier League.

We have lost a lot of quality players since I was last really involved and that is bound to be a factor. Peter Reid had to do what he could by bringing in loan players, so we have a very new team here that is taking time to bed in.

MORALE

Of course events and results have an effect on players' morale and it seems open season on Leeds United at the moment. Every day there is something new.

I'd only been in the job one day when I picked up the paper and read that I'd squashed Mark Viduka's fine. The truth was that I hadn't even spoken to him about it.

That's how it seems to go at the moment, but we have to buckle down and concentrate on what we can affect – what happens on the field.

Partly that is down to attitude. I heard some people

4   www.leedsunited.com

BOLTON WANDERERS 22.11.03

We have to get it into our minds that nobody is going to come to Elland Road and have an easy time. Because of recent results, teams fancy their chances, but we have to dig deep and make sure they know this is not the place to come for an easy three points.

The big problem for our team is that we have been letting in too many goals. We've lost a lot of players who can score goals like Bowyer, Keane and Kewell, and you have to be realistic and say we are not going to get as many as we have in the past, so we have to stop conceding.

It's up to me to instil a bit of confidence and get the lads playing with belief in their ability. We've had some good training sessions. Occasionally they've run over and we've gone back in the afternoon for a bit more.

We've been working on our shape and most of all on keeping the ball. When things aren't going well the tendency is to try to make something happen quickly. Then you give the ball away. Every team in the Premiership has at least one player who can hurt you if you allow them too much of the ball.

EXPERIENCE

In our case it's Mark Viduka. Things obviously didn't work out between him and Peter but whatever that was all about, it's now up to me to get Mark playing again. If he is fit to play today, he will play.

I'm looking for our experienced people like Mark, Gary Kelly and David Batty to use their know-how to lead from the front and help the players around them play with confidence and to the best of their ability.

We know it's not going to be easy today against Bolton. They are always a hard side to beat and as well as a few injuries, we are without two of our most influential players, Dominic Matteo and Alan Smith.

That gives me some selection problems but we have to be positive. We are at home and this is our chance to show what we are made of.

I know we can count on your support and I promise that however long I am here, we will all be doing our best to make sure you enjoy being a Leeds United fan.

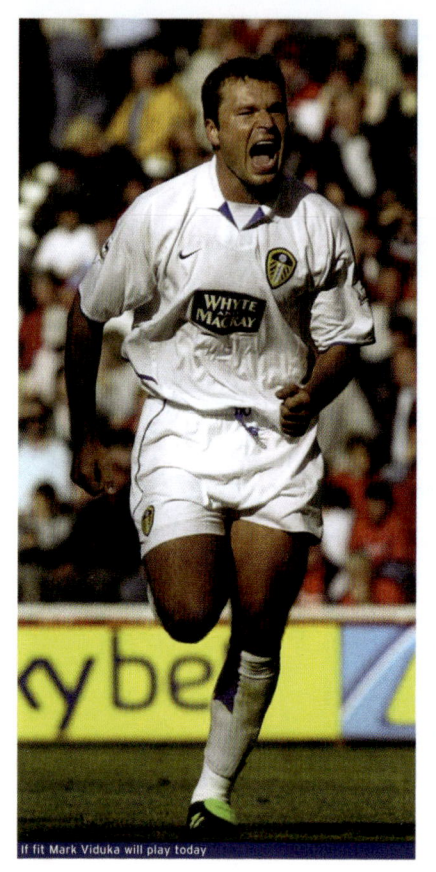

If fit Mark Viduka will play today

say that we couldn't expect to pick up any points last month because we were playing Arsenal, Liverpool and Manchester United.

I don't go along with that. We've still got to play them again, so are we going to write those games off as well?

Every time we play we have to go out and match the opposition. We've got to try and get results, especially at home. We've done that in the past and we've got to do it now.

5

in front of the Sky cameras, Gray made it seven points from nine with a late win at home to Fulham. Sadly that would be the last win for Leeds and Gray until a relegation six pointer at home to Wolverhampton Wanderers at Elland Road. Leeds produced a brilliant performance, winning 4-1, and suddenly the Whites were level on points at the bottom of the table with

350

their visitors. They followed this up with encouraging draws away at champions Manchester United and at home to Liverpool. A loss away at Fulham was followed up by a win over Manchester City, thanks to a penalty from Mark Viduka, but they lost again at Birmingham City. Gray then achieved back-to-back wins at home to Leicester City (3-2) and Blackburn Rovers (2-1) at Ewood Park, and all of sudden it looked like Leeds could pull off the great escape. However, three loses in the next four, which culminated in a 4-1 loss at Bolton, saw the side drop out of the top flight for the first time in 14 years. Gray parted company with the club for a second time after a 3-3 draw at home to Charlton Athletic in the penultimate game of an awful season.

Eddie Gray's first line up: Bolton Wanderers (H) 22 November 2003: Robinson, Camara, Harte, Radebe, Duberry, Batty (Chapuis), Seth Johnson (Barmby), Morris (Olembe), Milner, Viduka, Sakho. Subs not used: Carson, Domi.

Eddie Gray's last line up: Charlton Athletic (H) 8 May 2004: Robinson, Kelly (Wilcox), Harte, Kilgallon, Matteo, Duberry, McPhail, Richardson (Radebe), Pennant, Milner, Smith. Subs not used: Carson, Barmby, Winter.

KEVIN BLACKWELL

First game in charge: Chelsea (A) 15 May 2004 (as caretaker)
First game in charge: Derby County (H) 7 August 2004 (as permanent manager)
Last game in charge: Barnet (H) 19 September 2006
Games: 115
Won: 44
Drawn: 37
Lost: 34

Kevin Blackwell took on the role as caretaker for the last game in the Premier League away at Chelsea. He was given the task of rebuilding the side from square one: 'It was extremely difficult, the club had been in the Champions League semi-finals and every player had all but left. The first game against Derby, we were welcoming all the players, it took about six months to stabilise everything. The media had tipped us to go down, anything that could go wrong would. It was the worst financial state in the history of the club, they were £120 million in debt and we had to try and rebuild the club.'

Leeds started the season with a 1-0 win over Derby County thanks to a Frazer Richardson

AT LAST, THE MAIN EVENT!

This is what it has all been about. All the work of the summer has been leading to this moment – the start of a new season and a new era at Leeds United. I am delighted it is here at last. That is partly for selfish reasons. It has been a long and, at times, very hard summer and I'm hoping that many of the things I have had to concentrate on up to now will begin to fall away so we can concentrate even more on the football.

But the start of a new campaign is always a great occasion, a time of optimism and hope, a moment when we all feel that special buzz that only match day brings. We are probably something of an unknown quantity this season because we have sold some great players and the team that kicks off against Derby is totally unrecognisable from the one that finished at Chelsea.

It's a fresh start. We are putting the foundations back in place ready to go forward again. The sooner we do that the better.

Like everybody else my ambition is promotion. That's what we all want. But I am aware that we kick-off today with a team of players who have only played together in two full games. Before that many of them had not even met each other, let alone played together.

People in football say it takes two or three years to develop a team – we've had two or three weeks. So it's going to be a real test of everyone's patience – not least my own. I expect the team to develop more understanding as the season develops, to get better and stronger as a unit.

But we cannot allow ourselves to use the problems as excuses. We need to work hard from the very first whistle today. The fans have been exceptional in showing they appreciate what has been happening. The players have been delighted with the reception they've been given and I think the fans are starting to take to the players. I hope that traditional Leeds rapport will soon be at its strongest again because it will help the players settle quickly.

I'm confident we've made some good signings this summer. I didn't want to think short term by investing only in older players because that would leave the club in a position where we have to start all over again two years down the line. I've been trying to get a mixture so there are young players who will develop along with our talented home-grown youngsters like Frazer Richardson, Matthew Kilgallon, Aaron Lennon, Simon Walton and Scott Carson.

We've now got eight or nine challenging for first team places under the age of 23. We know we have to develop them but there is a lot of good potential there and I'll have no hesitation about playing them. But we also needed some older hands, like Paul Butler, who have been around and know what it takes to win at this level.

I was delighted Neil Sullivan decided to join us He will add that little bit of experience that we needed and provide a good role model for Scott Carson. Michael Ricketts is a proven goalscorer and has already scored on our trip to Sweden and at Hibs so I'm hoping he will be a real thorn in people's sides. Julian Joachim is only 29 and at the peak of his career. He overcame injury last season to finish with nine goals in 11 games. Eric Black was his manager at Coventry and he told me that if he got another job, Julian would

strike, and the new manager commented after the game, 'I think it was important because the side put together is brand new and the understanding and confidence can only come from winning games.' Blackwell was right in that it would take six months to rebuild the club from scratch. They were some high points, including a 4-2 win at Preston North End, in which new signing David Healy scored a brace against his former club, and a famous 6-1 win at home to Queens Park Rangers, in which Brian Deane scored four and had a fifth

JERMAINE WRIGHT REALLY EXCITES ME IN MIDFIELD. I HAD TO FIGHT VERY HARD WITH EVERTON TO GET HIM HERE AND I WAS DELIGHTED WHEN HE AGREED TO SIGN.

be the first player he would sign. You can't ask for a better reference than that. Jermaine Wright really excites me in midfield. I had to fight very hard with Everton to get him here and I was delighted when he agreed to sign.

But then I have been pleased with the reaction of all the players I have spoken to about joining us. Leeds is still a massively respected club round the country and players were eager to come here. They are hungry to do well. None of them mentioned money when we were talking and I know two of them took a pay cut when they came here.

We've had a busy pre-season that has gone very well and we have looked promising, especially given the problems we've had of constantly chopping and changing while we took a look at trialists. Even up to last weekend at Hibs, we were introducing new faces with Jermaine Wright and Neil Sullivan making their debuts. But now the turmoil of the summer is behind us, the pre-season is over and it's down to the real thing.

Thank you for the many good luck messages I've received and let's hope we are embarking on a season we can all enjoy.

kevinblackwell

ruled out for offside. 'The players were magnificent and we created the belief that we could stay in the league.' Leeds were struggling ahead of the Christmas period, but Blackwell led the side to three wins in four and up to 14th place. A takeover was then completed, with Ken Bates installed as chairman and there was stability at the football club. Blackwell finished his first season at the club in 14th and the following season saw the Whites in the top six from October onwards. Blackwell watched on as his side came back from 3-0 down to win at Southampton thanks to a late winner from the late Liam Miller. 'The Saints game made the players believe.' Leeds went on a run of eight wins in ten and, following a 2-1 win away at Crystal Palace at the start of March, looked set for a tilt at automatic promotion. A winless run of eight games saw the side miss out and end up in fifth place and a crack at the play-offs with a place in the Premier League at stake. Leeds drew the first leg in a packed Elland Road thanks to a free kick from former Preston man Eddie Lewis against his old club, and three days later they completed the job at Deepdale, with goals from Rob Hulse and Frazer Richardson. Sadly for Blackwell they lost out to Watford as they were outplayed in Cardiff, with the Hornets winning 3-0. Blackwell started his third season under pressure and with the club languishing in 23rd place and after a 1-0 defeat away at Coventry City he was sacked by the club.

Kevin Blackwell's first line up (as caretaker): Chelsea (A) 15 May 2004: Carson, Kelly, Harte, Radebe, Matteo, Dubbery, Richardson, Olembe (Barmby), Wilcox (Pennant), Milner, Smith. Subs not used: Allaway, Kilgallon, McPhail.

Kevin Blackwell's first line up (as manager): Derby County (H) 7 August 2004: Sullivan, Kelly, Kilgallon, Walton (Radebe), Butler, Duberry, Pugh, Richardson, Ricketts (Deane), Joachim, Wright. Subs not used: Carson, Crainey, Guppy.

Kevin Blackwell's last line up: Barnet (H): Sullivan, Kelly, Foxe, Kilgallon, Crainey, Nicholls (Derry), Stone (Howson), Douglas, Lewis, Blake, Horsfield (Moore). Subs not used: Westlake, Carole.

JOHN CARVER (CARETAKER)

First game in charge: Birmingham City (H) 23 September 2006
Last game in charge: Luton Town (A) 21 October 2006
Games: 5
Won: 1
Drawn: 0
Lost: 4

Following the dismissal of Blackwell after a League Cup win over Barnet, Leeds handed the role to Sir Bobby Robson's former assistant John Carver. Carver, who was born in Newcastle, was signed by his home-town club as an apprentice but never made his league debut, being released in 1985. He then spent a season in Wales, playing for Cardiff City before joining Gateshead as a semi-professional. His first job in management was as caretaker at Newcastle following the surprise sacking of Robson in August 2004. He oversaw a 3-0 win over Blackburn Rovers but left the club following the arrival of new manager Graeme Souness, who bought in his own staff. He was appointed first-team coach at Elland Road in July 2005 and helped Blackwell lead the side to the brink of promotion in 2006. He became caretaker following the departure of Blackwell and started with a thrilling 3-2 win over Birmingham

City at Elland Road, thanks to a late own goal from Olivier Tebily. He was quoted after the game: 'Going into the game against a side who are top of the league, full of confidence, only lost one game all season, to get off to a great start with a fantastic finish from David Healy, I'm absolutely delighted. I've made it my intention what I want to do and I think I've got off to a half-decent start, but I have to say it wasn't just about me. I've got fantastic staff behind me and this week they've been brilliant.' Sadly for Carver, things went wrong very quickly; they lost 4-2 at West Bromwich Albion, 4-0 at home Stoke City in an embarrassing performance, 2-1 at home to Leicester City and to top it off a 5-1 hammering away at Luton Town. Carver left the club two days later. He went on to manage Toronto FC, Sheffield United as caretaker, Newcastle United as an interim manager and Omonia in Cyprus.

John Carver's first line up: Birmingham City (H) 23 September 2006: Warner, Kelly, Butler, Kilgallon, Crainey, Derry (Stone), Douglas, Nicholls, Lewis (Westlake), Healy, Horsfield (Moore): Subs not used: Sullivan, Foxe

John Carver's last line up: Luton Town (A) 21 October 2006: Sullivan, Kelly, Foxe, Butler, Crainey, Westlake (Lewis), Douglas, Derry, A Johnson, Cresswell (Moore), Blake (Healy). Subs not used: Warner, Richardson.

CARETAKER MANAGER **JOHN CARVER**

WE MUST RE-GROUP AND FOCUS ON THE CHALLENGE AHEAD

It's back to the Championship this afternoon and hopefully we can continue where we left off by getting a win on Tuesday night.

Things have obviously happened since then – I've seen these situations before – but the main thing is that everyone re-groups and focuses fully on the challenge ahead of us. And that challenge is quite simple – winning football matches.

The 3-1 win against Barnet was obviously good from a confidence point of view because, no matter what the competition, when you have lost your last three games you want to get back to winning ways as soon as you can.

Barnet could have been a banana skin for us, but we were professional in the way we went about things – we treated them with respect – and, to borrow a well-known phrase from someone else, it was very much a case of job done.

It was all the more satisfying when I saw the results from elsewhere. Like the first round, a lot of the bigger teams suffered shock defeats or scraped their way through, and I think that puts these games into perspective a little bit. You have to give Barnet some credit as well because they didn't come here and put the shutters up. They had a go, particularly in the second half, and were a credit to themselves and their manager.

People talk about teams changing line-ups, and while we made quite a few, our starting line-up featured seven full internationals, one under-21 international and young substitute debutant Jonny Howson, who we as a club rate highly. That maybe shows the quality of players we have here, particularly as the injured lads start coming back.

The draw for the third round was made today and, by the time you are reading this we will hopefully be looking forward to a good draw against good opposition. The top end Premiership clubs come into the competition now so there are some good sides in there.

> *Our starting line-up featured seven full internationals, one under-21 international and young substitute debutant Jonny Howson, who we as a club rate highly.*

4   *Join the Leeds United Members Club, call 0845 121 1992*

Moving on to today, we were back out on the training ground on Thursday preparing for the game against Birmingham. In football you become used to changes and have to move with the flow. We all had a chat and then it was back to work at Thorp Arch. You can't dwell on things or look back. We have a big game this afternoon and that is the focus.

We were all bitterly disappointed against Sunderland in the last league game here, but felt there was an improvement at Coventry on Saturday when we maybe could have come away from the game with something to show for our efforts. The lads showed good spirit in the second half, they came back out a few minutes early at the break because they wanted to get straight back into it.

We were looking for a response after the Sunderland game and in the end we came close to Coventry but, as the old saying goes, we weren't close enough.

Birmingham come here this afternoon and, so far, they are living up to their credentials as one of the pre-season favourites for promotion. Steve Bruce kept the nucleus of his squad together and has added to it with players he believes can help him get back to the Premiership at the first attempt.

Birmingham did come unstuck at Cardiff, but given the way they have started the season that was no real surprise. Ninian Park can be a hard place to go at the best of times, but when they are top of the league and there's 20,000 plus in the ground, it's not the most inviting of places!

The biggest thing in the Championship so far, though, has been the inconsistent results that are flying about. There's nobody running away and looking invincible and there's been quite a few surprise results. It might be the old adage that anyone can beat anyone on their day. It certainly looks like that.

You only have to look at how tight the league table is from top to bottom to see that. A couple of wins can send you shooting up and a couple of defeats will see you shot down. It's still early days, but at this stage it looks like anyone's division.

From our point of view, today will be a tough game, but we wouldn't expect anything less from a team who were in the Premiership last season. We're looking forward to it. It's a challenge and a test, and that's what this game is all about.

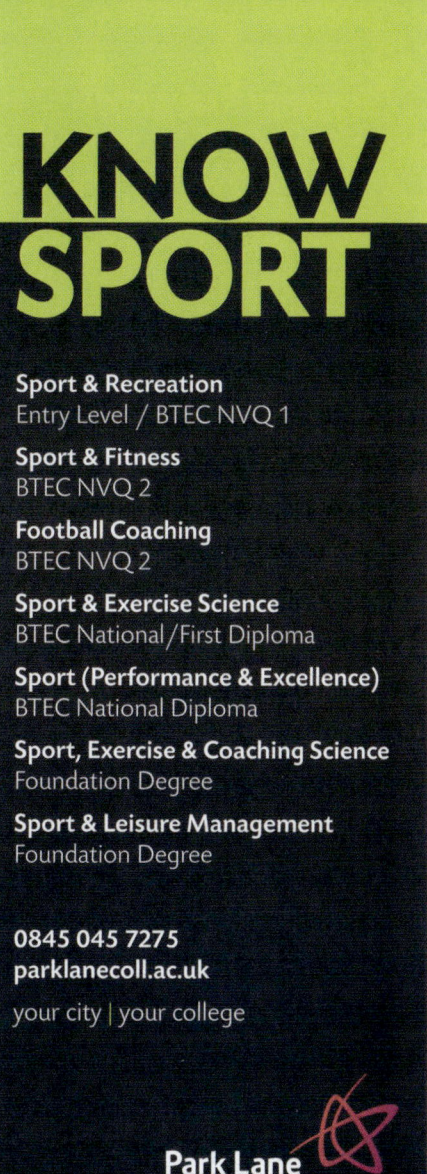

KNOW SPORT

Sport & Recreation
Entry Level / BTEC NVQ 1

Sport & Fitness
BTEC NVQ 2

Football Coaching
BTEC NVQ 2

Sport & Exercise Science
BTEC National/First Diploma

Sport (Performance & Excellence)
BTEC National Diploma

Sport, Exercise & Coaching Science
Foundation Degree

Sport & Leisure Management
Foundation Degree

0845 045 7275
parklanecoll.ac.uk

your city | your college

Park Lane
College Leeds

DAVE GEDDIS (CARETAKER)

First game in charge: Southend United (H) 24 October 2006
Last game in charge: Southend United (H) 24 October 2006
Games: 1
Won: 0
Drawn: 0
Lost: 1

Geddis took on the role for one game after John Carver had been dismissed following the 5-1 defeat at Luton Town and before Dennis Wise took over officially. Geddis, who was a former striker at clubs including Ipswich Town, Aston Villa, Barnsley and Birmingham City, took the team for a League Cup tie at home to Southend United, which they lost 3-1. He commented after the game, 'There are a lot of games to go in the league and realistically the play-offs are not a problem if they can raise their game. Momentum has to pick up sometime because it can't get any worse.'

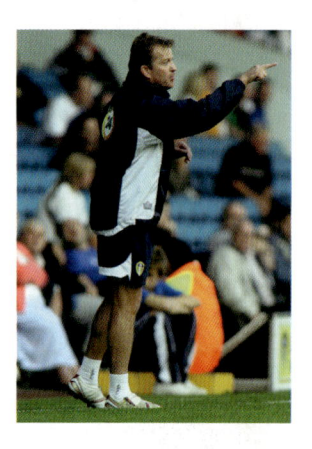

Dave Geddis's only line up: Southend United (H) 24 October 2006: Warner, Kelly, Butler, Kilgallon, Crainey (Cresswell), Douglas, Richardson, Westlake, Lewis (Bayly), Healy, Moore (Blake). Subs not used: Sullivan, Carole.

DENNIS WISE

First game in charge: Southend United (H) 28 October 2006
Last game in charge: Luton Town (A) 26 January 2008
Games: 68
Won: 30
Drawn: 12
Lost: 26

To many people's surprise, Leeds turned to former Chelsea player Dennis Wise to lift the doom and gloom around Elland Road. Wise had been part of the Blues side under Bates for 11 years and his former teammate Gus Poyet joined him as assistant manager.

Wise started his career at Wimbledon, being part of the infamous 'Crazy Gang', winning the 1988 FA Cup against overwhelming favourites Liverpool at Wembley. He joined Chelsea in July 1990 and was made captain at the start of the 1993-94 season. At Stamford Bridge he was an integral part of the side that won the FA Cup in 1997 and 2000, the League Cup in 1998, the Cup Winners' Cup in 1998, the Super Cup in 1998 and the Charity Shield in 2000. He left for Leicester City in 2001 before joining Millwall, first as a player then as a manager.

Wise led the side to the FA Cup Final in 2004 and European qualification. He left at the end of the 2004-05 season, joining Southampton as a player, and he then had a six-month spell at Coventry City.

   He was appointed manager of Swindon Town in May 2006, but his stay in Wiltshire was a short one as Leeds came calling in October of that year. He watched on as his new side lost 3-1 in a League Cup tie at home to Southend United, but just four days later he had a winning start against the same opposition thanks to goals from Ian Moore and Robbie Blake. 'I was more pleased about the clean sheet than anything because we've been leaking goals in the last few weeks and there were some tired legs. The whole team needs a lot of work but we are taking it a bit at a time.' Wise was right, Leeds results were inconsistent to say the least and following a 1-0 defeat away at Ipswich Town on 16 December they were 23rd in the Championship and looking like they were heading to League One. Wise did make changes in the January transfer window, bringing in Tore Andre Flo, Robbie Elliott, Alan Thompson and Armando Sa, but despite a morale boosting 2-1 win at Hull City they went bottom of the league following Southend's win at Birmingham City. The former Chelsea captain's stint at Elland Road had its problems, with rumours of a current player giving away his team selection before a game at home to Crystal Palace. 'I found that out and it disappoints me immensely and I told the players before, and he won't play for the club again.'

By the start of March Leeds were rock bottom and needed to go on a winning run. A victory over Luton Town helped, as did draws against Leicester City and Southend United (in which Leeds had a last-minute penalty appeal turned down), and on cold Friday night at the end of March man of the moment David Healy scored the winning goal at home to his former club Preston. 'We looked at it and we're very confident with the team we have now. It's maybe eight players different from the last time we played Preston.' They followed it up with an Easter Saturday win over Plymouth Argyle but were bought back down to earth two days later at Colchester United losing 2-1 at Layer Road. A 1-1 draw at home to Ipswich Town on 28 April 2007 meant Leeds would be starting the following campaign in the third tier of English football for the first time in their history. 'It's a sad enough day as it is.' The club were then put into administration, losing ten points and they ended up finishing bottom of the pile.

Wise and Poyet were both retained by the club but worse was to come, with the side deducted 15 points for irregularities and they were playing catch up from the off. Leeds knew they had to start like a house on fire and they did just that, winning their first seven league games, and on Boxing Day they were even top the table following a 1-1 draw at Hartlepool United. Wise won two Manager of the Month awards but rumours were abound that he was about to take up a new position at Premier League Newcastle United. Having lost his right-hand man in Poyet to Tottenham Hotspur, Wise did move to join the Toon Army as an executive director. He has never returned to football management.

Dennis Wise's first line up: Southend United (H) 28 October 2006: Stack, Kelly, Butler, Kilgallon, Lewis, Douglas, A Johnson (Westlake), Moore (Richardson), Healy (Blake), Cresswell. Subs not used: Warner, Foxe.

Dennis Wise's last line up: Luton Town (A) 26 January 2008: Ankergren, Richardson, Huntington, Kenton, Parker, Hughes, Prutton, B. Johnson, Sweeney (Westlake), Kandol, Beckford (Flo). Subs not used: Heath, Carole, Sorsa.

THE MANAGER **DENNIS WISE**

I WANT TO WIN...
AND I WANT TO WIN HERE

Welcome all to Elland Road for this afternoon's game against Southend United.

As you are all aware it's been a hectic week, but I have to say that I am simply delighted to be here. The same goes for Gus and Andy who have also joined the club from Swindon and together, with the existing staff, we will be giving our all to turn the situation at this great club.

I see the job as a real challenge and I have to admit as soon as I knew of the chairman's interest, I felt it was right. The club hasn't enjoyed the best of times in recent years – it's one of the most documented stories in football – and I'm looking forward to playing a part in turning things around.

I'm no under illusions about the size of the job or the expectations of the fans. I know a lot of people will already have their own perceptions about me (enough has been written and said!) but one thing I can say – and I'm sure you will all see this for yourselves in the coming weeks and months – I want to win. I'm not going to make daft promises, but believe me, I want to win, and I want to win here.

I watched Tuesday's game from the stand – thanks to the supporters who we met who wished us all the best – and started work officially on Wednesday morning. I watched the friendly against Sunderland and met the full squad for the first time that afternoon. I'm not going to go into the ins and outs of what was said, but the main thing I want is to see pride in the shirt.

This club's history is that of winning and competing at the highest level and that is what we all want to bring back here. From the legendary sides of the 60s through to the recent

> *As you will all probably be aware, I have already made some changes and will continue to do so as I assess things. Probably the biggest change so far is the changing of club captain. Kevin Nicholls will be our new captain, assisted by Shaun Derry who will lead the side in Nicko's absence.*

Kevin Nicholls has been handed the captain's armband by our new manager

Join the Leeds United Members Club, call 0845 121 1992

team of a few years ago, there's always been something about Leeds, and I want to see an edge about us.

As you will all probably be aware, I have already made some changes and will continue to do so as I assess things. Probably the biggest change so far is the changing of club captain. Kevin Nicholls will be our new captain, assisted by Shaun Derry who will lead the side in Nicko's absence. That is no slight on Paul Butler, who has captained the side for almost three years, it's simply a case of how I want to do things.

The chairman has been very supportive and will allow me to do what I think needs doing and what I believe is right. I'll look at the playing side and make my own decisions on that front as well. All the players start with a clean sheet and have to earn the right to wear the shirt. Those who are not with me will be shown the door.

The hardest thing about coming somewhere new is that your feet don't touch the ground. I don't think I've had a minute since Monday and I can't see that changing for the foreseeable future. In time, I hope to get to know people and will hopefully settle in the area.

Vinnie Jones has already been on at me telling what a brilliant city this so I can't wait to find out for myself. I also know that the support here can really be something else. It's not long ago I was coming here and playing in front of intimidating crowds who never let up on you. That's what I'd love to see here again.

I can tell you all – and this goes for a lot of players out there – Elland Road is not a place people used to look forward to going to. You knew you were in for a rough ride and it was all about character standing up to it. Is it like that now? I don't honestly know, but I want to get it back to being like that. I don't want teams to enjoy coming here or enjoy playing against Leeds!

For the moment, though, our first priority is getting away from where we are in the Coca-Cola Championship. League points are of the utmost importance starting this afternoon against Southend.

This a challenge I'm looking forward to and I hope you are too. Let's enjoy the ride, let's stick together and let's show them all that Leeds United are on the move again.

Dennis.

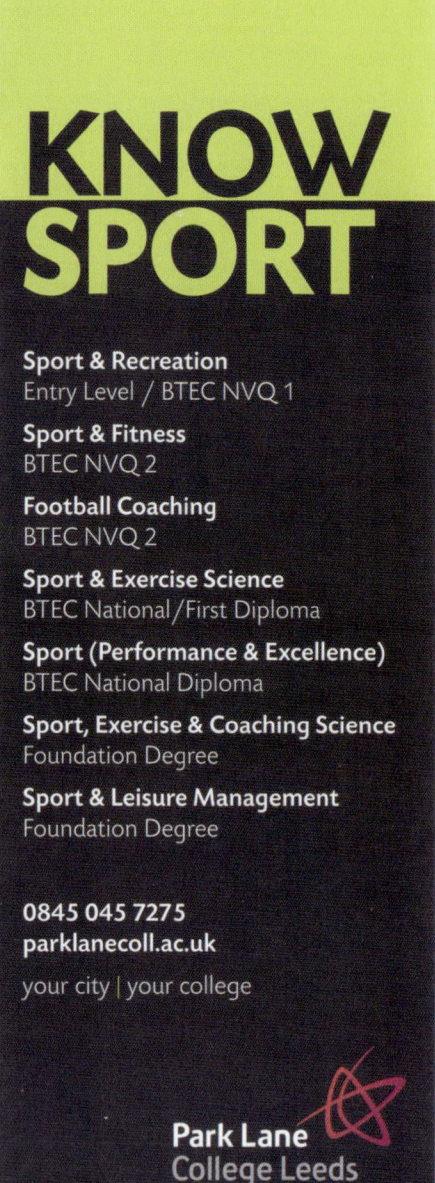

KNOW SPORT

Sport & Recreation
Entry Level / BTEC NVQ 1

Sport & Fitness
BTEC NVQ 2

Football Coaching
BTEC NVQ 2

Sport & Exercise Science
BTEC National/First Diploma

Sport (Performance & Excellence)
BTEC National Diploma

Sport, Exercise & Coaching Science
Foundation Degree

Sport & Leisure Management
Foundation Degree

0845 045 7275
parklanecoll.ac.uk

your city | your college

Park Lane College Leeds

Join the Leeds United Members Club, call 0845 121 1992

GWYN WILLIAMS (CARETAKER)

First game in charge: Southend United (A) 29 January 2008
Last game in charge: Southend United (A) 29 January 2008
Games: 1
Won: 0
Drawn: 0
Lost: 1

Technical director Gwyn Williams managed the side for one game following Dennis Wise's move to Newcastle United at the end of January 2008 and before Gary McAllister took the reins. Williams said after the loss at Roots Hall, 'It was disappointing. We started really well, created a couple of chances, but gave away a goal just before half-time. It was a needless free kick – Jermaine apologised in the dressing room at half-time. David Lucas saw it late and they finished it well. But the longer the game went on we were chasing. We huffed and puffed but didn't get to grips with it in the end.'

Gwyn Williams's only line up: Southend United (A) 29 January 2008: Ankergren, Richardson, Huntington, Kenton, Parker, Hughes, Prutton (Flo), B Johnson, Sweeney (Westlake), Kandol, Beckford (Flo): Subs not used: Heath, Howson.

GARY MCALLISTER MBE

First game in charge: Tranmere Rovers (H) 2 February 2008
Last game in charge: Milton Keynes Dons (A) 20 December 2008
Games: 50
Won: 25
Drawn: 8
Lost: 17

The question would be who would replace Wise, who left the club in fifth position in League One. They would turn to former title winner and captain Gary McAllister. Since leaving Leeds in 1996, McAllister joined Coventry City in the summer of 1996 and ended up playing under his former skipper Gordon Strachan at Highfield Road. Despite constant battles against the drops, McAllister was never relegated with the Sky Blues and joined Liverpool in July 2000. He proved to be an inspired signing at Anfield, helping the side to win an unprecedented cup treble, winning the Worthington Cup, the FA Cup and the UEFA Cup in his first season at the club. He left the red half of Merseyside to take up his first role in management at his former club Coventry in May 2002, but he left the side to care for his wife who was battling illness.

After almost four years out of the game, he returned to Elland Road, looking to carry on the work that former boss Dennis Wise had done in the first half of the campaign. McAllister had a difficult start, losing 2-0 at home to Tranmere Rovers: 'It's obvious there's work to be done. We've got a free week and we'll be spending a lot of time on the training ground.' It took till his fifth game to gain his first win, with striker Tresor Kandol scoring the winning goal. 'When you come back into the game after being out for a while, there's nothing like winning.'

Despite a surprising 2-1 home loss against Cheltenham Town and a 3-3 draw away at Port Vale, Leeds took 13 points from the next 15 available and ended up finishing in fifth place leading to a play-off match against Carlisle United. Leeds lost the first leg 2-1, but thanks to a goal deep into stoppage time from loan signing Dougie Freedman hopes were kept alive heading to Cumbria. Three days later, a brace from local boy Jonny Howson, with the second coming in the 90th minute, sent Leeds back to Wembley for the first time since 1996, when McAllister captained the side against Aston Villa in the League Cup Final.

Just like two years previously, Leeds seemed to freeze on the big stage and a James Hayter goal was enough to send Rovers up to the Championship and Leeds had to face the prospect of a second season in League One. McAllister said after the game, 'What I'm trying to impress on the guys in the dressing room is that myself and the coaching staff are very proud of them. Each individual should be proud of what they have done. To start the campaign with such a hefty handicap and get right to the final play-off match, they deserve to be applauded. They've continually picked themselves up and got on with it. It's simple. That group of players won 27 games, gained 91 points and barring the handicap would have been promoted.' Leeds responded in the summer by bringing in Andy Robinson from Swansea City (who was signed before the play-off final), Robert Snodgrass, Enoch Showunmi and an unknown striker called Luciano Becchio. Leeds were one of the pre-season favourites and produced some sparkling football, and following a 5-2 win over Crewe Alexandra McAllister said, 'we were clinical, we scored some good goals and I was pleased.' The boss saw the emergence of youngster Fabian Delph who was influential in a 3-0 win over Walsall at Elland Road. 'There were two fantastic goals from Fabian.' Unfortunately for McAllister, conceding goals from set pieces was an issue and they went on an awful run from the end of November through to the middle of December. They suffered an embarrassing cup defeat to non-league Histon and four consecutive league losses, which left the side in ninth place. With chairman Ken Bates in attendance at Stadium MK, McAllister's days were numbered and he was sacked a day later. He had a caretaker spell at Aston Villa following Gerard Houllier's illness and he is currently assistant to Steven Gerrard at Glasgow Rangers.

Gary McAllister's first line up: Tranmere Rovers (H) 2 February 2008: Lucas, Kenton (Carole), Michalik, Heath, Sheehan (Huntington), Hughes, Prutton, B. Johnson, Howson, Elding (Flo), Beckford. Subs not used: Martin, Sweeney.

Gary McAllister's last line up: Milton Keynes Dons (A) 20 December 2008: Lucas, Assoumani, Marques, Michalik (Richardson), Sheehan, Kilkenny, Delph, Douglas, Howson (Showunmi), Snodgrass, Becchio. Subs not used: Ankergren, Hughes, T. Elliott.

Gary Mac

I'm delighted to be back!

THE MANAGER

First things first. I'd just like to say how delighted I am to be back at Elland Road. There's no doubt I enjoyed my best years as a player here and to come back to the club once again is terrific. I couldn't wait to get started.

As you'll understand it's been a pretty hectic week. From receiving a telephone call on Sunday night, to meeting Shaun Harvey and the Chairman, to arriving at Thorp Arch for my first day in the job on Wednesday. Everything happened so quickly.

It's an unusual situation coming back here when the club is doing well. In January, managers usually come into jobs to pick up the pieces of failure, but what's gone here this season has been the talk of football, and we are well-placed in this division. Dennis and the players obviously deserve the credit for that.

My brief is to take us that extra mile now and go on and win promotion. That's the aim. And that's the message that I put across to the players when I met them for the first time. Everyone here has done well, now we have to kick on.

Results lately haven't been what people would have liked, or probably what people would have expected after such a terrific start, and we have to get back to winning matches. Hopefully I can fire up the lads a little, help get things back on track, and we can go on from there.

Gwyn Williams took charge of team affairs at Southend on Tuesday, and after that we immediately switched our attentions towards today's game against Tranmere. I know, from the start to the season and from the players that are here, that we have the potential to go on and finish the job that's been started.

We will give all our opponents the utmost respect, but we'll be focusing on what we can do and how we can win games.

There are a few butterflies as I write this, but that's only normal and you have to use that to your advantage. It will be a very proud moment for me today. This club has a proud history and having spent six years here as a player, living in Yorkshire, I'm excited about the prospect of what lies ahead.

The whole challenge is exciting, but I'm hoping we have some fun along the way, too.

A lot of people have asked me what my philosophy is. Well, I like to see football played in the right way. I like to pass the ball, but the most important thing is winning games.

We have to be brave and by that I mean getting in positions to receive the ball and taking responsibility.

The support here is obviously a big help and I know all about the support you can offer us. I can still remember the noise levels inside Elland Road – and away from here – from when I was a player. Teams never used to like coming here and I know it's been said before, but this place has to be a fortress for us.

Looking at the crowds this season, your support is still as strong as it always was, and I hope we can reward you. I'd just like to say thanks to the many of you have sent in messages of support. We all have to pull together, and together we can do this.

Last but not least I'd like to welcome Ronnie Moore and his Tranmere Rovers side to Elland Road. I've got to know Ronnie over the years and am expecting a good, competitive match from him.

Enjoy the game this afternoon and get behind the lads,

Gary

"I like to see football played in the right way. I like to pass the ball, but the most important thing is winning games"

Below: **The 12th man:** *"Looking at the crowds this season, your support is still as strong as it always was."*

www.co-star.co.uk
01423 340 066

LEEDS UNITED ON YOUR MOBILE... LEEDSUNITED.WAP.COM

SIMON GRAYSON

First game in charge: Leicester City (H) 26 December 2008
Last game in charge: Birmingham City (H) 31 January 2012
Games: 169
Won: 84
Drawn: 40
Lost: 45

It was a case of going from one former player to another as Leeds turned to Simon Grayson, who was appointed just before Christmas 2008. 'It was a club I had supported from a young age and it was a perfect opportunity for me. I was prepared to leave Blackpool and drop down a division. I needed to restore confidence with little steps.' A late Robert Snodgrass goal earned a share of the spoils in Grayson's first game against Leicester City and two days later he had a winning team thanks to a 3-1 win away at Stockport County. 'To get four points from the first two games is a good start. The players showed plenty of resolve and character.' Results were improving but there was a blip when they side slipped to a 2-0 defeat away at Hereford United. Everything that could go wrong did, it was very hurtful and we had a long discussion about attitude and desire.'

It proved to be the turning point as Leeds went on an unbeaten run of ten games, winning eight of them. Leeds again finished in the play-off places, meeting with Millwall. Leeds lost the first leg 1-0 at the Den thanks to a goal from Neil Harris, but hopes were high that they could turn it round in the second leg. Sadly for Leeds, and despite a goal from Luciano Becchio which bought the roof down at Elland Road, a strike from Djimi Abdou took the Lions to Wembley. Grayson said after, 'I thought we'd go on and get the winner, but now I'll sit down with the chairman. We had plans for Championship football and League One football, we know where we are with players and budgets. So we'll get over it, start again and give it a real good go for automatic promotion next season.' It would be prophetic words from Grayson as Leeds set off like a house on fire, winning their first six league games and topping the table after a 0-0 draw away at Southend United. They took Liverpool all the way in a League Cup tie towards the end of September and a 2-1 televised win over Norwich City kept them top of the pile thanks to a stoppage-time winners from Jermaine Beckford. They stayed top of the pile and on 3 January 2010 they produced one of the greatest upsets in FA Cup history as they defeated the Premier League Champions in their own backyard thanks to a winner from Beckford. 'We had 9,000 fans, we had to give them everything. We knew we could hurt them today and this signalled how well we've been playing all season. This win is for the fans, who have stuck by us in every game. Once again, they were great and they deserve this.' However, the win at Old Trafford seemed to have a detrimental effect on the League form: 'It was emotionally draining and it did affect us.' The side made it through to the latter stages of the Johnstone's Paint Trophy, only to lose to Carlisle United on penalties in the Northern Area Final. Leeds hit a rocky patch in March, losing four games on the bounce, but hit back with three straight wins. After a 1-0 loss at Charlton Athletic, Leeds went into the last game of the season at home to Bristol Rovers needing a win to secure promotion back to the Championship. Leeds being Leeds, they had to do things the hard way, Max Gradel was sent off for an alleged stamp on Daniel Jones: 'Jermaine had to get him off the pitch and I said to Jones good luck getting off the pitch.' Leeds went one down through a strike from Darryl Duffy, but hit back thanks to a brilliant goal from Jonny Howson, and it was left to captain for the day Beckford to win promotion in the 63rd minute.

Grayson had secured promotion in his first full season and attention quickly turned to life in the Championship. Leeds made a decent start back in the second tier and were in sixth

Simon Says...

"I'm not one for shouting about what we're looking to do – I prefer just to get things done"

First of all I'd like to take this opportunity to say a belated hello, and give my thanks for what was a terrific welcome at the Boxing Day game against Leicester City.

Returning to the club almost 20 years on from playing here it was a great feeling seeing over 33,000 people inside the ground, and it only further demonstrated what sort of club this is.

That game came at the end of what was one of the busiest weeks I have ever experienced in football. I came in here on the Tuesday, met the players and the staff for the first time in the afternoon, and then after two days training – on Christmas Eve and Christmas Day – we were straight into it against Leicester on Boxing Day.

We were joined by Ian "Dusty" Miller on Christmas Day and he is the first addition to the coaching staff. Ian is a good character who I know well and he brings a wealth of experience to the club.

I like to think I know what this club is all about and what it is looking to achieve. This club is in this division for a reason, but the one thing I can guarantee is that myself, my staff, and the players will be working very hard on a daily basis to try and get this football club back to where it belongs.

Looking back at that Leicester game, I thought the players showed a lot of character to come back and get a point against one of the best organised sides in this league. They stuck at it, and scoring so late in the game gave the feeling of a win rather than a draw. I actually felt if there had been longer left we would have gone on to win, but it was just the start we needed.

It gave the players a big lift in terms of confidence and, despite going an early goal down at Stockport a couple of days later, I thought we again showed good character and spirit. We played some good stuff at times, but just as importantly, we defended well when we came under pressure.

In this division you have to match your opponents and win the battle, and then hopefully our quality will come through in the games.

Coming in at this stage of the season isn't the time to start making radical changes. The single biggest thing is restoring a little bit of belief and confidence into the players, and making sure we get the basics right.

You start getting to know the players straight away, whether it's in training, matches, or even on the coach and at the hotel when we are away, and over the next few weeks I'll be looking at everyone and assessing strengths and weaknesses.

The transfer window is open and I'll make my own judgements on what needs to be done. I know the chairman likes to keep any business quiet and I like that. I'm not one for shouting about what we're looking to do – I prefer just to get things done. Actions speak louder than words!

Last, but by no means least, I'd like to welcome Greg Abbott and his Carlisle United side to Elland Road today. Hopefully we will have the backing of another great support, and we will be looking to build on the last two games.

There's still 23 games to go and it's all to play for and together, as a team and you the fans, we all have a part to play in making this club successful again.

Simon

LEEDS UNITED ON YOUR MOBILE... LEEDSUNITED.WAP.COM

---

place after a 2-1 win over Swansea City at the start of September. There was an extraordinary game that took place on Tuesday, 28 September 2010, with Leeds surrendering a 4-1 lead at home to Preston North End to somehow lose 6-4. 'I still had a go at the players at half-time, because we had given them far too many opportunities. When we were 4-1 up, we needed to be more professional but we gave them a chance to get back into the game. To lose 6-4 at home is unbelievable really, and embarrassing.' Leeds did bounce back to go on a 12-match unbeaten run that propelled the side into the play-off places. In that run was a 2-0 win over league leaders Queens Park Rangers thanks to a brace from Max Gradel. 'We were getting on a roll and were difficult to play against.' In the end away form cost the side a top six place as they finished in seventh.

It was a difficult summer for Leeds, but following a 3-0 win in front of the Sky Sports cameras against Doncaster Rovers, they moved up to fifth place. There was another horror show for Grayson as a Paul Rachubka disaster saw Blackpool win 5-0 at Elland Road in mid-November. Rachubka never played again for Leeds. Tragically for Grayson, the news of the death of his best friend Gary Speed shook everyone at Elland Road: 'It was on the Sunday, Alan Sutton [former physio] told me, I was stunned with what happened. On the Tuesday at Forest I left the team talk to Glyn Snodin and it was written that Snodgrass would score the opening goal.' Four days later, his former midfield colleagues Gordon Strachan, Gary McAllister and David Batty paid tribute to Speed at the home game against Millwall. Results fluctuated in the next few weeks, with another embarrassing visit to Barnsley as Leeds lost 4-1. Leeds showed their metal to bounce back with a late show at home to Burnley in a game which Grayson celebrated Ross McCormack's winning goal with a run down the West Stand touchline. Following a 4-1 defeat at home to Birmingham City on the final day of January in a game which Leeds started really well, Grayson was sacked and Neil Redfearn was placed in caretaker charge. He was close to coming back when Thomas Christiansen was sacked in February 2018, but the club went with Paul Heckingbottom.

Simon Grayson's first line up: Leicester City (H) 26 December 2008: Ankergren, Richardson, Marques, Sheehan, Prutton (Hughes), Douglas (Snodgrass), Delph, Robinson (Howson), Beckford, Becchio.

Simon Grayson's last line up: Birmingham City (H) 31 January 2012: Lonergan, Thompson, Lees, O'Dea, White, Clayton. Delph, Snodgrass, Townsend, McCormack, Becchio: Subs not used: M. Taylor, Bruce, Brown, Pugh, Nunez.

PREMIERSHIP

2000–01

Date	Opposition	Competition	Score
09/08/2000	1860 Munich	Champions League 3rd Qualifying Round 1st Leg	2-1
19/08/2000	Everton	Premiership	2-0
23/08/2000	1860 Munich	Champions League 3rd Qualifying Round 2nd Leg	1-0
26/08/2000	Middlesbrough	Premiership	2-1
05/09/2000	Manchester City	Premiership	1-2
09/09/2000	Coventry City	Premiership	0-0
13/09/2000	Barcelona	Champions League Phase 1 Group H	0-4
16/09/2000	Ipswich Town	Premiership	1-2
19/09/2000	AC Milan	Champions League Phase 1 Group H	1-0
23/09/2000	Derby County	Premiership	1-1
26/09/2000	Besiktas	Champions League Phase 1 Group H	6-0
30/09/2000	Tottenham Hotspur	Premiership	4-3
14/10/2000	Charlton Athletic	Premiership	3-1
18/10/2000	Besiktas	Champions League Phase 1 Group H	0-0
21/10/2000	Manchester United	Premiership	0-3
24/10/2000	Barcelona	Champions League Phase 1 Group H	1-1
29/10/2000	Bradford City	Premiership	1-1
31/10/2000	Tranmere Rovers	Worthington Cup 3rd Round	2-3
04/11/2000	Liverpool	Premiership	4-3
08/11/2000	AC Milan	Champions League Phase 1 Group H	1-1
12/11/2000	Chelsea	Premiership	1-1
18/11/2000	West Ham United	Premiership	0-1
22/11/2000	Real Madrid	Champions League Phase 2 Group D	0-2
26/11/2000	Arsenal	Premiership	1-0
02/12/2000	Leicester City	Premiership	1-3
05/12/2000	Lazio	Champions League Phase 2 Group D	1-0
09/12/2000	Southampton	Premiership	0-1
16/12/2000	Sunderland	Premiership	2-0
23/12/2000	Aston Villa	Premiership	1-2
26/12/2000	Newcastle United	Premiership	1-2
01/01/2001	Middlesbrough	Premiership	1-1
06/01/2001	Barnsley	FA Cup 3rd Round	1-0
13/01/2001	Manchester City	Premiership	4-0
20/01/2001	Newcastle United	Premiership	1-3
24/01/2001	Aston Villa	Premiership	2-1
27/01/2001	Liverpool	FA Cup 4th Round	0-2
31/01/2001	Coventry City	Premiership	1-0
03/02/2001	Ipswich Town	Premiership	2-1
07/02/2001	Everton	Premiership	2-2
10/02/2001	Derby County	Premiership	0-0
13/02/2001	Anderlecht	Champions League Phase 2 Group D	2-1
21/02/2001	Anderlecht	Champions League Phase 2 Group D	4-1
24/02/2001	Tottenham Hotspur	Premiership	2-1
03/03/2001	Manchester United	Premiership	1-1
06/03/2001	Real Madrid	Champions League Phase 2 Group D	2-3
14/03/2001	Lazio	Champions League Phase 2 Group D	3-3
17/03/2001	Charlton Athletic	Premiership	2-1
31/03/2001	Sunderland	Premiership	2-0
04/04/2001	Deportivo La Coruna	Champions League QF 1st Leg	3-0
07/04/2001	Southampton	Premiership	2-0
13/04/2001	Liverpool	Premiership	2-1
17/04/2001	Deportivo La Coruna	Champions League QF 2nd Leg	0-2
21/04/2001	West Ham United	Premiership	2-0
28/04/2001	Chelsea	Premiership	2-0
02/05/2001	Valencia	Champions League SF 1st Leg	0-0
05/05/2001	Arsenal	Premiership	1-2
08/05/2001	Valencia	Champions League SF 2nd Leg	0-3
13/05/2001	Bradford City	Premiership	6-1
19/05/2001	Leicester City	Premiership	3-1

Team	Pld	W	D	L	GF	GA	Pts
Manchester United	38	24	8	6	79	31	80
Arsenal	38	20	10	8	63	38	70
Liverpool	38	20	9	9	71	39	69
Leeds United	38	20	8	10	64	43	68
Ipswich Town	38	20	6	12	57	42	66
Chelsea	38	17	10	11	68	45	61
Sunderland	38	15	12	11	46	41	57
Aston Villa	38	13	15	10	46	43	54
Charlton Athletic	38	14	10	14	50	57	52
Southampton	38	14	10	14	40	48	52
Newcastle United	38	14	9	15	44	50	51
Tottenham Hotspur	38	13	10	15	47	54	49
Leicester City	38	14	6	18	39	51	48
Middlesbrough	38	9	15	14	44	44	42
West Ham United	38	10	12	16	45	50	42
Everton	38	11	9	18	45	59	42
Derby County	38	10	12	16	37	59	42
Manchester City	38	8	10	20	41	65	34
Coventry City	38	8	10	20	36	63	34
Bradford City	38	5	11	22	30	70	26

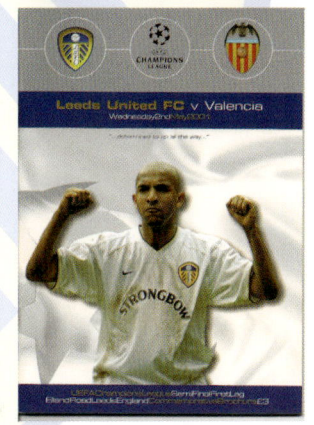

Only 138 Leeds United fans travelled to Besiktas following the tragic incident in Istanbul last April.

Tony Hackworth and Danny Hay both made their Leeds United debuts in the away game at Barcelona.

When Leeds United travelled to play Manchester United in October 2000, they had 11 players out injured. Martyn/ Mills/Radebe/Duberry/Harte/ Wilcox/Dacourt/Bakke/Battty/ Kewell/Bridges.

Alan Smith made his England debut v Mexico following an impressive season with Leeds United.

When Rio Ferdinand made his Leeds United debut away at Leicester, he was the only centre-back to finish the game.

2001–02

PREMIERSHIP

Team	Pld	W	D	L	GF	GA	Pts
Arsenal	38	26	9	3	79	36	87
Liverpool	38	24	8	6	67	30	80
Manchester United	38	24	5	9	87	45	77
Newcastle United	38	21	8	9	74	52	71
Leeds United	38	18	12	8	53	37	66
Chelsea	38	17	13	8	66	38	64
West Ham United	38	15	8	15	48	57	53
Aston Villa	38	12	14	12	46	47	50
Tottenham Hotspur	38	14	8	16	49	53	50
Blackburn Rovers	38	12	10	16	55	51	46
Southampton	38	12	9	17	46	54	45
Middlesbrough	38	12	9	17	35	47	45
Fulham	38	10	14	14	36	44	44
Charlton Athletic	38	10	14	14	38	49	44
Everton	38	11	10	17	45	57	43
Bolton Wanderers	38	9	13	16	44	62	40
Sunderland	38	10	10	18	29	51	40
Ipswich Town	38	9	9	20	41	64	36
Derby County	38	8	6	24	33	63	30
Leicester City	38	5	13	20	30	64	28

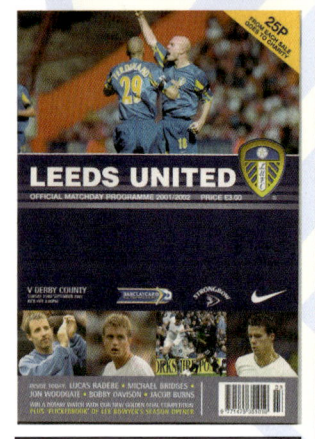

Date	Opposition	Competition	Score
18/08/2001	Southampton	Premiership	2-0
21/08/2001	Arsenal	Premiership	2-1
25/08/2001	West Ham United	Premiership	0-0
08/09/2001	Bolton Wanderers	Premiership	0-0
16/09/2001	Charlton Athletic	Premiership	2-0
20/09/2001	Maritimo	UEFA Cup 1st Round 1st Leg	0-1
23/09/2001	Derby County	Premiership	3-0
27/09/2001	Maritimo	UEFA Cup 1st Round 2nd Leg	3-0
30/09/2001	Ipswich Town	Premiership	2-1
09/10/2001	Leicester City	Worthington Cup 3rd Round	6-0
13/10/2001	Liverpool	Premiership	1-1
18/10/2001	Troyes	UEFA Cup 2nd Round 1st Leg	4-2
21/10/2001	Chelsea	Premiership	0-0
27/10/2001	Manchester United	Premiership	1-1
01/11/2001	Troyes	UEFA Cup 2nd Round 2nd Leg	2-3
04/11/2001	Tottenham Hotspur	Premiership	2-1
18/11/2001	Sunderland	Premiership	0-2
22/11/2001	Grasshoppers	UEFA Cup 3rd Round 1st Leg	2-1
25/11/2001	Aston Villa	Premiership	1-1
28/11/2001	Chelsea	Worthington Cup 4th Round	0-2
02/12/2001	Fulham	Premiership	0-0
06/12/2001	Grasshoppers	UEFA Cup 3rd Round 2nd Leg	2-2
09/12/2001	Blackburn Rovers	Premiership	2-1
16/12/2001	Leicester City	Premiership	2-2
19/12/2001	Everton	Premiership	3-2
22/12/2001	Newcastle United	Premiership	3-4
26/12/2001	Bolton Wanderers	Premiership	3-0
29/12/2001	Southampton	Premiership	1-0
01/01/2002	West Ham United	Premiership	3-0
06/01/2002	Cardiff City	FA Cup 3rd Round	1-2
12/01/2002	Newcastle United	Premiership	1-3
20/01/2002	Arsenal	Premiership	1-1
30/01/2002	Chelsea	Premiership	0-2
03/02/2002	Liverpool	Premiership	0-4
09/02/2002	Middlesbrough	Premiership	2-2
21/02/2002	PSV Eindhoven	UEFA Cup 4th Round 1st Leg	0-0
24/02/2002	Charlton Athletic	Premiership	0-0
28/02/2002	PSV Eindhoven	UEFA Cup 4th Round 2nd Leg	0-1
03/03/2002	Everton	Premiership	0-0
06/03/2002	Ipswich Town	Premiership	2-0
17/03/2002	Blackburn Rovers	Premiership	3-1
23/03/2002	Leicester City	Premiership	2-0
30/03/2002	Manchester United	Premiership	3-4
01/04/2002	Tottenham Hotspur	Premiership	1-2
07/04/2002	Sunderland	Premiership	2-0
13/04/2002	Aston Villa	Premiership	1-0
20/04/2002	Fulham	Premiership	0-1
27/04/2002	Derby County	Premiership	1-0
11/05/2002	Middlesbrough	Premiership	1-0

Leeds were the last Premiership side to lose their unbeaten record, following their 2-0 defeat at Sunderland in November.

For the second time in two seasons, Leeds had two players sent off in a game, this time at Arsenal, with Lee Bowyer and Danny Mills seeing red.

Newcastle United were the only side to do the double over Leeds in the space of three weeks, 4-3 at Elland Road and 3-1 at St James Park.

Leeds had two hat-tricks both from Robbie's (Keane at Leicester) and (Fowler at Bolton), both were whilst Leeds played in yellow.

Leeds were unbeaten in the blue/yellow away kit, winning at Arsenal and Charlton Athletic and drawing at Manchester United.

PREMIERSHIP

2002–03

Date	Opposition	Competition	Score
17/08/2002	Manchester City	Premiership	3-0
24/08/2002	West Bromwich Albion	Premiership	3-1
28/08/2002	Sunderland	Premiership	0-1
31/08/2002	Birmingham City	Premiership	1-2
11/09/2002	Newcastle United	Premiership	2-0
14/09/2002	Manchester United	Premiership	1-0
19/09/2002	Metalurg Zaporizhia	UEFA Cup 1st Round 1st Leg	1-0
22/09/2002	Blackburn Rovers	Premiership	0-1
28/09/2002	Arsenal	Premiership	1-4
03/10/2002	Metalurg Zaporizhia	UEFA Cup 1st Round 2nd Leg	1-1
06/10/2002	Aston Villa	Premiership	0-0
19/10/2002	Liverpool	Premiership	0-1
26/10/2002	Middlesbrough	Premiership	2-2
31/10/2002	Hapoel Tel Aviv	UEFA Cup 2nd Round 1st Leg	1-0
03/11/2002	Everton	Premiership	0-1
06/11/2002	Sheffield United	Worthington Cup 3rd Round	1-2
10/11/2012	West Ham United	Premiership	4-3
14/11/2002	Hapoel Tel Aviv	UEFA Cup 2nd Round 2nd Leg at the Artemio Franchi Stadium	4-1
17/11/2002	Bolton Wanderers	Premiership	2-4
24/11/2002	Tottenham Hotspur	Premiership	0-2
28/11/2002	Malaga	UEFA Cup 3rd Round 1st Leg	0-0
01/12/2002	Charlton Athletic	Premiership	1-2
07/12/2002	Fulham	Premiership	0-1
12/12/2002	Malaga	UEFA Cup 3rd Round 2nd Leg	1-2
16/12/2002	Bolton Wanderers	Premiership	3-0
21/12/2002	Southampton	Premiership	1-1
26/12/2002	Sunderland	Premiership	2-1
28/12/2002	Chelsea	Premiership	2-0
01/01/2003	Birmingham City	Premiership	2-0
04/01/2003	Scunthorpe United	FA Cup 3rd Round	2-0
11/01/2003	Manchester City		1-2
18/01/2003	West Bromwich Albion	Premiership	0-0
25/01/2003	Gillingham	FA Cup 4th Round	1-1
28/01/2003	Chelsea	Premiership	2-3
01/02/2003	Everton	Premiership	0-2
04/02/2003	Gillingham	FA Cup 4th Round Replay	2-1
08/02/2003	West Ham United	Premiership	1-0
16/02/2003	Crystal Palace	FA Cup 5th Round	2-1
22/02/2003	Newcastle United	Premiership	0-3
05/03/2003	Manchester United	Premiership	1-2
09/03/2003	Sheffield United	FA Cup QF	0-1
15/03/2003	Middlesbrough	Premiership	2-3
23/03/2003	Liverpool	Premiership	1-3
05/04/2003	Charlton Athletic	Premiership	6-1
12/04/2003	Tottenham Hotspur	Premiership	2-2
19/04/2003	Southampton	Premiership	2-3
22/04/2003	Fulham	Premiership	2-0
26/04/2003	Blackburn Rovers	Premiership	2-3
11/05/2003	Aston Villa	Premiership	3-1

Team	Pld	W	D	L	GF	GA	Pts
Manchester United	38	25	8	5	74	34	83
Arsenal	38	23	9	6	85	42	78
Newcastle United	38	21	6	11	63	48	69
Chelsea	38	19	10	9	68	38	67
Liverpool	38	18	10	10	61	41	64
Blackburn Rovers	38	16	12	10	52	43	60
Everton	38	17	8	13	48	49	59
Southampton	38	13	13	12	43	46	52
Manchester City	38	15	6	17	47	54	51
Tottenham Hotspur	38	14	8	16	51	62	50
Middlesbrough	38	13	10	15	48	44	49
Charlton Athletic	38	14	7	17	45	56	49
Birmingham City	38	13	9	16	41	49	48
Fulham	38	13	9	16	41	50	48
Leeds United	38	14	5	19	58	57	47
Aston Villa	38	12	9	17	42	47	45
Bolton Wanderers	38	10	14	14	41	51	44
West Ham United	38	10	12	16	42	59	42
West Bromwich Albion	38	6	8	24	29	65	26
Sunderland	38	4	7	27	21	65	19

Leeds beat Manchester United for the first time in five seasons thanks to a Harry Kewell header in September 2002.

Jamie McMaster become the fourth Australian to make his debut for the club following Harrry Kewell, Mark Viduka and Jacob Burns.

When James Milner scored away at Sunderland, he became the youngest-ever goalscorer in the Premier League, beating Wayne Rooney in the process.

Professor John Mckenzie took over the reins of chairman of the football club following the departure of Peter Ridsdale.

Mark Viduka single-handedly kept Leeds in the Premier League with 14 goals in his last ten game of the season.

373

2003–04

PREMIERSHIP

Team	Pld	W	D	L	GF	GA	Pts
Arsenal	38	26	12	0	73	26	90
Chelsea	38	24	7	7	67	30	79
Manchester United	38	23	6	9	64	35	75
Liverpool	38	16	12	10	55	37	60
Newcastle United	38	13	17	8	52	40	56
Aston Villa	38	15	11	12	48	44	56
Charlton Athletic	38	14	11	13	51	51	53
Bolton Wanderers	38	14	11	13	48	56	53
Fulham	38	14	10	14	52	46	52
Birmingham City	38	12	14	12	43	48	50
Middlesbrough	38	13	9	16	44	52	48
Southampton	38	12	11	15	44	45	47
Portsmouth	38	12	9	17	47	54	45
Tottenham Hotspur	38	13	6	19	47	57	45
Blackburn Rovers	38	12	8	18	51	59	44
Manchester City	38	9	14	15	55	54	41
Everton	38	9	12	17	45	57	39
Leicester City	38	6	15	17	48	65	33
Leeds United	38	8	9	21	40	79	33
Wolverhampton W	38	7	12	19	38	77	33

Date	Opposition	Competition	Score
17/08/2003	Newcastle United	Premiership	2-2
23/08/2003	Tottenham Hotspur	Premiership	1-2
26/08/2003	Southampton	Premiership	0-0
30/08/2003	Middlesbrough	Premiership	3-2
15/09/2003	Leicester City	Premiership	0-4
20/09/2003	Birmingham City	Premiership	0-2
24/09/2003	Swindon Town	Carling Cup 2nd Round	2-2 (4-3 ON PENS)
28/09/2003	Everton	Premiership	0-4
04/10/2003	Blackburn Rovers	Premiership	2-1
18/10/2003	Manchester United	Premiership	0-1
25/10/2003	Liverpool	Premiership	1-3
28/10/2003	Manchester United	Carling Cup 3rd Round	2-3
01/11/2003	Arsenal	Premiership	1-4
08/11/2003	Portsmouth	Premiership	1-6
22/11/2003	Bolton Wanderers	Premiership	0-2
29/11/2003	Charlton Athletic	Premiership	1-0
06/12/2003	Chelsea	Premiership	1-1
14/12/2003	Fulham	Premiership	3-2
22/12/2003	Manchester City	Premiership	1-1
26/12/2003	Aston Villa	Premiership	0-0
28/12/2003	Wolverhampton Wanderers	Premiership	1-3
04/01/2004	Arsenal	FA Cup 3rd Round	1-4
07/01/2004	Newcastle United	Premiership	0-1
10/01/2004	Tottenham Hotspur	Premiership	0-1
17/01/2004	Southampton	Premiership	1-2
31/01/2004	Middlesbrough	Premiership	0-3
07/02/2004	Aston Villa	Premiership	0-2
10/02/2004	Wolverhampton Wanderers	Premiership	4-1
21/02/2004	Manchester United	Premiership	1-1
29/04/2004	Liverpool	Premiership	2-2
13/03/2004	Fulham	Premiership	0-2
22/03/2004	Manchester City	Premiership	2-1
27/03/2004	Birmingham City	Premiership	1-4
05/04/2004	Leicester City	Premiership	3-2
10/04/2004	Blackburn Rovers	Premiership	2-1
13/04/2004	Everton	Premiership	1-1
16/04/2004	Arsenal	Premiership	0-5
25/04/2004	Portsmouth	Premiership	1-2
02/05/2004	Bolton Wanderers	Premiership	1-4
08/05/2005	Charlton Athletic	Premiership	3-3
15/05/2004	Chelsea	Premiership	0-1

Leeds started the season in decent form, finding themselves 11th at the end of August.

When Paul Robinson scored at home to Swindon Town, he became the first-ever goalkeeper to do so for Leeds.

When Dominic Matteo scored at home to Fulham it was his first goal for the Whites since that night at AC Milan.

When Michael Duberry scored at home to Fulham it was his first goal for the side since May 2000.

Leeds achieved only one double, against Blackburn Rovers winning both games 2-1.

374

CHAMPIONSHIP

2004–05

Date	Opposition	Competition	Score
07/08/2004	**Derby County**	**Championship**	**1-0**
10/08/2004	Gillingham	Championship	1-2
14/08/2004	Wolverhampton Wanderers	Championship	0-0
21/08/2004	**Nottingham Forest**	**Championship**	**1-1**
24/08/2004	**Huddersfield Town**	**Carling Cup 1st Round**	**1-0**
29/08/2004	Sheffield United	Championship	0-2
11/09/2004	**Coventry City**	**Championship**	**3-0**
14/09/2004	Plymouth Argyle	Championship	1-0
18/09/2004	Crewe Alexandra	Championship	2-2
21/09/2004	**Swindon Town**	**Carling Cup 2nd Round**	**1-0**
24/09/2004	**Sunderland**	**Championship**	**0-1**
28/09/2004	**Stoke City**	**Championship**	**0-0**
02/10/2004	Cardiff City	Championship	0-0
16/10/2004	**Preston North End**	**Championship**	**1-0**
19/10/2004	Reading	Championship	1-1
23/10/2004	Brighton & Hove Albion	Championship	0-1
26/10/2004	Portsmouth	Carling Cup 3rd Round	1-2
31/10/2004	**Wigan Athletic**	**Championship**	**0-2**
03/11/2004	**Burnley**	**Championship**	**1-2**
06/11/2004	Preston North End	Championship	4-2
13/11/2004	Ipswich Town	Championship	0-1
20/11/2004	**Queens Park Rangers**	**Championship**	**6-1**
24/11/2004	**Watford**	**Championship**	**2-2**
29/11/2004	Rotherham United	Championship	0-1
04/12/2004	**Leicester City**	**Championship**	**0-2**
10/12/2004	West Ham United	Championship	1-1
19/12/2004	**Millwall**	**Championship**	**1-1**
26/12/2004	Sunderland	Championship	3-2
28/12/2004	**Plymouth Argyle**	**Championship**	**2-1**
01/01/2005	**Crewe Alexandra**	**Championship**	**0-2**
03/01/2005	Coventry City	Championship	2-1
08/01/2005	Birmingham City	FA Cup 3rd Round	0-3
15/01/2005	**Cardiff City**	**Championship**	**1-1**
22/01/2005	Stoke City	Championship	1-0
26/01/2005	Derby County	Championship	0-2
29/01/2005	**Brighton & Hove Albion**	**Championship**	**1-1**
05/02/2005	Burnley	Championship	1-0
12/02/2005	**Reading**	**Championship**	**3-1**
19/02/2005	Wigan Athletic	Championship	0-3
26/02/2005	**West Ham United**	**Championship**	**2-1**
06/03/2005	Millwall	Championship	1-1
12/03/2005	**Gillingham**	**Championship**	**1-1**
16/03/2005	Nottingham Forest	Championship	0-0
02/04/2005	**Wolverhampton Wanderers**	**Championship**	**1-1**
05/04/2005	**Sheffield United**	**Championship**	**0-4**
09/04/2005	Watford	Championship	2-1
16/04/2005	Queens Park Rangers	Championship	1-1
23/04/2005	**Ipswich Town**	**Championship**	**1-1**
01/05/2005	Leicester City	Championship	0-2
08/05/2005	**Rotherham United**	**Championship**	**0-0**

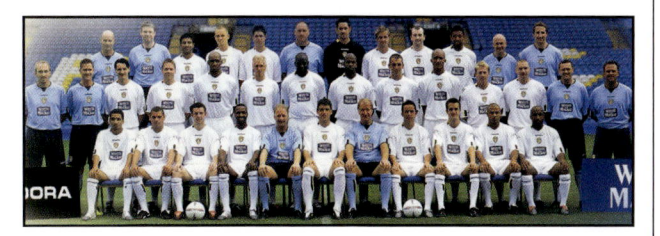

Team	Pld	W	D	L	GF	GA	Pts
Sunderland	46	29	7	10	76	41	94
Wigan Athletic	46	25	12	9	79	35	87
Ipswich Town	46	24	13	9	85	56	85
Derby County	46	22	10	14	71	60	76
Preston North End	46	21	12	13	67	58	75
West Ham United	46	21	10	15	66	56	73
Reading	46	19	13	14	51	44	70
Sheffield United	46	18	13	15	57	56	67
Wolverhampton W	46	15	21	10	72	59	66
Millwall	46	18	12	16	51	45	66
Queen's Park Rangers	46	17	11	18	54	58	62
Stoke City	46	17	10	19	36	38	61
Burnley	46	15	15	16	38	39	60
Leeds United	46	14	18	14	49	52	60
Leicester City	46	12	21	13	49	46	57
Cardiff City	46	13	15	18	48	51	54
Plymouth Argyle	46	14	11	21	52	64	53
Watford	46	12	16	18	52	59	52
Coventry City	46	13	13	20	61	73	52
Brighton & Hove Albion	46	13	12	21	40	65	51
Crewe Alexandra	46	12	14	20	66	86	50
Gillingham	46	12	14	20	45	66	50
Nottingham Forest	46	9	17	20	42	66	44
Rotherham United	46	5	14	27	35	69	29

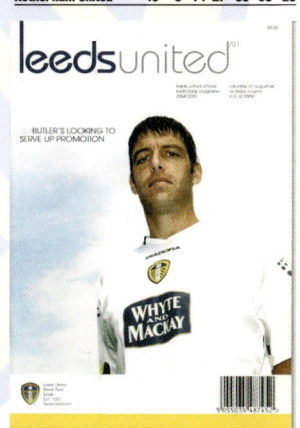

Leeds had seven debutants in the starting XI at home to Derby, with a second debutant in Brian Deane coming off the bench.

Leeds made their first-ever visits to Gresty Road, Madjeski Stadium, Withdean Stadium, JJB Stadium and The Den.

Leeds named five different goalkeepers this season, with Neil Sullivan an ever-present. Scott Carson, Paul Harrison, Kevin Pressman and Sasa Ilic unused on the bench.

Leeds handed squad numbers to an astonishing 47 players.

Included in those squad numbers were four different number 14s, Serge Branco, John Oster, Leandre Griffit and Marlon King.

2005–06

CHAMPIONSHIP

Team	Pld	W	D	L	GF	GA	Pts
Reading	46	31	13	2	99	32	106
Sheffield United	46	26	12	8	76	46	90
Watford	46	22	15	9	77	53	81
Preston North End	46	20	20	6	59	30	80
Leeds United	46	21	15	10	57	38	78
Crystal Palace	46	21	12	13	67	48	75
Wolverhampton W	46	16	19	11	50	42	67
Coventry City	46	16	15	15	62	65	63
Norwich City	46	18	8	20	56	65	62
Luton Town	46	17	10	19	66	67	61
Cardiff City	46	16	12	18	58	59	60
Southampton	46	13	19	14	49	50	58
Stoke City	46	17	7	22	54	63	58
Plymouth Argyle	46	13	17	16	39	46	56
Ipswich Town	46	14	14	18	53	66	56
Leicester City	46	13	15	18	51	59	54
Burnley	46	14	12	20	46	54	54
Hull City	46	12	16	18	49	55	52
Sheffield Wednesday	46	13	13	20	39	52	52
Derby County	46	10	20	16	53	67	50
Queen's Park Rangers	46	12	14	20	50	65	50
Crewe Alexandra	46	9	15	22	57	86	42
Millwall	46	8	16	22	35	62	40
Brighton & Hove Albion	46	7	17	22	39	71	38

Date	Opposition	Competition	Score
07/08/2005	Millwall	Championship	2-1
09/08/2005	Cardiff City	Championship	1-2
13/08/2005	Luton Town	Championship	0-0
20/08/2005	Wolverhampton Wanderers	Championship	2-0
23/08/2005	Oldham Athletic	Carling Cup 1st Round	2-0
27/08/2005	Norwich City	Championship	1-0
10/09/2005	Brighton & Hove Albion	Championship	3-3
13/09/2005	Sheffield Wednesday	Championship	0-1
17/09/2005	Queens Park Rangers	Championship	1-0
20/09/2005	Rotherham United	Carling Cup 2nd Round	2-0
24/09/2005	Ipswich Town	Championship	0-2
28/09/2005	Derby County	Championship	3-1
01/10/2005	Watford	Championship	0-0
15/10/2005	Burnley	Championship	2-1
18/10/2005	Southampton	Championship	2-1
21/10/2005	Sheffield United	Championship	1-1
25/10/2005	Blackburn Rovers	Carling Cup 3rd Round	0-3
29/10/2005	Reading	Championship	1-1
01/11/2005	Crewe Alexandra	Championship	0-1
05/11/2005	Preston North End	Championship	0-0
19/11/2005	Southampton	Championship	4-3
22/11/2005	Burnley	Championship	2-0
26/11/2005	Millwall	Championship	1-0
03/12/2005	Leicester City	Championship	2-1
10/12/2005	Cardiff City	Championship	0-1
17/12/2005	Wolverhampton Wanderers	Championship	0-1
26/12/2005	Coventry City	Championship	3-1
28/12/2005	Stoke City	Championship	1-0
31/12/2005	Hull City	Championship	2-0
02/01/2006	Plymouth Argyle	Championship	3-0
07/01/2006	Wigan Athletic	FA Cup 3rd Round	1-1
14/01/2006	Brighton & Hove Albion	Championship	1-2
17/01/2006	Wigan Athletic	FA Cup 3rd Round Replay	3-3 (2-4 on pens)
21/01/2006	Sheffield Wednesday	Championship	3-0
31/01/2006	Ipswich Town	Championship	1-1
04/02/2006	Queens Park Rangers	Championship	2-0
11/02/2006	Derby County	Championship	0-0
14/02/2006	Watford	Championship	2-1
18/02/2006	Leicester City	Championship	1-1
25/02/2006	Luton Town	Championship	2-1
04/03/2006	Crystal Palace	Championship	2-1
11/03/2006	Norwich City	Championship	2-2
18/03/2006	Coventry City	Championship	1-1
21/03/2006	Crystal Palace	Championship	0-1
25/03/2006	Stoke City	Championship	0-0
01/04/2006	Hull City	Championship	0-1
08/04/2006	Plymouth Argyle	Championship	0-0
15/04/2006	Reading	Championship	1-1
18/04/2006	Sheffield United	Championship	1-1
22/04/2006	Crewe Alexandra	Championship	1-0
30/04/2006	Preston North End	Championship	0-2
05/05/2006	Preston North End	Championship Play Off SF 1st Leg	1-1
08/05/2006	Preston North End	Championship Play Off SF 2nd Leg	2-0
21/05/2006	Watford	Championship Play Off Final	0-3

at the Millennium Stadium

David Healy scored his first goal for the club since February with a brace on day one.

Leeds had four different penalty takers, all four strikers took spot kicks, David Healy, Richard Cresswell, Rob Hulse and Robbie Blake.

After beating Leicester City at Elland Road in December, Leeds achieved four straight league wins for only the second time since the start of the 2000-01 season.

Leeds were involved in a penalty shoot-out in the FA Cup for the first time in the club's history when they drew 3-3 in a third-round replay against Wigan Athletic.

Jermaine Beckford made his debut for the club in the home League game against Crystal Palace following his move from Wealdstone.

CHAMPIONSHIP

2006–07

Date	Opposition	Competition	Score
05/08/2006	Norwich City	Championship	1-0
08/08/2006	Queens Park Rangers	Championship	2-2
13/08/2006	Crystal Palace	Championship	0-1
19/08/2006	Cardiff City	Championship	0-1
22/08/2006	Chester City	Carling Cup 1st Round	1-0
27/08/2006	Sheffield Wednesday	Championship	1-0
10/09/2006	Wolverhampton Wanderers	Championship	0-1
13/09/2006	Sunderland	Championship	0-3
16/09/2006	Coventry City	Championship	0-1
19/09/2006	Barnet	Carling Cup 2nd Round	3-1
23/09/2006	Birmingham City	Championship	3-2
30/09/2006	West Bromwich Albion	Championship	2-4
14/10/2006	Stoke City	Championship	0-4
17/10/2006	Leicester City	Championship	1-2
21/10/2006	Luton Town	Championship	1-5
24/10/2006	Southend United	Carling Cup 3rd Round	1-3
28/10/2006	Southend United	Championship	2-0
31/10/2006	Preston North End	Championship	1-4
04/11/2006	Barnsley	Championship	2-3
11/11/2006	Colchester United	Championship	3-0
18/11/2006	Southampton	Championship	0-3
25/11/2006	Plymouth Argyle	Championship	2-1
28/11/2006	Burnley	Championship	1-2
02/12/2006	Barnsley	Championship	2-2
09/12/2006	Derby County	Championship	0-1
16/12/2006	Ipswich Town	Championship	0-1
23/12/2006	Hull City	Championship	0-0
26/12/2006	Sunderland	Championship	0-2
30/12/2006	Stoke City	Championship	1-3
01/01/2007	Coventry City	Championship	2-1
06/01/2007	West Bromwich Albion	FA Cup 3rd Round	1-3
20/01/2007	West Bromwich Albion	Championship	2-3
30/01/2007	Hull City	Championship	2-1
03/02/2007	Norwich City	Championship	1-2
10/02/2007	Crystal Palace	Championship	2-1
17/02/2007	Cardiff City	Championship	0-1
20/02/2007	Queens Park Rangers	Championship	0-0
24/02/2007	Wolverhampton Wanderers	Championship	0-1
27/02/2007	Birmingham City	Championship	0-1
03/03/2007	Sheffield Wednesday	Championship	2-3
10/03/2007	Luton Town	Championship	1-0
13/03/2007	Leicester City	Championship	1-1
17/03/2007	Southend United	Championship	1-1
31/03/2007	Preston North End	Championship	2-1
07/04/2007	Plymouth Argyle	Championship	2-1
09/04/2007	Colchester United	Championship	1-2
14/04/2007	Burnley	Championship	1-0
21/04/2007	Southampton	Championship	0-1
28/04/2007	Ipswich Town	Championship	1-1
05/05/2007	Derby County	Championship	0-2

Team	Pld	W	D	L	GF	GA	Pts
Sunderland	46	27	7	12	76	47	88
Birmingham City	46	26	8	12	67	42	86
Derby County	46	25	9	12	62	46	84
West Bromwich Albion	46	22	10	14	81	55	76
Wolverhampton	46	22	10	14	59	56	76
Southampton	46	21	12	13	77	53	75
Preston North End	46	22	8	16	64	53	74
Stoke City	46	19	16	11	62	41	73
Sheffield Wednesday	46	20	11	15	70	66	71
Colchester United	46	20	9	17	70	56	69
Plymouth Argyle	46	17	16	13	63	62	67
Crystal Palace	46	18	11	17	59	51	65
Cardiff City	46	17	13	16	57	53	64
Ipswich Town	46	18	8	20	64	59	62
Burnley	46	15	12	19	52	49	57
Norwich City	46	16	9	21	56	71	57
Coventry City	46	16	8	22	47	62	56
Queen's Park Rangers	46	14	11	21	54	68	53
Leicester City	46	13	14	19	49	64	53
Barnsley	46	15	5	26	53	85	50
Hull City	46	13	10	23	51	67	49
Southend United	46	10	12	24	47	80	42
Luton Town	46	10	10	26	53	81	40
Leeds United*	46	13	7	26	46	72	36

*Leeds United deducted 10 points

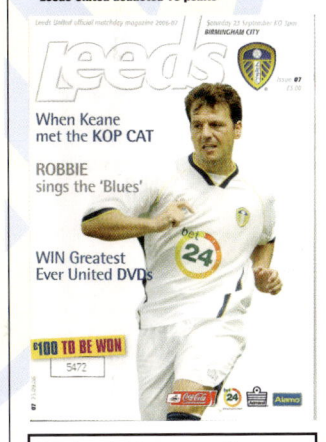

For the eighth consecutive season the Whites started the new campaign at Elland Road, they were also unbeaten in the previous seven.

Leeds gave debuts to 24 players in season 2006-07.

The club handed out squad numbers to 51 different players.

The Whites only achieved one double this season, against Plymouth Argyle, winning 2-1 on both occasions.

Leeds had eight different captains, Paul Butler, Sean Gregan, Gary Kelly, Shaun Derry, Jonathan Douglas, David Healy and Alan Thompson.

2007-08

LEAGUE ONE

Team	Pld	W	D	L	GF	GA	Pts
Swansea	46	27	11	8	82	42	92
Nottingham Forest	46	22	16	8	64	32	82
Doncaster Rovers	46	23	11	12	68	41	80
Carlisle United	46	23	11	12	64	46	80
Leeds United*	46	27	10	9	72	38	76
Southend United	46	22	10	14	70	55	76
Brighton & Hove Albion	46	19	12	15	57	49	69
Oldham Athletic	46	18	13	15	58	46	67
Northampton Town	46	17	15	14	60	55	66
Huddersfield Town	46	20	6	20	50	62	66
Tranmere Rovers	46	18	11	17	52	47	65
Walsall	46	16	16	14	51	45	64
Swindon Town	46	16	13	17	62	56	61
Leyton Orient	46	16	12	18	49	62	60
Hartlepool United	46	15	9	22	63	66	54
Bristol Rovers	46	12	17	17	45	56	53
Millwall	46	14	10	22	45	60	52
Yeovil Town	46	14	10	22	38	59	52
Cheltenham Town	46	13	12	21	42	64	51
Crewe Alexandra	46	12	14	20	47	65	50
Bournemouth**	46	17	7	22	62	72	48
Gillingham	46	11	13	22	44	73	46
Port Vale	46	9	11	26	47	81	38
Luton Town***	46	11	10	25	43	63	33

*Leeds United deducted 15 points
**Bournemouth deducted 10 points
***Luton Town deducted 10 points

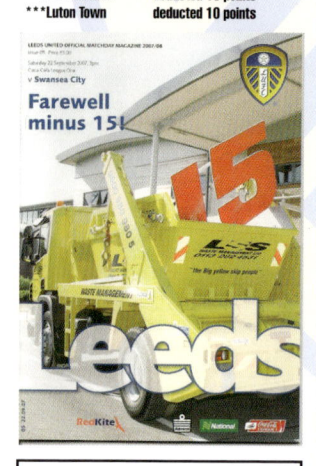

Date	Opposition	Competition	Score
11/08/2007	Tranmere Rovers	League One	2-1
14/08/2007	Macclesfield Town	Carling Cup 1st Round	1-0
18/08/2007	Southend United	League One	4-1
25/08/2007	Nottingham Forest	League One	2-1
28/08/2007	Portsmouth	Carling Cup 2nd Round	0-3
01/09/2007	Luton Town	League One	1-0
08/09/2007	Hartlepool United	League One	2-0
14/09/2007	Bristol Rovers	League One	3-0
22/09/2007	Swansea City	League One	2-0
29/09/2007	Gillingham	League One	1-1
02/10/2007	Oldham Athletic	League One	1-0
06/10/2007	Yeovil Town	League One	1-0
09/10/2002	Darlington	JPT Northern Section 2nd Round	1-0
13/10/2007	Leyton Orient	League One	1-1
20/10/2007	Brighton & Hove Albion	League One	1-0
27/10/2007	Millwall	League One	4-2
03/11/2007	Carlisle United	League One	1-3
06/11/2007	AFC Bournemouth	League One	3-1
09/11/2007	Hereford United	FA Cup 1st Round	0-0
13/11/2007	Bury	JPT Northern Section QF	1-2
17/11/2007	Swindon Town	League One	2-1
20/11/2007	Hereford United	FA Cup 1st Round Replay	0-1
25/11/2007	Cheltenham Town	League One	0-1
04/12/2007	Port Vale	League One	3-0
08/12/2007	Huddersfield Town	League One	4-0
15/12/2007	Walsall	League One	1-1
22/12/2007	Bristol Rovers	League One	1-0
26/12/2007	Hartlepool United	League One	1-1
29/12/2002	Swansea City	League One	2-3
01/01/2008	Oldham Athletic	League One	1-3
05/01/2008	Northampton Town	League One	3-0
14/01/2008	Crewe Alexandra	League One	1-0
19/01/2008	Doncaster Rovers	League One	0-1
26/01/2008	Luton Town	League One	1-1
29/01/2008	Southend United	League One	0-1
02/02/2008	Tranmere Rovers	League One	0-2
09/02/2008	Northampton Town	League One	1-1
12/02/2008	Nottingham Forest	League One	1-1
23/02/2008	Crewe Alexandra	League One	1-1
01/03/2008	Swindon Town	League One	1-0
08/03/2008	AFC Bournemouth	League One	2-0
11/03/2008	Cheltenham Town	League One	1-2
15/03/2008	Port Vale	League One	3-3
22/03/2008	Walsall	League One	2-0
29/03/2008	Brighton & Hove Albion	League One	0-0
01/04/2008	Doncaster Rovers	League One	1-0
05/04/2008	Leyton Orient	League One	2-0
12/04/2008	Carlisle United	League One	3-2
15/04/2008	Huddersfield Town	League One	0-1
19/04/2008	Millwall	League One	2-0
25/04/2008	Yeovil Town	League One	1-0
03/05/2008	Gillingham	League One	2-1
12/05/2008	Carlisle United	League One Play Off SF 1st Leg	1-2
15/05/2008	Carlisle United	League One Play Off SF 2nd Leg	2-0
25/05/2008	Doncaster Rovers	League One Play Off Final at Wembley	0-1

Matt Heath wrote his name in history when he scored the Whites' first-ever goal in the third tier of English football away at Tranmere Rovers.

The club won their first seven league games for only the second time in their history after they did this in season 1973-74.

Leeds made their debut in the Johnstone Paints Trophy, losing in the Northern Area quarter-final stage at home to Bury.

Leeds also made their first apperance in the first round of the FA Cup for the first time since season 1923-24.

15 players scored their first goals for the clubs, Paul Huntington, Rui Marques, David Prutton, Jermaine Beckford, Leon Constantine, Ian Westlake, Bradley Johnson, Sebastien Carole, Andy Hughes, Curtis Weston, Mark De Vries, Alan Sheehan, Neil Kilkenny, Dougie Freedman and Antony Elding.

LEAGUE ONE 2008–09

Date	Opposition	Competition	Score
09/08/2008	Scunthorpe United	League One	2-1
12/08/2008	Chester City	Carling Cup 1st Round	5-2
16/08/2008	**Oldham Athletic**	**League One**	**0-2**
23/08/2008	Yeovil Town	League One	1-1
26/08/2008	**Crystal Palace**	**Carling Cup 2nd Round**	**4-0**
30/08/2008	**Bristol Rovers**	**League One**	**2-2**
02/09/2008	**Bradford City**	**JPT North East Section 1st Round**	**2-1**
06/09/2008	**Crewe Alexandra**	**League One**	**5-2**
13/09/2008	Swindon Town	League One	3-1
20/09/2008	Carlisle United	League One	2-0
23/09/2008	**Hartlepool United**	**Carling Cup 3rd Round**	**3-2**
27/09/2008	**Hereford United**	**League One**	**1-0**
04/10/2008	Peterborough United	League One	0-2
08/10/2008	Rotherham United	JPT Northern Section 2nd Round	2-4
11/10/2008	**Brighton & Hove Albion**	**League One**	**3-1**
18/10/2008	Millwall	League One	1-3
21/10/2008	**Leyton Orient**	**League One**	**2-1**
25/10/2008	**Walsall**	**League One**	**3-0**
28/10/2008	Southend United	League One	0-1
01/11/2008	Cheltenham Town	League One	1-0
07/11/2008	**Northampton Town**	**FA Cup 1st Round**	**1-1**
11/11/2008	Derby County	Carling Cup 4th Round	1-2
15/11/2008	**Huddersfield Town**	**League One**	**1-2**
17/11/2008	Northampton Town	FA Cup 1st Round Replay	5-2
22/11/2008	**Hartlepool United**	**League One**	**4-1**
25/11/2008	Northampton Town	League One	1-2
30/11/2008	Histon	FA Cup 2nd Round	0-1
06/12/2008	Tranmere Rovers	League One	1-2
13/12/2008	**Colchester United**	**League One**	**1-2**
20/12/2008	Milton Keynes Dons	League One	1-3
26/12/2008	**Leicester City**	**League One**	**1-1**
28/12/2008	Stockport County	League One	3-1
10/01/2009	**Carlisle United**	**League One**	**0-2**
17/01/2009	Brighton & Hove Albion	League One	2-0
24/01/2009	**Peterborough United**	**League One**	**3-1**
27/01/2009	**Southend United**	**League One**	**2-0**
31/01/2009	Walsall	League One	0-1
09/02/2009	**Millwall**	**League One**	**2-0**
14/02/2009	Huddersfield Town	League One	0-1
17/02/2009	Hereford United	League One	0-2
21/02/2009	**Cheltenham Town**	**League One**	**2-0**
28/02/2009	**Scunthorpe United**	**League One**	**3-2**
02/03/2009	Oldham Athletic	League One	1-1
07/03/2009	Bristol Rovers	League One	2-2
10/03/2009	**Yeovil Town**	**League One**	**4-0**
14/03/2009	**Swindon Town**	**League One**	**1-0**
21/03/2009	Crewe Alexandra	League One	3-2
28/03/2009	**Milton Keynes Dons**	**League One**	**2-0**
04/04/2009	Colchester United	League One	1-0
07/04/2009	Leyton Orient	League One	2-2
11/04/2009	**Stockport County**	**League One**	**1-0**
13/04/2009	Leicester City	League One	0-1
18/04/2009	**Tranmere Rovers**	**League One**	**3-1**
25/04/2009	Hartlepool United	League One	1-0
02/05/2009	**Northampton Town**	**League One**	**3-0**
09/05/2009	Millwall	League One Play Off SF 1st Leg	0-1
14/05/2009	**Millwall**	**League One Play Off SF 2nd Leg**	**1-1**

Team	Pld	W	D	L	GF	GA	Pts
Leicester City	46	27	15	4	84	39	96
Peterborough United	46	26	11	9	78	54	89
Milton Keynes Dons	46	26	9	11	83	47	87
Leeds United	46	26	6	14	77	49	84
Millwall	46	25	7	14	63	53	82
Scunthorpe United	46	22	10	14	82	63	76
Tranmere Rovers	46	21	11	14	62	49	74
Southend United	46	21	8	17	58	61	71
Huddersfield Town	46	18	14	14	62	65	68
Oldham Athletic	46	16	17	13	66	65	65
Bristol Rovers	46	17	12	17	79	61	63
Colchester United	46	18	9	19	58	58	63
Walsall	46	17	10	19	61	66	61
Leyton Orient	46	15	11	20	45	57	56
Swindon Town	46	12	17	17	68	71	53
Brighton & Hove Albion	46	13	13	20	54	69	52
Yeovil Town	46	12	15	19	41	66	51
Stockport County*	46	16	12	18	59	57	50
Hartlepool United	46	13	11	22	66	79	50
Carlisle United	46	12	14	20	56	69	50
Northampton Town	46	12	13	21	60	64	49
Crewe Alexandra	46	12	10	24	59	82	46
Cheltenham Town	46	9	12	25	51	91	39
Hereford United	46	9	7	30	42	79	34

*Stockport County deducted 10 points

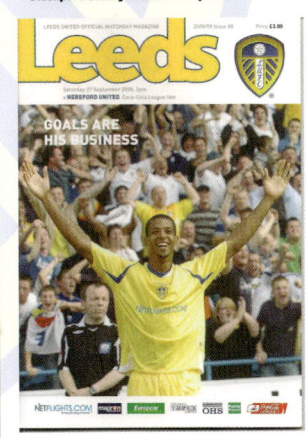

Leeds kept up their unbeaten start on day one of the new campaign following a 2-1 win at Scunthorpe United, the last time they tasted defeat on the opening day was in 1989 at Newcastle United.

Jermaine Beckford achieved the remarkable feat of scoring hat-tricks in the league (Yeovil Town), League Cup (Chester City) and FA Cup (Northampton Town).

When Leeds defeated Crystal Palace in the second round of the League Cup it was the first time since March 1987, when they defeated QPR, they had beaten a team in a higher league.

When Crewe Alexandra were defeated 5-2 at Elland Road, it was only the third time in the decade that Leeds had scored at least five goals in a league game at Elland Road.

Mansour Assoumani joined the one appearance club following his only game away at Milton Keynes Dons in Gary McAllister's last game in charge.

2009–10

LEAGUE ONE

Team	Pld	W	D	L	GF	GA	Pts
Norwich City	46	29	8	9	89	47	95
Leeds United	46	25	11	10	77	44	86
Millwall	46	24	13	9	76	44	85
Charlton Athletic	46	23	15	8	71	48	84
Swindon Town	46	22	16	8	73	57	82
Huddersfield Town	46	23	11	12	82	56	80
Southampton*	46	23	14	9	85	47	73
Colchester United	46	20	12	14	64	52	72
Brentford	46	14	20	12	55	52	62
Walsall	46	16	14	16	60	63	62
Bristol Rovers	46	19	5	22	59	70	62
Milton Keynes Dons	46	17	9	20	60	68	60
Brighton & Hove Albion	46	15	14	17	56	60	59
Carlisle United	46	15	13	18	63	66	58
Yeovil Town	46	13	14	19	55	59	53
Oldham Athletic	46	13	13	20	39	57	52
Leyton Orient	46	13	12	21	53	63	51
Exeter City	46	11	18	17	48	60	51
Tranmere Rovers	46	14	9	23	45	72	51
Hartlepool United**	46	14	11	21	59	67	50
Gillingham	46	12	14	20	48	64	50
Wycombe	46	10	15	21	56	76	45
Southend United	46	10	13	23	51	72	43
Stockport County	46	5	10	31	35	95	25

*Southampton deducted 10 points
**Hartlepool United deducted 3 points

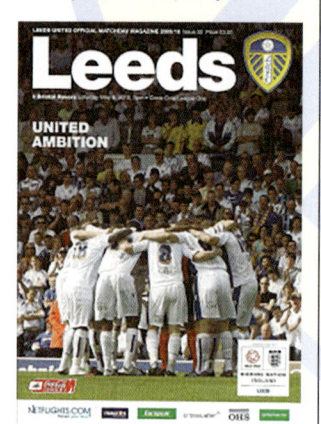

Date	Opposition	Competition	Score
08/08/2009	Exeter City	League One	2-1
10/08/2009	Darlington	Carling Cup 1st Round	1-0
15/08/2009	Wycombe Wanderers	League One	1-0
18/08/2009	Walsall	League One	2-1
22/08/2009	Tranmere Rovers	League One	3-0
25/08/2009	Watford	Carling Cup 2nd Round	2-1
29/08/2009	Colchester United	League One	2-1
05/09/2009	Stockport County	League One	2-0
11/09/2009	Southend United	League One	0-0
19/09/2009	Gillingham	League One	4-1
22/09/2009	Liverpool	Carling Cup 3rd Round	0-1
26/09/2009	Milton Keynes Dons	League One	1-0
29/09/2009	Carlisle United	League One	1-1
03/10/2009	Charlton Athletic	League One	0-0
06/10/2009	Darlington	JPT North East Section 2nd Round	2-1
19/10/2009	Norwich City	League One	2-1
24/10/2009	Millwall	League One	1-2
27/10/2009	Bristol Rovers	League One	4-0
31/10/2009	Yeovil Town	League One	4-0
07/11/2009	Oldham Athletic	FA Cup 1st Round	2-0
10/11/2009	Grimsby Town	JPT Northern Section QF	3-1
21/11/2009	Brighton & Hove Albion	League One	3-0
24/11/2009	Leyton Orient	League One	1-0
29/11/2009	Kettering Town	FA Cup 2nd Round	1-1
01/12/2009	Oldham Athletic	League One	2-0
05/12/2009	Huddersfield Town	League One	2-2
08/12/2009	Kettering Town	FA Cup 2nd Round Replay	5-1
12/12/2009	Brentford	League One	0-0
15/12/2009	Accrington Stanley	JPT Northern Section SF	2-0
19/12/2009	Southampton	League One	1-0
26/12/2009	Hartlepool United	League One	3-1
28/12/2009	Stockport County	League One	4-2
03/01/2010	Manchester United	FA Cup 3rd Round	1-0
09/01/2010	Wycombe Wanderers	League One	1-1
16/01/2010	Exeter City	League One	0-2
19/01/2010	Carlisle United	JPT Northern Section Final 1st Leg	1-2
23/01/2010	Tottenham Hotspur	FA Cup 4th Round	2-2
26/01/2010	Swindon Town	League One	0-3
30/01/2010	Colchester United	League One	2-0
03/02/2010	Tottenham Hotspur	FA Cup 4th Round Replay	1-3
06/02/2010	Hartlepool United	League One	2-2
09/02/2010	Carlisle United	JPT Northern Section Final 2nd Leg	3-2 (5-6 on pens)
13/02/2010	Leyton Orient	League One	1-1
16/02/2010	Walsall	League One	1-2
20/02/2010	Brighton & Hove Albion	League One	1-1
23/02/2010	Oldham Athletic	League One	2-0
27/02/2010	Huddersfield Town	League One	2-2
06/03/2010	Brentford	League One	1-1
09/03/2010	Tranmere Rovers	League One	4-1
13/03/2010	Southampton	League One	0-1
22/03/2010	Millwall	League One	0-2
27/03/2010	Norwich City	League One	0-1
03/04/2010	Swindon Town	League One	0-3
05/04/2010	Yeovil Town	League One	2-1
10/04/2010	Southend United	League One	2-0
13/04/2010	Carlisle United	League One	3-1
17/04/2010	Gillingham	League One	2-3
24/04/2010	Milton Keynes Dons	League One	4-1
01/05/2010	Charlton Athletic	League One	0-1
08/05/2010	Bristol Rovers	League One	2-1

Leeds made history when they faced Oldham Athletic in the first round of the FA Cup when the game was broadcast live on the FA website.

David Martin was another member of the one appearance club when he made his only start for the side in the Johnstone's Paint Trophy at home to Accrington Stanley.

When Leeds defeated Manchester United at Old Trafford in the third round of the FA Cup, it was the Whites first win there since February 1981.

The Whites made their first-ever league visit to Exeter City's St James Park in January 2010, sadly they were on the end of a 2-0 defeat.

In his last game for the club Jermaine Beckford was handed the captain's armband by Simon Grayson, Becks scored the winning goal v Bristol Rovers as Leeds won promotion.

THE 2010s
CHANGES, CHANGES AND MORE CHANGES

Following promotion at the third attempt, no one quite knew what to expect back in the Championship. Jermaine Beckford left for Premier League football at Everton, but in came Max Gradel on a permanent transfer, Paul Connolly, Alex Bruce, Lloyd Sam, Sanchez Watt, Billy Paynter, Kasper Schmeichel, Federico Bessone and Ross McCormack. Early season form was good and following a 2-1 win over eventual play-off winners Swansea City, Leeds were in the dizzy heights of sixth position. Form after that was inconsistent to say the least, summed up in a 6-4 defeat at home to Preston North End in which Leeds were 4-1 up just before the interval.

After a 4-0 home defeat to Cardiff City, Leeds were 16th in the Championship and needed a pick me up, which came in the form of debutant Andy O'Brien and a hat-trick from captain Jonny Howson away at Scunthorpe United. Leeds then went on a 12-game unbeaten run before defeat away at Cardiff City proceeded an excellent 1-1 draw in the FA Cup third round away at Arsenal. Leeds were eventually knocked out 3-1 by Arsene Wenger's side, which left them to concentrate on clinching a play-off place at the very least. A 5-2 win over Yorkshire rivals Doncaster Rovers and 2-1 win over Preston North End at Deepdale left the side in fifth place. Sadly that win in Lancashire was the last away win until the final day of the campaign at Queens Park Rangers. By that time Leeds had fallen to seventh and despite a win in west London they were left to a rue a missed opportunity.

In the close season, Schmeichel was sold to Leicester City and was replaced by Andy Lonergan, Michael Brown joined from Portsmouth, Darren O'Dea came on loan from Celtic and Andy Keogh returned for a second spell on loan from Wolverhampton Wanderers. Leeds

Leeds United, 2010-11.

made a poor start by their standard and following a defeat by Ipswich Town at the end of August they were in 19th place. Fans' favourite Max Gradel was sold to Saint-Etienne, which didn't help matters, but results did improve and following a 3-0 win away at Doncaster Rovers in which Danny Pugh came back for a second spell and scored the opening goal, Leeds were fifth in the Championship table.

The next month was one to forget, especially for new goalkeeper Paul Rachubka, who had a dreadful night in a 5-0 drubbing at home to Blackpool. He never played a first-team game again. Tragically for the club, the events of Sunday 27 November 2011 will go down as a day that anyone connected with the club, as well as football, will never forget as news came through of the untimely death of Leeds United title-winner Gary Speed. The Billy Bremner statue was turned into a shrine and the 4-0 win at Nottingham Forest was dedicated to the Welshman. The next game at home against Millwall saw his former midfielders Gary McAllister, David Batty and Gordon Strachan all return to Elland Road as the club played tribute to him. It was somewhat ironic that Robert Snodgrass, who played in Speed's position, would score both goals.

The form over Christmas was dire and summed up in a 4-1 dismal defeat away at Barnsley. Pressure was starting to mount on Grayson and he needed a 2-1 win at home to Burnley days later thanks to a late, late goal from Ross McCormack. Leeds met Arsenal again in the FA Cup and were beaten thanks to a Thierry Henry winner, but a league win over ten-man Ipswich eased the pressure. Following a 4-1 defeat at home to Birmingham City, Grayson was

Kasper Schmeichal tries in vain to recuce the deficit as Arsenal come out 1-3 winners at Elland Road in the FA Cup third-round replay, 19 January 2011.

Leeds United fans line-up patiently outside Elland Road to pay their respects to Gary Speed in the first home game since his untimely death, a 2-0 win over Millwall, 3 November 2013.

Leeds United, 2011-12.

gone and replaced in the interim by Neil Redfearn. Redfearn oversaw two wins, but Leeds needed a new manager and quick, so they turned to promotion specialist Neil Warnock. Warnock's first game was a 0-0 draw at Portsmouth. He achieved his first win in an impressive 2-0 victory at Middlesbrough, but a 1-1 draw at home to West Ham United and a crazy 3-7 defeat at Elland Road to Nottingham Forest all but ended any play-off chances. Leeds would finish the season in 14th place, with Warnock knowing he would have his work cut out to turn Leeds into contenders for promotion.

The off season saw the likes of Paul Green, Adam Drury, Luke Varney, Paddy Kenny, Lee Peltier, Rudy Austin, David Norris, Jason Pearce, Andy Gray and El Hadji Diouf all join the club as Warnock got to work on moulding Leeds into a promotion-winning side. Despite winning two out of his opening three league games, that was a good as it would get all season. League performances were inconsistent and a 6-1 home hammering against Watford saw Leeds drop to 17th. Fortunes in both cup competitions were better though and Leeds did make it through to the last eight of the Capital One Cup before losing 5-1 at home to Champions League holders Chelsea.

Following the loan signings of Jerome Thomas and Alan Tate, results took an upturn and four wins in six saw the club in eighth place leading up to the festive season. Despite home wins against Bolton Wanderers and Bristol City, Leeds couldn't win away from Elland Road and that would cost them a proper challenge at the play-off places. Leeds made headway in the FA Cup before losing to Premiership champions Manchester City and questions were being asked of Warnock.

Following a 2-1 defeat at home to Derby County he left the club, replaced initially by Redfearn once again. The former Barnsley captain presided over a 2-1 defeat away at Charlton Athletic before Brian McDermott was named permanent manager a day before the visit of

Sheffield Wednesday. A brace from Luke Varney and a winner from Rudy Austin at home to Burnley was enough to see Leeds safe from any relegation talk and the focus would turn to next season. Leeds finished in 13th place, and a year earlier McDermott had led Reading to promotion so hopes were high that he could do the same with Leeds.

Matt Smith from Oldham Athletic, Luke Murphy from Crewe Alexandra and Noel Hunt from Reading all joined in the summer of 2013 and early results looked promising, with Leeds in fifth place following their first win at Ipswich Town since September 2001. Like previous seasons, Leeds were hit by inconsistency and never really looked like they were going to mount a serious promotion challenge, but results did pick up in October at home to Birmingham City (4-0), at home to Yeovil Town (2-0) and away at Charlton Athletic (4-2) in which McCormack scored all four. Leeds were in eighth place.

Following a 3-0 victory at Doncaster Rovers, there was talk of a play-off place, but the side only took two points from the next 12 and would never regain their form. An embarrassing 2-0 defeat away at Rochdale in the FA Cup third round was followed by a shameful 6-0 defeat away at Sheffield Wednesday and all of a sudden there was talk of McDermott leaving. What happened next will go down in folklore as Italian businessman Massimo Cellino looked to complete his move to buy the football club from GFH capital. On transfer deadline day Cellino allegedly completed his buyout of the club and subsequently 'sacked' McDermott. To add insult to injury, star striker Ross McCormack went on to Sky Sports News looking for a move. The next day Nigel Gibbs took charge of the team against Huddersfield Town and McCormack scored a hat-trick, you could not have written it! McDermott was back in charge the following day as the EFL were yet to ratify the deal of Cellino's buyout. League form suffered and following another embarrassing defeat 5-1 at home to Bolton Wanderers, Leeds were suddenly nervously looking over their shoulder. In the end they took ten points from the last 15 available and ended up in 15th place, but McDermott's days were numbered.

To everyone's amazement, McDermott was replaced by David Hockaday, a former Forest Green Rovers boss and an influx of foreign players joined the club, with the likes of Guiseppe Bellusci, Mirco Antenucci, Soluyamane Doukara, Marco Silvestri and Tomassi Bianchi all signing. Long time target Billy Sharp also joined the Whites, as did Liam Cooper from Chesterfield. However, Hockaday was on a hiding to nothing and an opening day defeat to Millwall set alarm bells ringing.

Despite victories over Accrington Stanley and Middlesbrough, in which Sharp scored the winning goal on his debut, Hockaday was sacked following a 2-1 defeat in the Capital One Cup at Bradford City and Redfearn was placed in temporary charge – again! It had the desired effect and he won three of his four games in charge. Slovenian Darko Milanic was then handed the manager's job but became the first-ever Leeds United manager to fail to win a game in charge. Just like Hockday, he had six games as head coach before being sacked

Jimmy Kebe celebrates scoring as Leeds United come from behind to beat local rivals Huddersfield Town 5-1 at Elland Road, 1 February 2014.

following a 2-1 home to defeat to Wolverhampton Wanderers. This time Redfearn was given the job on a permanent basis and his first job was to lift the players leading up to Christmas.

An impressive win over Derby County in which Antenucci scored both goals, saw Leeds into 15th place. The side's form then took a nosedive with only one point from the next 15, which saw them drop to 20th place and fears of a relegation battle. Redfearn changed things around for the FA Cup tie at Sunderland and performances improved. A double over Huddersfield Town, a win of over AFC Bournemouth, a win at Reading and back-to-back wins over Millwall (1-0) and away at Middlesbrough (1-0), saw Leeds climb to 11th place and relative safety. Leeds finished the season in 15th place, which after a flirtation with relegation was a decent return. The question now was, would Redfearn be in charge for the following season?

The answer would be no, as he was replaced by former Brentford and Wigan Athletic boss Uwe Rosler. In came Sol Bamba following his loan move the previous season, as well as Stuart Dallas from Brentford, Chris Wood from Leicester City and Tom Adeyemi on loan from Cardiff City. Leeds started with four draws before an impressive 2-1 win away at Derby County with a wonderful winner from Wood. Rosler took only three points from the next 18 and was subsequently sacked following a 2-1 home loss to Brighton & Hove Albion. Former Crawley Town and Rotherham United boss Steve Evans was next in line and his first two games ended in 1-1 draws away at Fulham and Bolton Wanderers respectively. His first home game was one to forget as Blackburn won 2-0 with both goals in the first five minutes.

Results did improve with back-to-back wins over Cardiff City 1-0 at Elland Road and 3-0 away at Huddersfield Town. Progress was slow with a 1-0 defeat at home to Neil Redfearn's Rotherham United and a 1-0 defeat away at Neil Warnock's Queens Park Rangers. Results improved slightly and Leeds were in 12th position heading into 2016. Toumani Diagouraga was bought in from Brentford, with results being inconsistent. After a 4-0 drubbing away at Brighton & Hove Albion shown in front of a live TV audience, Leeds bounced back with three straight wins, 2-1 at home to Bolton Wanderers, 2-0 away at Cardiff City and

Alex Mowatt is congratulated for scoring the only goal of the game as Leeds United beat Millwall at Elland Road, 14 February 2015.

Kyle Bartley (second from the right) celebrates Leeds United's penalty shoot-out win against Fleetwood Town in the League Cup, 10 August 2016.

2-1 away at Blackburn Rovers. Leeds again finished in 13th place, and like the previous campaign questions were being asked about whether the head coach would be in charge for the following season.

The answer would be the same as the previous season as Evans was relieved of his duties and replaced by former Swansea City boss Garry Monk. Signings over the summer included former England keeper Rob Green, defender Kyle Bartley, Kemar Roofe, Matt Grimes and the influential Pablo Hernandez. Despite a penalty shoot-out win over former manager Uwe Rosler's Fleetwood Town in the League Cup early league form was a struggle, with only one win in the opening six games. There were rumours abound that Monk's position was looking shakey, but back-to-back over wins against Cardiff City (2-0) and Blackburn Rovers (2-1) eased the pressure and the Whites never really looked back. New Zealander Wood was scoring for fun and by the start of October Leeds found themselves in 11th place. A hard working win at Molineux thanks to a Silvio own goal set Leeds on a run that would see them in the play-off places after a fine 3-2 win on Bonfire Night away at Norwich City.

Cup form seem to go hand in hand with Leeds reaching the last eight of the EFL Cup before being knocked out by Liverpool 2-0 at Anfield. Following an impressive 4-1 win at Preston North End on Boxing Day, Leeds were handily placed in fifth and looked set for a play-off place. A shocking display away at non-league Sutton United in the FA Cup fourth

Chris Wood after scoring one of his brace for Leeds United in a 2-0 win against Brighton at Elland Road, 18 March 2017.

round saw Leeds exit the competition, in which the likes of Paul Mackay, Billy Whitehouse and Malik Wilks made their debuts for the club. They did back this up with a win over Blackburn Rovers thanks to a late goal from new fans' favourite Pontus Jansson, but this was followed by back-to-back defeats away at Huddersfield Town and at home to Cardiff City. Following an impressive win over Brighton & Hove Albion thanks to a brace from Chris Wood, looked to have sealed a play-off place, but poor form in the end put paid to that and like they had in 2010-11, they missed out by one place. Garry Monk left the club in May and yet again the club would start a new campaign with a new man at the helm. During the close season, Andrea Radrizanni completed his buyout from Massimo Cellino.

The new head coach would be a relatively unknown Thomas Christensen, who had previously managed at AEK Larnaca and APOEL in the Cypriot league. In came Caleb Ekuban, Felix Wiedwald, Matthew Pennington, Ezjgan Alioski and Samuel Saiz. Early form was superb and following a 2-0 win over Birmingham City at Elland Road, Leeds went top of the Championship table for the first time since winning promotion back in 1990. Chris Wood joined Burnley and was replaced by Pierre-Michel Lassoga, who scored a brace on his debut in a 5-0 demolition of Burton Albion. However, a defeat at Millwall, despite keeping Leeds top of the pile, set the side back and following back-to-back defeats away at Sheffield Wednesday (3-0) and at home to Reading (1-0), the side dropped to sixth. A 3-0 win at Bristol City in which

Samuel Saiz scored a brace saw Leeds climb back up to fourth. However, the side suffered three consecutive defeats and the pressure intensified on Christensen, but form did pick up through November and December, and a 2-1 win at Burton Albion on Boxing Day saw Leeds in fifth position. However, a disastrous January in which the side were knocked out of the FA Cup by League Two side Newport County and a run of two points in twelve saw the pressure rise back up again and Christiansen was sacked following a 4-1 home loss against Cardiff City.

He was replaced by Barnsley boss Paul Heckingbottom and Leeds were in 10th place when he started, so he knew he had to get off to a fast start to keep those faint hopes of a play-off place alive. Sadly for Leeds, it took him till his fourth game to achieve his first win as head coach, a 1-0 win over Brentford thanks to a Liam Cooper header. By the end of March, hopes of a play-off place were gone and it was a question of getting some wins under the belt in preparation for next season. Leeds yet again finished in 13th position and for the fourth consecutive season there were questions marks over who would be head coach.

Many names were linked with the job, but no one could have imagined who would take over. On 15 June 2018, former Argentinian manager Marcelo Bielsa was named as the new head coach of the football club. No one knew what to expect or what lay ahead in the up and coming months. Leeds brought in Barry Douglas from Wolverhampton Wanderers, Jack Harrison on loan from Manchester City, Lewis Baker on loan from Chelsea and Patrick Bamford from Middlesbrough.

Kemar Roofe fends off Fikayo Tomori (Derby County) in a resounding 4-1 win to Leeds United at Pride Park - a great start for Marcelo Bielsa, 11 August 2018.

The impact that Bielsa had was instant and he became the first head coach/manager to win his first four games in charge. Leeds topped the table at the end of August and Bielsa won the Manager of the Month award, the first time a Leeds incumbent had won it since Simon Grayson in December 2010. League form was extremely consistent, despite a 4-1 reverse at West Bromwich Albion. The side bounced back with seven straight league wins, including a famous 3-2 comeback win at Aston Villa in which Kemar Roofe scored the winner in the 95th minute. A further comeback win was achieved at home to Blackburn Rovers on Boxing Day, in which Roofe scored twice in injury time to overturn a 2-1 deficit. Despite back-to-back league defeats at home to Hull City and Nottingham Forest, Leeds bounced back with a superb Friday night win over

Patrick Bamford celebrates after scoring one of his two goals in a 4-0 demolition of West Bromwich Albion at Elland Road, 1 March 2019.

Patrick Bamford (Leeds United) scores one of his two goals in a 4-0 demolition of West Bromwich Albion at Elland Road, 1 March 2019.

Derby County at Elland Road. League form was up and down, proved by a disappointing defeat away at Queens Park Rangers, but Leeds returned to winning ways with a season's best 4-0 win over West Bromwich Albion in which Pablo Hernandez scored after 17 seconds. The side followed it up with away wins at Bristol City (1-0) and Reading (3-0), before Sheffield United overtook Leeds in the promotion spots with a 1-0 win at Elland Road. The Blades and Leeds were then involved in an intriguing promotion battle that lasted until the penultimate weekend of the season.

Going into the last four games of the campaign, Leeds had their fate in their own hands, but following defeats at home to Wigan Athletic 2-1 at Elland Road on Good Friday and Brentford 2-0 on Easter Monday, Sheffield United joined Norwich City in the Premier

Leeds United supporters show the strength of their support in a powerful display prior to in the 2019 Championship play-off semi-final second leg against Derby County.

League the next season. As for the Whites, they were forced to face the lottery of the play-offs for the first time in ten years, where they would face Derby County o ver a two-leg tie. Leeds won the first leg away at Pride Park thanks to a winner from Kemar Roofe, but the Rams came back from a 2-0 aggregate deficit after Stuart Dallas had doubled the Leeds advantage to win the game 4-2 and book a trip to Wembley. The good news from a Leeds perspective was that Marcelo Bielsa agreed to the take the club on for a second season, leading them into their centenary campaign.

DEBUTANTS IN 2010 ONWARDS

ROSS MCCORMACK

Debut: Watford (A) 28 August 2010
Appearances: 130 (28)
Goals: 58

The Glasgow-born striker started his career at his hometown club, joining them in 2002, before joining Motherwell at the start of the 2006-07 campaign. It was from Fir Park where he joined Cardiff City in the summer of 2008. Having had two seasons in the Welsh capital, he came to the attention of Leeds United and moved to west Yorkshire at the end of August 2010, making his debut as a substitute for Sanchez Watt away at Watford.

It was a frustrating first season for McCormack as he started only six games and came off the bench in another 15. He opened his Leeds United account in the penultimate game of the season at home to Burnley and he followed this up with the winner away at Queens Park Rangers on the final day as Leeds just missed out on the play-offs. The following season proved to be much more productive for McCormack as he started 45 games and was a used substitute in four others. He also hit the back of the net on 19 occasions, with braces at home to Crystal Palace, away at Brighton & Hove Albion and at home to Peterborough United. His most memorable strike came deep, deep into stoppage time in the 2-1 win over Burnley at the start of 2012, which saw incredible scenes at Elland Road.

The 2012-13 season, which had seen Neil Warnock take over the reins from Simon Grayson the previous February, saw McCormack taken off injured away at his old club Cardiff City and that would rule him out for over two months. It took him a while to find his goalscoring touch again after that, but he ended up scoring eight goals, including a fantastic solo goal in the 2-1 win over Tottenham Hotspur in the FA

Cup at Elland Road. He also scored the goal that would help Hull City win promotion to the Premier League on the final day away at Watford, under new Leeds boss Brian McDermott. The 2013-14 season, which was to be McCormack's last at Elland Road, proved to be the best of his four-year stay. He started with the equaliser at home to Brighton and never stopped scoring all the way through the season, including a four-goal haul away at Charlton Athletic on a rain sodden day in s outh London. He ended up with 29 goals and took over the captaincy from Rudy Austin. He joined Fulham in the summer of 2014.

SAM BYRAM

Debut: Shrewsbury Town (H) 11 August 2012
Appearances: 122 (21)
Goals: 10

Byram, who was born in Essex and educated in York, was offered full-time professional terms at Elland Road in May 2012. Expecting to be amongst the juniors for the 2012-13 campaign, Byram featured in a pre-season friendly away at Farsley in mid-July and never looked back. He featured in all of the pre-season games and scored away at Preston North End. He was thrust into competitive action at home to Shrewsbury Town and made his league bow a week later at home to Wolverhampton Wanderers, broadcast live on Sky Sports.

Byram's first goal came when he chipped the Oxford United goalkeeper in the second round of the Capital Cup. He ended this first season as a professional featuring in 53 out of

56 games, scoring a further three goals, away at Bolton Wanderers, away at Leicester City and at home to Peterborough United. In July 2013 he was named in Sky Sports Football League players to watch out for.

Frustratingly for Byram, a hip injury sustained at the back end of the previous season kept him out until September and he only played 27 times without hitting the back of the net in season 2013-14.

After numerous managerial changes came the arrival of Neil Redfearn on a permanent basis in October 2014. The emphasis was on the academy and Byram would go on to play an important role till the end of that season. Redfearn moved Byram into a midfield position as he changed the formation and he responded with vital goals away at Huddersfield Town, away at Reading and away at Fulham respectively. However, Redfearn was not kept on and was replaced by German Uwe Rosler ahead of the 2015-16 season, with Byram starting that campaign as a right midfield-forward. Rosler lasted until mid-October before being replaced by former Rotherham United manager Steve Evans, and the Essex-born player started the first three games under Evans amid contract talks. He scored a brace in a rare away win at Wolverhampton Wanderers 3-2 and he followed this up with the equaliser away at Nottingham Forest. He made his last appearance in a Leeds United shirt away at Ipswich Town before signing for West Ham United on a four-year contract for an undisclosed fee and a career down south.

LEWIS COOK

Debut: Millwall (A) 9 August 2014
Appearances: 78 (7)
Goals: 2

A true Yorkie, Cook was first discovered by the club playing for a junior club in his very early years, and he slowly graduated through the Leeds United academy. By the time he was 15 years old he was playing for the under 18s. He scored in a 3-1 loss away at Liverpool in a FA Youth Cup, broadcast live on Liverpool TV. He didn't feature in the 2013-14 season, but the following year would be his breakthrough one.

Under then head coach David Hockaday he featured in all of the side's pre-season games, starting in games at Guiseley and Chesterfield and coming off the bench in the others. He made his competitive debut in the 2-0 loss away at Millwall, coming off the bench for Soulyamane Doukara, and three days later he made his first start in the 2-1 Capital One Cup win over Accrington Stanley. He came off the bench in the 1-0 win over Middlesbrough and the 2-0 loss at home to Brighton & Hove Albion, before starting under Neil Redfearn in the 1-0 win over Bolton Wanderers at Elland Road. He kept his place for the next three games under Redfearn, including the memorable 3-1 win over AFC Bournemouth, and started the first game under new boss Darko Milanic away at Brentford.

Cook featured in five out of the six games under Milanic, missing the 1-1 draw at home to Sheffield Wednesday, and he was an instrumental part of the midfield under Neil Redfearn, after Milanic had departed after only six games at the helm. He played in every league game up to the draw at Blackpool in mid-March and subsequently went on to win the Championship Apprentice of the Year award and was named runner-up to Alex Mowatt in the *Yorkshire Evening Post* Player of the Year. He did however win the Leeds United Young Player of the Year at the start of May.

Cook signed a new contract tying him to the club until June 2017 and scored his first goal for the side in a cup defeat away at Doncaster Rovers. The youngster went on to feature 47 times that season under both Uwe Rosler and Steve Evans and scored a wonderful equaliser at home to Fulham from 35 yards. He went on to win the Football League Young Player of the Year award and for the second consecutive season went away with the Leeds United Young Player of the Year. Interest was growing in Cook and he joined AFC Bournemouth in July 2016 for an undisclosed fee.

LIAM COOPER

Debut: Middlesbrough (H) 16 August 2014
Appearances: 150 (10)
Goals: 6

Cooper who was born and bred in Hull and joined his hometown club at under-12 level. Having had loan spells at Carlisle United, Huddersfield Town and Chesterfield, he signed a two-and-half-year deal with the Spireites in January 2013. Fast forward to the summer of 2014, and following a pre-season game between Chesterfield and Leeds it was announced that his current club had rejected two bids from Leeds before a deal was agreed on 13 August.

Cooper made his debut in a 1-0 win over Middlesbrough and would go to feature 31 times in his first season at the club, scoring a brilliant volley in the 3-1 win at home to Blackpool. He also captained the side in the absence of Jason Pearce, Stephen Warnock and Sol Bamba. The following campaign saw the Hull-born defender start in 41 games, scoring at home to Brighton in what proved to be Uwe Rosler's last game in charge, and again he deputised as captain in place of Sol Bamba.

Under new head coach Garry Monk, the following season proved to be a difficult one for Cooper, with the signings of Pontus Jansson and Kyle Bartley (on loan from Swansea City) and he only played in 18 games. But when called upon he never failed to disappoint, including a brilliant performance in the 2-0 win over Brighton in mid-March 2017 as Leeds looked for a play-off place. With Bartley now back in South Wales, Cooper started the new campaign as first choice and was the chosen captain for the 2017-18 season, a role that he deservedly still keeps today. He featured in 32 games under both Thomas Christiansen and Paul Heckingbottom, scoring the winner at home to Brentford in February 2018.

The 2018-19 season saw another new head coach in former Argentinian World Cup coach Marcelo Bielsa, and he took Cooper's game to a new level. He started the season with the third goal on the opening day against Stoke City and followed this up with strikes at home to Preston North End and Ipswich Town. In the game away at Bristol City, he captained the side for the 100th time and by the end of the season he had made 160 appearances for the club. He also had the honour of being named in both the EFL Championship Team of the Year and the PFA Championship Team of the season.

KALVIN PHILLIPS

Debut: Wolverhampton Wanderers (A) 6 April 2015
Appearances: 106 (25)
Goals: 10

The Wortley-born midfielder signed his first professional deal with Leeds United in the summer of 2014 when he penned a one-year contract. When the team was announced for the FA Cup third-round tie away at Sunderland, the bench read: Sharp, Doukara, Stuart Taylor, Thompson, Dawson, Killock and a certain Kalvin Phillips. It was the first time he was named in a matchday squad and he was also an unused substitute away at Wigan Athletic and in home games against Nottingham Forest and Blackburn Rovers respectively. He made his debut in front of the Sky cameras in a thrilling 4-3 loss at Wolverhampton Wanderers before scoring his first goal for the club in his very next game at home to Cardiff City.

Under both Uwe Rosler and Steve Evans, the youngster only featured on ten occasions, although he was an unused sub in 19 games, but his big breakthrough campaign came under Garry Monk in the 2016-17 season. He scored his second goal for the club with a brilliant free kick away at Nottingham Forest and was named the EFL Championship Young Player of the Month for October 2016. He featured 40 times under Monk before the former Swansea boss left the club in May 2017.

Phillips went from strength to strength, scoring a brace on the opening day of the following season away at Bolton Wanderers under new boss Thomas Christiansen, and he scored in wins over Burton Albion (5-0), Ipswich Town (3-2) and the 2-1 loss at home to Sheffield United. He ended the season under Paul Heckingbottom with goals against Norwich City and Queens Park Rangers and kept up his brilliant form under new head coach Marcelo Bielsa the following season. He played a starring role under the Argentinian, picking up numerous Man of the Match awards with his outstanding displays as Leeds battled for a place in the Premier League.

He made his 100th appearance in a Leeds United shirt away at Swansea City in August 2018 in an exciting 2-2 draw and he went down in the club's history books by scoring the latest-ever goal (excluding extra time) when he popped up with an equaliser away at Middlesbrough in the 101st minute to salvage a deserved point for the side. The plaudits kept coming in for Phillips as he was named in the EFL Championship Team of the Season as well as being named the *Yorkshire Evening Post* Player of the Year.

CHRIS WOOD

Debut: Burnley (H) 8 August 2015
Appearances: 78 (10)
Goals: 44

Wood who was in born in Auckland in New Zealand and started his youth and senior career with Cambridge FC in his own country, came to the attention of West Bromwich Albion in 2009. He went on to have numerous loan spells at Barnsley, Brighton & Hove Albion,

Birmingham City, Millwall and Leicester City, before joining the Foxes at the start of 2013. He had a further loan spell at Ipswich Town in 2015 before returning to the Midlands.

Wood joined Leeds at the start of July 2015 for an undisclosed fee and made his debut in the sides 1-1 draw at home to Burnley on the opening day of that season. He scored his first goal for the side in the 2-2 draw away at Bristol City and followed this up with goals at home to Sheffield Wednesday and a brilliant winner at Derby County, which helped Leeds win at Pride Park for the first time since April 2002. He ended his first season in west Yorkshire featuring 37 times (33 starts, four substitute appearances), scoring 13 goals. He missed around three months of the campaign under Steve Evans due to injury, but bounced back with goals at home to Queens Park Rangers, a brace at home to Reading and one each away at Hull City and Preston North End respectively. The following season, under new head coach Garry Monk and new striking coach James Beattie, proved to be the best of the New Zealander's career. Despite not scoring on the opening day away at Queens Park Rangers, he grabbed a penalty in the League Cup game away at Fleetwood Town, then he just kept on scoring and scoring. He scored a brilliant bicycle kick to salvage a point at home to Fulham and followed it up with the second in a 2-0 away win at Sheffield Wednesday. He scored in four successive games in September to help Leeds up the Championship table and carried on the form right through the season.

Notable strikes included goals in wins at Norwich City, the second in a famous 2-0 win over Aston Villa, a brace at home to Brighton and the equaliser away at Newcastle United on Good Friday which produced magical scenes in the away end. He finished with 30 goals and became the first Leeds United player to do so since Jermaine Beckford in 2009-10.

Wood started the following campaign with a goal in the 3-2 away win at Bolton Wanderers, but rumours were abound that Wood was to leave, which in the end proved to be true as he joined Burnley for an undisclosed record fee.

KEMAR ROOFE

Debut: Queens Park Rangers (A) 7 August 2016
Appearances: 92 (31)
Goals: 32

The Walsall-born player started his footballing career with the West Bromwich Albion academy and had numerous loan spells at Vikingur Reykjavik (in Iceland), Northampton Town, Cheltenham Town, Colchester United and Oxford United, before joining the U's at the end of the 2014-15 season. It was during the following season that Roofe hit the headlines, scoring 26 goals for Oxford and being voted as League Two's Player of the Year and also being named in the League Two PFA Team of the Year.

In the summer of 2016 Roofe joined Leeds in a four year deal for an undisclosed fee and was handed the number seven shirt. He was played in various attacking position's under Garry Monk and after he hit the post in a League Cup tie at Liverpool, he tweeted 'pray4Roofe'. It seemed to have the desired effect as he notched his first goal in the 2-0 televised win over Aston Villa. He marked his first season at Elland Road with a half century of appearances and three goals to his name, the others coming in both wins over Preston North End, 4-1 at Deepdale and 3-0 at Elland Road.

The 2017-18 season saw a new head coach in Dane, Thomas Christiansen and Roofe started scoring with a hat-trick in the League Cup win over Newport County as well as goals in wins away at Nottingham Forest and one in the 5-0 win over Burton Albion, as Leeds started the campaign like a house on fire. He scored his second hat-trick for the club in a 3-1 win at Queens Park Rangers, and Roofe finished the year with a goal in the 2-1 win away at Burton Albion. He finished the season with 14 goals, the last of which came on the last day of the season at home to Queens Park Rangers. Under new boss Marcelo Bielsa, Roofe started the 2018-19 season with four goals and was awarded the Championship Player of the Month for August. He finished the campaign with 15, which was one better than the previous campaign, with memorable last minute winners away at Aston Villa and at home to Blackburn Rovers in successive games and scored the only goal in the play-off first leg away at Derby County. With that goal against the Rams, he scored in every game against them that season, having hit a brace in August as well as the opening goal in Leeds's 2-0 win in January 2019. With only year left of his contract, Roofe joined Belgian side Anderlecht in August 2019.

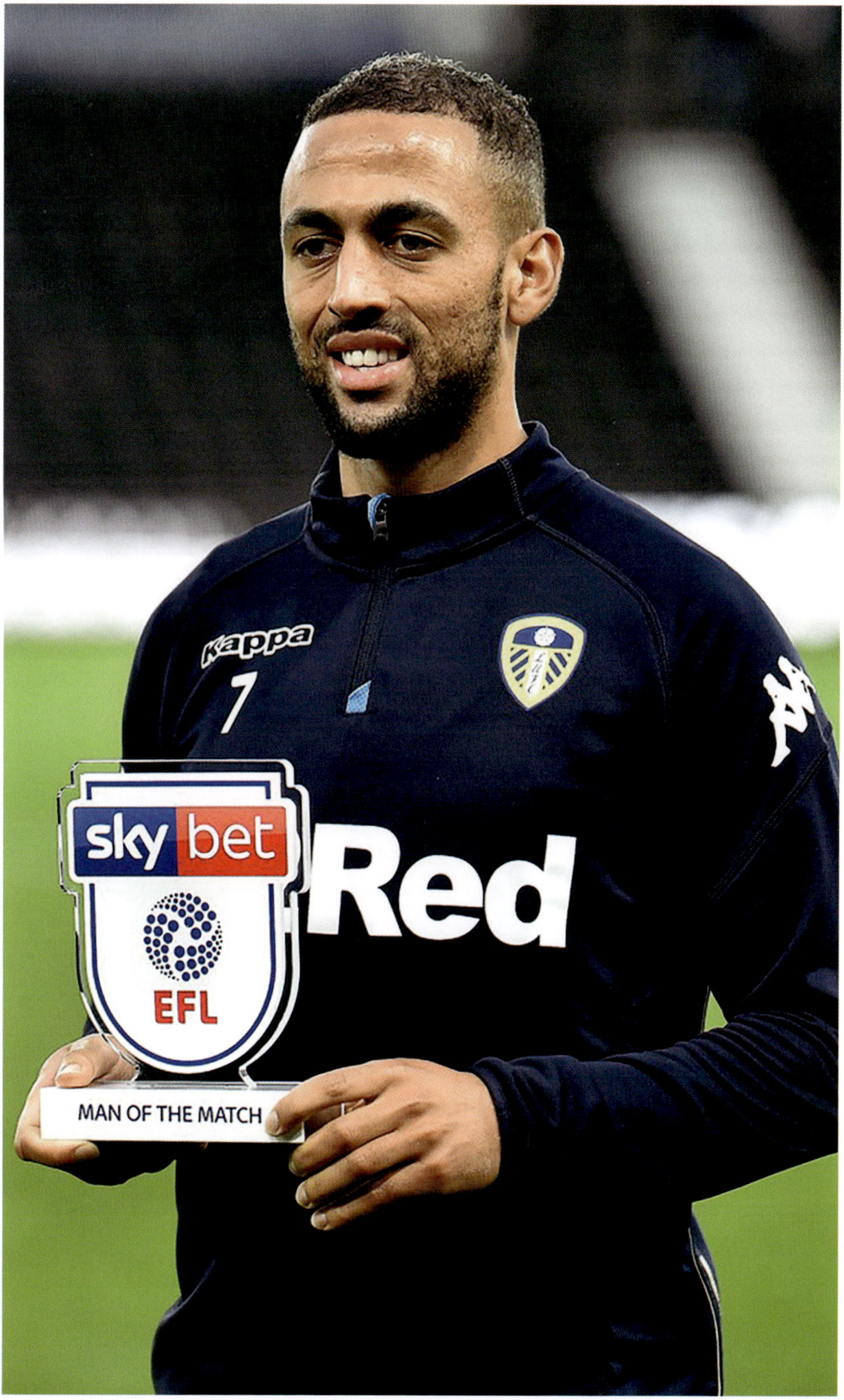
Kappa
7
sky bet
EFL
MAN OF THE MATCH
Red

KYLE BARTLEY

Debut: Queens Park Rangers (A) 7 August 2016
Appearances: 49 (1)
Goals: 6

Despite only being at the club for a season, Bartley became a fans' favourite for his all-action displays at the heart of the defence with Sol Bamba, Liam Cooper and Pontus Jansson. Signed on loan from Swansea City by former manager Garry Monk, Bartley made such an impact during the 2016-17 season that there were calls from supporters to sign him on a permanent basis ahead of both the 2017-18 and 2018-19 seasons respectively. Bartley, who was born in Stockport, started out at Arsenal captaining the reserves and he was also part of the side that won both the Premier Academy League and FA Youth Cup in 2009. It was in north London where he forged a friendship and partnership with Luke Ayling. He did make one appearance for the Gunners in a Champions League tie away at Olympiakos. He then spent the 2009-10 campaign on loan to Sheffield United before returning to Bramall Lane the following season. He also had loan spells at Rangers during both the 2010-11 and 2011-12 season as well as at Birmingham City during the 2013-14 term. He joined Swansea in August 2012 and Leeds ahead of the 2016-17 season on a season long loan deal. He made his debut in a disappointing 3-0 loss away at Queens Park Rangers and scored his first goal in a vital 2-1 win at home to Blackburn Rovers in mid-September and captained the side on numerous occasions in place of the two Liam's, Bridcutt and Cooper. He scored his second goal for the side in a 2-1 Yorkshire derby at home to Barnsley at the start of October 2016 and followed it up with a vital late winner at home to Brentford just before Christmas as Leeds made strides up the Championship table.

Another goal and another win followed as the Whites took apart Rotherham United in a superb second-half display at home to the Millers and he and his best mate, Ayling played a starring role in a 1-0 win in front of the Sky Sports cameras at home to Derby County in mid-January 2017. His other two goals for the side came in a 2-1 loss away at Burton Albion and a 3-3 draw at home to Norwich City, which saw the side subsequently miss out on a top six place at the end of the season. In total Bartley started 45 out of the 46 league games, missing out against Aston Villa just after Christmas. He started four out of five League Cup ties, missing the game away at Luton, in which head coach Garry Monk made 11 changes from the side that had started against Sheffield Wednesday three days earlier. He featured in the FA Cup tie at Cambridge United, coming on for Liam Cooper, but wasn't involved away at Sutton United. He signed a new contract in South Wales ahead of the 2017-18 season but joined West Bromwich Albion on a three-year deal less than a year later. He missed the game at the Hawthorns against Leeds in November 2018 and was an unused substitute in the reverse at Elland Road at the start of March 2019.

PABLO HERNANDEZ

Debut: Fleetwood Town (A) 10 August 2016
Appearances: 108 (14)
Goals: 27

The Castellon-born attacking midfielder/winger started his career at Valencia with loan spells at Onda and Cadiz and a permanent spell at Getafe before joining Swansea City in August 2012. He helped the Swans to win the League Cup in 2013, before joining Qatari club Al-Arabi in July 2014.

Whilst at Al-Arabi he had further loan spells at Al-Nasr and Rayo Vallecano before joining Leeds United on loan in August 2016, playing for his former Swansea City manager Garry Monk. He made his debut in a League Cup tie away at Fleetwood Town and would go on to become an integral part of the side for the next three seasons.

In his first season in west Yorkshire, he featured 34 times in total, scoring six goals from midfield. He scored his first in Leeds colours with a brilliant curling shot away at Cardiff City and followed it up with strikes at home to Barnsley, away at Preston North End, at home to Bristol City, at home to Preston and a brilliant free kick at home to Norwich City. That January he signed a permanent six-month contract and agreed a new one year deal at the end of the season. The following campaign would be even better for Hernandez, both on and off the pitch. He featured in 42 games, scoring nine goals and captaining the side in the absence of Liam Cooper. He scored in both game against Burton Albion, as well as strikes in the League Cup away at Burnley and Leicester City, and vital goals in home wins against Middlesbrough and Hull City. At the start of May, he won both the Player of the Year and the Players' Player of the Year and by this time had agreed a new two year deal running until the end of the 2019-20 season.

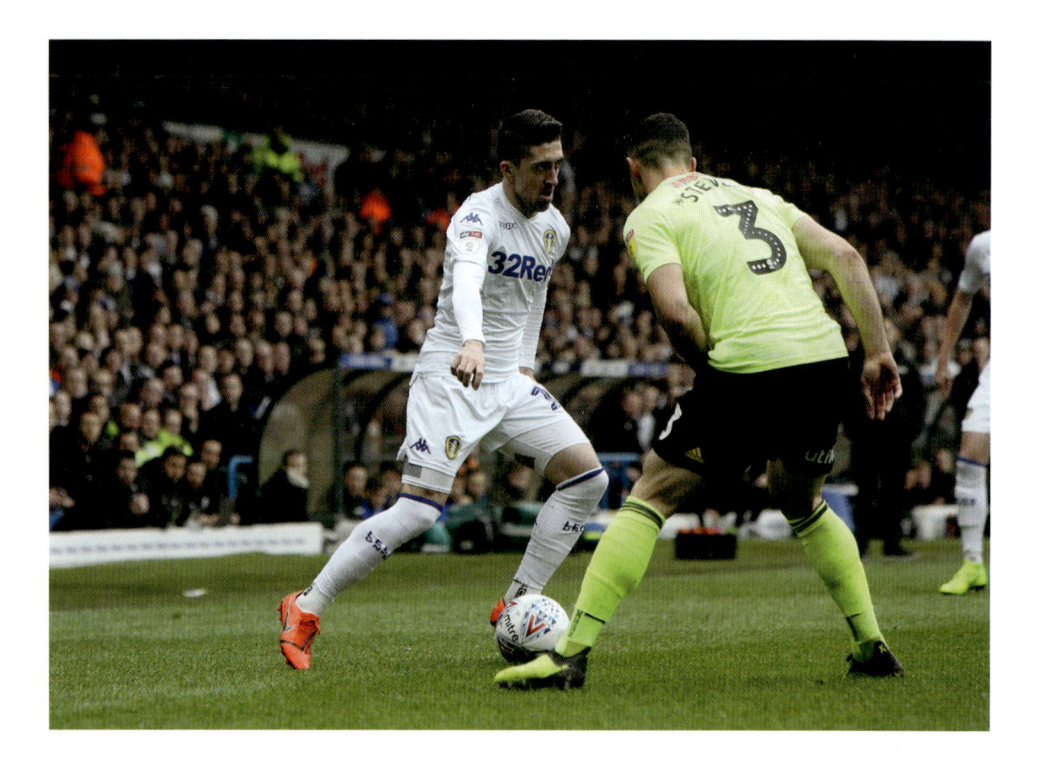

Under new head coach Marcelo Bielsa, Hernandez had a brilliant start to the 2018-19 campaign and in September he won the PFA Championship Player of the Month for August. He would feature heavily as Leeds were in the top two for the majority of the season before dropping into the play-offs and finishing third before losing to Derby County over two legs. The personal accolades kept coming, being voted into the PFA Team of the Year and for the second consecutive season walking away with both the Leeds United Player of the Year and the Players' Player of the Year.

LUKE AYLING

Debut: Birmingham City (H) 13 August 2016
Appearances: 114 (2)
Goals: 2

Ayling started his career at Arsenal after joining them aged 10 and progressed through the youth teams, playing with Jack Wilshere and Kyle Bartley before signing scholarship forms.

He was an unused substitute for the Gunners in the Champions League away at Olympiakos, but it would be the only time Ayling would feature in an Arsenal first team.

Originally from north London, he moved to Somerset to join Yeovil Town on loan, before agreeing a permanent contract at the end of the 2009-10 season. From Yeovil, where he had won promotion to the Championship in 2013, he joined Bristol City and again won promotion in 2015. Ayling joined Leeds in August 2016 (despite playing in Bristol City's opening game of the season against Wigan Athletic) under Garry Monk and would play a massive part under the former Swansea player and manager.

Ayling made his debut at home to Birmingham City and went on to make the right-back slot his own. He featured 43 times for the side and became a firm fans' favourite. On 7 November, following the Whites impressive 3-2 win at Norwich City, the right-back was named in EFL's Team of the Week. He helped the Whites finish in seventh place under Monk. But an even bigger honour was to await Ayling the following season under new head coach Thomas Christiansen as he captained the side for the first time in the 4-1 League Cup win over Port Vale. He also skippered the side in matches at home to Fulham, Newport County, away at Millwall, away at Burnley, away at Sheffield Wednesday and at home to Derby County.

Unfortunately, his season was cut short following an ankle ligament injury at home to Nottingham Forest on New Year's Day 2018, but he did return to play the full 90 minutes on the last day of the season at home to Queens Park Rangers. He broke his goalscoring duck in the 2-0 home win against Rotherham United in mid August and was a regular in the first team until another injury against Nottingham Forest would rule him out for seven games. He returned in the dramatic 3-2 win at Aston Villa, playing a huge part as Leeds finished in third place, only to lose out to Derby County in the end of season play-off lottery. He scored his second goal for the club in the nerve shredding 3-2 win over Millwall at the end of March.

MANAGERS APPOINTED IN THE 2010s

NEIL REDFEARN (CARETAKER)

First game in charge: Bristol City (A) 4 February 2012
Last game in charge: Doncaster Rovers (H) 18 February 2012
Games: 4
Won: 2
Drawn: 0
Lost: 2

Leeds turned to reserve team manager Neil Redfearn to hold the fort whilst on the lookout for a new number one. You can read about Redfearn's managerial career below as he took over from Darko Milanic in October 2014. As for his first spell in charge, it couldn't have started any better, with a 3-0 win over nine-man Bristol City. Leeds took the lead through Robert Snodgrass and made the game safe with goals from Ross McCormack and Luciano Becchio. Redfearn said after the game, 'When we got the goal and got a foothold there was only going to be one winner and it was a very professional performance.' Next up at Elland Road was the visit of former assistant manager Gus Poyet's Brighton & Hove Albion side, who took all three points thanks to a winner a minute into stoppage time from Alan Navarro. 'It was about being professional and as daft as it seems if it had finished 1-1 it would

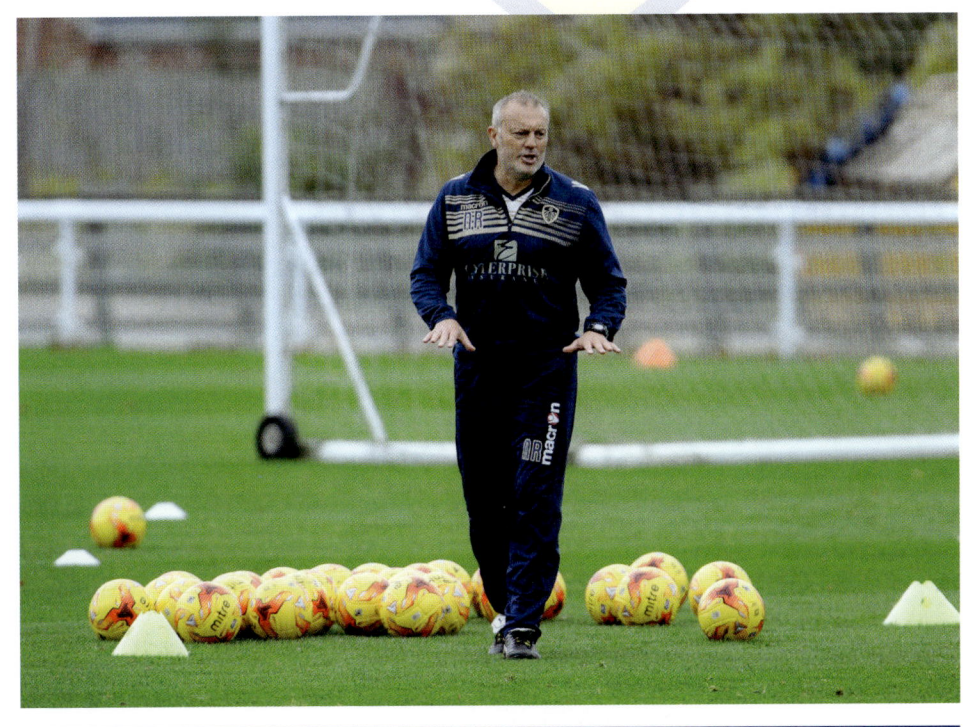

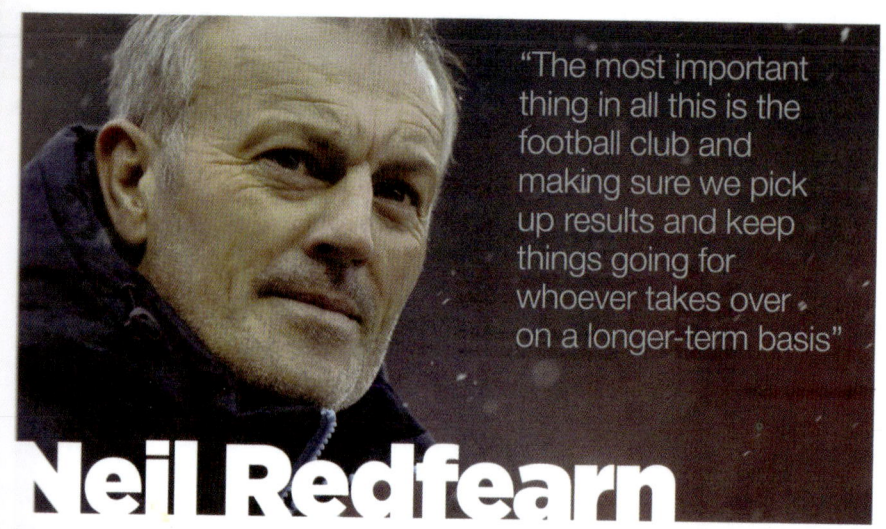

"The most important thing in all this is the football club and making sure we pick up results and keep things going for whoever takes over on a longer-term basis"

Neil Redfearn

Hello everyone and welcome back to Elland Road. I'd like to welcome Gus Poyet and his staff from Brighton.

It's a proud honour for me to be writing these notes for the first time today and we are looking to build on our performance at Bristol City last weekend and pick up another three points against a good Brighton side.

There's obviously been a lot written and said about the changes that have been made here since our last home game against Birmingham City, and when I was asked to take the job on a temporary basis after Simon departed then I naturally said yes.

Times like this can always be difficult at a football club, particularly when a manager has been here as long as Simon had and had achieved what he had over that period of time. He took the club out of League One and to a seventh place finish last season.

But, when you're in football, you become used to change and I have to say I have been delighted with the way the players have adapted. We approached things slightly differently before the Bristol City game last weekend and I was pleased to see what we had worked on come to fruition.

It was important we were solid and hard to beat and after the first 20 minutes or so at Bristol I felt we came into our own and, in the end, we won the game comfortably after laying down those foundations early on.

A lot of people have asked me about the job and whether I would like the opportunity, but I've always maintained this isn't about me. I am an employee of the football club who has been asked to take up the job in the short-term. What happens beyond that will happen.

The most important thing in all this is the football club and making sure we pick up results and keep things going for whoever takes over on a longer-term basis. I'm sure decisions will be made by the people at the top and, as I've always done while I've been here, I will support whatever decisions are made.

As it stands, we are two points away from the Play-Offs and it's important that we keep picking up points to stay in touch with the leading pack. We've got a pretty big week with two more important games after today, against Coventry and Doncaster, and we have a real opportunity to come out of the next three games in a very good position indeed.

On a slightly different note, some of you will have noticed Andy O'Brien in the dug-out at Bristol last weekend. Andy is now training again and we're delighted to have him back among the lads. We were hoping he would get the opportunity to have a run-out in the reserves in midweek, but unfortunately the game against Middlesbrough was called off due to the weather.

A few other senior players would have also played on Tuesday to keep their match fitness levels up because it's important everyone is available and ready if needed.

We have a good squad of players here, a squad that is capable of making a challenge, and equally, a squad that believes they have every chance. I said when I was asked to take up the job that we're starting with a blank canvas again, and everyone has that opportunity to stake their claims – be it in games, training, or reserve matches.

Finally, I'd like to thank the staff at the club for all their help and support over the past week or so, and also you the fans for your good wishes and your support. The 1,900 at Bristol last weekend travelled in awful conditions, and I'm glad we could reward you with the win.

Today, we're back on home soil with a bigger support, and by coming together and working together, there's no reason why we can't keep moving onwards and upwards.

---

have been fair.' Worse was to follow on Valentine's Day as two penalties from former loan player Gary McSheffrey won the day for the Sky Blues at the Ricoh Arena. Rumours then started about the arrival of Neil Warnock as the new manager ahead of the Doncaster Rovers game four days later, and these proved to be true and the former Sheffield United boss was confirmed just before the game. He watched on as Leeds came from 2-0 down to win a thrilling encounter nine minutes into stoppage time (the game had been held up due to a nasty injury to Robbie Rogers) with a goal from Luciano Becchio. 'I have to say the lads have been fantastic for me, even if a couple of the performances weren't what we wanted and were disappointing for the fans.' It was a case of one Neil to another.

Neil Redfearn's first line up: Bristol City (A) 4 February 2012: Lonergan, Smith, O'Dea, Lees, White, Clayton, Pugh, Delph, Snodgrass, McCormack, Becchio. Subs not used: M. Taylor, Bruce, Rogers, Brown, Townsend.

Neil Redfearn's last line up: Doncaster Rovers (H) 18 February 2012: Lonergan, Bruce, Lees, O'Dea, White, Pugh (Brown), Clayton, Townsend (Rogers, Forssell), Snodgrass, McCormack, Becchio. Subs not used: M. Taylor, Connolly.

NEIL WARNOCK

First game in charge: Portsmouth (A) 25 February 2012
Last game in charge: Derby County (H) 1 April 2013
Games: 63
Won: 23
Drawn: 15
Lost: 25

Leeds turned to promotion specialist Neil Warnock to guide them out of the wilderness and back into the top flight. The Sheffield-born manager started his playing career at Chesterfield and had spells at Rotherham United, Hartlepool United, Scunthorpe United, Aldershot, Barnsley, York City and finally Crewe Alexandra, but it would be as a manager that his career would really take off.

He started out at non-league Gainsborough Trinity, followed by a spell at Burton Albion. It was at non-league Scarborough that Warnock began to make a name for himself. He won promotion to the Football League with the Seadogs in 1987 and then moved to Notts County in

1989, where he achieved a double promotion with the Magpies, winning the Third Division play-offs in 1990 and the Second Division play-offs a year later. He turned down the advances of Ken Bates to stay with Notts County before being sacked at Meadow Lane in January 1993. He helped Torquay stay in the Football League before moving to Huddersfield Town in the summer of 1993. He was at it again with the Terriers, winning the Second Division play-offs in 1995, and he repeated the act with Plymouth Argyle a year later, this time winning the Third Division play-offs. He had spells at both Oldham Athletic and Bury before taking his dream job at Sheffield United in 1999.

Warnock had a brilliant campaign in 2002-03, reaching two cup semi-finals (defeating Leeds in both) and the play-off final before losing to Wolverhampton Wanderers in Cardiff. Three years later he won his sixth promotion as the Blades finished second in the Championship behind winners Reading. He failed to keep them in the Premier League and resigned a day after their relegation was confirmed. He then had a spell at Crystal Palace, where he lost in the lottery of the play-offs to Bristol City over two legs, before joining Queens Park Rangers in March 2010. Warnock completed his seventh promotion of his career, winning the Championship in season 2010-11, but he was sacked at Loftus Road in January 2012.

But he wasn't out of the game long, agreeing to take on the Leeds job up until the end of the 2012-13 season. His first game saw Leeds draw 0-0 at Portsmouth, and despite having the majority of play at home to Southampton they again lost 1-0. He had to wait till his fourth game in charge for his first win, which came in a 2-0 victory away at Middlesbrough thanks to goals from Snodgrass (his new captain) and Becchio. 'It doesn't get much better than that, does it? We were at it from the first whistle,' Warnock said afterwards, but it proved to be false hope, as the Whites' challenge filtered out which included an abysmal 7-3 home defeat to Nottingham Forest: 'I am embarrassed by the result, I don't think anyone could look in the

Neil Warnock

"From a personal point of view, I would like to thank all the fans who welcomed me… The level of support has even managed to surprise someone as long in the tooth as me!"

I'd like to give a big welcome to Nigel Adkins and his table-topping team today.

It's appropriate that for my first game officially in charge we welcome the league leaders to Elland Road. Southampton have shown tremendous consistency over the past couple of years and they have improved their squad on a regular basis. That is something that we have to try and attain in the coming months. I do wish Nigel Adkins all the very best in what he is doing down there – apart from today, of course!

From a personal point of view, I would like to thank all the fans who welcomed me when I arrived here for the Doncaster game a couple of weeks and to all those who travelled down to Portsmouth last week. The level of support has even managed to surprise someone as long in the tooth as me!

I can assure everyone that while I'm in charge of your team nothing less than 100 per cent will be given by everyone connected with the club. I know there have been one or two issues over the past few months, but I have to say I've been delighted to see everyone getting behind the team. I hope that continues for the rest of the season because who knows what we can achieve with such wonderful support and backing?

And if you think our chairman is difficult here, then tune in to BBC2 tomorrow night at 11.15pm and watch a programme called *The Four Year Plan* about the last four years at QPR. It makes my current chairman look like an angel!

Back to football, and having been around for the Doncaster game I have to say that if we defend like that today Southampton could get into double figures! But the lads have worked very, very hard on the training ground and to come away from Portsmouth with a clean sheet last weekend was very pleasing. I know they've had some problems off the field, but there's a very good squad of players there.

The Portsmouth game was an opportunity to look at the defensive side of things more closely and I was pleasantly surprised. This will be another good test today. I am learning all the time too, and by 8pm tonight, I'm sure I will have learnt a few more things.

Staying on Portsmouth for a moment, it was nice to pop into the Hampshire Whites' Leeds On The Road event at Fareham on the Friday night before the game. I'm usually superstitious and never go out the night before a game, but superstitions haven't really helped me this season, have they?! So I decided to surprise a few people. I enjoyed it, and I think a good night was had by all.

In the end, I was disappointed that we didn't actually win the game down there and pick up what would have been good three points. Ross McCormack had a goal disallowed which was well over the line, and the sooner goal-line technology comes in the better it will be for everyone concerned, including referee and linesmen.

Looking at today, I don't know what size the crowd will be, but it would be great if we could beat our biggest league crowd at some stage this season and push to the 30,000 mark, especially when our next game here is against a West Ham side, who are doing well and will bring a good support.

I remember visiting this place on a few occasions when there's been 30,000-plus crowds and it's some place when it's like that. I always remember the club's reputation for looking after visiting managers and at one game I came to I found myself at the top of one of the stands and needed a pair of binoculars to see the game. I hope we keep that tradition going!

But, it is a fantastic ground and when there's 30,000 here it's absolutely deafening. I'd like to think we can better that this season, although the players have their part to play by giving you something to shout about. I saw it and heard it in the second half against Doncaster and that was down to you. You spurred on the players that day and you did a great job.

You got the players going and it was fantastic to see. You have a big, big part to play, and hopefully you can all lift the roof this evening.

mirror after the goals we've conceded. Going back to my Sunday league days, I'd have been disappointed to concede two or three of those.' Leeds finished in 14th position and attention quickly turned to the summer and recruitment at Elland Road.

Warnock brought in Jason Pearce, Adam Drury, Paul Green, Paddy Kenny, Andy Gray (for his second spell), Jamie Ashdown, Luke Varney, David Norris, Rudy Austin and Lee Peltier. To the surprise of many, he also added El-Hadji Diouf to his new squad. Leeds started the new league campaign with a 1-0 win over newly relegated Wolverhampton Wanderers at Elland Road, thanks to a header from Luciano Becchio. 'You have to do what we did today. The Championship is a different league to the top level. The players loved the atmosphere and playing in front of a big crowd. That was something I didn't think we had about us last year,' Warnock said after the deserved 1-0 win. League form proved to be erratic and Leeds turned their attention to the cups, reaching the last eight of the Capital One Cup, before losing at home to European Champions Chelsea, and the last 16 of the FA Cup, losing out to Premier League champions Manchester City. Rumours were abound that Warnock was to leave the club, but he stayed on until the start of April when, following a televised defeat to Derby County, he parted company with the side, leaving them in 12th place. Neil Redfearn was asked again to take the reins on a caretaker basis.

As for Warnock, he had a second spell at Crystal Palace, was caretaker at Queens Park Rangers, saved Rotherham United from relegation in 2016 and won his eighth promotion in 2018, guiding Cardiff City back the Premier League.

Neil Warnock's first line up: Portsmouth (A) 25 February 2012: Lonergan, Bruce (Bromby), Lees, O'Dea, White, Pugh, Clayton, Brown, Snodgrass, McCormack, Becchio. Subs not used: Paynter, Sam, Forssell, Thompson.

Neil Warnock's last line up: Derby County (H) 1 April 2013: Kenny, Byram, Peltier, Pearce, S. Warnock, Green, Austin, Dawson (McCormack), Varney, Diouf (White), Morison. Subs not used: Ashdown, Tonge, Norris, Habibou.

NEIL REDFEARN (CARETAKER)

First game in charge: Charlton Athletic (A) 6 April 2013
Last game in charge: Charlton Athletic (A) 6 April 2013
Games: 1
Won: 0
Drawn: 0
Lost: 1

Redfearn was asked to take the game away at Charlton Athletic, assisted by former captain Richard Naylor, and despite equalising through Luke Varney nine minutes from time, they lost the game thanks to Jonathan Obika's stoppage-time header. Redfearn said afterwards,

"Hard work has been the motto since I was asked to take care of things on a caretaker basis"

NEIL REDFEARN

Good afternoon everyone and welcome to today's opponents Sheffield Wednesday for our final Yorkshire derby of the season.

Derby games are always something special, I played in plenty of different ones as a player, and it's true that form does go out of the window in these games.

In both our cases today, we have plenty to play for. Wednesday had a good win at Millwall in midweek to ease their own concerns and, like us, they will be looking for what could prove to be a decisive three points.

We should have been in a slightly better position than we are, but for Charlton's late winner at The Valley last weekend. I said before I didn't think the game would be pretty by any stretch – like a lot of pitches at the moment, the surface down there is awful – but having got ourselves back into it I felt we should have come away with a point at the very least.

Losing Lee Peltier in the final minutes didn't help us all at all, but I'm not going to start complaining about bad luck. I'm a believer that you make your own luck, and the harder you work the greater your rewards are. That's been the theme this week on the training ground; hard work.

Hard work has been the motto since I was asked to take care of things on a caretaker basis. I said at the start that however long it was for, I didn't want the position full-time but was happy to step up and help. I'm proud of the work we have done with the Academy over the past 12-18 months and that is where my focus is.

Another facet of the Academy has been developing our own coaches and, having Richard Naylor alongside me for a few games, and Leigh Bromby working with Chris Coates with the Under-18s and Under-21s, can only be good for them all. Developing players is why the Academy is there, but if we can develop our own coaches from within – particularly good people who care about the club and understand the club – that can only be for the best.

Having endured a difficult run, today's game is welcome in that we will have a big crowd and, on top of the three points, there is local pride at stake. It has all the ingredients of being a good game and hopefully we can pick up the win we want and move into Tuesday's game against Burnley and look for a positive finish to the season.

Luke Varney scoring at Charlton last weekend.

'From a performance point of view, I thought we went a goal down against the run of play – we were doing well up to that point. Whenever the manager leaves, it's upsetting – these are players that Neil Warnock signed. But they've applied themselves well. It was a good performance without being spectacular, it was a poor surface. They will be disappointed, but they've been professional at what they've done.' Former Reading boss Brian McDermott was announced as the new manager a day before the visit of Sheffield Wednesday to Elland Road.

Neil Redfearn's only line up: Charlton Athletic (A) 6 April 2013: Kenny, Byram, Peltier (Austin), Pearce, Warnock, Green, Tonge (Brown), White (Varney), Norris, McCormack, Morison. Subs not used: Ashdown, Diouf, Habibou, Poleon.

BRIAN MCDERMOTT

First game in charge: Sheffield Wednesday (H) 13 April 2013
Last game in charge: Derby County (H) 3 May 2014
Games: 54
Won: 20
Drawn: 9
Lost: 25

Brian McDermott had just been sacked from Reading when Leeds came calling. He started his playing career with Arsenal, making his debut for the Gunners in 1979. He had loan spells at Fulham and IFK Norkoping in Sweden, before joining Oxford United in December 1984. Whilst at the Manor Ground he had loan spells at Huddersfield Town and Djurgardens before moving to Cardiff City and later having stints at Exeter City, Yeovil Town, South China and Slough Town. It was at the latter that McDermott started his managerial career, finishing 17th in the Conference in season 1995-96 and 16th the following campaign. He then guided Slough to eighth place before leaving in the summer of 1998. His next job was at Woking, taking the job at the Cardinals in September 1998. He was sacked in February 2000, with the side struggling in 20th place.

McDermott then joined Reading in September of that year as chief scout and also became the under 19s manager as well as reserve team manager before taking on the role as caretaker manager in December 2009. Having defeated Liverpool on their own patch in an FA Cup replay in January 2010, he was handed the reins on a permanent basis. In season 2010-11 he led the Royals to the play-off final, where they lost to Swansea City at Wembley before he guided them to the Championship title a year later. After promotion to the top flight and being named Manager of the Month in February 2013, he was sacked a month later after a run of four successive league defeats.

He was appointed manager of the Whites a day before they took to the field in a local derby at home to Sheffield Wednesday. 'I had just left Reading and I was talking to Neil Redfearn. I was going to come in the summer, but at the time Shaun Harvey was talking to me, we decided best come now, I was before talking to Redders, and decided to come. The results were a little bit dicey and there were five games left so I decided to come straight away.' It had the desired impact as a Luke Varney double saw off the Owls: 'I was really pleased. It was hard in the first half and we knew we shouldn't have gone in a goal down but there was a good response after the interval, which was really important.' McDermott said afterwards.

He steered the side to 13th place and attentions turned to the 2013-14 campaign. He bought in Luke Murphy from Crewe Alexandra, Matt Smith from Oldham Athletic and Noel

"My philosophy with any successful group is that it is all about the team. Nothing comes before the team"

BRIAN
McDERMOTT

Good evening everyone and welcome back to Elland Road.
I'd like to welcome Sean Dyche, who brings his Burnley side here tonight. I've known Sean a long time and, going back, we did our Pro Licence course together. He did a really good job at Watford and, in my opinion he is one of the country's up-and-coming managers.

Officially, I'd like to say what a great honour it is for me to become Leeds United manager, and I'd like to thank Shaun Harvey who made it possible for me to come here.

I wasn't planning on going anywhere before the summer, but having had discussions with Shaun and spoken to Gwyn Williams I had a feeling that this was the right place to come, and even after just a couple of days here, I know that it is.

Nigel Gibbs has come with me and for anyone who doesn't know Nigel, he is a real football man. He is a fantastic coach, but first and foremost he is also a really, really good person. He's always been very, very popular and the work that he does is always player-orientated. I'm delighted to have him by my side, and he is equally delighted to be here.

Neil Redfearn will be working with us, too. Neil is someone else I've known for quite a while now. He had a fantastic reputation and before I came to Leeds I had a couple of discussions with Neil, and he told me all about the club and the good people here.

He was certainly right in that the people are very friendly and have made us feel very welcome.

When I first went to the training ground on Friday morning, I had a good feeling about the club. You could see that the players wanted to do well. When you look into their eyes you can see that they want to work hard, and that can only be good for us going forward.

My philosophy with any successful group is that it is all about the team. Nothing comes before the team. We as a staff are facilitators for the players to be the best they can be, and that is what we will strive to do, each and every day.

Looking back to Saturday's game against Sheffield Wednesday, that was a good result and good start for all of us. Going 1-0 behind was difficult to take because we didn't feel that they had really hurt us, but to come back from that showed the character of the boys.

When it got back to 1-1 I loved the reaction of our supporters. I felt the way you got behind the boys made a massive difference. It was a fantastic experience and a great day for all of us.

Hopefully we can have many, many more days like Saturday.

Goldenfry

Hunt from his former club Reading. The new season got off to a winning start thanks to a goal deep into stoppage time from Murphy at home to Brighton, and hopes were high of a promotion charge. Leeds were in sixth place heading into 2014, but the wheels were soon to fall off, with talks of a takeover by Italian businessman Massimo Cellino. The start to 2014 was disastrous as Leeds were dumped out of the FA Cup by lower league Rochdale before being hammered 6-0 away at Sheffield Wednesday. 'After that in a local derby it's public humiliation, as far as I'm concerned.' Cellino turned up at Elland Road and McDermott was allegedly sacked: 'I got a phone call from Chris Farnell who had been working with Massimo Cellino; I had been sacked. I rang up both Neil Redfearn and Nigel Gibbs and told them I had been sacked. Massimo didn't own the club and Nigel took the game against Huddersfield and I came back on the Monday. I knew that my time was numbered after that, I always felt that in the long run.' McDermott proved to be right despite finishing in 15th place. 'I was very proud to have managed Leeds, the supporters are everywhere and looked after me so well.' He had a second spell managing the Royals before being sacked at the end of the 2015-16 season.

Brian McDermott's first line up: Sheffield Wednesday (H) 13 April 2013: Kenny, Byram, Pearce, Warnock (Tonge), Drury, Green, Norris (Diouf), Austin, Varney, McCormack, Morison (White). Subs not used: Ashdown, Poleon, Somma, Hall.

For the record, the line up away at Yeovil Town on 8 February 2014 was: Kenny, Byram, Pearce, Lees, Warnock, Austin, Murphy, Kebe, Mowatt (Smith), Stewart, McCormack. Subs not used: Cairns, Peltier, Hunt, Wootton, Pugh, Brown, Wootton.

Brian McDermott's last line up: Derby County (H) 3 May 2014: Butland, Lees, Pearce, Wootton, Pugh, Austin, Tonge, Murphy (White), McCormack, Smith: Subs not used: Cairns, Hunt, Thompson, Poleon, Dawson, Walters.

Note: With the alleged sacking of McDermott, Nigel Gibbs took the team at home to Huddersfield Town on 1 February 2014, before McDermott returned to the dugout for the away game at Yeovil Town on 8 February 2014. With all that was going on around the club, the side produced a brilliant performance to defeat their local rivals 5-1 at Elland Road. The Terriers took the lead through Danny Ward after 25 minutes, but after that it was one-way traffic as a Ross McCormack hat-trick, one from Jimmy Kebe and a first for Alex Mowatt, ensured all three points in front of a jubilant crowd.

Nigel Gibbs's only game in charge: Huddersfield Town (H) 1 February 2014: Kenny, Byram, Pearce, Lees, Warnock, Austin (Brown), Murphy, Kebe, Mowatt (Tonge), Stewart, McCormack. Subs not used: Cairns, Peltier, Hunt, Wootton, Poleon.

DAVID HOCKADAY

First game in charge: Millwall (A) 9 August 2014
Last game in charge: Bradford City (A) 27 August 2014
Games: 6
Won: 2
Drawn: 0
Lost: 4

Massimo Cellino's takeover of the club was ratified by the Football League on 5 April 2014 and McDermott was sacked at the end of that season. To the shock of everyone in the football world, he appointed former Forest Green Rovers manager David Hockaday as his first permanent head coach. 'I had a phone call from an Italian voice asking if I would be interested in talking to his sponsor and that he had a strong influence at an English football club. I did my research and had a meeting in London and in walked Massimo Cellino. We were there for about five hours, playing around with salt and pepper pots and he asked me if I would be interested in becoming his head coach. I was pinching myself, it was a dream come true, the biggest football club in the United Kingdom. I had a very good relationship with Massimo.' Hockaday couldn't have wished for a harder start to life at Leeds, being thrown into the lion's den quite literally in an away game at Millwall. Leeds lost the game 2-0 and question marks were already been asked after only one game. The Whites did bounce back to beat Accrington Stanley 2-1 in the League Cup, and Hockaday recorded his first and only league win thanks to a late goal from new signing Billy Sharp against Middlesbrough. 'It was a tough game. There were quite a few chances and it took a goal poacher to sneak the win. I am fortunate to be given this chance and the players worked their socks off today. Nobody can say we didn't sweat blood for that white shirt. I've been in football for 40 years and pressure is my middle name.' Hockaday said afterwards, 'I

HEAD COACH

DAVID
HOCKADAY

Good evening and welcome to tonight's Capital One Cup tie against Accrington Stanley. I would like to welcome James Beattie, his players, staff and supporters to Elland Road. I hope you enjoy your experience here in Yorkshire and have a safe journey home.

On Saturday we were all disappointed with the result at Millwall. Our first-half performance was not up to the standard we would expect and to concede a poor goal from a corner certainly didn't help. At half-time we changed things about and the second period saw us play with more purpose.

Over the course of the whole 90 minutes we had the better chances but were unable to capitalise on any of these. We really should have come back with a share of the spoils and know we know we can play a lot better. A big thanks to our travelling supporters who were magnificent as always.

The president and myself have had many conversations over strengthening the squad and this is something we will continue to look to improve. The current group of players are giving us everything they can and are working incredibly hard every day on their game. We know the areas where we need strengthening and over the next couple of weeks I am confident that we will see some new faces here at Elland Road.

Back to tonight's game where we will expect a tough test against Accrington Stanley. We will continue to look to play a passing game and hopefully get through to the next round of the Capital One Cup. It is massively important that you get behind the players and cheer them on to victory.

Enjoy the game.

> "We really should have come back from Millwall with a share of the spoils and know we know we can play a lot better"

organised some great players and we needed a warrior, Hudson was available from Cardiff, he went to Huddersfield, I've got someone better said Cellino. "Bellusci" not a patch on Hudson, I wanted Andre Gray, he wants too much money.' Sadly for the former Swindon Town player, the Middlesbrough win was the highest point as defeats to Brighton (2-0) and Watford (4-1) ensured the pressure was on, going into a League Cup tie away at local rivals Bradford City. With Leeds down to ten men following the dismissal of Luke Murphy, they took the lead through Matt Smith eight minutes from time, but goals from Billy Knott and James Hanson saw Hockaday sacked less than 24 hours later and for the third time Neil Redfearn picked up the pieces.

David Hockadays's first line up: Millwall (A) 9 August 2014: Silvestri, Byram, Warnock, Austin, Wootton, Pearce, Tonge, Murphy, Hunt (Smith), Doukara (Cook), Ajose (Poleon). Subs not used: S. Taylor, Berardi, Killock, Benedicic.

David Hockadays's line up: Bradford City (A) 27 August 2014: S. Taylor, Wootton, Warnock, Tonge, Cooper, Pearce, Bianchi, Murphy, Norris (Poleon), Sharp, Smith. Subs not used: Silvestri, C. Taylor, Ajose, Cook, Benedicic, Antenucci.

NEIL REDFEARN (CARETAKER)

First game in charge: Bolton Wanderers (H) 30 August 2014
Last game in charge: Huddersfield Town (H) 20 September 2014
Games: 4
Won: 3
Drawn: 1
Lost: 0

Cellino turned to Redfearn with the club in 21st place in the Championship after four games and it couldn't have gone any better. Redfearn started with a 1-0 win over Bolton Wanderers thanks to a winner from Stephen Warnock and said afterwards, 'I love coaching and working with players. The most important thing is that the appointment is right for the football club. I will have a chat with the president and see what he is thinking. It is his decision but the club needs a settled set of circumstances.' Redfearn carried on after the international break and followed it up with a 1-1 draw away to Birmingham City thanks to an equaliser from Alex Mowatt before two excellent performances away to AFC Bournemouth and at home to Huddersfield Town.

Despite falling behind to an early Andrew Surman goal, Leeds turned the game on its head in the second period with goals from Doukara, Bellusci and Antenucci, ensuring a joyous journey back up north. 'I am enjoying being in charge and the club is in a far better position than when I took over. The lads are playing with confidence,' Redfearn said after. Even better was to come following an impressive 3-0 win over Huddersfield Town at Elland Road. Many expected him to get the job on a permanent basis, but Cellino appointed former Yugoslavian and Slovenian international Darko Milanic.

Neil Redfearn's first line up: Bolton Wanderers (H) 30 August 2014: Silvestri, Wottoon, Warnock (C. Taylor), Bianchi, Bellusci, Pearce, Sloth (Benedicic), Cook, Mowatt, Sharp, Antenucci. Subs not used: S. Taylor, Smith, Tonge, Dawson, Cooper.

CARETAKER HEAD COACH

NEIL
REDFEARN

Welcome to Elland Road for today's Yorkshire derby against Huddersfield Town.

Firstly, I'd like to congratulate the lads for the attitude, commitment and professionalism they have show during the last couple of weeks. We have a big squad here at the moment and I include all the lads as one, whether they are in the starting line-up on a Saturday or not. They have all mucked in and have showed a great togetherness and fighting spirit. It is this spirit that will get this team further up the league, because I believe they are good enough.

Being the Academy manager and head of coaching at the training ground I am so proud to see so many of our graduates in the first team here at Leeds United. This proves that the door is open for other young lads to make the step up into the first team. I'm biased, but I firmly believe that our Academy is one of the best in the country. We have great staff and some incredible young players. The likes of Sam Byram, Alex Mowatt and Lewis Cook are just the tip of the iceberg.

I'd like to welcome Chris Powell and his Huddersfield squad, staff and supporters. I've known Chris a long time now as we were in the same team at Charlton Athletic and he was also an apprentice when I was in the first team at Crystal Palace. He had a great playing career and I'm sure he will continue that into management.

At the moment we are an ongoing process and we all have to stick together. I believe this will be a case of two steps forward and one step back, but I know that we will get there. The supporters have to stick with the club and you will see an improvement and the progress being made. We have players here that are proud to wear the Leeds United badge and that will take us a long way.

Enjoy the game.

"I'd like to congratulate the lads for the attitude, commitment and professionalism they have show during the last couple of weeks"

WWW.LEEDSUNITED.COM / 5

Neil Redfearn's last line up: Huddersfield Town (H) 20 September 2014: Silvestri, Berardi, Warnock, Bianchi, Bellusci, Pearce, Austin (Tonge), Cook, Sloth (Byram), Doukara (Morison), Antenucci. Subs not used: S. Taylor, Sharp, Adryan, Cooper.

DARKO MILANIC

First game in charge: Brentford (A) 27 August 2014
Last game in charge: Wolverhampton Wanderers (H) 25 October 2014
Games: 6
Won: 0
Drawn: 3
Lost: 3

Born in Yugoslavia, Milanic started his playing career at Partizan Belgrade between 1986 and 1993, before joining Sturm Graz in Austria where he won the Austrian Bundesliga twice in 1997-98 and 1998-99, the Austrian Cup in season 1995-96, 1996-97 and 1998-99 and finally the Austrian Supercup in 1996, 1998 and 1999. He first represented Yugoslavia at international level and earned caps for Slovenia, playing for them in Euro 2000. His managerial career started with NK Primorje in Slovenia before moving to Gorica at the start of the 2007-08 season. He guided them to third place before joining Maribor ahead of the 2008-09 campaign. At Maribor he won four PrvaLiga titles, three Slovenian Cups and two Slovenian Supercups. He re-joined Sturm Graz, this time as a manager, in June 2013 and led them to a fifth-place finish during his first season. He announced on 21 September 2014 that he was joining Leeds after they had agreed to buy out his contract. Two days later he was appointed the Whites' new head coach. His first game was a disappointment as the side lost 2-0 away to Brentford: 'I want to play

HEAD COACH

DARKO
MILANIČ

Hello everyone and welcome back to Elland Road for today's Yorkshire derby with Sheffield Wednesday.

Welcome to Stuart Gray, his staff, players and the Sheffield Wednesday fans that have come here today for this early kick-off.

I'd like to thank all of you who were here on Wednesday evening, just three days ago, for giving me such a warm welcome. It was a special evening for me to make my Elland Road debut.

This is a special stadium and the energy you all showed made it special for me and the team. I hope that you show the same energy today and that we can reward you for that.

On Wednesday night the team showed great improvement from my first game last Saturday. On Wednesday we saw a better team performance. The players were focused and perhaps more importantly they were together as a team.

We know that there is still space for improvement and we need to be more dangerous in the final third of the pitch. But the players did show a will to win and we need to maintain that as well as our discipline and our mentality.

Back to today... Let's make this a special game and come away with an important win and three points before the international break.

Enjoy the game.

> "There is still space for improvement and we need to be more dangerous in the final third of the pitch"

offensively and we played with two strikers today, but it's not enough if you don't have offensive thoughts. That first game at Elland Road will be very important for us. With support and energy we can make it. But I have to know individual players in the division better and I need time.' Time was something he was not afforded, a goalless draw at home to Reading was followed up by an encouraging 1-1 draw at home to Sheffield Wednesday before a defeat at Rotherham and a draw away at Norwich City. In his sixth game, Leeds took the lead at home to Wolverhampton Wanderers thanks to a fine goal from Mirco Antenucci, but they again lost their way in the second half and lost 2-1. Milanic was sacked after the game and this time Cellino handed the job – until the end of the season at least – to Neil Redfearn.

Darko Milanic's first line up: Brentford (A) 27 September 2014: Silvestri, Byram, Warnock, Bianchi (Murphy), Bellusci, Pearce, Austin, Cook (Tonge), Mowatt (Sloth), Doukara, Antenucci. Subs not used: S. Taylor, Wootton, Morison, Cooper

Darko Milanic's last line up: Wolverhampton Wanderers (H) 25 October 2014: Silvestri, Beradi, Warnock, Bianchi (Montenegro), Bellusci, Pearce, Cook, Mowatt (Murphy), Adryan (Sloth), Morison, Antenucci. Subs not used: S. Taylor, Byram, Tonge, Cooper.

NEIL REDFEARN

First game in charge: Cardiff City (A) 1 November 2014
Last game in charge: Rotherham United (H) 2 May 2015
Games: 33
Won: 11
Drawn: 7
Lost: 15

Cellino then turned to Redfearn, who had done so well in his stint as caretaker earlier in the season. The Dewsbury-born player started on the books at Nottingham Forest before beginning his professional career at Bolton Wanderers. He then joined Lincoln City as well as Doncaster Rovers, before moving to Crystal Palace and later went on to play for both Watford and Oldham Athletic. His final full season at Boundary Park saw him convert a last minute penalty at home to Sheffield Wednesday to snatch the Second Division title from West Ham United.

In September 1991 Redfearn joined Barnsley, playing in most games and being appointed club captain. He had his best season in 1996-97 as he led the Tykes to the Premier League for the first time, scoring 17 goals along the way. He is also down in the record books as scoring the south Yorkshire side's first-ever top flight goal at home to West Ham United. Barnsley were relegated after just one season in the top tier, and Redfearn joined Charlton Athletic before returning north to join Bradford City. He went on to have spells at Wigan Athletic, Halifax Town (where he was caretaker manager on two occasions) Boston United, Rochdale, Scarborough (where he would manage) and a host of non-league sides. His first caretaker spell at the New Shay took place between August and October 2001 and he had a second spell between March and April the following year. His next spell as manager would be his first as he took over from Nick Henry at Scarborough. He had nine games in charge at Northwich Victoria and had a game in charge at York City. He moved to Leeds in December 2008 following the arrival of new boss Simon Grayson and took on the role of reserve team manager after the dismissal of Neil Thompson. In April 2012 he guided Leeds under-18s to a second place finish in the under-18s league and when Brian McDermott was sacked Redfearn continued his role of academy manager as well as reserve-team/development-squad manager. Following the sacking of Milanic, Redfean was appointed the Whites new head coach. He was confirmed on an initial 12-month contract with the option of a further 12 months. His first game saw Leeds lose 3-1 away at Cardiff City and then the side threw away a 1-0 and 2-1 lead at home to Charlton Athletic before winning his first game as permanent manager in a 3-1 win at home to Blackpool: 'I thought we were excellent in the first half, some of the movement and the passing was different class. That was as good as I've seen them play. It could have been anything. It wasn't just the pressure, it was good football culminating in three goals,' Redfearn said afterwards. It was a brief highlight as Leeds tumbled towards the wrong and end of the table but a change in formation and players saw a surge up the table and following a backs-against-the-wall win against Middlesbrough towards the end of February, Leeds were up to 11th. Three wins in four kept Leeds in the safety of mid-table, but his assistant Steve Thompson was then suspended by Leed's sporting director Nicola Salerno with Redfearn kept in the dark. Results suffered, with five consecutive league defeats and then there was the issue prior to the Charlton Athletic game when six of Massimo Cellino's signings (Antenucci, Bellusci, Doukara, Del Fabro, Silvestri and Cani)

HEAD COACH

"We still have a lot to learn and we need to be more thorough in games. That will come"

Welcome back to Elland Road. A warm welcome also to Bob Peeters, his staff, players and supporters at Charlton Athletic.

First of all, I am really proud to have been named as the head coach of Leeds United.

It is a fantastic thing for me and I am determined to do well for everybody – the players, supporters, staff and young players at this great club. We now need to kick on as a club.

Saturday's defeat to Cardiff was disappointing and I felt we only did half a job. We still have a lot to learn and we need to be more thorough in games. That will come.

The forthcoming international break will give me a proper chance to work with the players. We now have two tough home games, though, and we need to turn this run around.

I felt we lost a little bit of momentum after my caretaker spell earlier this season but I know the players are more than capable of getting back to winning ways.

Enjoy the game tonight.

NEIL REDFEARN

WWW.LEEDSUNITED.COM / 5

all pulled out a day before. In the end, Leeds finished in 15th place, but he was replaced by former Manchester City striker Uwe Rosler. Redfearn returned to management with Rotherham United, before spells at Doncaster Rovers Bells, Liverpool Women and he was recently appointed the Newcastle United under-23s coach.

Neil Redfearn's first line up: Cardiff City (A) 1 November 2014: Silvestri, Berardi (Byram), Warnock, Bianchi (Sloth), Bellusci, Pearce, Cook, Mowatt, Morison (Dawson), Doukara, Antenucci. Subs not used: S. Taylor, Tonge, Montenegro, Cooper.

Neil Redfearn's last line up: Rotherham United (H) 2 May 2015: S. Taylor, Wootton, C. Taylor, Austin, Cooper, Bamba, Berardi (Sharp), Mowatt (White), Murphy, Byram, Morison (Montenegro). Subs not used: Cairns, N'Goyi, Sloth, Phillips.

UWE ROSLER

First game in charge: Burnley (H) 8 August 2015
Last game in charge: Brighton & Hove Albion (H) 17 October 2015
Games: 12
Won: 2
Drawn: 6
Lost: 4

Into the hottest of hot seats came former Manchester City striker Uwe Rosler, who started his playing career in East Germany with Lokomotive Leipzig in 1987. From there he joined BSG Chemie Leipzig, 1 FC Magdeburg, Dynamo Dresden on two occasions and FC Nurnberg, before heading to England to join the blue half of Manchester. He scored five goals in 12 games whilst on loan and the move was made permanent that summer. He won the club's Player of the Year award at the end of the 1994-95 campaign and stayed at Maine Road until May 1998, following the side's relegation to the Second Division.

He returned to Germany for spells at Kaiserslautern and Borussia Berlin before landing back in England at Southampton. He had a brief loan spell at West Bromwich Albion before heading back to Germany to join Unterhaching. He then joined Lillestrom in Norway before taking a break from the game whilst in remission from cancer. After making a full recovery he took the manager's role in 2005, when he took the club to the Norwegian Cup Final and the Royal League Final, but was sacked in November 2006 alongside former Leeds player Gunnar Halle, who was his assistant. He then led Viking Stavanger to third place in 2007 but left in November 2009. He had a short term spell at Molde before being replaced by Ole Gunnar Solskjaer and heading back to England for his first managerial job in the country.

He was appointed manager of Brentford in June 2011 and he finished ninth in his first season with the Bees. The following year he led them to the play-offs, only to lose to Yeovil Town in the final. In December 2013 he moved to Wigan Athletic and again missed out in the play-offs, this time to Queens Park Rangers in the semi-finals. He was sacked just under a year later, and following six months out of the game he was named the new Head Coach of Leeds United. During his first summer at the club, in came Stuart Dallas from his former club Brentford, Chris Wood from Leicester City, Tom Adeyemi on loan from Cardiff City and

Ross Turnbull from Barnsley. Leeds became the draw specialist at the start of the 2015-16 season, drawing their first four league games before breaking their duck in a 2-1 win away at Derby County, with a brilliant goal from Chris Wood winning the day. Another draw at home to his former club Brentford soon followed before a mid week loss at home to Ipswich Town. Leeds did bounce back with a hard fought win at Milton Keynes Dons: 'the way we managed the first 15 to 20 minutes of the second half was very impressive. We went for another goal and we could have easily scored another goal in that period. You need to find a

HEAD COACH
UWE RÖSLER

The new Sky Bet Championship season is finally here and I would like to welcome you all to Elland Road for today's opening game against Burnley.

A warm welcome also goes to Sean Dyche, his backroom staff, players and the visiting Burnley supporters.

Our players and coaches have worked exceptionally hard over the summer to be ready for today and the next 10 months of football – and I feel we are well prepared to achieve our targets this season.

We come into this game on the back of a very strong week. Our intention is to carry that momentum into today when it really matters. The past week has been another step in the right direction for us and it has been the perfect way to sign off what has been a very pleasing and productive pre-season.

I thought the fans were excellent last Saturday. Having 17,000 people at any game is fantastic, let alone for a pre-season friendly. It was something new for me and it goes to show what a huge club this truly is. I felt it helped inspire the players to victory and it has really whetted my appetite for what is set to be an even bigger crowd today. It is such an asset having home support like that and you can be our extra man on the pitch this season.

Speaking of extra men on the pitch, apparently there was a streaker after Chris Wood's goal on Saturday but thankfully I was looking in the opposite direction!

Moving on, we are well-equipped and feeling confident going into today's game. Facing Burnley will be another chance for us to measure ourselves against what is really a Premier League club on and off the pitch.

Sol Bamba will be our captain this season and he is someone I have been very impressed with as a player and as a person since the day I met him. He is a unifying character who will be very important in the dressing room for us. You always want to have more than one leader on the pitch, though, and that's what I'm looking for from some of our other senior players this season.

We also added Stuart Dallas to our squad, a player I know well from my time at Brentford. Stuart will provide the natural width we have been looking for. He is a versatile player, which is a head coach's dream when you don't have the biggest of squads.. He did very well at this level last season and is a improving all the time. At 24 years old, he fits in with our young squad and I'm delighted to have him here.

Today should be a great occasion to start our season in front of the television cameras, so here's hoping for a memorable afternoon at Elland Road.

Marching on Together,
Uwe Rösler

> "Sol Bamba will be our captain this season and he is someone I have been very impressed with as a player and as a person since the day I met him"

---

way to win, even when you're not playing over 90 minutes prettily, and that's what we did,' Rosler said afterwards. It proved to be the last win he would achieve at Leeds as he was sacked following three consecutive defeats – 3-0 at Middlesbrough and back-to-back home defeats to Birmingham City 2-1 and by the same scoreline to Brighton & Hove Albion. He left the club in 18th position and was replaced by former Rotherham United boss Steve Evans. As for Rosler, he had a spell at Fleetwood Town and met Leeds in the first round of the EFL Cup in season 2016-17. He is the current manager of Malmo.

Uwe Rosler's first line up: Burnley (H) 8 August 2015: Silvestri, Berardi, Bellusci, Bamba, Taylor, Adeyemi, Mowatt (Doukara), Cook (Wootton), Byram, Dallas (Antenucci), Wood. Subs not used: Turnbull, Cooper, Erwin, Phillips.

Uwe Rosler's last line up: Brighton & Hove Albion (H) 17 October 2015: Silvestri, Berardi, Bamba, Cooper, Wootton, Adeyemi, Cook, Mowatt (Antenucci), Botaka (Byram), Dallas (Buckley), Wood. Subs not used: Horton, Bellusci, Murphy, Phillips.

STEVE EVANS

First game in charge: Fulham (A) 20 October 2015
Last game in charge: Preston North End (A) 7 May 2016
Games: 38
Won: 14
Drawn: 12
Lost: 12

With Rosler being sacked, Cellino then turned to former Boston United, Crawley Town and Rotherham United boss Steve Evans. The Glaswegian, who spent the majority of his playing career in Scotland with Clyde, Albion Rovers, Ayr United, Hamilton Academical and St Johnstone, first moved into management with non-league Stamford in 1994. He lead them to the United Counties Football League glory and promotion to the Southern League before joining Boston United in October 1998. He led them to the Football League in season 2001-02 but was banned from the game for contract irregularities. He returned to Boston in February 2004, resigning at the end of 2006-07 following relegation back to the Conference. He then joined Crawley Town and showed his promotion credentials, leading them to the Football League in the 2010-11 campaign. He left Sussex to join Rotherham United in April 2012 and was at it again, winning promotion to League One in 2012-13. He followed it up with a penalty shoot-out win over Leyton Orient in the League One play-off final at Wembley to guide the Millers to the Championship at the first attempt. He kept the side in the league but was sacked on 28 September 2015, to be replaced by former Leeds head coach Neil Redfearn. He was then appointed the Whites new head coach on 19 October 2015: 'I got a call before Uwe was appointed and they had seen my potential, it wasn't to be at the time, but they saw my potential. I went to the Blackpool v Coventry City game on the Saturday and got the call on the Sunday and jumped at the chance.' He found a club in 18th place and knew that confidence was an issue: 'I needed to freshen up the training and for the first game at Fulham, I felt very humble and it was an experience I will never forget.' Evans started with two 1-1 draws at Fulham and Bolton thanks to penalties from Chris Wood and Mirco Antenucci, but nothing could prepare him for his first home game against Blackburn Rovers the following Thursday night, when the side found themselves 2-0 down after five minutes. Evans commented, 'Oh my god, I can never feel like this, I had to make sure we don't concede a third goal and deliver a better performance in the second half.'

Thankfully for Evans and Leeds, things did get better in the next two games, with victories over Cardiff City at Elland Road thanks to a screamer from Alex Mowatt: 'Mowatt looked really lively in training leading up to the game and I sensed that the players were really confident.' Better was to follow for the Whites as the team clicked in an impressive performance away at Huddersfield in a 3-0 win with goals from Antenucci, Wood and another cracker from Mowatt: 'The team really clicked that day, Wood, Dallas and Antenucci were superb.' Leeds ended up in 13th place with some impressive performances away at Blackburn Rovers (2-1), Birmingham City (2-1) and back-to-back home wins against Reading (3-2) and Wolverhampton Wanderers (2-1). His contract was not renewed by Massimo Cellino, but he rarely had an issue with the owner: 'I only felt let down once, when we had both Lee Tomlin and Kyle Lafferty lined up to sign in January 2016 with the money from the sale of Sam Byram from West Ham United, but Mr Cellino didn't sanction the deals.' Steve Parkin from Clipper, one of the club's sponsors, was going to pay for the deals to go through, but Cellino decided against it. Evans knew of his fate a week after the last game of the season at Preston: 'Massimo did tell me I would be retained after the Preston game, but four days later after talks, the owner wanted a manager who had been in the Premier League, which was something I couldn't give him.' Evans had since had spells at Mansfield Town and Peterborough United and was recently installed as the boss of League One side Gillingham.

HEAD COACH
STEVE EVANS

Good evening and welcome to Elland Road for tonight's Sky Bet Championship clash with Blackburn Rovers.

Firstly, I would like to thank you all for the overwhelming support you have shown me since I arrived at the club last week. This is my first home match as the very proud manager of Leeds United Football Club, and it goes without saying it will be a very special moment for me.

I would like to extend my warm welcome to Gary Bowyer, his staff, players and travelling Blackburn supporters tonight.

A special mention also goes to Jordan Rhodes, because it's no hidden secret that I'm a family friend of his father. It will be nice to see Jordan but I certainly hope that it's not his night in front of goal!

Tonight's match is one of significant importance as two former English champions go head-to-head in front of the live Sky television cameras. When you look at the current Championship table, it's easy to identify that both teams need to secure the points.

Blackburn Rovers, with the quality of the players they have in their squad, are capable of beating anyone on their night. But rather than focus too much on the opposition, I want to focus on the undoubted quality we have got in the squad here at Elland Road.

It's been over seven months since we have won at home, though, and I've made my feelings clear about that statistic. That is the last remark I am going to make about it because we now have the opportunity to put it behind us.

The passion of the supporters here at this great club cannot go unnoticed, and neither can the huge numbers, described to me as "millions", in the club's worldwide fan-base. The away support at both Fulham – my first game in charge – and then again at Bolton at the weekend was nothing short of staggering for me. It was enlightening and inspiring to look across and see our fans getting right behind the team throughout both games, and then obviously enjoying themselves when we got the goals. They are the people we are working so hard every day to reward.

I hope that myself, my assistant Paul Raynor and all the staff, added together with our players, the president and most importantly you, the supporters, will regularly recall the words to our anthem "Marching On Together". Recently I studied the words and it's about sticking together, it's about coming through difficult periods together and it's about celebrating together. Let's be Marching on Together throughout the course of the evening.

Steve Evans's first line up: Fulham (A) 21 October 15: Silvestri, Byram, Bamba, Cooper, Berardi, Adayemi, Cook, Murphy (Botaka), Dallas (Phillips), Antenucci, Wood (Buckley). Subs not used: Horton, Wootton, Bellusci, Mowatt.

Pictures from the first training session with our new head coach.

The one thing I've noticed since I became a part of the Leeds United family is that – certainly within the club and inside the city – there is such fevered passion for the football club where everyone really does pull in the same direction.

Having won four promotions in the last five years, that had to be the case for me to achieve each one –

> **"This is my first home match as the very proud manager of Leeds United Football Club, and it goes without saying it will be a very special moment for me"**

even in the dark days. And there were some dark days in those promotions – when the team lost by five or six – but we all remembered at the end of it that there was a common cause to win the next game. By taking that approach, we delivered the promotions.

After the final whistle tonight, I can assure our supporters that the players will be working over the weekend to get ready to face Cardiff City, another club that has recently graced the Barclays Premier League, and another club that we are looking forward to hosting at Elland Road.

Finally, it's my 53rd birthday tomorrow and I want it to be a celebratory one – that would only feel right if we win the match tonight.

Marching on Together,
Steve Evans

WWW.LEEDSUNITED.COM » 5

Steve Evans's last line up: Preston North End (A) 7 May 2016: Silvestri, Coyle, Cooper (Wootton), Bamba, Taylor, Diagouraga, Murphy, Cook, Mowatt (Antenucci), Dallas (Ronaldo Vieira), Wood. Subs not used: Peacock-Farrell, Doukara, Botaka, Phillips.

GARRY MONK

First game in charge: Queens Park Rangers (A) 7 August 2016
Last game in charge: Wigan Athletic (A) 7 May 2017
Games: 53
Won: 25
Drawn: 11
Lost: 17

With Evans not having his contract renewed by Massimo Cellino, Leeds were on the lookout for another head coach and this time turned to former Swansea boss Garry Monk, who in season 2014-15 had seen his side do the double over both Arsenal and Manchester United. Monk began his career as a trainee at Torquay United before moving to Southampton, where he turned professional in May 1997. He had numerous loan spells whilst on the south coast, back at Torquay, at Stockport County, at Oxford United, Sheffield Wednesday and at Barnsley, who he went on to join on a free transfer. He didn't settle at Oakwell and moved to Swansea City in June 2004. It was during a successful playing spell in South Wales where he won the Football League Trophy in 2006, skippering the team to the League One title in 2008 and winning promotion to the Championship after defeating Reading 4-2 in the play-off final at Wembley. He came on as substitute as the Swans lifted their first ever League Cup in a 5-0 win over Bradford City. He was appointed interim player-manager following the sacking of Michael Laudrup and secured safety with one match to spare. He then became permanent manager in May 2014. His first full season in the dugout was an impressive one as the Swans ended the campaign in eighth place with a record points tally. However, he was sacked in December 2015 after only one win in 11 Premier League matches. He was announced as the new Leeds Head Coach at the start of June 2016 and set about doing his job, bringing in Pep Clotet, James Beattie and Darryl Flahavan as part of his backroom staff. Transfer wise, in came Kemar Roofe from Oxford United, Rob Green from QPR, Kyle Bartley on loan from Swansea, Matt Grimes also on loan from Swansea City, Marcus Antonsson from Kalmar, Luke Ayling from Bristol City, Hadi Sacko on loan from Sporting CP and attacking midfielder Pablo Hernandez from Al-Arabi. Defender Pontus Jansson also joined on loan from Torino.

Monk made a poor start, and following a defeat at Huddersfield Town there were rumours about his job. Monk said after, 'We have to get a real reaction now on Tuesday. We need to take the three points, it's as simple as that.' He did get a reaction, and following a memorable win at Norwich City on bonfire night, his side moved into the play-off places for the first time in the season: 'That's one for the fans to enjoy. It's a great result, but there is nothing to be won yet. We know we are not the finished article yet, but we are making good progress,' Monk commented after the win. He led Leeds to the last eight of the EFL Cup before bravely losing at Liverpool, but the league form was still consistent and they were up to third following an impressive win at Derby County in front of the Sky Cameras on a Friday night in January. The side left the FA Cup after Monk made numerous changes against non-league Sutton United, but following another fantastic display at home to Brighton & Hove Albion, in which Chris Wood scored both goals, Leeds looked a dead cert for the end-of-season lottery. Sadly for Monk, the dream disappeared in April

GARRY MONK

"The only thing I ask of you is to bring 'THE NOISE'. Give these players everything you have and back them with everything you've got for every minute of every game"

Hello and good afternoon to everyone here at Elland Road for our first home fixture of the new Sky Bet Championship season.

First of all, I must officially thank all of you for the incredible reception received by myself and my coaching staff since we arrived at the club just over two months ago.

I feel immensely proud to be managing this historic club and I am incredibly excited to be representing everyone connected with Leeds United this season. I will endeavour to bring success back to this fantastic club and to you, our loyal supporters.

So welcome back for our first of 23 cup finals here at Elland Road this season.

A warm welcome also goes to Gary Rowett, his staff, players and the Birmingham City supporters who have travelled over for today's game.

I'm fully aware, as are the players, of the huge importance of having strong home form this season. We must create performances that you enjoy watching and, if we can fuse together a good brand of football with, most importantly, winning matches, then I'm sure we can look forward to a successful season.

It's also important to recognise that we're at the beginning of this journey. As is the nature of this league, it's a journey that will have its ups and downs along the way, but I can assure you that myself, my staff and my players are going to fight with everything we have to make you, our passionate supporters, as proud as possible.

We have been asking the players to take on board a lot of new ideas this summer; ideas which are then worked on to refine and improve those principles on a daily basis. This is not an overnight process – it will take time to establish – but I'm also aware that we must work to have a team winning football matches in the here and now. That means it's crucial to strike a good balance between winning football matches and developing our long-term ideas with the players.

The attitude and desire shown by the players to work and improve has been very pleasing so far. They're a young group but one that I feel has huge potential. I know the work that we're doing will enable us to unlock that potential and bring it out in our performances.

This is where you, our loyal and famously passionate supporters, play a crucial role.

The only thing I ask of you is to bring "THE NOISE". Give these players everything you have and back them with everything you've got for every minute of every game, through the good and difficult moments. This is the only way the team will grow and, in turn, allow the club to grow.

We all have the same ambition; the club, myself, my staff, my players and you, the supporters – to get this club back to where it should be, which is the Premier League.

The aim is to meet that ambition as soon as possible but, however long it may take, the only way it can be achieved is by every single one of us connected to this great football club following our mantra: Marching on Together.

Garry Monk

FiRECREST CONSTRUCTION

following back-to-back defeats at home to Wolves and away to Burton Albion, and Leeds ended up in an agonising seventh place. By this time Andrea Radrizzani was in charge at the club and Leeds were set to activate a one-year contract extension for the head coach. Monk did not renew his contract and resigned on 25 May. He then had a spell in charge of Middlesbrough, before being sacked two days before Christmas 2017. He was sacked at the end of the 2018-19 season by Birmingham City.

Garry Monk's first line up: Queens Park Rangers (A) 7 August 2016: Green, Berardi (Coyle), Bamba, Bartley, Taylor, Diagouraga, Ronadlo Vieira, Grimes (Antonsson), Dallas, Roofe (Sacko), Wood. Subs not used: Turnbull, Cooper, Phillips, Mowatt.

Garry Monk's last line up: Wigan Athletic (A) 7 May 2017: Green, Coyle, Bartley, Ayling, Berardi, Ronaldo Vieira (Phillips), O'Kane, Dallas (Sacko), Hernandez (Pedraza), Roofe, Wood. Subs not used: Peacock-Farrell, Antonsson, Doukara, Denton.

THOMAS CHRISTIANSEN

First game in charge: Bolton Wanderers (A) 6 August 2017
Last game in charge: Cardiff City (H) 3 February 2018
Games: 35
Won: 15
Drawn: 6
Lost: 14

With Monk deciding to leave the club, Leeds then turned to relative unknown Thomas Christiansen, whose previous job had been with APOEL in the Cypriot League. The Dane started his playing career with Barcelona B, whilst having loan spells at Sporting Gijon, Osasuna and Racing Santander. He joined Real Oviedo in January 1996 and had spells

THOMAS CHRISTIANSEN

Good evening and welcome to our first competitive game of the season at Elland Road against Port Vale.

After a pleasing pre-season campaign building towards last Sunday's game at Bolton Wanderers, it was great to see our hard work throughout the summer rewarded with an opening day victory. I was really pleased with our attacking threat, especially in the first half, where we created many opportunities and scored three really good goals. There are still a number of areas we need to work and improve on, but as we play more games I am sure that will come.

Against Bolton it was disappointing to lose defenders Gaetano Berardi and Matthew Pennington to injury and I hope they will be available to return sooner rather than later. I am pleased on Monday that the club were able to complete the loan signing of Cameron Borthwick-Jackson, who adds further competition to our squad and will help fill the void left by Gaetano and Matthew.

It was fantastic to experience our away support for the first time at the Macron Stadium, I'd like to thank all of our supporters who made the trip to support us and I am glad we were able to send you back to Leeds happy with three points. Everyone in the squad is determined to repay your faith and loyalty.

This evening we welcome Port Vale and we are expecting another tough encounter. The Carabao Cup is an important competition for us and the club had a good run last season, reaching the quarter finals. We want to win as many games as possible for our supporters, especially on home soil, so the players will once again be giving everything to ensure we are in round two.

Port Vale have rebuilt over the summer under Michael Brown following their relegation to League Two and they will be striving to return to League One. They had a really good start at the weekend with a 3-1 victory over Crawley Town and will come to Elland Road with confidence, so we must ensure we put in a professional performance tonight.

Once again, thank you for coming to support us again this evening. I hope we can make it two victories out of two, to give us a great platform to go into the Preston North End game with on Saturday.

Marching on Together.
Thomas Christiansen

> "It was great to see our hard work throughout the summer rewarded with an opening day victory"

at Terrassa, Panionios in Greece and Herfolge in Denmark, before finishing his playing in Germany with VfL Bochum and Hannover 96. He started his coaching career in the UAE as assistant manager with Al Jazira before being appointed head coach of AEK Larnaca in April 2014. He led them to two second-place finishes before joining APOEL in May 2016. During his spell there he won his first managerial title in 2017, losing only two games, and reached the final of the Cypriot Cup, only to lose to Apollon Limassol. He left the side in May 2017.

He was appointed the new head coach of Leeds United in June of that year and brought in Felix Wiedwald from Werder Bremen, Mathew Pennington on loan from Everton, Ezgjan Alioski from Lugano, Samuel Saiz from Huesca, Cameron Borthwick-Jackson on loan from Manchester United, Vurnon Anita from Newcastle United, Mateusz Klich from FC Twente and Caleb Ekuban from Verona. Christiansen and Leeds started the season in brilliant form and topped the table after a Tuesday night win over Birmingham City: 'If you tell me it's the last game and we're in that position [first place] I would be happy, proud and all that you can say about that. But right now, don't give me anything. It puts a bit more pressure on the team because everyone now wants to beat Leeds,' the boss said after the win. They had reached the summit despite the sale of Chris Wood to Premier League side Burnley, who was replaced by Pierre-Michel Lasogga.

Leeds stayed in the top six until the start of November when a 3-1 defeat at Brentford, which was the side's third in row, dropped them to tenth. They responded with a 2-1 win over Garry Monk's Middlesbrough in front of a packed crowd at Elland Road and he lifted the side back into the top six after a Boxing Day win at Burton Albion. The wheels started to fall off following an FA Cup exit at the hands of Newport County and following three loses in the next four games, in which Leeds had players sent off in three of them, Christiansen was gone following a 4-1 defeat at home to Neil Warnock's Cardiff City. He has recently just been appointed the new coach of Royale Union Saint-Gilloise.

Thomas Christiansen's first line up: Bolton Wanderers (A) 6 August 2017: Wiedwald, Ayling, Pennington (Shaughnessy), Cooper, Berardi (Anita), O'Kane, Phillips, Hernandez, Alioski (Sacko), Roofe, Wood. Subs not used: Green: Saiz, Klich, Ekuban.

Thomas Christiansen's last line up: Cardiff City (H) 3 February 2018 Wiedwald, Berardi, Pennington, Jansson (Dallas), De Bock, Forshaw, Ronaldo Vieira (Grot), Hernandez, Alioski, Roofe, Lassoga (Sacko). Subs not used: Lonergan, Anita, Romario Vieira, Pearce.

PAUL HECKINGBOTTOM

First game in charge: Sheffield United (A) 10 February 2018
Last game in charge: Queens Park Rangers (H) 6 May 2018
Games: 16
Won: 4
Drawn: 4
Lost: 8

Leeds filled the gap with the appointment of Barnsley boss Paul Heckingbottom on an 18 month contract. Christiansen had been sacked with Leeds in tenth place on 44 points.

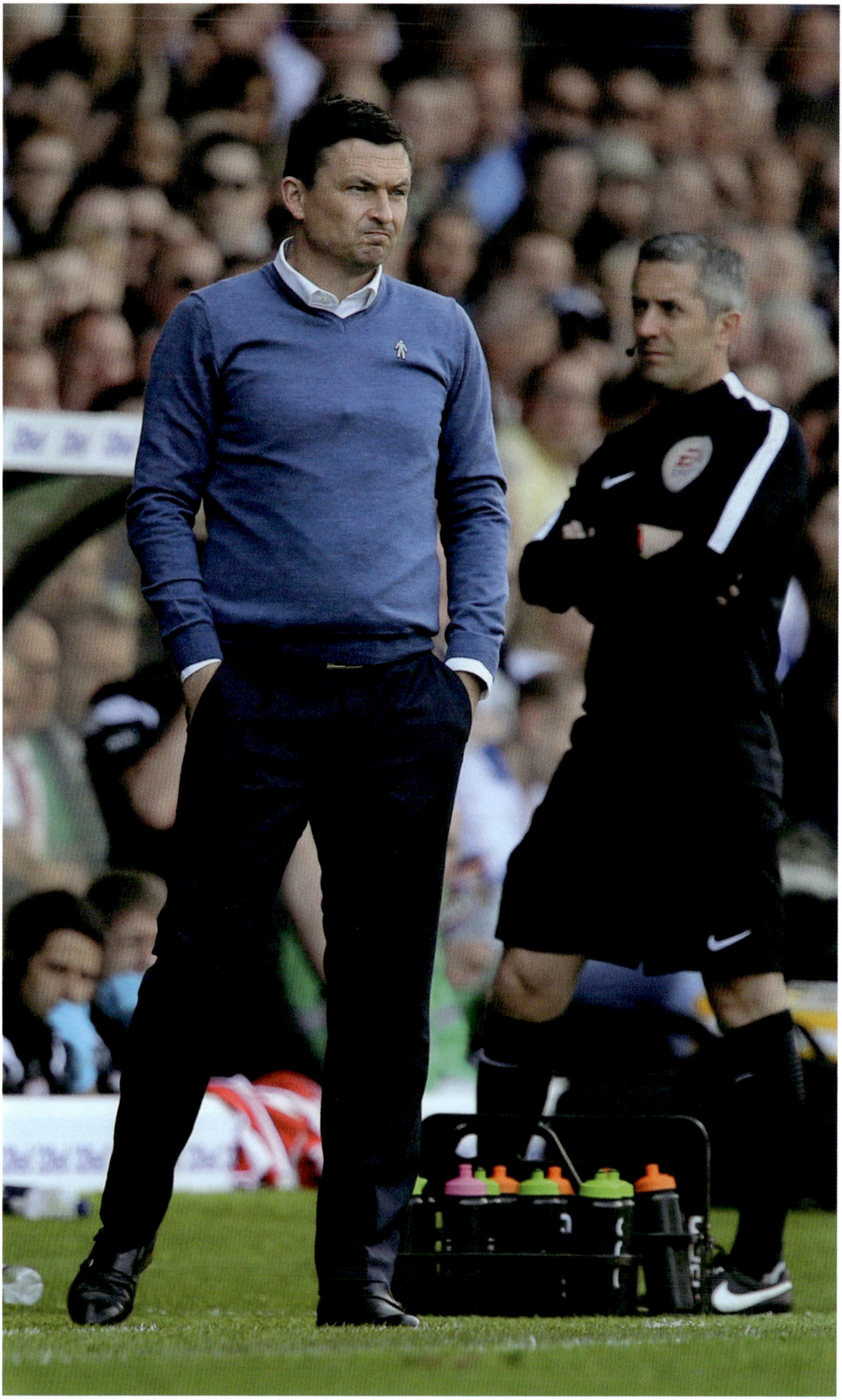

PAUL HECKINGBOTTOM

"Myself and the coaching team have inherited a talented squad and it is up to us to get the players to showcase that ability"

Good afternoon and welcome to today's Sky Bet Championship fixture with Bristol City.

Firstly, I would like to thank you all for the warm reception I have received since being appointed head coach of the club. I am really excited and pleased to be here, it is a real honour to have this opportunity. I know a lot about Leeds and the history of the club, along with the expectation levels and the potential it has and hopefully together we can unlock this.

Against Sheffield United last Saturday, I thought we were unlucky not to get anything out of the game. I was disappointed with the way we started the match, conceding so early on and with how we lost the goal. We were able to make a few tweaks at half-time and we managed to level the scores, which was pleasing. In the second half we played on the front foot, with more freedom, as Sheffield United had been doing in the first half and I think we can take a lot away from that. I thought the penalty decision which ultimately cost us the game was harsh on us, but we have to accept it and move on.

The first couple of days after being appointed head coach were a bit of a whirlwind, but I'm really pleased now to have had a full week of training with the group. Myself and the coaching team have inherited a talented squad here and it is up to us to get the players to showcase that ability on the pitch. We have our own concepts and ideas, which we have begun to implement and hopefully from this, as time goes on, we will be able to see improvements being made.

We know the games coming up in the rest of this month and March are going to define our season. We are facing teams we ultimately need to take points off, if we are to have a successful end to the campaign.

That starts with today's opponents Bristol City, who have had a really good season to date. I know their manager Lee Johnson well from our time at Barnsley together and he has done a great job at Ashton Gate. Like ourselves, Bristol have a lot of threats in their team and we know we are going to have to play very well to come away with the three points.

Finally, I'd like to urge you all to get behind the team today. I've been to Elland Road on a number of occasions with opposing teams and when the supporters are at full voice, backing the side, it is a really intimidating place which can make all the difference.

Marching on Together.

Paul Heckingbottom

FiRECREST CONSTRUCTION

Heckingbottom, who was born in Barnsley, started at Manchester United as a trainee before joining Sunderland in 1995 after failing to gain a professional contract at Old Trafford. He never featured for Sunderland and had loan spells at Scarborough, Hartlepool United and Darlington, before joining the latter in 1999. He was then snapped up by Norwich City before spells in Yorkshire at Barnsley, Sheffield Wednesday and his home-town club. Whilst at Oakwell he had a loan spell back at Bradford City before joining them on a permanent contract. From the Bantams, he had spells at Mansfield Town, Gateshead on loan and permanently, and finished his playing career at Harrogate Town. He took over as caretaker manager at Barnsley following the sacking of Danny Wilson and again was made caretaker following Lee Johnson's departure to Bristol City. In his second spell he led the Tykes to two Wembley appearances, winning the Football League Trophy against Oxford United and promotion to the Championship by defeating Millwall 3-1 in the play-off final. He was then appointed on a permanent basis and saw his side end 2016 in ninth place. Barnsley finished in 14th place and Heckingbottom signed a new rolling contract in February 2018, though four days later he left Oakwell for Elland Road. In his first game at the club he saw his new side lose 2-1 at Sheffield United and he saw the Whites show their battling qualities, coming from 2-0 down to earn a point at home to Bristol City. He had to wait until his fourth game for his first win, which came thanks to a Liam Cooper header against Brentford, and he said after the game, 'It's good to have the first win, it is a reward for the hard work of the players. There are lots of positives to take from the performance. Lots of organisation goes into it and to be successful in this league you have to be able to defend and stop teams as well as hurt teams.' He had to wait till the end of March for his next win, thanks to goals from Caleb Ekuban and Pablo Hernandez, which saw off Bolton Wanderers, but there was little left to play for with the play-offs a distant dream. He did see his side defeat his old club Barnsley at Elland Road and finish the season with a win at home to Queens Park Rangers. With little to play for, he did blood a number of youngsters, including Tom Pearce, Paudie O'Connor, Hugo Diaz and Ryan Edmondson but was shown the door at the start of June. He is currently the manager of Hibernian.

Paul Heckingbottom's first line up: Sheffield United (A) 10 February 2018: Wiedwald, Dallas, Jansson, Pennington, De Bock, Forshaw, O'Kane, Phillips (Ekuban), Alioski (Sacko), Lasogga, Roofe (Hernandez). Subs not used: Lonergan, Anita, Cibicki, Ronaldo Vieira.

Paul Heckingbottom's last line up: Queens Park Rangers (H) 6 May 2018: Peacock-Farrell, Ayling, Jansson (Pennington), Cooper, Pearce, Phillips, Forshaw (O'Kane), Ronaldo Vieira, Alioski, Roofe (Edmondson). Subs not used: Lonergan, Lassoga, Saiz, Sacko.

MARCELO BIELSA

First game in charge: Stoke City (H) 5 August 2018
Games: 51
Won: 27
Drawn: 8
Lost: 16

445

The question on everyone's lips was who would Leeds turn to ahead of the 2018-19 campaign and on 15 June 2018 the club announced that former Argentinean World Cup coach Marcelo Bielsa would be the new incumbent. Bielsa had a short playing career, as he retired at the age of 25, having played for Newell's Old Boys, Instituto and Argentino de Rosario. He returned to Newell's Old Boys to start his managerial career in 1990, where he won the top flight in 1991 and 1992 and finished runners-up in the Copa Libertadores in 1992. He then joined Atlas in Mexico followed by Club America before returning to Argentina with Velvez Sarsfield. He won his third title with Sarsfield in 1998 before a brief spell with Spanish La Liga side Espanyol. He was then offered the job to manage the Argentina national side, taking over from Daniel Passarella.

In his spell as national coach, he saw his side beaten 3-0 in a Copa America tie against Colombia in which Martin Palermo missed three penalties. He achieved qualification to the 2002 World Cup, but the team were knocked out in the group stages, losing 1-0 to England along the way. Argentina were runners-up in the 2004 Copa America and won the Olympic Games that year, but Bielsa resigned and went on to manage the Chilean national side. Bielsa saw Chile beat Argentina and qualify for the 2010 World Cup. He resigned in February 2011 and nine months later joined Athletic Bilbao, where he had double disappointment when he lost the 2012 Europa League Final to Atletico Madrid and the Copa Del Ray final to Barcelona.

He left the Spanish side in June 2013 and moved to Marseille the following May. He signed a two year contract with the French side and led them to a fourth place finish. After losing their opening Ligue One match to Caen, Bielsa announced his resignation. He had a two day stay at Lazio before another stint in France with Lille. He was suspended by the club after just 13 games in charge in November 2017 and in mid December Lille announced that his contract had been terminated.

His next stop would be Elland Road and what a journey the club and Bielsa went on in his first season in England. In came Barry Douglas from Wolverhampton Wanderers, Jack Harrison on loan from Manchester City, Lewis Baker on loan from Chelsea, Jamal Blackman also on loan from Chelsea and striker Patrick Bamford from Middlesbrough. Leeds made an outstanding to start to the new campaign and Bielsa became the first boss in the Whites' history to win his first four games in charge. He won his first Manager of the Month award at the end of August and Leeds weren't out of the top two until mid October. After a 4-1 loss at West Bromwich Albion, Bielsa and Leeds went on an incredible run of seven straight league wins that propelled them to the top of the Championship. Two games stand out in particular: Leeds were 2-0 down at Aston Villa after 17 minutes, two days before Christmas, but the side kept going and won it five minutes into stoppage time following a winner from Kemar Roofe. Three days later, Leeds did it again with the side 2-1 down at home to Blackburn Rovers and two goals into stoppage time from Roofe kept the winning run going. Bielsa

HEAD COACH
Marcelo Bielsa

Good afternoon and welcome to Elland Road for today's first Sky Bet Championship game of the season against Stoke City.

Firstly I would like to thank the Leeds United supporters for the warm reception I have received since being appointed head coach of the club. Leeds United has a great deal of history and I know how much the club means to the supporters and it has been really nice to meet a lot of fans during our preparation matches. We have had tremendous support at all of our pre-season games, despite many of them being far away, which everyone appreciates and we hope we will deserve it throughout the season.

Pre-season training has been very testing for the players and I am pleased with the fitness levels of the squad. It is really important to have a hard period of preparation, because with the 46-game schedule of the Championship, along with the extra cup matches involved, we need to have a big group with fit and available players to cope with the demands.

During the six games we played in July, we worked on many tactical elements. The players have been getting used to the style of play I want to implement and we will improve every day until this is perfected. There are still many areas that we wish to improve and work on, but I can tell that every player is taking on the messages we have been providing and we will continue to get better throughout the Championship.

It was good to experience the team playing at Elland Road for the first time last weekend against Las Palmas. I'd like to thank the fans who came to support us and I am looking forward to seeing the stadium at full capacity today and the atmosphere that brings.

I suppose Stoke City will be looking to get promoted back to the Premier League at the first attempt. Their squad possesses a lot of quality and they have a number of threats throughout their team and we know we will have to perform at our very best to come away with a positive result - which is what we are aiming to do.

Finally, I would like to pass my condolences to the family and friends of former Leeds United player Paul Madeley. Paul played a great role in helping this club achieve so much success and also epitomised everything about Leeds United.

Marching on Together

Marcelo Bielsa
Head coach

FIRECREST CONSTRUCTION

---

said after the game, 'It was moving for all of us. Football can give these emotions. That is why nothing compares to football. Late wins like this are important because it is not easy to win games in a tight league like the Championship.'

Leeds lost back-to-back games at home to Hull City and away at Nottingham Forest before exiting the FA Cup away at Queens Park Rangers before the visit of Derby County and the "spygate" drama. Bielsa admitted to sending a member of his staff to watch the Rams train ahead of the game, then watched his Leeds team dismantle Derby with a brilliant performance. Bielsa then gave an impromptu PowerPoint presentation in front of the watching media in which he showed how much work goes into analysing opponents. Leeds were handed a £200,000 fine for "spygate" and it lit the blue touch paper with Derby County.

Leeds continued their push for promotion and despite a 1-0 loss at QPR they bounced back with a magnificent performance in a 4-0 win at home to West Bromwich Albion. They followed it up with back-to-back away wins at Bristol City and Reading but dropped down to third after closest rivals Sheffield United won a tense encounter at Elland Road. They responded with three wins from their next four but a Good Friday defeat to ten-man Wigan Athletic and an Easter Monday loss at Brentford meant the side would have to settle for a place in the end of season lottery.

As fate would have it, Leeds met Derby County, with the Whites taking a massive step to Wembley, winning the first leg at Pride Park thanks to a Kemar Roofe goal. After taking the lead through a Stuart Dallas tap in, in the second leg at Elland Road it all went wrong as the Rams won 4-2 and 4-3 on aggregate and Leeds had to lick their wounds going into their centenary season.

Marcelo Bielsa's first line up: Stoke City (H) 5 August 2018: Peacock-Farrell, Ayling, Berardi, Cooper, Douglas, Phillips, Klich (Dallas), Hernandez, Saiz (Baker), Alioski (Harrison), Roofe. Subs not used: Blackman, Bamford, Roberts, Jansson.

CHAMPIONSHIP 2010–11

Date	Opposition	Competition	Score
07/08/2010	Derby County	Championship	1-2
10/08/2010	Lincoln City	Carling Cup 1st Round	4-0
15/08/2010	Nottingham Forest	Championship	1-1
21/08/2010	Millwall	Championship	3-1
24/08/2010	Leicester City	Carling Cup 2nd Round	1-2
28/08/2010	Watford	Championship	1-0
11/08/2010	Swansea City	Championship	2-1
14/08/2010	Barnsley	Championship	2-5
17/09/2010	Doncaster Rovers	Championship	0-0
25/09/2010	Sheffield United	Championship	1-0
28/09/2010	Preston North End	Championship	4-6
02/10/2010	Ipswich Town	Championship	1-2
16/10/2010	Middlesbrough	Championship	2-1
19/10/2010	Leicester City	Championship	1-2
25/10/2010	Cardiff City	Championship	0-4
30/10/2010	Scunthorpe United	Championship	4-1
06/11/2010	Coventry City	Championship	3-2
09/11/2010	Hull City	Championship	2-2
13/11/2010	Bristol City	Championship	3-1
20/11/2010	Norwich City	Championship	1-1
27/11/2010	Reading	Championship	0-0
04/12/2010	Crystal Palace	Championship	2-1
11/12/2010	Burnley	Championship	3-2
18/12/2010	Queens Park Rangers	Championship	2-0
26/12/2010	Leicester City	Championship	2-2
28/12/2010	Portsmouth	Championship	3-3
01/01/2011	Middlesbrough	Championship	1-1
04/01/2011	Cardiff City	Championship	1-2
08/01/2011	Arsenal	FA Cup 3rd Round	1-1
15/01/2011	Scunthorpe United	Championship	4-0
19/01/2011	Arsenal	FA Cup 3rd Round Replay	1-3
22/01/2011	Portsmouth	Championship	2-2
01/02/2011	Hull City	Championship	2-2
05/02/2011	Coventry City	Championship	1-0
12/02/2011	Bristol City	Championship	2-0
19/02/2011	Norwich City	Championship	2-2
22/02/2011	Barnsley	Championship	3-3
26/02/2011	Swansea City	Championship	0-3
05/03/2011	Doncaster Rovers	Championship	5-2
08/03/2011	Preston North End	Championship	2-1
12/03/2011	Ipswich Town	Championship	0-0
19/03/2011	Sheffield United	Championship	0-2
02/04/2011	Nottingham Forest	Championship	4-1
09/04/2011	Millwall	Championship	2-3
12/04/2011	Derby County	Championship	1-2
16/04/2011	Watford	Championship	2-2
22/04/2011	Reading	Championship	0-0
25/04/2011	Crystal Palace	Championship	0-1
30/04/2011	Burnley	Championship	1-0
07/05/2011	Queens Park Rangers	Championship	2-1

Team	Pld	W	D	L	GF	GA	Pts
Queen's Park Rangers	46	24	16	6	71	32	88
Norwich City	46	23	15	8	83	58	84
Swansea	46	24	8	14	69	42	80
Cardiff City	46	23	11	12	76	54	80
Reading	46	20	17	9	77	51	77
Nottingham Forest	46	20	15	11	69	50	75
Leeds United	46	19	15	12	81	70	72
Burnley	46	18	14	14	65	61	68
Millwall	46	18	13	15	62	48	67
Leicester City	46	19	10	17	76	71	67
Hull City	46	16	17	13	52	51	65
Middlesbrough	46	17	11	18	68	68	62
Ipswich Town	46	18	8	20	62	68	62
Watford	46	16	13	17	77	71	61
Bristol City	46	17	9	20	62	65	60
Portsmouth	46	15	13	18	53	60	58
Barnsley	46	14	14	18	55	66	56
Coventry City	46	14	13	19	54	58	55
Derby County	46	13	10	23	58	71	49
Crystal Palace	46	12	12	22	44	69	48
Doncaster Rovers	46	11	15	20	55	81	48
Preston North End	46	10	12	24	54	79	42
Sheffield United	46	11	9	26	44	79	42
Scunthorpe United	46	12	6	28	43	87	42

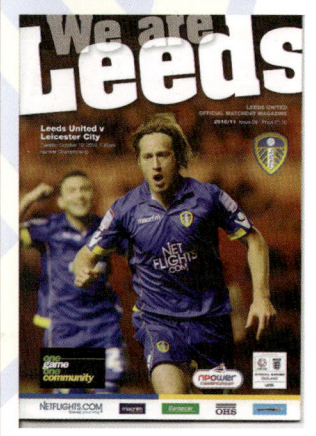

When Leeds kicked off the new campaign at home to Derby County it was the first time the club was broadcast live on the BBC since Partizan Belgrade away in September 1999.

It was also the fourth time since season 1996-97 that Leeds United and Derby County had met on the opening day of the new season.

When Jonny Howson scored a hat-trick away at Scunthorpe United he became the first Leeds United player since Rob Hulse to score a treble at this level.

The White's new number nine, Billy Paynter had to wait till the end of October to make his Leeds United debut. His first goal came in his 17th game away at Preston North End.

Having been so consistent away from home all season, the Whites suffered four straight league defeats away from Elland Road between March and April that cost them a play-off place.

2011–12 CHAMPIONSHIP

Team	Pld	W	D	L	GF	GA	Pts
Reading	46	27	8	11	69	41	89
Southampton	46	26	10	10	85	46	88
West Ham United	46	24	14	8	81	48	86
Birmingham	46	20	16	10	78	51	76
Blackpool	46	20	15	11	79	59	75
Cardiff City	46	19	18	9	66	53	75
Middlesbrough	46	18	16	12	52	51	70
Hull City	46	19	11	16	47	44	68
Leicester City	46	18	12	16	66	55	66
Brighton	46	17	15	14	52	52	66
Watford	46	16	16	14	56	64	64
Derby County	46	18	10	18	50	58	64
Burnley	46	17	11	18	61	58	62
Leeds United	46	17	10	19	65	68	61
Ipswich Town	46	17	10	19	69	77	61
Millwall	46	15	12	19	55	57	57
Crystal Palace	46	13	17	16	46	51	56
Peterborough	46	13	11	22	67	77	50
Nottingham Forest	46	14	8	24	48	63	50
Bristol City	46	12	13	21	44	68	49
Barnsley	46	13	9	24	49	74	48
Portsmouth	46	13	11	22	50	59	40
Coventry City	46	9	13	24	41	65	40
Doncaster	46	8	12	26	43	80	36

Date	Opposition	Competition	Score
06/08/2011	Southampton	Championship	1-3
09/08/2011	**Bradford City**	**Carling Cup 1st Round**	**3-2**
13/08/2011	**Middlesbrough**	**Championship**	**0-1**
16/08/2011	**Hull City**	**Championship**	**4-1**
21/08/2011	West Ham United	Championship	2-2
23/08/2011	Doncaster Rovers	Carling Cup 2nd Round	2-1
28/08/2011	Ipswich Town	Championship	1-2
10/09/2011	**Crystal Palace**	**Championship**	**3-2**
17/09/2011	**Bristol City**	**Championship**	**2-1**
20/09/2011	**Manchester United**	**Carling Cup 3rd Round**	**0-3**
23/09/2011	Brighton & Hove Albion	Championship	3-3
01/10/2011	**Portsmouth**	**Championship**	**1-0**
14/10/2011	Doncaster Rovers	Championship	3-0
18/10/2011	**Coventry City**	**Championship**	**1-1**
22/10/2011	Peterborough United	Championship	3-2
26/10/2011	Birmingham City	Championship	0-1
30/10/2011	**Cardiff City**	**Championship**	**1-1**
02/11/2011	**Blackpool**	**Championship**	**0-5**
06/11/2011	Leicester City	Championship	1-0
19/11/2011	Burnley	Championship	2-1
26/11/2011	**Barnsley**	**Championship**	**1-2**
29/11/2011	Nottingham Forest	Championship	4-0
03/12/2011	**Millwall**	**Championship**	**2-0**
10/12/2011	Watford	Championship	1-1
17/12/2011	**Reading**	**Championship**	**0-1**
26/12/2011	Derby County	Championship	0-1
31/12/2011	Barnsley	Championship	1-4
02/01/2012	**Burnley**	**Championship**	**2-1**
09/01/2012	Arsenal	FA Cup 3rd Round	0-1
14/01/2012	Crystal Palace	Championship	1-1
21/01/2012	**Ipswich Town**	**Championship**	**3-1**
31/01/2012	**Birmingham City**	**Championship**	**1-4**
04/02/2012	Bristol City	Championship	3-0
11/02/2012	**Brighton & Hove Albion**	**Championship**	**1-2**
14/02/2012	Coventry City	Championship	1-2
18/02/2012	**Doncaster Rovers**	**Championship**	**3-2**
25/02/2012	Portsmouth	Championship	0-0
03/03/2012	**Southampton**	**Championship**	**0-1**
06/03/2012	Hull City	Championship	0-0
11/03/2012	Middlesbrough	Championship	2-0
17/03/2012	**West Ham United**	**Championship**	**1-1**
20/03/2012	Nottingham Forest	Championship	3-7
24/03/2012	Millwall	Championship	1-0
31/03/2012	**Watford**	**Championship**	**0-2**
06/04/2012	Reading	Championship	0-2
09/04/2012	**Derby County**	**Championship**	**0-2**
14/04/2012	**Peterborough United**	**Championship**	**4-1**
17/04/2012	Blackpool	Championship	0-1
21/04/2012	Cardiff City	Championship	1-1
28/04/2012	**Leicester City**	**Championship**	**1-2**

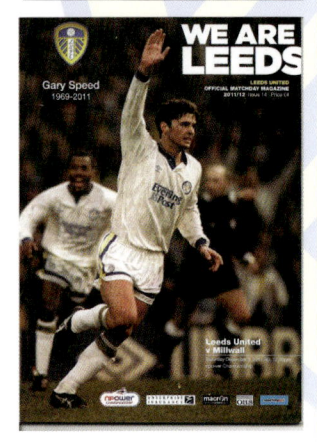

In January 2012, the opposition had players sent off in three out of four league games that Leeds played in.

One of the players sent off was Alex McCarthy for Ipswich who had a loan spell at Leeds earlier in the season.

Leeds were led out by Jonny Howson, Patrick Kisnorbo, Andy Lonergan and Robert Snodgrass

When Leeds won at Middlesbrough in March 2012, it kept up an unbeaten record at the Riverside of ten games.

Having conceded seven the previous mid-week, Andy Lonergan kept a clean sheet at Millwall four days later saving a penalty as well.

CHAMPIONSHIP

2012–13

Date	Opposition	Competition	Score
11/08/2012	Shrewsbury Town	Capital One Cup 1st Round	4-0
18/08/2012	Wolverhampton Wanderers	Championship	1-0
21/08/2012	Blackpool	Championship	1-2
25/08/2012	Peterborough United	Championship	2-1
28/08/2012	Oxford United	Capital One Cup 2nd Round	3-0
01/09/2012	Blackburn Rovers	Championship	3-3
15/09/2012	Cardiff City	Championship	1-2
18/09/2012	Hull City	Championship	2-3
22/09/2012	Nottingham Forest	Championship	2-1
25/09/2012	Everton	Capital One Cup 3rd Round	2-1
29/09/2012	Bristol City	Championship	3-2
02/10/2012	Bolton Wanderers	Championship	2-2
06/10/2012	Barnsley	Championship	1-0
19/10/2012	Sheffield Wednesday	Championship	1-1
23/10/2012	Charlton Athletic	Championship	1-1
27/10/2012	Birmingham City	Championship	0-1
30/10/2012	Southampton	Capital One Cup 4th Round	3-0
02/11/2012	Brighton & Hove Albion	Championship	2-2
06/11/2012	Burnley	Championship	0-1
10/11/2012	Watford	Championship	1-6
18/11/2012	Millwall	Championship	0-1
24/11/2012	Crystal Palace	Championship	2-1
27/11/2012	Leicester City	Championship	1-0
01/12/2012	Huddersfield Town	Championship	4-2
08/12/2012	Derby County	Championship	1-3
15/12/2012	Ipswich Town	Championship	2-0
19/12/2012	Chelsea	Capital One Cup 5th Round	1-5
22/12/2012	Middlesbrough	Championship	2-1
26/12/2012	Nottingham Forest	Championship	2-4
29/12/2012	Hull City	Championship	0-2
01/01/2013	Bolton Wanderers	Championship	1-0
05/01/2013	Birmingham City	FA Cup 3rd Round	1-1
12/01/2013	Barnsley	Championship	0-2
15/01/2013	Birmingham City	FA Cup 3rd Round Replay	2-1
19/01/2013	Bristol City	Championship	1-0
27/01/2013	Tottenham Hotspur	FA Cup 4th Round	2-1
02/02/2013	Cardiff City	Championship	0-1
09/02/2013	Wolverhampton Wanderers	Championship	2-2
12/02/2013	Middlesbrough	Championship	0-1
17/02/2013	Manchester City	FA Cup 5th Round	0-4
20/02/2013	Blackpool	Championship	2-0
23/02/2013	Blackburn Rovers	Championship	0-0
02/03/2013	Millwall	Championship	1-0
05/03/2003	Leicester City	Championship	1-1
09/03/2013	Crystal Palace	Championship	2-2
12/03/2013	Peterborough United	Championship	1-1
16/03/2013	Huddersfield Town	Championship	1-2
30/03/2013	Ipswich Town	Championship	0-3
01/04/2013	Derby County	Championship	1-2
06/04/2013	Charlton Athletic	Championship	1-2
13/04/2013	Sheffield Wednesday	Championship	2-1
16/04/2013	Burnley	Championship	1-0
20/04/2013	Birmingham City	Championship	0-1
27/04/2013	Brighton & Hove Albion	Championship	1-2
04/05/2013	Watford	Championship	2-1

Team	Pld	W	D	L	GF	GA	Pts
Cardiff City	46	25	12	9	72	45	87
Hull City	46	24	7	15	61	52	79
Watford	46	23	8	15	85	58	77
Brighton & Hove Albion	46	19	18	9	69	43	75
Crystal Palace	46	19	15	12	73	62	72
Leicester City	46	19	11	16	71	48	68
Bolton Wanderers	46	18	14	14	69	61	68
Nottingham Forest	46	17	16	13	63	59	67
Charlton Athletic	46	17	14	15	65	59	65
Derby County	46	16	13	17	65	62	61
Burnley	46	16	13	17	62	60	61
Birmingham City	46	15	16	15	63	69	61
Leeds United	46	17	10	19	57	66	61
Ipswich Town	46	16	12	18	48	61	60
Blackpool	46	14	17	15	62	63	59
Middlesbrough	46	18	5	23	61	70	59
Blackburn Rovers	46	14	16	16	55	62	58
Sheffield Wednesday	46	16	10	20	53	61	58
Huddersfield Town	46	15	13	18	53	73	58
Millwall	46	15	11	20	51	62	56
Barnsley	46	14	13	19	56	70	55
Peterborough United	46	15	9	22	75	–9	54
Wolverhampton	46	14	9	23	55	69	51
Bristol City	46	11	8	27	59	84	41

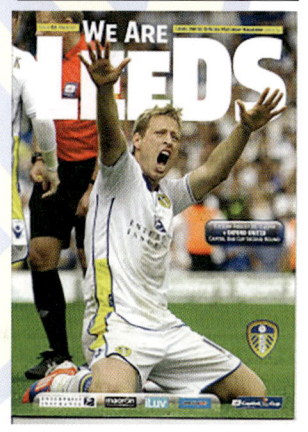

Luciano Becchio emerged as top scorer for the club despite moving to Norwich City in part-exchange for Steve Morison.

Leeds reached the League Cup last eight for the first time since season 1995-96.

Harrogate-born Andy Gray made his second debut for the club, almost 17 years after his first one.

Leeds also reached the fifth round of the FA Cup for the first time in ten years.

Leeds had five different penalty takers in Ross McCormack, Luciano Becchio, El Hadji Diouf, Michael Tonge and Stephen Warnock.

2013–14　　　　　　　　　　　　　　　　　　CHAMPIONSHIP

Team	Pld	W	D	L	GF	GA	Pts
Leicester City	46	31	9	6	83	43	102
Burnley	46	26	15	5	72	37	93
Derby County	46	25	10	11	84	52	85
Queens Park Rangers	46	23	11	12	60	44	80
Wigan Athletic	46	21	10	15	61	48	73
Brighton & Hove Albion	46	19	15	12	55	40	72
Reading	46	19	14	13	70	56	71
Blackburn Rovers	46	18	16	12	70	62	70
Ipswich Town	46	18	14	14	60	54	68
Bournemouth	46	18	12	16	67	66	66
Nottingham Forest	46	16	17	13	67	64	65
Middlesbrough	46	16	16	14	62	50	64
Watford	46	15	15	16	74	64	60
Bolton Wanderers	46	14	17	15	59	60	59
Leeds United	46	16	9	21	59	67	57
Sheffield Wednesday	46	13	14	19	63	65	53
Huddersfield Town	46	14	11	21	58	65	53
Charlton Athletic	46	13	12	21	41	61	51
Millwall	46	11	15	20	46	74	48
Blackpool	46	11	13	22	38	66	46
Birmingham City	46	11	11	24	58	74	44
Doncaster Rovers	46	11	11	24	39	70	44
Barnsley	46	9	12	25	44	77	39
Yeovil Town	46	8	13	25	44	75	37

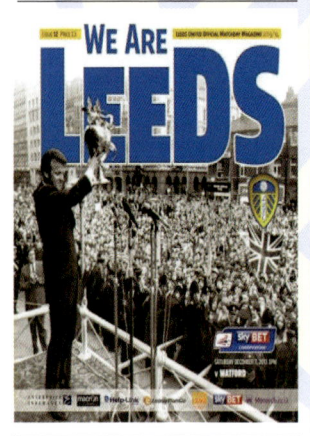

Date	Opposition	Competition	Score
03/08/2013	Brighton & Hove Albion	Championship	2-1
07/08/2013	Chesterfield	Capital One Cup 1st Round	2-1
11/08/2013	Leicester City	Championship	0-0
17/08/2013	Sheffield Wednesday	Championship	1-1
24/08/2013	Ipswich Town	Championship	2-1
27/08/2013	Doncaster Rovers	Capital One Cup 2nd Round	3-1
31/08/2013	Queens Park Rangers	Championship	0-1
14/09/2013	Bolton Wanderers	Championship	1-0
18/09/2013	Reading	Championship	0-1
21/09/2013	Burnley	Championship	1-2
25/09/2013	Newcastle United	Capital One Cup 3rd Round	0-2
28/09/2013	Millwall	Championship	0-2
01/10/2013	AFC Bournemouth	Championship	2-1
05/10/2013	Derby County	Championship	1-3
20/10/2013	Birmingham City	Championship	4-0
26/10/2013	Huddersfield Town	Championship	2-3
02/11/2013	Yeovil Town	Championship	2-0
09/11/2013	Charlton Athletic	Championship	4-2
23/11/2013	Middlesbrough	Championship	2-1
30/11/2013	Blackburn Rovers	Championship	0-1
04/12/2013	Wigan Athletic	Championship	2-0
07/12/2013	Watford	Championship	3-3
14/12/2013	Doncaster Rovers	Championship	3-0
21/12/2013	Barnsley	Championship	0-0
26/12/2013	Blackpool	Championship	1-1
29/12/2013	Nottingham Forest	Championship	1-2
01/01/2014	Blackburn Rovers	Championship	1-2
04/01/2014	Rochdale	FA Cup 3rd Round	0-2
11/01/2014	Sheffield Wednesday	Championship	0-6
18/01/2014	Leicester City	Championship	0-1
28/01/2014	Ipswich Town	Championship	1-1
01/02/2014	Huddersfield Town	Championship	5-1
08/02/2014	Yeovil Town	Championship	2-1
11/02/2014	Brighton & Hove Albion	Championship	0-1
22/02/2014	Middlesbrough	Championship	0-0
01/03/2014	Queens Park Rangers	Championship	1-1
08/03/2014	Bolton Wanderers	Championship	1-5
11/03/2014	Reading	Championship	2-4
15/03/2014	Burnley	Championship	1-2
22/03/2014	Millwall	Championship	2-1
25/03/2014	AFC Bournemouth	Championship	1-4
29/03/2014	Doncaster Rovers	Championship	1-2
01/04/2014	Charlton Athletic	Championship	0-1
05/04/2014	Wigan Athletic	Championship	0-1
08/04/2014	Watford	Championship	0-3
12/04/2014	Blackpool	Championship	2-0
19/04/2014	Barnsley	Championship	1-0
21/04/2014	Nottingham Forest	Championship	0-2
26/04/2014	Birmingham City	Championship	3-1
03/05/2014	Derby County	Championship	1-1

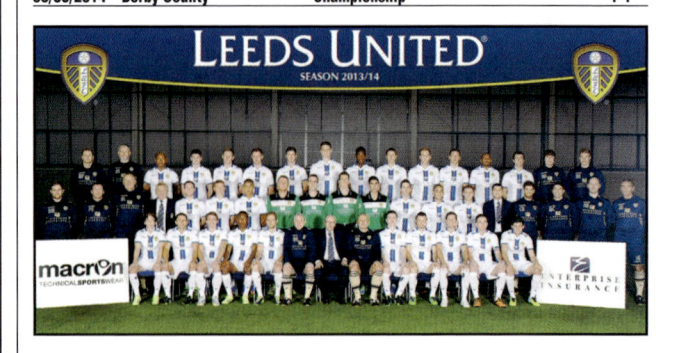

Leeds used four captains in season 2013-14, Lee Peltier, Paul Green, Rudy Austin and Ross McCormack.

When Ross McCormack scored four in the away win at Charlton, he became the first Leeds player since Alan Smith at Hapoel Tel Aviv to score four away from home.

Dexter Blackstock made an instant impact by scoring moments after coming off the bench at Huddersfield Town. Sadly his loan deal was cut short through injury.

The home game against Huddersfield Town saw assistant manager Nigel Gibbs take charge of the team following mad Friday!

When Leeds won at Birmingham in April, it was their first league win at St Andrews since April 1982.

CHAMPIONSHIP

2014–15

Date	Opposition	Competition	Score
09/08/2014	Millwall	Championship	0-2
12/08/2014	Accrington Stanley	Capital One Cup 1st Round	2-1
16/08/2014	Middlesbrough	Championship	1-0
19/08/2014	Brighton & Hove Albion	Championship	0-2
23/08/2014	Watford	Championship	1-4
27/08/2014	Bradford City	Capital One Cup 2nd Round	1-2
30/08/2014	Bolton Wanderers	Championship	1-0
13/09/2014	Birmingham City	Championship	1-1
16/09/2014	AFC Bournemouth	Championship	3-1
20/09/2014	Huddersfield Town	Championship	3-0
27/09/2014	Brentford	Championship	0-2
01/10/2014	Reading	Championship	0-0
04/10/2014	Sheffield Wednesday	Championship	1-1
17/10/2014	Rotherham United	Championship	1-2
21/10/2014	Norwich City	Championship	1-1
25/10/2014	Wolverhampton Wanderers	Championship	1-2
01/11/2014	Cardiff City	Championship	1-3
04/11/2004	Charlton Athletic	Championship	2-2
08/11/2014	Blackpool	Championship	3-1
22/11/2014	Blackburn Rovers	Championship	1-2
29/11/2014	Derby County	Championship	2-0
06/12/2014	Ipswich Town	Championship	1-4
13/12/2014	Fulham	Championship	0-1
20/12/2014	Nottingham Forest	Championship	1-1
26/12/2014	Wigan Athletic	Championship	0-2
30/12/2014	Derby County	Championship	0-2
04/01/2015	Sunderland	FA Cup 3rd Round	0-1
10/01/2015	Bolton Wanderers	Championship	1-1
17/01/2015	Birmingham City	Championship	1-1
20/01/2015	AFC Bournemouth	Championship	1-0
31/01/2015	Huddersfield Town	Championship	2-1
07/02/2015	Brentford	Championship	0-1
10/02/2015	Reading	Championship	2-0
14/02/2015	Millwall	Championship	1-0
21/02/2015	Middlesbrough	Championship	1-0
24/02/2015	Brighton & Hove Albion	Championship	0-2
28/02/2015	Watford	Championship	2-3
04/03/2015	Ipswich Town	Championship	2-1
07/03/2015	Wigan Athletic	Championship	1-0
14/03/2015	Nottingham Forest	Championship	0-0
18/03/2015	Fulham	Championship	3-0
21/03/2015	Blackpool	Championship	1-1
04/04/2015	Blackburn Rovers	Championship	0-3
06/04/2015	Wolverhampton Wanderers	Championship	3-4
11/04/2015	Cardiff City	Championship	1-2
14/04/2015	Norwich City	Championship	0-2
18/04/2015	Charlton Athletic	Championship	1-2
25/04/2015	Sheffield Wednesday	Championship	2-1
02/05/2015	Rotherham United	Championship	0-0

Team	Pld	W	D	L	GF	GA	Pts
Bournemouth (C, P)	46	26	12	8	98	45	90
Watford	46	27	8	11	91	50	89
Norwich City	46	25	11	10	88	48	86
Middlesbrough	46	25	10	11	68	37	85
Brentford	46	23	9	14	78	59	78
Ipswich Town	46	22	12	12	72	54	78
Wolverhampton	46	22	12	12	70	56	78
Derby County	46	21	14	11	85	56	77
Blackburn Rovers	46	17	16	13	66	59	67
Birmingham City	46	16	15	15	54	64	63
Cardiff City	46	16	14	16	57	61	62
Charlton Athletic	46	14	18	14	54	60	60
Sheffield Wednesday	46	14	18	14	43	49	60
Nottingham Forest	46	15	14	17	71	69	59
Leeds United	46	15	11	20	50	61	56
Huddersfield Town	46	13	16	17	58	75	55
Fulham	46	14	10	22	62	83	52
Bolton Wanderers	46	13	12	21	54	67	51
Reading	46	13	11	22	48	69	50
Brighton & Hove Albion	46	10	17	19	44	54	47
Rotherham United	46	11	16	19	46	67	46
Millwall	46	9	14	23	42	76	41
Wigan Athletic	46	9	12	25	39	64	39
Blackpool	46	4	14	28	36	91	26

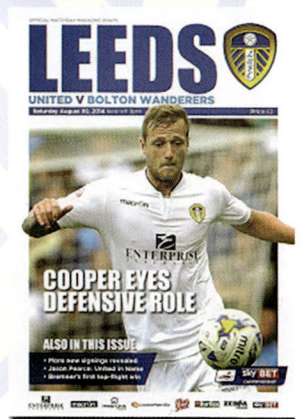

Leeds had three different managerial changes this season, David Hockaday (19 June 2014 to 28 August 2014), Neil Redfearn (28 August 2014 to 23 September 2014), Darko Milanic (23 September 2014 to 25 October 2014), Neil Redfearn (1 November 2014 to 2 May 2015).

Leeds completed a League double over Huddersfield Town for the first time since season 1937-38.

Darko Milanic became the first-ever Leeds United manager not to win a game in charge of the club.

When Steve Morison scored away at Charlton, it was his first goal for the Whites in over two years when he netted a double away at Crystal Palace in March 2013.

Leeds had four captains this season, Jason Pearce, Stephen Warnock, Liam Cooper and Sol Bamba.

2015–16　　　　　　　　　　　　　　　　　　　CHAMPIONSHIP

Team	Pld	W	D	L	GF	GA	Pts
Burnley	46	26	15	5	72	35	93
Middlesbrough	46	26	11	9	63	31	89
Brighton & Hove Albion	46	24	17	5	72	42	89
Hull City	46	24	11	11	69	35	83
Derby County	46	21	15	10	66	43	78
Sheffield Wednesday	46	19	17	10	66	45	74
Ipswich Town	46	18	15	13	53	51	69
Cardiff City	46	17	17	12	56	51	68
Brentford	46	19	8	19	72	67	65
Birmingham City	46	16	15	15	53	49	63
Preston North End	46	15	17	14	45	45	62
Queens Park Rangers	46	14	18	14	54	54	60
Leeds United	46	14	17	15	50	58	59
Wolverhampton	46	14	16	16	53	58	58
Blackburn Rovers	46	13	16	17	46	46	55
Nottingham Forest	46	13	16	17	43	47	55
Reading	46	13	13	20	52	59	52
Bristol City	46	13	13	20	54	71	52
Huddersfield Town	46	13	12	21	59	70	51
Fulham	46	12	15	19	66	79	51
Rotherham United	46	13	10	23	53	71	49
Charlton Athletic	46	9	13	24	40	80	40
Milton Keynes Dons	46	9	12	25	39	69	39
Bolton Wanderers	46	5	15	26	41	81	30

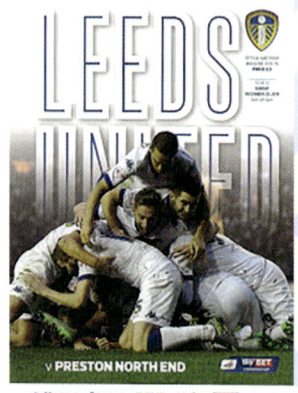

Date	Opposition	Competition	Score
08/08/2015	**Burnley**	**Championship**	**1-1**
13/08/2015	Doncaster Rovers	Capital One Cup 1st Round	1-1 (2-4 on pens)
16/08/2015	Reading	Championship	0-0
19/08/2015	Bristol City	Championship	2-2
22/08/2015	**Sheffield Wednesday**	**Championship**	**1-1**
29/08/2015	Derby County	Championship	2-1
12/09/2015	**Brentford**	**Championship**	**1-1**
15/09/2015	**Ipswich Town**	**Championship**	**0-1**
19/09/2015	Milton Keynes Dons	Championship	2-1
27/09/2015	Middlesbrough	Championship	0-3
03/10/2015	**Birmingham City**	**Championship**	**0-2**
17/10/2015	**Brighton & Hove Albion**	**Championship**	**1-2**
21/10/2015	Fulham	Championship	1-1
24/10/2015	Bolton Wanderers	Championship	1-1
29/10/2015	**Blackburn Rovers**	**Championship**	**0-2**
03/11/2015	**Cardiff City**	**Championship**	**1-0**
07/11/2015	Huddersfield Town	Championship	3-0
21/11/2015	**Rotherham United**	**Championship**	**0-1**
28/11/2015	Queens Park Rangers	Championship	0-1
05/12/2015	**Hull City**	**Championship**	**2-1**
12/12/2015	Charlton Athletic	Championship	0-0
17/12/2015	Wolverhampton Wanderers	Championship	3-2
20/12/2015	**Preston North End**	**Championship**	**1-0**
27/12/2015	Nottingham Forest	Championship	1-1
29/12/2015	**Derby County**	**Championship**	**2-2**
02/01/2016	**Milton Keynes Dons**	**Championship**	**1-1**
09/01/2016	**Rotherham United**	**FA Cup 3rd Round**	**2-0**
12/01/2016	Ipswich Town	Championship	1-2
16/01/2016	Sheffield Wednesday	Championship	0-2
23/01/2016	**Bristol City**	**Championship**	**1-0**
26/01/2016	Brentford	Championship	1-1
30/01/2016	Bolton Wanderers	FA Cup 4th Round	2-1
06/02/2016	**Nottingham Forest**	**Championship**	**0-1**
15/02/2016	**Middlesbrough**	**Championship**	**0-0**
20/02/2016	Watford	FA Cup 5th Round	0-1
23/02/2016	**Fulham**	**Championship**	**1-1**
29/02/2016	Brighton & Hove Albion	Championship	0-4
05/03/2016	**Bolton Wanderers**	**Championship**	**2-1**
08/03/2016	Cardiff City	Championship	2-0
12/03/2016	Blackburn Rovers	Championship	2-1
19/03/2016	**Huddersfield Town**	**Championship**	**1-4**
02/04/2016	Rotherham United	Championship	1-2
05/04/2016	**Queens Park Rangers**	**Championship**	**1-1**
09/04/2016	Burnley	Championship	0-1
12/04/2016	Birmingham City	Championship	2-1
16/04/2016	**Reading**	**Championship**	**3-2**
19/04/2016	**Wolverhampton Wanderers**	**Championship**	**2-1**
23/04/2016	Hull City	Championship	2-2
30/04/2016	**Charlton Athletic**	**Championship**	**1-2**
07/05/2016	Preston North End	Championship	1-1

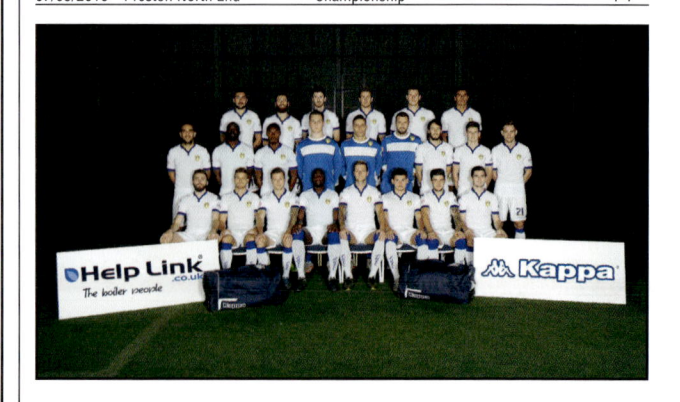

Leeds recorded their first away win at Derby County for the first time since April 2002.

When Leeds faced Rotherham at Elland Road, the Leeds head coach was Steve Evans who used to manage The Millers, whilst the away head coach was Neil Redfearn who used to manage Leeds.

When Leeds defeated Wolverhampton Wanderers at Molineux in December 2015, it was their first league win in the Black Country since December 1984.

Leeds handed squad numbers to five different keepers over the season, Marco Silvestri, Ross Turnbull, Charlie Horton, Bailey Peacock-Farrell and Eric Grimes.

Steve Evans presided over a double over Cardiff City for the first time since season 1983-84.

CHAMPIONSHIP
2016–17

Date	Opposition	Competition	Score
07/08/2016	Queens Park Rangers	Championship	0-3
10/08/2016	Fleetwood Town	EFL Cup 1st Round	2-2 (5-4 on pens)
13/08/2016	**Birmingham City**	**Championship**	**1-2**
16/08/2016	**Fulham**	**Championship**	**1-1**
20/08/2016	Sheffield Wednesday	Championship	2-0
23/08/2016	Luton Town	EFL Cup 2nd Round	1-0
27/08/2016	Nottingham Forest	Championship	1-3
10/09/2016	**Huddersfield Town**	**Championship**	**0-1**
13/09/2016	**Blackburn Rovers**	**Championship**	**2-1**
17/09/2016	Cardiff City	Championship	2-0
20/09/2016	**Blackburn Rovers**	**EFL Cup 3rd Round**	**1-0**
24/09/2016	**Ipswich Town**	**Championship**	**1-0**
27/09/2016	Bristol City	Championship	0-1
01/10/2016	**Barnsley**	**Championship**	**2-1**
15/10/2016	Derby County	Championship	0-1
18/10/2016	**Wigan Athletic**	**Championship**	**1-1**
22/10/2016	Wolverhampton Wanderers	Championship	1-0
25/10/2016	**Norwich City**	**EFL Cup 4th Round**	**2-2 (3-2 on pens)**
29/10/2016	**Burton Albion**	**Championship**	**2-0**
05/11/2016	Norwich City	Championship	3-2
20/11/2016	**Newcastle United**	**Championship**	**0-2**
26/11/2016	Rotherham United	Championship	2-1
29/11/2016	Liverpool	EFL Cup 5th Round	0-2
03/12/2016	**Aston Villa**	**Championship**	**2-0**
09/12/2016	Brighton & Hove Albion	Championship	0-2
13/12/2016	**Reading**	**Championship**	**2-0**
17/12/2016	**Brentford**	**Championship**	**1-0**
26/12/2016	Preston North End	Championship	4-1
29/12/2016	Aston Villa	Championship	1-1
02/01/2017	**Rotherham United**	**Championship**	**3-0**
09/01/2017	Cambridge United	FA Cup 3rd Round	2-1
13/01/2017	**Derby County**	**Championship**	**1-0**
21/01/2017	Barnsley	Championship	2-3
25/01/2017	**Nottingham Forest**	**Championship**	**2-0**
29/01/2017	Sutton United	FA Cup 4th Round	0-1
01/02/2017	Blackburn Rovers	Championship	2-1
05/02/2017	Huddersfield Town	Championship	1-2
11/02/2017	**Cardiff City**	**Championship**	**0-2**
14/02/2017	**Bristol City**	**Championship**	**2-1**
18/02/2017	Ipswich Town	Championship	1-1
25/02/2017	**Sheffield Wednesday**	**Championship**	**1-0**
03/03/2017	Birmingham City	Championship	3-1
07/03/2017	Fulham	Championship	1-1
11/03/2017	**Queens Park Rangers**	**Championship**	**0-0**
18/03/2017	**Brighton & Hove Albion**	**Championship**	**2-0**
01/04/2017	Reading	Championship	0-1
04/04/2017	Brentford	Championship	0-2
08/04/2017	**Preston North End**	**Championship**	**3-0**
14/04/2017	Newcastle United	Championship	1-1
17/04/2017	**Wolverhampton Wanderers**	**Championship**	**0-1**
22/04/2017	Burton Albion	Championship	1-2
29/04/2017	**Norwich City**	**Championship**	**3-3**
07/05/2017	Wigan Athletic	Championship	1-1

Team	Pld	W	D	L	GF	GA	Pts
Newcastle United	46	29	7	10	85	40	94
Brighton & Hove Albion	46	28	9	9	74	40	93
Reading	46	26	7	13	68	64	85
Sheffield Wednesday	46	24	9	13	60	45	81
Huddersfield Town	46	25	6	15	56	58	81
Fulham	46	22	14	10	85	57	80
Leeds United	46	22	9	15	61	47	75
Norwich City	46	20	10	16	85	69	70
Derby County	46	18	13	15	54	50	67
Brentford	46	18	10	18	75	65	64
Preston North End	46	16	14	16	64	63	62
Cardiff City	46	17	11	18	60	61	62
Aston Villa	46	16	14	16	47	48	62
Barnsley	46	15	13	18	64	67	58
Wolverhampton	46	16	10	20	54	58	58
Ipswich Town	46	13	16	17	48	58	55
Bristol City	46	15	9	22	60	66	54
Queens Park Rangers	46	15	8	23	52	66	53
Birmingham City	46	13	14	19	45	64	53
Burton Albion	46	13	13	20	49	63	52
Nottingham Forest	46	14	9	23	62	72	51
Blackburn Rovers	46	12	15	19	53	65	51
Wigan Athletic	46	10	12	24	40	57	42
Rotherham United	46	5	8	33	40	98	23

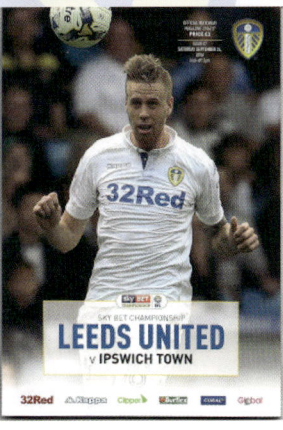

When Leeds defeated Fleetwood Town in the EFL Cup first round, they won a penalty shoot-out for the first time since defeating Swindon Town in September 2003.

Leeds used the all-yellow kit on only three occasions, on day one of the new campaign at Queens Park Rangers at Brighton and the last day of the season at Wigan Athletic.

Leeds were awarded seven penalties, scoring them all, with Chris Wood scoring six and Souleymane Doukara scoring the other.

If you include penalty shoots-outs, Leeds scored 15 out of 17 from the spot, with only Kalvin Phillips and Matt Grimes missing in the shoot-out v Norwich City.

Chris Wood became the first Leeds United player to hit 30 goals in either of the top two tiers of English football for the first time since Lee Chapman in season 1990-91 for Leeds.

2017–18 CHAMPIONSHIP

Team	Pld	W	D	L	GF	GA	Pts
Wolverhampton	46	30	9	7	82	39	99
Cardiff City	46	27	9	10	69	39	90
Fulham	46	25	13	8	79	46	88
Aston Villa	46	24	11	11	72	42	83
Middlesbrough	46	22	10	14	67	45	76
Derby County	46	20	15	11	69	48	75
Preston North End	46	19	16	11	58	45	73
Millwall	46	19	15	12	56	45	72
Brentford	46	18	15	13	62	52	69
Sheffield United	46	20	9	17	62	55	69
Bristol City	46	17	16	13	67	58	67
Ipswich Town	46	17	9	20	57	60	60
Leeds United	46	17	9	20	59	64	60
Norwich City	46	15	15	16	49	60	60
Sheffield Wednesday	46	14	15	17	59	60	57
Queens Park Rangers	46	15	11	20	58	70	56
Nottingham Forest	46	15	8	23	51	65	53
Hull City	46	11	16	19	70	70	49
Birmingham City	46	13	7	26	38	68	46
Reading	46	10	14	22	48	70	44
Bolton Wanderers	46	10	13	23	39	74	43
Barnsley	46	9	14	23	48	71	41
Burton Albion	46	10	11	25	35	81	41
Sunderland	46	7	16	23	52	80	37

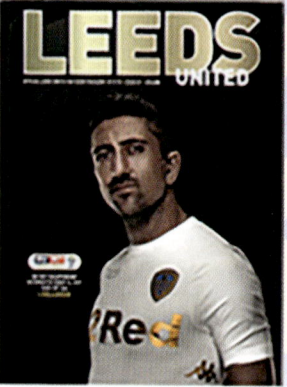

Date	Opposition	Competition	Score
06/08/2017	Bolton Wanderers	Championship	3-2
09/08/2017	**Port Vale**	**Carabao Cup 1st Round**	**4-1**
12/08/2017	**Preston North End**	**Championship**	**0-0**
15/08/2017	**Fulham**	**Championship**	**0-0**
19/08/2017	Sunderland	Championship	2-0
22/08/2017	**Newport County**	**Carabao Cup 2nd Round**	**5-1**
26/08/2017	Nottingham Forest	Championship	2-0
09/09/2017	**Burton Albion**	**Championship**	**5-0**
12/09/2017	**Birmingham City**	**Championship**	**2-0**
16/09/2017	Millwall	Championship	0-1
19/09/2017	Burnley	Carabao Cup 3rd Round	2-2 (5-3 on pens)
23/09/2017	**Ipswich Town**	**Championship**	**3-2**
26/09/2017	Cardiff City	Championship	1-3
01/10/2017	Sheffield Wednesday	Championship	0-3
14/10/2017	**Reading**	**Championship**	**0-1**
21/10/2017	Bristol City	Championship	3-0
24/10/2017	Leicester City	Carabao Cup 4th Round	1-3
27/10/2017	**Sheffield United**	**Championship**	**1-2**
31/10/2017	**Derby County**	**Championship**	**1-2**
05/11/2017	Brentford	Championship	1-3
19/11/2017	**Middlesbrough**	**Championship**	**2-1**
22/11/2017	Wolverhampton Wanderers	Championship	1-4
25/11/2017	Barnsley	Championship	2-0
01/12/2017	**Aston Villa**	**Championship**	**1-1**
09/12/2017	Queens Park Rangers	Championship	3-1
16/12/2017	**Norwich City**	**Championship**	**1-0**
23/12/2017	**Hull City**	**Championship**	**1-0**
26/12/2017	Burton Albion	Championship	2-1
30/12/2017	Birmingham City	Championship	0-1
01/01/2018	**Nottingham Forest**	**Championship**	**0-0**
07/01/2018	Newport County	FA Cup 3rd Round	1-2
13/01/2018	Ipswich Town	Championship	0-1
20/01/2018	**Millwall**	**Championship**	**3-4**
30/01/2018	Hull City	Championship	0-0
03/02/2018	**Cardiff City**	**Championship**	**1-4**
10/02/2018	Sheffield United	Championship	1-2
18/02/2018	**Bristol City**	**Championship**	**2-2**
21/02/2018	Derby County	Championship	2-2
24/02/2018	**Brentford**	**Championship**	**1-0**
02/03/2018	Middlesbrough	Championship	0-3
07/03/2018	**Wolverhampton Wanderers**	**Championship**	**0-3**
10/03/2018	Reading	Championship	2-2
17/03/2018	**Sheffield Wednesday**	**Championship**	**1-2**
30/03/2018	**Bolton Wanderers**	**Championship**	**2-1**
03/04/2018	Fulham	Championship	0-2
07/04/2018	**Sunderland**	**Championship**	**1-1**
10/04/2018	Preston North End	Championship	1-3
13/04/2018	Aston Villa	Championship	0-1
21/04/2018	**Barnsley**	**Championship**	**2-1**
28/04/2018	Norwich City	Championship	1-2
06/05/2018	**Queens Park Rangers**	**Championship**	**2-0**

When Samuel Saiz scored a hat-trick v Port Vale, he became the first Leeds United debutant to do so since Carl Shutt on 1 April 1989.

When Leeds beat Birmingham City on 12 September, they topped the Championship table for the first time since 5 May 1990.

Leeds were only awarded three penalties all season, two were scored at home to Burton Albion and away at Burnley and one missed at home to Reading.

Leeds achieved their first win at Oakwell since November 1997, following a 2-0 win over the Tykes at the end of November 2017.

Gaetano Berardi scored his first goal for the club in 102 appearances in the 2-1 FA Cup defeat away at Newport County.

Paul Heckingbottom.

456

CHAMPIONSHIP 2018–19

Date	Opposition	Competition	Score
05/08/2018	Stoke City	Championship	3-1
11/08/2018	Derby County	Championship	4-1
14/08/2018	Bolton Wanderers	Carabao Cup 1st Round	2-1
18/08/2018	Rotherham United	Championship	2-0
21/08/2018	Swansea City	Championship	2-2
25/08/2018	Norwich City	Championship	3-0
28/08/2018	Preston North End	Carabao Cup 2nd Round	0-2
31/08/2018	Middlesbrough	Championship	0-0
15/09/2018	Millwall	Championship	1-1
18/09/2018	Preston North End	Championship	3-0
22/09/2018	Birmingham City	Championship	1-2
28/09/2018	Sheffield Wednesday	Championship	1-1
02/10/2018	Hull City	Championship	1-0
06/10/2018	Brentford	Championship	1-1
20/10/2018	Blackburn Rovers	Championship	1-2
24/10/2018	Ipswich Town	Championship	2-0
27/10/2018	Nottingham Forest	Championship	1-1
04/11/2018	Wigan Athletic	Championship	2-1
10/11/2018	West Bromwich Albion	Championship	1-4
24/11/2018	Bristol City	Championship	2-0
27/11/2018	Reading	Championship	1-0
01/12/2018	Sheffield United	Championship	1-0
08/12/2018	Queens Park Rangers	Championship	2-1
15/12/2018	Bolton Wanderers	Championship	1-0
23/12/2018	Aston Villa	Championship	3-2
26/12/2018	Blackburn Rovers	Championship	3-2
29/12/2018	Hull City	Championship	0-2
01/01/2019	Nottingham Forest	Championship	2-4
06/01/2019	Queens Park Rangers	FA Cup 3rd Round	1-2
11/01/2019	Derby County	Championship	2-0
19/01/2019	Stoke City	Championship	1-2
26/01/2019	Rotherham United	Championship	2-1
02/02/2019	Norwich City	Championship	1-3
09/02/2019	Middlesbrough	Championship	1-1
13/02/2019	Swansea City	Championship	2-1
23/02/2019	Bolton Wanderers	Championship	2-1
26/02/2019	Queens Park Rangers	Championship	0-1
01/03/2019	West Bromwich Albion	Championship	4-0
09/03/2019	Bristol City	Championship	1-0
12/03/2019	Reading	Championship	3-0
16/03/2019	Sheffield United	Championship	0-1
30/03/2019	Millwall	Championship	3-2
06/04/2019	Birmingham City	Championship	0-1
09/04/2019	Preston North End	Championship	2-0
13/04/2019	Sheffield Wednesday	Championship	1-0
19/04/2019	Wigan Athletic	Championship	1-2
22/04/2019	Brentford	Championship	0-2
28/04/2019	Aston Villa	Championship	1-1
05/05/2019	Ipswich Town	Championship	2-3
11/05/2019	Derby County	Championship Play Off Semi Final 1st Leg	1-0
15/05/2019	Derby County	Championship Play Off Semi Final 2nd Leg	2-4

Team	Pld	W	D	L	GF	GA	Pts
Norwich City	46	27	13	6	93	57	94
Sheffield United	46	26	11	9	78	41	89
Leeds United	46	25	8	13	73	50	83
West Bromwich Albion	46	23	11	12	87	62	80
Aston Villa	46	20	16	10	82	61	76
Derby County	46	20	14	12	69	54	74
Middlesbrough	46	20	13	13	49	41	73
Bristol City	46	19	13	14	59	53	70
Nottingham Forest	46	17	15	14	61	54	66
Swansea City	46	18	11	17	65	62	65
Brentford	46	17	13	16	73	59	64
Sheffield Wednesday	46	16	16	14	60	62	64
Hull City	46	17	11	18	66	68	62
Preston North End	46	16	13	17	67	67	61
Blackburn Rovers	46	16	12	18	64	69	60
Stoke City	46	11	22	13	45	52	55
Birmingham City	46	14	19	13	64	58	52
Wigan Athletic	46	13	13	20	51	64	52
Queens Park Rangers	46	14	9	23	53	71	51
Reading	46	10	17	19	49	66	47
Millwall	46	10	14	22	48	64	44
Rotherham United	46	8	16	22	52	83	40
Bolton Wanderers	46	8	8	30	29	78	32
Ipswich Town	46	5	16	25	36	77	31

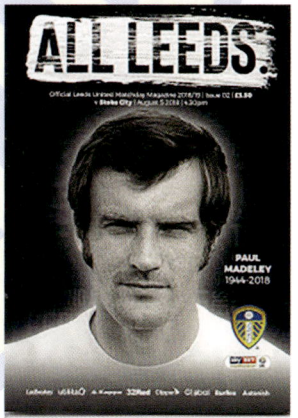

Patrick Bamford is challenged by Derby County Captain Richard Keogh at Pride Park.

Head coach Marcelo Bielsa became the first-ever head coach/manager to win his first four games in charge of the football club.

When Bielsa won the Manager of the Month award for August 2018, he became the first Leeds boss to do so since Simon Grayson in December 2010.

Leeds scored first in 25 games, winning 22, drawing one and losing just two

The Whites won seven straight league games for the first time since the start of the 2007-08 season when in League One.

In the win at Sheffield United in December, Leeds had three captains, Liam Copper, Pablo Hernandez and Stuart Dallas.

SHIRTS, SHORTS AND ALL
A HISTORY OF THE LEEDS UNITED FOOTBALL KIT
BY JOHN DEVLIN

It seems every team has a kit creation myth somewhere in their history; from Arsenal's experiments with white sleeves in the early 1930s to Liverpool's adoption of red shorts in 1965, there are countless tales of sides adopting a brand-new kit style in an attempt to change their fortunes or wipe the historical slate clean by forging a new identity.

One of the most famous of such tales has Elland Road as its backdrop when, in 1961, new manager Don Revie reviewed the blue and gold (OK, to all intents and purposes, yellow) in the current kitbag and decided it was time for a change …

EARLY YEARS

But before we get to Revie's kit revolution (and the commercial masterstroke he pulled a decade later), let's go back a little further and trace the Leeds kit history prior to that momentous date.

When the club's predecessors, Leeds City, controversially collapsed in 1919, the chairman of local rivals Huddersfield Town, J Hilton Crowther, proposed a merger with the newly formed Leeds United, with Elland Road suggested as the club's home. Not a popular decision with the Terriers, Crowther ended up being ousted from Huddersfield, allowing him to take full control of the brand new Leeds. Quite possibly as a parting shot, he dressed his new side in the blue and white stripes of Huddersfield and it was in this kit that the club played for the first 14 years of their life – complete with the standard lace-up neck design of the era – creating a very rare example of local football rivals playing in the same colours.

The ghost of Leeds City re-materialised in 1934 when United decided to resurrect the blue and gold of its predecessors and adopted a brand-new halved jersey in the colour scheme, paired with white shorts and blue socks with gold turnover. The kit was ahead of its time for a couple of reasons: firstly, although it was constructed in the familiar long-sleeved style of the day, it curiously did not feature as standard a commonplace button-up placket to accompany the collar. Instead, a more open 'v-neck' design, similar to that made popular in the late 1970s, was generally featured; and, secondly, in an era where team badges tended to be only worn for special matches or cup finals, a club badge comprising the city crest was regularly included on the shirt.

In 1948, following the arrival of new manager Major Frank Buckley, Leeds switched to a plain, button up gold/yellow shirt with Arsenal-style blue sleeves. Legend has it that the eccentric Buckley believed the side, who were then in Division Two, were playing badly due to difficulties in picking out their teammates on the pitch and blamed the kit for the problem. The striking new shirt was paired with white at first, and then a couple of years later black shorts and rather dashing hooped socks.

By the mid-50s the lightweight continental kit style, which first came into the football spotlight courtesy of Hungary's incredible win over England in 1954, was rampant throughout the British game and Leeds ditched the heavy, cotton collared shirts that had dominated the football world pretty much since Victorian times and adopted a new short sleeved v-neck design in a solid royal blue, with gold reduced to merely a supporting role as trim. The blue shirts were produced by Umbro and lasted for five years until the dawn of the Don Revie era.

459

THE SWITCH TO WHITE

Revie took over the reins of the side when they were struggling in Division Two and immediately began looking at ways to improve the team's fortunes. Free from the commercial sportswear obligations and ties that exist today, managers then were still able to take a more active role in the 'off-the-field' activities that are a necessary part of running a football club. The myth claims that Revie decided a brand-new kit and colour scheme was necessary to lift and reinvent the side and looked to the mighty Real Madrid for inspiration. In came a sparkling, all-white strip … and the now familiar Leeds kit was born.

However, quite how much of this aesthetic change was Revie's idea is perhaps up for debate as it appears that Leeds had sported white as a first-choice outfit in the previous season, under the managerial control of Jack Taylor, when the club began preferring their regular away kit of white with blue and gold trim.

Taking all the facts into account, one can assume that maybe both of the above stories are true. Although an all-white strip was seemingly very much on the Leeds agenda, it was Revie's cunning rhetoric of channelling the power and reputation of Read Madrid that gave meaning to the new outfits and made the change permanent in an attempt to inspire both players and fans alike. As Don's son, Duncan, is quoted as saying, 'The players thought he was mad when he ditched the blue and gold, but he replied "We are going to be the best in the world, just like Real Madrid".'

Apart from the Madrid connection, it should be noted that Revie was a fan of white kits in general, believing they gave an added advantage to player visibility on the pitch, as Jack Charlton pointed out when discussing Don's decision: 'When you have only a split second to make a pass before the tackle comes in, you're more likely to pick up the right man if he's wearing not red or blue or green but white.'

It's interesting to observe that despite Revie's effective dismantlement of four decades of Leeds history, apparently little fuss was made by the club board of the switch at the time. Such was Don's charisma and presence within the club, the men in suits totally bought into his heroic vision.

The first Revie white strip (produced again by Umbro) was all-white … and when I say all-white I MEAN all-white, with no additional colour present in any way whatsoever, not even via a team badge. In fact, a badge wasn't to reappear on a Leeds shirt until four years later with the introduction of the roundel owl design. The typical 60s football style saw a move back to long sleeves, topped off with a neat crew neck, although the club did occasionally make appearances in cooler, short sleeved/v-neck incarnations in warmer weather.

The next major change to the Leeds strip came with the introduction of the iconic LUFC script monogram that replaced the owl crest, and it was first worn in the 1971 Fairs Cup Final. Although it's since become part of Leeds folklore (despite the controversial lack of 'A' in the acronym!), this particular design nuance was actually a pretty standard early 70s trend that was rolled out by Umbro through much of their current roster as a way of effectively branding and bringing some bespoke character to shirts that, quite often at this point, still didn't regularly feature a team crest.

As Don's side gathered in power in their pristine white kits, it's interesting and not a little bewildering to look at the club's away outfits at the time. When a clash occurred, the side turned out in an array of change colours, including blue, yellow and, brace yourselves, red. Even orange made one appearance in a forgettable 3-0 defeat to Stoke City in 1970 (although perhaps unsurprisingly the kit was never seen again). All these alternate outfits followed the simple crew necked, long sleeved design of the first-choice kit and often utilised a mix and match approach to shorts and socks, even occasionally throwing in a contrasting neck/cuffs combination for good measure. Three, or sometimes four, kits were frequently worn in a single season, casting shade on the often-believed doctrine that third kits are a modern-day invention.

Ever the showman looking for a gimmick, Revie also introduced, via sportswear company Mileta, the short-lived, but fondly remembered, fad of sock tags. His thinking was that the numbered sock tags (with dainty tassles at the end) could be thrown into the ground after games, creating a bond between players and supporters. To be fair, although Leeds persevered with the trend for a further two years, few other teams took the bait and soon sock tags were ditched and filed under 'failed football fashions of the 70s'.

Sock tags aside, the game *was* changing in the early 70s though … and so were the kits. With colour TV growing in popularity and the nation embracing the glam-rock period of the first part of the decade, suddenly strips moved away from the plainer, monochromatic appearance of the 1960s and became increasingly flamboyant with more extravagant palettes and design choices. Umbro, who had been Leeds's long-term apparel incumbents, were about to be ousted by the new kit kids on the block – a company who were to revolutionise the entire way people showed their support for their team, not just in the UK but around the world: Admiral.

And Don Revie's Leeds were at the heart of this revolution.

THE ADMIRAL REVOLUTION

With no restrictions at the time on ownership of club's kits and colours, Admiral head honcho Bert Patrick had been producing children's football strips in the various colour combinations made famous by the major clubs of the day for some years. In a flash of genius, Patrick realised, however, that if he were to create distinctive and specially designed strips that were clearly branded then he could create 'authentic' and 'official' kits which could be copyrighted. Then, via exclusive rights deals that involved Admiral paying the clubs for the right to supply their kit, he would be able to produce and market replica versions, targeting young fans (it's worth remembering that the target audience were still just children back then; I mean, who can imagine grown men wearing replica football shirts?!)

Patrick understood that children wouldn't want to be seen in any old knock-off football shirt copy, and that only by buying the official, licensed Admiral replica version could they be seen in a shirt that was, give or take, identical to that worn by their heroes. Plus, of course, it gave his brand huge exposure.

Patrick approached the biggest club in the land, Leeds, with the proposition and Don Revie, ever keen to earn a shilling, immediately saw the financial potential of the idea (as he subsequently did later on when he signed England up to Admiral in a similar deal the following year) and midway through the 1973 season he jilted Umbro and dressed his Leeds side in Admiral.

And so, from Admiral's Leicester offices and the kit room at Elland Road emerged the replica kit market that still dominates world football fandom today.

Although the first Admiral Leeds kits were still relatively somber in appearance, by the end of the 1973–74 season a sparkling new yellow away kit was launched with stunning blue and white stripes down each sleeve, creating the copyrightable and bespoke kit model Bert

Patrick yearned for and couldn't wait to sell to fans desperate to emulate Lorimer, Bremner et al. Leeds fully embraced the new design, promoting the kit in press shots. The sacred home kit was off limits for the time being, however, and still remained plain in appearance … but all that was to change a couple of seasons later.

Admiral's master plan gathered pace in 1976 when a new Leeds home kit was launched, bringing with it the biggest change to the team's appearance since the all-white change in 1961. The pure white was now liberally decorated with a contrasting, striped blue and yellow wing collar and blue stripes that housed multiple tiny Admiral logos, running down each sleeve and sides of the shorts. From a marketing perspective it was genius, as Admiral was now rammed down the throats of every supporter who devoured highlights on *Match of the Day* via their colour tellys. The tracksuits with huge 'ADMIRAL' text emblazoned across them may also have played a part in the branding parade! The baroque fashion perfectly fitted with the mood of the era and soon it felt like every side in the land were dressed in the frippery and flounces of bright colourful, and most importantly, distinctive Admiral outfits.

The side went through a variety of shirt crests at this point, with the fondly remembered 'smiley' badge (in a variety of orientations and colours) taking over from the LUFC monogram before being eventually replaced by the peacock design that respectfully doffed its cap to the club's old nickname.

By 1981, though, Admiral were in financial disarray, having flown too close to the sun and burning themselves badly, perhaps not realising that for their model to be successful longer term, new designs needed to be introduced on a regular basis. Almost overnight, with the company bankrupt, Admiral kits virtually disappeared from the football world, with only England continuing to wear their strips. Leeds re-signed with the prodigal old hands Umbro, who had still been quietly going about their business while the young upstarts Admiral attempted to depose them from their position of THE football kit company to turn to. Umbro's first new kit for the side dispensed with the wing collars of the previous Admiral design and dressed the side in a modernist, slick, and typically 80s, shirt featuring dual-coloured pinstripes. A plain yellow away strip was launched with raglan sleeves and blue piping that was to last for five years.

Replica shirts were now the norm in playgrounds up and down the land, and the 1980s was the first decade to really experience the situation of a regularly updated team kit designed to constantly stimulate replica sales. Or as nonsensical, angry letters to the *Daily Mail* prefer to think, to 'rip off parents'. And so it was that shadow stripes, wrapover collars, side panels, piping and trim all came to adorn the famous white shirt during this period, each in line with the fashions of the day and all expertly crafted by Umbro's designers. The palette didn't alter: white = home and yellow = away, although eyebrows were raised in 1986 when a change kit that included a large blue upper half was introduced. An all-yellow third kit was hastily introduced to compensate when the blue/yellow second-choice outfit didn't quite provide enough colour differentiation when a clash occurred.

Of course, the 80s can't be discussed in kit terms without mentioning the arrival of shirt sponsors. Liverpool were the first English professional side to sport a third-party sponsor logo on their shirt in the shape of Hitachi in 1979, but by the early 80s virtually every top-flight side's shirt now housed an additional brand, which, according to the more purist and traditional football fans, turned the sanctity of the team shirt to nothing more than a billboard.

Leeds's first sponsor was electrical company RF Winder, who partnered up with the side in 1981. Since then no less than 16 other brands have featured on the front of the Leeds kit. A full roster is … deep breath … Systime, WGK, Lion Cabinets, Burton, Top Man, *Yorkshire Evening Post*, Admiral Sportswear (more about their return in a moment), Thistle Hotels, Packard Bell, Strongbow, Whyte & Mackay, Bet24, Red Kite, Netflights.com, Enterprise Insurance and 32Red.

The team's kits from the 1990–92 seasons were amongst Umbro's best, incorporating the new-look, baggier fit and featuring tasteful trim and complex shadow patterns and adornments that cleverly never overwhelmed the integrity of the shirt. Fittingly they were to accompany Howard Wilkinson's boys in their magnificent 1991–92 league triumph. The *Yorkshire Evening Post* struck it lucky, choosing that season to be their solitary year adorning the Leeds jersey.

THE DAWN OF THE PREMIER LEAGUE

After going through various ownership issues, Admiral returned to the then league champions in 1992 as Leeds prepared to do battle in the inaugural Premier League season. Although honouring the classic simplicity of the club's home kit, the designers went to town with the change kits, sprinkling them extravagantly with fractal-like yellow and white patterns on the blue away strip (a notable move away from yellow as first-choice change outfit) and blue and white on the third yellow strip.

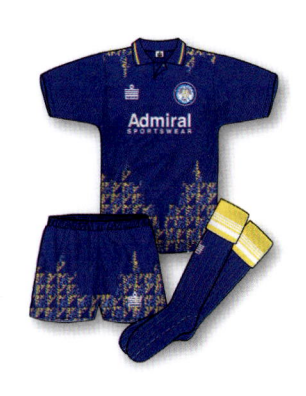

Perhaps to the relief of supporters struggling to embrace their wacky change outfits, the Admiral return lasted for just one season before Japanese sportswear firm Asics took over the Leeds contract in a three-year deal. They were responsible for some superb designs during their short stint at Elland Road, including the elegant 1993–95 pairings: a home jersey with smart collar and dynamic blue and yellow bands and a highly effective blue and yellow striped change shirt … not to mention their last home kit for the side that faithfully recreated the early 70s crew neck look, even bringing back the iconic LUFC monogram. Asics's crisp and stylish strips managed to give the side a class look – no mean feat given that shirts were now bigger and baggier then they had ever been and shorts were back to 1930s length. Controversy occurred, however, with the green and navy striped third/away kit that Asics first introduced in 1994. Manager George Graham eventually binned the kits in 1996 during an evening game at Bolton, complaining about player visibility and angrily exclaiming that his players disappeared from view as they blended into the crowd. A new yellow third kit with a superb button-up placket neck was hurriedly introduced and became a real favourite with the Leeds faithful.

The Asics era also coincided with the Premier League upping the branding and marketing ante of its most prized product and introducing squad numbers and names that, naturally, could also be affixed to replica shirts. The replica market no longer just catered for children and more and more adults began buying team jerseys. As the trend became more socially acceptable on the high street, sportswear designers began tailoring team kits specifically to the replica market. Of course, it's no coincidence that children who grew up in those first Admiral shirts were now adults themselves.

Puma, followed by Nike, became Leeds's technical suppliers as the pace of change commercially and sartorially increased. Puma ran into a spot of bother in 1998 when their repeated logos on the sleeves and shorts were removed in order to comply with UEFA Cup rules, creating an instant rarity for match-worn shirt collectors. A highlight, though, of Puma's time at the club was their 1997–99 away kit that faithfully paid tribute to the halved shirts worn by the team in the 1930s and 40s.

Puma were also responsible for another big visual change of direction in 1999. With the team growing in stature and one ambitious eye firmly fixed on lucrative

European competition, a more continental aesthetic was installed in the Elland Road changing room. A new club shield was introduced, replacing the Yorkshire rose design that had been introduced back in 1984, and was joined by a brand-new set of identically designed change strips complete with horizontal navy chest band – with the regular away option in an unfamiliar, but very demure, sky blue and a third kit in the more historically palatable yellow. It was a bold statement of the club's intent to become part of the furniture in European football.

THE ITALIAN CONNECTIONS

As the new millennium took hold, kits began to become more minimalist in appearance, with more effort and time being spent developing new lightweight, sweat-wicking fabrics and technological advances. Nike's set of outfits from the era have to be regarded as modern-day highlights in Leeds kit history – simple, clean and effortlessly suave … with just the right amount of yellow and blue trim. The 2000–02 home strip proved to be the last Leeds first-choice design to last for two seasons; the increasing speed of change meant that now one-season outfits were standard.

After a single year (2004–05) with Italian firm Diadora, whose major input into the Whites kit canon was a reintroduction of a sky blue change strip, incredibly Admiral rose from the ashes and returned for a third and, to date, final sojourn at the club. It has to be said, though, that apart from their first home kit that effortlessly resurrected the dual colour pinstripes of the early 80s, their strips were not the most memorable worn by the side. This period is also noted for introducing a new darker shade of blue to the by now well-established all white strip. With leisurewear beginning to have an increased influence on apparel colour choices (navy and black always being popular casual colours), darker hues were being spotted in clubs throughout the land, arguably giving sides a more sophisticated look. Navy formed the primary colour choice for the club's next away kit, continuing a theme started by Nike in 2003.

467

The shirt sponsorship merry-go-round continued and a sign of the times saw an increase in betting companies making their mark on the English game. At Leeds, Bet24 replaced the five-year association the club had enjoyed with alcohol brands (Strongbow and Whyte & Mackay) and lasted for a single campaign. Today, of course, 32Red continue the gambling association as official primary shirt sponsors at the club.

The sponsorship stakes moved up a notch in 2004 with the introduction of 'secondary kit sponsors' within the Football League and, ever the trendsetters, Leeds became the first Coca-Cola Championship club to take up this new commercial opportunity when asbestos abatement company Rhodar seized the chance to include their logo on the back of the club's shirts and shorts.

Another Italian company, Macron, began supplying the club in 2008 and were to remain at Elland Road for seven years. Their catalogue of Leeds strips varies wildly in style from the sparsely decorated 2010–11 shirt that again sought inspiration from the classic crew necks of the 1960s, and the 2012–14 efforts that threw everything bar the kitchen sink into the design – real bells and whistles strips with a plethora of panels, piping, trim and even go-faster stripes all featuring on the outfits.

Replica sales were driving design decisions more than ever as the club entered the 2010s, and in an effort to generate interest and stimulate replica purchases away kit colour choices began to stray more and more from the established palettes most clubs employed. Black was introduced for the first time in 2011 and a very pale gold with navy accoutrements made its debut two years later.

The Italian influence continued in 2015 when Leeds controversially ended their relationship with Macron early and took up with their fellow countrymen Kappa. Their first outfits for the side, who as no one will need reminding were still unable to break out of football's second tier, brought a touch of swagger and confidence to the side with broad, but considered use of blue (but no yellow) trim, asymmetrical badge/manufacturer logo placement and, incredibly, NO sponsor! The shirts with their elegant simplicity were snapped up by supporters, eager perhaps to relive those days of football kits before commercialism took hold. But the decision to keep the shirts plain and clean came not from a purist design sensibility but a legal dispute with previous shirt sponsors Enterprise Insurance, whose logo had appeared on the club jerseys for the past four years. A by-product of this unpleasantness, though, was the creation of a kit many quite rightly regarded as the best in England that year. Every cloud …

Kappa's five-year deal with the club has, to date, seen them dress the team in their typically slim-fitting, elegant, simple but well-designed outfits, all falling within the brand's solid template kit philosophy with an emphasis on performance. Kit design trends run in cycles and, although it wasn't long ago that supporters looked back at Admiral's 'fractal' away kits of the 1992 with some derision, today we see football apparel again adorned with all manner of bold and brassy abstract patterns. The Kappa 2018 change kit clearly follows this ethos, the navy design decorated with a wild array of white, light blue and yellow bars and splashes.

As the team move forward, it is difficult to predict where the precious team kit will go next. Will it stay clean and minimalist? Or embrace the trend of visual cacophony that the football apparel world is heading towards?

The Leeds kit story is more than just that famous early 60s adoption of a brand new visual identity. It includes some of the very best football outfits of the last 50+ years, plus, of course, it places the club as a key player at the heart of the replica shirt market – one of the most important cultural fashion trends of the modern age, a trend that aimed to bridge the gap between players and supporters and give Leeds fans a chance to experience the thrill of pulling on their team's heroic white jersey.

LEEDS UNITED 100 YEARS CONCERT

INTRODUCTION:

On Saturday, 8 June 2019, Elland Road kicked off the centenary celebrations with a major music festival. Headlined by the legendary Leeds band the Kaiser Chiefs, over 16,000 fans packed into the home of Leeds United for some of the best music around.

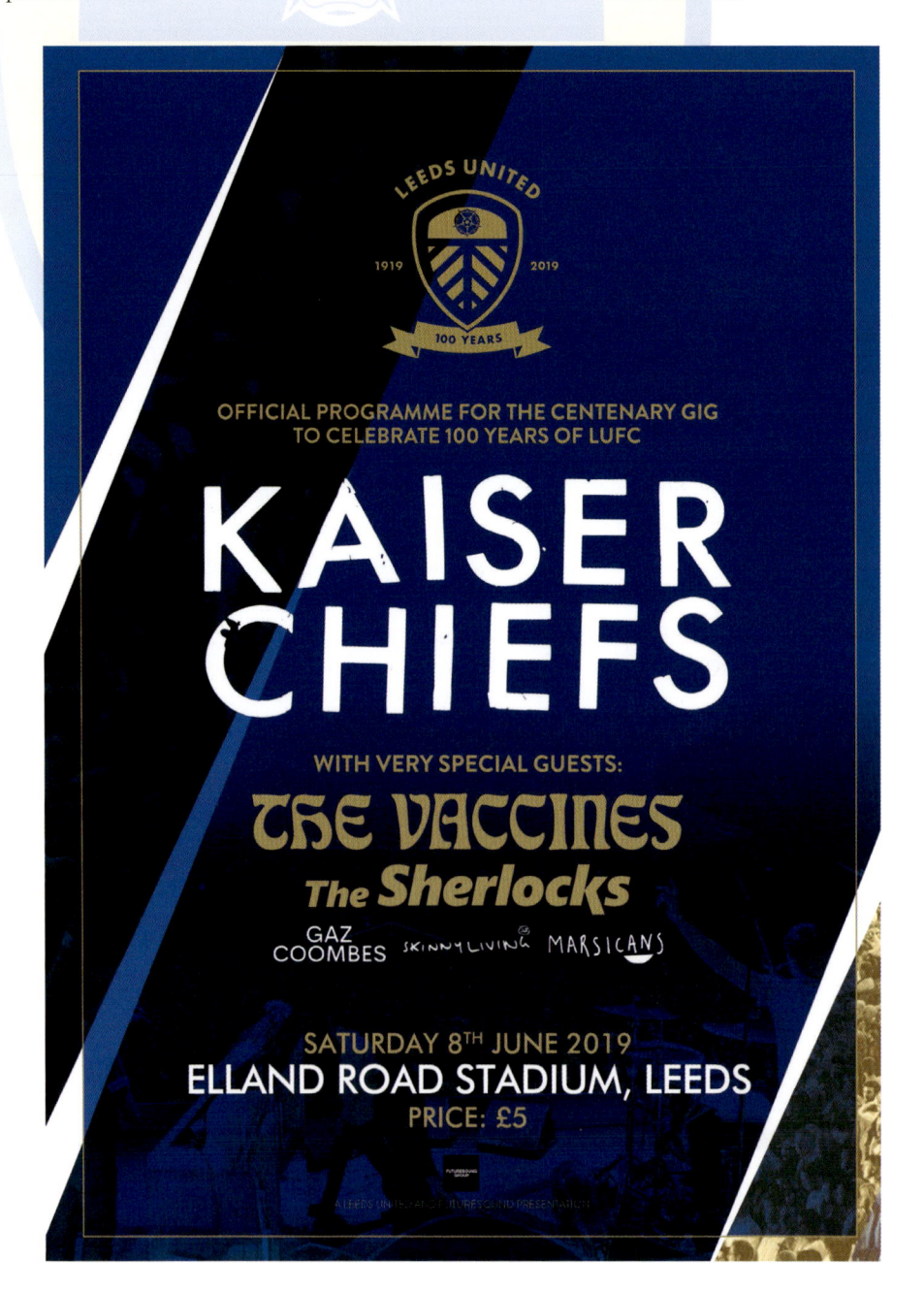

Despite the day starting in the rain, the crowd, made up of many sporting Leeds United shirts and scarves, enjoyed an afternoon and evening of great entertainment.

Before the gig, the Kaiser Chiefs bass player Simon Rix told Duncan Seaman from the *Yorkshire Post*,

'Similar to when we played at Elland Road 11 years ago, I think it will be a big event for the city, for everyone to show how brilliant Leeds is, what a great atmosphere we can create on the day, so we're hoping to do that again … to be asked to do this concert and be part of the celebrations for the centenary I think it's really great. I'm not a footballer, I'm never going to be able to play at that level, so to be able to sew my way into the Leeds United fabric in a different way is something very special to me.'

Ex-Leeds United legend and Sky Sports presenter Chris Kamara came on stage to introduce the Kaiser Chiefs and led the crowd in a rousing version of 'Marching on Together'. On stage he said 'It is an honour and a privilege for me to introduce the band tonight'.

Chris Kamara introducing The Kaiser Chiefs at Leeds United 100 Years concert on 8 June 2019. A great festival of music was enjoyed by all.

MARSICANS

The Marsicans ('MAR-sick-anz') kicked off the show, an upcoming band made up of James Newbigging (lead vocals), Oliver Jameson (guitar and vocals), Rob Brander (bass, keys and vocals) and Matthew McHale (drums and vocals). The band were formed in Leeds, three of whom were school mates, and they released their first single in 2015. They describe their style as 'Upbeat indie meets dirty pop from the north of England' which is proving popular as they have had over one million hits on Spotify for their EP 'Absence' and the band have played big stages such as Leeds Festival and Manchester's 'Dot-to-Dot Festival'.

The band tweeted after the show '*MARCHING ON TOGETHER. Big love to everyone who braved the rain to get the party started early at @LUFC yesterday. Huge thanks to @KaiserChiefs for having us on and putting in a performance none of us will forget*'.

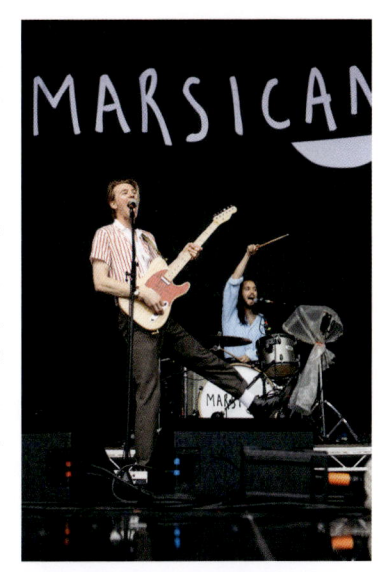

SKINNY LIVING

Soulful vocals, four-part harmonies and original sounds with influences from many genres, Skinny Living, from Wakefield, provided the second set of the day. With Ryan Johnston – Vocals, Will Booth - Guitar / Vocals, Danny Hepworth - Guitar / Vocals and Rhys Anderton - Cajon / Vocals, the band sang tracks from their debut album 'My Blood'.

GAZ COOMBS

Third on stage, former frontman Gaz Coombs's solo career kicked off in 2010 when famous indie rockers Supergrass disbanded. The Oxford-born singer has released three solo albums 'Here Comes the Bombs' (2012), 'Matador' (2015), and 'World's Strongest Man' (2018).

Coombs's second solo album, Matador was nominated for a Mercury Prize and an Ivor Novello award. 'World's Strongest Man' talks about modern politics, masculinity and mental health.

THE SHERLOCKS

As the weather started to brighten and the rain died away, The Sherlocks took to the stage. They posted on Facebook before the gig, 'We are buzzing for our biggest ever gig in Yorkshire.' And they didn't disappoint.

Consisting of two sets of brothers: Kiaran and Brandon Crook and Andy and Josh Davidson, from Bolton upon Deane, Barnsley, The Sherlocks rocked the crowd with tracks from their debut album 'Live for the Moment' (2017) as well as from their new album 'Under your Sky' (2019).

After the euphoria of the gig the band tweeted 'LEEEEEEDS WE LOVE YOU!!'

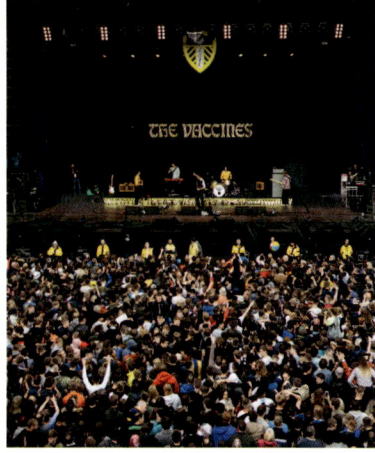

THE VACCINES

With four studio albums, 'What Did You Expect from The Vaccines?' (2011), 'Come of Age' (2012), 'English Graffiti' (2015) and 'Combat Sports' (2018) and a massive reputation in the music industry, The Vaccines played the penultimate slot to introduce the Kaiser Chiefs.

Formed in west London in 2010, Justin Hayward-Young (lead vocals, guitar), Freddie Cowan (lead guitar, vocals), Árni Árnason (bass, vocals) and Pete Robertson (drums, vocals) released the band's debut single 'If You Wanna' in 2010, which was named 'Hottest Record in the World'. Since then the band have released many noticeable singles including 'Post Break-Up Sex', 'Teenage Icon', 'All in White' and 'Handsome'.

A high-energy performance from the band was the perfect warm-up for the headliners.

KAISER CHIEFS

Leeds royalty Kaiser Chiefs returned to Elland Road to headline the show, 11 years after their last visit. The five-piece band, who were formed as 'Parva' in 2000 and later renamed in 2003, consists of Ricky Wilson (Lead Vocalist), Andrew 'Whitey' White (Guitar), Simon Rix (Bassist), Nick 'Peanut' Baines (Keyboard) and Vijay Mistry (Drummer, as of 2013).

The band have released six studio albums: 'Employment' (2005), 'Yours Truly, Angry Mob' (2007), 'Off with Their Heads' (2008), 'The Future Is Medieval' (2011), 'Education, Education, Education & War' (2014) and 'Stay Together' (2016) as well as a greatest hits album: 'Souvenir: The Singles 2004–2012' (2012).

Classics 'I Predict a Riot' (2004), 'Every day I Love You Less and Less' (2005) and 'Ruby' (2007) helped propel the band to the top of the indie-rock pyramid. They also treated the Elland Road crowd with newer material such as 'Coming Home' (2014), 'Hole in My Soul' (2016) and 'People Know How to Love One Another' (2019).

The band gave the home crowd exactly what they paid for with an energetic 20-song set list, filled with fan favourites. Ricky Wilson shouted out to the watching-on fans. 'We are the Kaiser Chiefs, we have been sent to entertain you … and we will.' They certainly delivered on expectations and wrapped up the centenary celebration in style.

MEMORABILIA

In the early days of football we saw simple memorabilia being produced to encourage fans to follow their teams and feel part of it. This included simple striped scarves, rosettes and football rattles in the club colours.

I'm sure most of you have a scarf, book or shirt bearing the badge of Leeds United. Club shops are now a staple at grounds across the country, and over time as memorabilia has become more popular and offered clubs the chance to make money, and the array of items on offer has drastically increased, including tankards, tracksuits, dog leads and even underwear.

Fans have collected souvenirs over the past 100 years, ranging from books, newspaper reports of memorable games to mugs, scarves and even calendars and some of them are pictured in this section. Some items may be worth more than others and some are more collectable than others, but to the fans who own them they are a part of the history of our great club.

The replica shirts, the souvenirs for cup wins, and even anniversary celebrations are all milestones in our history and these souvenirs all help to tell the story of Leeds United and help us feel a part of it.

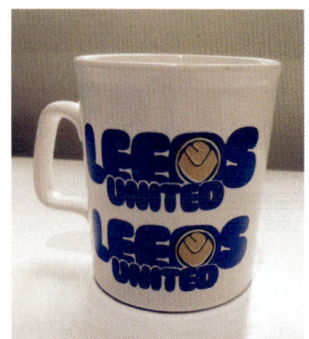

THE OFFICIAL PROGRAMME LEEDS UNITED FOOTBALL CLUB
A WEEKLY SOCCER SOUVENIR
LEEDS UNITED and OPPONENTS TEAMS Score Chart
2d
2d
1924
1925
THORNE'S
THE WORLD'S PREMIER TOFFEE
Extra Super Creme Assorted Almond Brazil Mint
6d. per Qr.
From all High-Class Confectioners
Insist on it!

2003
STRENGTH & SUCCESS
LEEDS UNITED

L.U.F.C

LEEDS UNITED
LEEDS UNITED

LEEDS UNITED
A·F·C

LEEDS UNITED
PROMOTION YEAR BOOK
Photographs, Records, History, and Blotter.

COLCHESTER UNITED FOOTBALL CLUB LTD.
F.A. CUP–5th ROUND
SATURDAY 13th FEBRUARY 1971
COLCHESTER UTD. v. LEEDS UTD.
KICK-OFF 3 p.m.
ADMISSION TO GROUND 12/6d.
ENTRANCE E
Nº 06457

FANS ON THEIR LEEDS UNITED

GARY BAKER (WEST MIDLANDS)

Leeds United has been a massive part of my life; I've been lucky enough to see us win the league in 1992 under Howard Wilkinson, and lucky enough to see us get to two European semi-finals in 2000 and 2001.

Since those days, I've grown up and what means most is me and my little boy Oliver, seven (nearly eight) going to games together. We're season ticket holders and go to as many away games we can get tickets for.

Watching our depleted club over the last 17 years finally become the club we know and love, the fans have always been here and we all know something wonderful is on the horizon.

Which leads me to Bielsa – every game is a school day and mesmerising to watch at times, the way football should be played. All we want to see is players play for each other and the fans and with Bielsa we see that.

Off we trot to Australia for the 100-year celebration with my family and Olly's godfather Roy, who is one of the biggest fans I know. We hope this can be our year so the younger generation can see some success.

RICKY GREENWOOD

My most memorable moment being a Leeds fan has to be promotion from League One. Seeing Beckford's goal hit the back of the net is something I'll never forget. That has been my favourite season so far following Leeds – 2009/10. The togetherness between the fans and players was great to see and the games we saw, like knocking our biggest rivals out of the FA Cup in their own back yard. Memories are made all the time with the best fans in the world. Win, lose or draw, we're all still there every week. Taking thousands everywhere we go, no matter whether it's a Tuesday night game in South Wales or a pre-season friendly abroad. Leeds United isn't just a football club, it means so much to so many. It's Our Life.

PAM FREER

There have been so many highlights.

Being League Champions in 1992 was a memorable week. It started with us winning at Bramall Lane then it being confirmed when Manchester United lost later that day. Six days later the team paraded the trophy at Elland Road followed by a brilliant night out and going to the Town Hall the following day to see the team with the trophy again.

The spell between 1998 and 2002 saw us qualify for Europe every season including one in the Champions League. There were many great away trips and fantastic football against the best teams in Europe. We went to some of the best grounds in Europe and to far flung places that we would have not gone to otherwise. One of the most memorable was to Moscow which was a great experience.

It's impossible to imagine my life without Leeds United.

LYNSEY LYON

My first Leeds United football match was at Elland Road against Shrewsbury Town on 9 November 1988 that Leeds won 3-1 which I went to with my dad and sister. I was hooked from then. My dad bought me my first season ticket in August 1990. I grew up watching football in the McAllister/Strachan/Speed/Batty era. The atmosphere was always electric and Leeds would completely bombard the opposing team, particularly in the first 20 minutes. David Batty was my hero for his tenacious playing skills in the centre of midfield.

I have lots and lots of memories following Leeds and one that always stands out for me is when my Dad took me to watch Leeds at the Nou Camp in Barcelona on 9 October 1992 against Stuttgart. A day out of school to travel to an amazing stadium to see my heroes … the only problem being that my dad had written a note for school and my teacher saw me on the local news in the Leeds end cheering Carl Shutt's goal! Was definitely worth it.

I took my daughter to her first Leeds match six seasons ago and have just purchased her sixth season ticket. All I want now if for her to experience the good times following Leeds that I did, hopefully that will happen with promotion next season … alwayskeepthefaith

JIM MULLINS - CORK WHITE

Shortly after 9.30pm on 15 May, I sat back and shed a tear or two, watching Derby County players and staff celebrate on the Elland Road pitch.

I said to myself if you ever want to sum up how Leeds Utd can break your heart look at one minute before half time and one minute after half time, the phrase self destruct sums it up perfectly. Next morning was an ordeal dragging myself out of bed and for a day or two it hurt like hell, but as time went on I realised the damage was done in the horrific run since christmas, losing games v QPR, Birmingham, Forest, Wigan, and particularly v Sheff Utd in the proverbial six pointer, when we had them by the throat in the first half. I have some great memories as a Leeds fan, promotions in 1989-90 and 2009-10 and of course the title in 1992, the great football played under O'leary, although we have no trophy to show for it.

I have made some lasting friendships as a leeds fan and that is something to be treasured, debates on the west of ireland facebook page are top class, great news Bielsa is staying and slowly but surely I am looking forward eagerly to next season, MOT

SUSAN SMITH

What does Leeds mean to me … I have supported Leeds since the age of 10, my brother and I collected football cards and one day I got Billy Bremner and decided from that day Leeds United were my team. Nothing much unusual about that apart from I lived in Weymouth in Dorset, but that didn't deter me and throughout the 90s I used to travel to home games – a 720-mile round trip and 11 hours of travelling. Then in 2001 I took the massive decision to leave my family and move near to my beloved club and have been ever since. Leeds United has always been and always will be the love of my life. I have many special memories supporting Leeds, meeting all the David O'Leary squad on a few occasions, meeting Olivier Dacourt, Norman Hunter and Allan Clarke, meeting Lucas Radebe and giving him a photo of my horse Lucas Radebe, and I got a kiss and a massive hug from him, which makes it very close to being my favourite highlight. But in all the years one special highlight is way and beyond any other and nothing will ever beat it and that was the day I met my all-time favourite player and my Leeds hero Nigel Martyn, that day will be in my heart always with my beloved club.

The photo is Susan with Nigel Martyn in 1999.

ANDREW BUTTERWICK

Leeds United, like many other football clubs, are like a family with traditions, customs and beliefs that go back generations. Many fans inherited their passion for the mighty Whites from their parents, grandparents, others just happened to be developing their love of football when Leeds were in one of their more successful stages of their evolution and fell in love with the team, the fans and the city. For me I was born at the top of Beeston hill and grew up with Revie's team of talents marching through Europe and what was then the English Division One, and so a lifetime of ups and many downs began. I was in the Boys Pen when a Mick Jones hat-trick helped destroy Best, Law, Charlton and the rest of the failing Reds 5-1. I was there when Leeds cruelly dismantled Southampton 7-0. Leeds were supreme and untouchable but not only that they were hated with a passion by the mainly southern press and opposition fans who couldn't stomach the fact that a bloody-minded Yorkshire team lead by an uncompromising and astute manager were infiltrating the football elite inhabited by Chelsea, Arsenal, Spurs, Man Utd and Liverpool.

All the anti-Leeds/Dirty Leeds agenda did was bond the fans and team together like the strongest super glue available. The siege mentality that is still evident today was born. Add in the injustices of Salonika and Paris, sprinkle with a little of Ray Tinkler and top off with the minus 15 points season you begin to get an understanding of why we still sing Waccoe, why we think the EFL is corrupt and why we ironically sing 'We all hate Leeds'. Leeds fans are a stubborn, loyal, passionate group who have no time for any of the modern trends that have infested football, such as clappers, drums and the worst of all nominated singing sections in grounds. We are proud to go to Elland Road, we are proud to wear our club colours and there is nothing like getting a Leeds salute from a fellow fan in some far flung corner of the world. In summary, being a Leeds fan is like an addiction. No matter how dreadful the experience or the performance we will always be there the following week with the unerring belief that one day we will be back at the top … and when we are we will make a very different impression on the Premier League.

VENNLIG HILSEN

I had no idea what I was walking into the first time I went to Elland Road. I was nine, me and my family flew over from Norway with my mate Fredrik and his parents. Fredrik's father, Thorbjørn, founded the Scandinavian supporters' club for Leeds United back in 1980, which 40 years later is 5,000 members strong. We just went along, I thought it would be fun. It was a shock, overwhelming and grabbed me with both arms! I had never been to a football match with more than a few hundred people attending, and here I was with 25,000 people to teach me how to cheer the lads on. We beat Wimbledon 4-0 too. It was the quickest brainwash possible and never been anything else since. Leeds has taken hold of my life completely; I moved there to be a season ticket holder for a year, it was a theme for the priest who married me and I'm doing my 50th match at Elland Road this centenary season. Life develops, and that 50th match will be my four-year-old son's first. Leeds until the world stops going around!

PAM FREER

I've always been obsessed with football. As a kid I couldn't ever sit down, I just ran about. I refused to read. I just played football. Then I got really interested in Leeds United results (eight years old) and then my mother said I wanted to learn so I could understand Ceefax (I just used to stare at it). Football taught me to read. It still means everything to me.

My first game was the FA Youth Cup Final and we were playing Manchester United. Think we beat them 2-1, Jamie Forester scored an over-head kick. It was incredible! What an atmosphere, the crowd was a decent size considering it was a youth game! I was hooked. We were also the champions of England. What an introduction into football. I wish I'd been able to appreciate that season more than I did. I didn't understand just how special it was at the time. My team were the best. It was just normal to a kid.

I didn't get my first season ticket until Year 11 (1996-97) but I went sporadically. I remember my next-door neighbour took me to a home game against Liverpool, I witnessed the best volley anyone has ever scored anywhere ever. Yeboah! Yeboah! Yeboah! We were all obsessed by him. We've had some very exciting players over the years who've really captured our hearts.

I remember the excitement around the turn of the century. The Champions League. Wow. The whole city was buzzing. We talked about it constantly, everyone did. Everyone talked about Leeds. It was a magical time, football can do so much to affect your life, we were flying so high.

Then we dropped. And dropped. And we knew pain. We still know it all too well. When you grow up and your team is the best in England you develop a winner's mentality. Leeds United aren't meant to be anywhere near the second tier, never mind the third. It's hard to comprehend. We've suffered more than any other English team I can think of. We're the famous Leeds United, not so famous anymore. It's got that bad that even Man United fans are asking for us back. Don't worry scum, we're coming.

Recently, it's been brilliant once again. The old feeling is back. Pride is back. We've been restored. Finishing third was frustrating but in many ways it didn't matter. Football is about the journey. It's about loving your team and your team giving something back. It's about the togetherness. Marcelo Bielsa has given us something we've lacked for the best part of a generation. The buzz is back. We're famous again. This is the Leeds United I've grown up knowing and loving. I've written songs for him but they're really for us, the fans, the people of Leeds United, a fan base that stretches across the globe.

In 2018 I went on Britain's Got Talent. During the auditions the camera caught me doing a Leeds salute to the crowd when they mentioned I was from Leeds (it was in Manchester). The whole city went mental about it. People were stopping me in the street and hugging me. Everywhere I went smiling faces were saluting me and beeping car horns. It felt amazing. I got to the final but they wouldn't let me do the routine I originally planned and I had to change it at the last minute (it would have won as well, it's probably my strongest routine, this story is so Leeds). I went for something really risky (I didn't have anything else) and it totally flopped. It was shit mate. Despite that sorry fact, the whole Leeds United fan base got behind me. I got 70,000 votes and I know they all came from Leeds fans. Even though I'd messed up it didn't matter because I was part of the family. People came up to me and said nice things, they bought me drinks and they hugged me. It was so special, I just don't know any other club that would do that to a comedian on a talent show. I'll never forget it. The club got behind me when I needed them most and I've never been made to feel that special. There are some very loyal supporters at Leeds United, once you're in, they're with you all the way. Family.

I did a UK Tour off the back of being on TV. My first show was in Swindon. As I walked onto the stage I heard the crowd clapping as they announced my name and the first thing that caught my eye when I walked on stage were two LUFC shirts sat on the front row together. They were both saluting. MOT.

ADONIS STORR

Adonis Storr is a songwriter and guitarist in the band The Adelites. A life-long Leeds United fan. He has travelled the world but is currently living in Vienna.

On 30 April 1994 I was seven years old and my mum had asked if I wanted to go see Leeds, I was a kid born in the LGI, surrounded by football, of course I said 'yes'. Three goals and 90 minutes later I was not really sure what had happened, but I asked tentatively, 'Mum, can we go again?'

We wouldn't go to Elland Road again that season, and I didn't know but she had got us season tickets for the next season. So on 23 August I saw Noel Whelan score the winner in a 1-0 win over Arsenal; four days later we'd lose to Chelsea 3-2. But on 11 September 1994 we played Manchester United at home. Nobody can go to a Leeds v Manchester United game and not feel something, the sound was deafening, I was totally and completely besotted. At eight years old I was in love, I felt part of something huge.

The meaning of the United feeling of being part of that crowd, the real enormity of it, the emotion, wouldn't dawn on me until years later, as a kid I took it for granted. And it feels like it was a different world back then, but there was something special about England in the mid-90s. Oasis and Blur on the radio, Yeboah's thunderous strikes on the pitch and unforgettable long and glorious summers. Maybe it shines brighter in my mind because I didn't have to work and I still had that eternal optimism that comes with childhood.

My mum had a heavy duty job being a manager at BT, so after school I'd be with a child-minder until she finished work. And so Leeds was something that I could share with my mum, it was our time together. For the next eight seasons we stayed in the same seats for every home league and cup game, I feel like we missed maybe five games in total.

In our second season we saw the club make it all the way to Wembley for the Coca Cola Cup Final. It's still the only time I've seen Leeds at Wembley and the only time I've ever seen my mum cry. The women in my family are tough (and proud of it), much like most women from the North.

By the time Euro 96 came by the whole country was in the midst of a celebration of football. And these foundational years of my life built the cornerstone of who I am deep down. That summer confirmed the inseparability of myself and the game. And that definition of self is everything that means anything in life. I'd be playing football before school, during every break and after school.

As soon as I'd get home I'd do my homework, wolf down my food, chuck a Leeds shirt on and pretend to be Alan Smith in our cul-de-sac, jumpers for goal posts. Fists outstretched in celebration. I'd talk about Leeds United at breakfast, lunch, dinner; and during class. I dreamt about scoring the winning goal for Leeds.

If beating Man Utd was the loudest I had ever heard an Elland Road crowd, even that noise paled and wilted in the deafening roar of European nights. The sight of AC Milan lining up on a sodden night, with a last gasp desperate long shot fumbled into the net by 'Dida, Dida, dodgy keeper' and the chants of 'Lee Bowyer' echoing around. The excitement of welcoming Real Madrid from the moment we were drawn together, to the game. Seeing Roberto Carlos less than 20m away flick the ball over his head to take a throw-in – and the wolf whistles from a Yorkshire crowd who found his show boating slightly farcical.

I was 16 in 2003 when I moved to Australia, and though that move and life has pushed me in many different directions, there was always one thing which tied me back to my childhood. I have learnt the hard way that no matter how lost you can get upon the path, if you start to lose your way, all you have to do to remember who you are is to never forget where you come from.

When I was a child I wanted to be a footballer and play for Leeds United. When I was a teenager I wanted to be in a punk rock band and write songs like Kurt Cobain. In the last year I stopped trying to be anything else and tried to blend the two. It is defining my life, giving me purpose and a direction on the path to resolving the existentialism that comes with the life of a traveller.

What does Leeds mean to me?

The view out the window as the rain pours down, a grey morning, a northern town. Waiting for the weekend. My mum's hand on the way to the ground. Roast pork sandwiches at half time, the smell of beer and pies. And thirty thousand Leeds fans. Cold steel blue rail, warm blue plastic seat. The quiet before the storm of the refs whistle, the roar of urgent hope, the explosion of joy. Family, home, blood, life. Strachan, McCallister, Speed, Yeboah, Radebe, Bowyer, Kelly, Smith, Beckford, Becchio, Hernandez, Jansson, Phillips. Names that stand like landmarks defining eras of my life. Decades of pain and joy. One club, one city, one family. United by Leeds.

MEDIA MEMORIES

So when did it start...

I'm fourteen years old in Bradford and after watching a few games with my Dad and Uncle Fred I decided it was time to 'find' my team. I'd seen Huddersfield Town, Bradford PA and even Manchester United but I'd not seen Leeds.

So with a handful of friends I ventured to Elland Road for the very first time, if memory serves me right it was Derby County who were our opponents. Leeds won 2-0 and that season won the Division One championship and also won my heart, 13 months later I'd follow them to Paris as a 15-year-old schoolboy on his first trip out of England. The defeat still hurts like hell but the experience of travelling abroad with Leeds was one I'll take to my end.

That's how my 40-plus year 'love affair' with this club started and she's broken my heart on numerous occasions but I still come back for more every August and probably will until I pass from this mortal coil.

Through football I've had the opportunity to dip my toes in the media, I run, along with my son, a blog site called www.weallloveleeds.co.uk. We had written on it previously when a lad called Andy Gregory invited us to write a few articles for him. He's a teacher so eventually he offered us the site and after over three million views by people we are now in the press box at Elland Road and do match reports for our blog site.

Alongside this I've been on LUTV, Radio Leeds and the now defunct radio station that used to broadcast from Subway when Ken Bates was the owner of Leeds. I've met many people, Adam Pope, Noel Whelan, Simon Grayson, Eddie Gray and many others in the press room at Elland Road. When involved with LUTV we actually did a Leeds quiz inside 'church' alongside two superb Leeds United authors David Watkins and Heidi Haigh.

Media has changed so much in my time as a Leeds fan, from listening to the semi-final of the European Cup against Barcelona on a transistor radio to Sky's coverage of the game. I used to love listening to games on the radio when I was unable to get to games, particular games that stand out apart from Barcelona were the play-offs of 1987. Keith Edwards scoring in injury time to take Leeds through to the final, only to be reduced to tears when Peter Shirtliff scored two goals to break Billy's heart and mine too. For me the next best thing to actually being there was to listen to the action.

This season has probably been one of the most entertaining in a few years. The arrival of Marcelo Bielsa has instilled pride in the famous white shirt again and made players that looked on their way out of the club, to ones that can look back on the 2018-19 season with a lot of satisfaction. We fell away in the last couple of months of the season, so will once again be in the Championship. It will be 16 years since Leeds United were in the top division of English football, I'm hopeful that in its centenary season the club can finally achieve promotion.

My journey with my beloved club has been an adventure, some days when you really wonder why you still bother, other days when it's so fantastic you never want the day to stop.

I'm proud to be a Leeds United supporter.

Keith Ingham
weallloveleeds

Having begun writing for my beloved club at the age of 16 for a website I would end up part-owning a mere seven years later, my experiences with Leeds media and the people within the business have been mixed.

I've worked as a freelance journalist, as a blogger and as a media head for a term during the days of LFU.

My earliest memory was Paul Robinson's goal against Swindon and the radio coverage that ensued on that evening.

I'd never paid attention to the radio when football was on, if I couldn't kick it or watch it, football was boring, I'll add I was nine.

From that day, the entire spectrum of footballing coverage changed for me. If a Leeds game was on the radio, me and my dad would sit and listen in the kitchen and consequently go barmy when the goals went in.

My love for radio changed when BBC Radio Leeds were informed they could no longer cover the club. The club lost part of its soul when this happened, although the club lost a lot more during the tenure of Papa Smurf.

I've been lucky enough to work within Leeds at certain periods, with a large part of my experiences coming with Leeds Fans United.

From a simple idea to press interviews and meetings with the chairmen, the rollercoaster that was fans purchasing part of Leeds was definitely a story the media loved.

I remember the first press conference after what can only described as a high-pressure week in offices just next to Elland Road. Dylan Thwaites was sat at the top of a table and I was just in front of him.

Launch day had come, contracts and T&C's were sorted and it was time for the cameras to roll. Dylan looked up at my face and said, 'Ryan, stop being nervous, you're the one that wrote this.'

It was a brilliant premise, it had engaged fans, the club and the media. However, the latter seemed to lull after the first month and I believe if we had upped our media presence and kept fans involved, along with a less questionable and flappable owner, the fans would still hold a stake in the club.

Finally, my experiences with the owners, players and media heads of Leeds has been nothing but superb.

Since reaching accreditation for WeAllLoveLeeds, we have interacted with some fantastic people who are key within the Leeds media spectrum. Heidi Haigh has been a wonderful support figure along with Dave Watkins and Adam Pope.

The club have given us a press pass which increased our site's support and we were even able to double our figures over the final year.

Covering Leeds is never easy, it's something you love, your passion mixed with your one true love. But it can be so tiring when the times are hard and for fan sights that continue to push articles out and keep their readers informed, I commend you.

For a 22 year old and his father to take a site from an average 200,000 views a year website to a site that hit one million views in its first year and last year reached 1.5 million in a year shows how progressive the media has become for Leeds United.

And we're extremely proud to call ourselves part of it.

Ryan Ingham
Editor-In-Chief
WeAllLoveLeeds

MY MEMORIES OF FOLLOWING LEEDS UNITED – HEIDI HAIGH

My love affair with Leeds United started in 1965 when watching the 1965 FA Cup Final against Liverpool on the TV. This love affair has never diminished in all my 50+ years of following Leeds United despite our ups and downs. Having had seven years of not missing a Leeds United game home and away in the 70s and 80/90s and travelling abroad to see them play, I feel I am the lucky one. Having had the privilege to see the best team ever under Don Revie as well as my hero Billy Bremner playing for us, they have made me the loyal Leeds fan I am until this day. Billy Bremner always was and always will be my hero and I am now the proud owner of a Bremner stone right under the top of his statue at Elland Road.

During the 70s I kept a diary of my times of following Leeds which is what inspired me to write my first book *Follow Me and Leeds United*. Written as a girl in a man's world from a female's perspective, it tells of the lengths my friends and I went to when following our team despite all the troubles on the terraces in those days. With all the stories in it true, the reflection of times past are very real. I have since written four more Leeds books, including one as a co-author, and I am currently writing my sixth based on last season.

In the 70s I became a member of the Kop Committee after being invited by John in the Pools Office to help promote Peter Lorimer's testimonial year. Even after all these years we still have a great rapport with players of that era with Eddie Gray, Peter Lorimer and Paul Reaney who would always speak to us fans. Mick Jones, Allan Clark and Mick Bates as well were stalwarts when raising funds for the Don Revie statue to be built and were always available to talk to. Mick Jones remembered my friend Carole and I being his backing group at a supporter's club function at Fullerton Park when he sang a song to everyone, even having a photo of that event.

My social media presence to begin with started when I was marketing my book which then became the name of my blog *Follow Me and Leeds United*. My blog is written as a fan for the fans which has a different aspect to it. My love of following my club shines out in all my writing and I share my blog with fans all over the world and take photos at every game and many of fans who like to get their photos taken. The aim of my blog is to keep Leeds fans all over the world in touch with following the team on our travels both home and away. Having received feedback on more than one occasion makes it worthwhile when fans are saying that I make them feel as if they are at the game with me. There are many of my followers who cannot get to games anymore due to ill health or other reasons who benefit.

I swiftly found that BBC Radio Leeds would contact me to take part in many live radio shows and interviews and I have a good rapport with Adam Pope and Katherine Hannah the latter who interviewed me twice before and after the recent Derby away play-off game. LUTV and Thom Kirwin saw a video interview with me promoting my love of Leeds United make an appearance. Last season I did an interview for COPA90, a Dutch sports magazine, another Dutch sports site plus a French reporter interviewed me about Bielsa. When contacting the club this last season I have been pleased with the response shown to fans by Angus Kinnear. We may not see eye to eye on everything, but it is nice to see the club responding to fans once again as that was missing for many a year. I also took part in the Leeds United documentary that is still to be released, with the crew coming out to my house to interview me. I didn't realise until then that I still had lots of memorabilia left despite selling a lot of it a few years ago.

My favourite game was the 1972 FA Cup Final. Going to Wembley for the first time and to see Leeds United win the FA Cup in their Centenary year was a dream come true especially when seeing Billy Bremner lift the cup. It was a fantastic day from start to finish apart from Mick Jones getting injured at the end of the game. Joining in with the community singing with Tommy Steele (wearing white so he must have been a Leeds fan!) has made 'Abide with Me' my favourite hymn till this day. That along with singing the National Anthem alongside the whole stadium was awe inspiring and made it a day to savour. Despite being robbed of our rightful titles in 1973 in the European Cup Winners' Cup Final in Salonika and in 1975 in the European Cup Final, Paris, I am still so glad that I had the opportunities to travel to support my team. Our fans are what makes supporting Leeds special, they stay loyal through thick and thin.

Last season rekindled my love of the football side of following Leeds as we saw some of the best football we have seen for a long time. Sadly we didn't gain promotion this year but having had a taste of the chance this season, we have to aim for automatic promotion in our centenary year. Having Marcello Bielsa at the helm was great as he reminded me of Don Revie with his dossiers. His integrity and honesty is a breath of fresh air with this modern world of football and many of the people in football should take a leaf out of his book. Unfortunately some of the media/authorities still show they are biased against Leeds United, which happened a lot in my earlier days of following Leeds. What Bielsa has done alongside Leeds United is make our club noticed around the world even more. With social media now being at the forefront of keeping up to date with everything Leeds United, this side of football reporting has certainly come a long way from my early days of following them.

OSCAR MARRIOTT
Presenter and Content Creator for All Leeds TV

The change in media coverage over the years has been massive in regards to Leeds United. One of the biggest changes has been the growth of fan-generated content. I do feel with that there is a nice mixture of media at Leeds between fan-generated content, external media such as the *Yorkshire Evening Post* as well as plenty of media produced by the club themselves. If you go back to around eight to nine years ago there was very little supporter or club-generated content. It's good to have a mixture as they all provide different viewpoints and angles. Fan-generated content has the 'can speak right from the heart' element to it, external media provides a non-bias point of view and more insider information about what is going on at the football club, whilst club produced media gives an insight into the players and manager themselves. There are so many incredibly talented people who produce content in relation to this football club. Whether that's writers and journalists, presenters, you tubers, podcasters and social media influencers there is an abundance of quality in all areas and it's superb to see.

At All Leeds TV we have been very lucky over the last year to be able to produce content with former players, managers and coaching staff, mainly legends of the club from the Revie and Wilko eras. I have to say they have all been an absolute joy to film with and are incredibly humble. What I really like about the players from the Revie and Wilkinson eras is that they will speak their mind and say exactly what they think they won't give you the modern day standard answers. Footballers in general have this reputation of not being interested in that type of media but nothing could be further from the truth when it comes to ex-Leeds players.

There is a lot more access to the football club now than there was about five years ago and full credit to the football club and new ownership for that, it helps us massively when it comes to producing videos.

Modern media has had a massive impact on football. In the last ten to 15 years social media is the main one which has grown massively and social media is usually associated with giving fans a voice. Social media, like anything, has it's positives and negatives, I find social media a great source of information as long as you know whether the sources are reliable or not of course. It is much easier to find out about transfer news; for example, how often these days do we see transfers completely out of the blue? 99.9 per cent of transfers come as no surprise as the media is able to get the information on them to report to the public days/weeks sometimes even months before the official information has been announced. Even information such as team news and injury news is normally known about and shared before official confirmation. Social media has made football reporting more proactive when in the past it was reactive; for example, before social media the main function of external media in particular was to produce articles reacting to the news. Now the demands seem totally different people want to know what's happening at football clubs 24/7. Another advantage of social media in relation to football is it's a great way to share your opinion and debate. In the past the only real way of doing this was through football phone ins or forums; both very much still exist, social media has just provided an alternative. There are disadvantages though, the main one being social media can be used as a tool to attack individual players. There is nothing wrong with having a negative opinion on a player or in voicing this opinion over social media; however, the line can occasionally be crossed, particularly when it turns to personal abuse or tweeting directly to the said player – what good is that going to achieve? I think footballers these days are thoroughly aware of issues like this with social media. Even when tweeting themselves if word can be taken out of context it can land a player in hot water or historic tweets which could be seen as controversial or to an extent embarrassing may also be picked up on sometimes.

BEST AND MOST MEMORABLE GAMES

TRANMERE ROVERS 1-2 LEEDS 11 AUGUST 2007

Remember this game like it was yesterday, a quite incredible day, our first game in League One and perhaps it's a surprise that I've included this but it was a whirlwind of emotions that day. The plan to get to the game with my dad was to get two trains, one from Southport to Liverpool and then Liverpool to Birkenhead followed by a bus to the ground. In the build up to the game and season itself I don't think either of us had a clue what to expect. You looked at the squad going into the season and the calibre (at the time) of players we were going into League One with was incredible. Alan Thompson had been playing Champions League football little over a year before, Eddie Lewis was attracting Premier League interest (and went on to go to Derby a few weeks later) and had been playing at the World Cup for the USA the previous year, then we had players like Jermaine Beckford and David Prutton who had performed very well for other clubs in League One the season before. There was plenty of ability in the squad; however, the minus 15-point penalty we had been given was probably going to affect us we felt.

We arrived at Birkenhead station with no problems but there was no bus. The station was too far away to walk and there was no one around, literally no one, the roads were completely empty. So we took a guess about which way and started walking and by pure chance walked past an advertisement board for a local taxi firm. Now you may be questioning why didn't we just open google maps or google taxi firms around the area? This was before smart phones were really a thing so neither of us possessed one. One thing we couldn't get our heads around was the lack of traffic going to away games in League One in comparison to games at Elland Road and away grounds in the Championship. That's when it started to sink in we were in a league no one cared about unless there team was in it; we were at real risk of becoming irrelevant. We got to the ground and we were in the Tranmere end just behind the dugouts; the reason for this was that we were only given an away allocation of 2,000 so couldn't get tickets in the away end. We started the game very poorly; it was wave after wave of Tranmere attacks and we were very much chasing shadows for the first 20 minutes. The home fans couldn't believe it, they thought it was going to be an easy Leeds win, it was a cup tie atmosphere like most away games during the League One years were. We fell behind when Chris Greenacre tapped the ball into an empty net – it turned out Greenacre was a Leeds fan as well to rub salt into the wounds, as he unexpectedly did the Leeds salute to the away end after scoring. I remember thinking ok we will wake up now but we didn't, Tranmere looked the more likely to score again. We offered absolutely nothing in the first half. The players looked unfit, one or two clearly uninterested. We did at least have a shot in the first half through Jermaine Beckford, but sadly it hit a burger van at the corner of the ground (similar to Steve Morison's corner flag shot against Nottingham Forest a few years ago.) At half time it felt like the writing was on the wall, League One was going to be very difficult, the 15-point penalty and our finances being all over the place meant relegation again was a genuine possibility. It might sound like a massive exaggeration but words cannot express how bad the first half was and the club was a million miles away from being a going concern at the time, the very worst really was crossing people's minds. The second half started and we were better still, far from our best but we were at least trying to be more aggressive and more like a Leeds team, getting closer to Tranmere and not letting them have time to dictate play. We got a free kick, which Alan

Thompson stood over; the angle was too difficult to shoot from so he went for the cross. Matt Heath made a very late run into the back post, 1-1 against the run of play. Tranmere started to take control again, creating chances and very much outplaying us like the first half. It felt like a matter of time until Tranmere made it 2-1 and we would be leaving Prenton Park 15 points off safety. Then against the run of play Tresor Kandol managed to grab the winner thanks to some very poor goalkeeping. It's the only time I've been in the home end away from home and celebrated us scoring, I just couldn't contain my emotions. Considering Tranmere had lost the game in the last minute and I was there jumping up and down, we did well to get out of the ground in one piece. Safe to say I learnt a lesson: never celebrate goals in those situations. The second half was far from perfect from Leeds, but the workrate and aggression was there for all to see, the players did actually care. Dennis Wise gathered the players in a circle between the centre circle and the away end. It must have been an excellent half-time team talk I have to say because the change in work rate was quite incredible, never really seen anything like it. We went on to make an incredible start to that season after that and so nearly went up that year too. However, had we lost or drawn that game instead I think the season would have been totally different. Something clicked in that second half; it cannot be underestimated how much confidence we got from that game and to an extent it began the turnaround in our fortunes at that time in its own way.

MANCHESTER UNITED 0-1 LEEDS 3 JANUARY 2010

To really give this the full credit you have to go back to the second round of the FA Cup that year. After a routine 2-0 win at Oldham in the first round, we were then drawn to play non-league Kettering in the second round away from home, a year on from the defeat to Histon. We didn't start well, we went 1-0 down and were playing terribly. We somehow took the game to a replay after battling to a 1-1 draw, when a Beckford goal ten minutes from time kept us in the cup. I remember initially moaning, saying something along the lines of 'that's the last thing we needed, promotion is the only thing we need this season we don't need the extra game to play, I'd have rather got beat than draw that, it's all about going up,' then the cup draw was made. I remember trying to load the cup draw on my old Sony Ericsson phone and I was scrolling down the draw looking for who we were going to be playing and I couldn't find us. I kept scrolling and there it was bottom of the page: 'Manchester United vs Leeds United/Kettering.' I was shaking, this was special, I was too young to properly remember/recall any of our previous games against them, this was the first time I was going to properly witness Leeds playing Man Utd – it was unbelievable. So what was a needless replay against Kettering became a totally different proposition. We made a mess of things, 1-1 in normal time we went 1-0 up and Anthony Elding (remember him?) got an equaliser. Then extra time started and you could just sense in the crowd fear! After seven to eight years of constant pain this was an opportunity for Leeds to play and be equals with the enemy again – the fans really wanted this game. These were the type of games Leeds had totally been starved of since the 2004 relegation and still are to this day. The players responded – we scored four goals in extra time and won 5-1. Then in the four weeks after we booked our place in the third round, we strengthened our position at the top of League One, but were suffering an injury crisis. Shane Higgs, first-choice keeper that season, was out with a long-term injury, Leigh Bromby was suspended after an accumulation of yellow cards and Robert Snodgrass wasn't fully fit. So we were lining up at Old Trafford without our main keeper, right-back and had to play Jonny Howson out of position in Snodgrass's position on the right wing. For further context this was a Man Utd side that had won the champions league 18 months before and also won three consecutive Premier League titles. We put ourselves under a little bit of self-inflicted pressure at the start of the game, then started to settle down and then came that pass from Johnny Howson ... It still annoys me to an extent to this day. Howson's pass never really gets the praise it deserves with that goal. The first-half performance was incredible, we were in control, Michael Doyle and Neil Kilkenny were dominating the midfield battle, Bradley Johnson on the left wing was causing Gary Neville all sorts of problems, whilst Richard Naylor and Patrick Kisnorbo totally restricted the service in to Wayne Rooney (who at the time was at his peak and arguably the best striker in the world). The only time Man Utd had threatened was when Jason Crowe had to produce an incredible goal-line clearance. Half-time and we thoroughly deserved to be in the lead.

The second half followed much of the same pattern; we were so comfortable and were totally in control. Robert Snodgrass came on and with ten minutes to go hit the woodwork with a free kick and I just remember thinking that was the turning point and Man Utd's lifeline in the game. After that near miss, Man Utd did start to put pressure on us and it was one long ten minutes, last ditch heroics defensively mainly from Patrick Kisnorbo helped us to see the game out and I honestly can't remember a proper chance for Man Utd in the second half, it was incredible. Yes cup shocks happen all the time but it was the performance more than anything that stunned me – as a League One team we went to Old Trafford and dictated the game. I spoke to Glynn Snodin six months ago and one of the things I asked Glynn was what the tactical approach in the cup games was? He made the point it was exactly the same as it was in league games. Play without fear and on the front foot, cup shocks will always happen being a lower-league club but going to one of the top six clubs away from home and playing them off the park is a much rarer occurrence. You saw that play without fear approach throughout the cup ties that season; we had played Liverpool off the park in the league cup four months earlier and gave Tottenham a real scare across 180 minutes in the next round of the cup. Everyone was a hero that day, but a special mention has to go to Patrick Kisnorbo – in all my time supporting the football club I have not seen a better individual performance in the white shirt than the one Paddy produced that day. Rumour has it Wayne Rooney is still in Kisnorbo's pocket. You could have had Messi, R9 Ronaldo, Pele, Ronaldinho and Maradona all in their prime on the pitch that day, and none of them would have stood a chance of getting any change out of Kisnorbo. 'You'll never beat Kisnorbo' was the legendary chant at the time which rung around Old Trafford, and make no mistake about it no one did that season.

LEEDS UNITED 2-1 BRISTOL ROVERS 8 MAY 2010

Without doubt the best day I have ever had supporting this football club (so far I hope) but the stress was unimaginable. The whole 90 minutes summed up the season and Leeds United in general perfectly - if we are ever going to achieve it has to be done the hard way. 12 months previously was incredibly difficult to accept when we failed to win the play-offs in 2008-09. It was the only time I have ever felt confident in the play-offs. I was convinced we were going to get promoted that year. Our form was exceptional going into them, we had a manager who had got promoted through them two years previously with Blackpool and even though we lost the first leg against Millwall I still felt we would do it as we were in the middle of a record-breaking sequence of wins at Elland Road. The reason that needs mentioning was that if we didn't win that day, play-offs were very likely, but considering we couldn't win them the season previously with everything working in our favour I didn't fancy our chances this time around considering how bad our form had been since 3 January. It was very much a case of now or never, and in my time as a Leeds fan prior to that we had always bottled those occasions previously. We were also presented with a glorious chance to clinch promotion the week before at Charlton. Millwall lost very surprisingly 2-0 at a struggling Tranmere, we finished the game at Charlton with four strikers on the pitch desperately searching for a winner, only to lose the game in the last minute. Despite this we had the one-point cushion on Millwall but there were also two other teams who could still get promoted: Swindon and Charlton. I remember on the radio travelling to the game they were going through all the different permutations and the nerves were starting to build. It looked like we had blown are chances of promotion about five weeks earlier when we lost 3-0 to Swindon at home and slipped out of the automatic places for the first time all season. We fought back with four wins from six, but halfway through this winning run Simon Grayson probably made the biggest call of his managerial career and dropped Beckford to the bench in favour of a Becchio and Gradel partnership. Beckford, to be fair, was in the poorest form of his Leeds career at the time, but it was still a big big call. It was the right call, Gradel was a revelation up front and injected some much needed energy into the team, which was really struggling to stay in the promotion race at the time. And Beckford found form off the bench, becoming a super sub scoring almost every time he came onto the pitch, so built his confidence back that way. However, I remember being in the pavilion when the teams were announced and Beckford was back in the starting 11 to huge cheers, but also captain for the day, which left everyone amazed. This was the second biggest call of Simon's career – if this backfired it would be looked at the same way as David Healy being benched in the 2006 play-off final defeat to Watford. We knew at that point that if we were to get promoted it was near certain this would be Beckford's last game. I was in the East Stand and it's the only time from my memory when I have ever known the East Stand to have everyone stood up rather than sat down. I honestly can't think of an occasion since when that has happened. We started the game well; it felt like a matter of time until we would score. Beckford had a goal disallowed for a tight offside decision but then Max Gradel stamped on Rovers full-back Dan Jones – red card no doubt about it, but Gradel made matters worse by refusing to leave the pitch. This is where captain Beckford stood in, he somehow managed to calm Gradel and the whole situation down. Half-time 0-0 but down to ten men, then within three minutes of the restart we are one down after good work down the left, ironically from Jones. Grayson had to be brave and made a big decision – he switched to a 3-4-2 formation, bringing on Jonny Howson for Shane Lowry. And you know the rest – Howson produced a moment of magic as he did throughout his Leeds career on the big occasions, Carlisle away in the play-offs two years previously the biggest example. Four to five minutes later the ball deflects to Beckford; I'll be honest I wish I celebrated that goal a bit more than I did but the nerves were still there, we still had 30 minutes to play with ten men. Johnny Howson continued his Roy of the Rovers performance, filling in at right-back. Leigh Bromby hit the post with a header but the rest of the game was thankfully uneventful. Shane Higgs had to claim a few crosses under huge pressure but did just that with no hesitation. The final whistle went and I am not ashamed to admit I burst into tears of joy, and to this day I have never cried at Elland Road since I don't have a clue why I reacted like that, but the whole season was a rollercoaster and it so nearly was a season when despite a lot of excitement we didn't achieve anything. An incredible day, as much as getting promoted much earlier would have been nice I don't think it would have been half as memorable had there not been a bit of drama along the way, it was like a film that day.

TOP THREE FAVOURITE/BEST PLAYERS

ROBERT SNODGRASS

He arrived at Leeds as a striker struggling to get game time in Scotland but left Leeds as the best player in the championship. His first season saw him initially struggle to get into the starting 11, but he soon became the heartbeat of the side, even during the difficult last months of Gary McAlister's time as manager Snodgrass was still 8/10 every week and delivering even when his teammates were hiding. I think he got something like 20 assists in his first season; in fact, it took me about a year to work out which foot was his favourite, he was brilliant with both feet and very two footed. It also needs to be mentioned the quality of goals he was creating – he saw things no other player at that level saw, and it was clear from the off he was a class above League One level. A game where Snodgrass really stood out early on was a home League Cup tie against Liverpool, where he caused so many problems for the Liverpool backline, including Jamie Carragher, absolutely no one could get near him. His understanding with Becchio and Beckford was incredible, he was able to play to both of their individual strengths. He would swing in airborne crosses into Becchio for him to attack and would cut in and try and find a throughball or ball over the top into Beckford to allow him to use his pace to get one on one with the goalkeeper. Snodgrass is easily the most composed player Leeds have had in the last 15 years, Snods never wasted an opportunity to either create or score when he was fed the ball in dangerous areas. When Leeds got promoted to the Championship I think everyone questioned whether he could have the same level of success at Championship level as he did at League One level. His first season 2010-11 was a success, but he was slightly overshadowed by Gradel, Becchio and Howson's huge individual contributions. When Gradel and Howson left during the next season, Snodgrass stepped up and had his best season for the club. It was during that season I felt he became the best player in the Championship. He carried the team that season and delivered week after week. He was just the perfect winger in so many ways – reliable, consistent, hard-working, composed and unselfish. The only thing that stopped Snodgrass having an even better career after Leeds was a slight lack of natural pace, he more than had the technical quality to play at the top level as he demonstrated for Norwich, Hull and West Ham. Despite the slight lack of pace, his technical quality served him brilliantly at Leeds, he got past players with ease and always had time to lift his head and pick the right pass.

JERMAINE BECKFORD

When you score 85 goals in three full seasons you are always likely to be regarded as a legend, especially when two of those goals were the most important goals in Leeds United's recent history: one on 3 January and the other to clinch promotion. Beckford was actually at Leeds for five seasons but barely featured during the first two. He got his chance in 2007-08 and formed a good partnership with Tresor Kandol and towards the end of the season Dougie Freedman. From minute one it was clear his pace was going to cause big problems at League One level, and throughout his time at Leeds he always had creators supplying the passes over the top and through balls to allow him to make the most of his pace in behind. That's not to say he didn't have excellent technical quality as well, many of the goals he scored during the three seasons were out of this world. His first season delivered plenty of goals, but he didn't finish the season well and struggled to have an impact in the play-offs that year. Meaning there were still slight doubts with Beckford going into the second season. His start to 2008-09 confirmed he wasn't a one-season wonder. He improved season on season and became better at linking play and holding the ball up as his Leeds career went on. When Luciano Becchio and Robert Snodgrass arrived at the club, his game hit new levels and he had a telepathic understanding with both. The way Beckford and Becchio split defences open was incredible. Becchio would win the flick on, taking one centre-back out of the game straight away, and Beckford would race on to the flick on, always beating the centre-back for pace. Beckford's movement was his biggest strength, he would always get himself into positions to score goals. He did occasionally have games where he missed the big chances, but he never ever let his head drop and kept getting himself into positions to score goals, and through sheer determination he got himself onto the score sheet more often than not, even when things hadn't gone his way in the game. Nothing summed this up more than a 2-1 win over Norwich during his final season. He missed several chances in the game, including a glorious one with a minute to go which went out for a goal kick. The Norwich keeper (Fraser Forster) miskicked the clearance but Beckford was the most alive to the situation, kept his cool, took the chance and won the game – nothing summed up Beckford more than that. It was impossible to dishearten Beckford, he always backed himself from minute one to 90, stepped up at the most crucial moments and never hid. It's unlikely Leeds will ever see a striker as prolific as Beckford again.

PABLO HERNANDEZ

He just continues to improve season upon season. Initially it looked like a risky signing as he hadn't played much football in the years before his arrival at Leeds. He made his debut at Fleetwood and was head and shoulders above everyone else on the pitch and helped Leeds to avoid a cup upset. He was a massive part of the turnaround in fortunes during Garry Monk's season at Leeds. His understanding with Chris Wood was excellent and the two were able to combine regularly to help deliver one of the best seasons Leeds have had in recent years. Whilst his first season was inconsistent at times, I think it would be fair to link that to the more defensive set up under Monk and the lack of passing options didn't suit Pablo's game. The supply from midfield into Pablo himself was often poor, to get on the ball he would often have to drop deep and drive forward himself to start attacks. When Samu Saiz and Ezgjan Alioski arrived in his second season he had more passing options and he was able to build a far better understanding and level of consistency. He moved to the wing in his second season and was a one-man army and the shining light in a dismal season. In the season just gone he moved back to his old position at Valencia, the right-wing, and delivered an extraordinary season that earned him a second Player of the Season win in a row. Pablo has won the hearts and minds of supporters, and this is someone who has played week in week out alongside two of the best players of all time in David Silva and David Villa and has reached his mid 30s – how does he still have the motivation to train so well and display the athleticism of someone ten years his junior in the second division of English football. Pablo being so incredibly humble amongst the group, despite his superior achievements in the game compared to the rest of the team, makes him even more popular. Quite simply, when Pablo smiles everyone smiles with Pablo, when Pablo cries everyone cries with Pablo, there is a mutual respect between Pablo and the fans you don't tend to see very often these days. The fact fans were more upset by how hard Pablo took the Brentford defeat than the implications of the result itself sums up just how highly Pablo is thought of at this football club.

LUFC 2019 TWEETS

Right Leeds fans, would you like to be part of history and appear in my centenary book? If you do, send me a single tweet in 200 characters as to what Leeds United means to you and you shall be included! Please don't swear!

@paulbrace66
I was born & lived in London. Leeds wasn't just a team I supported, it ran deep in me. It moulded me as a young lad, teen & man. Just through meeting other supporters & having the same desire. It gave me confidence and pride in whatever I believed just through who I supported.

@andrAENOBEradzl
Leeds United is more than just a club, supporting Leeds is a way of life, legends come and go but we will stay with this club until the end of time. One life one club, marching on together.

@milesiam
What Leeds mean to me?
Monday-looking back at the weekends game
Tuesday-enjoying or enduring a midweek game.
Wednesday-complaining or complimenting about the game
Thursday-pre-match prezzer
Friday-looking forward to Saturdays game
Sat-enjoying or enduring again Sunday - repeat.

@Abi_Carpenter
Born and bred in London to two Leeds supporting parents, I've spent endless hours on the M1 but nothing beats driving round the M621 when Elland Road comes into sight: I feel like I'm home.

@APA_89
Our club is like one true love, it has its ups and its downs, but no matter what, you'll never stop loving them, that is Leeds United.

@Dave_Pez
My dad taking me to my first game in 1987, seen more down than ups since then. The feeling of being Leeds never subsides. Marching on together.

@BlightAlan
Supported Leeds United as long as I can remember. I travel from Whitehaven to every home game and believe me that's not easy with our roads in Cumbria. There is no feeling like it when we score. We have highs and massive lows but no fans in the world are as loyal as ours. MOT

@alexhullock
Some run that by the youngster, Parker. Robinson takes over. Good ball, BECCHIO WELL PLACED... You only need to listen to that noise to know that Leeds United aren't just a football club, we're a family and we'll be together forever until the world stops going round #ALAW #MOT

@LaceyJohn19
Leeds have been my consistent inconsistent for the past 30yrs. A Greek Tragedy for the most part, but like a true drama the highs are unbelievable, I wouldn't have it any other way ! My love, my Leeds, my life!

@andyclarke71
Leeds United has meant different things throughout my life. As a lad it meant being with my mates, then I moved away and it became my link to home, now it is where my son and I enjoy time together. It's a constant in a world of short-term instant gratification.

@andylimb
It's the Keep Fighting of Billy Brenner in the same team as the ballet of Eddie Gray; the grit of David Batty and the will to win of Gordon Strachan. It's Marching on Together at least until the world stops going round.

@astrogilly1
Leeds United are everything to me. I've been a supporter as far back as I can remember and my first game at Elland Road was in 1971. I've witnessed the best of times and the worst but nothing beats the excitement of waking up on a match day.

@sirbenimiles
My Dad was lucky enough to see John Charles and through the Don Revie era. I was lucky enough to see the Wilkinson to O'Leary era. My hope is my son sees the best from the Bielsa era and the return to where we belong. #LUFC is not just football, it's family. #MOT

@PhyllySucker52
Fortunate to see Leeds play under Don and also watching Tony Currie not only gracing Elland Road but that goal against Southampton was flipping marvellous.

@UpTheJansson
It's a reason to be proud, it helps to keep Leeds relevant, being a Leeds fan is bigger than just football it's about being proud of where you are from & who you are. It's about putting one foot in front of the other & marching on together, you keep fighting for what you believe in.

@bjLUFC
From playground fights over 70', Clarke 1.0, Super Leeds, 80s blows, Wilko's Army, Eddie & O'Leary Babes, crazy owners, Beckford winners & play-off hell, heroes met, loyal fans awide - 50yr of weekends ruined or enjoyed by LUFC - Get In!

@BullMick
My eldest daughter was three weeks old when we beat Blunts to become League champions - she's a Leeds fan and lives in Wortley. Been harder with rest when we've been rubbish - my son supports Liverpool (we live in NW) although we have 100% win record when he comes to ER.

@canilatwit
Being Leeds United is to understand something that no other fan of any other club will ever do. It's a way of life.

@carolineLUFC
Following in the footsteps of my Grandad and my parents. LUFC is family.

@wi1son79
Supporting Leeds is an emotion as the song goes we've had our ups and downs, when Leeds are up so are my spirits and vice versa we've had more downs than ups lately and it's time to rise again!

@tats180
Quite easy - Leeds United is life!!!!

@dansethi91
I grew up on stories from my dad about the mighty Leeds and instantly fell in love with them. I've only ever known Leeds as a Championship/League One club, but I wouldn't have it any other way. It's more than just a club, it's more than just its fans, it's something much deeper.

@falsenine_82
Leeds United quite simply are more than just a football team and of the place where I was born; they brought me hope when I had little, inspiration when I felt down and above all joy and experiences with people that I will never forget. #LUFC

@WorsnopD
First game back on 30 September 1987 v Stoke City. Dire game but was hooked. Still remember John Sheridan hitting the cross bar … then that was it, life of ups and down cemented!

@Daryl1706
From the first time being taken to a Leeds game by my dad's friend I have been in love ever since and feeling when Leeds win or score is just undescribeable and even when the hurt of losing players or relegation etc, I love my team and will forever follow the mighty Leeds.

@davidowenLUFC
When I met my now wife and took her to a game I said I may be a bit nuts at the game but that's what Leeds fans do. We had a son and we are all season ticket holders and when Roofe scored on Boxing Day all three of us went NUTS guess that's us just being Leeds.

@DigglerBarnes
Leeds United is the difference between a good mood, or a bad mood.

@deanbooth1985
Leeds United was bred into me as a boy. Hearing my dad mention Bournemouth beach, football specials and standing on the terraces hooked me. It has brought us closer in recent years more than ever. Our United love for this great club.

@Maldino
It means belonging to a family that mostly you never meet, but when you do it's as if you've just popped away for five mins. Through it all together, there's always someone there to help, who you've never met before!

@DebsHLUFC
We've been through it altogether and we've had our ups and downs. Stand up and sing for Leeds United. They are the greatest in the land. Every day we're all gonna say we love Leeds. Everywhere we're gonna be there. We're marching on together. That's what Leeds United means to me.

@rebeldee
First match v Lyn Oslo 10-0. Going to Paris to see us robbed. Eddie Gray, my legend. O'Leary's babes. A white rose at Billy's feet day of Mum's funeral. No more games together. Hearing MOT, tears of joy, tears of despair. My Leeds family. My half centenary 2019!

@gemma07
My heart is divided into sections a piece of that will forever be Leeds United, my mum a supporter for 73 years would tell great stories of watching the great John Charles, her love and passion for Leeds United passed now onto me it's a family thing ALAW.

@dianeLUFC
Started going to Elland Road when I was 13 am now 64 still love Leeds and always supported them can't wait to see them back in the premiership remember the Revie days with pride it was always fortress Elland Road then and everyone played for the shirt NOT the money MOT.

@DirtyLeeds49ers
Leeds United is everything to me. Most of my life's memories are Leeds. From Champions League and Premier League through high school to the lows of League One in my early 20's. I can't wait until my lad has his own United memories.

@EllandBack1
Although I live 238 miles away from Elland Road, it still feels like home away from home. Win, lose or draw that will never change.

@Elliott_MOT
Living in S Wales, Leeds always meant that much more, every match is like an away one. If we were gone tomorrow would I still live my life, Yes, but would it ever be the same, No. For always and forever, we'll be Marching on Together.

@FACupFactfile
The five best things in my life happened in 1992:
5. Holiday of lifetime in Sri Lanka
4. Obsessively favourite band The Smiths had biggest hit single
3. First company car - a BMW
2. Married my wife of 26 years
1. #LUFC won the Title.

@FollowMeAndLUFC
I'm privileged to have seen the best team ever play under Don Revie, including my hero Billy Bremner. Leeds United is in my blood; the camaraderie of our fantastic worldwide fans is second to none and I still love it even after all these years.

@glennmoran23
I was lucky enough to start going to Leeds in the 91-92 season, so started with a high, and seen lots of lows, with some highs in between and I'm still here following and still will be till the day I die. #ALAW #MOT #LUFC

@GrahamA74
Leeds United are my religion and Elland Road is my church. Forever Leeds and forever proud!

@GrumpySteve66
Long time suffering loudest singing never stopping we hate Leeds scumming always believing Man U hating beer swilling chip supper eating Leeds Leeds Leedsing Elland Road loving media loathing away ground filling together marching giant sleeping giant awakening EPL we are coming.

@gasgusler
1/2 I grew up in Chapeltown in the 80s. I was the only Asian youth who supported Leeds in the area back then. I got some stick for that as Leeds had bit of a far right following at the time. I was proud of where I lived and proud to support my team.

@Bielsasdisciple
My Uncle Steve was signed by Don Revie from Leeds City Boys in the 60s. His Mum, my Gran took me to ER in 1981 to my first game vs Liverpool. First season ticket aged 14 & I now take my two sons and sit with my Mum and Dad both 72 years young. Simply in the blood...Cheers Gran!

@austrianwhite
1966. As a 12 year old lad I got in for free at half-time. Stood at the back of the old kop 'Can't ya see lad' a big fella asked me. 'No' I replied. There and then he picked me up and shouted to the other fans ahead 'Lad coming down' The Kop body-surfed me right to the front.

@NeilMidasTHovey
Leeds United is life. If you cut me and my son in half it says L U F C. It's in our DNA. Marching On Together.

@Hughspence91
Leeds is not supporting a club it is a lifestyle, it is my religion.

@iainmcooke59
Leeds Utd, becomes part of your life and stays there beating away day by day and then year by year. Leeds Utd have had many great players lots of whom are celebrated everyday and I'm sure we have many more Legends to come! #LUFC MOT

@iancarnegieruns
My first match was in September 1967 and was Mick Jones's debut game. I went with a couple of mates to see what the fuss was all about! We were in the Scratching Shed and didn't see much! Fantastic! The rest as they say ...

@JimHutchy
14 years old when I saw my first @LUFC match, bonfire nite 1994, my Grandad took me as he was a Wimbledon fan and they were visiting the hallowed turf that is Elland Road, we won 3-1, goals from Wetherall, Speed & White ... and so my love affair with the mighty whites began #LUFC

@ramsden302
It was my dad's club, it is mine, and it will be my children's. All Leeds Aren't We?

@jimmyrimski
it means one divorce after she accused me of loving Leeds more than her, Leeds United appears on my divorce papers several times.

@El_Loco_JoJo
Leeds United is a journey I never get bored of. It's given me heartache and joy beyond belief, it's given me great friends and a huge football family that have pulled me through some pretty dark times.

@TwizzlerLUFC
Once Leeds are in your blood, that's it for life. Introduced my daughter when she was eight years old, she's now 16 and a season ticket holder. Legacy will live on.

@joehewitt86
Had LUFC ingrained into me since a young boy my first season was the title winning season. Amazing ups and horrible lows in my 30 years. But one thing always remained the love for the club and the immense pride to wear the white shirt at Elland Road and on many away days. MOT

@JBEddison
From my first season as a five year old we won the league & I was ruined, I fell in love with Leeds United thanks to my Dad and it will always be my first love. Leeds United makes me feel things my family can't. It's a part of me and a part of who I am.

@Johnnythetouch
Dad took me to Leeds v Burnley 1974, only ER game we lost on way to the title. Nine-year-old me was star struck, even in defeat the Don's men were like Gods. Leeds are my first love & ER will always be home for me.

@john959379
There's been some highs & some lows but I would never change it. It's something you can't switch off - Forever Leeds & proud of it.

@JTinning
'We've been through it all together, and we've had our ups and downs' is more than just a line in a song. Through everything, Leeds are and always will be there. MOT

@LUFCJON1
All my mates at school wore their Liverpool and Manchester shirts but I always marched into school in my white Leeds topman shirt with pride. Still wear them with pride. Always and Forever LUFC.

@JonnyPrice07
Leeds United is everything to me. I've supported them for 21 years. When I see the East Stand I still get excited now as I did 21 years ago. It hasn't always been smooth sailing but I'll never stop loving Leeds United.

@JordyP1993
Supporting Leeds United is a lot of things. Sometimes it's a chore. Other times it's a religiousesque cult unlike no other. Some may say it's just a sports team. But to many, myself included it is so much more than that. It's an identity. It's a passion. It's Leeds. United. #MOT

@JoJrl
'You're from Leeds, you support Leeds'. The words from my Dad. Then he took me to my first game... The walk up the stairs and then you see the stadium. It was a night game and the floodlights were on. My breath was taken away. That buzz that never leaves every time you go there.

@Joshstone23
Leeds to me is us against the world, a way of living knowing you're a part of something special, going on holiday knowing your gonna see another Leeds fan, we are huge the sleeping giant is rising being held up by the fans through the good and the bad and now we are ready to go!

@LUFCracing
Saturday would be useless without LUFC.
Awesome being part of something so massive.
What a family.

@JudeLUFC
I've been a Leeds fan for 40 years and I still get butterflies just like I did as a kid when I get to Elland Road. I'm from Middlesbrough but used to have the Leeds Utd crest on my blazer instead of the school badge.

@KaiserChief82
Leeds is a club that stirs emotion and creates discussion from the majority, like us or hate us, we don't really care. I love that everywhere you go you'll find Leeds fans. Passionate. Determined. Loyal.
My blood runs White, Yellow and Blue. M.O.T

@kam_mannx
They mean so much to me that if we win I end up out all night in shed, if we draw I might do half a night, but if we lose I'm in bed early doors sulking.

@sergeantdudfoot
In good and bad times it's so special being Leeds. It's a feeling I just can't imagine other fans of other teams having.

@mskelly1990
Leeds United means a lot more to me than just football. I've jumped 12,000ft tandem… But that high doesn't beat some of the atmospheres I've seen at Elland Road. Just lately I've made some cracking friends too. Buckinghamshire to Yorkshire all for the love of Leeds. #MOT

@landspater
A reason to get up in the morning.

@anyoldsport
Leeds United is in my blood. I've worked there, I've played there, I met my wife there, I drive past Elland Road twice a day. LUFC is woven into the fabric of me.

@LeedsUtdBalkan
I'm from Balkan and just a small group of people love Leeds Utd but I always supported them when I was kid, but when we scored against man utd I came out of my home half naked and dancing in the snow. Leeds Leeds Leeds.

@LUFCHistory
What Leeds United means to me.
My dad got me on to Leeds back in the early 70s, first game 74 when 7 yr old and loved them ever since.
Season ticket holder since 1984 I've lost a job & relationships because of this great club and called my son Bremner.
Live and breathe #LUFC

@LeedsPal19
Leeds for breakfast Leeds for lunch Leeds for dinner Leeds is my diet my sustenance it's what keeps me going Leeds win I'm full and happy Leeds lose I get indigestion and I'm miserable.

@georgemcluskey
THAT moment when Leeds score a winner/equalising goal in a big game and everyone around you loses it and at THAT very moment you love Leeds United more than anything or anyone and you remember why you put up with all the heartache & expense following them, because We Are Leeds.

@Whitey077
The siege mentality of us against them, no one likes us, plenty aspire to be us, plenty hate us! #LUFC

@fenit52
Moved from Bradford to Ireland and still followed Leeds, met guys in Ireland who followed Leeds and are still friends with same guys 30 years later.

@lukeyminsh
From strings of Yasmin
From Bremner and Baird.
Marching on Together in the blood since birth.
Elland Road atmosphere
My love for Leeds United - Established 1986!

@Lukiano92
Leeds are frustrating, Leeds are irritating, Leeds bring misery and rage…
Leeds are bad for your nerves, Leeds are bad for your health…Leeds make you want to be by yourself…
But, Leeds will reward, and we will applaud, when a 90th minute winner is added to the scoreboard.

@lyndseytruth
LUFC means to be proud to be Yorkshire. Proud of my roots, my community and most of all proud of the football club that I live for.

@lawrielee
It means everything. The club that represents the city I love.

@hannnah200
AC Milan Elland Road torrential chucking it down rain Bowyer shoots from 30 yards. I see keeper save it turn around and it's absolute bedlam ended up three rows down in East stand upper. Remember walking back to the dragon ph soaked to skin but blown away Leeds had just beaten AC Milan.

@MarkLeedsFoster
Leeds has a place in my heart that no other will claim. I've supported them through thick and thin, the fans have always been there to pick the club up off of their knees. It's not a club, it's a family. Marching on together.

@AllansonMark
I was at that game … the kop was silent we were losing 2-0 and in 2nd half … then all of a sudden a bloke shouted out … even tho were losing were still, BILLY BREMNERS BARMY ARMY … kop went mental for half an hour for rest of game.

@markdennett86
My life stops for 90 minutes every time Leeds United play. The result defining how I feel from that final whistle to the next first whistle. It's more than football to me and it's time to hit the highs again! #MOT

@morti59
With all the hurt and disappointment I'd swap it all again for my kids (don't have any but I would) #LUFC

@MarkTaylor1979
For me Leeds United is not just the team that I support but actually a part of me. Part of a special family. When you meet another fan there is always that immediate bond. We win together and we lose together. The lows hurt but the highs are indescribable. A life long commitment!

@markwright1967
From the minute I went from the back of the kop to near the front without my feet touching the floor I loved ER. I was a young kid, it was the late 70s but now, 40 years later I still get a buzz from the place.

@belsom04
Born and bred in LDN I am always asked why #LUFC and it's simple I didnt choose them it just happened! I just fell in Love! The white kit, the rose and ball badge! The atmosphere! I dont get to go every week but I swear there isn't a game I have missed either on radio/tv/live.

@mattym2011
Supporting Leeds is the feeling of excitement and anticipation when you see ER come into view on a matchday, it's the feeling of pride wearing an LUFC top anywhere in the world and receiving the salute, it's singing mot at the top of your lungs home & away come rain or shine!

@LUFC_mick
My mates brother took us to the Leeds Vs Hibernian FC Inter-Cities Fairs Cup second leg at ER in 1973-74 season under lights, hooked instantly, the rest they

say is history, still hooked and always will be, no matter what ups and downs we have MOT!

@mightywhite83
Born into it & bred into my boys, it's a feeling only a Leeds fan can feel when it's us against the world & everyone hates us, we are an odd bunch can be the nicest or most horrible fans in football but I wouldn't want to follow any other team or have any other fans walk beside me.

@mikexile
Saw my first game in 1958 0-0 draw v Aston Villa. Following season (1958-59) we were relegated. Clueless for most of the time. They signed this over the hill striker called Don Revie who rarely shone for Leeds. He was stylish but past it. Made him manager. The rest is history.

@mike_yorkie
Leeds United is in my family which makes me immensely proud. My great grandad was Harry Duggan who played for Leeds In the late 1920s and early 1930s. He scored a good few goals for the club, but just to think he graced the sacred turf makes me and my family very proud!

@nathanfordyy
I think the main part of being a Leeds fan is having such a big community around you, you could be anywhere in the world and there's no doubt you'd see one of us. It's hard to think what life would be like without our beloved Leeds United, it means so much to everyone of us. MOT

@royceyLUFC
What else is there in life?

@NickRodgersLUFC
Leeds United is not just a part of me, but a part of my family, our family. I never gave up through the ups and downs and still managed to keep my season ticket through 20 years in the Military. MOT

@simonc30
I was taken as an eleven year old by my two older cousins. It bounced it down with rain, stood in the open, soaked, Leeds beat Coventry 2-0. I was hooked, still supporting 48 years later.

@BuntyLUFC
To many Leeds United means never giving up. And it applies to every aspect of life not just our football club. Work hard and fight to be successful. And always know that there are others beside you. We are a family.

@x_ourania_x
Leeds United means family. It's the feeling of belonging at Elland Road. It's the bond I share with my Dad, my Uncle and my Nephew and close friends

@patcorraine
Ups and downs but always Leeds through the goodtimes and the bad there is no club like ours.

@kenty227
Everything.

@pcrooks94
Leeds means everything to me it's in my blood when I'm at a game win lose or draw the feeling I get when we score is like no other better then any drug there is.

@NakedFarang
From the utter despair of hearing a ground erupt around you at an away game when the home team score to the ecstasy of coming from behind to beat them on their own pitch, nothing comes close.

@TaylorPaul83
With reviled comes revered. We are Leeds. Passing that down to your son from your own father.

@paulwarrick3
Been thru the Don era, battled thru the 70s 80s eras, trains from London weekly using every penny I had & catching staff trains home. Enjoyed every last moment of a life with LUFC, slept on trains, in doorways, in cars, stranger's beds, pub cellars, side before self every time.

@UpThePeacocks
I try and make it to 2-3 games a year. Everytime I catch my first glance of the stadium I turn into a kid again! I took my teenage daughters to their first game this year, despite their reluctancy you can't help but get caught up in the Elland Road atmosphere, they loved it!!

@PhilMerrick
Born 3.5 miles from Elland Road, been going there since a small boy with my dad who died tragically when I was 19. Going there today is obviously very special. We're a great club, with a proud history and our fans are amazing. #LUFC #mot

@Whiteyorkist
Over 45 years of supporting Leeds United, for which I have to thank my dad. I'm extremely proud to be a part of such a wonderful club and its fantastic supporters. #MOT

@Fil1966
Grandad took me to Elland Road aged six, I fell in love with Leeds United, I was lucky to witness The Revie era and Leeds is in my blood #MOT

@LUFCPIP
Happiness, sadness, hope or despair. Pride, passion, white, yellow and blue. Revie, Bremner, Speed, Batty. My Dad. Leeds means Everything. We March On Together, win lose or draw, because WE ARE Leeds!

@QuinnB112
Leeds United means everything to me. I was born in Leeds, the only club my mother wanted me to support was Leeds. From the highs of the Champions League to the lows of being relegated to League One, I've always been there. The club have my unwavering support.

@rafiadd
To be Leeds is to belong to a tradition of grit, of warmth and of passion. Leeds United is the beating heart of a city that has been, and will continue to be, a home for people from all walks of life, brought together by their love of just one club. Leeds.
I luv the passion of the fans, none more passionate then us, we can make a 2000 away allocation sound like 5000 and full Elland Road sound like we've filled wembley, with all our history not won as much as we should of, but up there with the fan bases of the biggests clubs.

@richyboy2k10
Replying to '@LUFCstats
From my first game vs Newcastle when I was young, through the highs of the Champions League and the lows of league One, Leeds is life and will be until I die.

@Rich57H
First game my dad took me to was at Burnley but a few weeks later we were stood on the old Kop watching Leeds beat Sheff Utd 1-0, FA Cup Sixth round 1968, Paul Madeley scored. The white shirts stood out like a beacon and I've been hooked ever since.

@robcartwright6
Started going when I was about six in early 80s my step dad was a steward in H stand so sneaked me in was hooked after my first game no other stadium compares to ER spent more time praying there than anywhere me and now my four boys are Leeds never hide it always be proud of it #ALAW

@_RobsonParker
The first time I went to a match was with my dad, I loved every second of the roaring crowd and the feeling of having a huge family that you've never met that bonded over a sport. For me Leeds is a way of life, I'd be lost without it!

@Machen2203
The joy of Revie's super Leeds, the slow decline, Sgt Wilko's wonderful renaissance, O'Leary's babes, financial meltdown, shyster owners, mad Italians, stoic loyalty and the final realisation I'm stuck with this club until the day I die!!

@bobly44
What Leeds United mean to me, it runs in the family my father, brother and nephew support this great team, yes the 60s and 70s were good for United but what adversity they had bounced back from it. I support them too I'm always at ER for league games away it's Twitter for me.

@GrumpyGit9
Leeds United - the first thing I think about when I wake up in a morning and the last thing I think about before I go to sleep. (Do not tell the wife)

@Russharker
Leeds United are the fabric of the great city of Leeds. The fans would sweat blood to see the team win. That's how much it means.

@RyanLUFC91
Wether it's a European night against Barcelona and Real Madrid, midweek trips to Northampton and Darlington or being witness to the Biesla Revolution, there's no greater feeling then being a Leeds United Fan! It runs through your blood and is simply a part of life.
MOT

@salzwhites2
Although I'm from Bristol I became a Leeds fan 20yrs ago because of looking at Alan Smith'ßs bum on MOTD. I have been to a few games Home and away. 19 managers and scores of players come and gone. The ambience at Elland Road is magic and can't be beat. The best fans in the world.

@itssamwilson_
I'm only young, 14 to be exact, but Leeds is everything to me to be honest. I'm a CB myself and Jansson is my idol. I have been to quite a lot of ER games but all that I remember going to, we have won. Me and '@Wilbur4ce have a brick there and recently had a brill tour around ER.

@SamAdjeii
I have supported Leeds Utd since I was seven years old. Leeds United is a very important part of my life - It has given me both happy and sad moments. But this is the difference between simply following a club and a team being in your blood. No matter what we always #MOT!!

@Horbury56
Five generations, stories handed down, dejection, elation, devotion, moments that will never be forgotten, pride, glory and humiliation. Forever Marching on Together.

@Smallback1955
Leeds two from bottom of old Division Two on 1962 when moved to England from Italy. Couldn't pronounce bottom team (BHA) so went for Leeds - what a journey since then!

@spencer69asda
Nothing better than in 1978 as a nine year old pulling on that admiral shirt after school and being Allen Clarke for a few hours.

@allwaysatwit
Been supporting Leeds since I was a small kid, and when Leeds scored a goal in the Third Division to me it felt just the same as when we scored in the Champions League. FANTASTIC Leeds forever me MOT ALAW

@stoopo
I've followed Leeds since the Revie years and will never give up on them. My club, my city, my life.

@superLUFC1919
As a fan born in the late 90s, I don't have any memories of the good old days and being from Birmingham some may think it'd be better to support my local team, but Leeds is one special family, and that walk down to Elland Road and the sound of MOT always gives me goosebumps.

@pwhiteley41
In one word Devotion. I have flown across the world to watch matches at the church I call Elland Road.

@paul_gobin
My first game watching Leeds was a 2-1 home defeat against Charlton in 1987-88. It wasn't the greatest game but the Leeds fans were incredible. I don't get to as many games as I'd like these days, but when I do it's those same fans creating that same atmosphere that's special.

@eirewhite
Born an Irish white. Been going over with my father since my first game in 1997 (Leeds-Derby 4-3) I saw the highs of Europe & the lows of League One & never stopped supporting. Now my kids are Leeds fans & I hope they enjoy the rollercoaster as much as I have. #KEEPTHEFAITH #MOT

@tonypdickinson
Blue, yellow and white; a football in a Yorkshire Rose. The words Leeds United AFC.
Everywhere we go, people know our name, our club and want to talk about its history. Marching on together, saluting with pride. We always find a home wherever we go.

@VANDIESEL09
I was five years old on my first visit to ER in 1975. My dad took me into the Lowfields. Unknowingly stood with a percentage of the service crew. Was made to feel like family although extremely frightened I became part of the greatest club ever.

@AllLoveLeeds
Leeds Utd is a feeling, a passion, a belonging. A unique club. I fell in love the moment I set foot in Elland Road. From Billy, Baird, Shez, Batty, Sgt Wilko, Strachan, Vinnie, Speed, Macca, Yeboah, O'Leary's babies, Viduka, Matteo. Ups n downs. One thing remains. The fans #MOT

@WotzThatSound
Grandad ST, Dad took me to ER. Took own stool to stand on in Lowfields as a kid. Tumbling down the Kop as young teenager then South Stand. Survived hooligan era & fans being caged in at ER. Wrongly locked up in Holbeck one night game. ST when I can afford it. #LUFC man and boy.

@PerrySve
As a kid growing up in Norway I was sold after I as a nine year old on telly saw us beat Barcelona in 'that' semi final. After that I've checked Leed's line ups on a weekly basis. Trip over was on Batty's debut in '87. Trip #50 is soon approaching…

@Chriscleghorn4
Supported Leeds since the day I was born. known nothing else and I couldn't imagine supporting another team. This football club means the world to me and has given me memories that will last forever. I'll always love Leeds United. At least until the world stops going round!! MOT

@astrogilly1
I was taken kicking and screaming to Elland Road in 1971. It was a scary place for a young teenage girl. We played Liverpool and Peter Lorimer scores the only goal. The crowd surged forward and I went with it. I loved it! Now a season ticket holder in the more sedate west stand.

@mightywrites
Leeds gets under your skin and can make or break your mood for days. Win and everything becomes more tolerable, lose and the whole world turns grey and miserable. No matter the outcome, Leeds are my drug and I'll always need to return to get my next fix.

@adam_pawson
Throughout my time following Leeds United, I have experienced both unbeatable highs, and inexplicable lows. But even after crushing defeats and horrible performances, I will always come back for more, as nothing beats the emotional rollercoaster of LUFC #LUFC

@LUFCLDP1989
We are unique. No matter how low we stoop. No matter how bad we perform. We all still back our team. We all still love the club. Being Leeds isn't just being a fan of a football team. It's being part of something that hasn't lost its identity even though times have changed.

BIBLIOGRAPHY

Don Revie – Programme column, Leeds United v Everton, 25 August 1973, Charles Harrold Promotions Ltd

Brian Clough – Programme column, Leeds United v Queens Park Rangers, 21 August 1974, Charles Harrold Promotions Ltd

Maurice Lindley – Programme column, Leeds United v Huddersfield Town, 24 September 1974, Charles Harrold Promotions Ltd

Jimmy Armfield – Programme column, Leeds United v Wolverhampton Wanderers, 19 October 1974, Charles Harrold Promotions Ltd

Maurice Lindley – Programme column, Leeds United v Derby County, 28 October 1978, Leeds United AFC

Jock Stein – Programme column, Leeds United v Manchester United, 23 August 1978, Leeds United AFC

Jimmy Adamson – Programme column, Leeds United v Arsenal, 11 November 1978, Leeds United AFC

Maurice Lindley – Programme column, Leeds United v Tottenham Hotspur, 13 September 1980, Leeds United AFC

Allan Clarke – Programme column, Leeds United v Manchester United, 20 September 1980, Leeds United AFC

Eddie Gray – Programme column, Leeds United v Wolverhampton Wanderers, 4 September 1982, Leeds United AFC

Leslie Silver – Programme column, Leeds United v Grimsby Town, 19 October 1985, Leeds United AFC

Billy Bremner – Programme column, Leeds United v Aston Villa, 30 October 1985, Leeds United AFC

Peter Gunby – Programme column, Leeds United v Watford, 8 October 1988, Leeds United AFC

Howard Wilkinson – Programme column, Leeds United v Leicester City, 22 October 1988, Leeds United AFC

George Graham – Programme column, Leeds United v Darlington, 18 September 1996, Leeds United AFC

David O'Leary – Programme column, Leeds United v Bradford City, 28 October 1998, Leeds United Publishing

Terry Venables – Programme column, Leeds United v Manchester City, 17 August 2002, Green Park

Peter Reid – Programme column, Leeds United v Tottenham Hotspur, 12 April 2003, Green Park

Eddie Gray – Programme column, Leeds United v Bolton Wanderers, 22 November 2003, Green Park

Kevin Blackwell – Programme column, Leeds United v Derby County, 7 August 2004, CRE8 (UK) Limited

John Carver – Programme column, Leeds United v Birmingham City, 23 September 2006, Ignition Publications

Dennis Wise – Programme column, Leeds United v Southend United, 28 October 2006, Ignition Publications

Gary McAllister – Programme column, Leeds United v Tranmere Rovers, 2 February 2008, Ignition Publications

Simon Grayson – Programme column, Leeds United v Carlisle United, 10 January 2009, Ignition Publications

Neil Redfearn – Programme column, Leeds United v Brighton & Hove Albion, 11 February 2012, Ignition Publications

Neil Warnock – Programme column, Leeds United v Southampton, March 3rd 2012, Ignition Publications

Neil Redfearn – Programme column, Leeds United v Sheffield Wednesday, 13 April 2013, Ignition Publications

Brian Mcdermott – Programme column, Leeds United v Burnley, 16 April 2013, Ignition Publications

David Hockaday – Programme column, Leeds United v Accrington Stanley, 12 August 2014, Ignition Publications

Neil Redfearn – Programme column, Leeds United v Huddersfield Town, 20 September 2014, Ignition Publications

Darko Milanic – Programme column, Leeds United v Sheffield Wednesday, 4 October 2014, Ignition Publications

Neil Redfearn – Programme column, Leeds United v Charlton Athletic, 4 November 2014, Ignition Publications

Uwe Rosler – Programme column, Leeds United v Burnley, 8 August 2015, Ignition Publications

Steve Evans – Programme column, Leeds United v Blackburn Rovers, 29 October 2015, Ignition Publications

Garry Monk – Programme column, Leeds United v Birmingham City, 13 August 2016, Ignition Publications

Thomas Christensen – Programme column, Leeds United v Port Vale, 9 August 2017, Ignition Publications

Paul Heckingbottom – Programme column, Leeds United v Bristol City, 18 February 2018, Ignition Publications

Marcelo Bielsa – Programme column, Leeds United v Stoke City, 5 August 2018, Ignition Publications

OTHER PROGRAMMES:

Season 1989-90
Leeds United v Sheffield United, 16 April 1990, Leeds United AFC

Season 1999-91
Leeds United v Manchester United, 28 August 1990, Leeds United AFC

Season 2007-08
Leeds United v Nottingham Forest, 12 February 2008, Ignition Publications
Leeds United v AFC Bournemouth, 8 March 2008, Ignition Publications

Season 2008-09
Leeds United v Huddersfield Town, 15 November 2008, Ignition Publications

Season 2011-12
Leeds United v Doncaster Rovers, 18 February 2012, Ignition Publications
Leeds United v West Ham United, 17 March 2012, Ignition Publications
Leeds United v Nottingham Forest, 20 March 2012, Ignition Publications
Leeds United v Watford, 31 March 2012, Ignition Publications

WEBSITES:

www.bbc.co.uk/sport

www.leedsunited.com

http://www.ozwhitelufc.net.au/

http://sheridan-dictates.com/historical-statistics.php

www.soccerbase.com

www.twitter.com

http://www.wafll.com/

http://www.leedsunitedprogrammeguide.co.uk/

BOOKS:

And we've had our ups and downs (Vertical Editions) by David Saffer and Gary Shepherd

Leeds United The Complete Record (The Derby Books Publishing Company Limited) by Martin Jarred and Malcolm MacDonald

The Who's Who of Leeds United (Breedon Books) by Martin Jarred and Malcolm MacDonald

Final Whistle, Every Club, Every Player, Every Match, Every Minute, 2004-05 (Sidan Press)

Inside Leeds United, The Story of the Millennium Season (Leeds United Publishing) Don Waters Limited

2001, A European Odyssey: Leeds United's Champions League season (Leeds United Publishing Limited) by Don Waters

MAGAZINE BIBLIOGRAPHY

Leeds, Leeds, Leeds, September 1999, Polar Print Group
Leeds, Leeds, Leeds, October 1999, Polar Print Group
Leeds, Leeds, Leeds, November, 1999, Polar Print Group
Leeds, Leeds, Leeds, February 2000, Polar Print Group
Leeds, Leeds, Leeds, April 2000, Polar Print Group
Leeds, Leeds, Leeds, June 2000, Polar Print Group
Leeds, Leeds, Leeds, October 2000, Polar Print Group

Leeds, Leeds, Leeds, November 2000, Polar Print Group
Leeds, Leeds, Leeds, December 2000, Polar Print Group
Leeds, Leeds, Leeds, January 2001, Polar Print Group
Leeds, Leeds, Leeds, May 2001, Polar Print Group
Leeds, Leeds, Leeds, September 2001, Polar Print Group
Leeds, Leeds, Leeds, November 2001, Polar Print Group
Leeds, Leeds, Leeds, October 2002, IFG – Publishers
Leeds, Leeds, Leeds, May 2003, IFG – Publishers
Leeds, Leeds, Leeds, June 2003, IFG – Publishers
Leeds, Leeds, Leeds, October 2003, IFG – Publishers
Leeds, Leeds, Leeds, November 2003, IFG – Publishers
Leeds, Leeds, Leeds, January 2004, GreenPark Publishing
Leeds, Leeds, Leeds, May 2004, GreenPark Publishing
Leeds, Leeds, Leeds, September 2004, GreenPark Publishing
Leeds, Leeds, Leeds, December 2004, GreenPark Publishing
Leeds, Leeds, Leeds, January 2005, GreenPark Publishing
Leeds, Leeds, Leeds, February 2005, GreenPark Publishing
Leeds, Leeds, Leeds, April 2005, GreenPark Publishing
Leeds, Leeds, Leeds, January 2006, GreenPark Publishing
Leeds, Leeds, Leeds, April 2006, GreenPark Publishing
Leeds, Leeds, Leeds, June 2006 GreenPark Publishing
Leeds, Leeds, Leeds, Feb/March 2007, Ignition Publications
Leeds, Leeds, Leeds, Apr/May 2007, Ignition Publications
Leeds, Leeds, Leeds, Summer 2007, Ignition Publications
Leeds, Leeds, Leeds, Oct/Nov 2007, Ignition Publications
Leeds, Leeds, Leeds, Feb/March 2008, Ignition Publications
Leeds, Leeds, Leeds, Apr/May 2008, Ignition Publications
Leeds, Leeds, Leeds, Summer 2008, Ignition Publications
Leeds, Leeds, Leeds, Oct/Nov 2008, Ignition Publications
Leeds, Leeds, Leeds, Feb/March 2009, Ignition Publications
Leeds, Leeds, Leeds, April/May 2009, Ignition Publications
Leeds, Leeds, Leeds, Dec 2009/Jan 2010, Ignition Publications
Leeds, Leeds, Leeds, Feb/March 2010, Ignition Publications
Leeds, Leeds, Leeds, June/July 2010, Ignition Publications
Leeds, Leeds, Leeds, June/July 2010, Ignition Publications
Leeds, Leeds, Leeds, February/March 2011, Ignition Publications